# ENCYCLOPEDIA OF EDUCATION

## SECOND EDITION

# EDITORIAL BOARD

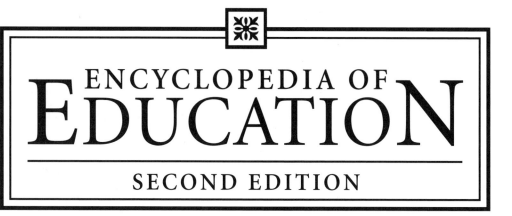

# ENCYCLOPEDIA OF EDUCATION

## SECOND EDITION

James W. Guthrie, Editor in Chief

VOLUME

# 6

Race–State

**MACMILLAN
REFERENCE
USA ™**

**THOMSON**
————✴————™
**GALE**

New York • Detroit • San Diego • San Francisco • Cleveland • New Haven, Conn. • Waterville, Maine • London • Munich

# Encyclopedia of Education, Second Edition

James W. Guthrie, Editor in Chief

For permission to use material from this product, submit your request via Web at http://www.gale-edit.com/permissions, or you may download our Permissions Request form and submit your request by fax or mail to:

*Permissions Department*
The Gale Group, Inc.
27500 Drake Road
Farmington Hills, MI 48331-3535
Permissions Hotline: 248-699-8006 or
800-877-4253 ext. 8006
Fax: 248-699-8074 or 800-762-4058

**LIBRARY OF CONGRESS CATALOGING-IN-PUBLICATION DATA**

Encyclopedia of education / edited by James W. Guthrie.—2nd ed.
    p. cm.
Includes bibliographical references and index.
    ISBN 0-02-865594-X (hardcover : set : alk. paper)
1. Education—Encyclopedias. I. Guthrie, James W.
    LB15 .E47 2003
    370'.3—dc21                                                    2002008205

ISBNs
Volume 1: 0-02-865595-8
Volume 2: 0-02-865596-6
Volume 3: 0-02-865597-4
Volume 4: 0-02-865598-2
Volume 5: 0-02-865599-0
Volume 6: 0-02-865600-8
Volume 7: 0-02-865601-6
Volume 8: 0-02-865602-4

Printed in the United States of America
10 9 8 7 6 5 4 3 2 1

# R

## RACE, ETHNICITY, AND CULTURE

## CULTURAL EXPECTATIONS AND STUDENT LEARNING

Students learn—whether in school or out. Of significance for the educational and scholarly communities is the extent to which certain kinds of learning are conducive to mainstream academic achievement within the context of formal educational institutions. The presumption is that a student's ability to acquire mainstream academic content and then demonstrate mastery of the content (often defined as learning and usually measured by standardized assessments) will lead to greater knowledge and to social and economic benefits in the dominant society. In multiracial and multiethnic societies such as the United States, a pressing issue is the various ways in which race, ethnicity, and culture might influence student learning in formal educational settings. This concern emanates from the fact that scores of students from some racial and ethnic minority groups do not "achieve" in schools at rates comparable either to those of European-American students or to those of students from other racial and ethnic minority groups. In order to examine how students'

race, ethnicity, and culture might influence learning, however, one must first examine the assumptions that underlie these concepts.

Race is not a biological category but a social construction that is given meaning and significance in specified historical, political, and social contexts. Historically, race has been predicated on phenotypic characteristics that mark "racial differences" in order to legitimate prejudice and discrimination on the basis of these supposed differences. As noted by Michael Omi and Howard Winant in their influential book *Racial Formation in the United States* (1994), the formation of race is social and historical in nature. At the dawn of the twenty-first century, most within the scholarly community no longer use biosocial terms such as *race* and embrace *ethnicity* instead. In the United States and Europe, ethnicity is commonly associated with membership in a non-dominant group (not of predominant European ancestry) and is perceived as constituting a different culture—in terms of language, style of dress, political consciousness and worldview, foods, music, and so on—than that of the dominant group. Membership status within ethnic groups can sometimes be negotiated, situational, or optional, particularly for some white ethnics. In comparison to the concept of race, ethnicity is a mutable and more flexible category.

Embracing ethnicity in place of race has shifted the discourse around human difference from one that is biological in nature to one that is greatly shaped by nurture, culture, and historical experiences. The change in terminology, however, does not automatically change the privileges and social disadvantages of being identified and categorized as a member of a particular group. Historically, such identities and categories shaped a number of theoretical perspectives that attempted to explain academic school success or failure among various groups of students. While these perspectives are chronologically outlined below, the fact that one particular paradigm was the dominant paradigm during a particular time period does not mean that other (and equally convincing) paradigms did not also exist. Nor does it mean that theories that once predominated are no longer appropriated as explanatory models.

## Theoretical Explanations of Differing Academic Achievement and Learning

Of the proponents of different theoretical perspectives used to explain student achievement, the ones that have provoked the greatest degree of controversy—the geneticists—place ethnicity and race at the center of their thesis. In general, geneticists view race as static and as a major determinant of one's intellectual capabilities.

**Geneticists.** The geneticists consider the differences in academic achievement among various groups of students (often measured by test scores) as indicative of the innate intelligence of certain groups, rather than a product of socioeconomic, historical, and cultural factors. During the first half of the twentieth century, geneticists such as Lewis Terman and Henry Goddard considered the low performance on intelligence tests of some racial, ethnic, and linguistic minorities to be a reflection of these groups' genetic inferiority. These theorists attempted to "prove" that some European ethnic minorities (Jews, Hungarians, Italians, and Russians) and Native Americans, Mexican Americans, and African Americans were inferior. This perspective, however, did not go unchallenged. African-American social scientists, in particular Horace Mann Bond, W. E. B. Du Bois, and Allison Davis, critiqued the studies that tried to prove African-American intellectual inferiority. Nevertheless, remnants of this belief continue to germinate within the academy, as exemplified by Richard J. Herrnstein and Charles H. Murray's 1996 book, *The Bell Curve.* For instance, in this book the authors assert that a major reason why some groups in society today do not achieve in schools might be connected more to rank-and-file notions of intellectual inferiority than to persistent economic, structural, cultural, and historic forces.

**Cultural deprivation.** Emanating out of the thrust to eradicate poverty in the United States and rejecting the geneticists' arguments, cultural deprivation theorists during the 1960s viewed academic differences on standardized measures as a result of nurture—or lack thereof—rather than nature. Proponents of cultural deprivation theories attributed the academic failure among some ethnic and racial minorities to the failure of some students' families to transmit the values and cultural patterns necessary for the students to achieve in mainstream academic institutions. The deprivation paradigm guided the formulation of most programs and pedagogies for low-income populations during the 1960s such as Head Start and other compensatory educational programs.

Considered enlightened during its time, cultural deprivation theorists believed that schools should assist low-income and racial and ethnic minority students in overcoming deficits caused by their families and communities; the best time to intervene was early childhood. A landmark Research Conference on Education and Cultural Deprivation convened in Chicago, Illinois, in 1964 and included participants such as Benjamin Bloom, Erik Erikson, Edmund Gordon, and Thomas Pettigrew. Influential books that focused on addressing the needs of the "culturally deprived" included *The Culturally Deprived Child,* by Frank Riessman, published in 1962; *Education in Depressed Areas,* edited in 1963 by A. Harry Passow; and *Compensatory Education for Cultural Deprivation,* edited in 1965 by Benjamin Bloom, Allison Davis, and Robert Hess.

**Cultural difference and learning styles.** Also during the 1960s, anthropologists began to challenge cultural deprivation theories by positing an alternative view of the academic failures of ethnic and racial minority students. This new group of theorists argued that the extent to which students learned or did not learn in schools reflected the cultural differences of the groups, which were either congruent with or incongruent with the dominant culture of schools. Building on this view, sociolinguists during the 1970s followed by asserting that differences in culture resulted in cultural and linguistic conflicts between students and their teachers, many of whom were white. This shifted part of the discourse from the notion that some groups' cultures were deficient toward the notion that cultures varied. An assumption, therefore, was that racially and ethnically diverse students' learning could be enhanced if there was cultural congruence or synchronization between the home and the school, and if the schooling experiences resonated with the unique cognitive or learning styles and cultural patterns of students.

Examples of the scholarship that documented this variation among cultures include Manuel Ramírez III and Alfredo Castañeda's 1974 book *Cultural Democracy, Bicognitive Development, and Education,* which describes Mexican-American students as field-dependent learners, in comparison to white students who are described as field independent. Native American and African-American students are also considered field-dependent learners. The research on African-American students' cognitive styles has generated much debate in the scholarly community. Significant scholarly contributions include Janice Hale-Benson's 1986 book, *Black Children: Their Roots, Culture, and Learning Styles;* Barbara J. Shade's 1982 article, "Afro-American Cognitive Styles: A Variable in School Success?"; and A. Wade Boykin's 1986 chapter, "The Triple Quandary and the Schooling of Afro-American Children." In general, these scholars assert that the instructional strategies used in schools do not work well with African-American students, and consequently, many do not experience academic success. Teaching strategies proposed to increase students' academic achievement include creating settings that are conducive to their learning styles such as cooperative environments, informal class discussions, a focus on larger concepts, and the de-emphasis of competition. Nevertheless, while these scholars find great value and potential in the research into learning styles for enhancing the achievement of students from diverse cultural backgrounds, Jacqueline Jordan Irvine and Darlene Eleanor York, in their exhaustive literature review from 1995, "Learning Styles and Culturally Diverse Students: A Literature Review," cautioned against using this body of research to automatically categorize students' styles of learning primarily on the basis of cultural characteristics.

Nevertheless, the cultural difference view of students' schooling experiences will remain a viable explanation because of an increasingly heterogeneous student population in which nonwhite students accounted for more than 30 percent of the school-age population at the end of the twentieth century. On the other hand, the teaching force in the United States is more than 90 percent white. Whereas proponents of the cultural difference paradigm would not assume that all white teachers are unable to teach these students, they would, however, continue to assert that for some students, this imbalance fos-

ters the kind of cultural incongruence that leads to school failure. The curriculum and the school environment serve as major areas in which this incongruence becomes manifested.

**Multicultural perspective.** With roots in the ethnic studies movement of the 1960s, multicultural education and cultural-centered approaches suggest infusing a multicultural ethos into schooling experiences, so as to reaffirm the social, cultural, and historical experiences of students from diverse cultural backgrounds. Though varied in the extent of the infusion and the scope of their critique of mainstream education, in general, multiculturalists such as James A. Banks, Geneva Gay, and Carl Grant, as well as proponents of ethnic-centered paradigms such as Molefi Asante (an advocate of Afrocentric education), assert that the European-American culture of schools distorts the history, culture, and background of students from non-European backgrounds. They note that the knowledge that school officials and society expect children to acquire often invalidates these students' cultural experiences. These scholars believe that an infusion of multicultural education and/or cultural-centered education can be part and parcel of the solution to improving the academic achievement of students from these diverse cultural backgrounds. They propose teaching students in ways that are culturally synchronized, culturally centered, empowering, and culturally relevant. This infusion would move beyond an additive approach and would transform the entire schooling experiences for students. Published sources that capture the arguments and critiques of multicultural and cultural-centered education include *Multicultural Education: Transformative Knowledge and Action,* edited by Banks and published in 1996, and *Handbook of Research on Multicultural Education,* edited by Banks and Cherry A. McGee Banks and published in 1995.

**Structural explanations.** Still another view subscribes to the notion that larger societal forces are key determinants of student learning, as are the cultural forces within a particular ethnic or racial community. For example, this view asserts that race, ethnicity, and culture are more likely to predict what educators and schools expect of students, rather than whether students will learn and achieve in schools. Proponents of this view note how some educators often create a self-fulfilling prophecy in relation to students from diverse racial and ethnic backgrounds: Teachers' expectations of students greatly shape student learning and achievement. Structural inequalities that can have deleterious consequences for students' learning may entail the limited access to knowledge and resources, the systematic denial of formal schooling, state-sanctioned discrimination, and gross disparities in the level of school funding. Moreover, proponents of this view assert that contemporary examples of structural inequalities include differential levels of quality teaching for some students, as well as the disproportionate placement of some racial and ethnic minority group members into the lowest academic tracks. African-American and Latino students are disproportionately placed in lower academic tracks, in comparison to white and Asian students. Jeannie Oakes's book on academic tracking, *Keeping Track: How Schools Structure Inequality,* published in 1985, and Kenneth J. Meier, Joseph Stewart Jr., and Robert E. England's 1989 book on second-generation discrimination, *Race, Class, and Education: The Politics of Second-Generation Discrimination,* were pivotal in bringing to light the structural inequalities embedded in schooling students from diverse racial and ethnic groups.

**Differing cultural expectations and the impact on school experiences.** Another position within this range of theories suggests that students' learning and achievement in schools reflect the values, beliefs, and traditions of some racial/ethnic groups, which may place a greater or lesser emphasis on achieving in the dominant educational context. John U. Ogbu's scholarship captures the essence of this view by asserting that the extent to which many members of some minority groups fail in mainstream schools can be linked to the way different minority groups enter into a society and, thereby, approach schooling. Ogbu's comparative research on immigrant and nonimmigrant minorities radically shifted the discourse by suggesting that a macro level of analysis should be considered when investigating why students from some minority groups achieve in school at greater rates than others.

Using a cultural ecological model to explain school failure, Ogbu developed a typology of ethnic groups based on the groups' entry into the dominant society: voluntary or immigrant minorities (which include Asian Americans, recent African immigrants, and immigrants from the Caribbean) and involuntary or nonimmigrant minority groups such as African Americans and Native Americans. In general, Ogbu noted that voluntary immigrant groups are more likely to accept the dominant achievement ideology, which holds the meritocratic view that hard work and motivation pay off. For example, although Asian-American students might come from different countries and also embrace cultural practices that starkly contrast with the dominant Anglo-American culture of schools, in general these students are more likely to be academically successful in the host society because of the way they approach the schooling process. On the other hand, students from nonimmigrant or involuntary minority groups are least likely to accept the dominant achievement model and are, therefore, more likely to resist schooling.

Building on Ogbu's theory were two 1986 publications: the highly cited article "Black Students' School Success: Coping with the Burden of Acting White," written by Signithia Fordham and Ogbu, and the book *To Be Popular or Smart: The Black Peer Group,* written by Jawanzaa Kunjufu. The latter work asserted that dominated (involuntary) minority groups develop secondary cultural characteristics as a resistive measure to a dominant white framework. Because of secondary cultural characteristics, some of these students do not achieve for fear of being labeled as trying to "act white." For many of these students, schooling becomes a culturally subtractive, rather than an additive, process.

Ogbu's thesis has been criticized as a "blaming the victim" approach because of its heavy emphasis on those factors and practices of the cultural group that contribute to school failure. Some scholars criticize Ogbu's model for being overly deterministic, note that it fails to capture the variation within groups, and assert that it overgeneralizes about some populations of students. In particular, Carla O'Connor posited in 1999 that ethnographic studies of involuntary immigrant groups (e.g., African-American students) should address the multiplicity of ways that students approach schooling, by also noting the heterogeneity that is present within social groups.

## The Future

The literature on how race, ethnicity, and culture affect the learning of students from non-European minority groups in the United States has overwhelmingly focused on school failure, rather than resilience. Nevertheless, an understanding of the various theoretical perspectives that have been used to explain the school performance of students from some racial and ethnic groups provides a backdrop for anticipating future schooling prospects for these children. The issues are complicated because notions of race, ethnicity, and culture are not static concepts and are not so easily definable. Therefore, proceeding with caution is essential when appropriating any one particular paradigm to explain how these concepts influence student learning. Clearly some paradigms can be dismissed, while others might be most appropriate given certain contexts. Nevertheless, the influence of race, ethnicity, and culture on students' schooling experiences will continue to be debated well into the twenty-first century.

*See also:* COMPENSATORY EDUCATION; INDIVIDUAL DIFFERENCES, *subentry on* ETHNICITY; LITERACY AND CULTURE; MULTICULTURAL EDUCATION; MULTICULTURALISM IN HIGHER EDUCATION.

## BIBLIOGRAPHY

BANKS, JAMES A., ed. 1996. *Multicultural Education, Transformative Knowledge, and Action: Historical and Contemporary Perspectives.* New York: Teachers College Press.

BANKS, JAMES A., and BANKS, CHERRY A. McGEE, eds. 1995. *Handbook of Research on Multicultural Education.* New York: Macmillan.

BLOOM, BENJAMIN; DAVIS, ALLISON; and HESS, ROBERT, eds. 1996. *Compensatory Education for Cultural Deprivation.* Chicago: University of Chicago.

BOYKIN, A. WADE. 1986. "The Triple Quandary and the Schooling of Afro-American Children." In *The School Achievement of Minority Children,* ed. Ulric Neisser. Hillsdale, NJ: Erlbaum.

FOLEY, DOUGLAS E. 1991. "Reconsidering Anthropological Explanations of School Failure." *Anthropology and Education Quarterly* 22:60–86.

FORDHAM, SIGNITHIA, and OGBU, JOHN U. 1986. "Black Students' School Success: Coping with the Burden of Acting White." *Urban Review* 18:176–206.

HALE-BENSON, JANICE E. 1986. *Black Children: Their Roots, Culture, and Learning Styles.* Baltimore: Johns Hopkins University Press.

HERRNSTEIN, RICHARD J., and MURRAY, CHARLES. 1996. *The Bell Curve: Intelligence and Class Structure in American Life.* New York: Simon and Schuster.

IRVINE, JACQUELINE JORDAN, and YORK, DARLENE ELEANOR. 1995. "Learning Styles and Culturally Diverse Students: A Literature Review." In *Handbook of Research on Multicultural Education,* ed. James A. Banks and Cherry A. McGee Banks. New York: Macmillan.

KUNJUFU, JAWANZAA. 1986. *To Be Popular or Smart: The Black Peer Group.* Chicago: African American Images.

MEIER, KENNETH J.; STEWART, JOSEPH, JR.; and ENGLAND, ROBERT E. 1989. *Race, Class, and Education: The Politics of Second-Generation Discrimination.* Madison: University of Wisconsin Press.

OAKES, JEANNIE. 1985. *Keeping Track: How Schools Structure Inequality.* New Haven, CT: Yale University Press.

O'CONNOR, CARLA. 1999. "Race, Class, and Gender in America: Narratives of Opportunity among Low-Income African American Youths." *Sociology of Education* 72:137–157.

OGBU, JOHN U. 1978. *Minority Education and Caste: The American System in Cross-Cultural Perspective.* New York: Academic Press.

OGBU, JOHN U. 1991. "Immigrant and Involuntary Minorities in Comparative Perspective." In *Minority Status and Schooling: A Comparative Study of Immigrant and Involuntary Minorities,* ed. John Ogbu and Margaret Gibson. New York: Garland.

OMI, MICHAEL, and WINANT, HOWARD. 1994. *Racial Formation in the United States,* 2nd edition. New York: Routledge.

PASSOW, A. HARRY, ed. 1963. *Education in Depressed Areas.* New York: New York Bureau of Publications, Teachers College, Columbia University.

RAMÍREZ, MANUEL, III, and CASTAÑEDA, ALFREDO. 1974. *Cultural Democracy, Bicognitive Development, and Education.* New York: Academic Press.

RIESSMAN, FRANK. 1962. *The Culturally Deprived Child.* New York: Harper.

SHADE, BARBARA J. 1982. "Afro-American Styles: A Variable in School Success?" *Review of Educational Research* 52:219–244.

TERMAN, LEWIS. 1916. *The Measure of Intelligence: An Explanation of and a Complete Guide for the Use of the Stanford Revision and Extension of the Binet-Simon Intelligence Scale.* Boston and New York: Houghton Mifflin.

WATERS, MARY C. 1990. *Ethnic Options: Choosing Identities in America.* Berkeley: University of California Press.

JEROME E. MORRIS

## LATINO GROWTH

The 2000 U.S. census counted 35.3 million Latinos in the fifty states (and counted 39.1 million if the Commonwealth of Puerto Rico is included). By 2010, the Latino population of the United States is projected to be 45.1 million, at which time this country will have a larger Spanish-speaking population than Spain, Colombia, or Argentina, and will trail only Mexico. By 2050, the U.S. Latino population is projected to be around 96.5 million, and one out of every four U.S. residents will be a Latino.

During the last half of the twentieth century, the Latino population was concentrated in nine states. In 2000, these nine states still had the largest Latino population (11.0 million in California, 6.7 million in Texas, 3.8 million in Puerto Rico, 2.9 million in New York, 2.7 million in Florida, 1.5 million in Illinois, 1.3 million in Arizona, 1.1 million in New Jersey, and 1.0 million in New Mexico), and 82 percent of all Latinos in the United States lived in those areas. However, Latino population growth has occurred in many states not traditionally thought of as Latino population strongholds, such as Georgia, Iowa, and Pennsylvania.

Most Latino population growth is due to births, rather than immigration. As a result, the school-age population in many areas will have a higher percentage of Latinos than the overall population. In California, 43.8 percent of all children age eighteen and under are Latino; 40.5 percent in Texas; 50.8 percent in New Mexico; and 36.1 percent in Arizona.

Immigration has been a secondary, but important, factor in Latino population growth. Some states such as California and Florida received a large number of Latino immigrants from 1960 through 2000, while others such as New Mexico and Colorado received relatively few.

### Educational Attainment

The educational attainment of the Latino population in 2000 was generally lower than non-Latino populations in the same area. Nationally, a lower percentage of Latino adults (57.0%) age twenty-five and older have graduated from high school, compared with 88.4 percent of non-Hispanic whites. However, the Latino figure needs to be taken with caution, for it combines the educational attainment of two very different Latino groups: the U.S.-born and immigrant Latino adults.

Generally, Latino immigrants have far lower educational attainment than U.S.-born Latinos. In the 1998 California Current Population Survey conducted by the U.S. Census, 75.1 percent of U.S.-born Latinos age twenty-five and older had graduated from high school, while only 38.1 percent of immigrant Latino adults had done so. In California, of Latino adults age 20 to 39, 62.2 percent are immigrants. Combining the educational attainment levels of both groups gives a blended picture that misses important educational dynamics: Latino immigrants tend to be young adults who do not immigrate to seek education, but to join the labor force. Hence, even though they have low educational levels, their behavior—high labor force participation, low welfare utilization, strong family formation—is not typical of high school dropouts. U.S.-born Latinos who do not complete high school are closer to the image of the high school dropout, in that their labor force participation is lower, welfare utilization rates higher, and family formation lower than immigrants with far lower educational levels.

### Language

U.S.-born Latinos are usually either monolingual English speaking or are bilingual, but with an ability to speak English very well. Immigrant Latinos usually start as monolingual Spanish speakers, but over the course of the years acquire some facility in English. School-age Latino children are overwhelmingly U.S.-born; 90.2 percent of Latino children age five through nine in California were U.S.-born in 2000. Not surprisingly, most Latino children speak English well, in addition to speaking Spanish. In the 1990 census, 85 percent of Latino children age five through seventeen in Los Angeles spoke English well, as did 87 percent of children in Miami, 86 percent of children in Chicago, 92 percent of children in San Antonio, and 88 percent of Latino children in New York.

While Latino children are predominantly U.S.-born, in states such as California, Texas, Florida, and New York, the parents are largely immigrant (in 2000, 62% of Latino children in California had at least one immigrant parent). These largely immigrant parents are less fluent in English. As measured by the 1990 census indicator of limited English proficiency (not to speak English at all, or not to speak it very well) in Latino adults age nineteen to sixty-four, 37 percent in Los Angeles, 35 percent in Miami, 32 percent in Chicago, and 28 percent in New York were not functional in English. Only in San Antonio were few parents—12 percent—not able to communicate well in English.

Latino parents want their children to learn English. A survey conducted in Los Angeles County in 2000 showed that 98 percent of U.S.-born Latino parents and 96 percent of immigrant Latino parents agreed that their children should be taught English in the schools. However, Latino parents also want their children to know how to speak Spanish. In the same Los Angeles county survey, 96 percent of U.S.-born Latino parents and 98 percent of immigrant Latino parents wanted their children to speak Spanish. Interestingly, 86 percent of non-Hispanic white parents and 90 percent of African-American parents also wanted their children to learn to speak Spanish. In that population-based survey, the only group that did not agree with the notion of children learning to speak Spanish were non-Hispanic whites who were not parents of children.

## Latinos and Race

The largely "mixed race" (or mestizo) Latino population has never fit comfortably into the U.S. biracial algorithm. In the 1930 census, Latinos of Mexican origin were considered a separate race, distinct from white, black, Indian, or Asian. Certainly, racial exclusion policy such as segregated schools, segregated public facilities, and restricted residential areas treated Latinos as a race. But in 1940, the Census Bureau reversed itself and counted Latinos as members of the white race. In spite of being classified racially as white, Latinos were still subject to racial restrictions.

In 1973 the Federal Office of Management and Budget developed a definition of the word *Hispanic* that was not a racial category, nor a national origin category, but a sui generis category, defined by the U.S. Census in 1993 as "those who indicated that their origin was Mexican, Puerto Rican, Cuban, Central or South American, or some other Hispanic origin." In the 1980 and 1990 censuses, a person had to chose first a racial category, then declare if he or she were Hispanic, in addition to the chosen racial category. In the 2000 census, all respondents were asked first to determine if they were Hispanic, then later to select a race, or combination of races. As La-

tinos may be any combination of Indian, European, African and Asian, the majority in many states (such as California) did not choose any of the racial categories offered (white, black, Indian, or Asian) but instead chose the residual category "Other," often writing in terms such as *mestizo* or "*raza*." In 1993 the U.S. census reported that "it should be noted that persons of Hispanic origin may be of any race." The Mexican author Carlos Fuentes best summed up the mestizo background of many Latinos when he described that he was "Indo-Afro-Ibero-American."

## Latinos and Culture

Modern Latino culture is the outgrowth of the meeting of indigenous, Iberian, African, and some Asian populations in most of the western hemisphere. The proportion of these elements varies from place to place in Latin America, with some regions more markedly indigenous (Mexico, Peru, Bolivia), others more markedly African (Dominican Republic, Puerto Rico, Cuba) others more markedly European (Argentina, Uruguay, Chile). Unlike the "Indian removal" policy followed in the United States, during the colonial period the Spanish Crown sought to incorporate indigenous populations into its realms, where they provided a population base for cultural development. The devastating smallpox epidemics of the sixteenth and seventeenth centuries reduced the native populations by nearly 95 percent. The hemisphere became gradually repopulated, but with an increasingly mestizo population that embodied a fusion of the various population, hence cultural, inputs. While Castilian Spanish was imposed as an official language spoken by a small ruling minority shortly after the Conquest, it is spoken by around 95 percent of residents of Latin America in the early twenty-first century, but with distinctive vocabulary and accents in various regions, again reflecting the process of cultural fusion unique to each region.

In the southwest United States, Latino culture antedated the arrival of Atlantic-American culture, hence the names of many towns are in Spanish, such as Los Angeles, San Antonio, Nogales, and Santa Fe. The meeting of Latino and Atlantic-American cultures in that region gave rise to the "cowboy culture," often considered worldwide to be the quintessential American image. In the northeast, Latino culture arrived during the last half of the twentieth century, along with the waves of immigrants from Latin America. Modern communications such as television, radio, telephones, coupled with a globalization of population made possible by modern transportation, allow Latino cultural regions in the United States to communicate with one another, with the rest of the hemisphere, and with Atlantic-American cultural communities.

While the expectation in the mid-twentieth century was that Latinos would assimilate as had other immigrant groups, the perhaps unique dynamics and nature of Latino culture (a culture of fusion) coupled with population and economic growth, makes it unlikely that it will simply disappear. Instead, it will likely have a two-way dialogue with Atlantic-American culture, which will probably result in some new cultural fusions wherever there are large Latino populations.

*See also:* BILINGUALISM, SECOND LANGUAGE LEARNING, AND ENGLISH AS A SECOND LANGUAGE; INDIVIDUAL DIFFERENCES, *subentry on* ETHNICITY; LANGUAGE AND EDUCATION; LANGUAGE MINORITY STUDENTS; LITERACY AND CULTURE; MULTICULTURAL EDUCATION; MULTICULTURALISM IN HIGHER EDUCATION.

### BIBLIOGRAPHY

U.S. CENSUS BUREAU. 1994. "The Hispanic Population in the United States: March 1993," *Current Population Reports, Population Characteristics,* Series P20-475. Washington, DC: U.S. Government Printing Office.

DAVID E. HAYES-BAUTISTA

## RACIAL AND ETHNIC MINORITY STUDENTS IN HIGHER EDUCATION

Since the 1960s, profound changes have occurred in minority-student patterns of college attendance and degree attainment in the United States. This change has led to a growing number of racial and ethnic minority students making up a considerable amount of the student population on American college campuses. In 1997 the National Center for Education Statistics (NCES) reported that African-American students, Hispanic students, Asian or Pacific Islander students, and Native American/Native Alaskan students constituted approximately 27 percent of the total college enrollment at degree-granting institutions. African-American students, Hispanic students, Asian or Pacific Islander students, and Native American /Native Alaskan students constituted 11

percent, 9 percent, 6 percent, and 1 percent, respectively, of all college students attending two-year and four-year institutions.

According to the U.S. Department of Education, the number of racial and ethnic minority students who were awarded degrees increased dramatically between the years of 1976 and 1998. Specifically, the number of bachelor's degrees awarded to racial and ethnic minority students increased as follows: African Americans, 58,636 to 98,132; Native American/ Native Alaskan students, 3,326 to 7,894; Asian or Pacific Islander students, 13,793 to 71,592; and Hispanic Americans, 18,743 to 65,937. In 1997, 19.4 percent of all bachelor's degrees were awarded to racial and ethnic minority students. In 1998, 20.5 percent of all bachelor's degrees were awarded to racial and ethnic minority students.

Due to the growth in racial and ethnic minority participation in higher education, institutions of higher learning are being asked to provide optimal learning environments, equitable admission standards, and a welcoming environment for students representing a variety of multicultural and ethnic backgrounds. To that end, colleges and universities are confronted with many complex issues, such as addressing the diverse academic and social needs of racial and ethnic minority students in higher education, improving the admission process to account for past legally sanctioned discrimination, helping minority students cope with issues they may face on campus, and offering suitable programs and instituting appropriate policies to help racial and ethnic minority students make successful transitions to college from high school.

### The Admissions Process for Racial and Ethnic Minority Students

To be sure, the admissions process for racial and ethnic minority students is similar to the admissions process for all students and includes such phases as making the initial decision to attend college, selecting the type of college to attend, and completing the necessary applications and admissions test required by the college or university. However, due to past racial discrimination and previous legal barriers, colleges and universities have had to consider innovative ways of trying to level the playing field in order to increase the number of racial and ethnic minority students in higher education—and to diversify the U.S. workforce to make it more representative of American society. Accordingly, colleges and universities have instituted two types of programs to aid in the enrollment of racial and ethnic minority students: enrollment programs and transition programs.

Enrollment programs are based on legislative mandates or statues (e.g., Civil Rights Act of 1964, Higher Education Act of 1965). Enrollment programs are primarily instituted to ensure that a percentage of college or university incoming enrollments are members of a racial or ethnic minority group. An example of an enrollment program is the education component of the One Florida Initiative, which mandates that 20 percent of each high school senior class in Florida will receive guaranteed admission to any of the state-supported colleges or universities in Florida. This enrollment program makes it possible to enroll racial and ethnic minority students from low-performing high schools, as well as students that may not otherwise gain admission to college.

Transition programs are defined as programs and related services designed to assist students who may not gain admittance to a college or university through traditional channels. The College Transition Program at Virginia Commonwealth University is an example of a summer transition program designed for high school students who have low scores on admission tests and low high school grade point averages. Transition programs, which enroll a large number of racial and ethnic minority students, also offer cultural enrichment activities that promote college readiness and social integration on campus. Though transition programs vary in type and length, most of them offer a study skills component and courses in mathematics, reading, and/or English composition, which gives students a jump-start on earning college credit. Students who complete a transition program at a particular university are usually guaranteed admission into that university. As such, transition programs also serve to increase the enrollment of racial and ethnic minority students by offering preparatory college instruction to students who may not otherwise be admitted to college.

## Issues Faced by Racial and Ethnic Minority Students on Campus

Prior to 1973, the overwhelming majority of African-American college students were enrolled in historically black colleges and universities. In the early twenty-first century, however, predominantly white institutions grant the majority of baccalaureate de-

grees awarded to African Americans (and other racial and ethnic minority students). This dramatic shift in postsecondary education patterns among minority students naturally leads to questions about their educational experiences and outcomes.

Racial and ethnic minority students face a considerable number of problems once they arrive on campus. Research evidence suggests that racial and ethnic minority students are more likely to experience problems of alienation, marginalization, and loneliness than white students are. Additional evidence suggests that these and other challenges on campus may have either a direct or indirect impact on their academic performance and social development. These students continue to be severely disadvantaged, relative to white students, in terms of persistence rates, academic achievement levels, enrollment in advanced degree programs, and overall psychological adjustments. Some other problems include monocultural curricula, professors' expectations and attitudes, cultural conflicts, institutional racism, lack of support services, isolation, and problems involving socialization and motivation. While college students of all races face many of these challenges, minority students face them in a compounded manner, resulting in higher dropout rates.

## Programs and Services for Racial and Ethnic Minority Students on Campus

Many services exist on college campuses to help facilitate a smooth transition for racial and ethnic minority students on campus. These services can be divided into two groups: campus-based programs and federally funded programs.

**Campus-based programs.** Inequality in higher educational attainment between different racial and ethnic groups continues to be a critical problem. Accordingly, many institutions have developed programs and implemented policies to address the academic and social challenges that many minority students encounter. Though it is the case that minority students are less likely to persist in college than white students are, the persistence gap can be traced to differences in legal discrimination and in the quality of secondary education of both groups. As a group, minority students are more likely to come from poorer backgrounds and have experienced inferior education than their white counterparts. This is not to suggest that all racial and ethnic minority students are disadvantaged, or that all disadvantaged students are members of racial and ethnic minority groups. Some racial and ethnic minority groups (e.g., Asian Americans) have higher rates of educational success than do groups commonly classified as belonging to the ethnic and racial majority. Thus, it is sometimes necessary for institutions to develop programs targeted to the needs of distinct groups of students.

Early contact and transition programs are important not only because they help cement personal affiliations that tie students into the fabric of student culture, but also because they enable the students to acquire useful information about the informal character of institutional life. Thus, to ensure successful programs, it is critical that institutions integrate programs and services within the mainstream of the institution's academic, social, and administrative life. One important component to successful retention programs for racial and ethnic minority students is the establishment of specialized advising and counseling services. Several institutions have established advising programs and designated offices to which racial and ethnic minority students go for many different services. An example of such a program is the New Vision Program at the University of New Orleans. This retention program focuses on academically at-risk students and students who have not met the university's academic standards and subsequently left the institution. To increase graduation and retention rates, these students are allowed to re-enroll at the University of New Orleans and participate in special academic development programs that offer advising sessions, orientations, and instructional assistance.

Having counselors and advisers of like ethnicity is not a requirement of these programs; however, experience has shown that racial and ethnic minority students are inclined to utilize these services when people of color are present. To the degree that racial and ethnic minority students represent a distinct minority on campus, they also face distinct problems in seeking to become integrated into the life of what may appear to be a foreign and hostile college community. The use of support programs and mentor programs has proven to be quite effective in increasing student retention. In many cases, these programs are designed to provide racial and ethnic minority students with faculty mentors or advisers who can provide useful information and advice. In other instances, faculty, and sometimes upper-class students, of similar ethnicity are asked to guide newly arrived racial and ethnic minority students through

the institution, or at least through the first year of college. For example, ALANA—which is an acronym for Asian, Latin, African, and Native American—is a mentoring program developed at St. Clair County Community College in Port Huron, Michigan. This multifaceted support program focuses on providing academic and social support to freshman students of color through the use of peer mentors.

Many of the challenges that racial and ethnic minority students face on a predominantly white campus reflect the behaviors and attitudes that the students, faculty, and staff have about them. For that reason, an increasing number of institutions have instituted programs designed to educate the broader community on issues of racism and the diversity of cultural traditions that mark American life. Some institutions have even established programs to broaden the repertoire of teaching skills faculty use in the education of diverse student bodies. For example, the Center for Research on Learning and Teaching at the University of Michigan offers consulting services, seminars, and workshops to faculty members who seek to learn more about how to integrate multiculturalism in the college classroom and how to develop a welcoming and inclusive learning environment. Realizing the many possible categories of institutional types, there is much to be gained from understanding how similar types of institutions have successfully addressed the issue of retention. However, it falls upon the individual institution to assess for itself the most effective approach. The beginning point of any institutional policy consists of an assessment of institutional mission and institutional priorities, as well as an assessment of racial and ethnic minority students' experiences on campus.

**Federally funded programs.** There are many types of proactive intervention strategies for racial and ethnic minority students. Some are long-term; others focus on the first-year experience. Many of these programs seek to encourage capable students to pursue postsecondary degrees. One such initiative is the federally supported Upward Bound program, established in 1965. Upward Bound was designed to help disadvantaged students enroll in and graduate from postsecondary institutions. A product of the Economic Opportunity Act of 1964, Upward Bound targets youth between thirteen and nineteen years of age who have experienced low academic success. High school students from low-income families whose parents have not earned a bachelor's degree and military veterans with only a high school diploma are eligible to participate. The program provides fundamental support, such as help with the college admissions process and assistance in preparing for college entrance examinations. It engages students in an extensive, multiyear program designed to provide academic, counseling, and tutoring services, along with a cultural enrichment component—all of which enhance their regular school program prior to entering college.

Most Upward Bound programs also provide participants with college experience through a five- to eight-week, full-time residential summer program at a postsecondary institution. The summer experience is reinforced with weekly tutorial and mentoring services during the school year. Upward Bound, along with four other federal initiatives that are collectively called the *TRIO programs,* receive funding under Title IV of the Higher Education Act of 1965. Upward Bound currently supports more than 560 projects serving approximately 41,000 students nationwide. The other TRIO initiatives are Talent Search, the Student Support Services program, Educational Opportunity Centers, and the Ronald E. McNair Postbaccalaureate Achievement program. These programs have much to offer institutions of higher education that seek to improve the educational outcomes of first-generation college students, racial and ethnic minority students, and low-income students.

Taken as a whole, the demographic in institutions of higher education has been changing and becoming increasingly more diverse. There is still a great need for innovative programming and policies to provide realistic guidance and counseling to assist minority students in dealing with academic, social, and economic challenges in college. Minority students come from different backgrounds with different orientations, ideologies, and perspectives—and with different perceptions of success and failure. When institutions properly recognize these differences and deal with them constructively, then they will be better able to address the problems faced by racial and ethnic minority students.

*See also:* ADJUSTMENT TO COLLEGE; AFFIRMATIVE ACTION COMPLIANCE IN HIGHER EDUCATION; COLLEGE STUDENT RETENTION; LANGUAGE MINORITY STUDENTS; MULTICULTURALISM IN HIGHER EDUCATION; UPWARD BOUND.

## BIBLIOGRAPHY

ALLEN, WALTER R., and HANIFF, NESHA Z. 1991. "Race, Gender, and Academic Performance in U.S. Higher Education." In *College in Black and White: African American Students in Predominantly White and in Historically Black Public Universities,* ed. Walter R. Allen, Edgar G. Epps, and Nesha Z. Haniff. Albany: State University of New York Press.

ANDERSON, JAMES D. 1988. *The Education of Blacks in the South, 1860–1935.* Chapel Hill: University of North Carolina Press.

BENNETT, CHRISTINE I. 2001. "Research on Racial Issues in American Higher Education." In *Handbook of Research on Multicultural Education,* ed. James A. Banks and Cherry A. McGee Banks. San Francisco: Jossey-Bass.

FLEMING, JACQUELINE. 1984. *Blacks in College: A Comparative Study of Students' Success in Black and in White Institutions.* San Francisco: Jossey-Bass.

HOSSLER, DON; BRAXTON, JOHN; and COOPERSMITH, GEORGIA. 1989. "Understanding College Choice." In *Higher Education: Handbook of Theory and Research,* Vol. 5, ed. John C. Smart. New York: Agathon.

LANG, MARVEL, and FORD, CLINITA A. 1988. *Black Student Retention in Higher Education.* Springfield, IL: Charles C. Thomas.

MCELROY, EDWARD J., and ARMESTO, MARIA. 1998. "TRIO and Upward Bound: History, Programs, and Issues: Past, Present, and Future." *Journal of Negro Education* 67(4):373–380.

TINTO, VINCENT. 1993. *Leaving College: Rethinking the Causes and Cures of Student Attrition.* Chicago: University of Chicago Press.

WALKER, DAVID A., and SCHULTZ, ANN M. 2001. "Reaching for Diversity: Recruiting and Retaining Mexican-American Students." *Journal of College Student Retention* 2(4):313–325.

ZULLI, REBECCA A.; FRIERSON, HENRY T., JR.; and CLAYTON, JOYCE D. 1998. "Parents' Perceptions of the Value and Nature of Their Children's and Their Own Involvement in an Upward Bound Program." *Journal of Negro Education* 67(4):364–372.

SHEDERICK A. MCCLENDON
LAMONT A. FLOWERS

# RANKINGS, COLLEGE

*See:* College Rankings.

# READABILITY INDICES

For several decades researchers have been concerned with the question of determining how easy or difficult a text will be for a particular reader to comprehend. For example, if a teacher is assigning a textbook to an eighth-grade class, how would the teacher determine whether the class will actually comprehend the book? Writers may also want to consider the comprehensibility of their texts during the writing and revision process. To address these goals, researchers have developed readability indices, which are tools or methods that provide assessments of the comprehensibility of texts. The term *readability indices* has also been used to describe the legibility of writing or the interest value of texts, but these aspects of readability will not be discussed here. The most effective readability indices for assessing comprehensibility are those that take into account how people actually go about processing the information in texts.

## Readability Formulas

Beginning in the 1920s, many efforts were undertaken to describe the readability of texts in terms of objective characteristics that could be measured and analyzed. First, researchers tabulated surface characteristics of written texts that may be related to how difficult the texts would be to comprehend. Some examples of these characteristics are the difficulty or frequency of the words in a text, the average number of syllables per word, and measures of the length or complexity of sentences. These data were then compared with predetermined standards, such as the average grade level of students who could correctly answer a certain percentage of questions generated from the text passage. Text characteristics that provided the most accurate predictions of the standards were judged to be indices of readability. These characteristics were then developed into readability formulas, which were equations that specified how much weight to assign to each characteristic. Probably the most widely used readability formula was one of Rudolf Flesch's, which used the number of syllables per 100 words and the average number of words per sentence.

Readability formulas also gained favor as guidelines for revising texts to improve comprehensibility. The Flesch formula, for example, implies that texts can be made more comprehensible by using shorter words and shorter sentences. Such guidelines have been used in many contexts and are appealing at least in part because they provide concrete feedback and can be automated. The value of readability formulas is limited, however, because these surface characteristics do not *cause* texts to be easy or difficult to comprehend. Long words and sentences simply happen to be typical characteristics of texts that are hard to comprehend. This limitation is particularly problematic when considering text revision. In fact, George R. Klare, in a 1963 book titled *The Measurement of Readability,* reviewed efforts to improve comprehensibility by revising texts to lower the readability scores, and he found this method to be ineffective.

## Readability and Comprehension Processes

Since the 1970s, researchers have made great advances in understanding the psychological processes that are involved in reading, and thus the factors that make a text comprehensible. As readers take in information from a text, they attempt to construct a coherent mental representation of the information. Semantic and causal coherence are critical factors that contribute to this process. When current text information is not coherent with previous text information, a reader must generate an inference in order to make sense out of the new information. More coherent texts require fewer inferences and are therefore easier to comprehend. Walter Kintsch and colleagues developed an index of semantic coherence based on the extent to which concepts are repeated across sentences. Tom Trabasso and colleagues have indexed events in a text according to the extent to which they are integral to the causal structure described in the text. Both of these indices of coherence are highly predictive of comprehension. In addition, generating inferences requires readers to use their own knowledge, such that readers with a lot of relevant knowledge will find texts more readable than readers with little knowledge. Readability is therefore not just determined by the text itself but is a product of the interaction between the text and reader.

Semantic and causal indices of readability can also be effectively used in revising texts to make them more readable. According to their 1991 article

Bruce K. Britton and Sami Gülgöz revised a textbook passage by repairing semantic coherence breaks (which incidentally did not alter the readability formula score). In another revision, they shortened words and sentences to lower the score on readability formulas. Comprehension improved for the coherence revision but not for the readability revision, indicating that readability indices based on psychological processes provide better guidance for revision than readability formulas.

Although textual coherence and reader knowledge can be effective readability indices, they are quite labor intensive to analyze and are impractical for use with long texts. Thomas Landauer and his colleagues, however, developed a computer model that provides a potential solution to this problem: Latent Semantic Analysis (LSA) estimates the semantic similarity of words and sets of words derived from their use in the context of large amounts of natural language. As reported in a 1998 article, Peter W. Foltz, Landauer, and Kintsch used LSA to assess the semantic coherence of texts by calculating the similarity between adjacent sentence pairs. The LSA model showed very high correlations between semantic coherence and comprehension, thereby suggesting an automatic measure of readability based on coherence. LSA has also been used to automatically assess knowledge about a particular topic by calculating the similarity between the content of short essays and standard texts on the topic. These LSA knowledge assessment scores were also predictive of comprehension, according to a 1998 article by Michael B. W. Wolfe and colleagues. LSA can therefore provide readability indices related both to the coherence of a text itself and to the interaction between the text and the knowledge of a particular reader.

In order to be truly useful, a readability index should be grounded in the psychological processes of reading. The LSA model represents a promising new technique for determining the readability of texts because it has psychological validity and can be automated. Nevertheless, LSA has not yet been developed into a practical index of readability for particular texts and readers. Only further testing on a broad range of texts and readers will reveal its potential.

*See also:* READING, *subentry on* COMPREHENSION.

## BIBLIOGRAPHY

BRITTON, BRUCE K., and GÜLGÖZ, SAMI. 1991. "Using Kintsch's Computational Model to Improve Instructional Text: Effects of Repairing Inference Calls on Recall and Cognitive Structures." *Journal of Educational Psychology* 83:329–345.

FLESCH, RUDOLF. 1948. "A New Readability Yardstick." *Journal of Applied Psychology* 32:221–233.

FOLTZ, PETER W.; KINTSCH, WALTER; and LANDAUER, THOMAS K. 1998. "The Measurement of Textual Coherence with Latent Semantic Analysis." *Discourse Processes* 25:285–307.

KLARE, GEORGE R. 1963. *The Measurement of Readability.* Ames: Iowa State University Press.

LORCH, ROBERT F., and O'BRIEN, EDWARD J., eds. 1995. *Sources of Coherence in Reading.* Hillsdale, NJ: Erlbaum.

MILLER, JAMES R., and KINTSCH, WALTER. 1980. "Readability and Recall of Short Prose Passages: A Theoretical Analysis." *Journal of Experimental Psychology: Human Learning and Memory* 6:335–354.

WOLFE, MICHAEL B. W.; SCHREINER, M. E.; REHDER, BOB; LAHAM, DARRELL; FOLTZ, PETER W.; KINTSCH, WALTER; and LANDAUER, THOMAS K. 1998. "Learning from Text: Matching Readers and Texts by Latent Semantic Analysis." *Discourse Processes* 25:309–336.

MICHAEL B. W. WOLFE

# READING

VALUE OF READING ENGAGEMENT FOR CHILDREN
Anne Cunningham

# BEGINNING READING

Beginning reading encompasses acquisition of the multiple acts, skills, and knowledge that enable individuals to comprehend the meaning of text. Reading is a complex psycholinguistic activity and thus beginning reading is a lengthy and complex process whereby the learner acquires expertise in the various perceptual, sensory, linguistic, cognitive, metacognitive, and social skills that are involved in literate behavior. Through this process the child gains functional knowledge of the purposes, uses, and principles of the writing system.

## Experiences before Formal Reading Instruction

Although a large portion of literacy acquisition occurs within the context of formal reading instruction, literacy-related awareness and knowledge start developing long before formal schooling, through pre-reading activities and interactions with print in the home and environment. The accomplishments before formal schooling prepare the child for later school-related literacy development.

There are important differences among children's early literacy experiences. Some children are exposed to a wide array of early literacy experiences. They are frequently and regularly read to, they are exposed to oral and written language activities such as playing on the computer or playing word games, they experience the functional use of print materials in their home and preschool environments, and they have model adults who value reading and use reading in various purposeful ways. In 1990 Marilyn J. Adams estimated that children from these mainstream homes are exposed to thousands of hours of pre-reading activities before they enter first grade. In contrast, there are children who are never or rarely read to, live in homes with few books, are rarely exposed to rich oral and written language activities, and interact with few adult models who use reading and writing for their own purposes. These two groups of children differ widely in their awareness and knowledge of literacy-related concepts.

**Concepts about print.** Through repeated interactions with literacy materials and activities children develop an awareness of the nature and function of text. Social routines practiced during one-on-one book reading between parents and children facilitate children's acquisition of concepts about print. Very early on children learn about the way books are handled, the differences between pictures and print, the directionality of print, and the characteristics of written-language-like routines. Shared book reading allows children to develop a sense of story structure where characters, the setting, and the plot make up the story. By observing adults' functional use of literacy, children also learn the different purposes of different literacy activities such as writing a grocery list versus writing a letter. So, by the time they are four years old, children also learn quite a lot about the nature of print, including the names and sounds of some letters, and will pretend to "write" by scribbling as part of play activities.

The acquisition of the concepts about print is important, and several studies have shown that such awareness predicts future reading achievement and is correlated with other measures of reading achievement. Thus, the development of concepts about print early in life seems to create the foundation upon which more sophisticated skills are built.

**Language development.** Spoken language develops naturally and effortlessly within the context of social interactions in a community. With the exception of those who have some physical challenges all children can produce and comprehend spoken language naturally early in life. They exhibit developments in phonology, morphology, syntax, semantics, and vocabulary. Engagement in literacy activities provides children with added opportunities to experience and experiment with language. Book reading, for instance, offers multiple opportunities for the child to use language at a more abstract and complex level than would be possible through spoken language experiences. Children learn to have a decreased reliance on immediate context for communication. This decontextualized language is the language that they will need to rely on in most school activities later on. Early literacy experiences also set the ground for growth in meta-linguistic skills. Children learn to think about, play with, talk about, and analyze language in addition to using it effectively.

**Phonological awareness.** Alphabetical writing systems are based on the representation of speech sounds by letters. In order to understand the alphabetic principle, children need to be aware that the spoken message can be broken down into smaller units such as words, syllables, and phonemes. Phonological awareness is the awareness of and the ability to manipulate phonological segments such as syllables, phonemes, and other intrasyllabic units such as onset-rimes in words. When phonological awareness refers to children's sensitivity to the phonemes in words, it is called phonemic awareness.

Tasks in which children are asked to isolate, segment, blend, or combine phonological segments have been typically used to assess phonological awareness. Phonemic segmentation and phonemic manipulation tasks yield particularly strong predictions of and correlations with beginning reading acquisition. There are also studies on phonemic awareness that point out that there is a bidirectional relationship between learning to read and phonemic awareness.

While studies on children's early experiences with print converge on the conclusion that these experiences and phonological awareness facilitate and set the ground for further development in the acquisition of reading, other research has investigated the relationship between IQ and reading achievement. These studies conclude that IQ is only weakly related to early reading achievement.

## Instruction in Reading

Children are immersed in formal instruction in reading once they enter kindergarten. Children come to school with different levels of awareness about print, and they encounter in school new expectations, new routines, and new experiences that dramatically broaden their concept of literacy. For children whose language and literacy experiences are closer to those in the school setting, this transition to school is relatively easy.

**Understanding the alphabetic principle.** Before formal instruction in reading begins, children can already recognize certain words, especially those occurring frequently in their environment, such as Coca-Cola or McDonald's. Nevertheless, a 1984 study by Patricia E. Masonheimer and colleagues investigating the features to which children attend to when they recognize these words showed that when the words were presented without the contextual cues, such as logos, most children up to five years of age failed to correctly identify them. Other studies also suggest that young children recognize words based on selective parts of the printed word. Thus, before formal reading instruction has begun, most young children cannot grasp how the writing system functions.

A dramatic change occurs when children are exposed to systematic reading instruction. Before they

begin to decode independently, children start using the phonetic values of letter names in identifying words. Although this is not yet an efficient word recognition strategy, it is a big step toward using the systematic relationships that exist between speech and the printed word. Full decoding becomes possible when children begin to use the full array of letters in words and map them unto phonemes, thus demonstrating an understanding of the alphabetic principle.

**Productivity and automaticity in word recognition.** It is not possible to characterize children's reading as productive unless they can recognize words that they have not encountered before. As children experience a growing number of letter patterns during reading, they gradually accumulate a large number of orthographic representations. Thus, instead of using single letters for word recognition they begin relying on letter strings and their corresponding phonologies. This growing knowledge of letter sequences and spelling patterns gradually allows readers to process words quickly and easily.

Every time a reader encounters a spelling pattern and attends to the particular sequence of letters in it, the pattern acquires more strength and is thus recognized faster and more efficiently during the next encounter. If on the other hand instead of focusing on the entire sequence, the reader's concentration is focused on resolving a single letter, or if one or some of the letters in the sequence cannot be correctly identified, the sequence may not be remembered as an entity. As the young reader's knowledge of the relationships between spelling and sound grows, this knowledge allows the child to form stronger associations between visual and phonological representations. Through experience with words in print, especially those of increasing complexity, word recognition becomes an automatic psychological process, enabling the reader to gain increasing levels of fluency. Thus, differences in exposure to print lead to differences in reading skill.

**Comprehension.** Reading comprehension is a complex skill that requires an active interaction between text elements and the reader. Since comprehension of text is the ultimate goal in reading, understanding comprehension processes is critical to the study of beginning reading.

Children beginning to read already have a well-developed system for oral language comprehension. By the end of preschool most children have well-developed vocabulary and world knowledge as well as morphological, semantic, and syntactic processes that make oral language comprehension possible.

There is considerably less research on comprehension processes in beginning readers, compared to studies on word processing. One of the consistent findings in comprehension research is that compared to more skilled comprehenders, unskilled comprehenders are also less skilled in decoding. In fact, during the early stages of beginning reading, text comprehension is limited to children's skill in decoding. Until decoding processes are rapid and efficient, high-level comprehension processes are severely limited. There is now converging evidence that for both children and adults, difficulties in comprehension are related to difficulties in decoding as well as to problems with working memory.

Besides being better at decoding, skilled comprehenders also have better global language skills than less skilled comprehenders. Studies have shown a causal relationship between vocabulary and comprehension. There is evidence showing that vocabulary instruction leads to gains in comprehension and improvement on semantic tasks. It is also clear that both direct and indirect instruction in vocabulary lead to comprehension gains.

Skilled comprehenders also have better metacognitive skills than less skilled comprehenders. Skilled comprehenders are aware of how well they are comprehending and use various comprehension strategies that guide them as they attempt to understand text.

Young readers benefit from cognitive strategy instruction. Instruction in cognitive strategies usually involves helping students be aware of their own cognitive processes in reading. Usually a teacher either models the use of comprehension strategies or guides the students in the use of strategies. Many approaches to cognitive strategy instruction allow readers to practice their newly acquired cognitive strategies with the teacher until the readers master their use.

In short, beginning reading instruction needs to focus on children's acquisition of letter-sound relationships, as well as comprehension strategies to assure that both word recognition and comprehension skills can develop simultaneously.

*See also:* CHILDREN'S LITERATURE; LANGUAGE ACQUISITION; LITERACY, *subentry on* EMERGENT LIT-ERACY; LITERACY AND CULTURE; LITERACY AND READING; READING, *subentry on* TEACHING OF.

## BIBLIOGRAPHY

ADAMS, MARILYN J. 1990. *Beginning to Read: Thinking and Learning about Print.* Cambridge, MA: MIT Press.

CLAY, MARIE M. 1979. *The Early Detection of Reading Difficulties,* 3rd edition. Portsmouth, NH: Heinemann.

GOUGH, PHILIP B., and JUEL, CONNIE. 1991. "The First Stages of Word Recognition." In *Learning to Read,* ed. Laurence Rieben and Charles A. Perfetti. Hillsdale, NJ: Erlbaum.

LIBERMAN, ISABEL Y.; SHANKWEILER, DONALD; FISCHER, F. WILLIAM; and CARTER, BONNIE. 1974. "Explicit Syllable and Phoneme Segmentation in Young Children." *Journal of Experimental Child Psychology* 18:201–212.

LOMAX, RICHARD G., and McGEE, LEA M. 1987. "Young Children's Concepts about Print and Reading: Toward a Model of Reading Acquisition." *Reading Research Quarterly* 22:237–256.

MASONHEIMER, PATRICIA E.; DRUM, PRISCILLA A.; and EHRI, LINNEA C. 1984. "Does Environmental Print Identification Lead Children into Word Reading?" *Journal of Reading Behavior* 16:257–271.

MEDO, MARY A., and RYDER, RANDALL J. 1993. "The Effects of Vocabulary Instruction on Readers' Ability to Make Causal Connections." *Reading Research and Instruction* 33:119–134.

PALINSCAR, ANNEMARIE S., and BROWN, ANN. 1984. "Reciprocal Teaching of Comprehension-Monitoring Activities." *Cognition and Instruction* 2:117–175.

PARIS, SCOTT G.; SAARNIO, DAVID A.; and CROSS, DAVID R. 1986. "A Metacognitive Curriculum to Promote Children's Reading and Learning." *Australian Journal of Psychology* 38:107–123.

PERFETTI, CHARLES A. 1985. *Reading Ability.* New York: Oxford University Press.

SHARE, DAVID L. 1995. "Phonological Recoding and Self-Teaching: Sine Qua Non of Reading Acquisition." *Cognition* 55:151–218.

SNOW, CATHERINE E., and NINIO, ANAT. 1986. "Contracts of Literacy: What Children Learn from Learning to Read Books." In *Emergent Literacy: Writing and Reading,* ed. Elizabeth Sulzby and William H. Teale. Norwood, NJ: Ablex.

STANOVICH, KEITH E.; CUNNINGHAM, ANNE E.; and FREEMAN, D. J. 1984. "Intelligence, Cognitive Skills, and Early Reading Progress." *Reading Research Quarterly* 19:278–303.

STANOVICH, KEITH E., and WEST, RICHARD F. "Exposure to Print and Orthographic Processing." *Reading Research Quarterly* 24:402–433.

SULZBY, ELISABETH, and TEALE, WILLIAM H. 1991. "Emergent Literacy." In *Handbook of Reading Research,* ed. Rebecca Barr, Michael L. Kamil, Peter Mosenthal, and P. David Pearson. New York: Longman.

BANU ÖNEY

# COMPREHENSION

From 1997 to 2000 the National Reading Panel (NRP) carried out a review of research-based knowledge about reading and instruction, especially in the early elementary grades. The research topics relevant to early reading and instruction that the NRP concentrated on were phonemic awareness instruction, phonics instruction, fluency, vocabulary instruction, text comprehension instruction, teacher preparation, and comprehension strategies instruction.

The group that focused on text comprehension instruction located more than 500 studies on the teaching of comprehension instruction. Using scientific criteria such as whether a study of a strategy instruction included a control group, they found that just over 200 of these studies were conducted sufficiently well to be confident that the conclusions based on them are scientifically trustworthy.

Comprehension strategy instruction fosters active reading. The strategies are designed to guide a reader to become more self-aware of one's self-understanding during reading, to become more in control of that understanding, to create images related to contents, to make graphic representations, to write summaries, and to answer or to make up questions. Depending on what type it is, a strategy can be implemented *before, during,* or *after* the reading of a text.

Skilled readers may invent strategies that help them understand and remember what they read. Most readers, however, do not spontaneously invent these strategies. Unless they are explicitly taught to apply cognitive procedures they are not likely to learn, develop, or use them. Readers at all levels, in fact, can benefit from explicit comprehension strategy instruction. A teacher begins by demonstrating or modeling a strategy. In some cases, the instruction is *reciprocal* or *transactional,* meaning that the teacher first performs the procedures and then the students gradually learn to implement them on their own. The process by which a student adopts the strategy—a process that is called "scaffolding"—is often a gradual one. Readers are first able to experience the construction of meaning by an expert reader, the teacher. As readers learn to take control of their own reading by practicing and acquiring cognitive strategy procedures, they gradually internalize the strategies and achieve independent mastery.

## History of Comprehension Strategy Instruction

Interest in reading comprehension strategies began to grow as a part of the new scientific understanding of cognition that emerged in the latter decades of the twentieth century. In 1978 Walter Kintsch and Teun A. van Dijk observed that a reader is an active participant with a text and that a reader "makes sense" of how ideas based on the text relate to one another by interpretive interactions between what the reader gleans from the text and what the reader already knows. They proposed that a reader actively builds meaning as *mental representations* and stores them as semantic interpretations held in memory during reading. These representations enable the reader to remember and use what had been read and understood.

In a landmark 1979 study Ellen M. Markman wondered whether readers would detect obvious logical contradictions in passages they read. She gave readers a passage about ants that indicated that when ants forage away from their hill they emit an invisible chemical with an odor that they use to find their way home. The passage also indicated, however, that ants have no nose and are unable to smell. Would readers notice that the passage did not make sense? Would they recognize that they did not understand the passage? What would they do? Her disturbing finding was that young and mature readers alike overwhelmingly failed to notice either logical or semantic inconsistencies in the texts. What instruction would help readers to be more conscious of their understanding and to learn strategies that would overcome these comprehension failures?

At about the same time Dolores Durkin observed reading instruction in fourth-grade classrooms over the course of a school year. For many student readers, fourth grade is a transition year from "learning to read" to "reading to learn." In a 1979 article Durkin reported that there was very little comprehension instruction in the classrooms. Teachers assigned questions and told students about content. But in seventy-five hours of reading instruction Durkin observed that year, teachers devoted only twenty minutes, less than 1 percent of the time, to teaching readers how to comprehend and learn new information from reading. Her studies and the others cited above anticipated an intense interest in helping students learn strategies to comprehend and learn from reading.

In the 1970s and early 1980s investigators generally focused on teaching an individual strategy to help readers construct meaning. There were literally hundreds of studies of individual comprehension strategies. One example is Abby Adams and colleagues' 1982 research applying the SQ3R (survey, question, read, recite, and review) technique to fifth-grade classrooms. SQ3R is a text pre-reading *graphic organizer* instruction developed in 1941 for World War II military personnel undergoing accelerated courses. It is considered a "text previewing" comprehension strategy instruction in that it guides readers to look for the meaning *before* reading the text. In this instruction, readers learn to use the text's headings, subheads, introductions, and summaries to construct graphic schemata of the text content. As did many of the other comprehension strategy instruction researchers, Adams and her colleagues obtained positive results, finding that students with the pre-reading instruction performed significantly higher on factual short-answer tests than did control group students.

Generally, many types of individual comprehension strategy instructions appeared to be successful in improving readers' ability to construct meaning from text. With the observed success of various individual strategy applications, there were several reviews of this growing body of scientific literature. In 1983 P. David Pearson and Margaret C. Gallagher categorized cognitive strategies by what teachers do to teach the strategies, and Robert J. Tierney and James W. Cunningham's 1984 review subdivided the cognitive strategies into pre-reading, during-reading, and post-reading activities.

With the success of individual strategy instruction in improving reading comprehension measures documented by research, focus shifted to using combinations of strategies to facilitate text comprehension, primarily in experimental situations rather than in natural classrooms. Among these was a very influential 1984 study of "reciprocal teaching" of comprehension by Annemarie S. Palincsar and Ann L. Brown. Reciprocal teaching is a method that involves the gradual release of responsibility for carrying out a strategy to the readers. It combines teacher modeling and student practice on four cognitive strategies: prediction, clarifying, summarizing, and question generation. Students who received this instruction showed marked improvement on a number of comprehension measures.

Success of teaching multiple strategies led to the study of the effectiveness of preparing teachers to teach comprehension strategies in natural, classroom settings. Two approaches are noteworthy, namely Gerald G. Duffy and Laura R. Roehler's 1987 direct explanation model and Rachel Brown, Michael Pressley, and colleagues' 1996 transactional instruction approach. Direct explanation emphasizes teacher-directed problem solving, whereas transactional instruction, similar to reciprocal teaching, employs teacher-directed actions with interactive exchanges with students in classrooms. Both direct and transactional approaches to training teachers have produced positive results.

**Strategies that Work**

The NRP identified twelve categories of comprehension instruction that have scientific support for the conclusion that they help readers to construct meaning and thereby improve reading comprehension, including two categories involving the preparation of teachers in cognitive strategy instruction. These strategies stimulate both audio and visual perception, activate memory and semantic processing, enhance perception, engage syntactic knowledge and processing, teach narrative structure, and promote reasoning. The strategies of active listening, comprehension monitoring, and prior knowledge use all serve to promote listening and awareness of one's thinking or "inner speech," a process emphasized by the Russian psychologist Lev Vygotsky in the 1920s. Mental imagery, mnemonic, and graphic organizer instruction, on the other hand, make use of readers' visual imagination and memory. Vocabulary instruction increases word and semantic knowledge and problem solving. Question answering and question generation require the access of what is known or understood and the prediction of future events. Story structure and summarization instruction create awareness of the organization of ideas and what is important. Finally, multiple strategy instruction combines the use of several of these processes together in flexible and appropriate ways. Research conducted in the late 1990s also suggests that teachers can learn to integrate these kinds of strategy instructions in classroom settings and that peers working in cooperative learning situations can effectively tutor each other in comprehension strategies.

**Active listening.** To instruct active listening, teachers guide readers in learning to listen while others read. The listening reader follows the text as another student reads aloud. The teacher may also pose questions for the readers to answer while they listen. Active-listening training improves listening and reading comprehension. It increases a reader's participation in discussions, engenders more thoughtful responses to questions, increases memory for the text, and focuses the reader's attention and interest on material. For example, in Gloria M. Boodt's 1984 study of training critical-listening strategies with fourth-grade to sixth-grade remedial readers, there was a gradual increase over the eighteen weeks of the study in students' willingness to participate in group discussions and provide more thoughtful responses to direct questions. Overall, four studies of this strategy met NRP scientific criteria. The students in the active listening studies ranged from first grade through sixth grade; they improved in critical listening, critical reading, and general reading comprehension.

**Comprehension monitoring.** One can learn to listen to one's own reading and to monitor one's own comprehension. Instruction in comprehension monitoring during reading helps readers manage their inner speech as they read. Self-listening and self-monitoring of one's own understanding during reading promote more careful reading and better comprehension.

To teach comprehension monitoring, a teacher, when reading aloud to a class, demonstrates the strategy by interrupting her own reading to "think aloud." She articulates to the class her own awareness of difficulties in understanding words, phrases, clauses, or sentences in a text. When a text poses potential comprehension breakdowns, such as unfamiliar concepts or logical inconsistencies in a passage, the teacher might look back in the text to try to solve a problem, restate the text content in more familiar terms, or look forward in the text to find a solution. After observing a teacher model the

comprehension monitoring strategy, readers are encouraged to carry out the same procedures—first with teacher scaffolding and then on their own. Eventually the student readers take responsibility for recognizing comprehension difficulties and for demonstrating ways to overcome them (e.g., by guessing and looking back or reading forward in the text).

The teaching of comprehension monitoring is very effective. The NRP found twenty studies of comprehension monitoring instruction with readers in grades two through six that met scientific criteria. In them, readers who were taught to self-monitor comprehension improved one of the following: their detection of text inconsistencies, their memory for the text, or their performance on standardized reading comprehension tests.

**Prior knowledge.** Prior knowledge instruction is designed to assist readers in bringing to mind their own knowledge that is relevant to understanding the text. A teacher can activate prior knowledge by asking students to think about topics relevant to the passage, by teaching the requisite relevant knowledge, by using pre-reading activity on related but better-known topics, by having the readers predict what will happen in the text based on personal experience, by having readers make associations during reading, and by previewing the story or text.

In fourteen studies with students spanning grades one through nine reviewed by the NRP, prior knowledge instruction helped readers improve on recall, in question answering, and in content area and standardized reading comprehension performance. For example, in a 1988 study, Teresa A. Roberts found that prior knowledge instruction had a positive effect on both factual and inferential comprehension performance with students in grades five and nine.

**Mental imagery.** Mental imagery instruction teaches readers to construct images that closely represent the content of what was read and understood. In 1986, after instructing less-skilled fourth- and fifth-grade readers in imagery training, Linda B. Gambrell and Ruby J. Bales had them read stories with inconsistencies like those in the 1979 Markman study mentioned above and instructed them "to make a picture in your mind to help determine if there is anything that is not clear and easy to understand about the story." Control students, that is, those without the imagery training, were simply asked to "do whatever you can do to help determine if anything is not clear and easy to understand about the story." The results were that imagery-trained readers were more likely to detect inconsistencies than the controls. In four studies with students in grades two through eight, the NRP found that mental imagery instruction led to modest increases in memory for the text that was imaged and improved reader detection of text inconsistencies.

**Mnemonics.** Like mental imagery instruction, mnemonic instruction teaches readers to use an external memory aid, but unlike mental imagery instruction, the mnemonic image can be one that does not necessarily closely represent the text. A teacher demonstrates how to construct a picture, keyword, or concept as a proxy for a person, concept, sentence, or passage—such as using an image of a "tailor" to remember the name "Taylor." These keywords and images aid later recall. In five studies examined by the NRP, mnemonic instruction improved reader memory of the assigned keywords and recall for the passages read. For example, in 1986 Ellen E. Peters and Joel R. Levin gave mnemonic instruction to good and poor readers and then gave them passages about "famous" people. As compared to the control subjects, the mnemonic-trained students were more likely to learn and remember information about new concepts and people who were unfamiliar to them.

**Graphic organizers.** Graphic organizer instruction shows readers how to construct displays that organize one's ideas based on a reading of the text. Graphic organizers aim at creating awareness of text structures, concepts and relations between concepts, and tools to represent text relationships visually. They also assist readers in writing well-organized summaries. Diagrams, pictorial devices, and story maps can all be used to outline the relationships among text ideas. This instruction is useful for expository texts in content areas such as science or social studies.

In eleven studies reviewed by the NRP that used graphic organizers with readers in grades four through eight, readers generally benefited in remembering what they read, in improved reading comprehension, or in improved achievement in social studies or science courses. For example, in 1991 Bonnie Armbruster and her colleagues compared the effectiveness of a graphic organizer instruction that taught fourth- and fifth-grade social science students to visually represent the important ideas in a social science text. In contrast, the control students' instruction consisted of workbook activity directions recommended in the teacher's edition of the social science textbook. The fifth-, but not necessarily the fourth-grade students, who received the graphic organizer cognitive strategy instruction scored higher on recall and recognition measures than the controls who received the workbook activity instruction.

**Vocabulary instruction.** There are many studies on teaching vocabulary but few on the relationship between vocabulary instruction and comprehension. In the context of comprehension strategy instruction, vocabulary instruction promotes new word meaning knowledge by teaching readers semantic processing strategies. For example, students learn to generate questions about an unknown word by examining how it relates to the text or noticing how a word changes meaning depending on the context in which it occurs. The teacher may model being a "word detective," looking for contextual clues to find a word's meaning, analyzing words and word parts, and looking at the surrounding text for clues to a word's meaning. For instance, the word *comprehension* combines *com,* meaning "together" with *pre-hension,* meaning "able to grasp in one's hand." From this, an operational definition of *comprehension* can be constructed (e.g., putting together individual word meanings to grasp an idea).

In three studies of vocabulary instruction in a cognitive strategy context with fourth-grade students reviewed by the NRP, the instruction led to success in learning words, in use of word meanings, and in increased story comprehension. For example, in a 1982 study involving fourth-graders receiving vocabulary instruction, Isabel L. Beck and her colleagues taught the students to perform tasks designed to require semantic processing. These students performed at a significantly higher level than pre-instruction matched controls on learning word meanings, on processing instructed vocabulary more efficiently, and in tasks more reflective of comprehension. In the three NRP-reviewed studies, however, learning to derive word meanings did not always improve standardized comprehension performance.

**Question answering.** Question answering focuses the reader on content. *Why* or *how* questions lead the student to focus on causes and consequences. Question answering guides students and motivates them to look in the text to find answers. Instruction on question answering leads to improvement in memory for what was read, to better answering of questions after reading, or to improvement in finding answers to questions in the text during reading.

In a 1985 study, Taffy E. Raphael and Clydie A. Wonnacott trained fourth-grade and sixth-grade readers to analyze questions, distinguishing those questions that could be answered by information in the passage from questions that required prior knowledge or information not in the text. The results were that students who had received this instruction provided higher quality responses to questions than a control group of students. In seventeen studies examined by the NRP for this strategy, the results were usually specific to experimenter tests of question answering and were greater for lower-grade than for upper-grade readers and greater with average and less-skilled readers than with high-achieving readers.

**Question generation.** Teachers demonstrate this strategy by generating questions aloud during reading. Readers then practice generating questions and answers as they read the text. Teachers provide feedback on the quality of the questions asked or assist the student in answering the question generated. Teachers teach the students to evaluate whether their questions covered important information, whether questions related to information provided in the text, and whether they themselves could answer the questions.

The scientific evidence that question generation cognitive strategy instruction is effective is very strong. In 1996 Barak Rosenshine and his colleagues conducted meta-analysis of twenty-six question generation studies with students from third grade through college. Like individual experimental studies, a meta-analysis applies scientific criteria to obtain a quantitative assessment of an instruction's effectiveness. A meta-analysis differs from single studies, however, in that it obtains a quantitative impact of a particular strategy by looking at effectiveness across a group of studies. In addition to the Rosenshine meta-analysis, the NRP examined twenty-seven question generation studies with students from grades three through nine. Question generation instruction during reading benefited reading comprehension in terms of improved memory, in accuracy in answering questions, or in better integration and identification of main ideas. The evidence that it improved performance on standardized comprehension tests is mixed.

**Story structure.** Story structure instruction is designed to help readers understand the who, what,

where, when, and why of stories, what happened, and what was done and to infer causal relationships between events. Readers learn to identify the main characters of the story, where and when the story took place, what the main characters did, how the story ended, and how the main characters felt. Readers learn to construct a story map recording the setting, problem, goal, action, and outcome of the story as they unfold over time.

Story structure instruction improves the ability of readers to answer questions, to recall what was read, and to improve standard comprehension test performance. The instruction also benefits recall, question answering, and identifying elements of story structure. For example, in 1983 Jill Fitzgerald and Daisy L. Spiegel found that instruction in narrative structure enhanced story structure knowledge and had a strong positive effect on reading comprehension with average and below-average fourth-grade students who had been identified as lacking a keen sense of narrative structure.

The NRP examined seventeen studies using story structure instruction with readers ranging from third grade through sixth grade. Story structure instruction improved readers' ability to answer short-answer questions and retell the story. In three of the studies, standardized tests were used for assessment. Story structure instruction led to improved reader scores in two of those studies.

**Summarization.** Teaching readers to summarize makes them more aware of how ideas based on the text are related. Readers learn to identify main ideas, leave out details, generalize, create topic sentences, and remove redundancy. Through example and feedback, a reader can be taught to apply these summarization rules to single- or multiple-paragraph passages by first summarizing individual paragraphs and then constructing a summary or spatial organization of the paragraph summaries.

In eighteen studies on summarization with students from grades three to eight examined by the NRP, readers improved the quality of their summaries of text not only by identifying the main ideas but also by leaving out detail, including ideas related to the main idea, generalizing, and removing redundancy. Further, the instruction of summarization improves memory for what is read, both in terms of free recall and answering questions. For example, in 1984 Thomas W. Bean and Fern L. Steenwyk examined whether training sixth-grade readers in rules for summarization developed in 1983 by Ann L. Brown and Jeannie D. Day would improve comprehension. They found that readers receiving summarization instruction either by rule-governed or intuitive-summarization techniques performed better than controls who were told to find main ideas but who had no explicit instruction. The summarization-trained students significantly outperformed the control group in the quality of their summaries and on a standardized test.

**Multiple-strategy instruction.** Readers can learn and flexibly coordinate several comprehension strategies to construct meaning from texts. Palincsar and Ann L. Brown's reciprocal teaching method, described in 1984, instructs readers to use four main strategies during reading: generating questions, summarizing, seeking clarification, and predicting what will occur later in the text. Additional strategies may also be introduced, including question answering, making inferences, drawing conclusions, listening, comprehension monitoring, thinking aloud, and question elaborating. The teacher models strategies and, in some cases, explains them as they are modeled. Then the reader, either alone or as a leader of a group, applies the strategies.

The evidence indicates that demonstration and repeated use of the strategies leads to their learning by readers and improvement in comprehension. In 1994 Rosenshine and Carla Meister conducted a meta-analysis of sixteen reciprocal teaching studies with students in grades one through eight. Most of the readers were above grade three. Weaker and older readers benefited most from reciprocal teaching. In eleven studies of reciprocal teaching in grades one through six reviewed by the NRP but not covered by Rosenshine and Meister, reciprocal teaching produced clear positive improvement on tasks that involve memory, summarizing, and identification of main ideas.

Multiple-strategy programs that do not use reciprocal teaching mainly have the student practice strategies with modeling and/or feedback from the teacher. In explicit, direct approaches, the teacher always explains a strategy before the teacher models it during reading.

**Teacher preparation for text comprehension instruction.** Teachers have to learn strategy instruction in order to interact with students at the right time and right place during the reading of a text. Teachers also need to know about cognitive process-es in reading and how to teach strategies through explanation, demonstration, modeling, or interactive techniques; how to allow readers to learn and use individual strategies; and how to teach a strategy in conjunction with several other strategies.

Four studies conducted in the late 1980s and 1990s indicated that teachers who learn multiple comprehension strategy instruction and use it in their classrooms improve the reading comprehension of their students, especially those who are below average in skill. Improvements occurred in subject matter learning and in performance on standardized reading comprehension tests. In 1996 Rachel Brown, Michael Pressley, and colleagues taught teachers to use transactional strategy instruction in a yearlong program where students made comprehension gains. Transaction instruction involves teacher-directed actions with interactive exchanges with students in classrooms.

**Cooperative learning by peers.** Readers may learn best when they are in social situations in which they are actively engaged with other learners who are near their same level of understanding. Cooperative learning involves readers reading together with a partner or in small groups. As they read aloud and listen to others, the teacher can guide them to use any of the various strategies for effective reading comprehension. At first the teacher may model reading through her demonstrated use of a strategy. Then the student readers carry out the demonstrated activities with a partner or in small reading groups. Readers take turns reading and listening, asking questions, answering questions, summarizing, recognizing words, predicting, and clarifying. The readers are encouraged to tutor each other on strategies. Group cooperative instruction has been found to promote intellectual discussion, increased student control over their learning, increased social interaction with peers, and savings in teacher time.

For example, in 1998 Janette K. Klingner, Sharon Vaughn, and Jeanne S. Schumm investigated the effectiveness of a cooperative learning approach designed to encourage culturally and linguistically diverse general education fourth-grade students to use strategic reading by employing various summarization and clarification procedures during reading. Students in the cooperative learning classes made greater gains in reading comprehension and equal gains in content knowledge than controls in measures that included a standardized reading test, a social studies unit test, and audiotapes of group work.

In ten studies on cooperative learning of comprehension strategies reviewed by the NRP, students successfully learned the reading strategies. Cooperative learning can also be effective for integrating students with academic and physical disabilities into regular classrooms. The social interaction increases motivation for learning and time spent by the learners on tasks.

## Implications for Future Research and Practice

Instruction of cognitive strategies for reading comprehension has been successful across a wide number of studies for readers in grades three to eleven. Despite these successful demonstrations, there are many unanswered questions. Among these are whether certain strategies are more appropriate than others for readers of certain ages or different abilities, whether comprehension strategy instruction would improve performance and achievement in all content areas, whether successful instruction generalizes across different types of texts, and whether comprehension strategies work better if what is being read engages the readers' interests. Researchers also need to find out more about important teacher characteristics that influence successful instruction of reading comprehension, especially in regard to decision-making processes (e.g., knowing when to apply what strategy with which particular student[s]). Finally, there has been little research that directly compares different methods of teaching comprehension. More needs to be known about "best approaches" to comprehension instruction and the circumstances under which they are successful. How does one best develop independent readers who have the abilities to understand what they read on their own?

## Conclusion

Cognitive strategy instruction does work to improve readers' comprehension performance. In her 2000 address to teachers, Carol Minnick Santa, president of the International Reading Association, noted that "teaching [comprehension] is a lot harder and more abstract than teaching phonemic awareness or language structures. Moreover, effective comprehension instruction . . . demands extensive teacher knowledge." In 1993, after a five-year study of teaching teachers to implement comprehension strategy instruction, Gerald G. Duffy, a developer of the direct-instruction approach to cognitive strategy instruction, concluded that teaching students to acquire and use strategies requires a fundamental "change in how teacher educators and staff developers work with teachers and what they count as important about learning to be a teacher" (p. 244). Successful comprehension teachers must be strategic themselves, coordinating individual strategies and altering, adjusting, modifying, testing, and shifting tactics appropriately until readers' comprehension problems are resolved. For readers to become good reading strategists requires teachers who have appreciation for reading strategies.

*See also:* LITERACY, *subentry on* VOCABULARY AND VOCABULARY LEARNING; LITERACY AND READING; MEMORY; READING, *subentries on* BEGINNING READING, CONTENT AREAS, INTEREST, LEARNING FROM TEXT, PRIOR KNOWLEDGE, BELIEFS, AND LEARNING, TEACHING OF; READING DISABILITIES.

### BIBLIOGRAPHY

ADAMS, ABBY; CARNINE, D.; and GERSTEN, R. 1982. "Instructional Strategies for Studying Content Area Texts in the Intermediate Grades." *Reading Research Quarterly* 18:27–55.

ARMBRUSTER, BONNIE; ANDERSON, THOMAS H.; and MEYER, JENNIFER L. 1991. "Improving Content-Area Reading Using Instructional Graphics." *Reading Research Quarterly* 26:393–416.

BEAN, THOMAS W., and STEENWYK, FERN L. 1984. "The Effect of Three Forms of Summarization Instruction on Sixth Graders' Summary Writing and Comprehension." *Journal of Reading Behavior* 16:297–306.

BECK, ISABEL L.; PERFETTI, CHARLES A.; and McKEOWN, MARGARET G. 1982. "Effects of Long Term Vocabulary Instruction on Lexical Access and Reading Comprehension." *Journal of Educational Psychology* 74:506–521.

BOODT, GLORIA M. 1984. "Critical Listeners Become Critical Readers in Remedial Reading Class." *Reading Teacher* 37:390–394.

BROWN, ANN L., and DAY, JEANNIE D. 1983. "Macro Rules for Summarizing Texts: The Development of Expertise." *Journal of Verbal Learning and Verbal Behavior* 22:1–14.

BROWN, RACHEL; PRESSLEY, MICHAEL; VAN METER, PEGGY; and SHUDER, TED. 1996. "A Quasi-Experimental Validation of Transactional Strategies Instruction with Low-Achieving Second Grade Readers." *Journal of Educational Psychology* 88:18–37.

Duffy, Gerald G. 1993. "Rethinking Strategy Instruction: Four Teachers' Development and Their Low Achievers' Understandings." *Elementary School Journal* 93:231–247.

Duffy, Gerald G.; Roehler, Laura R.; Sivan, Eva; Rackliff, Gary; Book, Cassandra; Meloth, Michael S.; Vavrus, Linda G.; Wesselman, Roy; Putnam, Joyce; and Bassiri, Dina. 1987. "Effects of Explaining the Reasoning Associated with Using Reading Strategies." *Reading Research Quarterly* 22:347–368.

Durkin, Dolores. "What Classroom Observations Reveal About Reading Comprehension." *Reading Research Quarterly* 15:481–533.

Fitzgerald, Jill, and Spiegel, Daisy L. 1983. "Enhancing Children's Reading Comprehension through Instruction in Narrative Structure." *Journal of Reading Behavior* 15:1–17.

Gambrell, Linda B., and Bales, Ruby J. 1986. "Mental Imagery and the Comprehension Monitoring Performance of Fourth- and Fifth-Grade Poor Readers." *Reading Research Quarterly* 21:454–464.

Kintsch, Walter, and van Dijk, Teun A. 1978. "Toward a Model of Discourse Comprehension and Production." *Psychological Review* 83:363–394.

Klingner, Janette K.; Vaughn, Sharon; and Schumm, Jeanne S. 1998. "Collaborative Strategic Reading during Social Studies in Heterogeneous Fourth-Grade Classrooms." *Elementary School Journal* 99:3–22.

Levin, Joel R.; Shriberg, Lawrence D.; and Berry, Jill K. 1983. "A Concrete Strategy for Remembering Abstract Prose." *American Educational Research Journal* 20:277–290.

Markman, Ellen M. 1977. "Realizing that You Don't Understand: A Preliminary Investigation." *Child Development* 46:986–992.

Markman, Ellen M. 1981. "Comprehension Monitoring." In *Children's Oral Communication Skills,* ed. W. Patrick Dickson. New York: Academic Press.

McCormick, Christine B., and Levin, Joel R. 1984. "A Comparison of Different Prose-Learning Variations of the Mnemonic Keyword Method." *American Educational Research Journal* 21:379–398.

National Institute of Child Health and Human Development. 2000. *Report of the National Reading Panel: Teaching Children to Read: An Evidence-Based Assessment of the Scientific Research Literature on Reading and Its Implications for Reading Instruction.* Washington, DC: National Institutes of Health, National Institute of Child Health and Human Development.

Palincsar, Annemarie S., and Brown, Ann L. 1984. "Reciprocal Teaching of Comprehension-Fostering and Comprehension-Monitoring Activities." *Cognition and Instruction* 1:117–175.

Pearson, P. David, and Gallagher, Margaret C. 1983. "The Instruction of Reading Comprehension." *Contemporary Educational Psychology* 8:317–344.

Peters, Ellen E., and Levin, Joel R. 1986. "Effects of a Mnemonic Imagery Strategy on Good and Poor Readers' Prose Recall." *Reading Research Quarterly* 21:179–192.

Raphael, Taffy E., and Wonnacott, Clydie A. 1985. "Heightening Fourth-Grade Students' Sensitivity to Sources of Information for Answering Comprehension Questions." *Reading Research Quarterly* 20:282–296.

Roberts, Teresa A. 1988. "Development of Pre-instruction versus Previous Experience: Effects on Factual and Inferential Comprehension." *Reading Psychology* 9:141–157.

Rosenshine, Barak, and Meister, Carla. 1994. "Reciprocal Teaching: A Review of the Research." *Review of Educational Research* 64:479–530.

Rosenshine, Barak; Meister, Carla; and Chapman, Saul. 1996. "Teaching Students to Generate Questions: A Review of the Intervention Studies." *Review of Educational Research* 66:181–221.

Tierney, Robert J., and Cunningham, James W. 1984. "Research on Teaching Reading Comprehension." In *Handbook of Reading Research,* Vol. 1, ed. P. David Pearson, Rebecca Barr, Michael L. Kamil, and Peter B. Mosenthal. New York: Longman.

Trabasso, Tom, and Bouchard, Ed. 2000. "Teaching Readers How to Comprehend Text: A Scientific Review of the Experimental Research Literature on Reading Comprehension." *Report of the National Reading Panel: Teaching Children to Read: An Evidence-Based Assessment of the Scientific Research Literature on Reading and Its Im-*

*plications for Reading Instruction: Reports of the Subgroups.* Washington, DC: National Institute of Health and Human Development.

TRABASSO, TOM, and BOUCHARD, ED. 2002. "Teaching Readers How to Strategically Comprehend Text." In *Comprehension Instruction: Research-Based Best Practices,* ed. Cathy Collins Block and Michael Pressley. New York: Guilford.

VYGOTSKY, LEV S. 1986. *Thought and Language* (1934), ed. Alex Kozulin. Cambridge, MA: MIT Press.

**INTERNET RESOURCE**

SANTA, CAROL MINNICK. 2000 (February/March). "President's Message: The Complexity of Comprehension: Effective Comprehension Instruction Requires Extensive Teacher Knowledge." *Reading Today.* International Reading Association. <www.reading.org/publications/rty/archives/feb_president.html>.

ED BOUCHARD
TOM TRABASSO

## CONTENT AREAS

Reading in content areas is also referred to as subject matter reading and disciplinary reading and embodies what educators call "reading to learn." These terms refer to reading, understanding, learning, and using content area, subject matter, or disciplinary texts such as texts in science, history, or literature, for the purpose of gaining, demonstrating, and possibly creating knowledge in that discipline. Proficiency in reading content area materials is influenced by: (1) the dispositions of individuals who read in the disciplines (including such influences as their levels of background and strategy knowledge, their understanding of the discipline, their attitudes and interest in the subject matter, and their ability levels); (2) the goals that students adapt for learning and the degree to which those goals are similar to the goals that their teachers have for their learning; (3) the structure, difficulty level, and tone of the texts; (4) the level of understanding required of the individuals (for example, memorization versus critical thinking); and (5) the form in which that understanding is displayed (such as written versus oral or recall versus recognition). Thus, reading content area materials involves complex processes.

Educators often state that "reading to learn" is different from "learning to read." When students learn to read, the focus is often on the pronunciation and comprehension of narrative texts. Comprehension of these narratives does not usually require expertise in literary criticism and interpretation, although teachers seek literal, inferential, and evaluative/applied understandings. Reading to learn, however, focuses on the understanding and use of largely informational texts in disciplines such as history and science and a mix of informational and literary texts in English. Reading to learn *does* require disciplinary expertise. When reading a literary text, for example, students benefit from knowing how literary critics think about and discuss literature as a guide to their own interpretation and discussion of that text. When reading a history text, students benefit from understanding the way that historians gather and interpret data and write about historical events. Reading to learn science requires a different set of understandings than reading to learn history, literature, or any other subject matter.

Level of background knowledge, interest, goals, and other student characteristics make a difference in how well students are able to understand and use the information in texts, but content area reading specialists disagree about the degree to which the approach to reading differs depending upon the discipline. Strategies for understanding and applying what is read will have some commonalties across disciplines; generally, however, the understanding of disciplinary texts is inextricably tied to understandings of the discipline.

In a 1997 article Patricia Alexander posited that disciplinary expertise is gained as a function of three interdependent influences—knowledge, interest, and strategy use. That is, as one increases, the others do as well. Alexander described three levels of disciplinary expertise. At the level of *acclimation,* knowledge is unorganized, strategies are general, and interest is extrinsic. At the level of *competency,* knowledge becomes organized (such as into processes in science), strategies become more specific, and interest becomes more intrinsic. At the level of *proficiency,* one may even create knowledge, strategies will not only be more specific but also become fluid and very efficient, and interest will be very closely tied to one's inner desires. Students may move from acclimation to competency because they get hooked on a topic and that hook helps them become more interested in other topics, because they develop strategies that help them learn more effectively, or because they may learn more and, thus, understand how better to use strategies for learning. In any event, knowledge, interest, and strategy use are tied to the discipline rather than being seen as general constructs.

## Reading in Three Disciplines: History, Science, and Literature

Disciplines differ in their methods for creating and displaying knowledge. In addition, teachers in the disciplines expect students to understand those differences and to use them in learning information from texts.

**The case of history.** History texts are traditionally written as narratives that are sometimes interspersed with interpretation. For example, an event such as the Tonkin Gulf incident of the Vietnam War may be described sequentially, followed by a paragraph discussing the importance of the event in determining U.S. involvement in the war. Students often read historical texts as if they were "baskets of facts" to be memorized in sequential order, but this strategy is naive. Historians, when asked to read historical texts, read them differently. In a 1992 article Samuel Wineburg reported that historians read historical texts as arguments. When reading several historical documents, they engaged in *sourcing* (determining the expertise of the author and the source of the material), *contextualization* (determining when it was written and what surrounding influences there might be), and *corroboration* (determining whether or not the texts agreed).

The differences in the way students and historians read the documents can be attributed to differences in disciplinary expertise. That is, historians know the way that historical evidence is collected. They understand that there is the danger of bias in the selection process of that evidence. They also know that original documents are sometimes difficult to interpret. The documents are like pieces of a puzzle that must be assembled without a preexisting border, with the final picture being a creation of the historian. In interpreting those original documents historians are influenced by the time period in which they live, the political and philosophical approaches they have embraced, and past historical interpretations, to name a few influences. In addition, historians understand the power relations that exist among historians. They know what counts as good historical writing, model their own writing on that of oth-

ers, and examine the writing of their fellow historians accordingly. Historians understand the elements of their discipline and thus read historical texts with a critical eye.

But the processes of selecting and interpreting historical evidence and writing about historical events is hidden from the reader of historical texts. In presenting history as a coherent story, this information is obscured. Therefore, it is up to teachers of history to call to the attention of students the elements of the discipline that will help them engage in reading history.

What are students required to do when they read history texts? Typically, students are expected to engage in several levels of understanding of history as a result of reading historical texts. These include a mastery of the "facts" of history. They include understanding consensual interpretations of history, such as understanding various historians' ideas of the causes and effects of important events. They also include students' engagement in thinking about these interpretations for themselves. Students in history classes are often asked to make comparisons and contrasts and to discuss possible cause-and-effect relationships that have not been made explicit in the texts. Students are also often required to synthesize information across several texts. For instance, they may be required to read Benjamin Franklin's writings and decide in what ways his ideas had embodied the principles of the Enlightenment. Sometimes students are asked to look at history from different perspectives. For instance, they may be required to read several versions of an event to consider how the context of those writings influenced understanding about it. Students sometimes are asked to engage in the gathering of and interpretation of historical evidence and to write their interpretations in report form, such as in a term paper. Finally, students are sometimes required to engage in thinking about the philosophical aspects of historical understanding. For example, they may be asked to consider whether important people create noteworthy events or whether noteworthy events create important people.

The tradition in history classes for demonstrating these various understandings turns increasingly toward essay writing as students move from naivete to expertise and from lower-level mastery of factual information to higher-level critical thinking and interpretation. Thus, students need to have a complex array of strategies for understanding historical texts and for demonstrating that understanding. These include strategies for remembering the facts of historical events, engaging in historical research, making comparisons and contrasts, synthesizing information across texts, writing essays, and thinking critically about the nature of history and historical writing. Whereas these strategies share common elements with strategies needed for other disciplines, they are, in the end, discipline specific.

**The case of science.** The hard sciences such as physics and biology rest on the assumptions of the scientific method. Scientists understand and use the scientific method in their search for "truth." They adhere to the principle of objectivity, understanding that their own biases and perceptual shortcomings may cause misinterpretations of evidence. Thus they engage in experimentation using controlled conditions whenever possible and rely on numerical rather than qualitative assessments of data as the main determinants of scientific principles. Yet, as scientists, they are still influenced by several constraining elements. The selection of research topic, the use of certain measurement devices, the importance assigned to various scientific findings, and the previous understandings of the research topic are all examples of constraints that are in part culturally and socially based. Which topics get studied and which findings gain acceptance in the scientific community are functions of power relations among scientists, of necessity, and of the veracity of the findings. As an example, consider that it took hundreds of years for the ideas of the seventeenth century Italian astronomer and physicist Galileo Galilei to be accepted by the scientific community, or that sterilization procedures were staunchly resisted by the scientific community despite evidence that such procedures were necessary.

Also in science, information is always partial and relational. Because the workings of the natural world are obscured for individuals by the limits of their perceptual and sociocultural understandings, scientific understandings are always in a state of flux. For example, the ideas about gravity and motion formulated by the English mathematician and physicist Isaac Newton (1642–1727) are functional on Earth but have become outmoded based upon newer conceptions of quantum physics. Scientists understand this flux; they have the disciplinary knowledge necessary to help them critically read and evaluate scientific texts. They also know what counts as written proof of a scientific finding. For example, they know

that the reporting of a scientific finding in the journal *Science* requires adherence to certain traditional rules for scientific reporting and has been anonymously reviewed (refereed) by a group of distinguished scientists. They know that such a report counts more than the accounting of similar findings in a local, nonrefereed publication. Students, however, do not have the disciplinary knowledge necessary to make these evaluations. Skillful reading of science is in part dependent upon students gaining that disciplinary knowledge.

What are students required to do as they read science texts? Typically, they are required to master a knowledge base that represents the current understandings of the scientific community. These understandings involve the identification of various elements and their function in carrying out common processes. For example, students are required to identify the parts and understand the workings of the human digestive system. They are also often required to solve problems or to make predictions about processes based upon their scientific understandings. For example, a student who understands the path of a projectile and how it is calculated might be asked to determine the time it would take a projectile to reach the ground if it were launched at a certain speed at a certain trajectory from a certain height. In other words, students must be able to understand the vocabulary and concepts of what they read and apply that understanding in new contexts.

In trying to understand the processes of science, students may need to suspend their own ideas in favor of scientific evidence. In the study of gravity, for example, students often have erroneous conceptions of how gravity works based upon their intuitive but scientifically disproven assumptions. Students may believe that a heavier object will fall faster than a lighter one, when, in reality, weight or mass do not influence the speed of a projectile as it falls to Earth. Scientists know that weight has no influence because they have performed controlled experiments. Students must suspend their intuitive beliefs to learn the scientific information, and those who understand the assumptions of the scientific method will more likely engage in that learning than students who do not.

Science texts are often seen as difficult to understand. Students complain that concepts are not sufficiently elaborated, the material assumes a level of background information that exceeds theirs, the vocabulary is too dense, and the content is dull. Texts are even harder to understand when students begin their reading harboring misconceptions about the content that interfere with their understanding. Researchers have found that refutational text, or text that explicitly describes erroneous understandings and explains why they are erroneous, is more effective at helping students to learn counterintuitive ideas.

The procedures in science classes for demonstrating students' understandings are varied, including answering literal, inferential, and applied questions on multiple-choice tests; solving numerical problems; writing descriptive essays; writing field notes; making charts, graphs, and diagrams; and writing scientific reports. Students are required to have elaborative understandings of current conceptions of the working of the natural world, and they must have a number of strategies for learning at their disposal.

**The case of literature.** Literature has its own disciplinary traditions. Knowledge of the way that literary experts refer to such elements as genre, characterization, theme, conflict, symbolism, and language use is important. In addition, experts in literature often engage in various kinds of interpretation, for example, putting a feminist, Marxist, Freudian, or postmodern spin on the interpretation of a piece of literature. Experts in literature understand the different perspectives that are part and parcel of the field. They understand that literary criticism has evolved over time; that the relationship of the author, the text, and the reader and their importance in interpretation have fluctuated; and that arguments rage over what is important for students to read (the canon versus multicultural literature, for example). Students may not have this disciplinary knowledge but would benefit by it.

Students need to develop a common language with which they can discuss and write about their interpretations of text, and the tradition in literature classes is for the demonstration of disciplinary expertise to be in essay form. In addition, they are often expected to apply their knowledge of the elements of certain genres by engaging in writing literary texts themselves, such as in writing poetry or short stories. And they are sometimes required to write reports about authors or certain literary traditions. The strategies for engaging in these activities are quite complex, and, although they require literal, interpretive, and applied/evaluative thinking, the way in which this thinking is used is different from the way it is used in history and science.

The three disciplines—science, history, and literature—are similar in that all require thinking at literal, inferential, and applied/evaluative levels. In addition, reading texts in these disciplines requires vocabulary knowledge and strategic effort. But the disciplines are different. For example, science is well-structured, history less well-structured, and literature relatively unstructured in relation to what is agreed upon as being "known."

## Strategies for Reading Content Area Texts

When discussing strategy use, educators find it useful to make a distinction between teacher-generated and student-generated strategies. In both cases, however, content area specialists argue about whether general strategies can be used and applied across subject areas or whether strategies must be discipline specific. In reality, probably both ideas are true.

An example of a teacher-directed strategy is list-group-label. In this pre-reading strategy, the teacher solicits and makes a list of all the information students already know about the content of what they are about to read. Then, she directs the students to group the items in the list into meaningful groups and to label each meaningful group. From this activity, the teacher finds out what the students already understand and can, thus, be more effective in bridging any gaps between information in the text and student knowledge. In addition, the activity can be used to generate a list of questions that might be answered by the text. These questions would then make reading a more directed and interesting activity. The strategy can be applied across contents, but the lists that are generated and the way the lists are used might differ depending upon the discipline. For example, in a history class, groups may include events, policies, and people. In science they may include patterns of behavior or processes.

Regarding student-generated strategies, to be successful in classes in any discipline, students must read with the purpose of understanding and thinking about the information at deep levels, organizing the information into meaningful units, remembering the information, and displaying their knowledge in various ways. Strategies such as previewing, annotating, and outlining help students identify important information to study; strategies such as charting, mapping, and concept cards help students to organize material across sources in meaningful ways; strategies such as verbal rehearsal help students to remember and think about the material; and strategies such as predicting and answering exam questions help students prepare for displaying their knowledge. If students think at literal, inferential, and applied/evaluative levels, they will be more likely to truly learn new information. But even though all of these strategies can be applied across content areas, they will, in practice, be different depending upon the content of the material. Evidence that strategy use in one discipline can be transferred to other disciplines without explicit instruction in strategy modification is rare, and so it seems necessary that students should get explicit strategy modification instruction in each discipline.

In conclusion, the more discipline knowledge they possess, the more content knowledge they have, the more they are interested in the subject matter, the more familiarity they have with the way knowledge is created and structured in a particular discipline, and the more closely their goals for learning match disciplinary goals, the more likely it is that students will be able to adapt general strategies or create new ones to meet their discipline-specific needs for learning and applying the information in their content area texts.

*See also:* CHILDREN'S LITERATURE; HISTORY; READING, *subentries on* COMPREHENSION, INTEREST, LEARNING FROM TEXT, PRIOR KNOWLEDGE, BELIEFS, AND LEARNING, TEACHING OF; READING DISABILITIES; SCIENCE EDUCATION; SCIENCE LEARNING.

#### BIBLIOGRAPHY

ALEXANDER, PATRICIA A. 1997. "Mapping the Multidimensional Nature of Domain Learning: The Interplay of Cognitive, Motivation, and Strategic Forces." *Advances in Motivation and Achievement* 10:213–250.

WINEBURG, SAMUEL S. 1991. "On the Reading of Historical Texts: Notes on the Breach between School and Academy." *American Educational Research Journal* 28:495–519.

CYNTHIA HYND

## INTEREST

The powerful facilitative effect of interest on academic performance in general has been well estab-

lished. For the purpose of this entry, the current conceptualization of interest is overviewed, followed by a review of interest research on reading.

### The Conceptualization of Interest

Among the many conceptualizations of interest the most common are to consider interest as a state and/or as a disposition. It has also been demonstrated that interest has both cognitive and affective (emotional) components. Researchers also distinguish between individual and situational interest, with the former targeting personal interest and the latter focusing on creating appropriate environmental settings.

Individual interest has been viewed as a relatively long-lasting predisposition to reengage with particular objects and events. Increased knowledge, value, and positive affect have been connected with individual interest. Students bring to their academic experience a network of individual interests, some similar to and some incompatible with classroom learning. Social categories such as gender and race also function as individual interest factors that may affect classroom engagement.

Situational interest refers to a psychological state elicited by environmental stimuli. The state is characterized by focused attention and an immediate affective reaction. The affective component is generally positive, although it may also include some negative emotions. Once triggered, the reaction may or may not be maintained. Situational sources of interest in learning contexts may be particularly relevant for educators working with students who do not have preformed individual interests in their school activities.

Although differences exist between situational and individual interest, they are not dichotomous phenomena. First, both situational and individual interest include an affective component and culminate in the psychological state of interest. Such a state is characterized by focused attention, increased cognitive functioning, and increased and persistent activity. Second, investigators concede that both types of interest are content specific and emerge from the interaction of the person and aspects in the environment. Third, numerous researchers recognize that situational and individual interests may interact. In the absence of the other, the role of individual or situational interest may be particularly important. For example, individual interest in a subject may help individuals deal with relevant but boring texts, while situational interest generated by texts may sustain motivation even when individuals have no particular interest in the topic. In addition, situational interest may develop over time into individual interest.

It has been found that topic interest has both situational and individual components. Topic interest may have an especially significant role in reading and writing in schools because students usually have to deal with text on the basis of topics provided by teachers.

## Interest and Reading Research

The most important questions raised in the literature on interest and reading concerned the influence of interest on readers' text processing and learning, the factors that contribute to readers' interest, and the specific processes through which interest influences learning. These issues are considered next.

**The influence of interest on readers' text processing and learning.** Up to the early 1980s, the prevalent view in educational research was that proficient readers process and recall text according to its hierarchical structure. Thus it was believed that readers could recall best the more important ideas at the higher levels of text structures. Since the early 1980s, however, research has shown that readers' well-formed individual interests and their situational interests (evoked by topics and text segments) contributed to their reading comprehension and learning. Several studies have demonstrated that personally interesting text segments and passages written on high-interest topics facilitate children's as well as college students' comprehension, inferencing, and retention.

Researchers have also demonstrated that interest affects the type of learning that occurs. Specifically, beyond increasing the amount of recall, interest seems to have a substantial effect on the quality of learning. Interest leads to more elaborate and deeper processing of texts. In 2000 Mark McDaniel, Paula Waddill, Kraig Finstad, and Tammy Bourg found that readers engaged with uninteresting narratives focused on individual text elements, such as extracting proposition-specific content, whereas readers of interesting texts tended to engage in organizational processing of information. Furthermore, their research suggests that text differing in interest may affect the degree to which processing strategies benefit memory performance.

**Factors contributing to readers' interest.** Another important educational issue is to increase the amount of interesting reading that students engage in. The bulk of the research in this area examined text characteristics that contribute to making reading materials more interesting. In his seminal 1979 paper, Roger Schank indicated that certain concepts (e.g., death, violence, and sex) can be considered "absolute interests" that almost universally elicit individuals' interest. In 1980 Walter Kintsch, referring to these interests as "emotional interests," distinguished them from cognitive interests, which result from events that are involved in complex cognitive structures or contain surprise. Subsequent research has suggested that a variety of text characteristics contribute in a positive way to the interestingness and memorability of written materials. Features that were found to be sources of situational interest include novelty, surprising information, intensity, visual imagery, ease of comprehension, text cohesion, and prior knowledge.

Text-based interest can also be promoted by altering certain aspects of the learning environment such as modifying task presentations, curriculum materials, and individuals' self-regulation. For example, in 1994 Gregg Schraw and R. S. Dennison were able to change the interestingness and recall of text materials by assigning for reading various perspectives on the same topic. In addition, research has indicated that presenting educational materials in more meaningful, challenging, and/or personally relevant contexts can stimulate interest. Modifying the presence of others in the learning environment can also elicit interest. For example, German researchers Lore Hoffman and P. Haussler demonstrated that mono-educational classes in physics can contribute to girls' increased interest in the subject area. Finally, Carol Sansone and colleagues in a series of studies showed that individuals can self-regulate in order to make tasks more interesting and subsequently to develop individual interest in activities initially considered uninteresting. Although these studies did not deal specifically with interest in reading, they indicated that interest in reading could also be increased by similar methods.

**Specific processes through which interest influences learning.** Gregg Schraw and colleagues suggested in 1995 that interest should be thought of as a complex cognitive phenomenon affected by multiple text and reader characteristic. A critical question is how the elicitation of interest leads to improved recall. One possibility is that interest activates text-processing strategies that result in readers being engaged in deeper-level processing. Suzanne Wade and colleagues reported in 1999 that the connections readers made between information and their prior knowledge or previous experience increased their interest.

Mark Sadoski and colleagues suggested in 1993 that interacting but separate cognitive systems (verbal and nonverbal) can explain the relationships among interest, comprehension, and recall. When verbal materials are encoded through both of these systems, comprehension and memory increase. The dual coding suggested by Sadoski and colleagues seems to account for the effects of some of the sources of interest that have been found to be associated with increased comprehension and memory, such as the processing of concrete, high-imagery materials. Nevertheless, some highly concrete and easily imaginable information is more interesting than other similar information. In addition, the informational significance of intensity, novelty, surprise, high personal relevance, and character identification reported in the literature to elicit interest do not seem to promote dual encoding prompted by concrete language and mental imagery. Another factor that has been associated with interest, reading, and increased learning is attention. Suzanne Hidi argued that interest is associated with automatic attention that facilitates learning. More specifically, she argued that such attention frees cognitive resources and leads to more efficient processing and better recall of information. In 2000 McDaniel, Waddill, Finstad, and Bourg reported empirical data supporting this position. Finally, as interest undoubtedly has a strong emotional component, this aspect may play a critical role in how interest influences learning. The effect of emotions on interest, however, is yet to be fully investigated in educational research.

*See also:* EFFORT AND INTEREST; LITERACY AND READING; READING, *subentries on* COMPREHENSION, CONTENT AREAS, LEARNING FROM TEXT, PRIOR KNOWLEDGE, BELIEFS AND LEARNING.

## BIBLIOGRAPHY

ALEXANDER, PATRICIA A. 1997. "Mapping the Multidimensional Nature of Domain Learning: The Interplay of Cognitive, Motivational, and Strategic Forces." In *Advances in Motivation and Achievement,* Vol. 10, ed. Martin L. Maehr and Paul R. Pintrich. Greenwich, CT: JAI Press.

ALEXANDER, PATRICIA A.; JETTON, T. L.; and KULIKOWICH, JONNA M. 1995. "Interrelationship of Knowledge, Interest, and Recall: Assessing a Model of Domain Learning." *Journal of Educational Psychology* 87:559–575.

ANDERSON, RICHARD C.; SHIRLEY, L. L.; WILSON, P. T.; and FIELDING, L. G. 1987. "Interestingness of Children's Reading Material." In *Aptitude, Learning and Instruction: Vol III: Cognitive and Affective Progress Analyses,* ed. Richard E. Snow and Marshall J. Farr. Hillsdale, NJ: Erlbaum.

BERGIN, DAVID A. 1999. "Influences on Classroom Interest." *Educational Psychologist* 34:87–98.

HARACKIEWIEZ, JUDITH M.; BARRON, KENNETH E.; CARTER, S. M.; LEHTO, A. T.; and ELLIOT, ANDREW J. 1997. "Predictors and Consequences of Achievement Goals in the College Classroom: Maintaining Interest and Making the Grade." *Journal of Personality and Social Psychology* 73:1284–1295.

HARACKIEWIEZ, JUDITH M.; BARRON, KENNETH E.; TAUER, JOHN M.; CARTER, S. M.; and ELLIOT, ANDREW J. 2000. "Short-Term and Long-Term Consequences of Achievement: Predicting Continued Interest and Performance over Time." *Journal of Educational Psychology* 92(2):36–330.

HIDI, SUZANNE. 1990. "Interest and Its Contribution as a Mental Resource for Learning." *Review of Educational Research* 60:549–571.

HIDI, SUZANNE. 2000. "An Interest Researcher's Perspective on the Effects of Extrinsic and Intrinsic Factors on Motivation." In *Intrinsic and Extrinsic Motivation: The Search for Optimum Motivation and Performance,* ed. Carol Sansone and Judith M. Harackiewicz. New York: Academic Press.

HIDI, SUZANNE. 2001. "Interest and Reading: Theoretical and Practical Considerations." *Educational Psychology Review* 13(3):191–208.

HIDI, SUZANNE, and HARACKIEWIEZ, JUDITH M. 2000. "Motivating the Academically Unmotivated: A Critical Issue for the 21st Century." *Review of Educational Research* 70(2):151–179.

HOFFMAN, LORE, and HAUSSLER, P. 1998. "An Intervention Project Promoting Girls' and Boys' Interest in Physics." In *Interest and Learning: Proceedings of the Seeon Conference on Interest and Gender*, ed. Lore Hoffman, Andreas Krapp, K. Ann Renninger, and Jürgen Baumert. Kiel, Germany: Institute for Science Education (IPN).

HOFFMAN, LEON; KRAPP, ANDREAS; RENNINGER, K. ANN; and BAUMERT, JÜRGEN, eds. 1998. *Interest and Learning: Proceedings of the Seeon Conference on Interest and Gender*, ed. Lore Hoffman, Andreas Krapp, K. Ann Renninger, and Jürgen Baumert. Kiel, Germany: Institute for Science Education (IPN).

KINTSCH, WALTER. 1980. "Learning from Texts, Levels of Comprehension, Or: Why Anyone Would Read a Story Anyway." *Poetics* 9:87–98.

KRAPP, ANDREAS. 1999. "Interest, Motivation and Learning: An Educational-Psychological Perspective." *European Journal of Psychology in Education* 14:23–40.

KRAPP, ANDREAS; HIDI, SUZANNE; and RENNINGER, K. ANN. 1992. Interest, Learning and Development." In *The Role of Interest in Learning and Development*, ed. K. Ann Renninger, Suzanne Hidi, and Andreas Krapp. Hillsdale, NJ: Erlbaum.

MCDANIEL, MARK A.; FINSTAD, KRAIG; WADDILL, PAULA J.; and BOURG, TAMMY. 2000. "The Effects of Text-Based Interest on Attention and Recall." *Journal of Educational Psychology* 92(3):492–502.

MITCHELL, M. 1993. "Situational Interest: Its Multifaceted Structure in the Secondary School Mathematics Classroom." *Journal of Educational Psychology* 85:424–426.

MEYER, BONNIE J. F.; TALBOT, A.; and STUBBLEFIELD, R. A. 1998. "Interest and Strategies of Young and Old Readers Differently Interact with Characteristics of Texts." *Educational Gerontology* 24:747–771.

RENNINGER, K. ANN. 1992. "Individual Interest and Development: Implications for Theory and Practice." In *The Role of Interest in Learning and Development*, ed. K. Ann Renninger, Suzanne Hidi, and Andreas Krapp. Hillsdale, NJ: Erlbaum.

RENNINGER, K. ANN. 2000. "Individual Interest and Its Implications for Understanding Intrinsic Motivation." In *Intrinsic Motivation: Controversies and New Directions*, ed. Carol Sansone and Judith M. Harackiewicz. New York: Academic Press.

RENNINER, K. ANN, and HIDI, SUZANNE. 2002. "Student Interest and Achievement: Developmental Issues Raised by a Case Study." In *The Development of Achievement Motivation*, ed. Allan Wigfield and Jacquelynne S. Eccles. New York: Academic Press.

SADOSKI, MARK. 2001. "Resolving the Effects of Concreteness on Interest, Comprehension, and Learning Important Ideas from Text." *Educational Psychology Review* 13(3).

SADOSKI, MARK; GOETZ, ERNEST T.; and FRITZ, J. 1993. "Impact of Concreteness on Comprehensibility, Interest, and Memory for Text: Implications for Dual Coding Theory and Text Design." *Journal of Educational Psychology* 85:291–304.

SANSONE, CAROL, and SMITH, JESSI L. 2000. "Self-Regulating Interest: When, Why and How." In *Intrinsic Motivation: Controversies and New Directions*, ed. Carol Sansone and Judith M. Harackiewicz. New York: Academic Press.

SANSONE, CAROL; WEIR, C.; HARPSTER, L.; and MORGAN, C. 1992. "Once a Boring Task Always a Boring Task? Interest as a Self-Regulatory Mechanism." *Journal of Personality and Social Psychology* 63:379–390.

SCHANK, ROGER C. 1979. "Interestingness: Controlling Inferences." *Artificial Intelligence* 12:273–297.

SCHIEFELE, ULRICH. 1998. "Individual Interest and Learning, What We Know and What We Don't Know." In *Interest and Learning: Proceedings of the Seeon Conference on Interest and Gender*, ed. Leon Hoffman, Andreas Krapp, K. Ann Renninger, and J. Baumert. Kiel, Germany: Institute for Science Education (IPN).

SCHIEFELE, ULRICH, and KRAPP, ANDREAS. 1996. "Topic Interest and Free Recall of Expository Text." *Learning and Individual Differences* 8:141–160.

SCHRAW, GREGG, and DENNISON, R. S. 1994. "The Effect of Reader Purpose on Interest and Recall." *Journal of Reading Behavior* 26(1):1–18.

SCHRAW, GREGG; BRUNING, R.; and SVOBODA, C. 1995. "Sources of Situational Interest." *Journal of Reading Behavior* 27:1–17.

SCHRAW, GREGG; FLOWERDAY, TERRI; and LEHMAN, STEVE. 2001. "Increasing Situation Interest in the Classroom." *Educational Psychology Review* 13(3):211–224.

WADE, SUZANNE E.; BUXTON, WILLIAM M.; and KELLY, MICHELLE. 1999. "Using Think-Alouds to Examine Reader-Text Interest." *Reading Research Quarterly* 34:194–216.

SUZANNE HIDI

# LEARNING FROM TEXT

Text allows people to communicate their ideas with one another across time and space. Indeed, a large part of what each person knows comes from reading texts. People who never discover how to learn from text have strong constraints on what they can know and do. On careful reflection, however, learning from text is a more controversial topic than is readily obvious. Learning may be of higher quality when students experience the world directly rather than read about it. Fourth graders who construct electric circuits or twelfth graders who enact a mock trial may well understand more about the underlying principles of electricity or the judicial system than if they had read chapters from their science or social studies textbooks. As appealing as learning by doing may seem, it has its own limitations. It is unrealistic to assume that students would be able to acquire the understanding of electricity that the nineteenth-century German physicist Georg Ohm had or the understanding of the law that John Marshall, chief justice of the U.S. Supreme Court from 1801 to 1835, had by repeating the same school activities even countless times. Through reading, students can experience the thinking of these experts and come to know some of what they knew or know without completing the same years of study or possessing equal amounts of academic insight. Successful learning depends on a close match among reader goals, text characteristics, reader proficiencies, and instructional context.

## Reader Goals

People read for many reasons. A mystery lover reads a new novel to be intrigued and entertained. A cook reads a recipe to prepare a new dish successfully. A caller reads the telephone book to find a telephone number. The mystery lover, cook, and caller will have connected the words, sentences, and paragraphs of their texts together to be entertained, follow the set of prescribed steps, or locate the information they seek. In other words, they will have comprehended successfully. Nevertheless, they probably will not have learned much. The goal of the mystery lover is to be entertained, not to learn. While the cook and caller read to find information, this information probably will remain in the text where it can be accessed again when needed rather than become a part of each reader's knowledge.

Comprehension, memorizing, and learning require different processes and different amounts of effort. Walter Kintsch, a cognitive psychologist who has studied text comprehension and learning, has shown that children can comprehend, or recall, an arithmetic problem without being able to solve it correctly and that adults can recall a set of directions without being able to find a particular location. To comprehend, readers connect the separate ideas in a text into a coherent whole that resembles the text. They know the meanings of most words and are able to draw necessary inferences between sentences, paragraphs, and larger sections of a text. As they draw these inferences, they distinguish superordinate topics or ideas from details. If asked to recall a text soon after reading it, they will tend to remember the superordinate topics, but not the details.

Memorizing requires rehearsal and therefore more effort than comprehension. Readers who re-read a text several times, focusing attention on the superordinate ideas and some of the details, will be better able to reproduce what they have rehearsed, particularly if prompted. Memorization is often what students do when they study for an exam. If the test has multiple choice or true and false questions, memorization can be an effective strategy. Neither text comprehension nor memorization alone, however, will result in learning, according to Kintsch.

Kintsch found that children were able to solve a problem if they could apply what they know about arithmetic and life in general to imagine a situation that represents the details in the problem. He suggested that learning occurs when readers can use their own relevant knowledge to think about, perhaps rearrange, critique, and retain or discard the content in a text. Picture the master chef following a new recipe for a type of dish that she has cooked many times. Because of her knowledge about ingredients, preparation choices, cooking temperatures, and heat sources, this chef would notice any new features, critique the recipe, keep what she likes, and add to what she already knows about preparing the dish. Learning brings about a change in what readers know, understand, and can do rather than simply what they remember or comprehend.

**Texts for Learning**

Learning requires more from a text than comprehensibility. To be sure, comprehensibility serves as a gatekeeper. Readers who comprehend a text have a chance at learning from it. Those who fail to comprehend will learn little without substantial intervention from the teacher. Centuries of scholarship on the features of effective writing accompanied by decades of comprehension research have revealed the characteristics of comprehensible text. Organization is important. Coherent texts are easier to comprehend than incoherent, poorly organized texts. In coherent texts sentences and paragraphs are organized around clear subtopics, and the overall text follows a well-known genre, such as argument or explanation. If the text has introductions, transitions, conclusions, paragraph topic sentences, and signal words that highlight this organization, readers will comprehend it better than they will a text without these features. In addition to organization, comprehension is affected by familiarity and interestingness. Readers comprehend texts better that are maximally informative, neither too familiar nor too unfamiliar, and that include vivid details and examples to capture interest. As important as text comprehensibility is, however, it does not address *what* students will learn from their reading or *whether* they will learn anything at all.

What is worth learning? The philosopher Alfred North Whitehead saw in schooling the potential to teach important understandings that students could use to make sense of the chaotic stream of events that make up experience. In his 1974 book *The Organisation of Thought,* he warned educators, "Do not teach too many subjects, [and] what you teach, teach thoroughly, seizing on the few general ideas which illuminate the whole, and persistently marshalling subsidiary facts round them" (Whitehead, p. 3.) The difficulty, of course, arises in choosing the few understandings to teach.

Ralph W. Tyler, in his classic 1949 book *Basic Principles of Curriculum and Instruction,* proposed five types of important understandings. First, subject specialists believe that the major understandings should come from the design of the knowledge domains themselves. Second, progressives and child psychologists maintain that the goal of education is to produce well-adjusted adults and that student needs should guide the choice of understandings. Third, sociologists, aware of the needs of society, argue that the understandings should be based on whatever the pressing societal problems are; the goal of schooling is to produce good citizens. Fourth, educational philosophers point to important basic life values as a guide, because they believe that the goal of education is to produce an ethical populace. Fifth, educational psychologists explain that the understandings must be developmentally appropriate; the goal of schooling is to teach something. No curriculum could effectively incorporate everything worthwhile. Therefore, Tyler suggested that curriculum designers use their philosophy of education and what they know about educational psychology to decide which understandings to include from student needs, society needs, and the domain.

Besides being comprehensible and presenting valuable content, certain types of texts are intentionally instructional, designed specifically to enhance reader learning. Argument and explanation, two familiar genres, are particularly effective instructional text types. Both genres marshal subsidiary facts around general ideas, the optimal instructional approach for teaching important understandings according to Whitehead. Argument offers facts and examples to support a claim, or general statement. Twelfth graders studying the judiciary might read a text that presents details about court decisions in order to argue, "Through its decisions, the Supreme Court has a major influence on how the trials in lower courts are conducted." Explanation presents facts, examples, illustrations, and analogies ordered logically to guide a reader from an everyday understanding toward the understanding of an expert. Fourth graders might read an explanation of electricity that introduces the scientific model of electric circuits. The explanation could begin by describing the everyday experience of turning a light switch on and off. Next it could present the steps for building a simple circuit and examples of circuits that light lamps, houses, and entire towns. The explanation could display diagrams with arrows that show how electricity moves in each of the circuits. It could conclude with a description of the atomic model and accompanying diagrams. Text features can substantially affect student learning.

**Reader Characteristics**

In order to comprehend a text, integrate the ideas in the text with what they already know and understand, and then construct a model of the situation in the text, readers must be able to capitalize on a text's comprehensibility and instructional features.

Reader knowledge is crucial. Readers who are familiar with a text's topic can rely on what they know to recognize important ideas and distinguish them from details. They can readily identify the meanings of familiar words in the text and can use what they already know to infer the meanings of unknown words. If they also know common text patterns and how they are signaled in introductions, conclusions, transitions, and topic sentences, readers can connect the separate ideas in the text into a coherent whole that resembles the text. Knowledge about arguments and explanations may be particularly important. Readers who expect to recognize and learn new ideas from reading these two genres will be far more likely to learn the ideas than readers who are oblivious to them.

But learning requires special reading strategies beyond what readers must know to be able to comprehend. In a 1997 article Susan R. Goldman, a cognitive psychologist, reviewed the extensive work on learning strategies, including some of her own work. She concluded that readers who explain and elaborate what they are reading and who have flexible comprehension strategies learn more from reading than readers who do not. The effective explainers actively search for the logical relationships among the ideas in a text. Thinking about the relationships reminds successful learners of related facts and examples from their own knowledge. These strategies lead readers to construct a model of the situation in the text closely intertwined with what they already know.

### The Learning Context

Contexts that effectively promote learning from text set learning as the goal for reading, provide students with comprehensible and "learnable" texts, draw connections between student knowledge and reading, and support and promote student thinking about text. Students may read to complete tasks, to understand activities more fully, to teach ideas to one another, to figure out the important ideas in a text, and to prepare reports, arguments, and explanations. Each of these learning goals requires that readers connect the ideas in the texts to what they already know. Teachers can promote connections by brainstorming with the students, reminding them of relevant experiences in and outside of class, encouraging them to read from several related texts, and pairing reading and experiential activities. Learning also requires readers to search for the logical

relationships among ideas in a text. Contexts that encourage students to formulate questions, summarize, explain, construct graphic organizers, and apply generic writing patterns teach students to seek out and identify the logical organization in a text. Because these strategies require conscious effort, successful learning contexts include time for students to reflect on the connections that they are making, the logical relationships that they are identifying, and whether they are successfully learning from the text.

The same instructional features that promote learning in general will also support successful learning from text. The text must be comprehensible and present significant content, however, and at least some of the instruction must focus on the ideas presented in the text. For fourth graders learning about electric circuits or twelfth graders learning about the judicial system, whether they learn from reading text will depend on the match among their goals for reading, the characteristics of the text, their reading strategies, and the entire instructional context within which their reading occurs.

*See also:* CHILDREN'S LITERATURE; LITERACY, *subentry on* INTERTEXTUALITY; LITERACY AND READING; READING, *subentries on* COMPREHENSION, CONTENT AREAS, INTEREST, PRIOR KNOWLEDGE, BELIEFS, AND LEARNING, TEACHING OF; TEXTBOOKS.

#### BIBLIOGRAPHY

CHAMBLISS, MARILYN J., and CALFEE, ROBERT C. 1998. *Textbooks for Learning: Nurturing Children's Minds.* Oxford, Eng., and Malden, MA: Blackwell Publishers.

GOLDMAN, SUSAN R. 1997. "Learning from Text: Reflections on the Past and Suggestions for the Future." *Discourse Processes* 23:357–398.

KINTSCH, WALTER. 1986. "Learning from Text." *Cognition and Instruction* 3:87–108.

TYLER, RALPH W. 1949. *Basic Principles of Curriculum and Instruction.* Chicago: University of Chicago Press.

WHITEHEAD, ALFRED N. 1974. *The Organisation of Thought.* Westport, CT: Greenwood Press.

MARILYN J. CHAMBLISS

# PRIOR KNOWLEDGE, BELIEFS, AND LEARNING

For most students, the process of learning is strongly dependent on their ability to make sense of linguistic information presented in either written or oral form. That is, for most students the process of learning is fundamentally the process of learning from text. The importance of text-based learning is as old as formal education. Yet, during the last three decades of the twentieth century, the concepts of text and learning underwent transformations that significantly influenced the nature of student academic development.

Traditionally, *text* has been viewed as the linear connected discourse typified by textbooks, magazines, or newspapers. This textual form remains a centerpiece of human learning and the source of most of the research in text-based learning. In the 1980s and 1990s other forms of text became increasingly important components in school learning. Specifically, students were also required to learn from the less linear, more dynamic, and more transient messages encountered daily in discussions and online. Thus, students must become conversant with all modalities of text if they are to learn effectively in the decades to come.

Moreover, when considering student *learning,* one must think beyond simple notions about the acquisition of declarative (i.e., factual) knowledge and procedural knowledge (i.e., knowing how to do something). Instead, learning is essentially the process of instigating deep and enduring changes in students' knowledge, beliefs, motivations, and problem-solving abilities. The focus in this entry is on the dimensions of knowledge and belief and their relationship to learning from text. As will become evident, learning from any text is a process inevitably intertwined with one's knowledge and beliefs, both in terms of the knowledge and beliefs one brings *to* the text, as well as the knowledge and beliefs one derives *from* it.

## The Text

Not surprisingly, the process of learning from text depends significantly on the genre, structure, and quality of the messages students encounter in books, in discussions, and online. For example, students must deal with texts written to tell a story (i.e., narrative), those that convey information (i.e., exposition), and those that are some combination of both (i.e., mixed text). Each of these genres affects student learning in different ways. Further, some texts offer only one perspective on a topic or issue, whereas others present multiple, competing views. These varied structures have been shown to influence students' knowledge and beliefs differently. Finally, whether narrative or expository and whether one-sided or multisided in perspective, texts can be comprehensible and coherent or difficult and inconsiderate of their audiences. Such qualities can facilitate or frustrate student learning.

**Text genres.** Research has shown that text genre influences student learning. Narratives, such as myths and novels, are expressions of actual or fictitious experiences. Because of their common story structure and overall appeal, narratives are often easier forms of text to process. Also in narration, interesting segments are often important ideas to be learned. This perhaps explains why most students learn to read using narrative texts.

In contrast, expository texts (e.g., newspapers, encyclopedias) present information that explains principles and general behavioral patterns. Many subject-matter textbooks employ exposition. They are characteristically dense with facts and concepts and are often considered to be rather dry in style. Also, interesting and important content are likely to diverge in exposition. While exposition becomes increasingly prevalent as students move out of the early elementary grades, students are given little explicit instruction in how to learn from such texts, which might help explain students' difficulties in learning from their course textbooks.

A mixed text, by comparison, possesses properties of both narration and exposition, as when textbooks incorporate personally involving information about central figures. Biography is one of the most common examples of mixed text. One problem with mixed texts is that students are often uncertain about what is factual versus what is fiction. Interesting and important content might also diverge in mixed texts as it does in exposition.

**Argument structure.** Within each genre, texts can be written to conform to particular text structures (e.g., essay or argument). Texts characterized by an argument structure, for example, often open with a claim about a topic and then follow with supporting evidence. This format closes with a warrant, restatement, or summary of the claim and supporting evidence. Texts with an argument structure are often employed to alter students' knowledge and beliefs, so studies employing various forms of argument structure appear in the literature on changing knowledge and beliefs.

In addition, a given text can have multiple arguments embedded in it. For instance, a substantive finding in the change literature is that texts presenting both sides of an argument and then refuting one side of the argument (i.e., two-sided refutational texts) are more likely to influence students' knowledge and beliefs than other argument structures. By comparison, texts that present only one side of the argument or present both sides in a more neutral fashion may be less likely to alter students' conceptions. Finally, the content or supporting evidence within a given argument also plays a significant role in learning. Students are more likely to believe and comprehend the argument if the supporting evidence comes in multiple forms (e.g., graphs, stories, and examples) or if the evidence includes personally relevant scenarios rather than consisting only of graphs and statistical data.

**Textual quality.** Among the multiple factors that contribute to text quality and subsequent learning are comprehensibility and text credibility. Simply put, when students understand the intended message in the text, text-based learning is more likely to take place. In a 1996 article Patricia A. Alexander and Tamara L. Jetton suggested that problems in text comprehension limit the acquisition of knowledge. Also, students must be able to judge the communication as coming from a reliable source. While students will likely judge textbooks as credible, this may not be the case for online materials, magazines, or newspapers. Text credibility is enhanced, however, when the message is judged as unbiased and if the author or communicator is perceived as an expert.

### The Learner

In addition to the genre, structure, content, and quality of the text, characteristics of the learner also play an influential role in text-based learning. Specifically, learning from text is mediated by a number of variables including one's prior knowledge and preexisting beliefs.

**Knowledge.** Of all the factors relevant to text-based learning, none exerts more influence on what students understand and remember than the knowledge they already possess. This background or prior knowledge serves as a scaffold for obtaining new knowledge. The term *prior knowledge*, in effect, rep-

resents individuals' mental histories or their "personal stock of information, skills, experiences, beliefs, and memories" (Alexander, Schallert, and Hare, p. 317).

Moreover, both the accuracy and extent or depth of one's knowledge seem to be critical factors in learning from text. For instance, changing students' understanding about a rather well-defined concept (e.g., the speed of falling objects) is more difficult when an individual's prior knowledge is less sophisticated or runs counter to the scientific knowledge presented in the text. The use of a two-sided refutational text that specifically counters students' naive or ill-formed concepts has proven effective under such circumstances.

The amount or level of an individual's knowledge also plays an influential role in the learning. It is relatively easier to change individuals' ideas about a particular topic if they possess some, but not too much, relevant knowledge. Individuals who are or who believe they are quite knowledgeable about a topic may feel that they have less to gain from engaging with a text message on that topic. Indeed, several studies have found that readers' perceptions of what they know (i.e., perceived knowledge) is critical and possibly even more predictive of learning than the amount of relevant knowledge they actually display (i.e., demonstrated knowledge).

**Beliefs.** Like knowledge, beliefs play a fundamental role in what students learn from text. One's beliefs are idiosyncratic, the result of the accumulation of experiences over the course of one's life. Unlike knowledge, however, definitions of beliefs vary widely from philosophy to psychology to education. Most agree that beliefs generally pertain to psychologically held understandings, premises, or propositions about the world that are felt to be true. As such, beliefs have much in common with concepts such as attitudes, values, judgments, opinions, dispositions, implicit theories, preconceptions, personal theories, and perspectives. In fact, the word *belief* is often used interchangeably with these terms. Also, the valence of truthfulness often associated with beliefs seems to give them even greater importance within text.

Perhaps one of the most important aspects about beliefs and text is the degree to which one is aware of them. While students have many beliefs that guide their actions, these beliefs may reside at the tacit level, and students may be unaware of their existence. Indeed, researchers contend that beliefs are organized in such a way that certain beliefs—the more central ones—become connected to other beliefs and are more resistant to change. Further, beliefs may be organized in clusters, allowing incompatible beliefs to be held apart in separate clusters and thus protected from each other.

The more embedded individual beliefs or clusters of beliefs become in one's belief system, the more difficult it is to change them. Nevertheless, when individuals are presented with causal explanations concerning people, objects, or events, they are likely to change or alter their beliefs, even if they are deeply embedded. It would seem that the reading and discussing of argument texts helps to bring embedded beliefs to an explicit level where they are more open to alteration. Finally, as is the case for changing or altering one's knowledge, belief change is more likely to occur when individuals read well-written, comprehensible texts. Certainly, the learning and processing of written or oral text is an intricate endeavor involving the interaction of the learner *with* the text.

*See also:* LITERACY, *subentry on* INTERTEXTUALITY; LITERACY AND READING; READING, *subentries on* COMPREHENSION, CONTENT AREAS, INTEREST, LEARNING FROM TEXT, TEACHING OF.

**BIBLIOGRAPHY**

ALEXANDER, PATRICIA A. 1996. "The Past, Present, and Future of Knowledge Research: A Reexamination of the Role of Knowledge in Learning and Instruction." *Educational Psychologist* 31:89–92.

ALEXANDER, PATRICIA A., and JETTON, TAMARA L. 1996. "The Role of Importance and Interest in the Processing of Text." *Educational Psychology Review* 8:89–122.

ALEXANDER, PATRICIA A., and MURPHY, P. KAREN. 1998. "The Research Base for APA's Learner-Centered Principles." In *Issues in School Reform: A Sampler of Psychological Perspectives on Learner-Centered School,* ed. Nadine M. Lambert and Barbara L. McCombs. Washington, DC: American Psychological Association.

ALEXANDER, PATRICIA A.; MURPHY, P. KAREN; BUEHL, MICHELLE M.; and SPERL, CHRISTOPHER T. 1998. "The Influence of Prior Knowledge, Beliefs, and Interest in Learning from Persuasive Text." In *Forty-Seventh Yearbook of the National Reading Conference,* ed. Timothy Shanahan and Flora Rodriguez-Brown. Chicago: National Reading Conference.

ALEXANDER, PATRICIA A.; SCHALLERT, DIANE L.; and HARE, VICTORIA C. 1991. "Coming to Terms: How Researchers in Learning and Literacy Talk about Knowledge." *Review of Educational Research* 61:315–343.

AXELROD, RISE B., and COOPER, CHARLES R. 1996. *The Concise Guide to Writing.* New York: St. Martin's Press.

GRAESSER, ARTHUR C.; GOLDING, JONATHAN M.; and LONG, DEBORAH L. 1991. "Narrative Representation and Comprehension." In *Handbook of Reading Research,* ed. Rebecca Barr, Michael L. Kamil, Peter B. Mosenthal, and P. David Pearson. White Plains, NY: Longman.

MURPHY, P. KAREN. 1998. "Toward a Multifaceted Model of Persuasion: Exploring Textual and Learner Interactions." Ph.D. diss., University of Maryland.

PEARSON, P. DAVID; GALLAGHER, MEG Y.; GOUDVIS, ANNE; and JOHNSTON, P. 1981. "What Kinds of Expository Materials Occur in Elementary School Children's Textbooks?" Paper presented at the annual meeting of the National Reading Conference, Dallas, TX.

TOULMIN, STEVEN E. 1958. *The Uses of Argument.* Cambridge, Eng.: Cambridge University Press.

P. KAREN MURPHY
PATRICIA A. ALEXANDER

## TEACHING OF

Reading instruction began in the United States in the early and mid-1600s with the ABC method exemplified by the hornbook, a paddle-shaped board on which were inscribed the alphabet, a few syllables, and the Lord's Prayer. *Webster's Blue-Backed Speller* replaced the hornbook, but instruction retained an emphasis on the alphabet and the Bible. *Webster's* remained at the center of reading instruction for more than a century and served mainly the upper class, as few others attended school. Those who did not attend received their education by being read to by those who did. Thus, a focus of instruction was on oral reading skills.

When the United States expanded westward, the widely dispersed people could not be serviced by a few who attended school, and everyone, those on the eastern seaboard and elsewhere, needed to learn geography and history. In 1842, in an effort to make learning to read easy for the diverse students who now attended school, Horace Mann introduced his word-to-letters approach, which employed the opposite sequence for instruction as the letters-to-words approach (that of the ABC method and *Webster's*). Eventually Mann's approach became the whole-word approach, where little attention was given to letters.

The most common texts during this time were the McGuffey Readers, 122 million copies of which were sold between 1836 and 1920. The selections not only taught history and geography but also praised the virtues of hard work and honesty. They were read orally in classrooms and were the only source of knowledge and literature for many Americans.

In 1875 Francis Parker entered the picture with his emphasis on silent reading for the purpose of greater understanding. The pronunciation of words while reading orally was no longer a sign of a good reader. When World War I began, however, 24.9 percent of the soldiers could not read and write well enough to perform the simple tasks assigned to them. Instruction needed to change, and John Dewey led the way with an emphasis on a child-centered curriculum designed to accommodate individual differences.

Discontent with the numbers of students who continued to experience difficulty in learning to read, however, led William S. Gray to move away from student-centered instruction to a model where all students received identical lessons. He developed basal readers and created the first manuals with instructional advice for teachers. His "Dick and Jane" series, launched in 1930s, consisted of passages with increasingly difficult words instead of selections of literature. His characters, drawn from successful, suburban families, became the symbols of reading instruction at the time when the United States was emerging from the depths of World War II.

In the 1960s many reading instructors, worried about the students who continued to experience difficulty, started to return to a version of the old ABC method; they placed great importance on the sounding out of words. Phonetically spelled words in reading instructional materials became increasingly popular. Selections became even further removed from the literature selections that were favored in previous decades.

Also in the 1950s and 1960s, the differences among students expanded dramatically, and the civil rights movement brought African Americans into the mainstream public schools. As always, the evolution of the nation influenced reading instruction; many students experienced difficulty, and the search for the best method of instruction continued. In 1968 Robert Dykstra conducted a nationwide survey to find the most effective means of reading instruction, but he concluded that teacher behaviors were more influential than any particular instructional method in determining student success as a reader.

A few years earlier, in 1965, Kenneth S. Goodman's report on miscue analysis practices started to influence instruction; teachers were no longer to correct every error a student made when reading orally. If an error did not affect meaning, it was considered a sign of good comprehension. In the late 1970s Dolores Durkin, in an effort to further refine comprehension instruction, observed in classrooms and found that teachers were not teaching students strategies to use in order to compose meaning as they read. Instead, teachers asked students questions to find out if they understood what they read.

Instruction in comprehension evolved as schema theorists studied the influence of students' previous experiences on their comprehension. Teachers started to focus more attention on the inferences students needed to draw between their prior knowledge and the texts they were reading. By the late 1990s dual emphases on phonemic awareness and composition brought both comprehension (the act of composing meaning) and skills (attention to the details of letters and words) to the forefront of reading instruction.

## Research on Reading Instruction

The first research on reading instruction was in the form of surveys of teaching methods and was begun in the early 1900s. In 1915 the results of reading tests were first used to compare teaching methods, and in 1933 Gray used reading tests to measure improvements in several Chicago schools.

In 1963 researchers Mary C. Austin and Coleman Morrison surveyed more than 1,000 U.S. school administrators about reading instruction and found a high reliance on basal readers and ability grouping (separating students into reading groups based upon their reading achievement levels). They recommended that teachers use a wider variety of instructional approaches and more flexible grouping plans, as differences will exist in any group despite efforts to achieve homogeneity. This survey was modified and replicated in 2000 by James F. Baumann and colleagues, and the results were compared to the original. The results of the 2000 surveys showed that basals were being used in combination with trade books and that the predominant mode for instruction had become whole-class instruction. Thus, the 2000 survey hearkened back to the earlier study where the researchers found "teachers who ignore the concept of individual difference" (Austin and Morrison, p. 219).

Large-scale, systematic comparisons of various approaches to beginning reading instruction, using objective measures of outcomes, were conducted in the 1960s and 1970s. The U.S. Office of Education sponsored the Cooperative Research Program in First Grade Reading Instruction, finding that no one program or single instructional method was superior for all classrooms or teachers. Project Follow Through, a second government study of the same era, sought specifically to determine which instructional approaches worked best to foster and maintain the educational progress of disadvantaged children through the primary grades. Again, no one instructional approach was strong enough to raise reading test scores everywhere it was implemented.

The quest for the best methods of reading instruction has continued into the twenty-first century. In 1997 the U.S. Congress authorized a national panel to assess the effectiveness of various instructional approaches to teaching reading. The National Reading Panel (NRP) conducted a meta-analysis of the effects of scientific research (experimental or quasi-experimental research) on reading instruction. The NRP limited their review to the major domains of instruction deemed essential to learning to read by the National Research Council. These domains included alphabetics (phoneme awareness, phonics instruction), fluency (oral reading accuracy, speed, and expression), and comprehension (vocabulary instruction, text comprehension instruction, strategy instruction).

In the domain of alphabetics, the NRP reported that teaching children to manipulate phonemes in words was highly effective under a variety of teaching conditions with a variety of children. In addition, systematic phonics instruction produced significant benefits for students in kindergarten through the sixth grade. In the domain of fluency, the panel concluded that guided, repeated oral reading procedures yielded significant and positive impacts on word recognition, fluency, and comprehension across a range of grade levels. In the domain of comprehension, the panel concluded that vocabulary instruction led to gains in reading comprehension and that seven types of comprehension instruction were supported by the scientific research.

Another form of research in reading instruction consists of qualitative, descriptive research within classroom settings. It includes observational studies that link classroom procedures and interactions to student outcomes and teacher behavior. Such research has the potential to distinguish between the characteristics of an instructional method and how it is actually used. According to Rebecca Barr, descriptive research "complements the research on effectiveness by revealing how an instructional approach works and how teachers differ in using it" (2001, p. 406).

Classroom observational research linked critical features of the Project Follow Through studies to student outcomes. These studies revealed high correlations between the amount of time that students were engaged in academic tasks and their academic growth. The work of these researchers influenced much of the research on effective teaching practices conducted in the late 1970s and 1980s.

Ethnographic, sociolinguistic, and other descriptive studies of reading instruction view teaching and learning as responsive, interactive forms of socially constructed activity, and such studies capture a more complete picture of instructional contexts than research labeled scientific does. Qualitative, descriptive research has revealed that interactive learning produces more growth than instruction in which students are passive. Active engagement appears to be more important that the exact method of reading instruction.

### Reading Instruction within the Overall Curriculum

Prior to the 1980s reading instruction barely existed within the content areas of the curriculum; reading was taught during times of the day called *reading* and/or *language arts*. Within the content areas, students were given textbooks and were expected to be able to read them. But because one textbook did not accommodate the reading levels of all learners, secondary teachers often used the textbooks to determine the content they would teach and delivered lectures accordingly. Elementary students often engaged in round-robin reading as their way of using the text. At all levels, students wrote answers to end-of-the-chapter questions, so that teachers could assess their student's retention of the content.

During the early 1980s the textbook began to lose its position as the sole source of subject area knowledge. Teachers started to use manipulatives (small objects such as beans and buttons that students count and move about into various groupings) to teach math, hands-on activities to teach science, and community resources to teach social studies. They supported this instruction with a variety of children's literature, rather than a single textbook. Based upon a new view of reading largely influenced by theories on meaning-making in reading that Goodman and Frank Smith put forth, even the basal readers used to teach reading started to contain more natural-sounding language.

In the 1990s falling test scores and a new political climate forced a reexamination of reading instruction within the curriculum. Researchers, teachers, administrators, and government officials formed a set of national education goals called Goals 2000. They did not agree, however, upon the approaches needed to meet these goals. Various approaches, therefore, continue to influence the direction of reading instruction in the curriculum.

One of these approaches advocates the teaching of a specific body of knowledge found within state curriculum standards. Educators create these standards to reflect the content they believe is essential to the formation of a common knowledge, and teachers use these standards to guide their instruction. Teachers across grade levels work in collaboration to ensure that the content builds in a manner that allows students to use prior knowledge and make meaningful connections across the curriculum. Teachers access online resources and handbooks for a multitude of instructional suggestions.

Thus, reading instruction related to state-directed content involves the use of textbooks, trade books, computer programs, lectures, demonstrations, specific writing models, and hands-on activities, thereby providing students with opportunities to learn the material in a variety of ways. Reading materials on many reading levels address much of this content, and schools provide additional support to students who struggle. In these various instruc-

tional arrangements, students learn the reading and writing strategies they need in order to learn about and share knowledge.

Another approach to reading instruction across the curriculum focuses on the contexts present in the classroom, rather than upon a body of content. Researchers and teachers explore interactions among the learners, the teacher, the classroom, and the texts. These interactions lead to instructional arrangements unique to individual classrooms, in which the students use their own knowledge, interests, and personal cultures to make the curriculum meaningful and to create new understandings.

In 1998 Vivian Gadsden endorsed this contextual approach in response to the increasing diversity of classroom populations. In her collaborations with primary-grade teachers, the teachers incorporated a wide range of literacy experiences specific to the cultures of the students and involved students' extended families and community in planning the endeavors. These literacy events crossed the curriculum, becoming part of the family histories students wrote with family members. Students compared their histories to texts found in the classroom, building critical literacy.

Similarly, students in some urban high schools study U.S. history in accordance with their personal histories. They move beyond textbooks, using personal artifacts, historical documents, magazine articles, and photographs in their compositions. In these different grade level contexts, reading instruction involves learners in making connections among various texts, themselves, and the world.

Text-based and context-based approaches continue to define the role of reading instruction in the curriculum during the early part of the twenty-first century. New programs advocating a core curriculum, developed outside the classroom, arise at the same time that teachers and researchers develop new instructional arrangements based upon classroom contexts. In 1992 Judith A. Langer and Richard L. Allington urged researchers to reconceptualize reading and writing instruction within the curriculum, to abandon fragmentation of study, and to consider "the relative roles of content, skills, discipline-specific thinking, and the student in the instructional agenda" (p. 717).

**Trends, Issues, and Controversies**

Increased immigration in the early twenty-first century is bringing more changes to U.S. schools. In

1993 Kathryn H. Au wrote about the need for teachers to consider the various forms of literacy that are significant in the lives of students of diverse backgrounds and to include critical literacy in their instruction.

Paulo Freire, a Brazilian educator, brought the notion of critical literacy to his country in the late 1960s, and at the turn of the millennium his work began to influence reading instruction in the United States. It is becoming increasingly important for students to critique power relationships within U.S. society.

In 2002 Arlette Ingram Willis reported on her study of the complex relationships among literacy, knowledge, privilege, and power through the lens of one institution, the Calhoun Colored School in Alabama from 1892 to 1945. She showed how the school's white founders controlled the aspirations of the school's students. Willis acknowledged the failure of countless attempts to discover the best methods of reading instruction but implored educators to remember the relationship between knowledge and power. She urged literacy instructors to critically examine the ways by which they provide opportunity for all.

This call for complexity in instruction becomes even more complicated when the nature of research enters the picture. Of the three types of research on reading instruction, the scientific method has predominated since the early twentieth century. Increases in the quantity of experimental studies have paralleled increases in immigration and scientific advances, from the beginning (the Industrial Revolution) to the end (the Technological Revolution) of the twentieth century.

According to Barr, however, this methodology treats teaching as a unidirectional variable, "an activity introduced to observe its effect on some outcome" (2001, p. 406). While outcome-based research on reading instruction yields important information about the effectiveness of instructional approaches, it does not reveal how the instructional approach works and how teachers differ in using it. Observations are necessary to elucidate the reality that scientific methods are supposed to discover. Socioconstructivist approaches to research in reading instruction examine teaching and learning in an interactive context and allow interactions among the teacher, student, and text to be seen.

These approaches have their dangers too, for if all classrooms are unique, then teachers will never

benefit from the generalizations made possible from broad-based conceptualizations of teaching that guide the critical decisions teachers make in providing instruction. Detailed descriptions are helpful when they show the day-to-day decisions teachers make when they select appropriate reading materials; achieve an effective balance of reading, writing, and word study instruction; differentiate instruction to meet diverse student needs; and empower students to take ownership of their own learning.

This call becomes complicated in the context of the standardized tests that influence reading instruction across the curriculum at the beginning of the twenty-first century. Given that many states use the results of the tests to determine school funding, teachers and school administrators often base the curriculum on the knowledge needed to answer specific items found within the tests. Teachers choose reading materials pertinent to the test content and focus reading instruction on retention of this material in the subject areas.

Educators use various kinds of reading materials to teach the above information, but textbooks occupy an important position in many classrooms. In 2000, however, Suzanne E. Wade and Elizabeth B. Moje reported on the lack of engagement of secondary school students in textbook reading. Wade and Moje advocated change and described classrooms that integrate the textbook with government documents, magazines, student-generated texts, novels, and hypermedia to provide students with opportunities to expand their perspectives on curricular concepts.

Also in 2000, the National Reading Panel reported on the lack of research into the use of technology in reading instruction in the curriculum. Given the workplace emphasis on accessing, processing, and communicating information via computers, and the increasing number of schools and homes with computers and Internet access, the roles of hypermedia and the Internet remain important areas for future exploration.

*See also:* ELEMENTARY EDUCATION, PREPARATION OF TEACHERS; LANGUAGE ARTS, TEACHING OF; READABILITY INDICES; READING, *subentries on* BEGINNING READING, COMPREHENSION, CONTENT AREAS, INTEREST, LEARNING FROM TEXT; TEACHER EDUCATION; SPELLING, TEACHING OF; WRITING, TEACHING OF.

**BIBLIOGRAPHY**

Au, Kathryn H. 1993. *Literacy Instruction in Multicultural Settings.* Fort Worth, TX: Harcourt Brace Jovanovich.

Austin, Mary C., and Morrison, Coleman. 1963. *The First R: The Harvard Report on Reading in Elementary Schools.* New York: Macmillan.

Barr, Rebecca. 2001. "Research on the Teaching of Reading." In *Handbook of Research on Teaching,* 4th edition, ed. Virginia Richardson. Washington, DC: American Educational Research Association.

Barr, Rebecca; Kamil, Michael L.; and Mosenthal, Peter, eds. 1984. *Handbook of Reading Research.* New York: Longman.

Baumann, James F.; Hoffman, James V.; Duffy-Hester, Ann M.; and Ro, Jennifer Moon. 2000. "*The First R* Yesterday and Today: U.S. Elementary Reading Instruction Practices Reported by Teachers and Administrators." *Reading Research Quarterly* 35:338–377.

Bond, Guy L., and Dykstra, Robert. 1967. "The Cooperative Research Program in First-Grade Reading Instruction." *Reading Research Quarterly* 2:5–142.

Durkin, Dolores. 1978–1979. "What Classroom Observations Reveal about Comprehension Instruction." *Reading Research Quarterly* 14:481–533.

Dykstra, Robert. 1968. "Summary of the Second-Grade Phase of the Cooperative Research Program in Primary Reading Instruction." *Reading Research Quarterly* 4:49–71.

Freire, Paulo. 1970. *Pedagogy of the Oppressed.* New York: Continuum.

Gadsden, Vivian L. 1998. "Family Cultures and Literacy Learning." In *Literacy for All: Issues in Teaching and Learning,* ed. Jean Osborn and Fran Lehr. New York: Guilford Press.

Goodman, Kenneth S. 1965. "A Linguistic Study of Cues and Miscues in Reading. *Elementary English* 42:639–643.

Goodman, Kenneth S. 1968. *The Psycholinguistic Nature of the Reading Process.* Detroit, MI: Wayne State University Press.

Gray, William S. 1948. *On Their Own in Reading.* Chicago: University of Chicago Press.

Langer, Judith A., and Allington, Richard L. 1992. "Curriculum Research in Writing and Reading." In *Handbook of Research on Curriculum: A Project of the American Educational Research Association,* ed. Philip W. Jackson. New York: Macmillan.

Mathews, Mitford M. 1966. *Teaching to Read: Historically Considered.* Chicago: University of Chicago Press.

National Institute of Child Health and Human Development. 2000. *Report of the National Reading Panel: Teaching Children to Read: An Evidence-Based Assessment of the Scientific Research Literature on Reading and Its Implications for Reading Instruction.* Washington DC: National Institutes of Health, National Institute of Child Health and Human Development.

Smith, Frank. 1979. *Reading without Nonsense.* New York: Teachers College Press.

Snow, Catherine E.; Burns, Marilyn S.; and Griffin, Peg, eds. 1998. *Preventing Reading Difficulties in Young Children.* Washington, DC: National Academy Press.

Venezky, Richard L. 1984. "The History of Reading Research." In *Handbook of Reading Research,* ed. Rebecca Barr, Michael L. Kamil, and Peter Mosenthal. New York: Longman.

Wade, Suzanne E., and Moje, Elizabeth B. 2000. "The Role of Text in Classroom Learning." In *Handbook of Reading Research,* Vol. III, ed. Michael L. Kamil, Peter B. Mosenthal, P. David Pearson, and Rebecca Barr. Mahwah, NJ: Erlbaum.

Willis, Arlette Ingram. 2002. "Literacy at Calhoun Colored School, 1892–1945." *Reading Research Quarterly* 37:8–44.

Wilson, Paul T., and Anderson, Richard C. 1986. "What They Don't Know Will Hurt Them: The Role of Prior Knowledge in Comprehension." In *Reading Comprehension: From Research to Practice,* ed. Judith Orasanu. Hillsdale, NJ: Erlbaum.

Jane Hansen
Marcia Invernizzi
Jenesse Wells Evertson

# VALUE OF READING ENGAGEMENT FOR CHILDREN

Educators have become increasingly interested in the role that reading engagement or volume—the amount of print children are exposed to—plays in the growth of academic achievement. In the early twenty-first century, it is believed that reading activity itself serves to increase the achievement differences among children. Children who are exposed to more literacy experiences early in their development are positioned to take advantage of the educational opportunities presented to them in preschool and elementary school. In contrast, children who are largely unfamiliar with print find themselves less able to take advantage of those same educational opportunities. This reciprocal relationship is observed in the social and cognitive contexts of school and home. A model of these effects in reading has been emerging in the literature. Reading engagement is thought to be deeply intertwined and a contributing factor to the escalating differences observed among children in their reading achievement. Thus, on the basis of available evidence, there appears to be a strong rationale for educators and policymakers alike to call for increased amounts of reading volume or engagement in young children as means to improve their reading achievement.

## The Importance of Reading Aloud to Children

Reading aloud to children has been broadly advocated as an important educational practice in which to foster reading volume. Parents and teachers have been increasingly encouraged to read aloud to young children as a developmentally appropriate practice by professional societies such as the International Reading Association for the Education of Young Children. These reading experiences have been shown to provide a host of benefits to the young child. In addition to the socioemotional benefits of sitting in a parent's lap, many aspects of language and cognitive development are thought to be facilitated. For example, reading aloud to children has been found to facilitate the growth of vocabulary in preschool-age children and elementary-age students. Reading aloud has been shown to promote children's understanding of academic language of text, which differs significantly from oral language. This practice also introduces novel concepts of text structure and story grammar and provides an important avenue for learning about the world. One of the most commonly held beliefs regarding the value of reading aloud to young children is that such exposure will introduce them to the world of print and motivate them to seek out these experiences on their own. These outcomes are all important predictors of children's reading achievement, yet it appears the effects of reading aloud to children are limited to certain facets of language and literacy.

## Does Reading Aloud to Children Teach Them How to Learn to Read?

A common hypothesis, held by many educators and parents, is that one of the primary benefits of reading aloud to children is the promotion of children's literacy development. Specifically, some researchers have argued that reading aloud to children is an effective and natural way for them to learn to read. Via a series of successive approximations while being read to, the young child will learn how to decode and recognize words. That is, the practice of reading aloud to children is thought to be an important mechanism (and for some the primary one) in learning to read and can explain individual and group differences in literacy growth among children. Although it makes sense intuitively that reading aloud should facilitate general literacy development, this hypothesis merits empirical investigation to understand under what conditions and for what readers reading aloud facilitates children's reading development. While it is difficult to isolate the literacy gains that accrue from reading aloud to children, one must attempt to compare this variable to the impact of other educational practices or experiences when inferring causality about certain practices.

Although many studies have shown a strong to moderate relation between reading aloud to children and their subsequent reading achievement, these studies failed to control for numerous mediating variables. The studies that attempted to tease apart the relative contribution of the time parents spend reading aloud to their children and determine the effect of this practice have demonstrated relatively low correlations when compared with other predictors such as promoting phonemic awareness (the ability to attend to the sounds of language and manipulate them) and letter-name knowledge (the ability to quickly name letters). David Share and colleagues' comprehensive study from 1984 indicted that parents reading aloud to their children made a weak indirect contribution to developing literacy and that children's phonemic awareness was a far more potent indicator. In the early 1990s Hollis Scarborough and her colleagues determined that other variables— such as early language, interest in solitary book reading, and emergent literacy skills—were significantly more predictive of later reading achievement. The results of yet another large-scale study by Jana Mason suggested that when compared to other individual differences in children's abilities, reading aloud to children was a less direct and relatively weaker predictor of children's reading achievement. Parallel results have been observed through the examination of the contribution of teachers' reading aloud to their students and the students' subsequent growth in decoding and word recognition skills. Many of the studies demonstrate weak or moderately facilitative effects, whereas a few have even observed negative effects of reading aloud to children, which should be interpreted as largely owing to the displacement effect of reading to children instead of teaching them to read.

In the domain of children's beginning word recognition skills, the research is demonstrating that read-alouds by parents and teachers play a limited role. Yet when parents and teachers scaffold or help a child's attempts to read the words in a story (compared to reading the words out loud to the child), stronger effects are observed. The National Reading Panel Report in 2000 summarized the research demonstrating that the primary mechanism for acquiring fluent word recognition skills (e.g., letter knowledge, sound-symbol correspondences, decoding words and recognizing them automatically) is not through being read to but via methods that entail guided or direct instruction.

## Guided Reading and Reading Aloud to Children

In addition to direct instruction, guided oral reading is emerging as an important form of reading volume, particularly for beginning readers. Guided oral reading encourages children to read text orally and includes systematic, explicit guidance and feedback from their parent or teacher. In 1999 Linda Meyer and colleagues juxtaposed the practice of teachers reading *with* children (guided oral reading) versus reading *to* them (read-alouds) as different mechanisms for increasing reading engagement. In contrast to reading aloud to children, reading with children is a more effective practice for promoting reading skill and fluency. In 1997 Steve Stahl and colleagues provided further support for this conjecture. They observed significant differences in students' reading fluency and comprehension levels as a result of teacher-guided reading practices in a comprehensive study of second-grade students. Meta-analyses of guided oral reading have further demonstrated the value of this instructional practice

in promoting word recognition, fluency, and reading comprehension across a range of grade levels.

In conclusion, the emphasis on immersing children in literature and increasing their exposure to print is an educational practice that makes sense. Nonetheless, there are multiple purposes and mechanisms for fostering reading engagement and volume that must be considered. When discussing the value of reading engagement and volume, one should attempt to specify the purposes of these practices, especially when making causal attributions. Reading aloud to children is an important educational practice that promotes vocabulary growth, understanding of text and genre, general knowledge, and hopefully motivation to read. In contrast, guided oral reading is a practice that has been found to be a more effective method of promoting children's word recognition, fluency, and comprehension. The primary aim of these educational practices is to foster independent reading.

The variability in children's levels of reading volume serves to further exacerbate the growing disparities between good and poor readers. It is therefore essential to provide multiple reading experiences for young children: reading aloud to them from a variety of genres, reading with them and facilitating their oral reading with tailored feedback and guidance, and promoting extended independent reading opportunities at home and after school. If reading makes one smarter (as some research has found) and if reading is important for a child to get off to a successful early start for future reading ability and engagement, then the value of early reading engagements, as Anne Cunningham and Keith Stanovich have found, and volume across a variety of venues cannot be overestimated.

*See also:* CHILDREN'S LITERATURE; EARLY CHILDHOOD EDUCATION; READING, *subentries on* BEGINNING READING, INTEREST.

### BIBLIOGRAPHY

ADAMS, MARILYN J. 1990. *Beginning to Read: Thinking and Learning about Print.* Cambridge, MA: MIT Press.

ARNOLD, DAVID S., and WHITEHURST, GROVER J. 1994. "Accelerating Language Development through Picture Book Reading: A Summary of Dialogic Reading and Its Effects." In *Bridges to Literacy: Children, Families, and Schools,* ed.

David K. Dickinson. Cambridge, MA: Basil Blackwell.

BAKER, LINDA; SCHER, DEBORAH; and MACKLER, KIRSTEN. 1997. "Home and Family Influences on Motivations for Reading." *Educational Psychologists* 32(2):69–82.

BUS, A. G., and VAN IJZENDOORN, M. H. 1995. "Mothers Reading to Their Three Year Olds: The Role of Mother-Child Attachment Security in Becoming Literate." *Reading Research Quarterly* 40:998–1,015.

CHALL, JEANNE S.; JACOBS, VICKI A.; and BALDWIN, LUKE E. 1990. *The Reading Crisis: Why Poor Children Fall Behind.* Cambridge, MA: Harvard University Press.

CUNNINGHAM, ANNE E., and STANOVICH, KEITH E. 1997. "Early Reading Acquisition and Its Relation to Reading Experience and Ability Ten Years Later." *Developmental Psychology* 33:934–945.

CUNNINGHAM, ANNE E., and STANOVICH, KEITH E. 1998. "What Reading Does for the Mind." *American Educator* 22(1–2):8–15.

DICKINSON, DAVID K., and SMITH, MIRIAM W. 1994. "Long-Term Effects of Preschool Teachers' Book Readings on Low-Income Children's Vocabulary and Story Comprehension." *Reading Research Quarterly* 29:104–122.

EHRI, LINNEA C., and ROBBINS, C. 1992. "Beginners Need Some Decoding Skill to Read by Analogy." *Reading Research Quarterly* 27:13–26.

ELLER, REBECCA G.; PAPPAS, CHRISTINE C.; and BROWN, ELGA. 1988. "The Lexical Development of Kindergartners: Learning from Written Context." *Journal of Reading Behavior* 20:5–24.

ELLEY, WARWICK B. 1989. "Vocabulary Acquisition from Listening to Stories." *Reading Research Quarterly* 24:174–187.

FEITELSON, D.; GOLDSTEIN, Z.; IRAQI, U.; and SHARE, D. 1993. "Effects of Listening to Story Reading on Aspects of Literacy Acquisition in a Diglossic Situation." *Reading Research Quarterly* 28:70–79.

HAYES, DONALD P., and AHRENS, MARGARET G. 1988. "Vocabulary Simplification for Children: A Special Case of 'Motherese'?" *Journal of Child Language* 15:395–410.

JUEL, CONNIE. 1994. *Learning to Read and Write in One Elementary School.* New York: Springer-Verlag.

MASON, JANA M. 1992. "Reading Stories to Preliterate Children: A Proposed Connection to Reading." In *Reading Acquisition,* ed. Philip B. Gough, Linnea C. Ehri, and Rebecca Treiman. Hillsdale, NJ: Erlbaum.

MASON, JANA M.; STEWART, J. P.; PETERMAN, C. L.; and DUNNING, D. 1992. *Toward an Integrated Model of Early Reading Development.* Urbana-Champaign, IL: Center for the Study of Reading.

McCORMICK, CHRISTINE E., and MASON, JANA M. 1986. "Intervention Procedures for Increasing Preschool Children's Interest in and Knowledge about Reading." In *Emergent Literacy: Writing and Reading,* ed. William H. Teale and Elizabeth Sulzby. Norwood, NJ: Ablex.

MEYER, LINDA A.; STAHL, STEVEN A.; WARDROP, JAMES L.; and LINN, ROBERT E. 1999. "Reading to Children or Reading with Children?" *Effective School Practices* 17(3):56–64.

NATIONAL INSTITUTE OF CHILD HEALTH AND HUMAN DEVELOPMENT. 2000. *Report of the National Reading Panel: Teaching Children to Read: An Evidence-Based Assessment of the Scientific Research Literature on Reading and Its Implications for Reading Instruction.* Washington, DC: National Institutes of Health, National Institute of Child Health and Human Development.

NICHOLSON, TOM, and WHYTE, B. 1992. "Matthew Effects in Learning New Words while Reading." In *Literacy Research, Theory, and Practice: Views from Many Perspectives,* ed. Charles K. Kinzer and Donald J. Leu. Chicago: National Reading Conference.

OLSON, DAVID R. 1986. "Intelligence and Literacy: The Relationships between Intelligence and the Technologies of Representation and Communication." In *Practical Intelligence,* ed. Robert J. Sternberg and Richard K. Wagner. Cambridge, Eng.: Cambridge University Press.

SCARBOROUGH, HOLLIS S. 1990. "Very Early Language Deficits in Dyslexic Children." *Child Development* 61:1728–1743.

SCARBOROUGH, HOLLIS S. 1991. "Early Syntactic Development of Dyslexic Children." *Annals of Dyslexia* 41:207–220.

SCARBOROUGH, HOLLIS S., and DOBRICH, WANDA. 1994. "On the Efficacy of Reading to Preschoolers." *Developmental Review* 14:245–302.

Scarborough, Hollis S.; Dobrich, Wanda; and Hager, M. 1990. "Preschool Literacy Experience and Later Reading Achievement." *Journal of Learning Disabilities* 24:508–511.

Senechal, Monique. 1997. "The Differential Effect of Storybook Reading on Preschoolers' Acquisition of Expressive and Receptive Vocabulary." *Journal of Child Language* 24:123–138.

Senechal, Monique; LeFevre, J.; Hudson, E.; and Lawson, E. P. 1996. "Knowledge of Storybooks as a Predictor of Young Children's Vocabulary." *Journal of Educational Psychology* 88:520–536.

Senechal, Monique; LeFevre, J.; Smith-Chant, B.; and Colton, K. 2001. "On Refining Theoretical Models of Emergent Literacy: The Role of Empirical Evidence." *Journal of School Psychology* 39:439–460.

Share, David L. 1995. "Phonological Recoding and Self-Teaching: Sine Qua Non of Reading Acquisition." *Cognition* 55:151–218.

Share, David L.; Jorm, Anthony F.; Maclean, R.; and Matthews, R. 1984. "Sources of Individual Differences in Reading Acquisition." *Journal of Educational Psychology* 76:1,309–1,324.

Snow, Catherine E.; Burns, M. Susan; and Griffin, Peg, eds. 1998. *Preventing Reading Difficulties in Young Children.* Washington, DC: National Academy Press.

Stahl, Steven A; Heubach, K.; and Cramond, B. 1997. *Fluency-Oriented Reading Instruction. Reading Research Report No. 79.* Athens, GA: National Reading Research Center.

Stanovich, Keith E. 1986. "Matthew Effects in Reading: Some Consequences of Individual Differences in the Acquisition of Literacy." *Reading Research Quarterly* 21:360–407.

Stanovich, Keith E. 1993. "Does Reading Make You Smarter? Literacy and the Development of Verbal Intelligence." In *Advances in Child Development and Behavior,* ed. Hayne W. Reese. San Diego, CA: Academic Press.

Stanovich, Keith E. 2000. *Progress in Understanding Reading: Scientific Foundations and New Frontiers.* New York: Guilford Press.

Stanovich, Keith E., and Cunningham, Anne E. 1992. "Studying the Consequences of Literacy within a Literate Society: The Cognitive Correlates of Print Exposure." *Memory and Cognition* 20:51–68.

Stanovich, Keith E., and Cunningham, Anne E. 1993. "Where Does Knowledge Come From? Specific Associations between Print Exposure and Information Acquisition." *Journal of Educational Psychology* 85:211–229.

Sulzby, Elizabeth, and Teale, William H. 1991. "Emergent Literacy." In *Handbook of Reading Research,* Vol. 2, ed. Rebecca Barr, Michael L. Kamil, Peter Mosenthal, and P. David Pearson. White Plains, NY: Longman.

Teale, William H. 1984. "Home Background and Young Children's Literacy Development." In *Emergent Literacy: Writing and Reading,* ed. William H. Teale and Elizabeth Sulzby. Norwood, NJ: Ablex.

Walberg, Herbert J., and Tsai, Shiow-Ling. 1983. "Matthew Effects in Education." *American Educational Research Journal* 20:359–373.

Wigfield, Allan, and Asher, Steven R. 1984. "Social and Motivational Influences on Reading." In *Handbook of Reading Research,* Vol. 1, ed. P. David Pearson, Rebecca Barr, Michael L. Kamil, and Peter Mosenthal. New York: Longman.

Anne Cunningham

# READING DISABILITIES

The concept of reading disability, while widely accepted, is not clearly understood. Traditionally, reading disability has been defined as unexpected underachievement characterized as a discrepancy between achievement and intellectual aptitude, despite adequate opportunity to learn and in the absence of sensory difficulties or cultural deprivation. This discrepancy is typically defined operationally in terms of a difference between IQ and scores on a test of reading achievement. The specific discrepancy necessary to qualify varies from state to state. Children who conform to this definition qualify for special education services under the learning disabilities label, whereas children who do not conform do not qualify, even though they may experience serious difficulties in becoming competent readers. While some low-achieving students who do not demonstrate the stipulated achievement-aptitude discrepancy may receive supplemental reading instruction in compensatory education or dyslexia programs, in many locations they receive no extra attention. A small number of schools qualify students as having learning disabilities based on professional judgment rather than IQ-achievement discrepancies, so that these students can receive reading assistance.

## Historical Context

The concept of unexpected underachievement has appeared in the literature since the middle of the nineteenth century. The term *learning disability* (LD) first appeared in 1962, when Samuel Kirk applied it to unexpected difficulties in the areas of language, learning, and communication. In 1969 the Learning Disabilities Act made special education services available to students with LD. The category was reaffirmed in 1975 with the passage of the Education for All Handicapped Children Act. The concept of LD remains basically unchanged in the current authorization of the Individuals with Disabilities Education Act (IDEA). In the early twenty-first century more than 80 percent of students classified as learning disabled are identified as having a reading disability.

## Types of Reading Disabilities

The most widely recognized and researched reading disability is associated with difficulty with reading single words. This type of difficulty is the most pervasive characteristic of dyslexia. These single-word-reading problems are thought to be based on an underlying phonological processing core deficit. Persons with dyslexia experience great difficulty in applying the alphabetic principle to decode words quickly and efficiently. The result is that decoding is labored, fluency is poor, and comprehension is negatively affected.

A less common and poorly researched reading disability is associated with poor language comprehension. While much less frequent than decoding difficulty, this disability affects some persons who have normal phonological processing skills but who demonstrate difficulty in formulating main ideas, summaries, and inferences. This difficulty is demonstrated when listening to, as well as reading, text.

A third group of students who experience great difficulty in learning to read are those who experience both decoding problems and language comprehension problems. So far, little research has been conducted with these students. It can be argued, however, that students in this last category have the greatest needs and the most severe reading disabilities.

## Validity of the Discrepancy Model

Educational leaders and researchers have been questioning the validity of the definition of reading disability in terms of an aptitude-achievement discrepancy. Proposals under study in the early twenty-first century would identify a student as having a reading disability based on the growth of reading performance across time in response to quality instruction.

A convergence of research evidence has called into question the validity of the discrepancy models. Three groups of researchers have conducted meta-analyses of studies addressing the question of differences between students identified as having LD and other struggling readers.

Doug Fuchs and his colleagues examined seventy-nine studies that compared poor readers with and without the LD label. Across studies, and across many substantive and mythological variables associated with the studies, the mean-weighted effect size describing the difference between students identified as having LD and other low-achieving readers was 0.6 of a standard deviation. In other words, the LD-identified students on average performed worse on measures of reading than other low-achieving readers. The effect sizes were more pronounced on timed reading tests, and they were larger for students at higher grade levels. Interestingly, the difference between LD and low-achieving readers was greatly diminished when analyses were run only on researcher-identified LD samples, thereby eliminating school-identified samples. This finding suggests that schools identify LD as the lowest of the low performers.

The difference between school-identified and researcher-identified LD samples is an important distinction. Researchers are much more likely to apply IQ-achievement discrepancy criteria. Schools, however, are more likely to identify students who have IQs in a range that identifies them as having mild mental retardation or to use professional judgment, despite lack of a discrepancy, to label students as having LD. Thus, it would seem that schools are actually identifying more seriously impaired readers as having LD than strict application of the definitions would permit.

Looking specifically at the validity of discrepancy models, Maureen Hoskyn and H. Lee Swanson (2000) coded nineteen studies that met certain criteria for the definition of the IQ-discrepant and

IQ-consistent (nondiscrepant low-achieving) groups. Hoskyn and Swanson found that students in the two groups had minimal differences on measures of reading and phonological processing and had larger differences on measures of vocabulary and syntax.

Similarly, K. K. Stuebing and colleagues, in another study, coded forty-six studies that clearly defined groups of readers as IQ-discrepant or IQ-consistent, with the primary research question focusing on the validity of the use of aptitude-achievement discrepancies to categorize struggling readers. The researchers found little support for the validity of discrepancies for the classification of students as LD. There were negligible differences between the IQ-discrepant and IQ-consistent groups on measures most closely associated with reading. Taken together, these three syntheses suggest that there is little basis for continuing to base qualifications for special services on current discrepancy models.

Beyond the fact that the current model lacks validity, it tends to favor students with higher IQs, as it is difficult for a student with a low IQ to exhibit achievement scores low enough to qualify for the discrepancy. There is at best, however, a questionable relationship between IQ and the way students respond to early intervention. Five studies conducted between 1997 and 2000 found no relationship between IQ and intervention outcomes. One study found a small relationship between IQ and outcome on one of three outcome measures. David Francis and colleagues found in 1996 that IQ-discrepant and IQ-consistent groups had no significant differences in progress from kindergarten through high school.

Further, the use of the exclusionary criteria in the current definition of LD can result in the withholding of services to students from culturally different or impoverished backgrounds. Given the strong correlation between oral language development and socioeconomic level, it is likely that many children from impoverished families would experience difficulties with phonological processing and in language comprehension. Further, factors associated with inadequate instruction, emotional disturbance, and poverty may actually cause differences in neurological and cognitive development that lead to severe learning difficulties. The current definition of LD makes it all too likely that students experiencing difficulties stemming from these situations will be excluded from receiving services.

Another problem with using a discrepancy model to identify reading disabilities is that it is very difficult to detect discrepancies early. Typically, children have to fall behind before the discrepancy is identified. Thus, the use of IQ-achievement discrepancy is inherently a "wait to fail" model. The problem with waiting until a child fails is that reading problems become intractable as children age. Thus, it is important to begin intervention with children very early.

## Changing Criteria for Reading Disability

Rather than focus on whether a child has an IQ-achievement discrepancy, current proposals recommend that determination of reading disabilities be made based on an examination of response to quality intervention. This response to treatment would be determined using ongoing, frequent measures of word recognition, fluency, vocabulary, and comprehension, as well as subskills that correlate strongly with reading development, including phonological awareness (the ability to blend and segment sounds in speech), rapid naming, and phonological working memory.

A convergence of research indicates that early intervention in the primary grades is effective in preventing reading problems for most children and that, for those who continue to experience difficulty, the depth of the reading problem can be greatly reduced. In their 2001 analysis of response rates to interventions in five studies, G. Reid Lyon and colleagues estimated that the number of students experiencing serious reading problems could be reduced from about 20 percent to 5 percent or less of the school population through quality early intervention.

## A Three-Tiered Approach to Intervention

Current proposals recommend a three-tiered model of reading intervention. On the first tier, classroom-level general education instruction is improved. Research suggests that this first level of intervention is adequate to reduce substantially the large numbers of struggling readers. For example, in 1998 Barbara Foorman and colleagues found that classroom-level explicit instruction in phonological awareness and the alphabetic principle as part of a balanced approach to reading brought the majority of students in grades one and two in eight Title I schools to national averages. More recently, in 2002, Joseph Torgesen and colleagues demonstrated that the vast majority of struggling first-grade readers in middle-class schools could attain above-average reading performance through quality classroom reading instruction alone.

Children who still experience difficulty after quality classroom-level instruction move into the second tier, which incorporates more intense interventions presumably delivered within general education in small groups. There are many examples of successful secondary-level interventions. In 1997 Torgesen and colleagues identified children in kindergarten who had poor phonological awareness. By second grade, intervention brought 75 percent of these children to grade-level reading. Frank Vellutino and colleagues in 1996 identified middle-class children with very low word recognition skills at the beginning of first grade. After one semester of intervention, 70 percent were reading at grade level. After two semesters, more than 90 percent were at grade level.

In the three-tiered intervention model, only after these two levels of interventions have failed would a child be considered reading disabled, requiring tertiary intervention. Tertiary intervention is typically described as having greater intensity and duration than secondary intervention. Presumably, at this point special education services would be provided.

Under this three-tiered model, there would be provisions for (1) early identification of children at risk for reading failure, followed by (2) carefully designed intense early reading instruction incorporating an emphasis on systematic, explicit instruction in alphabetic reading skills balanced with meaningful experiences with authentic texts and writing, and (3) continued support beyond the initial acquisition of reading skill to ensure continued academic growth into the upper grades. Thus, all students who are identified as at risk for possible reading problems would be provided with intervention within general education. Only children who do not make adequate progress would be considered for a reading disabilities label. This label, however, would not be based on IQ-achievement discrepancies, but rather on inadequate response to intervention.

## Quality of Intervention

The success of the three-tier model hinges on ensuring that instruction at each of the three levels is of high quality. As a result, it would unify general, special, and compensatory education services into one adaptable unit and would require that all teachers involved in the process be provided with ongoing staff development and mentoring in the critical content of effective reading instruction. This critical content includes instruction that supports the development of phonological awareness, letter knowledge, and concepts of print in emergent readers. This type of curriculum ensures acquisition of accurate and quick word recognition skills and increases the speed and ease of reading connected text. Instruction linked to extensive engagement with authentic literature gives students the opportunity to learn new vocabulary and to acquire strategies such as making inferences, identifying main ideas, and summarizing text.

## Lingering Questions

Although there is substantial research evidence regarding effective models of reading intervention at the primary (classroom) and secondary levels, it is not yet known whether a three-tiered reading intervention model can be consistently implemented to identify students in need of more intense special services. Further research is necessary to validate this model as practical and accurate. A primary question focuses on how such a model based on instructional practices that have been validated in research projects can be "scaled up" to be implemented successfully within many school contexts.

Research has focused on classroom-level and secondary-level intervention that impacts the majority of students. What is much less clear is the content of tertiary instruction. Little has been done to follow up and provide additional services with the few children who have made poor progress in secondary intervention models. Thus, there is little guidance as to what will be required to promote adequate progress among this small set of impaired readers.

Likewise, the bulk of research on the prevention of reading difficulties has focused on the most common type of reading problems, those associated with phonological processing problems. Much less is known about how to appropriately intervene with students who experience language comprehension problems.

## Conclusion

Knowledge about reading disability is evolving. It is clear that many students struggle to develop reading competence. Although most of these students exhibit common characteristics related to difficulties in processing the sounds of language, researchers have yet to satisfactorily answer the question, "When is a reading difficulty a serious reading disability?" The current practice of identifying reading disability according to a discrepancy between IQ and achievement scores, although relatively easy to implement, has the potential to underidentify many students who need special services. A more useful way to identify reading disability may be through the evaluation of a student's response to well-implemented, quality intervention. Much remains to be learned, however, regarding the implementation of this type of identification system.

*See also:* LEARNING DISABILITIES, EDUCATION OF INDIVIDUALS WITH; LITERACY AND READING; READING, *subentry on* COMPREHENSION.

## BIBLIOGRAPHY

BERNINGER, VIRGINIA W., and ABBOTT, ROBERT D. 1994. "Redefining Learning Disabilities: Moving beyond Aptitude-Achievement Discrepancies to Failure to Validate Treatment Protocols." In *Frames of Reference for the Assessment of Learning Disabilities,* ed. G. Reid Lyon. Baltimore: Brookes.

*Education for All Handicapped Children Act of 1975.* U.S. Public Law 94-142. *U.S. Code.* Vol. 20, secs. 1401 et seq.

*Education of the Handicapped Act of 1970.* U.S. Public Law 91-230. *U.S. Code.* Vol. 20, secs. 1401 et seq.

ELMORE, RICHARD F. 1996. "Getting to Scale with Good Educational Practice." *Harvard Educational Review* 66:1–26.

FOORMAN, BARBARA R.; FRANCIS, DAVID J.; FLETCHER, JACK M.; SCHATSCHNEIDER, CHRISTOPHER; and MEHTA, PARAS. 1998. "The Role of Instruction in Learning to Read: Preventing Reading Failure in At-Risk Children." *Journal of Educational Psychology* 90:38–55.

FOORMAN, BARBARA R.; FRANCIS, DAVID J.; WINIKATES, DEBBIE; MEHTA, PARAS; SCHATSCHNEIDER, CHRISTOPHER; and FLETCHER, JACK M. 1997. "Early Interventions for Children with Reading Disabilities." *Scientific Studies of Reading* 3:255–276.

FRANCIS, DAVID J.; SHAYWITZ, SALLY E.; STUEBING, K. K.; SHAYWITZ, BENNETT A.; and FLETCHER,

JACK M. 1996. "Developmental Lag versus Deficit Models of Reading Disability: A Longitudinal Individual Growth Curves Analysis." *Journal of Educational Psychology* 88:3–17.

FUCHS, DOUG; FUCHS, LYNN S.; MATHES, PATRICIA G.; LIPSEY, MARK W.; and EATON, SUSAN A. 2000. "Meta-analysis of Reading Differences between Underachievers with and without the Disabilities Label: A Brief Report." *Learning Disability: A Multidisciplinary Journal* 10(1):1–4.

FUCHS, DOUG; FUCHS, LYNN S.; MATHES, PATRICIA G.; and LIPSEY, MARK W. 2000. "Reading Differences in Low-Achievers with and without Learning Disabilities." In *Contemporary Special Education Research,* ed. Russell Gersten and Sharon Vaughn. Mahwah, NJ: Erlbaum.

FUCHS, DOUG; FUCHS, LYNN S.; MATHES, PATRICIA G.; LIPSEY, MARK W.; and ROBERTS, P. HOLLEY. 2001. "Is 'Learning Disabilities' Just a Fancy Term for Low-Achievement? A Meta-analysis of Reading Differences between Low Achievers with and without the Label." Paper presented at the Learning Disabilities Summit, Washington, DC.

FUCHS, DOUG; MATHES, PATRICIA G.; FUCHS, LYNN S.; and LIPSEY, MARK W. 1998. *Is Learning Disabilities Nothing More than an Oversophistication of Low Achievement? A Review of the Literature in Reading.* Technical report submitted to U.S. Department of Education, Washington, DC.

FUCHS, LYNN S., and FUCHS, DOUG. 1997. "Use of Curriculum-Based Measurement in Identifying Students with Disabilities." *Focus on Exceptional Children* 30:1–16.

GRESHAM, FRANK M. 2001. "Responsiveness to Intervention: An Alternative Approach to the Identification of Learning Disabilities." Paper presented at the Learning Disabilities Summit, Washington DC.

GRESHAM, FRANK M.; MACMILLAN, DONALD L.; and BOCIAN, KATHLEEN. 1996. "Teachers as 'Tests': Differential Validity of Teacher Judgment in Identifying Students at Risk for Learning Difficulties." *School Psychology Review* 26:47–60.

HART, BETTY, and RISLEY, TODD R. 1995. *Meaningful Differences in the Everyday Experience of Young American Children.* Baltimore: Brookes.

HATCHER, PETER, and HULME, CHARLES. 1999. "Phonemes, Rhymes, and Intelligence as Predictors of Children's Responsiveness to Reading Remediation." *Journal of Experimental Child Psychology* 72:130–155.

Hoskyn, Maureen, and Swanson, H. Lee. 2000. "Cognitive Processing of Low Achievers and Children with Reading Disabilities: A Selective Meta-analytic Review of the Published Literature." *School Psychology Review* 29:102–119.

*Individuals with Disabilities Education Act of 1997.* U.S. Public Law 105-17. *U.S. Code.* Vol. 20, secs. 1400 et seq.

Jenkins, J., and O'Connor, R. E. 2001. "Early Identification for Young Children with Reading/ Learning Disabilities." Paper presented at the Learning Disabilities Summit, Washington DC.

Juel, Connie. 1988. "Learning to Read and Write: A Longitudinal Study of Children in First and Second Grade." *Journal of Educational Psychology* 80:437–447.

Kavale, Kenneth A., and Reese, Jim H. 1992. "The Character of Learning Disabilities: An Iowa Profile." *Learning Disability Quarterly* 15:74–94.

Kirk, Samuel. 1962. *Educating Exceptional Children.* Boston: Houghton Mifflin.

Lerner, J. 1989. "Educational Intervention in Learning Disabilities." *Journal of the American Academy of Child and Adolescent Psychiatry* 28:326–331.

Lyon, G. Reid. 1995. "Toward a Definition of Dyslexia." *Annals of Dyslexia* 45:3–27.

Lyon, G. Reid; Fletcher, Jack M.; Shaywitz, Sally E.; Shaywitz, Bennett A.; Torgesen, Joseph K.; Wood, Frank B.; Schulte, Ann; and Olson, Richard. 2001. "Rethinking Learning Disabilities." In *Rethinking Special Education for a New Century,* ed. Chester E. Finn, Andrew J. Rotherham, and Charles R Hokanson, Jr. Washington, DC: Fordham Foundation.

Mathes, Patricia G., and Torgesen, Joseph K. 1998. "All Children Can Learn to Read: Critical Care for Student with Special Needs." *Peabody Journal of Education* 73:317–340.

National Institute of Child Health and Human Development. 2000. *Report of the National Reading Panel: Teaching Students to Read: An Evidence-Based Assessment of the Scientific Research Literature on Reading and Its Implications for Reading Instruction.* Washington, DC: National Institutes of Health, National Institute of Child Health and Human Development.

Snow, Catherine E.; Burns, M. Susan; and Griffin, Peg, eds. 1998. *Preventing Reading Difficulties in Young Children.* Washington, DC: National Academy Press.

Stanovich, Keith E. 1986. "Matthew Effects in Reading: Some Consequences of Individual Differences in the Acquisition of Literacy." *Reading Research Quarterly* 21:360–406.

Stanovich, Keith E. 1991. "Discrepancy Definitions of Reading Ability: Has Intelligence Led Us Astray?" *Reading Research Quarterly* 26:7–29.

Stanovich, Keith E., and Siegel, Linda S. 1994. "Phenotypic Performance Profile of Children with Reading Disabilities: A Regression-Based Test of Phonological-Core Variable-Difference Model." *Journal of Educational Psychology* 86:24–53.

Stuebing, K. K.; Fletcher, J. M.; LeDoux, J. M.; Lyon, G. R.; Shaywitz, S. E.; and Shaywitz, B. A. Forthcoming. "Validity of IQ-Discrepancy Classifications of Reading Disabilities: A Meta-Analysis." *American Educational Research Journal.*

Torgesen, Joseph K.; Alexander, Ann W.; Wagner, Richard K.; Rashotte, Carol A.; Voeller, Kytja K. S.; and Conway, Tim. 2001. "Intensive Remedial Instruction for Children with Severe Reading Disabilities: Immediate and Long-Term Outcomes from Two Instructional Approaches." *Journal of Learning Disabilities* 34:33–58.

Torgesen, Joseph K., and Burgess, S. R. 1998. "Consistency of Reading-Related Phonological Processes throughout Early Childhood: Evidence from Longitudinal-Correlational and Instructional Studies." In *Word Recognition in Beginning Literacy,* ed. Jamie Metsala and Linnea Ehri. Hillsdale, NJ: Erlbaum.

Torgesen, Joseph K.; Mathes, Patricia G.; and Grek, M. L. 2002. "Effectiveness of an Early Intervention Curriculum that Is Closely Coordinated with the Regular Classroom Reading Curriculum." Paper presented at the annual meeting of the Pacific Coast Research Conference, San Diego, CA.

Torgesen, Joseph K.; Wagner, Richard K.; Rashotte, Carol A.; Alexander, Ann W.; and Conway, Tim. 1997. "Preventive and Remedial Interventions for Children with Severe Disabilities." *Learning Disabilities: A Multidisciplinary Journal* 8:51–61.

TORGESEN, J. K.; WAGNER, RICHARD K.; RASHOTTE, CAROL A.; ROSE, ELAINE; LINDAMOOD, PATRICIA; CONWAY, TIM; and GARVAN, CYNDI. 1999. "Preventing Reading Failure in Young Children with Phonological Processing Disabilities: Group and Individual Responses to Instruction." *Journal of Educational Psychology* 91:579–594.

U.S. DEPARTMENT OF EDUCATION. 1992. *Assistance to States for the Education of Children with Disabilities Program and Preschool Grants for Children with Disabilities: Final Rule. Federal Register* 57(189):44,794–44,852.

VELLUTINO, FRANK R.; SCANLON, DONNA M.; and LYON, G. REID. 2000. "Differentiating between Difficult-to-Remediate and Readily Remediated Poor Readers: More Evidence against the IQ-Achievement Discrepancy Definition for Reading Disability." *Journal of Learning Disabilities* 33:223–238.

VELLUTINO, FRANK R.; SCANLON, DONNA M.; SIPAY, EDWARD R.; SMALL, S. G.; PRATT, A.; CHEN, R.; and DENCKLA, MARTHA B. 1996. "Cognitive Profiles of Difficult-to-Remediate and Readily Remediated Poor Readers: Early Intervention as a Vehicle for Distinguishing between Cognitive and Experiential Deficits as Basic Causes of Specific Reading Disability." *Journal of Educational Psychology* 88:601–638.

WISE, BARBARA W.; RING, JEREMIAH; and OLSON, RICHARD K. 2000. "Individual Differences in Gains from Computer-Assisted Remedial Reading." *Journal of Experimental Child Psychology* 77:197–235.

WISE, BARBARA W., and SNYDER, LYNN. 2001. "Judgments in Identifying and Teaching Children with Language-Based Reading Difficulties." Paper presented at the Learning Disabilities Summit, Washington DC.

PATRICIA G. MATHES

# RECORDS AND REPORTS, SCHOOL

The information presented here is based on the Family Educational Rights and Privacy Act of 1974 (FERPA or the Buckley Amendment) and the Illinois School Student Records Act.

Public school records fall into two general categories. The first is the organizational records of the school district, which parallel those that any business or organization would ordinarily keep. Financial and personnel records, minutes of meetings, contracts, and schedules are generally open to the public under the provisions of the Freedom of Information Act.

The second category is student records. Their administration is governed by FERPA, or as it is also known, the Buckley Amendment. FERPA is intended to protect the privacy and confidentiality of a student's school records and to allow parents, guardians, and students access to those records. It affords a wide range of rights and privileges to students and parents and places great responsibilities on the schools. Individual states have statutes that govern the administration of student records and individual school districts have student record management policies. These statutes and policies generally mirror the language of FERPA but may not change the intent of the federal legislation. The following are the key provisions that outline students' protections, parents' rights, and the school's obligations.

## Records Custodian

Each school must designate an official records custodian who is responsible for the maintenance, care, and security of student records, whether or not that person has actual physical control of the student records. The building principal generally serves as records custodian because he has the authority to meet the responsibilities of record maintenance and is specifically charged with assuring that school personnel are informed of the provisions of the law.

## Categories

Student records fall into three basic categories: permanent, temporary, and directory information.

Permanent records shall contain the following information:

- Basic identifying information, including both the student's and parent's names and addresses, and student birth date, birthplace, and gender
- Academic transcript, including grades, class rank, graduation date or grade level achieved, and scores on college entrance examinations
- Attendance record
- Health record and accident reports
- Record of release of permanent record information

- Honors and awards received
- Information concerning participation in school-sponsored activities or athletics, or offices held in school-sponsored organizations

No other information shall be placed in the student's permanent record. FERPA has no provision for the length of time permanent records must be maintained, but states generally do. Illinois, for example, requires they be kept for sixty years.

Temporary records must contain a record of release of temporary record information and may include the following:

- Family background information
- Intelligence test scores, both group and individual
- Aptitude test scores
- Elementary and secondary achievement level test results
- Reports of psychological evaluations, including information on intelligence, personality, and academic information obtained through test administration, observation, or interviews
- Participation in extracurricular activities, including any offices held in school sponsored clubs or organizations
- Honors and awards received
- Teacher anecdotal records
- Disciplinary information, including information regarding serious disciplinary infractions that resulted in expulsion, suspension, or the imposition of punishment or sanction
- Special education files, including the report of the multidisciplinary staffing on which placement or nonplacement was based and all records and recordings related to special education placement hearings and appeals
- Any verified reports or information from non-educational persons, agencies, or organizations
- Other verified information of clear relevance to the education of the student

Although FERPA does not specify, most states require that temporary records must be maintained for at least five years after the student transfers, graduates, or withdraws from the school.

Directory information is that information that may be released to the general public in publications such as athletic programs or news articles, and in school publications, such as yearbooks. This information is limited to the following:

- Identifying information to include name, address, gender, grade level, birth date and birthplace, and parents' names and addresses
- Academic awards and honors
- Information in relation to school-sponsored activities, organizations, and athletics
- Major field of study
- Period of attendance in the school

Parents have the right to request that any or all directory information not be released for their child. Prior to the release of directory information, school districts must notify affected parents in writing and the notification must include date of notification, parents' names, student's name, directory information to be released, and scheduled date of release.

Although not an official category under the language of the Family Education Rights and Privacy Act, personal anecdotal records should be mentioned here. These are the written notes that school personnel keep for their own use. A principal, for example, may make notes that record the details of a disciplinary situation to aid in future decisions concerning that student. As long as they are used only by that principal for that purpose, they remain personal anecdotal records outside of the provisions of the act. If, however, they are shared with other personnel, or are used to upgrade or annotate the student's discipline record, those notes must become part of the student's temporary record.

**Access**

The Freedom of Information Act has no bearing on student records, and only persons authorized by FERPA and the state's act shall be granted access. Access to student records is granted to parents or their designated representative and to the student. Access must be granted to students or parents within fifteen days of the request to inspect or copy records. All rights of access by parents cease and pass exclusively to the student when the student turns eighteen years of age, becomes legally emancipated, marries, graduates from high school, or enters into military service.

The following persons also have access to student records: (1) employees or officials of the school district on a "need to know" basis; (2) the records custodian of another school where the student is, or will become, enrolled; (3) legitimate researchers, provided no student is identified by name; (4) persons designated by court order; (4) persons required by state or federal law; (5) in connection with an emergency, when information contained in the records is necessary to protect the health or safety of the student or other persons; and (6) government or social agencies who are investigating the student's attendance in connection with the compulsory attendance law.

Notification of rights regarding student records include a number of specific administrative regulations that require, upon the student's initial enrollment or transfer, that the school shall notify the student and their parents of their rights under the act. The notification shall be in English and in the language of the child's primary speaking ability if they are of limited English-speaking ability. The notification must include definition of student records (permanent versus temporary), inspection rights and procedures, right to control access to records, challenge procedures, maintenance procedures, and destruction schedule.

Upon graduation, transfer, or permanent withdrawal of a student, the school must notify the student and parents of the destruction schedule for both permanent and temporary records, and of their right to request copies of the records anytime prior to their scheduled destruction. Notification must include the notification date, names of the student and parents, scheduled destruction date, and the name of the records custodian.

Policies for transfer of student records between schools specifies that within fourteen days of enrolling a transfer student, the enrolling school must request directly from the student's previous school a certified copy of the student's records. Within ten days of receiving a request for records, the school must forward an unofficial record. Within ten days after all fees and fines are paid, the official records shall be forwarded to the requesting school.

Before records are sent, the student and parents must be notified of their right to inspect, challenge, and copy records. They may not challenge academic grades or references to expulsions or out-of-school suspensions. Appropriate records must be kept of any transfer.

### Review

A review of records must be made every four years or upon a student's change in attendance centers, whichever occurs first. The purpose of the review is to verify entries and to eliminate or correct all out-of-date, misleading, inaccurate, unnecessary, or irrelevant information.

*See also:* GUIDANCE AND COUNSELING, SCHOOL; PRINCIPAL, SCHOOL; PSYCHOLOGIST, SCHOOL.

**BIBLIOGRAPHY**

BRAUN, BRIAN. 2000. *Illinois School Law Survey,* 6th edition. Springfield, IL: Illinois School Board Association.

*Illinois Administrative Code.* Vol. 23, chap. 1. *State Board of Education, Subchapter K: School Records, Part 375: Student Records.*

DAVID TURNER

# RECREATION PROGRAMS IN THE SCHOOLS

As early as 1918 the relationship between the school and recreation was identified when the National Education Association (NEA) adopted the "Seven Cardinal Principles of Education," one of which was the "worthy use of leisure." Today, schools are involved in the provision of recreation using three approaches: school-sponsored activities, community-sponsored activities, and school–community cooperative partnerships.

### School-Sponsored Recreation

School-sponsored recreation often relates to course material taught within the school system, but it provides learning experiences in addition to academic studies. Programs aimed at the school's student population are called *extracurricular activities* and include such things as bands, debating teams, choral groups, athletics and intramural activities, hobby groups, and interest clubs. For many students, these activities fill an important need in their school experience.

Schools also offer programs for adults within the community, and these are commonly referred to as *continuing education.* Historically, the intent of these programs was to enable adult learners to enhance career-related skills and knowledge. Continuing education programs have expanded, however, to include a variety of lifelong learning opportunities and currently include language classes, computer courses, fitness programs, auto mechanics classes, public speaking programs, and travelogues.

RECREATION PROGRAMS IN THE SCHOOLS

## Community-Sponsored Recreation

Community-sponsored programs are activities that are planned and implemented by various community groups for all residents within the community. Local schools are used as the program site during evening and weekend hours when the school would otherwise be empty. When one considers that the typical school timetable occupies only 18 percent of the hours available in the school year, the potential for increased use is obvious. Schools, situated in neighborhoods and close to residents, provide excellent satellite locations for community-based programs because of their accessibility. Examples of these types of programs include recreational sports leagues, ballroom dancing classes, card clubs, neighborhood festivals, and local theater groups.

## School-Community Cooperative Partnerships

Partnerships between schools and community agencies is a third way that leisure-related programs are aligned with the schools. The Kids at Hope program is one example of a national program where multiple community agencies form partnerships with the schools to develop extracurricular programs for youth. Sharing a belief that all children can succeed, the teachers and community volunteers, who implement the program, seek to affirm the skills, abilities, and talents of children to boost their self-esteem in a safe and supportive environment. Similarly, the Partnership for Civic Change (PCC) program in Waco, Texas, is a partnership among agencies and schools organized to provide positive after-school and summer recreation alternatives for youth. The programs offered through PCC are aimed at preventing at-risk youth from becoming involved in the juvenile justice system.

## Current Trends

There are three key trends emerging in the early twenty-first century that are affecting recreation programs in the schools: fiscal restraint in the public sector, changing family demographics, and the development of innovative programs.

**Fiscal restraint in the public sector.** The climate of fiscal restraint prevailing in the early twenty-first century presents a challenge for school administrators whose primary mandate is the delivery of academic programs. Increasingly, schools have fewer resources for school-based recreation, and there is a recognition that a decrease in recreation programs in the schools could result in an increase in activities that are commonly perceived to be a negative use of leisure time (drug use, vandalism, and high-risk activities). As a result, there is a growing impetus to find ways to ensure the future of recreation programs in the schools. Creative ways to meet this challenge are emerging and include such things as increased relationships with community agencies, the development of unique partnerships, the use of volunteers, and an increase in corporate support.

**Changing family demographics.** North American family structures are changing radically. With the increase of single-parent families and parents who hold jobs outside the home, schools and community agencies have a shared role in child care extending beyond the usual class times. Of particular concern are children and youth from economically disadvantaged households with few resources available to them for positive recreation activities or constructive play. For these families, dependence on extracurricular programs in the schools has been increasing.

**Innovations.** A number of innovations are emerging in regard to recreation programs in schools. In 1940 the NEA urged school districts to make their facilities available for community use. This has led to the common practice of joint facility planning. This trend is growing with the inclusion of a broader range of partners, including the school board, local government, community groups, individual donors, and the private sector. For example, a library may be planned so that the school and all members of the community have shared access to the collection and the library staff. Another common partnership is the development of parkland adjacent to school lands so that outdoor athletic fields can be developed for the use of both the school and community members.

In addition to joint facility and site planning initiatives, some schools and communities are developing funding partnerships so that building expenditures can be met. These partnerships can include funding from corporations, public sector organizations, local service clubs, and private donors.

It is apparent that recreation in the schools has grown beyond the traditional extracurricular programming. There is a greater understanding of the important role that recreation plays in the quality of community life. It is through the combined efforts of schools and community partners that recreation in the schools continues to play a key role in the provision of positive alternatives for children and families as they attempt to find channels for individual and creative expression.

*See also:* COMMUNITY EDUCATION; OUTDOOR AND ENVIRONMENTAL EDUCATION; PHYSICAL EDUCATION; SPORTS, SCHOOL.

### BIBLIOGRAPHY

BECK, TERESA; REYNOLDS, JOYCE; and GAVLIK, SALLY. 1995. "Partnerships for Civic Change." *Leisure Today* 66(4):14.

COMMISSION ON THE REORGANIZATION OF SECONDARY EDUCATION. 1918. *Cardinal Principles of Secondary Education.* Washington, DC: Bureau of Education.

CROMPTON, JOHN. 2000. "Sharing Space: Schools Can Serve as Recreation Facilities to Benefit the Community." *Parks and Recreation* 35(3):100–105.

KRAUS, RICHARD. 2001. *Recreation and Leisure in Modern Society,* 6th edition. Sudbury, MA: Jones and Bartlett.

MILLER, RICK. 2000. *From Youth at Risk to Kids at Hope.* Chicago: Chicago Education Alliance.

RUSKIN, HILLEL. 1995. "Conceptual Approaches to Policy Development in Leisure Education." In *Leisure Education Towards the Twenty-First Century,* ed. Hillel Ruskin and Atara Sivan. Provo, UT: Brigham Young University.

RANDY SWEDBURG
KATE CONNOLLY

# REGIONAL LABORATORIES AND RESEARCH AND DEVELOPMENT CENTERS

The U.S. government authorized formation of research and development (R&D) centers and regional educational laboratories (RELs) in 1965 under Title IV of the Elementary and Secondary Education Act (ESEA). Labs were reauthorized in 1994 under Title IX of the Goals 2000: Educate America Act.

During the Johnson administration's War on Poverty, the centers and laboratories were intended to be a network of institutions designed to revitalize American education through strategic research, development, and dissemination of new programs and processes. Since their inception, such external issues as the federal role in education and the allocation of funding, along with such internal issues as the challenge of applying research to real-world school settings, have significantly affected the mission and operation of these institutions. Nevertheless, laboratories and centers continue to house the federal government's most concentrated efforts to improve U.S. education through research and development.

### The 1960s and 1970s

At the outset, legislators envisioned R&D centers as conducting sustained scientific research concentrated on academic subject matter content (e.g., mathematics), skills (e.g., writing), or processes (e.g., instruction). In July 1964, John W. Gardner, then president of the Carnegie Foundation for the Advancement of Teaching, headed a presidential task force that proposed establishment of the RELs as a vital link to interpret, shape, and communicate the centers' research findings; tailor them for practical school use; and infuse them into the nation's classrooms, including college classrooms. This staged delivery system supplanted a diffused project-by-project strategy on research topics previously proposed for funding by university faculty.

Title IV of the Elementary and Secondary Education Act called for well-funded, large-scale institutions similar to atomic energy laboratories, the archetypes of R&D; however, appropriations for education R&D fell significantly short of that goal. Additionally, the legislation did not specify the number of laboratories and centers to be created, nor did it determine how they would be organized. By 1969, twenty RELs and eleven centers had been founded. The U.S. Office for Education closed fourteen of the laboratories in the next few years because of budget concerns and lack of confidence in their work.

In 1972 the National Institute of Education (NIE) was created, and the RELs and R&D centers were transferred to its jurisdiction. From 1973 to 1976, laboratories bid on individual projects defined by NIE through a program-purchase policy, rather than on contracts for institution-wide support. This process allowed for greater federal control, but reduced the laboratories' ability to address regional concerns. In 1979 education became a cabinet-level department. Laboratories and centers were placed under the jurisdiction of the Office of Education Research and Improvement (OERI) within the new Department of Education.

**The 1980s and Beyond**

In the 1980s a fundamental change occurred in the government's attitude towards educational research: while it had been assumed in the 1960s that the government should shape the research agenda, it was now felt that state departments of education and private foundations should take the lead. The new role of the laboratories was to work "with and through" these other agencies instead of pursuing their own programs (Guthrie, pp. 9–10).

In 1984 and 1985 the first recompetition since the founding of the labs in the 1960s was held. RELs were required to submit five-year plans for their research, development, and dissemination activities. This recompetition also ensured that nine RELs would cover all regions of the nation. A tenth REL, which served Hawaii and islands in the Pacific Basin, was awarded in 1990. The contract period of 1990 to 1995 saw development of the Laboratory Networking Program (LNP), which allows the RELs to share their knowledge and experience as they collaborate on common issues.

The Request for Proposal for projects to be conducted between 1995 and 2000 initiated laboratory specialty areas, requiring that each laboratory exert substantial effort and resources toward providing national leadership in an area that reflects the laboratory's expertise and that is of national importance. Another focus of the contract was assisting states in designing and implementing Comprehensive School Reform Demonstration (CSRD) programs. RELs provided technical assistance and created national resources, such as a database of all CSRD awards across the country and a catalog of school reform models. The 2001–2005 contract focused on developing and codifying knowledge about how to improve the academic achievement of students in low performing schools.

The number of R&D centers has fluctuated from eleven in 1966 to a high of twenty-five in 1990 and to twelve in 2001. At the outset of the twenty-first century, the university-based centers focus on such topics as at-risk students, testing, teaching, early development and learning, and improving student learning in the content areas. Descriptions of the centers and their areas of research are detailed on the National Research and Development Centers page of the U.S. government's Office of Educational Research and Improvement (OERI) website. A description of the labs and their national leadership areas may be found on the Regional Educational Laboratories page of the OERI website.

Besides the relatively low levels of funding for RELs and R&D centers compared to scientific laboratories, the laboratories and centers have "suffered from declining budgets: In 1973 NIE provided $80 million for their operations (in 1990 constant dollars); by 1979 that had declined to $52 million; and in 1991 the amount was $47 million. For individual laboratories and centers, the effect has been more dramatic because there are now twice as many of them as there were in 1973" (Atkinson and Jackson, pp. 96–97). As a consequence, laboratories have had to become entrepreneurial almost from the beginning in order to secure sufficient operational funding.

While critics have pointed to laboratories' shortcomings, as noted by reviewers, no "systematic assessment of the laboratories' work" has yet been produced (Atkinson and Jackson, p. 78). After more than three decades, with the support of their regions and congressional representatives, laboratories and centers continue to receive funding from Congress.

*See also:* FEDERAL FUNDING FOR ACADEMIC RESEARCH; RESEARCH UNIVERSITIES.

**BIBLIOGRAPHY**

ATKINSON, RICHARD C., AND JACKSON, GREGG B., eds. 1992. *Research and Education Reform: Roles for the Office of Education Research and Improvement.* Washington, DC: National Research Council, National Academy Press.

GUTHRIE, JAMES. 1989. *Regional Educational Laboratories: History and Prospect.* Washington, DC: U.S. Department of Education, Office of Educational Research and Improvement.

REGIONAL EDUCATIONAL LABORATORIES FOR RESEARCH, DEVELOPMENT, DISSEMINATION AND TECHNICAL ASSISTANCE. 1995. *Request for Proposal 95–040.* Washington, DC: U.S. Department of Education, Office of Educational Research and Improvement.

**INTERNET RESOURCES**

NATIONAL RESEARCH AND DEVELOPMENT CENTERS. 2002. <www.ed.gov/offices/OERI/ResCtr.html>.

REGIONAL EDUCATIONAL LABORATORIES. 2002. <www.ed.gov/offices/OERI/edlabs.html>.

PAMELA B. LUTZ
KATHERINE J. WORKMAN

# RELIGIOUS AFFILIATIONS, COLLEGES AND UNIVERSITIES WITH

*See:* COLLEGES AND UNIVERSITIES WITH RELIGIOUS AFFILIATIONS.

# RELIGIOUS SCHOOLS

*See:* PRIVATE SCHOOLING.

# RESEARCH AND TEACHING

*See:* TEACHING AND RESEARCH, THE RELATIONSHIP BETWEEN.

# RESEARCH GRANTS AND INDIRECT COSTS

During the later half of the twentieth century, the federal government of the United States invested heavily in research. Unlike other countries, such as Russia and Japan, which produce research within governmental laboratories, the research supported by the U.S. government primarily takes place within universities. To entice universities and their researchers to conduct the government's desired research projects, the federal government traditionally promises to cover much of the costs. The government pays the university the estimated cost of the project and allows the school to keep all funds whose occurrence can be documented.

This policy of cost-reimbursement is easy to implement for the expenses that are definitively associated with the particular project. These costs, often called direct costs, include such items as the equipment, materials, and personnel used during the project, and are relatively easy to measure and can be fully assigned to that project. Hence, the governmental policy toward direct costs receives little notice despite these expenditures accounting for 70 percent of the cost of research grants on average.

The other source of expenses in research grants are items that benefit other activities in the university, such as education or extension, as well as federally funded research. These costs, usually called indirect or overhead costs, are partially assigned to several activities and include items such as building maintenance, library materials, utility costs, and central administrative staff. Unfortunately, deciding which portion of these costs should be assigned to federally funded research grants is not a straightforward task. The complexity of indirect costs ensures that any method used to allocate them among activities is likely to receive some criticism, explaining why much of the debate over governmental policy for research funding focuses on overhead.

The system used in the United States to measure the costs of research grants has not changed in principle since 1958. For each grant, the direct costs are estimated and then multiplied by the indirect cost rate of the university to compute the total indirect costs. The method used to determine the indirect cost rate contains the complexity and controversy of the policy. Before 1958, the same rate was used for all universities, but this simple policy was abandoned because it ignored the varying character and resources among schools. To better account for these differences, the revised policy computes a unique indirect cost rate for each institution in two steps. First, each university estimates the level of indirect costs due to federal grants for the next year by conducting elaborate and complicated costing studies. Then, this total is divided by their expected level of direct costs (excluding some categories) to compute that year's rate. The average indirect cost rate in 1997 was 56 percent for private institutions and 47 percent for public institutions. The lower rate for public schools is partially due to weaker incentives for aggressive cost recovery caused by state policies that require public institutions to return indirect cost payments to the states.

Although the theory of cost-reimbursement guides the policy for research funding, the federal government uses alternative methods to purchase other products such as office furniture. For these other goods, the government selects a producer through a competitive bidding process and then pays the company by their level of output. This method is not used for research because it is impossible to accurately measure the output of research. Although one can measure the quantity and quality of furniture in an objectively verifiable fashion, one cannot do the same for most types of research.

Therefore, payment for research is based on inputs, which can be objectively measured, as opposed to outputs. As just discussed, measuring inputs is complicated because some inputs simultaneously benefit other activities in the university, such as education. It is important, however, for research grants to include these indirect costs because overhead reimbursement encourages quality research in the universities in two ways. First, the funds provide universities with the resources necessary to maintain a strong research infrastructure. Second, the extra compensation increases the value of research grants to universities, and subsequently, provides incentives for universities to devote their efforts toward building a strong reputation for quality research.

Partly for these reasons, most agree that indirect costs should be covered in research grants, but no similar consensus exists on the proper method of indirect cost measurement. Critics of the current system have several grievances; the most prominent criticism suggests that inappropriate items are sometimes included in research grants as overhead. Politicians wishing to lower governmental spending usually voice this complaint, or researchers concerned that high indirect cost rates at their university limit their ability to win grant funding. This grievance received much attention in the press in the early 1990s when federal auditors questioned some of the indirect costs claimed by Stanford University. While the costs questioned by auditors are only a small part of the total level of federally funded research, the publicity from the case caused the federal government to more closely scrutinize the costs suggested by universities and to enact additional regulations that more specifically outlined which costs are acceptable.

To much less fanfare, the method utilized in the early twenty-first century for measuring indirect costs is also criticized for encouraging cost increases in institutions of higher education. Universities incur large administrative costs when they determine their indirect cost rate because the computation requires periodic costing studies that are expensive. Because these rates vary little across institutions of similar types, the information obtained from the studies may not justify the costs. In addition to creating additional costs, the system may also not adequately encourage universities to limit other costs. Universities are not rewarded for cost containment and are sometimes penalized for frugal behavior through lower indirect cost rates. To minimize

these weaknesses in the system, economists Roger Noll and William Rogerson suggest a more simple approach where universities of the same type use a fixed indirect cost rate that is based on an audit of a sample of peer universities.

*See also:* FEDERAL FUNDING FOR ACADEMIC RESEARCH; RESEARCH UNIVERSITIES.

### BIBLIOGRAPHY

EHRENBERG, RONALD G., and MYKULA, JAROSLAVA K. 1999. *Do Indirect Costs Rates Matter?* National Bureau of Economic Research Working Paper 6976.

LIKINS, PETER, and TEICH, ALBERT H. 1994. "Indirect Costs and the Government-University Partnership." In *The Fragile Contract,* ed. David H. Guston and Kenneth Keniston. Cambridge, MA: MIT Press.

NOLL, ROGER G., and ROGERSON, WILLIAM P. 1998. "The Economics of University Indirect Cost Reimbursement in Federal Research Grants." In *Challenges to Research Universities,* ed. Roger G. Noll. Washington DC: Brookings Institution Press.

ROSENZWEIG, ROBERT M. 1991. "Debate over Indirect Costs Raises Policy Issues." *Chronicle of Higher Education* March 6.

JOHN J. CHESLOCK

# RESEARCH METHODS

## OVERVIEW

How do people learn to be effective teachers? What percentage of American students has access to computers at home? What types of assessments best measure learning in science classes? Do college admission tests place certain groups at a disadvantage? Can students who are at risk for dropping out of high school be identified? What is the impact of new technologies on school performance? These are some of the many questions that can be informed by the results of research.

Although research is not the only source used for seeking answers to such questions, it is an important one and the most reliable if executed well. Research is a process in which measurements are taken of individuals or organizations and the resulting data are subjected to analysis and interpretation. Special care is taken to provide *as accurate an answer as possible* to the posed question by subjecting "beliefs, conjectures, policies, positions, sources of ideas, traditions, and the like . . . to maximum criticism, in order to counteract and eliminate as much intellectual error as possible" (Bartley, pp. 139–140). In collecting the necessary information, a variety of methodologies and procedures can be used, many of which are shared by such disciplines as education, psychology, sociology, cognitive science, anthropology, history, and economics.

### Evidence—The Foundation of Research

In education, research is approached from two distinct perspectives on how knowledge should be acquired. Research using *quantitative* methods rests on the belief that individuals, groups, organizations, and the environments in which they operate have an objective reality that is relatively constant across time and settings. Consequently, it is possible to construct measures that yield numerical data on this reality, which can then be further probed and interpreted by statistical analyses. In contrast, *qualitative* research methods are rooted in the conviction that "features of the social environment are constructed as interpretations by individuals and that these interpretations tend to be transitory and situational" (Gall, Borg, and Gall, p. 28). It is only through intensive study of specific cases in natural settings that these meanings and interpretations can be revealed and common themes educed. Although debate over which perspective is "right" continues, qualitative and quantitative research share a common feature— *data* are at the center of all forms of inquiry.

Fundamentally, data gathering boils down to two basic activities: Researchers either *ask* individuals (or other units) *questions* or *observe behavior.* More specifically, individuals can be asked about their attitudes, beliefs, and knowledge about past or current behaviors or experiences. Questions can also tap personality traits and other hypothetical constructs associated with individuals. Similarly, observations can take on a number of forms: (1) the observer can be a passive transducer of information or an active participant in the group being observed; (2) those being observed may or may not be aware that their behavior is being chronicled for research purposes; and (3) data gathering can be done by a human recorder or through the use of technology (e.g., video cameras or other electronic devices). Another distinction that is applicable to both forms of data gathering is whether the data are developed afresh within the study (i.e., primary data) or stem from secondary sources (e.g., data archives; written documents such as academic transcripts, individualized educational plans, or teacher notes; and artifacts that are found in natural settings). Artifacts can be very telling about naturally occurring phenomena. These can involve trace and accretion measures— that is, "residue" that individuals leave behind in the course of their daily lives. Examples include carpet wear in front of exhibits at children's museums (showing which exhibits are the most popular), graffiti written on school buildings, and websites visited by students.

What should be clear from this discussion so far is that there exists a vast array of approaches to gathering evidence about educational and social phenomena. Although reliance on empirical data distinguishes research-based disciplines from other modes of knowing, decisions about what to gather and how to structure the data gathering process need to be governed by the purpose of the research. In addition, a thoughtful combination of data gathering approaches has the greater chance of producing the most accurate answer.

### Purposes of Research

The array of questions listed in the introductory paragraph suggests that research is done for a variety of purposes. These include exploring, describing, predicting, explaining, or evaluating some phenomenon or set of phenomena. Some research is aimed at replicating results from previous studies; other research is focused on quantitatively synthesizing a body of research. These two types of efforts are directed at strengthening a theory, verifying predictions, or probing the robustness of explanations by seeing if they hold true for different types of individuals, organizations, or settings.

**Exploration.** Very little may be known about some phenomena such as new types of settings, practices, or groups. Here, the research question focuses on identifying salient characteristics or features that merit further and more concerted examination in additional studies.

**Description.** Often, research is initiated to carefully describe a phenomenon or problem in terms of its structure, form, key ingredients, magnitude, and/or changes over time. The resulting profiles can either be qualitative or narrative, quantitative (e.g., *x* number of people have this characteristic), or a mixture of both. For example, the National Center for Education Statistics collects statistical information about several aspects of education and monitors changes in these indicators over time. The information covers a broad range of topics, most of which are chosen because of their interest to policymakers and educational personnel.

**Prediction.** Some questions seek to predict the occurrence of specific phenomena or states on the basis of one or more other characteristics. Short- and long-term planning are often the main rationale for this type of research.

**Explanation.** It is possible to be able to predict the occurrence of a certain phenomenon but not to know exactly why this relationship exists. In explanatory research, the aim is to not only predict the outcome or state of interest but also understand the mechanisms and processes that result in one variable causing another.

**Evaluation.** Questions of this nature focus on evaluating or judging the worth of something, typically an intervention or program. Of primary interest is to learn whether an organized set of activities that is aimed at correcting some problem (e.g., poor academic skills, low self-esteem, disruptive behavior) is effective. When these efforts are targeted at evaluating the potential or actual success of policies, regulations, and laws, this is often known as policy analysis.

**Replication.** Some questions revolve around whether a demonstrated relationship between two variables (e.g., predictive value of the SAT in college persistence) can be again found in different populations or different types of settings. Because few studies can incorporate all relevant populations and settings, it is important to determine how generalizable the results of a study to a particular group or program are.

**Synthesis.** Taking stock of what is known and what is not known is a major function of research. "Summing-up" a body of prior research can take quantitative (e.g., meta-analysis) and qualitative (narrative summaries) forms.

**Types of Research Methods**

The purpose or purposes underlying a research study guide the choice of the specific research methods that are used. Any individual research study may address multiple questions, not all of which share the same purpose. Consequently, more than one research method may be incorporated into a particular research effort. Because methods of investigation are not pure (i.e., free of bias), several types of data and methods of gathering data are often used to "triangulate" on the answer to a specific question.

**Measurement development.** At the root of most inquiry is the act of measuring key conceptual variables of interest (e.g., learning strategies, intrinsic motivation, learning with understanding). When the outcomes being measured are important (e.g., grade placement, speech therapy, college admission), considerable research is often needed prior to conducting the main research study to ensure that the measure accurately describes individuals' status or performance. This can require substantial data collection and analysis in order to determine the measure's reliability, validity, and sensitivity to change; for some measures, additional data from a variety of diverse groups must be gathered for establishing norms that can assist in interpretation. With the exception of exploratory research, the quality of most studies relies heavily upon the degree to which the data-collection instruments provide reliable and valid information on the variables of interest.

**Survey methodology.** Survey research is primarily aimed at collecting self-report information about a population by asking questions directly of some sample of it. The members of the target population can be individuals (e.g., local teachers), organizations (e.g., parent–teacher associations), or other recognized bodies (e.g., school districts or states). The questions can be directed at examining attitudes and preferences, facts, previous behaviors, and past experiences. Such questions can be asked by interviewers either face-to-face or on the telephone; they can also be self-administered by distributing them to groups (e.g., students in classrooms) or delivering them via the mail, e-mail, or the Internet.

High-quality surveys devote considerable attention to reducing as much as possible the major sources of error that can bias the results. For example, the target population needs to be completely enumerated so that important segments or groups are not unintentionally excluded from being eligible to participate. The sample is chosen in a way as to be representative of the population of interest, which is best accomplished through the use of probability sampling. Substantial time is given to constructing survey questions, pilot testing them, and training interviewers so that item wording, question presentation and format, and interviewing styles are likely to encourage thoughtful and accurate responses. Finally, concerted efforts are used to encourage all sampled individuals to complete the interview or questionnaire.

Surveys are mainly designed for description and prediction. Because they rarely involve the manipulation of independent variables or random assignment of individuals (or units) to conditions, they generally are less useful by themselves for answering explanatory and effects-oriented evaluative questions. If survey research is separated into its two fundamental components—sampling and data gathering through the use of questionnaires—it is easy to see that survey methods are embedded within experimental and quasi-experimental studies. For example, comparing learning outcome among students enrolled in traditional classroom-based college courses with those of students completing the course through distance learning would likely involve the administration of surveys that assess student views of the instructor and their satisfaction with how the course was taught. As another illustration, a major evaluation of *Sesame Street* that randomly assigned classrooms to in-class viewing of the program involved not only administering standardized reading tests to the students participating but also surveys of teachers and parents. So, in this sense, many forms of inquiry can be improved by using state-of-the-art methods in questionnaire construction and measurement.

**Observational methods.** Instead of relying on individuals' self-reports of events, researchers can conduct their own observations. This is often preferable when there is a concern that individuals may misreport the requested information, either deliberately or inadvertently (e.g., they cannot remember). In addition, some variables are better measured by direct observation. For example, in comparing direct observations of how long teachers lecture in a class as opposed to asking teachers to self-report the time they spent lecturing; it should be obvious that the latter could be influenced (biased upward or downward) by how the teachers believe the researcher wants them to respond.

Observational methods are typically used in natural settings, although, as with survey methods, observations can be made of behaviors even in experimental and quasi-experimental studies. Both quantitative and qualitative observation strategies are possible. Quantitative strategies involve either training observers to record the information of interest in a systematic fashion or employing audiotape recorders, video cameras, and other electronic devices. When observers are used, they must be trained and monitored as to what should be observed and how it should be recorded (e.g., the number of times that a target behavior occurs during an agreed-upon time period).

Qualitative observational methods are distinctly different in several ways. First, rather than coding a prescribed set of behaviors, the focus of the observations is deliberately left more open-ended. By using open-ended observation schemes, the full range of individuals' responses to an environment can be recorded. That is, observations are much broader in contrast to quantitative observational strategies that focus on specific behaviors. Second, observers do not necessarily strive to remain neutral about what they are observing and may include their own feelings and experiences in interpreting what happened. Also, observers who employ quantitative methods do not participate in the situations that they are observing. In contrast, observers in qualitative research are not typically detached from the setting being studied; rather, they are more likely to be complete participants where the researcher is a member of the setting that is being observed.

Qualitative strategies are typically used to answer exploratory questions as they help identify important variables and hypotheses about them. They also are commonly used to answer descriptive questions because they can provide in-depth information about groups and situations. Although qualitative strategies have been used to answer predictive, explanatory, and evaluative questions, they are less able to yield results that can eliminate all rival explanations for causal relationships.

**Experimental methods.** Experimental research methods are ideally suited for examining explanatory questions that seek to ascertain whether a cause-and-effect relationship exists among two or more variables. In experiments, the researcher directly manipulates the cause (the independent variable), assigns individuals randomly to various levels of the independent variable, and measures their responses (the expected effect). Ideally, the researcher has a high degree of control over the presentation of the purported cause—where, when, and in what form it is delivered; who receives it; and when and how the effect is measured. This level of control helps rule out alternative or rival explanations for the observed results. Exercising this control typically requires that the research be done under laboratory or contrived conditions rather than in natural settings. Experimental methods, however, can also be used in real-world settings—these are commonly referred to as field experiments.

Conducting experiments in the field is more difficult inasmuch as the chances increase that integral parts of the experimental method will be compromised. Participants may be more likely to leave the study and thus be unavailable for measurement of the outcomes of interest. Subjects who are randomly assigned to the control group, which may receive no tutoring, may decide to obtain help on their own—assistance that resembles the intervention being tested. Such problems essentially work against controlling for rival explanations and the key elements of the experimental method are sacrificed. Excellent discussions of procedures for conducting field experiments can be found in the 2002 book *Experimental and Quasi-Experimental Designs for Generalized Causal Inference,* written by William R. Shadish, Thomas D. Cook, and Donald T. Campbell, and in Robert F. Boruch's 1997 book *Randomized Field Experiments for Planning and Evaluation: A Practical Guide.*

**Quasi-experimental methods.** As suggested by its name, the methods that comprise quasi-experimental research approximate experimental methodologies. They are directed at fulfilling the same purposes—explanation and evaluation—but may provide more equivocal answers than experimental designs. The key characteristic that distinguishes quasi experiments from experiments is the lack of random assignment. Because of this, researchers must make concerted efforts to rule out the plausible rival hypotheses that random assignment is designed to eliminate.

Quasi-experimental designs constitute a core set of research strategies because there are many instances in which it is impossible to successfully assign participants randomly to different conditions or levels of the independent variable. For example, the first evaluation of *Sesame Street* that was conducted by Samuel Ball and Gerry Bogatz in 1970 was designed as a randomized experiment where individual children in five locations were randomly assigned to either be encouraged to watch the television program (and be observed in their homes doing it) or not encouraged. Classrooms in these locations were also either given television sets or not, and teachers in classrooms with television sets were encouraged to allow the children to view the show at least three days per week. The study, however, turned into a quasi experiment because *Sesame Street* became so popular that children in the control group (who were not encouraged to watch) ended up watching a considerable number of shows.

The two most frequently used quasi-experimental strategies are time-series designs and nonequivalent comparison group designs, each of which has some variations. In time-series designs, the dependent variable or expected effect is measured several times before and after the independent variable is introduced. For example, in a study of a zero tolerance policy, the number of school incidents related to violence and substance use are recorded on a monthly basis for twelve months before the policy is introduced and twelve or more months after its implementation. If a noticeable reduction in incidents occurs soon after the new policy is introduced and the reduction persists, one can be reasonably confident that the new policy was responsible for the observed increase if no other events occurred that could have resulted in a decline and there was evidence that the policy was actually enforced. This confidence may be even stronger if data are collected on schools that have similar student populations and characteristics but no zero tolerance policies during the same period and there is no reduction in illegal substance and violence-related incidents.

Establishing causal relationships with the nonequivalent comparison group design is typically more difficult. This is because when groups are formed in ways other than random assignment (e.g., participant choice), this often means that they differ in other ways that affect the outcome of interest. For example, suppose that students who are having problems academically are identified and allowed to choose to be involved or not involved in an after-school tutoring program. Those who decide to enroll are also those who may be more motivated to do well, who may have parents who are willing to help their children improve, and who may differ in other ways from those who choose not to stay after school. They may also have less-serious academic problems. Such factors all may contribute to these students exhibiting higher academic gains than their nontutored counterparts do when after-tutoring testing has been completed. It is difficult, however, to disentangle the role that tutoring contributed to any observed improvement from these other features. The use of well-validated measures of these characteristics for both groups prior to receiving or not receiving tutoring can help in this process, but the difficulty is to identify and measure all the key variables other than tutoring receipt that can influence the observed outcomes.

**Secondary analysis and meta-analysis.** Both secondary analysis and meta-analysis are part of the arsenal of quantitative research methods, and both rely on research data already collected by other studies. They are invaluable tools for informing questions that seek descriptive, predictive, explanatory, or evaluative answers. Studies that rely on secondary analysis focus on examining and reanalyzing the raw data from prior surveys, experiments, and quasi experiments. In some cases, the questions prompting the analysis are ones that were not examined by the original investigator; in other cases, secondary analysis is performed because the researcher disagrees to some extent with the original conclusions and wants to probe the data, using different statistical techniques.

Secondary analyses occupy a distinct place in educational research. Since the 1960s federal agencies have sponsored several large-scale survey and evaluation efforts relevant to education, which have been analyzed by other researchers to re-examine the reported results or answer additional questions not addressed by the original researchers. Two examples, both conducted by the National Center for Education Statistics, include the High School and Beyond Survey, which tracks seniors and sophomores as they progress through high school and college and enter the workplace; and the Schools and Staffing Survey, which regularly collects data on the characteristics and qualifications of teachers and principals, class size, and other school conditions.

The primary idea underlying meta-analysis or research synthesis methods is to go beyond the more traditional, narrative literature reviews of research in a given area. The process involves using systematic and comprehensive retrieval practices for accumulating prior studies, quantifying the results by using a common metric (such as the effect size), and statistically combining this collection of results. In general, the reported results that are used from studies involve intermediate statistics such as means, standard deviations, proportions, and correlations.

The use of meta-analysis grew dramatically in the 1990s. Its strength is that it allows one to draw conclusions across multiple studies that addressed the same question (e.g., what have been the effects of bilingual education?) but used different measures, populations, settings, and study designs. The use of both secondary analysis and meta-analysis has increased the longer-term value of individual research efforts, either by increasing the number of questions that can be answered from one large-scale survey or by looking across several small-scale studies that seek answers to the same question. These research methods have contributed much in addressing policymakers' questions in a timely fashion and to advancing theories relevant to translating educational research into recommended practices.

*See also:* FACULTY PERFORMANCE OF RESEARCH AND SCHOLARSHIP; RESEARCH METHODS, *subentries on* QUALITATIVE AND ETHNOGRAPHIC, SCHOOL AND PROGRAM EVALUATION.

### BIBLIOGRAPHY

BALL, SAMUEL, and BOGATZ, GERRY A. 1970. *The First Year of Sesame Street: An Evaluation.* Princeton, NJ: Educational Testing Service.

BARTLEY, WILLIAM W., III. 1962. *The Retreat to Commitment.* New York: Knopf.

BORUCH, ROBERT F. 1997. *Randomized Field Experiments for Planning and Evaluation: A Practical Guide.* Thousand Oaks, CA: Sage.

BRYK, ANTHONY S., and RAUDENBUSH, STEPHEN W. 1992. *Hierarchical Linear Models: Applications and Data Analysis Methods.* Newbury Park, CA: Sage.

COOK, THOMAS D.; COOPER, HARRISON; CORDRAY, DAVID S.; HARTMANN, HEIDI; HEDGES, LARRY V.; LIGHT, RICHARD J.; LOUIS, THOMAS A.; and MOSTELLER, FREDERICK, eds. 1992. *Meta-*

*analysis for Explanation: A Casebook.* New York: Russell Sage Foundation.

COOPER, HARRISON, and HEDGES, LARRY V., eds. 1994. *The Handbook of Research Synthesis.* New York: Russell Sage Foundation.

GALL, MERIDITH D.; BORG, WALTER R.; and GALL, JOYCE P. 1966. *Educational Research: An Introduction,* 6th edition. White Plains, NY: Longman

SHADISH, WILLIAM R.; COOK, THOMAS D.; and CAMPBELL, DONALD T. 2002. *Experimental and Quasi-Experimental Designs for Generalized Causal Inference.* Boston: Houghton Mifflin.

GEORGINE M. PION
DAVID S. CORDRAY

## QUALITATIVE AND ETHNOGRAPHIC

A qualitative approach to research generally involves the researcher in contact with participants in their natural setting to answer questions related to how the participants make sense of their lives. Qualitative researchers may observe the participants and conduct formal and informal interviews to further an understanding of what is going on in the setting from the point of view of those involved in the study. Ethnographic research shares these qualitative traits, but ethnographers more specifically seek understanding of what participants do to create the culture in which they live, and how the culture develops over time. This article further explores what it means to conduct qualitative and ethnographic research by looking at them historically and then by describing key characteristics of these approaches.

### The Context in Education

Qualitative and ethnographic research developed in education in the late 1970s. Ethnographic researchers drew on theory and methods in anthropology and sociology, creating a distinction between ethnography of education (work undertaken by anthropologists and sociologists) and ethnography in education (work undertaken by educators to address educational issues). Other forms of qualitative research drew on theories from the humanities and other social and behavioral sciences, adapting this work to educational goals and concerns, often creating new forms (e.g., connoisseurship, a field method approach, interview approaches, and some forms of action research).

In the early development of these traditions, educational researchers struggled for acceptance by both other professionals and policymakers. This phase was characterized by arguments over the value of qualitative methods in contrast to the dominant paradigms of the time—quantitative and experimental approaches. Qualitative and ethnographic researchers argued that questions important to education were left unexamined by the dominant paradigms. Some qualitative researchers argued for the need to include and represent the voices of people in their research, particularly voices not heard in other forms of research involving large-scale studies.

Questions asked by qualitative and ethnographic researchers generally focus on understanding the local experiences of people as they engage in their everyday worlds (e.g., classrooms, peer groups, homes, communities). For example, some researchers explore questions about ways in which people gain, or fail to gain, access to ways of learning in a diverse world; others focus on beliefs people hold about education and learning; while still others examine how patterns learned within a group are consequential for participation in other groups and situations.

A broad range of perspectives and approaches exist, each with its own historical tradition and theoretical orientation. A number of common dimensions can be identified across these perspectives and approaches. Qualitative and ethnographic researchers in education are concerned with the positions they take relative to participants and data collected. For example, many qualitative and ethnographic researchers engage in observations over a period of time to identify patterns of life in a particular group.

The theoretical orientation chosen guides the design and implementation of the research, including the tools used to collect (e.g., participant observation, interviewing, and collecting artifacts) and analyze data (e.g., discourse analysis, document analysis, content analysis, and transcribing video/audio data). Theory also guides other decisions, including how to enter the field (e.g., the social group, classroom, home, and/or community center), what types and how much data to collect and records to make (e.g., videotape, audiotape, and/or field notes), who to interview (formally and/or informally), how long to remain in the field (e.g., for ethnography, one or more years), and what literature is relevant. It also influences relationships researchers establish with people in local settings, which in turn influences what can be known. Some theoretical perspectives guide researchers to observe what is occurring from a distance by taking the role of passive observer, recording information for analysis once they leave the field. Such researchers often do not interview participants, preferring to "ground" their observations in patterns in the data, without concern for what members understand. These descriptions are called *etic,* or outsider descriptions, because the observer is not concerned with members' understandings.

This approach is in contrast with ones in which researchers join the group and become active participant-observers, at times participating directly in events. Such researchers also make videotape records that enable them to step back from what they thought was occurring to examine closely what resulted from those actions. Those not using video or audio records reconstruct events by constructing retrospective field notes, drawing on their memories of what occurred to create a written record to analyze when they leave the field. Just which type of approach and position researchers take depends on their research goal(s) and theoretical orientation(s) as well as what participants permit.

**Approaches to Research Questions**

Research questions in a qualitative study are generated as part of the research process. Qualitative and ethnographic researchers often begin a study with one or more initiating question(s) or an issue they want to examine. Qualitative and ethnographic research approaches involve a process of interacting with data, reflecting on what is important to members in the local setting, and using this to generate new questions and refine the initial questions. This interactive and responsive process also influences the data that are collected and analyzed throughout the study. Therefore, it is common for researchers to construct more detailed questions that are generated as part of the analysis as they proceed throughout the study, or to abandon questions and generate ones more relevant to the local group or issues being studied.

For example, in one study of a fifth-grade classroom, the initial research questions were open ended and general: (1) What counts as community to the students and teacher in this classroom? (2) How do the participants construct community in this classroom? and (3) How is participating in this classroom consequential for students and the teacher? As the study unfolded, the research questions became more

directed toward what the researcher was beginning to understand about this classroom in particular. After first developing an understanding of patterns of interactions among participants, the researcher began to formulate more specific questions: (1) What patterns of practice does the teacher construct to offer opportunities for learning? (2) What roles do the social and academic practices play in the construction of community in this classroom? and (3) What are the consequences for individuals and the collective when a member leaves and reenters the classroom community? This last question was one that could not have been anticipated but was important to understanding what students learned and when student learning occurred as well as what supported and constrained that learning. The shifts in questions constitute this researcher's logic of inquiry and need to be reported as part of the dynamic design of the study.

**Approaches to Design and Data Collection**

In designing qualitative studies, researchers consider ways of collecting data to represent the multiple voices and actions constituting the research setting. Typical techniques used in qualitative research for collecting data include observing in the particular setting, conducting interviews with various participants, and reviewing documents or artifacts. The degree to which these techniques are used depends on the nature of the particular research study and what occurs in the local group.

Some studies involve in-depth analysis of one setting or interviews of one group of people. Others involve a contrastive design from the beginning, seeking to understand how the practices of one group are similar to or different from another group. Others seek to study multiple communities to test hypotheses from the research literature (e.g., child-rearing practices are the same in all communities). What is common to all of these studies is that they are examining the qualities of life and experiences within a local situation. This is often called a situated perspective.

**Entering the Field and Gaining Access to Insider Knowledge**

Entering the research setting is one of the first phases of conducting fieldwork. Gaining access to the site is ongoing and negotiated with the participants throughout the study. As new questions arise, the researcher has to renegotiate access. For example, a researcher may find that the outcomes of standardized tests become an important issue for the teachers and students. The researcher may not have obtained permission to collect these data at the beginning of the study and must then negotiate permission from parents, students, teachers, and district personnel to gain access to these scores.

Qualitative research involves a social contract with those participating in the study, and informed consent is negotiated at each phase of the research when new information is needed or new areas of study are undertaken. At such points of renegotiation, researchers need to consider the tools necessary and the ways to participate within the group (e.g., as participant-observer and/or observer-participant, as interviewer of one person or as a facilitator of a focus group, or as analyst of district data or student products). How the researcher conducts observations, collects new forms of data, and analyzes such data is related to shifts in questions and/or theoretical stance(s) necessary to understand what is occurring.

## Research Tools

One of the most frequently used tools, in addition to participant observation, is interviewing. For ethnography and other types of field research, interviews occur within the context of the ongoing observations and collection of artifacts. These interviews are grounded in what is occurring in the local context, both within and across time. Some interviews are undertaken to gain insider information about what the researcher is observing or to test out the developing theory that the researcher is constructing.

In contrast, other forms of qualitative research may use interviews as the sole form of data collection. Such interviews also seek meanings that individuals or groups have for their own experience or of observed phenomena. These interviews, however, form the basis for analysis and do not require contextual information from observations. What the people say becomes the basis for exploration, not what was observed.

Other tools used by qualitative and ethnographic researchers include artifact and document analysis (artifacts being anything people make and use). The researcher in a field-based study collects artifacts produced and/or used by members of the group, identifies how these artifacts function for the individual and/or the group, and explores how members talk about and name these artifacts. For some theoretical positions, the artifacts may be viewed as a type of participant in the local event (e.g., computer programs as participants). Some artifacts, such as documents, are examined for links to other events or artifacts. This form of analysis builds on the understanding that the past (and future) is present in these artifacts and that intertextual links between and among events are often inscribed in such documents. In some cases, qualitative researchers may focus solely on a set of artifacts (e.g., student work, linked sets of laws, a photograph collection, or written texts in the environment–environmental print). Such studies seek to examine the range of texts or materials constructed, the patterned ways in which the texts are constructed, and how the choices of focus or discourse inscribe the views that members have of self and others as well as what is possible in their worlds.

Although some qualitative studies focus solely on the documents, field-based researchers generally move between document analysis and an exploration of the relationship of the document to past, present, and future actions of individuals and/or groups. These studies seek to understand the importance of the artifact or document within the lives of those being studied.

## Ongoing Data Analysis

While conducting fieldwork, researchers reread their field notes and add to them any relevant information that they were not able to include at the time of first writing the notes. While reviewing their field notes, researchers look for themes and information relevant to the research questions. They note this information in the form of theoretical notes (or write theoretical memos to themselves) that may include questions about repeated patterns, links to other theories, and conceptual ideas they are beginning to develop. They also make methodological notes to reconstruct their thinking and their logic of inquiry. Sometimes they make personal notes that reflect their thoughts and feelings about what they are observing or experiencing. These notes allow them to keep from imposing their own opinion on data, helping them to focus on what is meaningful or important to those with whom they are working.

Researchers constantly use contrast to build interpretations that are grounded in the data, within and across actors, events, times, actions, and activities that constitute the social situations of everyday life. Many qualitative (particularly ethnographic) researchers examine material, activity, semiotic (meaning-carrying), and/or social dimensions of everyday life and its consequences for members. The analytic principles of practice that they use include comparing and contrasting data, methods, theories, and perspectives; examining part-whole relationships between and among actions, events, and actors; seeking insider (*emic*) understandings of experiences, actions, practices, and events; and identifying through these what is relevant to the local group.

## Reporting Research Findings

The final step in qualitative and ethnographic research is writing an account. The researchers make choices about how to represent the data that illustrate what was typical about the particular group being studied. Another choice might be to highlight actions of the group that were illustrative of their particular patterns of beliefs. In some studies, several cases are chosen to make visible comparisons across different activities within the group, or across different groups that may have some activities in common. For example, researchers who study classroom interactions might bring together data from different classrooms to make visible principles of practice that are similar in general terms such as asking students to understand various points of view. However, in each classroom, the actions of juxtaposing points of view will be carried out differently due to the different experiences within each classroom.

Researchers also select genres for writing the report that best enable the intended audience to understand what the study made visible that was not previously known or that extended previous knowledge. The researcher does not seek to generalize from the specific case. Rather, qualitative or ethnographic researchers provide in-depth descriptions that lead to general patterns. These patterns are then examined in other situations to see if, when, and how they occur and what consequences they have for what members in the new setting can know, do, understand, and/or produce. In qualitative and ethnographic studies this is often referred to as transferability, in contrast to generalizability.

*See also:* RESEARCH METHODS, *subentries on* OVERVIEW, SCHOOL AND PROGRAM EVALUATION.

### BIBLIOGRAPHY

DENZIN, NORMAN, and LINCOLN, YVONNA, eds. 1994. *Handbook of Qualitative Research.* Thousand Oaks, CA: Sage.

ERICKSON, FREDRICK. 1986. "Qualitative Research." In *The Handbook of Research on Teaching*, 3rd edition, ed. Merle Wittrock. New York: Macmillan.

FLOOD, JAMES; JENSEN, JULIE; LAPP, DIANE; and SQUIRE, JAMES, eds. 1990. *Handbook of Research on Teaching the English Language Arts.* New York: Macmillan.

GEE, JAMES, and GREEN, JUDITH. 1998. "Discourse Analysis, Learning, and Social Practice: A Methodological Study." *Review of Research in Education* 23:119–169.

GILLMORE, PERRY, and GLATTHORN, ALAN, eds. *Children In and Out of School: Ethnography and Education.* Washington, DC: Center for Applied Linguistics.

GREEN, JUDITH; DIXON, CAROL; and ZAHARLICK, AMY. 2002. "Ethnography as a Logic of Inquiry." In *Handbook for Methods of Research on English Language Arts Teaching*, ed. James Flood, Julie Jensen, Diane Lapp, and James Squire. New York: Macmillan.

HAMMERSLEY, MARTIN, and ATKINSON, PAUL. 1995. *Ethnography: Principles in Practice*, 2nd edition. New York: Routledge.

KVALE, STEINAR. 1996. *Interviews: An Introduction to Qualitative Research Interviewing.* Thousand Oaks, CA: Sage.

LECOMPTE, MARGARET; MILLROY, WENDY; and PREISSLE, JUDITH, eds. 1992. *The Handbook of Qualitative Research in Education.* San Diego, CA: Academic Press.

LINDE, CHARLOTTE. 1993. *Life Stories: The Creation of Coherence.* New York: Oxford University Press.

OCHS, ELINOR. 1979. "Transcription as Theory." In *Developmental Pragmatics*, ed. Elinor Ochs and Bambi B. Schieffelin. New York: Academic Press.

PUTNEY, LEANN; GREEN, JUDITH; DIXON, CAROL; and KELLY, GREGORY. 1999. "Evolution of Qualitative Research Methodology: Looking beyond Defense to Possibilities." *Reading Research Quarterly* 34:368–377.

RICHARDSON, VIRGINIA. 2002. *Handbook for Research on Teaching,* 4th edition. Mahwah, NJ: Erlbaum.

SPRADLEY, JAMES. 1980. *Participant Observation.* New York: Holt, Rinehart and Winston.

STRIKE, KENNETH. 1974. "On the Expressive Potential of Behaviorist Language." *American Educational Research Journal* 11:103–120.

VAN MAANEN, JOHN. 1988. *Tales of the Field: On Writing Ethnography.* Chicago: University of Chicago Press.

WOLCOTT, HARRY. 1992. "Posturing in Qualitative Research." In *The Handbook of Qualitative Research in Education,* ed. Margaret LeCompte, Wendy Millroy, and Judith Preissle. New York: Academic Press.

LeANN G. PUTNEY
JUDITH L. GREEN
CAROL N. DIXON

# SCHOOL AND PROGRAM EVALUATION

Program evaluation is research designed to assess the implementation and effects of a program. Its purposes vary and can include (1) program improvement, (2) judging the value of a program, (3) assessing the utility of particular components of a program, and (4) meeting accountability requirements. Results of program evaluations are often used for decisions about whether to continue a program, improve it, institute similar programs elsewhere, allocate resources among competing programs, or accept or reject a program approach or theory. Through these uses program evaluation is viewed as a way of rationalizing policy decision-making.

Program evaluation is conducted for a wide range of programs, from broad social programs such as welfare, to large multisite programs such as the preschool intervention program Head Start, to program funding streams such as the U.S. Department of Education's Title I program that gives millions of dollars to high-poverty schools, to small-scale programs with only one or a few sites such as a new mathematics curriculum in one school or district.

## Scientific Research versus Evaluation

There has been some debate about the relationship between "basic" or scientific research and program evaluation. For example, in 1999 Peter Rossi, Howard Freeman, and Michael Lipsey described program evaluation as the application of scientific research methods to the assessment of the design and implementation of a program. In contrast, Michael Patton in 1997 described program evaluation not as the application of scientific research methods, but as the systematic collection of information about a program to inform decision-making.

Both agree, however, that in many circumstances the design of a program evaluation that is sufficient for answering evaluation questions and providing guidance to decision-makers would not meet the high standards of scientific research. Further, program evaluations are often not able to strictly follow the principles of scientific research because evaluators must confront the politics of changing actors and priorities, limited resources, short timelines, and imperfect program implementation.

Another dimension on which scientific research and program evaluation differ is their purpose. Program evaluations must be designed to maximize the usefulness for decision-makers, whereas scientific research does not have this constraint. Both types of research might use the same methods or focus on the same subject, but scientific research can be formulated solely from intellectual curiosity, whereas evaluations must respond to the policy and program interests of stakeholders (i.e., those who hold a stake in the program, such as those who fund or manage it, or program staff or clients).

## How Did Program Evaluation Evolve?

Program evaluation began proliferating in the 1960s, with the dawn of social antipoverty programs and the government's desire to hold the programs accountable for positive results. Education program evaluation in particular expanded also because of the formal evaluation requirements of the National Science Foundation–sponsored mathematics and science curriculum reforms that were a response to the 1957 launch of *Sputnik* by the Soviet Union, as well as the evaluation requirements instituted as part of the Elementary and Secondary Education Act of 1965.

## Experimentation versus Quasi-experimentation

The first large-scale evaluations in education were the subject of much criticism. In particular, two influential early evaluations were Paul Berman and Milbrey McLaughlin's RAND Change Agent 1973–

1978 study of four major federal programs: the Elementary and Secondary Education Act, Title VII (bilingual education), the Vocational Education Act, and the Right to Read Act; and a four-year study of Follow Through, which sampled 20,000 students and compared thirteen models of early childhood education. Some of the criticisms of these evaluations were that they were conducted under too short of a time frame, used crude measures that did not look at incremental or intermediate change, had statistical inadequacies including invalid assumptions, used poorly supported models and inappropriate analyses, and did not consider the social context of the program.

These criticisms led to the promotion of the use of experiments for program evaluation. Donald Campbell wrote an influential article in 1969 advocating the use of experimental designs in social program evaluation. The Social Science Research Council commissioned Henry Riecken and Robert Boruch to write the 1978 book *Social Experimentation,* which served as both a "guidebook and manifesto" for using experimentation in program evaluation. The best example of the use of experimentation in social research is the New Jersey negative income tax experiment sponsored by the Office of Equal Opportunity of the federal Department of Health, Education, and Welfare.

Experiments are the strongest designs for assessing impact, because through random sampling from the population of interest and random assignment to treatment and control groups, experiments rule out other factors besides the program that might explain program success. There are several practical disadvantages to experiments, however. First, they require that the program be a partial coverage program—that is, there must be people who do not participate in the program, who can serve as the control group. Second, experiments require large amounts of resources that are not always available. Third, they require that the program be firmly and consistently implemented, which is frequently not the case. Fourth, experiments do not provide information about how the program achieved its effects. Fifth, program stakeholders sometimes feel that random assignment to the program is unethical or politically unfeasible. Sixth, an experimental design in a field study is likely to produce no more than an approximation of a true experiment, because of such factors as systematic attrition from the program, which leaves the evaluator with a biased sample of participants (e.g., those who leave the program, or attrite, might be those who are the hardest to influence, so successful program outcomes would be biased in the positive direction).

When experiments are not appropriate or feasible, quasi-experimental techniques are used. Set forth by Donald Campbell and Julian Stanley in 1963, quasi-experimentation involves a number of different methods of conducting research that does not require random sampling and random assignment to treatment and control groups. One common example is an evaluation that matches the program participants to nonparticipants that share similar characteristics (e.g., race) and measures outcomes of both groups before and after the program. The challenge to quasi-experimentation is to rule out what Campbell and Stanley termed internal validity threats, or factors that might be alternative explanations for program results besides the program itself, which in turn would reduce confidence in the conclusions of the study. Unlike experimental design, which protects against just about all possible internal validity threats, quasi-experimental designs generally leave one or several of them uncontrolled.

## Implementation

In addition to focusing on the relative strengths and weaknesses of experiments and quasi-experiments, criticisms of early large-scale education evaluations highlighted the importance of measuring implementation. For example, McLaughlin and Berman's RAND Change Agent study and the Follow-Through evaluation demonstrated that implementation of a specific program can differ a great deal from one site to the next. If an evaluation is designed to attribute effects to a program, varying implementation of the same program reduces the value of the evaluation, because it is unclear how to define the program. Thus, it is necessary to include in a program evaluation a complete description of how the program is being implemented, to allow the examination of implementation fidelity to the original design, and to discover any cross-site implementation differences that would affect outcomes.

In 1967 Michael Scriven first articulated the idea that there were two types of evaluation—one focused on evaluating implementation, called formative evaluation, and one focused on evaluating the impact of the program, called summative evaluation. He argued that emerging programs should be the subject of formative evaluations, which are designed to see how well a program was implemented and to improve implementation; and that summative evaluations should be reserved for programs that have been well-established and have stable and consistent implementation.

Related to the idea of formative and summative evaluation is a controversy over the extent to which the evaluator should be a program insider or an objective third party. In formative evaluations, it can be argued that the evaluator needs to become somewhat of an insider, in order to become part of the formal and informal feedback loop that makes providing program improvement information possible. In contrast, summative evaluations conducted by a program insider foster little confidence in the results, because of the inherent conflict of interest.

## Stakeholder and Utilization Approaches

Still another criticism of early education evaluations was that stakeholders felt uninvolved in the evaluations; did not agree with the goals, measures, and procedures; and thus rejected the findings. This discovery of the importance to the evaluation of stakeholder buy-in led to what Michael Patton termed stakeholder or utilization-focused evaluation. Stakeholder evaluation bases its design and execution on the needs and goals of identified stakeholders or users, such as the funding organization, a program director, the staff, or clients of the program.

In the context of stakeholder evaluation, Patton in 1997 introduced the idea that it is sometimes appropriate to conduct goal-free evaluation. He suggested that evaluators should be open to the idea of conducting an evaluation without preconceived goals because program staff might not agree with the goals and because the goals of the program might change over time. Further, he argued that goal-free evaluation avoids missing unanticipated outcomes, removes the negative connotation to side effects, eliminates perceptual biases that occur when goals are known, and helps to maintain evaluator objectivity. Goals are often necessary, however, to guide and focus the evaluation and to respond to the needs of policymakers. As a result, Patton argued that the use of goals in program evaluation should be decided on a case-by-case basis.

## Theory-Based Evaluations

Besides stakeholder and goal-free evaluation, Carol Weiss in 1997 advocated for theory-based evaluations, or evaluations that are grounded in the pro-

gram's theory of action. Theory-based evaluation aims to make clear the theoretical underpinnings of the program and use them to help structure the evaluation. In her support of theory-based evaluation, Weiss wrote that if the program theory is outlined in a phased sequence of cause and effect, then the evaluation can identify weaknesses in the system or at what point in the chain of effects results can be attributed. Also, articulating a programmatic theory can have positive benefits for the program, including helping the staff address conflicts, examine their own assumptions, and improve practice.

Weiss explained that theory-based approaches have not been widespread because there may be more than one theory that applies to a program and no guidance about which to choose, and because the process of constructing theories is challenging and time consuming. Further, theory-based approaches require large amounts of data and resources. A theory-based evaluation approach does, however, strengthen the rigor of the evaluation and link it more with scientific research, which by design is a theory-testing endeavor.

## Data Collection Methods

Within different types of evaluation (e.g., formative, stakeholder, theory-based), there have been debates about which type of methodology is appropriate, with these debates mirroring the debates in the larger social science community. The "scientific ideal" of using social experiments and randomized experiments, which supports the quantification of implementation and outcomes, is contrasted with the "humanistic ideal" that the program should be seen through the eyes of the clients and defies quantification, which supports an ethnographic or observational methodology.

Campbell believed that the nature of the research question should determine the question, and he encouraged evaluations that have both qualitative and quantitative assessments, with these assessments supporting each other. In the early twenty-first century, program evaluations commonly use a combination of qualitative and quantitative data collection techniques.

## Does Evaluation Influence Policy?

Although the main justification for program evaluation is its role in rationalizing policy, program evaluation results rarely have a direct impact on decision-making. This is because of the diffuse and political nature of policy decision-making and because people are generally resistant to change. Most evaluations are undertaken and disseminated in an environment where decision-making is decentralized among several groups and where program and policy choices result from conflict and accommodation across a complex and shifting set of players. In this environment, evaluation results cannot have a single and clear use, nor can the evaluator be sure how the results will be interpreted or used.

While program evaluations may not directly affect decisions, evaluation does play a critical role in contributing to the discourse around a particular program or issue. Information generated from program evaluation helps to frame the policy debate by bringing conflict to the forefront, providing information about trade-offs, influencing the broad assumptions and beliefs underlying policies, and changing the way people think about a specific issue or problem.

## Evaluation in the Early Twenty-First Century

In the early twenty-first century, program evaluation is an integral component of education research and practice. The No Child Left Behind Act of 2001 (reauthorization of the U.S. government's Elementary and Secondary Education Act) calls for schools to use "research-based practices." This means practices that are grounded in research and have been proven through evaluation to be successful. Owing in part to this government emphasis on the results of program evaluation, there is an increased call for the use of experimental designs.

Further, as the evaluation field has developed in sophistication and increased its requirements for rigor and high standards of research, the lines between scientific research and evaluation have faded. There is a move to design large-scale education evaluations to respond to programmatic concerns while simultaneously informing methodological and substantive inquiry.

While program evaluation is not expected to drive policy, if conducted in a rigorous and systematic way that adheres to the principles of social research as closely as possible, the results of program evaluations can contribute to program improvement and can provide valuable information to both advance scholarly inquiry as well as inform important policy debates.

*See also:* RESEARCH METHODS, *subentries on* OVERVIEW, QUALITATIVE AND ETHNOGRAPHIC.

## BIBLIOGRAPHY

BERMAN, PAUL, and MCLAUGHLIN, MILBREY. 1978. *Federal Programs Supporting Educational Change,* Vol. IV: *The Findings in Review.* Santa Monica, CA: RAND.

CAMPBELL, DONALD. 1969. "Reforms as Experiments." *American Psychologist* 24:409–429.

CAMPBELL, DONALD, and STANLEY, JULIAN. 1963. *Experimental and Quasi-Experimental Designs for Research.* Chicago: Rand McNally.

CHELIMSKY, ELEANOR. 1987. "What Have We Learned about the Politics of Program Evaluation?" *Evaluation News* 8(1):5–22.

COHEN, DAVID, and GARET, MICHAEL. 1975. "Reforming Educational Policy with Applied Social Research." *Harvard Educational Review* 45(1):17–43.

COOK, THOMAS D., and CAMPBELL, DONALD T. 1979. *Quasi-Experimentation: Design and Analysis Issues for Field Settings.* Chicago: Rand McNally.

CRONBACH, LEE J. 1982. *Designing Evaluations of Educational and Social Programs.* San Francisco: Jossey-Bass.

CRONBACH, LEE J.; ABRON, SUEANN ROBINSON; DORNBUSCH, SANFORD; HESS, ROBERT; PHILLIPS, D. C.; WALKER, DECKER; and WEINER, STEPHEN. 1980. *Toward Reform of Program Evaluation: Aims, Methods, and Institutional Arrangements.* San Francisco: Jossey-Bass.

HOUSE, ERNEST; GLASS, GENE; MCLEAN, LESLIE; and WALKER, DECKER. 1978. "No Simple Answer: Critique of the Follow Through Evaluation." *Harvard Educational Review* 48:128–160.

PATTON, MICHAEL. 1997. *Utilization-Focused Evaluation,* 3rd edition. Thousand Oaks, CA: Sage.

RIECKEN, HENRY, and BORUCH, ROBERT. 1978. *Social Experimentation: A Method for Planning and Evaluating Social Intervention.* New York: Academic Press.

ROSSI, PETER; FREEMAN, HOWARD; and LIPSEY, MARK. 1999. *Evaluation: A Systematic Approach,* 6th edition. Thousand Oaks, CA: Sage.

SCRIVEN, MICHAEL. 1967. "The Methodology of Evaluation." In *Perspective of Curriculum Evaluation,* ed. Robert E. Stake. Chicago: Rand McNally.

SHADISH, WILLIAM R.; COOK, THOMAS; and LEVITON, LAURA. 1991. *Foundations of Program Eval-*

*uation: Theories of Practice.* Newbury Park, CA: Sage.

U.S. OFFICE OF EDUCATION. 1977. *National Evaluation: Detailed Effects.* Volumes II-A and II-B of the Follow Through Planned Variation Experiment Series. Washington, DC: Government Printing Office.

WEISS, CAROL. 1972. *Evaluation Research: Methods for Assessing Program Effectiveness.* Englewood Cliffs, NJ: Prentice Hall.

WEISS, CAROL. 1987. "Evaluating Social Programs: What Have We Learned?" *Society* 25:40–45.

WEISS, CAROL. 1988. "Evaluation for Decisions: Is Anybody There? Does Anybody Care?" *Evaluation Practice* 9:5–20.

WEISS, CAROL. 1997. "How Can Theory-Based Evaluation Make Greater Headway?" *Evaluation Review* 21:501–524.

LAURA DESIMONE

# VERBAL PROTOCOLS

Since the early 1900s, researchers have relied on verbal data to gain insights about thinking and learning. Over the years, however, the perceived value of verbal data for gaining such insights has waxed and waned. In 1912 Edward Titchener, one of the founders of structural psychology, advocated the use of introspection by highly trained self-observers as the only method for revealing certain cognitive processes. At the same time, this technique of observing and verbalizing one's own cognitive processes drew much criticism. Researchers questioned the objectivity of the technique and the extent to which people have knowledge of and access to their cognitive processes. With behaviorism as the dominant perspective for studying learning in the United States, verbal data were treated as behavioral products, not as information that might reveal something about cognitive processing. From about the 1920s to 1950s, most U.S. researchers abandoned the use of introspective techniques, as well as most other types of verbal data such as question answering.

While U.S. learning theorists and researchers were relying almost solely on nonverbal or very limited verbal (e.g., yes/no response) techniques, the Swiss cognitive theorist Jean Piaget was relying primarily on children's verbal explanations for gaining insights into their cognitive abilities and processes.

Piaget believed that children's explanations for their responses to various cognitive tasks provided much more information about their thinking than did the task responses alone. United States theorists, however, were not ready to consider Piaget's work seriously until about 1960, when cognitive psychology was beginning to emerge and there was declining satisfaction with a purely behavioral perspective.

With the rise of cognitive psychology beginning in the 1950s and 1960s, educational and experimental psychologists became interested once again in the usefulness of verbal data for providing information about thinking and learning. Cognitive researchers rarely use Titchener's original introspective technique in the early twenty-first century. Since the 1980s, however, researchers have increasingly used verbal protocol analysis, which has roots in the introspective technique, to study the cognitive processes involved in expert task performance, problem solving, text comprehension, science education, second language acquisition, and hypertext navigation.

## What Are Verbal Protocols?

Verbal protocols are rich data sources containing individuals' spoken thoughts that are associated with working on a task. While working on a particular task, subjects usually either think aloud as thoughts occur to them or they do so at intervals specified by the researcher. In some studies, researchers ask subjects to verbalize their thoughts upon completion of the task. The verbalizations are recorded verbatim, usually using a tape recorder, and are then coded according to theory-driven and/or empirically driven categories.

Verbal protocols differ from introspection. Subjects are not instructed to focus on the cognitive processes involved in task completion nor are they trained in the self-observation of cognitive processing. The goal is for subjects to express out loud the thoughts that occur to them naturally. Researchers use these data in conjunction with logical theoretical premises to generate hypotheses and to draw conclusions about cognitive processes and products.

## What Can Verbal Protocols Reveal about Thinking and Learning?

In order to verbalize one's thoughts, individuals must be aware of those thoughts and the thoughts must be amenable to language. Thus, verbal protocol analysis can reveal those aspects of thinking and learning that are consciously available, or activated in working memory, and that can be encoded verbally.

One major advantage of verbal protocol data is that they provide the richest information regarding the contents of working memory during task execution. In studies of reading comprehension, for example, verbal protocols have provided a detailed database of the types of text-based and knowledge-based inferences that might occur during the normal reading of narrative texts. Data using other measures such as sentence reading time and reaction time to single-word probes have corroborated some of the verbal protocol findings. For example, corroborating evidence for the generation of causal inferences and goal-based explanations exists. Verbal protocols have also provided information about the particular knowledge domains that are used to make inferences when reading narratives, and about differences in readers' deliberate strategies for understanding both narrative and informational texts.

Verbal protocols have been used extensively in the study of expert versus novice task performance across a variety of domains (e.g., cognitive-perceptual expertise involved in chess, perceptual-motor expertise such as in sports, science and mathematical problem-solving strategies, skilled versus less-skilled reading). While the specific insights about the differences between expert and novice approaches vary from domain to domain, some generalities across domains can be made. Clearly, experts have more knowledge and more highly organized knowledge structures within their domains than do novices. But the processes by which they solve problems and accomplish tasks within their domains of expertise also differ. Verbal protocols have revealed that experts are more likely to evaluate and anticipate the ever-changing situations involved with many problems and to plan ahead and reason accordingly. Knowledge about expert and novice problem-solving processes has implications for developing and assessing pedagogical practices.

Another advantage of verbal protocol analysis is that it provides sequential observations over time. As such, it reveals changes that occur in working memory over the course of task execution. This has been useful in studies of reading comprehension where the information presented and the individual's representation of the text change over time, in studies of problem solving where multiple steps are involved in reaching a solution and/or where multiple solutions are possible, in studies of expert versus novice task performance, and in studies of conceptual change.

## Limitations of Verbal Protocol Data

As is the case with most research methods, verbal protocols have both advantages and limitations. Obviously, subjects can verbalize only thoughts and processes about which they are consciously aware. Thus, processes that are automatic and executed outside of conscious awareness are not likely to be included in verbal protocols, and other means of assessing such processes must be used. Also, nonverbal knowledge is not likely to be reported.

Most authors of articles examining the think-aloud procedure seem to disagree with the 1993 contention of K. Anders Ericsson and Herbert A. Simon that thinking aloud does not usually affect normal cognitive processing. It is thought that the think-aloud procedure may lead to overestimates and/or underestimates of the knowledge and processes used under normal task conditions. The need to verbalize for the think-aloud task itself might encourage subjects to strategically use knowledge or processes that they might not otherwise use. Alternately, the demands of the think-aloud task might interfere with subjects' abilities to use knowledge and/or processes they might use under normal conditions. Self-presentation issues (e.g., desire to appear smart, embarrassment, introversion/extroversion) might affect subjects' verbal reports. Finally, the pragmatics and social rules associated with the perception of having to communicate one's thoughts to the researcher might also lead to overestimates or underestimates of knowledge and processes typically used.

Unfortunately, it is not possible to know if a verbal protocol provides a complete picture of the knowledge and processes normally used to perform a task. Typically, however, no single research technique provides a complete picture. Only the use of multiple measures for assessing the same hypotheses and for assessing various aspects of task performance can provide the most complete picture possible.

A final limitation of verbal protocol methodology is that it is very labor intensive. The data collection and data coding are extremely time consuming as compared with other methodologies. The amount of potential information that can be acquired about the contents of working memory during task performance, however, is often well worth the time required.

## Optimizing the Advantages and Minimizing the Limitations

Several suggestions have been put forth for increasing the likelihood of obtaining verbal protocol data that provide valid information about the contents of working memory under normal task conditions. The most frequent suggestions are as follows:

- Collect verbal protocol data while subjects are performing the task of interest.

- Ask subjects to verbalize all thoughts that occur. One should not direct their thoughts or processing by asking for specific types of information unless one wishes to study the planned, strategic use of that type of information.

- Make it clear to the subjects that task performance is their primary concern and that thinking aloud is secondary. If, however, a subject is silent for a relatively long period as compared to others during task execution, prompts such as "keep talking" may become necessary.

- To minimize as much as possible the conversational aspects of the think-aloud task, the researcher should try to remain out of the subject's view.

*See also:* LANGUAGE AND EDUCATION; LEARNING, *subentry on* CONCEPTUAL CHANGE; READING, *subentries on* COMPREHENSION, CONTENT AREAS; SCIENCE LEARNING, *subentry on* EXPLANATION AND ARGUMENTATION.

### BIBLIOGRAPHY

BERK, LAURA E. 2000. *Child Development,* 5th edition. Boston: Allyn and Bacon.

COTE, NATHALIE, and GOLDMAN, SUSAN R. 1999. "Building Representations of Informational Text: Evidence from Children's Think-Aloud Protocols." In *The Construction of Mental Representations during Reading,* ed. Herre van Oostendorp and Susan R. Goldman. Mahwah, NJ: Erlbaum.

CRUTCHER, ROBERT J. 1994. "Telling What We Know: The Use of Verbal Report Methodologies in Psychological Research." *Psychological Science* 5:241–244.

DHILLON, AMARJIT S. 1998. "Individual Differences within Problem-Solving Strategies Used in Physics." *Science Education* 82:379–405.

ERICSSON, K. ANDERS, and SIMON, HERBERT A. 1993. *Protocol Analysis: Verbal Reports as Data,* revised edition. Cambridge, MA: MIT Press.

HURST, ROY W., and MILKENT, MARLENE M. 1996. "Facilitating Successful Prediction Problem Solving in Biology through Application of Skill Theory." *Journal of Research in Science Teaching* 33:541–552.

LONG, DEBRA L., and BOURG, TAMMY. 1996. "Thinking Aloud: Telling a Story about a Story." *Discourse Processes* 21:329–339.

MAGLIANO, JOSEPH P. 1999. "Revealing Inference Processes during Text Comprehension." In *Narrative Comprehension, Causality, and Coherence: Essays in Honor of Tom Trabasso,* ed. Susan R. Goldman, Arthur C. Graesser, and Paul van den Broek. Mahwah, NJ: Erlbaum.

MAGLIANO, JOSEPH P.; TRABASSO, TOM; and GRAESSER, ARTHUR C. 1999. "Strategic Processing during Comprehension." *Journal of Educational Psychology* 91:615–629.

PAYNE, JOHN W. 1994. "Thinking Aloud: Insights into Information Processing." *Psychological Science* 5(5):241–248.

PIAGET, JEAN. 1929. *The Child's Conception of the World* (1926), trans. Joan Tomlinson and Andrew Tomlinson. London: Kegan Paul.

PRESSLEY, MICHAEL, and AFFLERBACH, PETER. 1995. *Verbal Protocols of Reading: The Nature of Constructively Responsive Reading.* Hillsdale, NJ: Erlbaum.

PRITCHARD, ROBERT. 1990. "The Evolution of Introspective Methodology and Its Implications for Studying the Reading Process." *Reading Psychology: An International Quarterly* 11(1):1–13.

TRABASSO, TOM, and MAGLIANO, JOSEPH P. 1996. "Conscious Understanding during Comprehension." *Discourse Processes* 21:255–287.

WHITNEY, PAUL, and BUDD, DESIREE. 1996. "Think-Aloud Protocols and the Study of Comprehension." *Discourse Processes* 21:341–351.

WILSON, TIMOTHY D. 1994. "The Proper Protocol: Validity and Completeness of Verbal Reports." *Psychological Science* 5(5):249–252.

ZWAAN, ROLF A., and BROWN, CAROL M. 1996. "The Influence of Language Proficiency and Comprehension Skill on Situation-Model Construction." *Discourse Processes* 21:289–327.

TAMMY BOURG

# RESEARCH MISCONDUCT

Research encompasses a broad range of activities that are bound together by the common goal of advancing knowledge and understandings. Its usefulness to society rests on the expectation that researchers undertake and report their work fairly, accurately, and honestly. Researchers who fail to fulfill this expectation lack integrity and can be accused of engaging in research misconduct.

## Policies and Procedures

In 1981 when Congress convened its first hearing to investigate fraud in biomedical research, researchers expressed confidence in their ability to police their own affairs. The fact that researchers who engaged in misconduct were caught seemingly justified this confidence. A few professional societies subsequently issued reports discussing the importance of integrity in research, including the Association of American Medical Colleges, which published *The Maintenance of High Ethical Standards in the Conduct of Research* in 1982, and the Association of American Universities, which published its *Report . . . on the Integrity of Research* in 1983. A small number of research universities also adopted research misconduct policies—primarily the ones directly affected by misconduct cases, such as Yale and Harvard universities. However, neither government nor the majority of research universities saw any pressing need to make major changes. Through the mid-1980s, research misconduct remained largely undefined on most university campuses and was policed only through the informal mechanisms of peer review and general policies governing academic conduct.

The Health Research Extension Act of 1985 changed this situation and required government and universities to take a more aggressive approach to investigating research misconduct. In response to this call for action, the Public Health Service (PHS) published an Interim Policy on Research Misconduct in 1986 and adopted a final policy in 1989. The latter established two offices to investigate and adjudicate research misconduct cases: the Office of Scientific Integrity (OSI) as part of the National Institutes of Health (NIH) and the Office of Scientific Integrity Review (OSIR), affiliated with the Office of the Assistant Secretary of Health (OASH). The National Science Foundation (NSF) also published *Final Regulations for Misconduct in Science and Engineering Research* (1987) and assigned administration of its regulations to the NSF Office of the Inspector General (OIG). These actions established policies and procedures for investigating research misconduct. They also required research universities to establish their own policies and procedures for handing research misconduct cases, which they slowly did over the course of the 1990s.

The responsibility for administering research misconduct policies on most university campuses is assigned to the chief research officer, although in a few cases universities have established research integrity or misconduct committees. On campuses with large research budgets, one staff person, sometimes called the "research integrity officer," is assigned primary responsibility for initiating inquiries, setting up investigation committees, making timely reports, and handling other matters relating to research misconduct. The process for determining whether misconduct has been committed usually follows the three-step model outlined by the federal government—inquiry, investigation, and adjudication. During inquires, charges are informally assessed to determine whether there is enough evidence to proceed with a formal investigation. If there is, a formal investigation follows, after which decisions about innocence or guilt and appropriate penalties or exoneration are made (adjudication).

Proper handling of misconduct cases proposes three challenges for universities. First, since state and federal governments provide no funds to comply with research misconduct regulations, other sources of support are needed. Second, misconduct cases often pit one university employee against another, making it difficult for the university to provide equal justice and protection to all concerned. Third, universities have conflicts of interest when they confront reports of research misconduct.

Several factors can make it tempting for universities to dismiss cases early in the process prior to fair and complete investigations. Investigations can be expensive and divisive. Findings of misconduct can require that funds be returned to a funding agency, even if some or all of the funds have already been spent. Reports of research misconduct can also erode public confidence in a university. However, in addition to the clear responsibility universities have to assure that public research funds are used properly, the costs of cover-ups can be high and may lead to further regulation. Therefore universities must take their responsibility for conducting fair and complete investigations seriously.

## Definitions

The first formal government definition of research misconduct was published in the 1986 PHS Interim Policy. This initial definition framed all subsequent discussions of research misconduct in two important ways. First, in rejecting the use of the term "fraud" for describing inappropriate behavior in research, PHS officials helped assure that all subsequent discussions would be framed in terms of "research misconduct." Second, the three key terms used in the Interim Policies to describe research misconduct—"fabrication, falsification, and plagiarism," or FFP—have been used in all subsequent federal and many university definitions.

As important and long-lasting as the framework established in the Interim Policy turned out to be, it raised points of contention that to this day continue to polarize discussions of research misconduct. Most importantly, PHS proposed and the National Science Foundation (NSF) soon officially included, in 1987, one additional phrase in the government definition of research misconduct: "other practices that seriously deviate from those that are commonly accepted within the scientific community for proposing, conducting, or reporting research." The "other practices" phrase turned out to be very controversial. Scientists worried that professional disagreements over methods or theories might be construed as *other practices that seriously deviate from those that are commonly accepted.* They wanted a tight, unambiguous definition that left no room for arbitrary interpretation. Government officials, particularly at NSF, felt they needed some flexibility to investigate behavior that did not constitute FFP but that nonetheless was clearly inappropriate and undermined the public's investment in research. NSF officials backed up their claim with several examples, including a widely publicized case of inappropriate sexual behavior by an anthropologist who had an NSF grant to train students in field research.

Two efforts to resolve disagreements over the definition of misconduct in the 1990s failed to produce a consensus. The first, led by a subcommittee of the National Academy of Sciences, dropped the "other practices" phrase from the formal definition of research misconduct, but agreed that there were "other questionable research practices" that needed to be investigated, not by government but by re-

search institutions and professional societies. The second effort to produce a consensus definition by a specially appointed PHS Commission on Research Integrity failed to win serious support and was largely ignored. The failure of these efforts and the lack of a common government definition led eventually to a new government effort to produce a uniform federal definition for research misconduct, coordinated this time by the Office of Science and Technology Policy (OSTP) in the Executive Office of the President.

The new OSTP policy, which was published in the *Federal Register* in December 2000, defines "research misconduct" as "fabrication, falsification, or plagiarism in proposing, performing, or reviewing research, or in reporting research results." It also sets three criteria for proving misconduct, which further narrow the definition of research misconduct. When adopted, the new definition will require evidence that the behavior:

- [represents a] significant departure from accepted practices of the relevant research community; and
- [was] committed intentionally, or knowingly, or recklessly; and
- [can be] proven by a preponderance of evidence.

With the publication of the OSTP Policy, nearly two decades of intense debate over the definition of research misconduct reached a tentative conclusion, assuming the federal agencies that fund research follow through and adopt the proposed OSTP definition.

## Misconduct Cases

The evolution of research misconduct policy has unquestionably been driven by a small number of prominent cases. In the early 1970s, William Summerlin, working at the Sloane Kettering Institute, tried to pass off black patches painted on white mice as genuine skin grafts that he had applied using a new technique. Elias Asabati, while at Temple University and Jefferson Medical College in Philadelphia and the Anderson Hospital in Houston, took published articles, replaced the authors' names with his own name, made occasional minor modifications in the text, and then submitted them to other journals for publication. His misdeeds, which eventually included the submission of eighty fraudulent articles, became public in 1978. A junior researcher at Yale

University, Vijay Soman, used information from an unpublished article from another laboratory being reviewed by his mentor, Philip Felig, to publish his own, supposedly original findings on the same topic. Yale initially ignored the charges of plagiarism and data falsification brought by the researcher whose work Soman used. The charges were confirmed in 1980 by an investigation conducted by the NIH. The 1981 Congressional hearings on fraud in biomedical research were convened specifically to investigate these cases.

Reports of new cases of research misconduct and the 1982 publication of *Betrayers of the Truth: Fraud and Deceit in the Hall of Science,* by *New York Times* writers William Broad and Nicholas Wade, guaranteed that the problem of research misconduct did not disappear after the 1981 hearings. One case, which involved data falsification by John Darsee, a promising young cardiovascular researcher at Harvard, dragged on for five years, due not to uncertainty about the actual misconduct but to a dispute over the responsibilities of others who oversaw Darsee's work. A paper by NIH researchers Walter Stuart and Ned Feder raised serious questions about the role of Darsee's chief mentor, Eugene Braunwald, in reviewing publications he coauthored with Darsee. Disagreement over the publication of Stuart and Feder's paper kept the Darsee case alive through most of the 1980s.

As the Darsee case was slowly coming to an end, two new cases assured continued public interest in research misconduct. The first involved disputed data published in an article in *Cell* in 1986, based on research conducted by Tufts University researcher Thereza Imanishi-Kari. A postdoctoral student working in Imanishi-Kari's laboratory, Margot O'Toole, raised questions about research misconduct when she was unable to replicate some of the results reported in the *Cell* article. Eventually, the article's most prominent co-author, Nobel scientist and Whitehead Institute Director David Baltimore, was drawn into the dispute. After numerous investigations by the Massachusetts Institute of Technology (MIT) and the Office of Scientific Integrity (renamed the Office of Research Integrity in 1992), the charges against Imanishi-Kari were dismissed by a Health and Human Services appeal board in 1996, ten years after the original article was published and five years after the article had been retracted by four of the five co-authors, including Baltimore. (David Baltimore was never formally charged with miscon-

duct.) The bitter dispute between Baltimore and his supporters on the one hand and Congressman John Dingell of Michigan and research critics on the other seriously polarized the debate over the importance of and ways to deal with research misconduct.

The second prominent case involved NIH AIDS researcher Robert Gallo, a researcher in his laboratory, Mikulas Popovic, and their 1984 article published in *Science* claiming discovery of the AIDS virus. At issue was whether Gallo's team had isolated the virus described in the article or whether they had improperly used samples supplied by the Institut Pasteur in France. A series of articles by *Chicago Tribune* reporter John Crewdson and reports issued by the ORI and a subcommittee headed by Representative John Dingell cast serious doubts on Gallo's claims. However, the charges against Popovic were dismissed in 1995 by the same HHS appeal board that had dismissed the charges against Imanishi-Kari. ORI therefore decided to drop its charges against Gallo, arguing that the appeal board had adopted a new definition of misconduct that ORI was not prepared to meet.

In the late 1990s the focus of interest in research misconduct shifted to clinical research, following the report of the death of a young subject, Jesse Gelsinger, in 1999, during a gene therapy trial at the University of Pennsylvania. In this and other cases involving clinical research, the questionable research behavior does not constitute research misconduct, narrowly defined as FFB, but rather raises questions about conflicts of interest, misleading or incomplete reports on past research, the failure to inform research subjects of risks, and noncompliance with federal rules. These new concerns have raised questions about the way researchers are trained and steps that can be taken to foster the "responsible conduct of research."

## Responsible Conduct of Research

Interest in instruction in the "responsible conduct of research" (RCR) emerged in the late 1980s as one solution to growing public concern about research misconduct. Although a number of earlier reports had stressed the importance of education in research training, few substantive changes in the way researchers are trained were made prior to the 1989 Institute of Medicine report *The Responsible Conduct of Research in the Health Sciences.* Within a year, NIH and the Alcohol, Drug and Mental Health Administration (ADAMHA) published rules that required researchers seeking a special type of award known as a "training grant" to include a description of "activities related to the instruction about the responsible conduct of research" in their applications.

Over the course of the 1990s the modest NIH/ADAMHA training grant requirement fostered the development of a growing number of RCR courses on university campuses and related instructional materials, such as textbooks, videos, and Internet resources. This development was given a considerable boost in 2000, when NIH implemented *Required Education in the Protection of Human Research Participants* and ORI published an RCR requirement that would have affected all PHS funded research, had it not been suspended due to Congressional questions about the way it was developed. However, even without the broad ORI RCR requirement, efforts continue on university campuses to formalize instruction in the responsible conduct of research, relying more and more on web-based training.

## Future Considerations

When research misconduct first emerged as a public concern in the late 1970s, it was seen primarily as an aberration that did not typify the conduct of most researchers. By implication, it was therefore assumed that most researchers adopted high standards for integrity in their work. Since the early 1980s, research misconduct has continued to occur, but its overall rate of occurrence is still small in comparison to the total number of active researchers. Research misconduct, defined as intentional FFP, still seems to be an aberration that does not typify the conduct of most researchers. However, based on a growing body of research on research integrity, it can no longer be assumed that most researchers do in fact adopt high standards for integrity in their work.

Studies of peer review, publication practices, conflicts of interest, bias, mentoring, and other elements of the research process consistently report that significant numbers of researchers (defined as 10% or higher) do not adhere to accepted norms for the responsible practice of research. Significant numbers inappropriately list their names on publications, are unwilling to share data with colleagues, use inappropriate statistical analyses, provide inaccurate references in publications, fail to list conflicts of interest, and engage in other practices that fall short of ideal standards for the responsible conduct of research. There has been widespread agreement that these other "questionable research practices" as

titled in the 1982 NAS report should not be considered research misconduct. However, whether classed as misconduct or not, these practices unquestionably waste public research dollars, undermine the integrity of the research record, and can even endanger public health. As a result, the focus of attention both in government and on university campuses is slowly shifting from confronting misconduct to fostering integrity through education and the serious appraisal of what it means to be a research university.

*See also:* ETHICS, *subentry on* HIGHER EDUCATION; FEDERAL FUNDING FOR ACADEMIC RESEARCH; MISCONDUCT AND EDUCATION.

## BIBLIOGRAPHY

ASSOCIATION OF AMERICAN MEDICAL COLLEGES. 1982. *The Maintenance of High Ethical Standards in the Conduct of Research.* Washington, DC: Association of American Medical Colleges.

ASSOCIATION OF AMERICAN UNIVERSITIES. 1983. *Report of the Association of American Universities Committee on the Integrity of Research.* Washington, DC: American Association of Universities.

BROAD, WILLIAM J., and WADE, NICHOLAS. 1982. *Betrayers of the Truth: Fraud and Deceit in the Halls of Science.* New York: Simon and Schuster.

BUZZELLI, DONALD E. 1993. "The Definition of Misconduct in Science: A View from NSF." *Science* 259:584–585, 647–648.

CREWDSON, JOHN. 2002. *Science Fictions: A Scientific Mystery, a Massive Cover-up, and the Dark Legacy of Robert Gallo.* Boston: Little, Brown.

*Health Research Extension Act of 1985.* U.S. Public Law 99–158.

HIXSON, JOSEPH. 1976. *The Patchwork Mouse.* Garden City, NY: Anchor Press/Doubleday.

INSTITUTE OF MEDICINE, AND COMMITTEE ON THE RESPONSIBLE CONDUCT OF RESEARCH. 1989. *The Responsible Conduct of Research in the Health Sciences.* Washington, DC: National Academy of Sciences.

KEVLES, DANIEL J. 1998. *The Baltimore Case: A Trial of Politics, Science, and Character,* 1st edition. New York: W.W. Norton.

NATIONAL ACADEMIC OF SCIENCE, COMMITTEE ON SCIENCE ENGINEERING AND PUBLIC POLICY, PANEL ON SCIENTIFIC RESPONSIBILITY AND THE

Conduct of Research. 1992. *Responsible Science : Ensuring the Integrity of the Research Process.* Washington, DC: National Academy Press.

National Institutes of Health, and the Alcohol, Drug and Mental Health Administration. 1989. "Requirement for Programs on the Responsible Conduct of Research in National Research Service Award Institutional Training Programs." *NIH Guide for Grants and Contracts* 18:1.

National Institutes of Health. 2000. "Required Education in the Protection of Human Research Participants." Washington, DC: National Institutes of Health.

National Science Foundation. 1987. *Misconduct in Science and Engineering Research: Final Regulations.* Washington, DC: National Science Foundation.

Office of the President and Office of Science and Technology Policy. 2000. *Federal Policy on Research Misconduct.* Washington, DC: Office of Science and Technology.

Sarasohn, Judy. 1993. *Science on Trial: The Whistle Blower, The Accused, and The Nobel Laureate.* New York: St. Martin's Press.

Steneck, Nicholas H. 1984. "The University and Research Ethics: Commentary." *Science, Technology, and Human Values* 94(September):6–15.

Steneck, Nicholas H. 1994. "Research Universities and Scientific Misconduct—History, Policies, and the Future."*Journal of Higher Education* 65(3):54–69.

Steneck, Nicholas H. 1999. "Confronting Misconduct in Science in the 1980s and 1990s: What Has and Has Not Been Accomplished?" *Science and Engineering Ethics* 5(2):1–16.

Steneck, Nicholas H., and Scheetz, Mary D., eds. 2002. *Investigating Research Integrity: Proceedings of the First ORI Research Conference on Research Integrity.* Washington, DC: Office of Research Integrity.

**INTERNET RESOURCE**

U.S. Department of Health and Human Services Office of Research Integrity. 2002. *Responsible Conduct of Research (RCR) Education.* <http://ori.dhhs.gov/html/programs/congressionalconcerns.asp>.

Nicholas H. Steneck

# RESEARCH UNIVERSITIES

Research universities are postsecondary institutions that devote a large portion of their mission, resources, and focus to graduate education and research. Currently, there are more than 250 of these institutions in the United States. Research universities such as Harvard, Stanford, Berkeley, and Michigan are often mentioned in the media due to their size, resources, status, and athletic teams. These are among the best-known, but there are many different kinds of research universities.

Research universities in the United States vary according to size, control, focus, selectivity, and the number of degree programs offered. They include public universities, such as the universities of Michigan and Virginia, and private universities, such as Duke University and MIT (Massachusetts Institute of Technology). They range in size from very large universities such as the University of Minnesota, which has almost 60,000 students enrolled at three campuses, to small universities such as Rice University in Houston, which has fewer than 4,500 students. A few research universities are very focused in mission and offer degree programs in specialized areas, such as The Rockefeller University, which offers graduate programs, including a Ph.D., in biomedical sciences only. Others, like Michigan State University, offer a dizzying portfolio of undergraduate and graduate degrees across seventeen colleges and hundreds of undergraduate and graduate degree programs. Some research universities embrace open admissions policies, while others are very selective and admit less than 20 percent of those students that apply.

What all research universities have in common—and what makes them research universities—is an emphasis on graduate education and research. All research universities offer advanced degrees, up to and including the doctorate. Most research universities also enroll a sizeable number of undergraduates in a comprehensive set of bachelor's degree programs.

## Faculty and Students

Research universities occupy a unique position within the United States higher education system. For example, unlike students enrolled at liberal arts colleges, undergraduate students attending research universities generally pursue a specialized curriculum with a very large number of requirements for the major and a smaller number of electives and general education requirements. Due to the large size of most research universities, students who attend these institutions are likely to have large lower-division classes, some of which may be taught by graduate students who serve as teaching assistants.

Faculty members at research universities are expected to devote a larger amount of their time to research than are faculty members at liberal arts colleges and comprehensive universities, where the faculty's primary role is that of teacher rather than researcher. At research universities, faculty members are sometimes researchers first and teachers second, and are expected to publish articles and books and secure research grants from external sources.

While these qualities have provoked some criticism of research universities, they remain a very popular option for postsecondary students. As of 1998, for example, research universities enrolled more than one out of every five students attending a college or university in the United States. Research universities also attract a large percentage of the best and brightest students. Annually, research universities enroll the largest numbers of National Merit Scholars. These students are attracted to research universities because of their high-profile faculty members, the prestige associated with these institutions, and their resources, including state-of-the-art labs and technology.

## Beyond Academics

The U.S. research university is much more than academics, however. The research university is a far-flung and complex organization with multiple campuses, extension centers, research centers and institutes, multiple campuses, student services and programming for diverse student groups, and often high-profile athletics teams. The Big Ten, Big 12, and PAC-10 athletic conferences consist entirely of research universities, for example. It is not unusual for research universities to establish their own research parks where private companies and the university engage in technology transfer and spin off new businesses. In the early twenty-first century, it is difficult to think of something in which research universities are not involved.

In this sense, Clark Kerr refers to the modern U.S. research university as a ''multiversity'' and a ''community of communities'' where the complexity and sheer number of goals the organization strives to achieve creates great specialization and multiple communities of actors who share little in common, except for the fact that they work for the university. Similarly, higher education researchers Michael Cohen and James March refer to research universities as ''organized anarchies'' where, at times, there appear to be no rules governing the organization, and no recognized leaders, only a sort of chaos that someone familiar with the research university can sort out.

## The History of the Research University

The lineage of the U.S. research university can be traced to the great German and English universities and their respective forms and traditions. In fact, throughout most of the nineteenth century, there were no true research universities in the country. It was during the latter portion of the 1800s that several influential higher education leaders, including Daniel Coit Gilman of Johns Hopkins University, William Rainey Harper of the University of Chicago, and G. Stanley Hall of Clark University, established universities devoted to the primacy of research and specialized graduate education. These universities were modeled after the German traditions and structures found at Berlin and Heidelberg, including the graduate seminar and academic freedom (*Lehrfreiheit*). Before this time, earned Ph.D.s were largely unheard of in the United States. These leaders and their universities adopted the Germanic university form, and other universities followed. Soon after the founding of Johns Hopkins, Chicago, and Clark, universities that were founded during the colonial period were adopting and adapting the forms legitimated by Johns Hopkins and others.

Yet the U.S. research university also functions like an English university in many ways. For example, the research university in the United States almost always features a comprehensive undergraduate curriculum with a residential component that is more akin to Oxford and Cambridge than it is to Berlin. Similarly, student development and providing student services occupies a significant focus for U.S. research universities. This is a function of the fact that colonial colleges were organized according to an Oxbridge model, and their graduate education and research functions were superimposed on this existing organizational structure and culture.

## Classifying and Ranking Research Universities

Given the variance in the characteristics of research universities, how can the different types of research universities be categorized? Traditionally, this has been accomplished by the Carnegie Foundation for the Advancement of Teaching through its *Classification of Institutions*. Begun in 1973, and continuing throughout the classifications of 1976, 1987, 1994, and 2000, this scheme categorized all postsecondary institutions in the United Stations. As part of this larger classification, the Carnegie Foundation placed research universities in one of two categories, Research Universities I and Research Universities II, prior to the 2000 classification. Research universities were placed within these two categories depending upon the number of doctorate degrees they awarded and the amount of federal research funding they received. For the 2000 classification, these categories were expanded and renamed Doctoral/Research Universities—Extensive and Doctoral/Research Universities–Intensive, respectively. According to this classification, there are 261 research universities in the United States.

There are other recognized ways of determining what a research university is, and which are of the highest quality. There are organizations such as the Association of American Universities, a prestigious, invitation-only group of sixty-one American and two Canadian universities, all of which are high-quality research universities. Historically, organizations such as the National Research Council have also worked to qualitatively and quantitatively describe the relative quality of research universities and their various academic departments. Most recently, magazines such as *U.S. News and World Report* have introduced very popular rankings of postsecondary institutions, including research universities. These rankings are quite controversial, however, because of the great weight they place on inputs and reputation, and because they attempt to rank what is arguably a very diverse set of colleges and universities.

*See also:* CARNEGIE CLASSIFICATION SYSTEM, THE; COLLEGE RANKINGS; HARVARD UNIVERSITY; HIGHER EDUCATION IN THE UNITED STATES; JOHNS HOPKINS UNIVERSITY; TEACHING AND RESEARCH, THE RELATIONSHIP BETWEEN; UNIVERSITY OF CHICAGO; UNIVERSITY OF VIRGINIA; YALE UNIVERSITY.

## BIBLIOGRAPHY

BIRNBAUM, ROBERT. 1980. *How Colleges Work.* San Francisco: Jossey-Bass.

BRUBACHER, JOHN S., and RUDY, WILLIS. 1976. *Higher Education in Transition: A History of American Colleges and Universities, 1636–1976.* New York: Harper and Row.

CLARK, BURTON R. 2001. *The Uses of the University.* Cambridge, MA: Harvard University Press.

COHEN, MICHAEL D., and MARCH, JAMES G. 1974. *Leadership and Ambiguity: The American College President.* New York: McGraw-Hill.

COLE, JONATHAN R.; BARBER, ELINOR G.; and GRAUBARD, STEPHEN R. 1994. *The Research University in a Time of Discontent.* Baltimore: Johns Hopkins University Press.

GRAHAM, HUGH D., and DIAMOND, NANCY. 1997. *The Rise of American Research Universities.* Baltimore: Johns Hopkins University Press.

KERR, CLARK. 2001. *The Uses of the University.* Cambridge, MA: Harvard University Press.

LUCAS, CHRISTOPHER J. 1994. *American Higher Education: A History.* New York: St. Martin's Press.

VEYSEY, LAURENCE R. 1965. *The Emergence of the American University.* Chicago: University of Chicago Press.

CHRISTOPHER C. MORPHEW

# RESIDENTIAL COLLEGES

Islamic in origin, the residential college may well be the oldest organizational model in Western higher education. Established as foundations to provide support for advanced students, residential colleges first appeared at the University of Paris and Oxford University in the twelfth century. From these medieval roots, the residential colleges of Oxford and Cambridge University evolved to become academic communities made up of students and faculty sharing living quarters, meals, and tutorial study. Oxford and Cambridge served as models for colleges and universities throughout the former colonies of England and beyond.

## Defining Residential Colleges and Related Terms

Residential colleges have evolved over the centuries and under different local conditions. As a consequence, there is a range of variation in their structures and a lack of consensus about the meaning of the term *residential college*. In its most generic sense, the term may be used to refer to an institution that houses most of its students on-campus as opposed to an institution with a large commuter or off-campus population. Many small, independent, liberal arts colleges conform to this definition of residential college. In a more restricted sense, the term residential college may be used interchangeably with terms such as *living-learning center, theme house,* and *residential learning community.* This usage, however, may obscure important differences between the classical model of residential college, conventional residence halls, and other types of contemporary residence education programs.

Conventional residence halls are on-campus facilities intended to provide low-cost, attractive, safe, and convenient living quarters for undergraduate students in close proximity to academic buildings. Residents may participate in dining plans provided by centralized dining facilities and services. Conventional halls are usually supervised by undergraduate resident advisers and professional staff members trained in student affairs administration. Staff members are trained to assist students with adjustment and developmental issues or to make appropriate referrals to other campus professionals. Conventional residence halls may offer a range of social, recreational, and educational programming organized by their staffs.

Contemporary residence education programs attempt to more completely integrate out-of-class experiences with in-class learning. In a 1998 opinion paper, the Residential College Task Force of the Association of College and University Housing Officers presented a number of models of existing residence education programs. There is considerable overlap among these models; the differences are often matters of emphasis. These programs are generally the result of partnerships between student affairs professionals, academic staff, and faculty.

Living-learning centers are programs with direct connections to specific academic programs such as foreign languages, premedical studies, or science. For instance, the McTyeire International House at Vanderbilt University clusters students interested in studying one of five foreign languages on halls with native speakers as program coordinators. Faculty advisers guide the programming of each language hall.

Theme houses offer opportunities for students with special interests to live and work together. Stanford University offers a variety of theme halls. Casa Zapata (Chicano/Mexican-American theme) and Ujamaa (black/African-American theme) are cross-cultural theme halls exploring issues of ethnic identity, culture, and history. Other halls offer programs for students with interests in community service and environmental issues.

*Academic residential programs* provide academic support services, such as academic advising, career planning, tutoring, and programming in study skills, to residential students. At Washington State University, the Academic Resource Center is located in the freshman residential complex. The center provides a computer lab, academic advising, tutoring, and programming on study skills, career planning, and time management. Specially trained, upper-level residents are assigned as academic peer advisers to freshmen.

Residential learning communities create opportunities for students attending the same classes to live in the same residence hall. Participants in the Scholars Program at the University of Maryland–College Park are grouped so that they can take fourteen to seventeen credits of curricular theme courses together over the first two years of college and participate in a colloquium on their theme.

*Freshman Year Experience housing* provides specialized housing configurations to focus delivery of student affairs and academic services to first-year students. At the University of Missouri–Columbia, groups of up to twenty freshmen take three courses together and live on the same floor with a peer adviser assigned to help first-year students with adjustment issues.

## The Classic Residential College

Residential colleges and the aforementioned forms of contemporary residence education programs share a common goal of seeking to integrate in-class learning with out-of-class experiences in residential settings. What distinguishes classic residential colleges from other forms of residence education is the level and quality of faculty involvement. In residential colleges found in leading universities, faculty and students live and work in shared residential facilities. Further, the program is staffed and directed by the affiliated and resident faculty. In rare instances, the college is itself a degree-granting institution.

While the functions, nomenclature, and organizational structures of colleges differ from university to university, leading institutions in the United States share certain general patterns. In institutions such as Harvard, Yale, Princeton, and Rice Universities, residential colleges are decentralized academic societies or associations composed of faculty and student members. They range in size from 250 to 500 members. A distinction is usually drawn between senior and junior members of the college. The senior membership includes faculty, selected staff, and distinguished members of the local community. The junior membership includes undergraduate and graduate students. Residential colleges are microcosms of their universities. Senior members are drawn from all schools and departments; care is taken to achieve a balance in disciplinary representation. The junior members of a college reflect the full range of academic interests and backgrounds present in the university as a whole. Some schools randomly assign junior members to their colleges. Others take into consideration the preferences of junior members but also take measures to ensure that students do not self-segregate on the basis of demographic characteristics.

A faculty member is appointed to serve as the master of the college and has oversight responsibility for the college as a whole. The master reports to the chief academic officer or the chancellor or president of the university. A college dean is also appointed from the faculty and is responsible for academic advising and the personal welfare of student members of the college. Affiliated senior members are expected to attend college functions, dine frequently at the college, and take an interest in the life of the college. Senior members are appointed for specific terms and periodically reviewed. Resident tutors are selected from the graduate student members of the college and serve as intellectual role models, mentors, and advisers for the undergraduate students. They are supervised by the dean.

In a residential college, the staff works to create an orderly, satisfying, and nurturing environment that fosters a sense of belonging, promotes positive relationships among all members of the community, and is organized around the experience of learning. The master, the dean, and, especially, the resident tutors are visible and available members of the community; they closely observe their students, listen to their concerns, and respond as needed. Colleges have active student governments and seek to provide leadership opportunities for all junior members. The senior members of the college and the resident tutors are expected to participate in the evening activities, both formal and informal, of the college.

A residential college has its own character and culture; a conscious effort is made to create and sustain a tradition and a sense of history. A college program has a measured temporal structure providing for regular interactions of its members and for special events with ritual significance. Colleges hold regular weekly, monthly, and annual meetings. A common meal plan for students and staff plays a central role in establishing the college community. Welcoming events are held for new members as well as commencement events for departing members. Colleges create unique identities by celebrating selected events such as specific holidays or anniversaries. The pattern of events and activities is intended to be meaningful for its members; the program fosters shared norms, values, and expectations. These shared meanings may even be embodied in artifacts such as murals, facebooks (containing photographs of and biographical information on the college's residents), commonplace books, insignia, and mascots.

The central purpose of the college is academic. Colleges may provide academic advising for their junior members, offer for-credit classes or not-for-credit study, and organize opportunities for formal and informal discussions with faculty and visiting scholars and artists. Social activities are organized around opportunities for learning. Poetry readings, recitals, theatrical productions, scientific experiments, reading groups, field trips, and attendance at cultural and artistic events are common activities in residential colleges.

The architecture of the classic residential college promotes its educational mission. College buildings and gardens generally demarcate some sort of an enclosed space, such as a quadrangle. The enclosure helps foster a sense of communal identity and can be used to create traffic patterns promoting positive interaction among the college's members. The master, the dean, the resident tutors, and their families are provided with living quarters. Each college has an office complex to support the master, dean, and resident tutors. Central to the life of a college is a dining commons large enough to seat all of the members of the college. The dining commons can be used for announcements, college meetings, social activities, and special events. Separate meeting or social rooms are provided for senior and junior members. Libraries, classrooms, guest apartments, art studios, computer labs, kitchens, and laundries are often included in college facilities.

## Benefits of Residential Colleges

The benefits for students derived from simply living on campus, as opposed to living off campus, are well documented. Living on campus has been linked to increases in aesthetic, cultural, and intellectual values; increases in self-concept, intellectual orientation, autonomy, and independence; gains in tolerance, empathy, and interpersonal skills; persistence in college; and degree attainment. According to a 1991 book by Ernest T. Pascarella and Patrick T. Terenzini, there is little evidence linking living in a conventional residence hall with knowledge acquisition or cognitive growth. A 1998 meta-analysis by Gregory Blimling of studies published from 1966 through June 1997 shows, however, that residential colleges, as compared to conventional halls, increase students' academic performance and retention and enhance the social climate of the living unit. Blimling's study does not distinguish clearly between classic residential colleges and living-learning centers.

According to studies conducted in 1991 by George D. Kuh and associates and in 1993 by Jerry A. Stark, faculty participating in residential colleges or living/learning centers report improvement in their teaching skills and enhanced relationships with faculty from other disciplines. Frances Arndt reported in 1993 that faculty also held positive attitudes about opportunities offered by residential colleges for teaching a variety of special and experimental courses.

## Challenges and Prospects

In the 1996 book *Importing Oxbridge,* Alex Duke analyzed factors affecting the failure of residential college systems in North America. While attempting to model their colleges after the exemplars of Oxford and Cambridge, North American educators did not understand the historical development or social context of these institutions. Further, the departmental organization of academic disciplines does not cohere with the interdisciplinary character of residential colleges. Finally, the rapid postwar growth in enrollment simply outstripped the ability of institutions to provide housing for students. In a chapter in the 1994 book *Realizing the Educational Potential of Residence Halls,* Terry B. Smith argued that institutional reward structures focus on disciplinary achievement in the form of scholarly research, publication, and grant awards. There is little incentive for faculty to work with students in out-of-class contexts. Will

Koch reported in a 1999 article in *College Student Affairs Journal* that students may prefer conventional housing assignment practices that permit self-segregation by demographic characteristics. Finally, residential colleges require considerable investments in personnel and facilities. Funding for programming and space requirements as well as compensation for participating faculty make residential college programs more expensive than conventional residence halls.

Since the publication of the landmark study *Involvement in Learning: Realizing the Potential of Higher Education,* published by the National Institute of Education in 1984, numerous reports have called for increased emphases on improving teaching and learning, increasing student involvement in learning, and integrating in-class and out-of-class learning. Residential colleges are clearly one way to achieve these goals. There is evidence of growing interest in living-learning centers and residential college models. The future of the residential college model may depend on its cost-effectiveness relative to other means for achieving these educational goals.

*See also:* ADJUSTMENT TO COLLEGE; COLLEGE AND ITS EFFECT ON STUDENTS; COLLEGE AND UNIVERSITY RESIDENCE HALLS; COLLEGE STUDENT RETENTION; LEARNING COMMUNITIES AND THE UNDERGRADUATE CURRICULUM; LIVING AND LEARNING CENTER RESIDENCE HALLS.

### BIBLIOGRAPHY

ARNDT, FRANCES. 1993. "Making Connections: The Mission of UNCG's Residential College." In *Gateways: Residential Colleges in the Freshman Year Experience,* ed. Terry B. Smith. Columbia, SC: National Resource Center for the Freshman Year Experience.

BLIMLING, GREGORY S. 1998. "The Benefits and Limitations of Residential Colleges: A Meta-Analysis of the Research." In *Residential Colleges: Reforming American Higher Education,* ed. F. King Alexander and Don E. Robertson. Lexington, KY: Oxford International Round Table.

DUKE, ALEX. 1996. *Importing Oxbridge: English Residential Colleges and American Universities.* New Haven, CT: Yale University Press.

KOCH, WILL. 1999. "Integration and De Facto Segregation in Campus Housing: An Analysis of Campus Housing Policy." *College Student Affairs Journal* 18(2):35–43.

KUH, GEORGE D.; SCHUH, JOHN H.; WHITT, ELIZA-
BETH J.; and ASSOCIATES. 1991. *Involving Colleges: Successful Approaches to Fostering Student
Learning and Development outside the Classroom.* San Francisco: Jossey-Bass.

LENNING, OSCAR T., and EBBERS, LARRY H. 1999.
*The Powerful Potential of Learning Communities:
Improving Education for the Future.* Washing-
ton, DC: George Washington University, Grad-
uate School of Education and Human
Development.

PASCARELLA, ERNEST T., and TERENZINI, PATRICK
T. 1991. *How College Affects Students: Findings
and Insights from Twenty Years of Research.* San
Francisco: Jossey-Bass.

RESIDENTIAL COLLEGE TASK FORCE. 1998. *The Residential Nexus: A Focus on Student Learning.* Columbus, OH: Association of College and
University Housing Officers-International.

RYAN, MARK. 1992. "Residential Colleges: A Legacy
of Living and Learning Together." *Change*
24(5):26–35.

SMITH, TERRY B., ed. 1992. *Proceedings of the First
Annual Conference of Residential Colleges and
Living-Learning Centers.* Kirksville: Northeast
Missouri State University.

SMITH, TERRY B. 1994. "Integrating Living and
Learning through Residential Colleges." In *Re-
alizing the Educational Potential of Residence
Halls,* ed. Charles C. Schroeder and Phyllis
Mable. San Francisco: Jossey-Bass.

STARK, JERRY A. 1993. "Putting the College Back in
University." In *Gateways: Residential Colleges in
the Freshman Year Experience,* ed. Terry B.
Smith. Columbia, SC: National Resource Center
for the Freshman Year Experience.

STUDY GROUP ON THE CONDITIONS OF EXCELLENCE
IN HIGHER EDUCATION. 1984. *Involvement in
Learning: Realizing the Educational Potential of
Higher Education.* Washington, DC: National
Institute of Education.

**INTERNET RESOURCE**

O'HARA, ROBERT J. 2001. "How to Build a Residential College." <http://collegiateway.org/howto.
html>.

MARK BANDAS

# RESOURCE ALLOCATION IN HIGHER EDUCATION

Institutions of higher education—be they large public universities or small private colleges—are not homogeneous organizations. Because of differing
missions, goals, programs, histories, traditions, laws,
and explicit procedures, they obtain and expend revenues, or financial resources, in myriad ways. Therefore, there is no universal model about the best way
to allocate financial resources within higher education. Nevertheless, there is general consensus within
the U. S. higher education community about the
meaning of certain terms pertaining to resource allocation, as well as a general consensus about certain
methods and processes for channeling financial resources into specific programs and projects.

## Budgetary Concepts and Terms

For the layperson, the terms *budget* and *allocation*
are often confused. Although the two terms are certainly related, and often synonymous, there are differences that one should be aware of in order to gain
an appreciation of the resource allocation process.

Broadly interpreted, the term *budget* represents
both an institution's revenue sources and its expenditures. For public institutions, this side of the coin
is usually comprised of legislative appropriations;
tuition based on the number of credit hours and
level of courses taken; contracts and grants—which
comprise revenues received from external sources
for research and certain types of off-campus program development; auxiliary operations—which
refer to on-campus operations that are self-
supporting, for-profit enterprises (such as the campus bookstore, cafeteria, and laundry); and local
funds. Local funds, particularly within public universities, refer to those revenue sources not kept
within the state treasury, but within local banks.
Local funds may be comprised of fees and assessments charged against students for the support of
campus-wide student activities, intercollegiate athletics revenues, concessions, and financial aid
monies.

Taken together, these revenue sources make up
an institution's operating budget. They represent the
totality of monies required to finance the institution's normal and recurring expenses (its core operations). However, this is not the complete picture,
for the operating budget does not include fund-
raising revenues, which are monies donated to the

institution by private donors, usually for specific purposes (such as endowed academic chairs, athletic scholarships, or a new academic program that is acceptable to the institution and a priority of the donor). Although fund-raising revenues have become ever more critical for institutional operations, they are rarely considered part of the traditional operating budget.

Expenditures represent the most common understanding of the term *budget*. In this sense, the budget formally represents the institution's strategic priorities and associated costs. That is, the budget is a detailed plan for expending revenues for various institutional purposes. Moreover, these purposes are, or should be, focused on long-term strategic imperatives that parallel and support the accomplishment of the institution's most critical needs and aspirations.

Traditionally, expenditures for the operating budget fall into certain main categories that apply to both public and private institutions. Certainly, the largest slice of the budget pie is earmarked for instruction and research (I & R)—the core activities of any college or university. At Florida State University, for example, approximately 70 percent of the operating budget is designated for I & R purposes. Other large slices of the budget pie include administrative support services, such as centralized computing and accounting services; student services, such as the registrar's office and financial aid; plant operations and maintenance, including grounds, building services, and utilities; and libraries.

Expenditures from the operating budget are generally *unrestricted*. That is, there is some flexibility in allocating resources within and between the various categories that make up the operating budget. However, there are also restricted budgets, both within and external to the operating budget. *Restricted* means just that—monies can only be expended for strict, narrowly defined purposes. For example, within I & R, a public university could receive a restricted legislative appropriation to fund a Title IX (gender equity) program. Likewise, restricted budgets outside the operating budget may include monies earmarked for sponsored research or financial aid monies received from external sources, such as the federal government.

For most core operations, whether financed by unrestricted or restricted budget expenditures, one should be aware of exactly how the monies are ear-

marked within the major expenditure categories. Generally, the monies fall into three main activities: (1) salaries and benefits, which are certainly the most costly activities; (2) capital outlay, which refers to major purchases of expensive equipment, such as computer systems; and (3) expense items, which include less expensive items and continuing costs such as office furniture, service contracts, expendable supplies, and travel.

One critical budgetary category that is not considered a part of the traditional operating budget is *fixed capital outlay*, which comprises the monies earmarked for major construction and renovation projects. The *auxiliary budget*, also kept separate from the core, concerns the receipt and expenditure of monies obtained from revenue producing campus enterprises (e.g., a bookstore). Institutions with medical schools and teaching hospitals often have separate budgets for these purposes.

Some institutions have service-center budgets, which refers to certain centralized services such as photography, printing, and copying. These services are not financed by operating budget expenditures. Rather, units under the umbrella of the service-center budget are reimbursed for their services by charging operating budgetary units, which, in turn, pay the service-center unit from operating budget expenditures, usually from the expense category.

## Allocation Concepts and Terms

For the purpose of understanding the differences (and nuances) between the concepts of *budget* and *allocation*, one could say that the formal budget is the architecture (or basic plan per category) of how monies will be expended. *Allocation*, however, refers to the actual funneling of dollars to various units within an institution. In some instances, allocation flows will exactly mimic the expenditure categories. However, were this always the case, the descriptive analysis of budgets and allocations would end here. Rather, allocations often do (and should) have an element of flexibility built within them to reflect changing environmental conditions—including both internal and external environments, such as political circumstances, economic exigencies, and the strategic direction of the institution.

Although most institutions do permit some flexibility within their allocation decisions, many eminent higher education leaders, such as Dr. James J. Duderstadt, the former president of the University of Michigan, have publicly noted that far too many allocation decisions have become overly mechanistic. This has become particularly true within large, public institutions, which have also publicly expressed their collective concern over the ineffective and inefficient ways that monies are allocated. In addition, the National Association of College and University Business Officers (NACUBO) has also publicly expressed concern about the deficiencies currently inherent within internal allocation systems and processes.

Before discussing normative issues concerning how such deficiencies may be corrected, one must first understand the basic processes of allocations, particularly within the unrestricted I & R category. Historically, both academic and administrative units have relied upon incremental budgeting for determining allocations. Incremental budgeting simply means that the unit will sum the dollars contained within its current (annual) salary and benefits, capital outlay, and expense activities, and then increase the sum by a percentage to cover inflation and other expected cost increases. Incremental budgeting certainly simplifies the allocation process and facilitates accounting. With limited exceptions, incremental budget requests are accepted as forwarded to the central budget authority, funds are allocated according to the three major activities, and the unit lives within the allocations. At some institutions, academic and administrative units, with approval of a central budget authority, are able to transfer a minimal percentage of funds among salaries and benefits, capital outlay, and expense—if critical exigencies so demand. Nevertheless, this type of allocation system remains basically static.

The problem with static allocation systems is that they are inherently unable to anticipate change. Duderstadt duly notes that within large public universities, legislative appropriations, in terms of real dollars, have continuously diminished since the 1970s. Diminishing public appropriations, coupled with the opportunities and threats posed by a volatile environment, limit an institution's ability to adapt. During extreme economic situations, static allocations based upon incremental budgeting could actually spell the death of a public institutions' major academic offerings.

Another allocation process, often coupled with incremental budgeting, is formula-based allocation. This can be more flexible than simple incremental budgeting, because such formulas are usually based upon total credit hours or full-time head count per academic unit. This type of allocation process rewards those academic units that are most popular with students, and therefore does provide flexibility to fund those programs that are most in demand. Conversely, if an academic program is critical to a university's mission, but does not attract large numbers of students, it is automatically punished by formula-based allocations. In short, this is a market-based allocation process. While a for-profit organization can and should allocate its resources into the maintenance and expansion of its most profitable offerings, higher education institutions are striving for both tangible and intangible successes that may not necessarily be popular among students.

Colleges and universities, recognizing the inadequacies of incremental and formula-based budgeting, have enacted certain allocation adjustments to enhance flexibility and the quality of certain programs. At one university, for example, a 1 percent flat tax was charged against the allocations to all academic units to replenish a central reserve fund and enhance certain graduate programs. However, according to a report by that university's provost, this type of allocation mechanism proved itself insufficient to meet most challenges facing the institution.

In order to meet institutional objectives, and depending upon the authority granted to an institution by its governing board or its state legislature, an institution may be required to reduce allocations in one area to cover allocation demands in another. In order to meet the salary needs of the faculty, for example, resource allocations may be significantly diminished for libraries, computing systems, or facilities maintenance.

Flat taxes and other short-term options, such as hiring adjunct faculty or downgrading positions, can only operate at the margin, however, because not enough financial resources are generated, particularly on a long-term basis, to solve problems resulting from a lack of allocation flexibility. Similarly, wholesale raiding of funds from one allocation category to fill the coffers of another, if permitted, can only serve to weaken the entire university structure over time. Whether the allocation process is incremental, formula-based, or stopgap in nature, such processes focus only upon short-term, year-to-year allocations.

In 1999, Drs. Edward Ray and William Shkurti, the provost and senior vice president for finance, respectively, at Ohio State University, succinctly stated the problems accruing to that particular institution as a result of allocation inefficiencies:

- Current practices were not supportive of the instructional mission.
- Current practices were not supportive of the research mission.
- Current practices did not provide sufficient incentives to reduce costs and/or generate additional revenues required to address academic priorities.
- Current practices did not provide sufficient accountability for the costs of individual unit decisions that impact the entire university.

### Achieving Normative Consensus

The problems inherent within traditional budgetary and allocation processes indicate the need for a new approach. Notwithstanding the fact that public institutions are further hampered by legislative mandates, private institutions also face the same problems inherent within incremental and formula-based allocations.

The challenge facing higher education is to embrace new philosophies and outlooks that take a long-term, wide-ranging view of what the institution is, what it should be, and how it can move from what is to what should be.

Appropriate, sufficient, and equitable resource allocation processes simply can no longer be based on what worked in the past. In this sense, most colleges and universities have embraced strategic planning—a long-range, holistic examination of what the overall mission of the institution should be; in other words, a vision. To better define this vision, one must further ascertain the specific goals that should be set to accomplish the mission, and what environmental factors exist—internally and externally—that can either enhance or inhibit the accomplishment of the vision. Specific questions need to be asked, such as: What does the university plan to accomplish over the next several years? How does the university plan to accomplish its goals and objectives? What resources are needed to carry out this plan? What are the funding sources from which the institution can obtain the necessary financial support?

To best answer these questions, institutions should first examine their decision-making struc-

tures. Colleges and universities are not pyramidal, hierarchical structures ruled by an autocracy at the top that transmits decrees downward through the chain of command. Conversely, colleges and universities cannot be anarchistic organizations where decision-making is randomly conducted by individual units. The problem, thus, is to create a decision-making structure that seeks consensus through participation.

At one Eastern university, for example, allocation decisions remain the basic prerogative of university executives, such as the president, provost, vice president for finance, and the deans. Nevertheless, to reach its highest-priority strategic objectives, faculty and staff members from colleges and departments are invited to submit their own ideas on how best to achieve the institution's overall mission, long-term strategic initiatives, and specific goals—all within the context of maintaining and enhancing the quality of priority programs identified by strategic planning. Specifically, faculty and staff members are requested to review the allocation and adequacy of resources vis-à-vis the quality of programs relative to peer institutions, the centrality of programs to the university's mission, and the cost-effectiveness of programs relative to the best practices of higher education and the private sector. To facilitate and direct this endeavor, a university-wide committee, the Strategic Plan Advisory Committee (SPAC) was formed. SPAC not only identified allocation problems in detail, it helped develop a long-term, multi-year plan that will enable the university to respond to special opportunities and eventually solve the most basic and continuing allocation problems.

Similarly, at the small, private-college level, Wheaton College in Massachusetts has set up a formal group—the Budget Advisory Committee—similar to the SPAC. Wheaton's committee, consisting of faculty and staff members, reports directly to the college president, and operates with the long-term view that allocations should be treated as strategic investments, not simply as annual costs. Hence, it has determined that allocations should regularly include reallocations from lower priorities to higher priorities, and that cost savings should be actively pursued in order to increase the college's strategic flexibility.

In short, if realistic and successful allocation processes are to be developed and accepted throughout the institution, structural arrangements must be designed to facilitate the participation of stakeholders and attainment of consensus.

Once consensus on basic allocation-decision parameters is achieved, a second consideration includes the formal allocation structures and processes that might be adopted. To help identify these means, decision-makers and participants in the decision-making process should be provided with feasible and workable alternatives.

One alternative, as suggested by Duderstadt, is an institution-wide, integrated resource-allocation model he calls *Responsibility Center Management*. Resource-allocation decisions are shared between academic units, administrative units, and the central administration. After determining strategic priorities, this alternative allows critically-important units to keep the resources they generate, makes them responsible for meeting costs they incur, and then levies a tax on a unit's expenditures to provide a central pool of resources for supporting central operations and facilitating flexibility funding. This alternative has the potential to reduce some of the inequities and inefficiencies inherent within formulaic or incremental allocation processes.

Another alternative is *substitution,* or the elimination or reduction of noncritical activities to release allocations for more critical, strategically oriented activities. This alternative not only reallocates resources to those programs deemed most critical for strategic purposes, it also alerts the public and the institution's stakeholders that the college or university has taken cost effectiveness very seriously.

Other structural and process alternatives for resource allocations include: differential tuition rates based upon program popularity; using foundation allocations to replace traditional allocations; permitting the carry-over of surpluses from one year to another; and permitting the most productive research units to retain a large portion of the overhead (indirect) costs assessed against their research awards. The point is that viable and reasonable alternatives should be presented at the start of the analysis in order to preclude time being wasted.

## Conclusion

Traditional budgetary and resource allocation procedures that have been utilized for decades in America's colleges and universities are rapidly losing their functionality. Indeed, reliance upon their continued use can cause irreparable damage to the system of higher education.

Budgets and resultant allocations are complicated subjects. Because of their complexity and a reliance on the fact that they worked well enough in the past, inertia exists. However, in light of the volatile higher education environment of the early twenty-first century, the increasing inequities and inefficiencies of current systems and processes, and greater demands for accountability by legislative bodies and institutional stakeholders, structures and procedures for budgeting and allocating financial resources must be re-examined. The task is not easy—the problems are complex, and consensus about what should be done is difficult to attain. Nevertheless, to ignore the problem can, and will, have a negative impact upon public and private higher education systems.

*See also:* ACCOUNTING SYSTEMS IN HIGHER EDUCATION; FINANCE, HIGHER EDUCATION.

### BIBLIOGRAPHY

CALLAN, PATRICK M., and FINNEY, JONI E., eds. 1997. *Public and Private Financing of Higher Education: Shaping Public Policy for the Future.* Phoenix, AZ: Oryx Press.

DUDERSTADT, JAMES J. 2000. *A University for the Twenty-First Century.* Ann Arbor: University of Michigan Press.

MEISENGER, RICHARD J., JR., and DUBECK, LEROY W. 1984. *College and University Budgeting: An Introduction for Faculty and Academic Administrators.* Washington, DC: National Association of College and University Business Officers.

### INTERNET RESOURCES

RAY, EDWARD J., and SHKURTI, WILLIAM J. 1999. "University Goals and Resource Allocation." <www.rpia.ohio-state/Budget_Planning/html>.

SCHWARTZ, JOHN E. 1999. <http://w3.Arizona.edu/~provost/issues/issues-5.html>.

SOUTHERN ILLINOIS UNIVERSITY. 2001. "What Is RAMP?" <www.siu.edu/~budget/rampint.html>.

UNIVERSITY OF MARYLAND-COLLEGE PARK. 1998. "Rationalizing Resource Allocation and Administrative Operations." <www.inform.umd.edu/EdRes/provost/StrategicPlanning/SPAC2_IV_Rationalizing.html>.

WHEATON COLLEGE. 2001. "College Priorities for 2001-2002." <www.wheatonma.edu/admin/finance/RA/Prior.html>

JOHN R. CARNAGHI

# RICE, JOHN A. (1888–1968)

Founder and first rector of Black Mountain College, a renowned experimental and progressive endeavor in higher education (1933–1956), John Andrew Rice Jr., was a major figure in debates during the 1930s and early 1940s among educators concerning the appropriate means and methods of a liberal education. Through magazine articles and his book *I Came Out of the Eighteenth Century* (1942), he became known as an eloquent and harsh critic of a variety of approaches to education such as lecture, over-reliance on "great books," memorization, and counting credits by time in seat; and a proponent of Progressive education philosophies concerning student centered curriculum and classroom community.

Born in Lynchburg, South Carolina, Rice was the son of John Andrew Rice Sr., a Methodist minister who eventually became the president of Columbia (South Carolina) College and a founding faculty member at Southern Methodist University (Dallas, Texas). His mother, Annabelle Smith, was the sister of U.S. Senator Ellison Durant ("Cotton Ed") Smith. Two years after her death in 1899, the senior Rice married Launa Darnell who became stepmother to Rice and his two younger brothers.

Rice attended the Webb School, a highly regarded college preparatory boarding school in Bell Buckle, Tennessee, from 1905 to 1908, where he encountered the teacher he would revere all his life, John Webb. Webb's penchant for open and wide-ranging classroom discussion sparked young Rice's first interest in learning. Rice then attended Tulane University and, after graduating in three years with a bachelor of arts degree, won a Rhodes scholarship to Oxford University.

At Oxford Rice met Frank Aydelotte, future president of Swarthmore College, and the latter's sister Nell. Rice and Nell Aydelotte were married in 1914, after Rice graduated from Oxford with first honors in jurisprudence. He began his teaching career at Webb School, but left after a year to pursue doctoral studies in classics at the University of Chicago.

Although Rice never completed his doctoral dissertation, he secured a faculty position at University of Nebraska, where he and Nell Rice and their two young children lived from 1920 to 1927. Rice proved brilliant in the classroom and in counseling individual students. His Socratic style and ability to provoke free-ranging conversations drew students to his courses in increasing numbers. His methods aimed at their emotional and intellectual maturity rather than their store of subject knowledge and he began writing articles that criticized American higher education for teaching unconnected course subjects with pedagogy that emphasized lecture and response. As he insisted in an article in Harper's in 1937, "What you do with what you know is the important thing. To know is not enough" (p. 590).

When Rice's candid and critical opinions extended to his immediate surroundings, he could seem audacious and insulting. His stay at the University of Nebraska ended when the president who hired and protected him fell ill. Next, at New Jersey College for Women, he quickly managed to rankle Dean Mabel Smith Douglass and was forced to resign after two years. After a year in England on a Guggenheim fellowship, he landed a faculty position at Rollins College in Winter Park, Florida.

At Rollins, Rice would eventually earn a national reputation as the subject of an early and highly publicized investigation by the American Association of University Professors (AAUP). He managed to polarize faculty and students by speaking out against fraternities and sororities and by objecting to various policies of Rollins president Hamilton Holt. Students and colleagues found him either brilliant and charismatic or argumentative and insulting. After three years, President Holt asked Rice to resign, an act that resulted in a nationally reported AAUP investigation that eventually censured Rollins and exonerated Rice. A number of supportive Rollins faculty and students resigned during the fracas and, along with Rice, began planning the learning community that would become Black Mountain College, located near Asheville, North Carolina, on the campus of a YMCA summer conference facility in the town of Black Mountain.

## Black Mountain College

The college opened in 1933 with twenty-one students and eventually grew to nearly 100 students. It quickly gathered national notice for testing a number of innovative ideas about the means and ends of

American higher education. Among these were the following: (1) the centrality of artistic experience to support learning in any discipline; (2) the value of experiential learning; (3) the practice of democratic governance shared among faculty and students; (4) the contribution of social and cultural endeavors outside the classroom; and (5) the absence of oversight from outside trustees.

Rice recruited artist Josef Albers and weaver Anni Albers from Germany's famed Bauhaus Art and Architecture Institute after it was closed by the Nazi regime. They were joined by Bauhaus stage designer and graphic artist Xanti Schawinsky. Although students might select economics, foreign languages, mathematics, or music as major areas in their individually tailored programs of study, all were required to take Josef Albers's drawing course and Rice's classics course. As the college gained national renown for its art program and its experimental approaches to education, numerous well-known visitors joined the community for days or weeks at a time, including John Dewey, Buckminster Fuller, Marcel Breuer, Thornton Wilder, Aldous Huxley, Henry Miller, and others.

Rice enjoyed incorporating visitors into classes, evening seminars, even campus dramatic productions or community work projects. He committed the college to the practice of participatory democracy among students, faculty, staff, and families in order to prepare students for life in a democratic society. Although formal degrees or graduation ceremonies were absent, students needed to pass oral examinations by outside examiners in their chosen areas of emphasis in order to complete their course of study. Those who did had little problem entering graduate programs at selective universities.

### Life as a Writer

Rice's outspoken and polarizing personality contributed to his resignation from the college, requested by the faculty, in 1940. He and Nell Rice divorced; he later married Dikka Moen with whom he had two children. Rice forged a second career in writing, starting with a collection in 1942 of his own memories and essays, *I Came Out of the Eighteenth Century,* named by his publisher as a winner of its one hundred and twenty-fifth anniversary prize for best nonfiction. Rice then turned to fiction, writing short stories mostly about life and race relations in the South for *The New Yorker, Saturday Evening Post, Collier's, Harper's,* and others. His stories also ap-

peared in several anthologies and were collected in his book *Local Color* (1957).

When financially struggling Black Mountain College closed in 1956, Rice exchanged correspondence with final rector Charles Olson in an attempted to retrieve books he had left for the college library. However, he was never directly involved with teaching or educational ideas after his departure from the college.

*See also:* HIGHER EDUCATION IN THE UNITED STATES, *subentry on* HISTORICAL DEVELOPMENT.

**BIBLIOGRAPHY**

ADAMIC, LOUIS. 1936. "Education on a Mountain." *Harper's* 172:516–530.

DUBERMAN, MARTIN. 1972. *Black Mountain College: An Exploration in Community.* New York: Dutton.

HARRIS, MARY EMMA. 1987. *The Arts at Black Mountain College.* Cambridge, MA: MIT Press.

LANE, MERVIN, ed. 1990. *Black Mountain College, Sprouted Seeds: An Anthology of Personal Accounts.* Knoxville: University of Tennessee Press.

REYNOLDS, KATHERINE C. 1998. *Visions and Vanities: John Andrew Rice of Black Mountain College.* Baton Rouge: Louisiana State University Press.

RICE, JOHN ANDREW. 1937. "Fundamentalism and the Higher Learning." *Harper's* 174:587–596.

RICE, JOHN ANDREW. 1942. *I Came Out of the Eighteenth Century.* New York: Harper.

RICE, JOHN ANDREW. 1955. *Local Color.* New York: Dell.

KATHERINE C. REYNOLDS

# RICE, JOSEPH MAYER (1857–1934)

Physician, journal editor, education critic, and originator of comparative methodology in educational research, Joseph Mayer Rice is recognized, along with Lester Frank Ward and John Dewey, as a major figure in the Progressive education movement in the United States.

Rice was born in Philadelphia, Pennsylvania, the son of Mayer and Fanny (Sohn) Rice, natives of Germany who immigrated to America in 1855. Rice attended public schools in Philadelphia and New York City, where his parents and older brother, Isaac Leopold Rice, relocated in 1870. He attended the City College of New York, and in 1881 received a degree in medicine from the College of Physicians and Surgeons of Columbia University. Rice, having established a successful private practice in pediatrics in New York City, became interested in the physical fitness programs offered by the New York City public schools. His research into these programs led to an interest in the schools as educational institutions.

In 1888, Rice traveled to Europe to observe the school systems of various countries. He settled in Germany for two years to study psychology and pedagogy at the universities of Jena and Leipzig. Although specific reasons for his decision to remain in Germany for these two years remain speculative, Rice's studies paralleled other American academics and educators who traveled to Germany during this time to learn the rudiments of empirical research and foundations for scientific pedagogy.

Rice observed the first laboratory of experimental psychology, directed by Wilhelm Wundt at the University in Leipzig, and studied Herbartism as it was conceptualized and enacted at the University of Jena and its laboratory school. The theories of German educator and philosopher Johann Freidrich Herbart, known as the originator of the science of education and of modern psychology, focused on the development of a cultured human being who strove to discover as well as be guided by the highest ethical values. Education, then, was a moral enterprise for Herbart. Although the corpus of Rice's writings extend well beyond this particular focus, Rice returned home from Germany in 1890, greatly influenced by his studies and with strong ideas about ways to improve elementary education in the United States.

An interview with Rice, focused on his school reform ideas, ran for three issues in the New York City weekly *Epoch* in July 1891, and the weekly published another series of articles by Rice from October through December of that same year. The *Forum,* a monthly magazine owned by Rice's brother, also published an article in 1891 in which Rice proposed two essentials for the natural development of the child: proper training of the teacher and a curriculum based on sound psychological principles. Rice maintained that these could be assured only when those who managed educational systems were themselves trained educators.

At the time, the *Forum* was edited by Walter Hines Page. Under Page, the monthly had published articles on education and social reform. Page was intrigued with Rice's ideas about pedagogy; thus, in 1892, under the sponsorship of the *Forum,* Rice conducted a six-month tour of thirty-six cities in the United States, visiting six to eight urban public elementary schools in each city. During this survey, Rice spent the school hours of every day observing actual classroom events. He talked with approximately twelve hundred teachers, met with school officials and school board members, interviewed parents, and visited twenty teacher-training institutions.

Rice devoted the summer of 1892 to the analysis of data from his survey of schools. From October 1892 through June 1893, the *Forum* published a series of nine articles by Rice, where he reported tedious, pedantic teaching in traditionally structured schools, unassisted superintendents responsible for the supervision of hundreds of teachers, and board of education reports portraying deplorable conditions of schools. As anticipated by Page, Rice's study generated outraged reactions among a public that heretofore had assumed a fully functioning and effective educational system. Rice's articles earned him a reputation (not a pleasant one among many professional educators) for bringing the topic of schooling into the public's eye, and, in effect, introducing muckraking to the field of education.

In the spring of 1893, Rice undertook a second survey of schools. This five-week tour focused on those schools said to represent new (Progressive) education. He visited schools in Indianapolis, Minneapolis, St. Paul, La Porte (Indiana), and Cook County (Illinois). These were schools that had expanded their curricula, as recommended by Herbartian theory, beyond the traditional "Reading, Writing, and Arithmetic," and had encouraged an integrated approach to curriculum and pedagogy. This study was reported in *The Public-School System of the United States* (1893) along with the nine original *Forum* essays, and continued Rice's critique of the public schools and their inadequate pedagogical knowledge.

Rice returned to the University of Jena in the summer of 1893. Upon his return, he was determined to further document his conviction that the wider curricula of the Progressive schools enhanced rather than detracted from students' overall achievement. Thus, Rice embarked on another *Forum-*

sponsored tour of classrooms in 1895. This time he was armed with the first comparative test—a school/student survey—ever used in American education or psychology. During sixteen months of study, Rice administered his survey to nearly 33,000 fourth- to eighth-grade children, and he carefully tabulated modifying conditions such as age, nationality, environment, and type of school system. The survey focused, in part, on the pedagogy of spelling. Rice found no link between the time spent on spelling drills and students' performance on spelling tests. His study was far ahead of its time, not only methodologically but also pedagogically, as he pointed to "the futility of the spelling grind."

Rice served as editor of the *Forum* from 1897 through 1907. He retired in Philadelphia in 1915, the same year that he published his last book, *The People's Government.* He had married Deborah Levinson in 1900; they had two children. He died in Philadelphia, June 1934.

*See also:* ASSESSMENT, CLASSROOM; EDUCATION REFORM; HERBART, JOHANN.

### BIBLIOGRAPHY

HOUSTON, CAMILLE M. E. 1965. "Joseph Mayer Rice: Pioneer in Educational Research." M.S. thesis, University of Wisconsin, Madison.

RICE, JOSEPH M. 1893. *The Public-School System of the United States.* New York: Century.

RICE, JOSEPH M. 1898. *The Rational Spelling Book.* New York: American Book.

RICE, JOSEPH M. 1913. *Scientific Management in Education.* New York: Hinds, Noble and Eldredge.

RICE, JOSEPH M. 1915. *The People's Government.* Philadelphia: Winston.

JANET L. MILLER

# RISK BEHAVIORS

**TABLE 1**

**Trends in alcohol, tobacco, or other drug use by twelfth graders, 1975–2000**

|  | 1975 | 1980 | 1985 | 1990 | 1995 | 2000 |
|---|---|---|---|---|---|---|
| **Tobacco** | | | | | | |
| lifetime | 73.6 | 71.0 | 68.8 | 64.4 | 64.2 | 62.5 |
| 30-day | 36.7 | 30.5 | 30.1 | 29.4 | 33.5 | 31.4 |
| **Alcohol** | | | | | | |
| lifetime | 90.4 | 93.2 | 92.2 | 89.5 | 80.7 | 80.3 |
| 30-day | 68.2 | 72.0 | 65.9 | 57.1 | 51.3 | 50.0 |
| **Other drugs** | | | | | | |
| lifetime | 55.2 | 65.4 | 60.6 | 47.9 | 48.4 | 54.0 |
| 30-day | 30.7 | 37.2 | 29.7 | 17.2 | 23.8 | 24.9 |

SOURCE: Adapted from University of Michigan News and Information Services. 2000. "'Ecstasy' Use Rises Sharply Among Teens in 2000: Use of Many Other Drugs Stays Steady, but Significant Declines Are Reported for Some." December 14 news release. Ann Arbor: University of Michigan News and Information Services.

## DRUG USE AMONG TEENS

Substance abuse is an international problem of epidemic proportions that has particularly devastating effects on youth because the early initiation of alcohol, tobacco, or other drug (ATOD) use within this population is linked to abuse and related problem behaviors among adults. The cost of alcohol abuse to society is estimated to be $250 billion per year in health care, public safety, and social welfare expenditures. Key trends in substance use by twelfth graders are displayed in Table 1.

### Causes

A number of models and theories address the causes of adolescent ATOD use. The most salient of these is the "Risk and Protective Factor" framework, which has identified a variety of psychosocial factors associated with ATOD use. In the *individual* domain, substance use has been linked to values and beliefs about and attitudes toward substances, genetic susceptibility, early ATOD use, sensation seeking, and various psychological disorders including antisocial, aggressive, and other problem behaviors. In the *family* domain, ATOD use has been associated with familial substance use, poor parenting practices including harsh or inconsistent discipline, poor intrafamilial communication, and inadequate supervision and monitoring of children's behaviors and peer associations. In the *peer* domain, substance use has been linked to social isolation and association with ATOD-using and otherwise deviant peer networks. In the *school* domain, ATOD use has been linked to poor academic performance and truancy, as well as a disorderly and unsafe school climate and lax school policies concerning substance use. In the *community* and *environmental* domains, ready social and physical access to ATODs has been associated with use, as has lack of recreational resources (especially during the after-school hours).

## Protective Factors

Protective factors, or factors that promote resiliency, have also been identified in these various domains. Among those most frequently cited are religiosity or spirituality, commitment to academic achievement, strong life skills, social competencies, and belief in self-efficacy. Protective factors in the family and school domains include strong intrafamilial bonds, positive family dynamics, and positive attachment to school. In the community and environmental domains, strongly held adult values antithetical to substance use constitute protective factors, as do clearly communicated and consistently enforced regulations concerning use.

## Prevention Strategies

A variety of strategies have demonstrated effectiveness in preventing or reducing ATOD use. Project Alert, described by Phyllis Ellickson and colleagues in a 1993 article, and Life Skills Training Program, described by Gill Botvin and colleagues in 1995, are the two most-prevalent effective *classroom-based curricula*. The "Reconnecting Youth" Program, described by Leona Eggert and colleagues in 1994, is designed for high school students who manifest poor academic achievement or who are at high risk for dropping out and other problem behaviors. In the family domain, the Iowa Strengthening Families Program, described by Richard Spoth and colleagues in 1999, has received considerable attention. In the community and environmental domains, strategies have been developed to increase the enforcement of public policies and ordinances that inhibit adolescent substance use. These include efforts targeting tobacco and alcohol outlets, including restrictions on their location and density and on alcohol and tobacco advertising. Also effective is the vigorous enforcement of laws governing sales to minors, including using underage youth to buy alcohol and tobacco products in "sting" operations. Increasing excise taxes on alcohol and tobacco products has also been associated with reductions in use, as has linking apprehension for infractions of laws related to purchasing and consuming ATODs to suspension or revocation of driver's licenses. Other preventive measures that target youth drivers include "zero tolerance" laws linking evidence of alcohol on the breath with suspension or revocation of driving privileges.

The results of two decades of evaluative research have yielded considerable information suggesting that a number of approaches to adolescent ATOD use prevention do *not* work. Scare tactics, designed to frighten adolescents into avoiding drugs, are often recognized as such by their target audiences and can even be counterproductive. Efforts to raise self-esteem as a drug prevention strategy have long been discredited given the lack of association between self-esteem and ATOD use. Strategies designed to increase knowledge and convey information about the risks and dangers of drug use are generally recognized to be failures, in part because of the lack of association between knowledge and use. Indeed, all largely didactic approaches to prevention education, such as Project "Drug Abuse Resistance Education" (Project DARE), are widely understood to be ineffective, especially if they concentrate on long-term risks. Mass media campaigns are of dubious value, especially if they are brief, aired in contexts that are unlikely to reach their target audience, and uncoordinated with a comprehensive, community-wide strategy.

Unfortunately, relatively little is also known about prevention on college campuses. Many college campuses have cultures that are at least covertly supportive of alcohol consumption, and many administrators treat the issue with benign neglect. While most drinking on college campuses occurs in neighborhood bars and residential contexts such as fraternities, relatively little has been done to develop and implement demonstration programs that increase enforcement of, and penalties for, selling or otherwise supplying liquor to underage students.

It is known that even the most effective and comprehensive school-based strategies, and even those that reinforce their messages across multiple grade levels, are only slightly more effective than school-based programs that are generally discredited in the early twenty-first century. There has evolved a consensus among both practitioners and researchers that school-based programs, by themselves, are insufficient. Such efforts should be part of a broad and comprehensive array of prevention approaches that integrate both supply and demand reduction strategies in the family and community, as well as the individual, domains.

*See also:* DRUG AND ALCOHOL ABUSE; GUIDANCE AND COUNSELING, SCHOOL; FAMILY COMPOSITION AND CIRCUMSTANCE, *subentry on* ALCOHOL, TOBACCO, AND OTHER DRUGS; OUT-OF-SCHOOL INFLUENCES AND ACADEMIC SUCCESS; RISK BEHAVIORS, *subentry on* SMOKING AND ITS EFFECT ON CHILDREN'S HEALTH.

### BIBLIOGRAPHY

BOTVIN, GILBERT J.; BAKER, ELI; DUSENBURG, LINDA; BOTVIN, ELIZABETH M.; and DIAZ, TRACY. 1995. "Long-Term Followup Results of a Randomized Drug Abuse Prevention Trial in a White Middle-Class Population." *Journal of the American Medical Association* 273:1106–1112.

CENTER FOR SUBSTANCE ABUSE PREVENTION. DIVISION OF KNOWLEDGE DEVELOPMENT AND EVALUATION. 1998. *Science-Based Practices in Substance Abuse Prevention: A Guide.* Washington, DC: Substance Abuse and Mental Health Services Administration, Center for Substance Abuse Prevention, Division of Knowledge Development and Evaluation.

CENTER FOR SUBSTANCE ABUSE PREVENTION. NATIONAL CENTER FOR THE ADVANCEMENT OF PREVENTION. 2000. *2000 Annual Summary: Effective Prevention Principles and Programs.* Rockville, MD: Center for Substance Abuse Prevention.

DUSENBURY, LINDA. 2000. "Implementing a Comprehensive Drug Abuse Prevention Strategy." In *Increasing Prevention Effectiveness,* ed. William B. Hansen, Steve M. Giles, and Melodia Fearnow-Kenney. Greensboro, NC: Tanglewood Research.

EGGERT, LEONA L.; THOMPSON, ELAINE A.; HERTING, JERALD R.; NICHOLAS, LIELA J.; and DICK-ER, BARBARA G. 1994. "Preventing Adolescent Drug Abuse and High School Dropout through an Intensive School-Based Social Network Development Program." *American Journal of Health Promotion* 8:202–215.

ELLICKSON, PHYLLIS L.; BELL, ROBERT M.; and McGUIGAN, KIMBERLEY. 1993. "Preventing Adolescent Drug Use: Long-Term Results of a Junior High Program." *American Journal of Public Health* 83:856–861.

ENNETT, SUSAN; TOBLER, NANCY S.; RINGWALT, CHRISTOPHER L.; and FLEWELLING, ROBERT L. 1994. "How Effective Is Drug Abuse Resistance Education? A Meta-Analysis of Project DARE Outcome Evaluations." *American Journal of Public Health* 84:1394–1401.

HAWKINS, J. DAVID; CATALANO, RICHARD F.; and MILLER, JANET Y. 1992. "Risk and Protective Factors for Alcohol and Other Drug Problems in Adolescence and Early Adulthood: Implications for Substance Abuse Prevention." *Psychological Bulletin* 112:64–105.

PACIFIC INSTITUTE FOR RESEARCH AND EVALUATION. 1999. *Strategies to Reduce Underage Alcohol Use: Typology and Brief Overview.* Washington, DC: U.S. Department of Justice, Office of Justice Programs, Office of Juvenile Justice and Delinquency Prevention.

SPOTH, RICHARD LEE; REDMOND, CLEVE; and LEPPER, H. 1999. "Alcohol Initiation Outcomes of Universal Family-Focused Preventive Interventions: One- and Two-Year Follow-Ups of a Controlled Study." *Journal of Studies on Alcohol* 13:103–111.

TOBLER, NANCY S. 1986. "Meta-Analysis of 143 Adolescent Drug Prevention Programs: Quantitative Outcome Results of Program Participants Compared to a Control or Comparison Group." *Journal of Drug Issues* 16:537–567.

UNIVERSITY OF MICHIGAN NEWS AND INFORMATION SERVICES. 2000. "'Ecstasy' Use Rises Sharply among Teens in 2000: Use of Many Other Drugs Stays Steady, but Significant Declines Are Reported for Some." December 14 news release. Ann Arbor: University of Michigan, News and Information Services.

### INTERNET RESOURCE

JOIN TOGETHER ONLINE. 1999. "Alcohol Abuse Costs Society $250 Billion Per Year."

<www.jointogether.org/sa/news/features/
reader/0,1854,261313,00.html>.

CHRISTOPHER L. RINGWALT

## HIV/AIDS AND ITS IMPACT ON ADOLESCENTS

Acquired immunodeficiency syndrome (AIDS) is a significant threat to youth and young adults. It is the seventh leading cause of death among U.S. youth aged fifteen to twenty-four. More than 126,000 cases of AIDS among individuals ages twenty to twenty-nine had been diagnosed in the U.S. through June 2000. Given the long latency period between infection and symptoms, most of these individuals were infected as adolescents. Estimates of human immunodeficiency virus (HIV) among adolescents range from 112,000 to 250,000 in the United States, although actual prevalence is not known because representative data are not available. Estimates of HIV incidence in the early twenty-first century suggest that at least 50 percent of the 40,000 new infections in the United States each year are among individuals under twenty-five years old, and 25 percent are among persons aged twenty-one or younger.

### HIV Transmission

The majority of HIV infections among adolescents are contracted through sexual activity. Among HIV positive thirteen to nineteen year-old females who had not developed AIDS, 49 percent of the cases were associated with exposure through sexual contact, 7 percent through injection drug use, 1 percent through blood exposure, and 43 percent through a risk not reported or identified. Among males in the same age group, 50 percent were associated with male to male sex, 5 percent with injection drug use, 5 percent with both male to male sex and injection drug use, 5 percent with hemophilia or coagulation disorder, 7 percent with heterosexual exposure, 1 percent with blood exposure, and 28 percent with an unreported or unidentified risk.

Many adolescents are sexually experienced, but the extent of experience and risk varies for different groups of adolescents. Youth Risk Behavior Survey (YRBS) data indicate that about half of all high school students report having engaged in intercourse at least once. Almost 10 percent of youth were younger than age thirteen at first sexual intercourse, and by twelfth grade, 65 percent of students have become

sexually active. Sexual risk increases with the number of partners and the failure to use condoms. In the YRBS data, about 16 percent of high school students report having had sex with four or more partners; 48 percent of adolescent African-American males report four or more sexual partners. Forty-two percent of sexually active respondents did not use a condom at last intercourse.

The presence of other sexually transmitted infections (STIs) can also facilitate HIV transmission. Adolescents and young adults are physiologically and behaviorally at higher risk for acquiring STIs. An estimated three million cases of STIs other than HIV are acquired each year among persons between ten and nineteen years old. Youth under the age of twenty-five account for two-thirds of the total number of cases of STIs diagnosed annually. Rates of chlamydia, gonorrhea, and human papillomavirus are particularly high among sexually active female teens. An individual's risk is affected by STI prevalence among the pool of potential sex partners. African-American and Hispanic teens, for example, are disproportionately overrepresented among AIDS cases and cases of other STIs. Given that sexual networks tend to be homogeneous by race, these youth are more likely to face greater prevalence of HIV among their sex partners.

Drug use also places young people at risk for HIV. The most direct route is through sharing needles. Addicts may engage in sex with multiple partners to obtain drugs or money to buy drugs, and may thus increase the spread of infection to otherwise low-risk individuals. Non-injected drugs may also reduce inhibitions, influencing the individual to engage in risky sexual activity. Studies show that there are positive relationships between substance use and various facets of sexual behavior, such as timing of initiation, frequency, persistence, and risk taking, for both adolescents and young adults. However, findings regarding this pathway are mixed and may vary by race/ethnicity. For example, the link between substance use and sexual activity may be less strong among African Americans. Alcohol consumption has been linked to sexual risk taking among white adolescents, but a more recent study found that young women's condom use patterns were not linked to pre-coital substance use.

### Pathways to HIV Prevention

Longitudinal studies that follow high-risk youth into adulthood provide a way for researchers to understand the developmental pathways of problem behavior. Greater involvement with problem behavior as a youth is predictive of greater involvement in young adulthood. However, problem behavior in the teen years does not necessarily lead to poor adult outcomes. For most adolescents, drug use and sexual activity reflect behavior that is experimental and socially normative. Longitudinal studies have shown that a "maturing out" process typically occurs, particularly if the individual is embedded in conventional institutions such as marriage.

Although most adolescents will grow out of many risk behaviors, prevention efforts are needed to reduce the risk of HIV infection during adolescence. As has been found with other risk behaviors, studies have demonstrated that knowledge about risk is not sufficient for the prevention of HIV risk behavior. This is not really surprising, given the variety of individual and contextual factors that contribute to motivation and the persistence of risk behaviors into young adulthood. For example, substance abuse, suicidality, and depression in adolescence are strong predictors of increasing or maintaining HIV high risk behaviors in young adulthood. Other contributing factors are problems in relationships with parents, friends' misbehaviors, stressful events, and neighborhood violence and unemployment.

Given the complexity of factors that contribute to risk behavior, prevention efforts that focus exclusively on knowledge are unlikely to be successful. However, there are effective school-based HIV prevention programs, which typically rely on principles of Social Cognitive (Learning) Theory. These principles include the use of experiential activities that allow for the modeling and practicing of skills, and the reinforcement of group norms against unprotected sex. A focus on reducing sexual risk behaviors and the use of trained motivated teachers enhance program effectiveness. However, adolescents live and learn in a variety of social contexts, and it is important to expand the scope of HIV prevention to include contextual interventions. For example, consistent adult monitoring can reduce opportunities for risky behaviors, and religious involvement protects adolescents from premature sex and drug use behaviors. Although they are currently very limited, school-based or school-linked clinic services, such as condom distribution and STI diagnosis and treatment, can be another important strategy for prevention.

*See also:* GUIDANCE AND COUNSELING, SCHOOL; HEALTH SERVICES; OUT-OF-SCHOOL INFLUENCES AND ACADEMIC SUCCESS; RISK BEHAVIORS, *subentries on* SEXUAL ACTIVITY AMONG TEENS AND TEEN PREGNANCY TRENDS, SEXUALLY TRANSMITTED DISEASES; SEXUALITY EDUCATION.

### BIBLIOGRAPHY

BANDURA, ALBERT. 1986. *Social Foundations of Thought and Action: A Social Cognitive Theory.* Englewood Cliffs, NJ: Prentice-Hall.

BERMAN, STUART M., and HEIN, KAREN. 1999. "Adolescents and STDs." In *Sexually Transmitted Diseases,* 3rd edition, ed. King K. Holmes et al. New York: McGraw-Hill.

CENTERS FOR DISEASE CONTROL AND PREVENTION. 2000. "U.S. HIV and AIDS Cases Reported through June 2000." *HIV/AIDS Surveillance Report* 12(1):1–44.

CENTERS FOR DISEASE CONTROL AND PREVENTION. 2000. *Be a Force for Change: Talk with Young People About HIV.* Washington, DC: U.S. Government Printing Office.

CENTERS FOR DISEASE CONTROL AND PREVENTION. 2000. "Youth Risk Behavior Surveillance—United States, 1999." *MMWR Morbidity and Mortality Weekly Reports* 49(5):1–96.

CENTERS FOR DISEASE CONTROL AND PREVENTION, HIV/AIDS PREVENTION RESEARCH SYNTHESIS PROJECT. 1999. *Compendium of HIV Prevention Interventions with Evidence of Effectiveness.* Atlanta, GA: Centers for Disease Control and Prevention.

COOPER, M. LYNNE; PEIRCE, ROBERT S.; and HUSELID, REBECCA FARMER. 1994. "Substance Use and Sexual Risk Taking among Black Adolescents and White Adolescents." *Health Psychology* 13(3):251–262.

DiCLEMENTE, RALPH J. 1996. "Adolescents at Risk for AIDS: AIDS Epidemiology, and Prevalence and Incidence of HIV." In *Understanding and Preventing HIV Risk Behavior: Safer Sex and Drug Use,* ed. Stuart Oskamp and Suzanne C. Thompson. Thousand Oaks, CA: Sage Publications.

DiCLEMENTE, RALPH J., and WINGOOD, GINA M. 2000. "Expanding the Scope of HIV Prevention for Adolescents: Beyond Individual-Level Interventions." *Journal of Adolescent Health* 26(6):377–378.

DIVISION OF STD PREVENTION–CENTERS FOR DISEASE CONTROL AND PREVENTION. 2000. *Sexually Transmitted Disease Surveillance, 1999.* Atlanta, GA: Centers for Disease Control and Prevention.

DUNCAN, SUSAN C.; STRYCKER, LISA A.; and DUNCAN, TERRY E. 1999. "Exploring Associations in Developmental Trends in Adolescent Substance Use and Risky Sexual Behavior in a High-Risk Population." *Journal of Behavioral Medicine* 22(1):21–34.

FORTENBERRY, J. DENNIS, et al. 1997. "Sex under the Influence: A Diary Self-Report Study of Substance Use and Sexual Behavior Among Adolescent Women." *Sexually Transmitted Diseases* 24(6):313–319.

GRAVES, KAREN L., and LEIGH, BARBARA C. 1995. "The Relationship of Substance Use to Sexual Activity among Young Adults in the United States." *Family Planning Perspectives* 27(1):18–22, 33.

HEIN, KAREN, and HURST, MARSHA. 1988. "Human Immunodeficiency Virus Infection in Adolescence: A Rationale for Action." *Adolescent and Pediatric Gynecology* 1:73–82.

HOYERT, DONNA L.; KOCHANEK, KENNETH D.; and MURPHY, SHERRY L. 1999. "Deaths: Final Data for 1997." *National Vital Statistics Reports* 47(19):1–104.

INSTITUTE OF MEDICINE—COMMITTEE ON PREVENTION AND CONTROL OF SEXUALLY TRANSMITTED DISEASES. 1997. *Hidden Epidemic: Confronting Sexually Transmitted Diseases.* Washington, DC: National Academy Press.

JESSOR, RICHARD; DONOVAN, JOHN EDWARD; and COSTA, FRANCES MARIE. 1991. *Beyond Adolescence: Problem Behavior and Young Adult Development.* New York: Cambridge University Press.

KIRBY, DOUGLAS. 1999. "Sexuality and Sex Education at Home and School." *Adolescent Medicine* 10(2):195–209.

LOWRY, RICHARD, et al. 1994. "Substance Use and HIV-related Sexual Behaviors among U.S. High School Students: Are They Related?" *American Journal of Public Health* 84(7):1116–1120.

RESNICK, MICHAEL D., et al. 1997. "Protecting Adolescents from Harm. Findings From the National Longitudinal Study on Adolescent Health." *Journal of the American Medical Association* 278(10):823–832.

ROTHERAM-BORUS, MARY JANE, et al. 2000. "Prevention of HIV Among Adolescents." *Prevention Science* 1(1):15–30.

STANTON, BONITA, et al. 1993. "Early Initiation of Sex and Its Lack of Association with Risk Behaviors among Adolescent African-Americans." *Pediatrics* 92(1):13–19.

STIFFMAN, ARLENE RUBIN, et al. 1995. "Person and Environment in HIV Risk Behavior Change between Adolescence and Young Adulthood." *Health Education Quarterly* 22(2):211–226.

INTERNET RESOURCE

CENTERS FOR DISEASE CONTROL AND PREVENTION. 2001. "Young People at Risk: HIV/AIDS Among America's Youth." <www.cdc.gov/hiv/pubs/facts/youth.htm>.

DENISE DION HALLFORS
CAROLYN TUCKER HALPERN
BONITA IRITANI

## SEXUAL ACTIVITY AMONG TEENS AND TEEN PREGNANCY TRENDS

Adolescent sexuality is often viewed from a negative perspective that focuses primarily on sexual behavior and its association with other high-risk behaviors. Youth are sometimes negatively viewed as sex-crazed, hormone-driven individuals who want the perceived independence of adulthood without the responsibility of adulthood. On the other hand, psychosexual development is a critical developmental process during adolescence. P. B. Koch has identified the need for research identifying healthy psychosexual development in adolescents. As children emerge into adolescence, their developing gender identity shapes whom they interact and associate with, especially peers. Negative media images that appear to promote lustful, irresponsible sexual behavior are often associated with early sexual activity among adolescents. However, it is crucial to identify what protective factors can shape positive psychosexual development, including delaying the onset of sexual activity. Research has yet to identify gender-specific strategies that can promote positive psychosexual development in boys and girls.

### Early Sexual Activity

Early sexual activity is a growing issue in adolescent development. According to both the National Survey of Family Growth and the Youth Risk Behavior Survey, adolescents are engaging in sexual activity at earlier ages. In general, older adolescents (age fifteen and older) demonstrate a reduction in early sexual activity, whereas adolescents younger than thirteen demonstrate an increase in sexual activity. In addition, two-thirds of high school students report having sex before graduating from high school. These findings persist in the face of an apparent leveling off of sexual activity in adolescents.

Peer pressure to engage in adult-like activities can encourage adolescents to engage in various levels of sexual experimentation. Adolescents who engage in sexual experimentation are at increased risk for sexually transmitted diseases, including HIV/AIDs, and pregnancy. Moreover, risk for early sexual experimentation is associated with other high-risk behaviors in adolescence, including sexual abuse and drug and alcohol use, and emotional adjustment.

In regard to puberty, early-maturing adolescents are more likely to engage in early sexual experimentation than are later-maturing adolescents. They confront their emerging sexuality at younger ages than their peers do, and are more likely to be pursued by older peers in social settings because they appear physically older than their chronological age.

For both male and female adolescents, adolescence represents, in part, a time for pressure to engage in sexual intimacy. As girls enter adolescence (typically a few years before boys), they begin to grow into womanhood and become sexualized objects. Within the media, images of sexuality and overly thin body images can socialize girls into seeing themselves as sexual objects. On the other hand, boys are pressured to exhibit their manhood through sexual conquests.

Much of the research on early sexual activity in adolescents does not address early patterns of noncoital sexuality. Noncoital sexuality is defined as involvement in sexual contact that does not include the exchange of body fluids. Research suggests that by middle adolescence most youths have begun to engage in sexual experimentation, including kissing, with 97 percent of adolescents experiencing their first kiss by age fifteen. Understanding the onset of noncoital sexuality and factors influencing its timing is vital to delineating patterns of early sexual activity in teenagers.

Adolescent condom use has increased for both males and females. The decline in teenage pregnancy is, in part, attributable to an increase in contraceptive use. However, since psychosexual development is a new challenge faced during adolescence, some youths are ill informed, and even though they may choose to use contraceptives, they may use these methods incorrectly.

**Teenage Pregnancy**

The association of early sexual activity with teenage pregnancy has been a societal concern for decades. For females, teenage pregnancy can complicate adolescent development and contribute to a troublesome transition to young adulthood, which involves a potential future as a single parent with limited educational and economic opportunities. Since the 1990s the overall teenage pregnancy rate has declined, though, according to the National Campaign to Prevent Teen Pregnancy, four out of ten girls still get pregnant before their twentieth birthday. The United States has the highest teen pregnancy, birth, and abortion rates of any industrialized nation.

Teenage mothers are at risk for poverty and school failure, while their offspring are at risk for low birthweight, poor access to health care, poverty, and early childhood developmental problems. Programs such as Aid to Families with Dependent Children (AFDC), which were created to support single parent mothers, have been criticized as being an incentive for the birth of children out of wedlock in poor communities. Consequently, poor teen mothers have sometimes been blamed for their circumstances and negatively portrayed within the media and the public arena. Yet the overall decline in teenage pregnancy has occurred across all ethnic groups, including the poor ethnic minority groups that are most likely to be demonized in the media as having excessive teenage pregnancy rates.

A significant risk factor for early sexual experimentation is a history of sexual trauma. This is true for both males and females, though the level of risk is increased for females. Adolescent girls who have a history of sexual trauma during childhood and/or adolescence may try to cope during their adolescent years by being sexually provocative. This coping mechanism is negative; however, victims of sexual abuse may try to control future sexual encounters by initiating sexual contact. This may influence the likelihood of their involvement in prostitution and other sexually exploitative illegal activities.

Girls with a history of sexual trauma are also at great risk for involvement in the juvenile justice system, particularly if they do not have supportive home environments that allow them the opportunity to heal from their traumas. Girls within the juvenile justice system are likely to exhibit runaway behaviors in an effort to get out of abusive home environments. Through these runaway patterns, some girls are introduced to sexual exploitation in their effort to survive on the street. Boys who are victims of sexual abuse are at risk for offending behaviors if they lack supportive home environments, and they are also at risk for involvement in the juvenile justice system.

The use of alcohol and drugs reduces inhibitions, and can therefore influence participation in unprotected sexual activity. Boys and girls with a history of smoking and alcohol use have an increased risk for early sexual activity, in part because the use of these substances can influence the decision making of adolescents in social contexts.

Efforts to conduct sexuality education within the home environment have been found to be insufficient. Parents need to provide supportive learning environments in which children can develop a healthy understanding of their sexuality, particularly during their adolescent years. Adolescence represents a time of fundamental change, as adolescents are introduced to new reproductive capacities that have to be understood cognitively, socially, and emotionally.

### Pregnancy Prevention

Adolescents receive most of their information about sexuality from peers, which often leads to misinformation. Adolescents need structured formal and informal learning environments with age-appropriate peers to address issues of sexuality. These programmatic models may be available within school and community-based settings. Most pregnancy prevention programs fall within three categories: knowledge interventions, access to contraception, and programs to enhance life options. Lisa Crockett and Joanne Chopack suggest three categories of programs: programs that focus on sexual antecedents, programs that focus on nonsexual antecedents, and programs that focus on a combination of both sexual and nonsexual antecedents. Programs that focus on sexual antecedents directly target sexual behavior and often focus on reducing sexual activity, minimizing the number of sexual partners, and contraceptive use. Programs that focus on nonsexual antecedents indirectly target sexual activity by focusing on other outcomes, such as academic achievement, youth development (including leadership skills), and service-learning models.

Joy Dryfoss has proposed the need for comprehensive health-promotion models as the best practice within sexuality education. This practice not only seeks to minimize risk, but to provide leadership and prosocial skills development to shape the changing lives of young people. Scholars and activists continue to debate the usefulness of abstinence versus education, including birth control strategies. Abstinence-based models show mixed results when rigorously researched, with a limited demonstrated effect on sexual behavior. Many abstinence-only proponents believe that birth control education increases the likelihood of teen sexual activity; however, the evaluations do not support this notion. Sex education models designed to support the psychosexual development of adolescents have been extensively debated, based on religious, moral, family, and community values and attitudes. Educational systems have been permitted to provide abstinence-based education to combat historically high teenage pregnancy rates. Those that propose that birth control education should include life-skills development assert that interventions need to be grounded in the realities of those who are at greatest risk for premature sexual activity and associated negative consequences.

Young people from poor, underserved, inner-city communities are at risk for poor access to health care, including health education, which increases their risk of negative developmental outcomes related to early sexuality activity. Programmatic efforts need to take into account the social context of these communities. Young people living in such an environment particularly need increased life options rooted in effective decision making, which may lead to a delay in early sexual activity in the adolescent years. According to Saul Hoffman, author of "Teenage Childbearing Is Not So Bad After All . . . Or Is It? A Review of the New Literature," teenage pregnancy prevention programs targeting teen mothers in poor, underserved communities may yield indirect effects in addition to reducing teen pregnancy. These programs may represent pathways out of poverty for these poor populations of teen mothers.

Within inner-city communities of color, program models such as the I Have a Future program founded by Dr. Henry Foster provide a supportive learning community for youths residing in economically deprived communities with high rates of multi-generational teen pregnancy and sexually transmitted diseases. Such families often remain trapped in poverty, poor health care systems, and economic deprivation. The I Have a Future model provides comprehensive adolescent health services, prosocial skills development, leadership development, alcohol and drug education, gender and ethnic identity development, and academic support. In addition, participants gain exposure to positive role models within the supportive staff and through community linkages to colleges and universities. This program represents a mixed-gender context in which both males and females adolescents can develop positive decision-making skills regarding delayed sexual activity, and it provides a promising framework for effective interventions for high-risk youth.

Positive psychosexual development is important in making a successful transition through adolescence. Adolescents need safe opportunities to relate to peers and develop meaningful attachments without bringing harm to themselves. Psychosexual development is shaped by media, family, community, and peer contexts, and comprehensive strategies that address these contexts are needed to fully support adolescent development. Media literacy can be incorporated into intervention models in order to increase understanding of gender stereotypes. Girls must confront the overwhelming stereotypes of thin, sexually provocative body images of females, whereas males must confront macho images reinforcing masculine control.

**The Role of Parents**

Parents need resources to support their vital role in shaping the lives of adolescents. Families, and parents in particular, need help in learning effective ways of supporting their adolescent's psychosexual development. In the face of declining teenage pregnancy rates, it is imperative that research focus on targeted evaluations of promising practices that can influence positive developmental outcomes. Some communities and individual programs are strapped for funds to establish and maintain programming, while evaluation goals are deferred because of limited funding. Academic communities can partner with local communities and health promotion agencies to assist in the development of rigorous research paradigms that can increase knowledge of effective interventions that can be potentially replicated in other communities.

In the face of community efforts to address teenage pregnancy, some parents may be apprehensive about other adults influencing their children regarding personal, sensitive issues. For parents who feel comfortable and equipped in addressing these issues with their children, the National Campaign to Prevent Teen Pregnancy offers several tips for parents, including being aware of their own personal values and attitudes regarding sexuality and how they want their children to be introduced to the sensitive topic of sexuality. Effective parent–child communication regarding love and intimacy, as well as family rules and standards about teenage dating, can provide needed support for adolescents who are confronting the social and emotional challenges related to puberty. Parents are encouraged to introduce the topic of sexuality and sex education early in a child's development. How early this occurs is again influenced by the personal values and attitudes of the parents. Parents can also assist as interpreters of negative media images that foster inconsistent and controversial attitudes toward early sexual activity and promiscuity.

In addition, parents are encouraged to become knowledgeable about their children's social contexts. Monitoring children's activities includes not only knowing where one's children are, but also who are the friends and peer associates of one's children. It is also important to provide life options that provide children with constructive, safe opportunities for personal growth.

Other effective models of service include gender-specific interventions that assist adolescents in understanding positive manhood and womanhood development. Through the development of positive gender identity, adolescents can fully consider their role in relationships with family, peers, and community.

There has been some debate regarding gender-specific versus mixed-gender programs to address the issue of teenage pregnancy. Programs are encouraged to be intentional in their efforts to maximize opportunities for education and life-skills development, whether in same-gender or mixed-gender environments. Same-gender programs can provide safe learning environments in which groups can fully consider the challenges facing adolescents to engage in early sexual activity. In particular, for girls who may have been traumatized by males, it is critical that they have opportunities to voice their concerns and experiences without any perceived threat by male counterparts. On the other hand, in the absence of trauma-related experiences, adolescents may benefit from healthy, mixed-gender programs that focus on the shared responsibility of both sexes in family planning. Otherwise, the burden for safe sex, including contraceptive use, is often perceived as the responsibility of the female. Even though females are more likely to experience pubertal changes earlier than their male counterparts, these females are not necessarily advanced in their emotional maturity to the point that they can assume sole responsibility for sexual behavior.

In order to address premature sexual activity among teenagers effectively, comprehensive community strategies are needed to address the myriad of issues involved and the diversity in social and community contexts. In 2002, thirteen community partnerships within eleven states were implementing comprehensive youth preventive interventions to combat teenage pregnancy. These partnerships distribute the responsibility for sexuality education across the family, community, and school.

*See also:* GUIDANCE AND COUNSELING, SCHOOL; HEALTH SERVICES; PARENTING; OUT-OF-SCHOOL INFLUENCES AND ACADEMIC SUCCESS; RISK BEHAVIORS, *subentry on* SEXUALLY TRANSMITTED DISEASES; SEXUALITY EDUCATION.

### BIBLIOGRAPHY

CROCKETT, LISA, and CHOPAK, JOANNE S. 1993. "Pregnancy Prevention in Early Adolescence: A Developmental Perspective." In *Early Adolescence: Perspectives on Research, Policy, and Intervention,* ed. Richard Lerner. Hillsdale, NJ: Erlbaum.

DRYFOSS, JOY. 1990. *Adolescents at Risk: Prevalence and Prevention.* New York: Oxford University Press.

HOFFMAN, SAUL D. 1998. "Teenage Childbearing Is Not So Bad After All . . . Or Is It? A Review of New Literature." *Family Planning Perspectives* 30(5):236–239, 243.

KIRBY, DOUGLAS. 2001. *Emerging Answers: Research Findings on Programs to Reduce Teen Pregnancy.* Washington, DC: National Campaign to Prevent Teen Pregnancy.

KOCH, P. B. 1993. "Promoting Healthy Sexual Development During Early Adolescence" In *Early Adolescence: Perspectives on Research, Policy, and*

*Intervention,* ed. Richard Lerner. Hillsdale, NJ: Erlbaum.

### INTERNET RESOURCES

ADVOCATES FOR YOUTH. 2002. "Adolescent Pregnancy and Childbearing." <www.advocates foryouth.org/publications/factsheet/ fsprechd.htm>.

NATIONAL CAMPAIGN TO PREVENT TEEN PREGNANCY. 2002. "Ten Tips for Parents to Help Their Children Avoid Teen Pregnancy." <www. teenpregnancy.org/resources/reading/tips/ tips.asp>.

NATIONAL CENTER FOR CHRONIC DISEASE AND HEALTH PROMOTION. 2002. "Preventing Teen Pregnancy." <www.cdc.gov/nccdphp/teen. htm>.

WERTHEIMER, RICHARD, and MOORE, KRISTIN. 2002. "Childbearing by Teens: Links to Welfare Reform." Urban Institute. <http://new federalism.urban.org/html/anf24.html>.

SHEILA PETERS

# SEXUALLY TRANSMITTED DISEASES

Sexually transmitted diseases (STDs) are viral and bacterial infections passed from one person to another through sexual contact. In 1960 there were two common STDs; by the beginning of the twenty-first century, there were more than twenty-five. In 1980 alone, eight new STD pathogens were recognized in the United States. In 1995 STDs accounted for 87 percent of cases reported among the top ten diseases in the United States.

The Institute of Medicine coined the phrase "the hidden epidemic" to describe the problem of STDs in the United States. STDs disproportionately affect women and young people. In 1996 an estimated 15 million new cases of STDs occurred in the United States, of which at least one-quarter were among adolescents between the ages of fifteen and nineteen. Adolescents are at a higher risk for contracting sexually transmitted disease because of biological and behavioral factors.

### Biological Factors

During each sexual encounter, women are at an inherently greater risk of acquiring an STD than men are. Young women are especially vulnerable to infection because of the increased amount of immature ectopic tissue on the endocervix, which increases the likelihood of acquiring certain STDs such as chlamydia, gonorrhea, and HIV. Adolescent women also have "immature" or unchallenged local immune systems that make them more vulnerable to STD infections. Most sexually transmitted diseases are asymptomatic and go undiagnosed, further promoting the spread of infection.

## Behavioral Risk

Behavioral risk factors that predispose individuals to STDs include age at initiation of sexual activity, having multiple sexual partners or a partner with multiple partners, use of barrier protection, and use of diagnostic and treatment services. Furthermore, risk of STDs may be compounded by additional socioeconomic factors, though this relationship is unclear. Many markers of STD risk (e.g., age, gender, race/ethnicity) are associated with fundamental determinants of risk status (e.g., access to health care, residing in communities with high prevalence of STDs) to influence adolescents' risk for STDs. Since the early 1980s the age of initiation of sexual activity has steadily decreased and age at first marriage has increased, resulting in increases in premarital sexual experience among adolescent women and an increasing number of women at risk. Multiple (sequential or concurrent) sexual partners rather than a single, long-term relationship increases the likelihood that a person may become infected. The Centers for Disease Control and Prevention (CDC) showed that almost 45 percent of women who initiated sexual activity before the age of sixteen had more than five lifetime sexual partners. Among women who delayed first sex until after the age of twenty, however, only 15 percent had more than five lifetime sexual partners. Of women who delayed their first sexual activity until after the age of twenty, close to 52 percent had only one lifetime sexual partner, compared with about 19 percent of women who had initiated sex before the age of sixteen. The risk of STDs increases with the total number of lifetime sexual partners, whether over a short time period or spread over a life course.

In addition to having more than one sexual partner, adolescents may be more likely to engage in unprotected intercourse or engage in high-risk sexual activities such as anal sex. They may also select partners at higher risk. For example, young women are more likely than women in other age groups to choose a partner who is older than themselves. Additionally, oral sex and mutual masturbation may also lead to the spread of infection and should be considered risky activities.

Studies have shown that adolescents who are involved in one risky behavior are more likely to be involved in others. Adolescent boys and girls who have had sex are also more likely to drink alcohol, take drugs, and smoke cigarettes than adolescents who have not had sex. A quarter of adolescents interviewed reported that they were under the influence of drugs or alcohol when they last engaged in sexual intercourse. There is evidence that young people who avoided risky behavior had positive influences in their lives, such as a strong relationship with their parents.

The high prevalence of STDs among adolescents may also reflect multiple barriers to quality STD prevention services. Adolescents may lack insurance or the ability to pay for such services. They may lack transportation to reach an adequate facility. Additionally, they may feel uncomfortable in facilities and with services designed for adults. Adolescents may also be concerned about the confidentiality of their visits. Most studies following adolescents who have been diagnosed and treated for STDs by health care providers show a high incidence of reinfection at follow-up visits.

## Prevalent Bacterial STDs

The most prevalent bacterial STDs are gonorrhea and chlamydia. Ongoing surveys of women in clinic settings has shown that adolescent women consistently have higher rates of chlamydia infection when compared to other age groups. In 2000 women aged fifteen to nineteen years old had the highest rates of chlamydia infection among all women even when overall prevalence declined. Chlamydia rates are low among men. Though the rates of gonorrhea decreased among adolescent women ages ten to nineteen years between 1996 and 2000, in 2000 the highest age-specific gonorrhea rates were among women in the fifteen- to nineteen-year-old age group. Adolescent men ages fifteen to nineteen years had the third-highest rates of gonorrhea when compared to other age groups of men.

## Prevalent Viral STDs

Genital herpes simplex virus (HSV-2) and human papillomavirus (HPV) are prevalent among sexually experienced adolescents. Furthermore, infection with HSV-2, HPV, or HIV may result in negative reproductive morbidity, including neonatal transmission of these infections, cervical and genital cancer, and even premature death. As of yet, there are no effective cures for these viral infections.

Studies indicate that one in six Americans is infected with HSV-2, reflecting a ninefold increase since the early 1970s. An estimated 4 percent of Caucasians and 17 percent of African Americans are infected with HSV-2 by the end of their teenage years. One study of low-income pregnant women found an HSV-2 infection rate as high as 11 percent in women fifteen to nineteen years of age and 22 percent in women twenty-five to twenty-nine years of age.

Based on data from twenty-five states with integrated HIV and AIDS reporting systems, the CDC reported that for the period from January 1996 to June 1999 young people (aged thirteen to twenty-four) accounted for a much greater proportion of HIV (13%) than AIDS cases (3%). Though the number of new AIDS cases diagnosed during the period declined, no decline was observed in the number of newly diagnosed HIV cases among youth. Because progression from HIV infection to AIDS may be on the order of years, the reported number of AIDS cases may not reflect the actual rate of HIV infection among adolescents. At least half of all new HIV infections in the United States are among people under age twenty-five, and the majority of young people are infected sexually. In 1999 there were 29,629 cumulative cases of AIDS among those aged thirteen to twenty-four years. The CDC further reported that in 1999, of the cases of AIDS in young men aged thirteen to twenty-four years, 50 percent were among men who have sex with men; 8 percent were among injection drug users; and 8 percent were among young men infected heterosexually. Among young women aged thirteen to twenty-four years, 47 percent of cases reported were acquired heterosexually and 11 percent were acquired through injection drug use.

**Impact**

STDs prevent adolescents from leading healthy lives. They lead to declines in school performance, increased poverty, and higher crime rates. The financial cost of STDs runs in the billions each year. As a consequence of STDs, many adolescents experience serious health problems that often alter the course of their adult lives, including infertility, difficult pregnancy, genital and cervical cancer, neonatal transmission of infections, and AIDS.

*See also:* GUIDANCE AND COUNSELING, SCHOOL; HEALTH SERVICES; OUT-OF-SCHOOL INFLUENCES AND ACADEMIC SUCCESS; RISK BEHAVIORS, *subentries on* HIV/AIDS AND ITS IMPACT ON ADOLESCENTS, SEXUAL ACTIVITY AMONG TEENS AND TEEN PREGNANCY TRENDS; SEXUALITY EDUCATION.

### BIBLIOGRAPHY

KAGAN, JEROME, and GALL, SUSAN B., eds. 1998. *The Gale Encyclopedia of Childhood and Adolescence.* Detroit: Gale.

MCILHANEY, J. S., JR. 2000. "Sexually Transmitted Infection and Teenage Sexuality." *American Journal of Obstetrics and Gynecology* 183:334–339.

### INTERNET RESOURCES

CENTERS FOR DISEASE CONTROL AND PREVENTION. NATIONAL CENTER FOR HIV, STD AND TB PREVENTION. DIVISION OF SEXUALLY TRANSMITTED DISEASES. 2002. "STDs in Adolescents and Young Adults: STD Surveillance, Special Focus Profiles." <www.cdc.gov/std/stats/PDF/SFAdoles2000.pdf>.

CENTERS FOR DISEASE CONTROL AND PREVENTION. NATIONAL CENTER FOR HIV, STD AND TB PREVENTION. DIVISION OF SEXUALLY TRANSMITTED DISEASES. 2002. "STD Surveillance 2000." <www.cdc.gov/std/stats/TOC2000.htm>.

ANGELA HUANG

# SMOKING AND ITS EFFECT ON CHILDREN'S HEALTH

The impact of tobacco use in the United States and worldwide is staggering. According to the World Health Organization, 1.1 billion people worldwide regularly smoke tobacco products, and smoking accounts for 10,000 deaths per day. In 1990 there were 418,000 deaths in the United States alone attributed to smoking and its effects. Smoking kills two and one-half times more people than alcohol and drug use combined. In the United States 25 percent of the population regularly uses tobacco, with 6,000 new adolescent smokers each day—half of whom will go on to be regular smokers. Every day more than 15 million children are exposed to smoke in their homes. Environmental tobacco smoke (ETS), also known as "second hand smoke," poses significant risks to children. The United States Environmental Protection Agency (EPA) has classified ETS as a class A carcinogen, which means that ETS is known to cause cancer in humans. Exposure to ETS before the age of ten will increase a child's chances of developing lymphoma and leukemia (i.e., cancers of the blood) as an adult. The effects of ETS are actually worse than those acquired from smoking cigarettes directly.

### Pregnancy/Perinatal/SIDS

It has been estimated that 19 percent to 27 percent of pregnant women smoke during their pregnancy. The pregnant woman who smokes not only affects her own health, but she harms the baby she is carrying as well. A major risk of smoking during pregnancy is the increased rate of premature delivery of the baby. Infants who are born prematurely can have many severe medical problems, including lung immaturity and brain injury. Maternal smoking contributes to 5 percent of all perinatal deaths (i.e., 2,800 deaths per year). Pregnant women who smoke are at a greater risk of miscarriage and low-birth-weight infants, as well as higher rates of long-term behavioral and mental problems in her child. Infants born to mothers who smoked during pregnancy have a much higher rate of Sudden Infant Death Syndrome (SIDS) than infants born to mothers who did not smoke during pregnancy. There is a dose-dependent relationship between ETS exposure during pregnancy and the rate of SIDS: The greater the exposure of cigarette smoke to an unborn baby, the higher their risk of SIDS. Cigarette smoke exposure is one of the few preventable risk factors for SIDS.

Newborn infants are in a unique situation when it comes to exposure to their mothers' smoke. Cotinine, a metabolite of nicotine, is found in newborn babies' blood at levels almost equivalent to their mothers'. There are significant levels of cotinine in a newborn's blood even if the mother herself does not smoke, but simply lives in a household where there is ETS exposure. There is a direct relationship between the maternal and newborn infant's blood levels of cigarette smoke products. The mother who smokes during pregnancy transfers the products in cigarette smoke to the fetus through the placenta, as well as to the newborn infant though breast-feeding. In fact, breast-fed infants have the same urinary cotinine levels as active adult smokers.

### Childhood Diseases

The risks of ETS are not simply restricted to the newborn infant. There are many childhood illnesses that are dramatically worsened by exposure to smoke. A 1994 study by Joan Cunningham and colleagues showed that there was an increased risk of colds, wheezing, shortness-of-breath, and emergency room visits by children living in households where there is a smoker. There is also a significant increase is the risk of ear infections in children who live in households where there are smokers. Children born to mothers who smoke have a higher risk of developing asthma. Along with an increased risk of asthma, children of mothers who smoked during pregnancy will be at a greater risk of have problems with environmental allergies (e.g., hay fever). These effects can be seen in newborn infants as well as school-aged children.

### Adolescence

Between 4 million and 5 million adolescents in the United States smoke daily. Each year more than 1 million people under eighteen years of age become daily smokers. Ninety percent of adults who regularly smoke began smoking before they were nineteen years of age. Throughout the 1990s the age at which children began smoking became increasingly younger. In 1990, 31 percent of all twelfth graders reported recent (within the last month) tobacco use while 21 percent were daily smokers. Shockingly, 8 percent of all eighth graders reported daily tobacco use. By the end of the 1990s the percentages of twelfth and eighth graders who recently used cigarettes was up to 36 percent and 21 percent, respectively. The younger and younger beginning smoker is reflected in the higher percentage of adolescent smokers as compared to the adult population. Besides the negative health effects of smoking itself, adolescents who smoke are fifteen times more likely to use drugs than their peers who do not smoke.

There are many reasons why a child or adolescent will begin to smoke. The most common influence is family and peer pressures, but the most potent factor is the media portrayal of "glamorous" smoking. The top three most popular brands of cigarettes amongst adolescents were the top three companies that spent the most on advertising. In 1993 these companies collectively spent $153 million dollars on advertising. Many popular sporting events are still sponsored by tobacco companies, and there is some evidence that advertising had been directed toward recruiting new child or adolescent smokers. To combat the draw of the media for adolescents to begin smoking, the Centers for Diseases Control and Prevention (CDC) began, in the fall of 2000, the *Surgeon General's Report for Kids on Smoking.* This was an attempt to enlist celebrities and sports figures to promote an antismoking message to young people. It involves posters and media advertisements directed toward children and adolescents, informing them of the health damages caused by cigarette smoking.

## Costs

The true cost of smoking is incalculable, but there are some very practical measures that can be seen. In 1997 American children made more than 500,000 doctor visits for asthma, and 1.3 million visits for cough that were directly attributed to smoke exposure. This does not include the 115,000 cases of pneumonia, 260,000 cases of bronchitis, and more than two million ear infections. The annual cost of ear infections in children in the United States caused by smoke exposure is $1.5 billion. The actual total financial costs, directly related to the exposure of American children to ETS, are broken into direct medical costs and the loss of life costs. In 1997 the total medical cost of the complications of cigarette smoke on American children was $4.6 billion. The loss of life cost (calculated based upon loss of earnings and costs needed to prevent disease) was $8.2 billion. The true cost of cigarette smoking, however, is in the impact smoking has on the health of infants and children.

*See also:* GUIDANCE AND COUNSELING, SCHOOL; HEALTH EDUCATION; HEALTH SERVICES; OUT-OF-SCHOOL INFLUENCES AND ACADEMIC SUCCESS; RISK BEHAVIORS, *subentry on* SEXUAL ACTIVITY AMONG TEENS AND TEEN PREGNANCY TRENDS.

**BIBLIOGRAPHY**

ALIGNE, C. ANDREW, and STODDARD, JEFFREY J. 1997. "Tobacco and Children: An Economic Evaluation of the Medical Effects of Parental Smoking" *Archives of Pediatrics and Adolescent Medicine* 171(7):648–653.

AMERICAN ACADEMY OF PEDIATRICS COMMITTEE ON SUBSTANCE ABUSE. 2001. "Tobacco's Toll: Implications for the Pediatrician." *Pediatrics* 107:794–798.

CENTERS FOR DISEASE CONTROL AND PREVENTION. 1997. "State-Specific Prevalence of Cigarette Smoking among Adults, and Children's and Adolescents' Exposure to Environmental Tobacco Smoke—United States, 1996." *Morbidity and Mortality Weekly Reports* 46:1038–1043.

CUNNINGHAM, JOAN, et al. 1994. "Environmental Tobacco Smoke, Wheezing, and Asthma in Children in Twenty-Four Mothers." *American Journal of Respiratory and Critical Care Medicine* 86:1398–1402.

DIFRANZA, JOSEPH R., and LEW, ROBERT A. 1997. "Morbidity and Mortality in Children Associated with the Use of Tobacco Products by Other People." *Pediatrics* 97:560–568.

JOAD, JESSE. 2000. "Smoking and Pediatric Respiratory Health." *Clinics in Chest Medicine* 21(1):37–46.

CHRISTOPHER S. GREELEY

# SUICIDE

School-age children can engage in many behaviors of concern to adults as a function of their development as well as the changing culture and environments in which they live. Perhaps the most concerning and baffling of these risk behaviors are the tendencies in some to consider ending their own lives at so young an age. Why children and adolescents consider these self-destructive actions is a complicated puzzle to understand and solve. Such behaviors must be considered in light of young people's vulnerability to external models, their increased anxiety related to issues of social acceptance, their desire to develop a unique identity, and the existence of unstable and abusive families.

In 1999 the surgeon general of the United States, David Satcher, issued a call to action to prevent suicide. Satcher noted the continuing increase in suicide rates among the young, with the rate tripling from 1952 to 1996. He stated that Americans under the age of twenty-five accounted for 15 percent of all completed suicides and that risk factors for suicide attempts among the young included depression, alcohol or drug use disorders, and aggressive and disruptive behaviors. Suicide was not just a mental health problem but a public health problem as well.

## Occurrence

Suicide rates for children and adolescents are regularly reported by the National Center for Health Statistics in the U.S. Department of Health and Human Services. These reports count only those for whom suicide is listed as the cause of death. For this reason it is believed that suicides may be underreported. Those who sign death certificates (family physicians, emergency room staff, and medical examiners) may not always list the cause of death as intentional in order to avoid stigma for the family or because evidence of suicide may not be immediately present. It is suspected that vehicular accidents and deaths related to substance abuse, for instance, may in some cases be suicides, but they may not be recorded as such.

A review of statistics regarding rates of suicide reveal a number of facts. For those aged fifteen to twenty-four, suicide stands as the third-leading cause of death behind accidents and homicides. As of 1996, the rate of suicide deaths for Americans aged ten to fourteen was 1.6 deaths per 100,000 population (2.3 per 100,000 for males and 0.8 per 100,000 for females). For fifteen- to nineteen-year-olds the rate was 9.7 deaths per 100,000 (15.6 per 100,000 for males and 3.5 per 100,000 for females), and for those aged twenty to twenty-four the rate was 14.5 deaths per 100,000 (24.8 per 100,000 for males and 3.7 per 100,000 for females). Young males (aged fifteen to nineteen) are more likely to succeed at killing themselves than females by a ratio of at least five to one. Reports from the surgeon general also suggest that gay and lesbian youth may be two to three times more likely to commit suicide. Although accomplished suicide rates were highest for white males, young African American males showed the greatest increase during the 1980s and 1990s. White females had the next highest rates, followed by African-American females. Research on Hispanic populations indicated that rates of suicide in young men and women may be higher than for whites.

Suicides can be completed using a variety of means. Nearly 63 percent of suicides occur using firearms. Most other deaths are a result of more passive means such as drug poisonings or hangings. Suicide attempts are less likely to involve firearms and may, therefore, provide opportunities for discovery and rescue.

In addition to completed or accomplished suicides, many young people attempt suicide. Accurate rates for this group of attempted suicides, often called *parasuicides,* are even more difficult to obtain. Hospitals and emergency rooms may identify attempters, but many parasuicides go completely un-

detected or are confided only to the closest of friends. Possible ratios of attempts to completions may range from 10:1 to 150:1, depending upon the research and the definition of attempts. The continuum of suicidal behaviors, which includes actual suicide on one end and attempted suicides in the middle, includes on the other end the least severe form of self-destructiveness, usually identified as suicidal ideation or intent. The idea of killing oneself may occur quite frequently in young people, but it becomes serious only when there is intent to actually act. Such suicidal intent often includes a plan and a timetable in the person's mind.

## Risk Factors

Many factors have been examined as contributors to the likelihood that a school-age child will become suicidal. Some factors appear to be historical or situational whereas others are psychological. A large percentage (perhaps as high as 90 percent) of those who are victims of suicide have diagnosable psychiatric disorders at the time of death. Many suffer from mood disorders, and a large percentage have made previous suicide attempts. Risk factors may include: psychiatric disorder, previous suicide attempt, co-occurring drug use and mental disorder, family history of suicide, impulsive or aggressive tendencies, feelings of hopelessness, loss of significant relationship, loss of job, physical illness, stress, lack of access to mental health treatment, availability of lethal means (e.g., guns or drugs), feelings of isolation and alienation, influence of peers or family members, unwillingness to seek help, cultural or religious beliefs or traditions, influence of the media, current epidemics of suicidal behaviors, and being a victim of bullying.

In the case of children and adolescents, two major themes related to increased risk for suicide are fears of humiliation by others and feelings of invisibility. Additional themes may also include general levels of stress, breakdown of psychological defenses, self-deprecatory thoughts, and a negative personal history.

## Protective Factors

Just as some factors seem to increase the incidence of self-destructive suicidal intent, so also there appear to be conditions that make these thoughts and behaviors less likely. Such circumstances or characteristics are considered to be protective. Among those cited by the surgeon general in 1999 were: effective and appropriate clinical care; access to treatment and support for seeking help; restricted access to lethal means; family and community support; ongoing medical and mental health care relationships; learned skills in problem solving, conflict resolution and nonviolent dispute management; and a belief system, either cultural or religious in nature, that discourages suicide. Skills in anger management, impulse control, and appropriate action in the face of victimization have been also cited as protective factors.

## Warning Signs

The warning signs of imminent suicidal behaviors can appear in many forms. They can be verbal, spoken to others; written as poems, songs, diary entries, or suicide notes; or made as threats directly ("I am going to kill myself") or indirectly ("You won't have me to kick around anymore"). Other warning signs include social withdrawal, getting things in order, giving things away, constant crying, or an angry or hostile attitude. Some signs occur in the person's environment, such as the death of someone close, family problems, or failure in school or at work. Lastly, some signs are those characteristic of depression or general mental and emotional difficulties. These latter signs might include sleep disturbance, feelings of despair, appetite change, or radical and abrupt changes in behavior or personality.

## Formulation of the Problem

According to Jerry Jacobs, writing in 1971, early research into suicide examined five major stages seen in suicidal children. These included a history of problems, an escalation of problems, the failure of coping, the experience of helplessness, and finally, a justification for taking a self-destructive action. Although these stages may be present, in many cases adults do not observe them, but rather they are shared with peers. Adults may merely see the final behaviors.

It is important to realize that suicidal behavior can best be seen not as a disease (although it may in some cases be the manifestation of one), but rather as a symptom with many different possible underlying causes. Just as a headache could be caused by many things, so the action to end one's own life can be a result of any number of causes: depression or other mental illness, stress, grief or loss, unresolved conflict, substance use, unexpressed anger or rage, social pressure, lack of problem-solving or conflict

resolution skills, hopelessness or frustration, chronic victimization, a desire for visibility or respect, the need to avoid humiliation, or the desire to be noticed.

## Prevention

The best strategies for the prevention of suicide are those that reduce the number of risk factors and increase protective factors. This means making resources available to families and schools to aid in this process. In some cases early intervention is needed. Prevention or primary interventions need to: develop strategies for detecting suicidal individuals, treat all threats seriously, educate those who work with kids about suicide, increase peer education about suicide, teach families and communities to look for warning signs, reduce the availability of lethal means, make twenty-four-hour hotlines available, and use the media to teach the public how to recognize those at risk.

Finally, it must be acknowledged that the problem of self-destructive behavior affects everyone. Parents, schools, and communities must make a commitment to work to end this behavior and its causes.

*See also:* Guidance and Counseling, School; Mental Health Services and Children; Parenting; Out-of-School Influences and Academic Success.

### BIBLIOGRAPHY

Berman, Alan L., and Jobes, David A. 1991. *Adolescent Suicide: Assessment and Intervention.* Washington, DC: American Psychological Association.

Fremouw, William J.; de Perczel, Maria; and Ellis, Thomas E. 1990. *Suicide Risk: Assessment and Response Guidelines.* New York: Pergamon Press.

Group for the Advancement of Psychiatry. 1996. *Adolescent Suicide.* Washington, DC: American Psychiatric Press.

Jacobs, J. 1971. *Adolescent Suicide.* New York: Wiley.

Peters, Kimberly D.; Kochanek, Kenneth D.; and Murphy, Sherry L. 1998. "Deaths: Final Data for 1996." *National Vital Statistics Reports* 47(9). Hyattsville, MD: National Center for Health Statistics.

ROBBINS, PAUL R. 1998. *Adolescent Suicide.* Jefferson, NC: McFarland.

SHAFFER, DAVID, and CRAFT, LESLIE. 1999. "Methods of Adolescent Suicide Prevention." *Journal of Clinical Psychiatry* 60(suppl. 2):70–74.

SHERAS, PETER L. 2001. "Depression and Suicide in Adolescence." In *The Handbook of Clinical Child Psychology,* 3rd edition, ed. Eugene Walker and Michael Roberts. New York: Wiley.

U.S. DEPARTMENT OF HEALTH AND HUMAN SERVICES, NATIONAL CENTER FOR HEALTH STATISTICS. 1998. *Vital Statistics of the United States.* Hyattsville, MD: U.S. Public Health Service.

U.S. PUBLIC HEALTH SERVICE. 1999. *The Surgeon General's Call to Action to Prevent Suicide.* Washington, DC: U.S. Public Health Service.

PETER L. SHERAS

# TEEN PREGNANCY

In the United States, teen pregnancy is an important problem. In 1997, the last year for which accurate estimates are available, about 896,000 young women under the age of twenty became pregnant. Among women aged fifteen to nineteen, 94 per 1,000 (or about 9%) became pregnant. This rate is much higher than that in other Western industrialized countries. In addition, according to a 1997 publication of the National Campaign to Prevent Teen Pregnancy, more than 40 percent of young women in the United States become pregnant one or more times before they reach twenty years of age.

The U.S. pregnancy rate is higher for females aged eighteen and nineteen (142 per 1,000) than for females fifteen to seventeen (64 per 1000). It is also higher for African Americans (170 per 1,000) and Hispanics (149 per 1,000) than for non-Hispanic whites (65 per 1,000). Much of this ethnic variation, however, reflects differences in poverty and opportunity.

On the positive side, the 1997 teen pregnancy rate in the United States was the lowest pregnancy rate since it was first measured in the early 1970s. The rate fluctuated considerably over the course of the 1970s, 1980s, and 1990s, however, reflecting both changing percentages of youth who have sex and improved use of contraception among those having sex.

While the teenage pregnancy rate is, by definition, based upon female teenagers, this does not mean that all the males involved in these pregnancies are teenagers. Indeed, in 1994, whereas 11 percent of fifteen- to nineteen-year-old females became pregnant, only 5 percent of fifteen- to nineteen-year-old males caused a pregnancy.

About four-fifths of teen pregnancies are unintended. Accordingly, in 1997, 15 percent of all teen pregnancies ended in miscarriages, 29 percent ended in legal abortions, and 55 percent ended in births.

Among mothers under the age twenty, the percentage of births that occur out of wedlock has risen dramatically—from 15 percent in 1960 to 79 percent in 2000. This large increase in and high rate of nonmarital childbearing has alarmed many people and motivated many efforts to reduce teenage pregnancy.

## Consequences of Teen Childbearing

According to a 1996 report written by Rebecca A. Maynard, when teenagers, especially younger teenagers, give birth, their future prospects decline on a number of dimensions. Teenage mothers are less likely to complete school, more likely to have large families, and more likely to be single parents. They work as much as women who delay childbearing for several years, but their earnings must provide for a larger number of children.

It is the children of teenage mothers, however, who may bear the greatest brunt of their mothers' young age. In comparison with those born to mothers aged twenty or twenty-one, children born to mothers aged fifteen to seventeen tend to have less supportive and stimulating home environments, poorer health, lower cognitive development, worse educational outcomes, higher rates of behavior problems, and higher rates of adolescent childbearing themselves.

Although the greatest costs are to the families directly involved, adolescent childbearing leads to considerable cost to taxpayers and society more generally. Estimates of these costs are in the billions.

## Adolescent Sexual and Contraceptive Behavior

Obviously, teens become pregnant because they have sex without effectively using contraception. In the United States, the proportion of teens who have ever had sexual intercourse increases steadily with age. In 1995, among girls, the percentage increased from 25 percent among fifteen-year-olds to 77 percent among nineteen-year-olds, while among males it increased from 27 percent among fifteen-year-olds to 85 percent among nineteen-year-olds. Among students in grades nine through twelve across the United States in 1999, 50 percent reported sexual experience.

Most sexually experienced teenagers use contraception at least part of the time. Condoms and oral contraceptives are the two most common methods, but small and increasing percentages of teens use long-lasting contraceptives such as Depo-Provera or Norplant. Like some adults, however, many sexually active teenagers do not use contraceptives consistently and properly, thereby exposing themselves to risks of pregnancy or sexually transmitted diseases (STDs).

### Factors Associated with Sexual Risk-Taking and Pregnancy

While nearly all youth are at risk of engaging in sex and thus girls becoming pregnant, many risk and protective factors distinguish between youth who engage in unprotected sex and sometimes become pregnant and those who do not. For example, when teens have permissive attitudes toward premarital sex, lack confidence to avoid sex or to use contraception consistently, lack adequate knowledge about contraception, have negative attitudes toward contraception, and are ambivalent about pregnancy and childbearing, then they are more likely to engage in sex without contraception.

Other more indirect environmental factors, however, also affect teen sexual risk-taking, either by decreasing motivation to avoid sex or through other mechanisms. For example, teens are more likely to engage in unprotected sex and become pregnant (1) when they live in communities with lower levels of education, employment, and income and thereby have fewer opportunities and encouragement for advanced education and careers; (2) when their parents also have low levels of education and income; (3) when they live with only one or neither biological parent and believe they have little parental support; (4) when they feel disconnected from their parents or are inappropriately supervised or monitored by their parents; (5) when they have friends who obtain poor grades and engage in nonnormative behaviors; and (6) when they believe their peers are having sex and are failing to use contraceptives consistently.

Furthermore, teens are more likely to engage in sex when they, themselves, (1) do poorly in school

and lack plans for higher education; (2) use alcohol and drugs, engage in other problem or risk-taking behaviors, and are depressed; (3) begin dating at an early age, go steady at an early age, have a large number of romantic partners, or have a romantic partner three or more years older (the latter being a particularly telling factor); or (4) were previously sexually abused. These individual and environmental, sexual and nonsexual, risk and protective factors are the factors that programs try to change when they attempt to reduce teen sexual risk-taking and pregnancy.

### Family Planning Services

The efforts most directly involved with preventing pregnancy among sexually experienced teens are family planning services. The primary objectives of family planning clinics or family planning services within other health settings are to provide contraception and other reproductive health services and to provide patients with the knowledge and skills to use their selected methods of contraception.

Large numbers of sexually active female teenagers obtain family planning services each year. Many of these young women receive oral contraceptives and to a lesser extent other contraceptives that are more effective than condoms or other nonprescription contraceptives. Accordingly, these family planning services prevent large numbers of adolescent pregnancies.

In addition to those practicing at family planning clinics, some clinicians in health clinics also focus upon the adolescent's sexual behavior. Several studies have found that these visits can increase contraceptive use when clinicians spend more time focusing upon the teen patients' sexual behavior; give a clear message about always using protection against pregnancy and STDs; show videos or provide pamphlets and other materials; discuss patients' barriers to avoiding sex or using contraception; and model ways to avoid sex or use condoms or contraception.

### Sex and HIV Education Programs

To reduce teen pregnancy and also STDs, including HIV, most schools have implemented sex and HIV education programs. Typically, these programs emphasize that abstinence is the safest method of avoiding pregnancy and STD, but they also encourage condom and contraceptive use if teens do have sex. Contrary to the fears of some people, a large number of studies have demonstrated that these programs do not have negative behavioral effects, such as increasing sexual behavior. To the contrary, many studies have demonstrated that some, but not all of these programs, delay the initiation of sex, decrease the frequency of sex, and increase the use of contraception once youth have sex. They thereby reduce risk of pregnancy, as well as STD. Some sex and HIV education programs have been found to be effective in multiple states in the country, and some have found positive behavioral effects for almost three years.

Programs that are short and that focus upon knowledge increase knowledge, but they tend not to change behavior. In contrast, programs that effectively reduce sexual risk-taking (1) focus on changing specific sexual or contraceptive behaviors; (2) are based on health theories that specify the risk and protective factors to be addressed by the program; (3) give a clear message about avoiding unprotected sex; (4) provide basic, accurate information about the risks of teen sexual activity and about methods of avoiding intercourse or using contraception; (5) address social pressures that influence sexual behavior; (6) provide modeling and practice of communication, negotiation, and refusal skills; (7) employ a variety of teaching methods designed to involve the participants and help them personalize the information; (8) are appropriate to the age, sexual experience, and culture of the participants; (9) last a sufficient length of time to complete important activities adequately; and (10) select teachers or peer leaders who believe in the program they are implementing and then provide them with training.

Many people have proposed abstinence-only programs as a solution to reducing teen pregnancy and STDs. Such programs emphasize that abstinence is the only acceptable method of avoiding pregnancy, and they either fail to discuss contraception or emphasis its limitations. Although some abstinence-only programs might delay sex, there is thus far simply too little research to know which abstinence-only programs are effective.

In an effort to reduce teen pregnancy and STDs, including HIV, hundreds of high schools have made condoms available or have opened school-based health centers that provide reproductive health services. Although studies have demonstrated that these services do not increase teen sexual behavior, they have also found inconsistent results on improved contraceptive use.

## Service-Learning Programs

Whereas the programs summarized above focus primarily on changing the sexual risk factors of adolescent sexual behavior, some programs focus primarily on the *nonsexual* risk and protective factors. In 1997 researchers Joseph P. Allen and associates found the strongest evidence for teen pregnancy reduction for one type of program, service learning.

By definition, service-learning programs include voluntary or unpaid service in the community (e.g., tutoring, working in nursing homes, helping fix up recreation areas) and structured time for preparation and reflection before, during, and after service (e.g., group discussions, journal writing, composing short papers). Often the service is voluntary, but sometimes it is prearranged as part of a class.

Although service learning does have strong evidence for reducing teen pregnancy, other youth development programs have not reduced teen pregnancy or childbearing (e.g., the Conservation and Youth Service Corps, the Job Corps, JOBSTART). Thus, it remains unclear why some programs are effective and others are not.

## Comprehensive and Intensive Programs

A few programs designed to reduce teen pregnancy have been designed for high-risk youth and are both intensive and comprehensive. One of them, the Children's Aid Society Carrera program, is an intensive program operating five days per week and lasting throughout high school. It includes family life and sex education, medical care including reproductive health services, individual academic assessment and tutoring, a job club, employment, arts, and sports. Research demonstrates that it reduced both pregnancy and birthrates over a three-year period.

## Conclusion

Despite declines in the teen pregnancy rate in the United States in the 1990s, teen pregnancy remains an important problem and diminishes the well-being of both teen mothers and their children. Fortunately, by the beginning of the twenty-first century there were a diverse group of programs that were demonstrated to be effective in reducing teen sexual risk-taking or pregnancy. These include reproductive health services and clinic protocols focusing upon patient sexual behavior, sex and HIV education programs, service-learning programs, and intensive and comprehensive programs for higher risk youth. The diversity of these programs increases the choices for communities. To reduce teen pregnancy, communities can replicate much more broadly and with fidelity those programs with the greatest evidence for success with populations similar to their own; replicate more broadly programs incorporating the common qualities of programs effective with populations similar to their own; and design and implement programs that effectively address the important risk and protective factors associated with sexual risk-taking in their communities.

*See also:* GUIDANCE AND COUNSELING, SCHOOL; HEALTH SERVICES; OUT-OF-SCHOOL INFLUENCES AND ACADEMIC SUCCESS; RISK BEHAVIORS, *subentries on* HIV/AIDS, SEXUAL ACTIVITY AMONG TEENS AND TEEN PREGNANCY TRENDS, SEXUALLY TRANSMITTED DISEASES; SEXUALITY EDUCATION.

### BIBLIOGRAPHY

ALAN GUTTMACHER INSTITUTE. 1994. *Sex and America's Teenagers.* New York: Alan Guttmacher Institute.

ALLEN, JOSEPH P.; PHILLIBER, SUSAN; HERRLING, SCOTT; and KUPERMINC, GABRIEL P. 1997. "Preventing Teen Pregnancy and Academic Failure: Experimental Evaluation of a Developmentally-Based Approach." *Child Development* 64:729–742.

BOEKELOO, BRADLEY O.; SCHAMUS, LISA A.; SIMMENS, SAMUEL J.; CHENG, TINA L.; O'CONNOR, KATHLEEN; and D'ANGELO, LAWRENCE J. 1999. "An STD/HIV Prevention Trial among Adolescents in Managed Care." *Pediatrics* 103(1):107–115.

CENTERS FOR DISEASE CONTROL AND PREVENTION. 2000. "CDC Surveillance Summaries." *Morbidity and Mortality Weekly Report* 49(SS-5).

CURTIN, SALLY C., and MARTIN, JOYCE A. 2000. "Births: Preliminary Data for 1999." *National Vital Statistics Reports* 48(14). Hyattsville, MD: National Center for Health Statistics.

DARROCH, JACQUELINE E., and SINGH, SUSHEELA. 1999. *Why Is Teenage Pregnancy Declining? The Roles of Abstinence, Sexual Activity, and Contraceptive Use.* New York: Alan Guttmacher Institute.

HENSHAW, STANLEY K. 1999. *U.S. Teenage Pregnancy Statistics with Comparative Statistics for Women Aged 20–24.* New York: Alan Guttmacher Institute.

KIRBY, DOUGLAS B. 2001. *Emerging Answers: Research Findings on Programs to Reduce Sexual Risk-Taking and Teen Pregnancy.* Washington, DC: National Campaign to Prevent Teen Pregnancy.

KIRBY, DOUGLAS B.; BARTH, RICHARD; LELAND, NANCY; and FETRO, JOYCE. 1991. "Reducing the Risk: A New Curriculum to Prevent Sexual Risk-Taking." *Family Planning Perspectives* 23:253–263.

MAYNARD, REBECCA A. 1996. *Kids Having Kids: A Robin Hood Foundation Special Report on the Costs of Adolescent Childbearing.* New York: Robin Hood Foundation.

MOORE, KRISTIN A.; DRISCOLL, ANNE K.; and LINDBERG, LAURA D. 1998. *A Statistical Portrait of Adolescent Sex, Contraception, and Childbearing.* Washington, DC: National Campaign to Prevent Teen Pregnancy.

NATIONAL CAMPAIGN TO PREVENT TEEN PREGNANCY. 1997. *Whatever Happened to Childhood? The Problem of Teen Pregnancy in the United States.* Washington, DC: National Campaign to Prevent Teen Pregnancy.

ORR, DONALD P.; LANGEFELD, CARL D.; KATZ, BARRY P.; and CAINE, VIRGINIA A. 1996. "Behavioral Intervention to Increase Condom Use among High-Risk Female Adolescents." *Journal of Pediatrics* 128:288–295.

TERRY, ELIZABETH, and MANLOVE, JENNIFER. 2000. *Trends in Sexual Activity and Contraceptive Use among Teens.* Washington, DC: National Campaign to Prevent Teen Pregnancy, 2000.

DOUGLAS B. KIRBY

# RISK MANAGEMENT IN HIGHER EDUCATION

During the late twentieth century, American society and higher education experienced a substantial increase in lawsuits resulting from some form of personal injury, according to John F. Adams and John W. Hall. A response to the trend of litigiousness, risk management seeks to control exposure to legal risk, thus limiting the negative impact of liability on the institution. In 1995 William A. Kaplin and Barbara A. Lee described four of the most common methods of risk management: risk avoidance, risk control, risk transfer, and risk retention. Risk avoidance entails an effort on the institution's part to limit risk by eliminating programs or activities or avoiding creating those that involve risk. A less extreme approach is risk control, which seeks to manage liability by structuring activities and programs in ways that reduce or limit institutional risk. There are several methods of transferring risk to other parties including insurance, indemnification agreements, and releases and waivers. Risk retention describes the self-insurance as a means to prepare for the financial implications of legal liability.

## Tort Liability

One of the primary areas of legal liability that risk management addresses is tort liability, which is generally defined as "a civil wrong, other than a breach of contract, for which the courts will allow a damage remedy" (Kaplin and Lee, p. 98). The area within tort liability with which institutions of higher education must most often deal is negligence. Most of these cases involve lawsuits by students and others who suffered injuries that they claim the institution should have prevented through the exercise of reasonable care. The four elements of negligence are duty, breach of that duty, injury (physical or emotional), and proximate cause.

In addition to duties commonly associated with any business enterprise, colleges and universities, according to some courts and authors, have a special relationship with students that demands a higher level of care. Many of the cases heard in the 1980s and 1990s rejected this claim of a higher duty. For example, in *Beach v. the University of Utah* (1986) the institution was freed from any legal responsibility for the injuries that befell Donna Beach while on a university-sponsored field trip where underage students, including Beach, were served alcohol in the presence of the faculty member supervising the trip. The Utah Supreme Court ruled that no special relationship existed between Beach and the university to prevent her injuries. This decision was not anomalous during this period. In rulings in such cases as *Bradshaw v. Rawlings* (1979), *Baldwin v. Zoradi* (1981), and *Rabel v. Illinois Wesleyan University* (1987), the courts continued to reject the idea that college and universities had any heightened duty for the safety of their students and others on campus.

These cases and a number of others led Robert D. Bickel and Peter F. Lake in 1999 to describe this

period and line of reasoning as the bystander university that "cast the university in the legal and cultural role of helpless 'bystander' to student life and danger" (p. 49). During this time, colleges and universities were often seen as having no duty to their students, and as a result no legal liability for the harm their students may suffer. However, not all courts embraced this no-duty reasoning. For example in *Mullins v. Pine Manor College* (1983) and *Tarasoff v. Board of Regents of the University of California* (1976), the courts clearly articulated heightened duties for colleges and universities to their students and others. In *Mullins* the Massachusetts Supreme Court found Pine Manor College liable for the rape of a student in a residence hall by a third party, noting that a residential college has a general duty to provide for campus security and noting that efforts by the college to provide for campus security (including fences around the campus) represented a voluntary assumption of a duty as well. A series of cases in the 1990s including *Furek v. The University of Delaware* (1991) and *Nero v. Kansas State University* (1993) continued in the view of earlier duty cases as courts ruled that institutions had an obligation in the prevention of foreseeable harm. In cases such as *Tanja H. v. Regents of the University of California* (1991), however, the courts continued to reject any heightened duty owed to students by the institution. In their analysis, Bickel and Lake suggested that cases such as *Furek* and *Nero* should be viewed as beginning a larger body of cases that redefine the duty that institutions owe their students, "Duty is owed if danger is foreseeable from prior indicia or assumption of duty and reasonable precautions could prevent harm" (p. 145). Throughout these cases from the 1970s to the early twenty-first century, several common sources of institution liability can be seen with multiple elements present in many cases such as those involving alcohol, fraternities, and campus crime—particularly sexual assault.

## Other Sources of Risk

Risk management in higher education does not end with the consideration of tort liability and negligence. Public and private institutions must address the issue of potential institutional contract liability in the enforcement of contracts in which its agents enter the institution. Public institutions may also face lawsuits brought under 42 USC 1983 for intentional violations of federal constitutional rights. Additionally, institutions must pay careful attention to compliance with federal legislation and regulations governing higher education, which expand and grow more complicated with each congressional session.

Much of the legislation directly affecting higher education passed in the late 1980s and 1990s must be viewed in the context of the negligence cases involving harm to students. Congress passed legislation related to both alcohol (Drug-Free Schools and Communities Act) and campus crime (Jeanne Clery Disclosure of Campus Security Policy and Campus Crime Statistics Act). In 1998 Congress authorized the use of fines by the Department of Education to enforce the Campus Security Act. Under federal law, another significant concern for institutions is sexual harassment, which is a form of sexual discrimination prohibited under Title IX of the Educational Amendments of 1972. The Supreme Court has allowed students to recover monetary damages for both quid pro quo (*Gebser v. Lago Vista Independent School District*, 1998) and hostile environment sexual harassment (*Davis v. Monroe County Board of Education*, 1999). In order to win monetary damages, the student must show that a school official with authority to take corrective action had actual knowledge of the sexual harassment and responded with deliberate indifference. However, the Department of Education's Office of Civil Rights holds institutions of higher education to even higher standard in administrative enforcement of the legislation.

Risk management is an issue that demands careful attention by all institutions of higher education. In the fall of 2000 the Massachusetts Institute of Technology settled the lawsuit brought by the parents of Scott Krueger, a freshman who died as a result of excessive alcohol consumption at a fraternity, for $6 million. This is a clear indication of the profound financial implications of educational institutions' lack of response to this important issue.

*See also:* DRUG AND ALCOHOL ABUSE, *subentry on* COLLEGE; TITLE IX; SUPREME COURT OF THE UNITED STATES AND EDUCATION.

### BIBLIOGRAPHY

ADAMS, JOHN F., and HALL, JOHN W. 1976. "Legal Liabilities in Higher Education: Their Scope and Management (Sections II–III)." *Journal of College and University Law* 3:337–448.

AIKEN, RAY J. 1976. "Legal Liabilities in Higher Education: Their Scope and Management (Section I)." *Journal of College and University Law* 3:127–334.

NATIONAL ASSOCIATION OF COLLEGE AND UNIVERSITY ATTORNEYS. 1989. *Am I Liable? Faculty, Staff and Institutional Liability in the College and University Setting.* Washington, DC: National Association of College and University Attorneys.

BAZLUKE, FRANCINE T. 1990. *Defamation Issues in Higher Education.* Washington, DC: National Association of College and University Attorneys.

BENNETT, BARBARA. 1990. *Risky Business: Risk Management, Loss Prevention and Insurance Procurement for Colleges and Universities.* Washington, DC: National Association of College and University Attorneys.

BICKEL, ROBERT D., and LAKE, PETER F. 1999. *The Rights and Responsibilities of the Modern University: Who Assumes the Risks of College Life?* Durham, NC: Carolina Academic Press.

HIGGINS, BYRON H., and ZULKEY, EDWARD J. 1990. "Liability Insurance Coverage: How to Avoid Unpleasant Surprises." *Journal of College and University Law* 17:123–147.

KAPLIN WILLIAM A., and LEE, BARBARA A. 1995. *The Law of Higher Education: A Comprehensive Guide to Legal Implications of Administrative Decision Making,* 3rd edition. San Francisco: Jossey-Bass.

JOHN W. LOWERY

## ROGERS, CARL (1902–1987)

American psychologist and therapist, Carl R. Rogers relied on personal experience as well as scientific inquiry to guide his methodology, much of which foreshadowed late-twentieth-century practice of psychotherapy.

Rogers was born in Oak Park, Illinois, to a prosperous and quite religiously conservative Protestant upper-middle-class family. He was a precocious child, reading bible stories before he entered school, achieving an A grade average through high school, and testing near the top of every intellectual aptitude test he took. As an adolescent some of his interests in science and agriculture were crystallized in working on his father's farm and reading a major book on scientific farming. A five-month YMCA trip to China while still a twenty-year-old college student confirmed his religious interests, but also gave him a chance to begin to formulate his own personal philosophy independent of his parents. During the following year, he remembered in 1967, he spoke of the trip as "the greatest experience of my life." After college (University of Wisconsin), he attended the liberal Union Theological Seminary, but he completed his Ph.D. at Teachers College, Columbia University, in 1931.

Intellectually Rogers was liberal, idealistic, and optimistic. In a very critical biography David Cohen, drawing on unpublished notes, letters, and essays in the 140 boxes of the Rogers archives in the Library of Congress, painted a different picture of Rogers: a troubled man, often in conflict with his parents, siblings, wife, children and their spouses, and a number of colleagues. Rogers, in more temperate terms, made public only an inkling of his problems, in some brief comments in his chapter in the *History of Psychology in Autobiography* by David Boring and Gardner Lindzey. In contrast, Howard Kirschenbaum in a biography based on many interviews with Rogers and others presents what he, Kirschenbaum, views as "a balanced picture of the man" (p. xvi).

**Counseling and Clinical Practice**

Rogers's concern for making clinical work in psychology scientific appeared early in his dissertation "Measuring Personality Adjustment in Children Nine to Thirteen Years of Age" (1931). He developed a paper and pencil objective test with six kinds of item formats, which were derived heavily from clinical interview questions and four subscales of adjustment, and summarized into an overall score. The test was empirically developed, cross-validated, and had norms based on elementary school children from New York City. One group of items required the children to rate perceived self versus ideal self, a conception that would be increasingly a part of Rogers's long-term view of personality.

The dozen years he spent doing clinical work and directing what became the Rochester Guidance Center resulted in the *Clinical Treatment of the Problem Child* (1939). He dealt with testing, interviewing, camps, foster homes, families, and schools, and the beginning of "relationship therapy," with an acknowledgment of the work of Otto Rank, Jessie Taft, and Frederick Allen. The comprehensiveness of the

book along with Rogers's developing point of view presages an intellectual and writing style in his later efforts.

He became a candidate for, and accepted, a full professorship at the Ohio State University, teaching courses in mental hygiene and counseling practices and guiding Ph.D. students in their dissertations. There he wrote what is arguably his most important and provocative book, *Counseling and Psychotherapy* (1942). Significantly it carried the subtitle, 'Newer concepts in practice,' which accented the shift from diagnosis to therapy that was occurring in several of the helping disciplines. The audience was broadly construed: psychologists, college counselors, marital advisers, psychiatrists, social workers, and high school guidance counselors. Methodologically, his intent was to present his extensive personal experience in the practical work of counseling in a number of settings over the 1930s and 1940s—increasingly important, personal experience as well as scientific research became a major baseline for his ideas and practices.

More recent theorists and methodologists might have labeled his efforts "action research," "a discovering/generating grounded theory," and "reconstruals." The seeds of nondirective and client-centered counseling are readily apparent, as are the beginnings of basic conceptions of fully functioning, authenticity/congruence, unconditional positive regard and acceptance, and empathy. Transcripts of phonographic recordings of counseling interviews document every idea in the text. The back-and-forth dialogue between the data and the conjectures is stimulating. The apex of the recording thrust appears in part four, "the case of Herbert Bryan." All eight counseling interviews were recorded, a full 178 pages. The verbatim transcripts carry interpolated reactions, thoughts, hunches, criticisms, and suggestions, and the reader is able to follow along and make his or her own interpretations.

Less than a decade later, Rogers edited *Client-Centered Therapy: Its Current Practice, Implications, and Theory* (1951), and was teaching at the University of Chicago. The preface acknowledges the large group of counselors at the Chicago Counseling Center whose thought and effort had contributed to his thinking. The preface, in emotional and near spiritual terms, thanks the clients from whose struggles and concerns he and his colleagues have learned. Mostly though, the book is a treatise on Rogers's evolving point of view, almost an intellectual autobiography.

Beyond the continuity and the elaboration of issues in nondirective counseling or client-centered therapy, several other aspects stand out: discussions of group-centered therapy and leadership, a move toward student-centered teaching, and a theory of personality and behavior. The chapter on theory of personality and behavior formalized much of Rogers's contribution to what came to be called "third force psychology," a complex set of alternatives to behaviorism and psychoanalysis. He commented: "Like Maslow, the writer would confess that in the early portion of his professional life he held a theoretical view opposed at almost every point to the view he has gradually come to adopt as a result of clinical experience and clinically oriented research" (Rogers 1951, p. 482).

## The Move beyond Individual Counseling

One of Rogers's most significant contributions involved his concern for the education of children and adolescents, as well as adults. *Freedom to Learn: A View of What Education Might Become* (1969), represents an attack on traditional formal schooling. In one chapter, Rogers based the work on a diary kept by a teacher about her efforts to refocus her sixth-grade class toward better learning. Interpreting her actions, Rogers recounted the realities of a class experiencing apathy, discipline problems, and parental concerns, and the teacher who, after reading an account of student-centered teaching—"an unstructured or non-directive approach"—worked to build a more exciting and stimulating classroom. The diary is supplemented with responses written to questions raised by Rogers.In another chapter Rogers extended his ideas to the college level, using a college professor's descriptive account and adding his own interpretations. Then he wrote of his personal experience in teaching a course, "Values in Human Behavior Including Sensitivity Training," at the Western Behavioral Sciences Institute. One of the most fascinating chapters in the book is a four and a half page statement, "Personal thoughts on teaching and learning," which was a very radical document that received major criticism. Rogers began, "I find it very troubling to think, particularly when I think about my own experiences and try to extract from those experiences the meaning that seems genuinely inherent in them." He then stated thirteen propositions/hypotheses with five consequences. His first proposition is "My experience has been that I cannot teach another person how to teach." His fourth is "I have come to feel that the only learning which significantly influences behavior is self-discovered, self-appropriated learning." After a baker's dozen of these, the consequences include doing away with teaching, examinations, and grades.

In 1970, he joined the faculty of the Western Behavioral Sciences Institute and later the Center for the Study of the Person, writing another major book *Carl Rogers on Encounter Groups* (1970). He and the times had shifted dramatically. The book continues his personal and autobiographical style, this time his experiences with the nature, process, and impact of groups on the lives of individuals. Quickly he grounds the reader in prior key figures (e.g., Kurt Lewin), in prior labels (e.g., T-groups), sensitivity training, and encounter groups. Notes, letters, stories, and individual accounts illustrate processes, changes, and personal experiences. He then turns autobiographical, "Can I be a facilitative person in a group?," to ward off a brief general statement that "would have to be so homogenized that every truth in it would also be so some extent a falsehood" and also to minimize "the flavor of expertise in it, that I did not want to emphasize" (p. 43). Then, too, the more traditional scientist in him leads to a chapter "What we know from research." The book has a persuasive rhetorical quality in the mix of vivid data, startling personal experiences from leaders and participants, and broad useful practical ideas and suggestions.

## An International Dialogue

Rogers was at the forefront of psychology, engaging in discussions with international scholars. He discussed individual psychotherapy as an approach to the "I-Thou" relationship with the eminent Jewish intellectual Martin Buber in 1957, asking him "How have you lived so deeply in interpersonal relationships and gained such an understanding of the human individual without being a psychotherapist? (Buber laughs)" (Kirschenbaum and Henderson, p. 45). A long elaborate answer followed and the dialogue continued. A discussion with the theologian Paul Tillich moved into a major give-and-take on the nature—multiple natures—of man. With the behaviorist psychologist B. F. Skinner, the issue of freedom and control in human life became central. Others would argue that the soul of psychology was in debate. Discussions with Gregory Bateson, Michael Polanyi, and Reinhold Niebuhr enlarged the scope of the discussions. With Rollo May, the role of evil and the daimonic and demonic came to the fore and cut to the heart of Rogers's central tenets of the goodness of man versus man having the potentiality for goodness and evil. In short, one finds Rogers, a brilliant psychologist and therapist, in contention with some of the most important minds of the twentieth century, over issues that have puzzled human beings for centuries—millennia, really.

*See also:* EDUCATIONAL PSYCHOLOGY; GUIDANCE AND COUNSELING, SCHOOL; PERSONAL AND PSYCHOLOGICAL COUNSELING AT COLLEGES AND UNIVERSITIES.

## BIBLIOGRAPHY

COHEN, DAVID. 1997. *Carl Rogers: A Critical Biography.* London: Constable.

KIRSCHENBAUM, HOWARD. 1979. *On Becoming Carl Rogers.* New York: Delacorte.

KIRSCHENBAUM, HOWARD, and HENDERSON, VALERIE LAND, eds. 1989. *Carl Rogers: Dialogues.* Boston: Houghton Mifflin.

ROGERS, CARL R. 1931. *Measuring Personality Adjustment in Children Nine to Thirteen Years of Age.* New York: Bureau of Publications, Teachers College, Columbia University.

ROGERS, CARL R. 1939. *The Clinical Treatment of the Problem Child.* Boston: Houghton Mifflin.

ROGERS, CARL R. 1942. *Counseling and Psychotherapy.* Boston: Houghton Mifflin.

ROGERS, CARL R. 1951. *Client-Centered Therapy.* Boston: Houghton Mifflin.

ROGERS, CARL R. 1967. "Autobiography." In *A History of Psychology in Autobiography,* Vol. 5, ed. Edwin Boring and Gardner Lindzey. New York: Appleton, Century, Crofts.

ROGERS, CARL R. 1969. *Freedom to Learn: A View of What Education Might Become.* Columbus, OH: Merrill.

ROGERS, CARL R. 1970. *Carl Rogers on Encounter Groups.* New York: Harper and Row.

LOUIS M. SMITH

# ROUSSEAU, JEAN-JACQUES (1712–1778)

A political and moral philosopher during the Enlightenment, Jean-Jacques Rousseau developed provocative ideas about human nature, education, and the desired relationship between individuals and the ideal society.

Born in the city of Geneva, Switzerland, Jean-Jacques Rousseau lost his mother hours after his birth and was abandoned by his father at the age of seven. After many years of failed apprenticeships and employments, Rousseau rose to intellectual prominence in 1750 upon winning first prize in an essay contest in France. This marked the beginning of a long period of scholarly production in which he authored a number of philosophical treatises that addressed the problem of individual and collective freedom—and how education might help to resolve the dilemma by producing enlightened citizens who would uphold an ideal state. Forced to flee France and Switzerland as a result of the social criticisms inherent in his work, Rousseau found temporary refuge in England and then surreptitiously returned to France where he remained until his death.

## Social Inequalities

Rousseau's discontent with contemporary society became evident in his *Discourse on the Arts and Sciences* (1750). Addressing the question of whether progress in the arts and sciences had abetted or detracted from morals, Rousseau portrayed civilization as evil, and he chastised scholars for pursuing knowledge for fame instead of social progress. Similarly, in his *Discourse on Inequality* and his article on political economy written for Denis Diderot's *Encyclopédie* (both published in 1755), Rousseau lamented man's departure from the state of nature and his consequent preoccupation with artificial social customs and institutions—all derived from vain and illusory desires to dominate others. Although he accepted individual or innate differences among human beings, Rousseau attacked the existence of social and civil inequalities in which people crushed the spirits of others in attempting to control them.

In the wake of these social criticisms, Rousseau sketched his vision for an ideal society. Particularly in *The Social Contract* and *Émile,* both published in 1762, Rousseau delineated a society without artificial social constraints or civil inequality. Ruled by a "general will" that encapsulated the essential commonality of all men, citizens would utilize reason to reconcile their individual interests with the laws of the state. Educated to be self-interested and self-reliant, a citizen would not measure himself against other people nor seek to control them. He would eschew selfish inclinations in favor of social equality. How, then, could such an ideal state emerge? For Rousseau, it required the complete education of a child.

### Émile

Echoing his disdain for contemporary culture and politics in *The Social Contract,* Rousseau begins *Émile* by declaring: "God makes all things good; man meddles with them and they become evil." Society held man hostage in artificial institutions and traditions, thereby corrupting the natural goodness of human nature. This proclamation contradicted the notion of original sin, widely accepted in eighteenth-century Europe. It implied that a complete social revolution—not mere pedagogical reform—was necessary to replace the artificial social mores of the bourgeoisie with a new class of natural, self-reliant citizens. In accordance with John Locke's empirical epistemology, moreover, Rousseau believed that children were born ignorant, dependent, impressionable, without rational thought, and gained all knowledge through direct contact with the physical world.

As a result, Rousseau removed his fictional pupil, Émile, from his family and placed him in rural isolation. The first three stages of a child's development (infancy, boyhood, and pre-adolescence) required a kind of "negative" education. Protected from the artificial and pernicious influences of contemporary society, Émile would not develop unrealistic ambitions and feelings of jealousy or superiority with regard to other men (*amour propre*). In such a way, the tutor would encourage the child's physical development, shield him from social and religious institutions, prevent the formation of bad habits and prejudices, and preserve his natural inclination of self-interest (*amour de soi*).

Educated free from the manipulations and desires of others up to this point, Rousseau wanted Émile to remain ignorant of social duty and only to understand what was possible or impossible in the physical world. In such a way, his student would learn to obey the immutable laws of nature. For instance, if Émile were to break the window to his room, he would face the consequences of sleeping with a cold draft. If Émile were to ignore his astronomy lesson, he would endure the panic of losing his way in the woods at night. Through this kind of trial and error, the child would gradually develop reason, adapt to different situations, and become an autonomous man.

The only appropriate book for Rousseau's future citizen was *Robinson Crusoe,* as it depicted the independent activities of a man isolated in a natural setting. And to abet Émile's self-reliance, Rousseau exposed his student to a variety of artisan trades. Thus, the child would not crave things he could not get, nor would he engage in a vain desire to control other people. An independent and rational young man, Émile learned to accept what was available to him. It is important to note, however, that although the tutor was always behind the scenes, he constantly manipulated conditions to give Émile the illusion of freedom.

Having developed the power to reason by the age of fifteen, the child then needed to develop his morality by understanding society and God. Through the safe and detached medium of historical study, Rousseau wanted his pupil to construct his understanding of human character. Detailed historical accounts of men's spoken words and actions would allow Émile to recognize the universality of natural human passion. As a self-confident and rational adolescent, he would neither envy nor disdain those in the past, but would feel compassion towards them.

This was also the time to cultivate Émile's religious faith. Rousseau did not want his pupil to become an anthropomorphic atheist. Nor did he want his pupil to fall under the authority of a specific religious denomination, with its formal rituals and doctrines. Such trappings smacked of the very artificial social institutions from which Émile was to be freed. Instead, Émile was to recognize the limitations of his senses and to have faith that God—the supreme intelligent will that created the universe and put it into motion—must in fact exist. In this respect, Rousseau deviated from the Enlightenment faith in man's reason as the sole vehicle for understanding God. Rousseau also alienated himself from formal religious institutions in demeaning their authority and asserting the original goodness of human nature. The corrupt codes and institutions of society had tarnished the purity of human nature, fueled a quest to rule over others, and made man a tyrant over nature and himself. The only salvation, however, rested not with God but society itself. A better society, with civil equality and social harmony, would restore human nature to its original and natural state and thereby serve the intent of God. In this way, Rousseau's brand of religious education attempted to teach the child that social reform was both necessary and consistent with God's will.

In Rousseau's final stage of education, his pupil needed to travel throughout the capitals of Europe to learn directly how different societies functioned. Émile also needed to find an appropriate mate, Sophie, who would support him emotionally and raise his children. Assuming that women possessed affectionate natures and inferior intellectual capacities, Rousseau relegated Sophie to the role of wife and mother. In direct contrast to Émile's isolated upbringing for developing his reason and preparing him as a citizen, Sophie's education immersed her in social and religious circles from the outset, thereby ensuring that she would not become a citizen. Despite this inequality, Rousseau believed that Émile and Sophie would comprise a harmonious and moral unit in the ideal state and produce future generations who would uphold it.

## Gender Considerations

Some scholars have explored the implications of Rousseau's gender-distinct education and have suggested that Émile's societal isolation rendered him inadequate as a husband and citizen. Raised in social isolation and without family, Émile developed the capacity to think rationally, but at the expense of affectionate and empathetic feelings necessary to sustain a relationship with his future wife or with the ideal state. As delineated in *The Social Contract*, Rousseau's ideal state required not merely rational thinkers, but citizens who empathized with one another and the state. Thus, according to this view, Rousseau's gender-distinct assumptions produced an inadequate education for Sophie (whose reason had not developed) and Émile (emotionally cold and prey to his wife's manipulations). The family, fragmented and incomplete, could not sustain the ideal state.

A number of scholars have doubted whether Émile's isolation in the countryside could necessarily be free of social forces and whether the tutor could exemplify abstract principles without alluding to examples from conventional society. On the other hand, generations since Rousseau have altered their child-rearing practices and adopted his developmental view of childhood as a period of innocence. Some have accused Rousseau, in his manipulation of Émile and stress on the general will, of advocating a proto-totalitarian state. On the other hand, many scholars

have identified Rousseau's faith in the agency of individuals to make rational and enlightened decisions both for themselves and their society as a precursor to democracy. Indeed, this lack of consensus about Rousseau's legacy speaks less to his inadequacies than to his profound contributions to the fundamental, enduring, and controversial questions about human nature, self, society, and education.

*See also:* PHILOSOPHY OF EDUCATION.

### BIBLIOGRAPHY

BLOOM, ALLAN. 1978. "The Education of Democratic Man: *Émile.*" *Daedalus* 107:135–153.

BOYD, WILLIAM. 1963. *The Educational Theory of Jean Jacques Rousseau.* New York: Russell and Russell.

CASSIRER, ERNST. 1954. *The Question of Jean-Jacques Rousseau,* trans. and ed. Peter Gay. New York: Columbia University Press.

MARTIN, JANE ROLAND. 1985. *Reclaiming a Conversation: The Ideal of the Educated Woman.* New Haven, CT: Yale University Press.

OWEN, DAVID B. 1982. "History and the Curriculum in Rousseau's *Émile.*" *Educational Theory* 32:117–129.

ROUSSEAU, JEAN-JACQUES. 1964. *The First and Second Discourses* (1750, 1755), ed. Roger D. Masters and trans. Roger D. Masters and Judith R. Masters. New York: St. Martins.

ROUSSEAU, JEAN-JACQUES. 1993. *Émile* (1762), trans. Barbara Foxley. London: Dent.

ROUSSEAU, JEAN-JACQUES. 1988. THE SOCIAL CONTRACT (1762), trans. George Douglas Howard Cole. Buffalo, NY: Prometheus.

SEVAN G. TERZIAN

# RUGG, HAROLD (1886–1960)

Harold Rugg, a longtime professor of education at Teachers College, Columbia University, was one of the best-known educators during the era of Progressive education in the United States. He produced the first-ever series of school textbooks from 1929 until the early 1940s.

Rugg was born in Fitchburg, Massachusetts, the son of a carpenter. His early poverty seemed to preclude his attending college. Nevertheless, he was able to matriculate at Dartmouth College, graduating in 1908 with a bachelor's degree in civil engineering and earning a graduate civil engineering degree from Dartmouth's Thayer School of Civil Engineering in 1909. Rugg worked briefly as a civil engineer, then taught civil engineering at Milliken University in Decatur, Illinois, where he grew interested in how students learn. This interest inspired him to gain a doctorate in education at the University of Illinois in 1915, and he began a college teaching career at the University of Chicago, where he taught until 1920. He then went to Teachers College at Columbia University, where he taught until his retirement in 1951. After his retirement he continued publishing books in education and also served as an educational consultant in Egypt and Puerto Rico.

The field of education was still in its formative stages when Rugg began his career, and he proceeded to have a major impact in a number of areas. Although Rugg was trained as an engineer and educational psychologist, his major initial impact was in the field of curriculum. Rugg applied his training to reassessing how curriculum was created. His editing of and writing in both the twenty-second and twenty-sixth yearbooks of the National Society for the Study of Education provided groundbreaking syntheses of the fields of social studies and general curriculum, respectively.

Rugg was a cofounder of the National Council for the Social Studies and edited yearbooks for a number of respected educational organizations. Rugg, however, did not get very involved in the duties and tasks of such organizations, instead concentrating on his own research and writing projects.

In 1922 Rugg assembled a team to create his Social Science Pamphlets, a series of booklets that comprised the social studies materials for junior high school (grades six to eight). These materials were adapted and published by Ginn and Company starting in 1929. Over the course of the next fifteen years Rugg and Ginn and Company would sell over 5 million textbooks, and the pattern of creating textbook series became a model in publishing still used in the early twenty-first century. With Louise Krueger, Rugg also developed an elementary education (grades one through eight) social studies textbook series in 1939. Unfortunately, Rugg's junior high textbooks were the subject of censorship efforts headed by the National Association of Manufacturers and the American Legion. In this controversy,

these groups accused Rugg of anti-Americanism, socialist or communist leanings, as well as anticapitalism. He was not the only target of such accusations, with other Progressive educators also being so accused. Rugg, however, gained more notoriety because of the enormous popularity of his textbooks. In the 1940s the texts ceased to be published.

In 1928 Rugg cowrote his first major work, *The Child-Centered School,* which described the historical and contemporary basis for "child-centered" education. This work had a major impact on Progressive educators and remains an excellent explanation and critique of this topic. It also was one of the first treatises on the two major emphases within Progressive education—child centeredness and social reconstruction.

As Rugg's career progressed he became as much a critic and discussant of contemporary American culture as an educator. He was an outspoken Social Reconstructionist and a strong advocate of the reform programs of President Franklin Roosevelt. Indeed Rugg was outspoken in much that he did. He was a large man with a commanding presence. People had strong feelings about him, both negative and positive. Despite criticism, he was not easily intimidated and remained confident and hard driving in his work.

Rugg directed his attention primarily toward teacher education and foundations of education in the last years before his retirement. His books in these areas were well respected and received but did not have the lasting impact of his curriculum work. At his death Rugg was attempting to understand and explain creative thought, and his last book, *Imagination,* focused on this area and was published posthumously, not fully completed.

***See also:*** CURRICULUM, SCHOOL; EDUCATION REFORM; ELEMENTARY EDUCATION, *subentry on* HISTORY OF; PHILOSOPHY OF EDUCATION; PROGRESSIVE EDUCATION; SOCIAL STUDIES EDUCATION.

## BIBLIOGRAPHY

CARBONE, PETER. 1977. *The Social and Educational Thought of Harold Rugg.* Durham, NC: Duke University Press.

JOHNSON, F. ERNEST. 1960. "Harold O. Rugg, 1886–1960." *Educational Theory* 10:176–181.

NELSON, MURRY R. 1977. "The Development of the Rugg Social Studies Program." *Theory and Research in Social Education* 5(3):64–83.

NELSON, MURRY R. 1978. "Rugg on Rugg: The Curricular Ideas of Harold Rugg." *Curriculum Inquiry* 8:119–132.

RUGG, HAROLD, ed. 1927. *The Foundations of Curriculum-Making: Twenty-Sixth Yearbook of the National Society for the Study of Education.* Bloomington, IL: Public School Publishing.

RUGG, HAROLD. 1929–1936. *Man and His Changing Society,* 6 vols. Boston: Ginn and Company.

RUGG, HAROLD. 1941. *That Men May Understand.* New York: Doubleday, Doran

RUGG, HAROLD, and SHUMAKER, ANN. 1928. *The Child-Centered School: An Appraisal of the New Education.* Yonkers-on-Hudson, NY: World Book.

MURRY NELSON

# RURAL EDUCATION

## OVERVIEW

Rural education reflects the circumstances, challenges, and context of places in America called "rural." Rural America has been and continues to be a vital part of the nation. As of 2001, rural America comprised 2,288 counties, contained 83 percent of the nation's land and was home to 21 percent of its population (51 million people). The United States, like the rest of the world, is steadily becoming more urban. Two national censuses illustrate the point dramatically. For the first 140 years of the nation's existence, most Americans lived in open country and small towns. The 1920 census was the first to record that urban people outnumbered those living in open country and small towns. Just seventy years later, the 1990 census recorded not only that most Americans lived in urban areas but also that they lived in metropolitan areas of 1 million or more people.

### The Changing Nature of Rural America

Rural America has changed in many ways. The rural economy in particular has changed—shifting from a dependence on farming, forestry, and mining to a striking diversity of economic activity. Improvements in communication and transportation between urban and rural areas have reduced rural isolation and removed many of the cultural differences between the two areas. Television, phone service, and transportation systems have helped bring rural and urban dwellers much closer together in terms of culture, information, and lifestyles. And while it continues to provide most of the nation's food and fiber, rural America has taken on additional roles, providing labor for industry, land for urban and suburban expansion, sites for hazardous activities and the storage of waste, and natural settings for recreation and enjoyment.

No one industry dominates the rural economy, no single pattern of population decline or growth exists for all rural areas, and no statement about improvements and gaps in well-being holds true for all rural people. Many of these differences are regional in nature. That is, rural areas within a particular geographic region of the country often tend to be similar to each other and different from areas in another region. Some industries, for example, are associated with different regions: logging and sawmills in the Pacific Northwest and New England, manufacturing in the Southeast and Midwest, and farming in the Great Plains. Persistent poverty also has a regional pattern, concentrated primarily in the Southeast. Areas that rely heavily on the services industry are located throughout rural America, as are rural areas that have little access to advanced telecommunications services. Many of these differences—regional and nonregional—are the result of a combination of factors including the availability of natural resources; distance from and access to major metropolitan areas and the information and services found there; transportation and shipping facilities; political history and structure; and the racial, ethnic, and cultural makeup of the population. As a result, rural areas differ in terms of their needs and the resources they possess to address those needs.

Understanding rural America is no easy task. It is tempting to generalize and oversimplify, to characterize rural areas as they once were or as they are now in only some places. Still, there is an overall pattern of economic disadvantage in rural areas. The historical and defining features of rural economies often constrain development. Regardless of other differences, efforts to assist rural areas must take into account three common rural characteristics: (1) rural settlement patterns tend to be small in scale and low in density; (2) the natural resource-based industries on which many rural areas have traditionally depended are declining as generators of jobs and income; and (3) low-skill, low-wage rural labor faces increasingly fierce global competition.

Connecting rural America to the digital economy and raising the skills of workers and leaders found there will be essential for rural America to compete more effectively. A third of all rural counties captured three-fourths of all rural economic gains in the 1990s. This concentration of economic activity is the result of powerful shifts in demographics, technology, and business practices. And while rural America has often based its development on relatively low labor costs, future opportunity will be based more on skilled workers and capital investments. Many rural schools need to raise their standards and become fully integrated into telecommunication networks.

Some observers point to technology as the driving force of the rural economy in the twenty-first century. Others believe a significant portion of today's rural America will be "metropolitanized" in the years ahead, continuing the trend in which the fastest growing portion of the U.S. economy from the 1970s into the twenty-first century was the part that was "formerly rural." That is, rural areas adjacent to the nation's metro areas, or ones growing fast enough to become a metro area in their own right, probably have very bright economic futures.

Rural areas suffer from the out-migration of both young and highly skilled workers, leaving an aging population and strained public services (including public education). Most areas have difficulty providing the capital and infrastructure to encourage and sustain new rural entrepreneurs. As a result, many rural areas are searching for local features that can spur new growth, such as scenic amenities, environmental virtues, or unique products that reflect the cultural heritage of a particular region. Expanding agricultural opportunities will be important, through value-added processing and new specialized crops. Better educated residents and improved rural economic networks are essential to the development of new rural businesses.

## Defining Rural Schooling

No single definition exists to define rural America and rural schools. All that is not metropolitan is often said to be rural. As noted earlier, one should remember that rural America is quite diverse from one part of the country to another. Issues and trends in rural education may be place (region) specific for any number of factors. Generalizations about education in one rural area of the United States may or may not be true for another. Nevertheless, generalizations can provide a foundation of information for examining issues and trends in a regional and local area.

The *Common Core of Data* (CCD), maintained by the National Center for Education Statistics, uses information on two locale classification schemes to identify every school and district in the nation. The first locale scheme consists of seven types of locale codes created in the late 1980s, ranging from a large city to rural. The categories of *rural* and *small town* are often used to describe the rural segment of American schooling. In 1997–1998, nearly 64 percent of all school districts were classified as rural or small-town districts. The second locale classification scheme in the CCD is *metropolitan location,* divided into three categories: a central city of a metropolitan area, metropolitan but not central city, and nonmetropolitan. About 53 percent of all districts were located in nonmetropolitan areas. Interestingly, in these two schemes, rural and small-town schools were found in both metropolitan and nonmetropolitan areas. Of the 9,249 districts identified as rural and small town, 1,693 were located in metropolitan areas. Lastly, fewer than 1,000 kindergarten through grade twelve unit schools remained in the United States, that is, schools with all grades—kindergarten through twelve—located in the same building.

In 1998 the National Education Association used data primarily from studies conducted by federal agencies to describe public education in rural areas and small towns compared to central city schools and urban fringe schools. A few of the findings were as follows:

- Approximately one-half of the nation's 80,000 public schools and approximately 40 percent of the 41.6 million public school students were located in rural areas and small towns. Rural schools were smaller, less likely to have minority students, and less likely to provide bilingual education, English as a second language, magnet schools, and job placement programs. But rural schools were more likely to offer remedial programs and Title I programs that serve high poverty populations.

• Of the approximately 2.56 million public school teachers, approximately 40 percent were in rural and small town schools. Compared to teachers in central city schools and urban fringe schools, rural teachers tended to be less well educated, slightly less experienced, younger, and less likely to belong to a minority group. Rural school principals were more likely to be male and less likely to belong to a minority group compared to principals in central city schools and urban fringe schools.

• Teachers in rural and small town schools spent more time with students at school and outside school hours, had smaller incomes, and were less likely to have benefits of medical insurance, dental insurance, group life insurance, and pension contributions.

• Teachers in rural and small town schools perceived student use of alcohol to be a more serious problem and were less likely to perceive a serious problem in student absenteeism, tardiness, verbal abuse of teachers, and student disrespect for teachers. Teachers in rural schools were less likely than teachers in central city schools, but more likely than teachers in urban fringe schools to perceive poverty as a serious problem in their schools.

In his 1982 book *Rural Education: In Search of a Better Way,* Paul Nachtigal contended that the important factors that differentiate a rural community in one part of the country from a community of similar size and isolation in another part of the country appear to be related to the availability of economic resources, cultural priorities of the local community, commonality of purpose, and political efficacy. Nachtigal described some basic differences between rural and urban areas, which are listed in Table 1.

Perceptions of all rural schools as inferior schools are incorrect. States with a predominance of small, community-centered schools do rather well. For example, on achieving the National Education Goals, in 1998, eight of the top ten states on math and science performance, six of the top seven on student achievement in the core subjects, and all top five on parent involvement were rural states. In fact, many of education's so-called best practices were born out of necessity long ago in the rural school. Examples include cooperative learning, multigrade classrooms, intimate links between school and community, interdisciplinary studies, peer tutoring,

**TABLE 1**

### Basic differences between rural and urban areas

| Rural | Urban |
|---|---|
| Personal/tightly linked | Impersonal/loosely coupled |
| Generalists | Specialists |
| Homogeneous | Heterogeneous |
| Nonbureaucratic | Bureaucratic |
| Verbal communication | Written memos |
| Who said it | What is said |
| Time measured by seasons of year | Time measured by clock |
| Traditional values | Liberal values |
| Entrepreneur | Corporate labor force |
| Make do/respond to environment | Rational planning to control environment |
| Self-sufficiency | Leave problem solving to experts |
| Poorer (in spendable income) | Richer (in spendable income) |
| Less formal education | More formal education |
| Smaller/less density | Larger/greater density |

SOURCE: Based on Nachtigal, Paul. 1982. *Rural Education: In Search of a Better Way.* Boulder, CO: Westview Press.

block scheduling, the community as the focus of study, older students teaching younger ones, site-based management, and close relationships between teachers and students.

## Challenges and Issues

Many of the challenges and issues that confront rural schools are not new, and in large measure they are linked to regional and local circumstances of change and reality in rural areas.

**Adequate funding.** Rural school districts, with their modest fiscal bases, usually cannot generate sufficient local resources to supplement adequately the state school finance programs the way that more affluent localities can. In at least sixteen states, supreme courts have ruled that their state system of school funding is unconstitutional and have ordered that new systems be developed. While equity and efficiency arguments have been prevalent in most of these cases, these court challenges also highlight the need to provide a level of funding for providing adequate educational opportunities if students are expected to meet state-mandated standards of performance.

**Setting standards.** Americans want schools where students must meet some standard of achievement. But who sets the standard is a critical issue being debated in rural schools and their communities. Local versus state (or federal) control of public schools is at the center of the controversy of setting standards. Rural schools and community advocates, such as the

Rural School and Community Trust, believe that standards should originate within the community in which the students live. Others argue that the state should set standards because local schools in some rural areas traditionally have low expectations for student achievement and because taxpayers in some rural areas have low interest in funding high standards for all students. Rural interests also argue that rural communities cannot afford to fund the requirements for state-mandated standards and that school consolidation—in the name of fiscal efficiency—is the likely result. Some policymakers also believe federal and state interests in having an educated citizenry for competing in a global economy compels standards be set at the state level, with local schools having flexibility to decide how to teach the content rather than what to teach.

**School size.** The majority of schools in rural settings are small, enrolling fewer than 400 students. Only 2 percent have enrollments exceeding 1,200 students. Research reveals that a high school with an enrollment of 400 is able to offer a reasonably comprehensive curriculum and that high schools ought not to enroll more than 600 to 1,000 students. Schools with high populations of students from low-income families do best academically in small schools. Public concerns regarding school safety issues also reinforce the need for small schools, where teachers know students well and students have a feeling of belonging in the school and community.

**School facilities.** While rural schools may be located in some of America's most beautiful areas, in 1996 about 4.6 million rural students were attending schools in inadequate buildings. Three out of ten rural and small-town schools have at least one inadequate building. One in two schools have at least one inadequate building feature, such as a roof, a foundation, or plumbing. Approximately one-half have unsatisfactory environmental conditions in the buildings. Approximately 37 percent have inadequate science laboratory facilities, 40 percent have inadequate space for large-group instruction, and 13 percent report an inadequate library/media center.

Technology needs also force building modifications. Many older schools lack conduits for computer-related cables, electrical wiring for computers and other communications technology, or adequate electrical outlets. Without the necessary infrastructure, schools cannot use technology to help overcome historical barriers associated with ruralness and isolation. In 1990 rural schools expressed a need for an estimated $2.6 billion for funding maintenance on existing buildings and almost $18 billion to replace obsolete rural schools.

**Diversity and poverty.** Addressing issues of education in rural areas includes confronting the realities of people in poverty and the growing diversity of rural America. Geographic diversity best defines the issue of diversity in rural America. Using 1990 census data, 333 of the 2,288 rural counties have a minority group that makes up one-third of the population. These counties contain only 12 percent of the total rural population. They are geographically clustered, however, according to the residents' race or ethnic group. Rural minorities often live in geographically isolated communities where poverty is high, opportunity is low, and the economic benefits derived from education and training are limited. Rural counties in which African Americans make up one-third or more of the total population are found only in the South. Native American (American Indian, Alaskan Native) counties are clustered in three areas: the northern High Plains, the Four Corners region in the Southwest, and Alaska. Most of the Hispanic counties lie near the Rio Grande, from its headwaters in southern Colorado to the Gulf of Mexico. Hispanics are the fastest growing rural minority group. Agricultural areas in Washington, ski resorts in Colorado, and meatpacking centers in Kansas, Nebraska, and Iowa saw new or greatly expanded Hispanic settlements in the 1990s.

Nearly 10 million poor people live in rural America, comprising almost one of every five rural residents. A poverty gap exists between rural minorities and the white population. Rural minorities are significantly more impoverished as a percentage of the population. Nevertheless, the overwhelming majority of poor people living in rural America are white (72.9%). Fewer than one-fourth (23.6%) are African Americans, and Hispanics make up only 5.4 percent of the total. Less than 5 percent are Native Americans. These facts contradict the widely held notion that poverty in the United States is a minority problem. These people are the working poor in rural America. Addressing rural education will require solutions to both the poverty gap of minority groups and the persistent impoverished conditions of all rural poor, especially those who work for low wages.

**School improvement capacity.** Major initiatives in the 1990s—such as the National Science Foundation's Rural Systemic Initiative, the federal government's Comprehensive School Reform Demonstration Program, the Annenberg Foundation's Rural Challenge (now the Rural School and Community Trust), and the U.S. Department of Education's Regional Educational Laboratory program—have each in their own way attempted to give assistance to rural school systems. Increasingly, rural school districts are relying on regional educational service agencies (ESAs) in their respective states as vital partners in school improvement efforts. In his 1998 book *Expanding the Vision: New Roles for Educational Service Agencies in Rural School District Improvement,* E. Robert Stephens called on ESAs to pursue strategic goals that will enable them to be the first line of school improvement support for their rural school districts. ESAs are particularly important in giving rural schools the capacity to educate students with special and exceptional learning needs. The Association of Educational Service Agencies is the national professional organization serving ESAs in thirty-three states.

**Teacher recruitment and retention.** Attracting and retaining quality teachers will be critical in creating and implementing higher standards for student academic achievement. According to Said Yasin's report "The Supply and Demand of Elementary and Secondary School Teachers in the United States," during the 1998–1999 school year there were 2.78 million teachers in public schools. More than a million of those teachers (approximately 40%) were in six states: California, Florida, Illinois, New York, Ohio, and Texas. These six states also have almost 1,400 rural school districts. The number of elementary and secondary school teachers was projected to increase by 1.1 percent annually to a total of 3.46 million by 2008. Urban and poor communities will have the greatest need for teachers, with more than 700,000 additional teachers needed by 2010.

The rural teacher shortage affects all subject areas but particularly math, science, and special education. According to the National Association of State Boards of Education, an adequate number of teachers is trained each year. The problem is one of distribution. Causes for a teacher shortage in rural areas include: social and cultural isolation, poor pay and salary differentials, limited teacher mobility, lack of personal privacy, rigid lockstep salary schedules and monetary practices, the luring of teachers away by higher paying private sector businesses and industries, strict teacher certification and licensure practices and tests, lack of reciprocal certification and licensure to enable teaching in another state, re-cruitment cost (time/costs to gather information), and a high rate of teacher turnover (30% to 50% in some areas).

**Leadership.** The most critical issues in managing and running small rural school districts are finances, regional economic conditions, state regulations, salaries, and providing an adequate variety of classes. The greatest turnover among superintendents occurs among the smallest districts, those with fewer than 300 students. An environment of high-stakes testing and increasing public accountability for student and school success is placing a premium on persons who can effectively lead schools (and school districts). As is noted in the 1999 book *Leadership for Rural Schools: Lessons for All Educators,* edited by Donald M. Chalker, being an effective principal in a rural area means building positive relationships with the people in the rural community. The school in the rural community is still a respected institution, with much more focus on people than on business. Building trust and finding ways to make the curriculum incorporate the strengths of the community are key features of successful school leaders in rural areas. In the decades ahead, leading rural schools and school systems in ways that contribute to community and economic development appear essential for sustaining a prosperous school and community in much of rural America.

**Policy action.** Lack of a precise demographic rural definition frustrates those who work in setting educational policy. In 2000, for the first time in history, an organization—the Rural School and Community Trust—systematically attempted to gauge and describe the relative importance of rural education in each state. This first effort used both *importance* and *urgency* gauges. The results revealed a cluster of seven states where rural education is crucial to the state's educational performance and where the need for attention is great: Alabama, Arkansas, Kentucky, Mississippi, North Dakota, South Dakota, and West Virginia. These states are in regions that are chronically depressed, suffer large areas of out-migration, and are deeply distressed by changes in the global economy. Louisiana, Montana, and Oklahoma rounded out the top ten states where rural education was important and the need for policy action was urgent. That twenty-five states now have affiliate organizations with the National Rural Education Association also reflects the growing trend for rural education interests to unite and seek solutions to public education issues.

**Research.** In 1991 Alan J. DeYoung pointed out in his book *Rural Education: Issues and Practices* that rural educational issues rarely attract the attention of prestigious colleges of education and their professorates. Part of the reason is that rural areas are places with traditions and cultures of labor and of working, rather than demand for intellectual understanding and for abstract scholarship. In 1996 rural education researchers Hobart L. Harmon, Craig B. Howley, and John R. Sanders reported in the *Journal of Research in Rural Education* that only 196 doctoral dissertations were written between 1989 and 1993 on the topic of rural education.

Since 1997, the U.S. Department of Education's Office of Educational Research and Improvement has operated Regional Educational Laboratories. These labs were authorized by federal law to devote 25 percent of their funding to meeting the needs of rural schools, part of which has been the conduct of applied research. In 1996 the Education Department designated one of the labs to operate the National Rural Education Specialty, a practice that ended with the start of a new five-year contact period for the labs in 2001. The need for research and evaluation of practice in rural education is likely to increase as more accountability and results are expected from public investments in education.

### Educational Services in Rural Areas

Public elementary and secondary schools are the greatest provider of educational services in most local rural communities, and often are the community's largest employer. In 1917, passage of the Smith-Hughes Act by the U.S. Congress provided funds for teaching agriculture to boys in high school, as well as to young farmers and to adults who came to school on a part-time basis. In the 1960s, Congress initiated many educational programs, including Title I of the Elementary and Secondary Education Act, which provided funds for educating disadvantaged children. In the 1970s, federal vocational funds helped establish regional vocational centers in rural areas. Federal school-to-work funds in the 1990s encouraged school systems, including rural school systems, to better connect the school curriculum with the workplace. By the mid-1990s, the U.S. Department of Education operated more than 140 elementary and secondary assistance programs, of which twelve specifically targeted or included rural schools.

Passage of the Morrill Act in 1862 provided an opportunity for persons interested in agriculture and the mechanical arts to attend a land-grant college. In 1914 Congress passed the Smith-Lever Act, which created the Cooperative Agricultural Extension Service, arguably the agency that has provided more educational opportunities for rural adults than any other agency. The Cooperative Extension's 4-H youth program has also been a leading educator of young people in rural America. Like much of rural America itself, these traditional agricultural-focused agencies have been responding to the need to serve a broader constituency in rural areas, in addition to agriculture.

Rapid expansion of community colleges in the 1960s and 1970s greatly expanded higher education and adult education opportunities to many rural communities. These efforts expanded the informal adult education opportunities made available by organizations such as the National Grange, the National Farmers Union, the American Farm Bureau Federation, and the National Farmers Organization.

In addition to the U.S. Department of Agriculture, the Appalachian Regional Commission, the U.S. Department of Health and Human Services, the U.S. Department of Labor, the U.S. Department of Commerce, and a host of other federal agencies operate programs serving the educational needs of rural America.

*See also:* AGRICULTURAL EDUCATION; COMMUNITY EDUCATION; FEDERAL EDUCATIONAL ACTIVITIES; FINANCIAL SUPPORT OF SCHOOLS; POVERTY AND EDUCATION; SCHOOL FACILITIES.

**BIBLIOGRAPHY**

BEAULIEU, LIONEL J., and MULKEY, DAVID, eds. 1995. *Investing in People: The Human Capital Needs of Rural America.* Boulder, CO: Westview.

BEESON, ELIZABETH, and STRANGE, MARTY. 2000. *Why Rural Matters: The Need for Every State to Take Action on Rural Education.* Randolph, VT: Rural School and Community Trust Policy Program.

CASTLE, EMERY N., ed. 1995. *The Changing American Countryside: Rural People and Places.* Lawrence: University Press of Kansas.

CHALKER, DONALD M., ed. 1999. *Leadership for Rural Schools: Lessons for All Educators.* Lancaster, PA: Technomic.

DeYoung, Alan J. 1987. "The Status of American Rural Education Research: An Integrated Review and Commentary." *Review of Educational Research* 57:123–148.

DeYoung, Alan J., ed. 1991. *Rural Education: Issues and Practices.* New York: Garland.

Dewees, Sarah, and Hammer, Patricia Cahape, eds. 2000. *Improving Rural School Facilities: Design, Construction, Finance, and Public Support.* Charleston, WV: AEL.

Galston, William A., and Baehler, Karen J. 1995. *Rural Development in the United States: Connecting Theory, Practice, and Possibilities.* Washington, DC: Island Press.

Gibbs, Robert M.; Swaim, Paul L.; and Teixeira, Ruy, eds. 1998. *Rural Education and Training in the New Economy: The Myth of the Rural Skills Gap.* Ames: Iowa State University Press.

Haas, Toni, and Nachtigal, Paul. 1998. *Place Value: An Educator's Guide to Good Literature on Rural Lifeways, Environments, and Purposes of Education.* Charleston, WV: ERIC Clearinghouse on Rural Education and Small Schools.

Harmon, Hobart L., and Branham, Dan H. 1999. "Creating Standards for Rural Schools: A Matter of Values." *High School Magazine* 7:14–19.

Harmon, Hobart L.; Howley, Craig B.; and Sanders, John R. 1996. "Doctoral Research in Rural Education and the Rural R&D Menu." *Journal of Research in Rural Education* 12:68–75.

Howley, Craig B. 2000. *School District Size and School Performance.* Charleston, WV: AEL.

Howley, Craig B., and Eckman, John M., eds. 1997. *Sustainable Small Schools: A Handbook for Rural Communities.* Charleston, WV: AEL.

Howley, Craig B., and Harmon, Hobart L. 2000. "K–12 Unit Schooling in Rural America: A First Description." *Rural Educator* 22:10–18.

Howley, Craig B., and Harmon, Hobart L., eds. 2000. *Small High Schools that Flourish: Rural Context, Case Studies, and Resources.* Charleston, WV: AEL.

McLaughlin, Donald H.; Huberman, Mette B.; and Hawkins, Evelyn K. 1997. *Characteristics of Small and Rural School Districts.* Washington, DC: U.S. Department of Education, National Center for Education Statistics.

Miller, Bruce A. 1995. "The Role of Rural Schools in Community Development: Policy Issues and Implications." *Journal of Research in Rural Education* 11:163–172.

Moore, Robert M., III, ed. 2001. *The Hidden America: Social Problems in Rural America for the Twenty-First Century.* Selinsgrove, PA: Susquehanna University Press.

Nachtigal, Paul. 1982. *Rural Education: In Search of a Better Way.* Boulder, CO: Westview Press.

Rural Challenge Policy Program. 1999. *Public School Standards: Discussing the Case for Community Control.* Randolph, VT: Rural Challenge Policy Program.

Seal, Kenna R., and Harmon, Hobart L. 1995. "Realities of Rural School Reform." *Phi Delta Kappan* 77:119–120, 122–124.

Sears, David W., and Reid, J. Norman, eds. 1995. *Rural Development Strategies.* Chicago: Nelson-Hall.

Stephens, E. Robert. 1988. *The Changing Context of Education in a Rural Setting.* Charleston, WV: AEL.

Stephens, E. Robert. 1998. *Expanding the Vision: New Roles for Educational Service Agencies in Rural School District Improvement.* Charleston, WV: AEL.

Stephens, E. Robert; Stern, Joyce D.; Collins, Timothy; and Sanders, John R. 2001. *Milestones in Rural Education, 1950–2000.* Greensboro: SERVE, University of North Carolina–Greensboro.

Stern, Joyce D., ed. 1994. *The Condition of Education in Rural Schools: Statistical Analysis Report.* Washington, DC: U.S. Department of Education, Office of Educational Research and Improvement.

U.S. Department of Agriculture. 1995. *Understanding Rural America.* Washington, DC: U.S. Department of Agriculture, Economic Research Service.

U.S. Department of Agriculture. 1996. "Value of Rural America." *Rural Development Perspectives* 12:1–28.

U.S. Department of Agriculture. 1999. "Socioeconomic Conditions." *Rural Conditions and Trends* 9:1–143.

**INTERNET RESOURCES**

ERIC Clearinghouse on Rural Education and Small Schools, Regional Educational Lab-

ORATORY AT AEL, and NATIONAL RURAL EDU-CATION ASSOCIATION. 2002. "Rural Education Directory." <www.ael.org/eric/ruraled>.

NATIONAL EDUCATION ASSOCIATION. 1998. "Status of Public Education in Rural Areas and Small Towns: Comparative Analysis." <www.nea.org/publiced/rural.htm>.

YASIN, SAID. 1999. "The Supply and Demand of Elementary and Secondary School Teachers in the United States." <www.ericsp.org/pages/digests/supply_damand_elem_teachers_99-6.html>.

HOBART L. HARMON

## INTERNATIONAL CONTEXT

Rural education is always considered in comparison to urban education. There are other dichotomies, including government versus private or mission schools; access to the first year of schooling for male versus female pupils; the standard of facilities and resources; the education and experience of teachers; and the quality of education offered and the language of instruction (the national language is often a foreign tongue to people in rural areas).

### The Challenges of Rural Education

When outside teachers who do not speak the local language staff rural schools, cultural conflict occurs. Often they feel superior to the local people and refuse to take the time to learn about the culture of their host community. Teachers posted to rural schools usually apply for transfers and if denied them simply "run away." Even when "at post," they often teach only a portion of their load, as they find excuses to leave—to collect their pay, to go to the health center, to attend funerals, and so on. Teacher absenteeism is a major problem in rural areas.

In the Majority World (or Third World, the South, where the majority of the peoples of the world live) there exists a range of possibilities that are encompassed by *rural*. Population densities vary but are usually small and scattered. The environment is also diverse, ranging from plains and deserts to mountain areas with deep valleys and flowing rivers, to places with small islands scattered across large areas of open sea. "Remote" and "isolated" are other categories of rural. Schools in rural areas tend to lack amenities. Electricity is either not available or limited. Where education systems rely on interactive radio and television to deliver primary school class-

es, the isolated schools are left out. Even if they have batteries for radios, the signal either does not reach them or is too weak to be understood. If the community must construct the classrooms and teachers' houses, they are often built out of local or temporary materials, which are perceived as inferior by outsiders. School supplies may never arrive, so teachers fall back on teaching from their kit from their training college days and rely more on rote learning.

Rural schools tend to harbor untrained or unqualified teachers. School inspectors do not like walking or riding in canoes for a number of days, so remote schools rarely get visited. Where population densities are small, rural schools tend to need only one or two teachers. This requires either staggered intakes—a class every two or three years—or multigrade teaching (as in the old one-room, one-teacher schoolhouses in rural America that went from kindergarten to grade twelve, which are now museums as they have been replaced by busing and regional schools).

The solution to this problem in the Majority World has been boarding schools or primary schools with hostels for students from remote communities. Most secondary schools still rely on boarding students from far away.

Some countries, such as Jamaica, Papua New Guinea, and Tanzania, have experimented with "quotas" to control the transition from primary to secondary school so that a fair proportion of those pupils in rural schools are able to continue their education (or to ensure that females are represented at the next level). Selection systems employing quotas have lasted for only a few years because urban elites, who make the decisions, find rural children taking places in schools where their children might have gone.

Where rural schools are inferior in facilities and the quality of teachers (for example, the majority of South African farm schools, which enroll 40 percent of the primary pupils), the consequence is that students tend not to get selected for the next level of schooling. The examinations—the item banks written by educators who live in cities—contain clear urban biases and favor the progression of urban children. "First-past-the-post" examination systems in rural areas have tended to favor the children of outsiders (such as health professionals, police officers, extension officers, and teachers) over local children.

It has been found, when intelligence tests have been administered, that bright rural children do not get admitted into secondary schools, whereas duller urban children do. This is because first-past-the-post selection systems based on formal primary-school-leaving examinations favor children from urban areas where there are better facilities, equipment, and teachers, and more diverse experiences. All of this contributes to the vicious cycle of rural poverty and neglect. The policy debates are never ending. Where successful, the best students who excel on examinations generally leave their communities, never to return. This results in a leadership vacuum in rural areas. Even youth who have been barred from further studies often migrate to gain experience or seek employment in unskilled jobs that are not available at home.

## Changing Strategies

Some policymakers believe that in order to keep young people in rural areas, rural education should be different from urban education. It is claimed that if schooling is more relevant to local conditions and designed to contribute to rural development, the youth may not want to migrate. They also assume, usually fallaciously, that teachers can become community development workers and assist in the transformation of rural areas. The change in name from primary to community schools, which has occurred in many countries, reflects this bias. Planners often ignore the aspirations that rural parents have for their children—to become educated, obtain a job in a city, and send remittances home to their aging parents.

Ways of adapting primary education to local conditions, while maintaining standards and permitting the quality of learning and supporting upward mobility for the brighter children, are being explored in many countries. An example is integrating school gardens with agricultural and nutrition education and school lunch programs. Another is new programs in minority education that address local needs without undermining quality or equality of opportunity.

Urban elites may clamor for "vocationalization," but for other people's children, not their own. Generally there has been a rejection of vocationalization of primary schooling. Rural education must not become "unequal" education. The conviction remains that primary schooling must be a firm foundation for further education, while being terminal for those who are unable to continue to the next level. This was the key message in the 1967 book *Education for Self-Reliance,* written by Julius Nyerere, president of Tanzania. The challenge of how to achieve both objectives at once continues to exist in the early twenty-first century.

The distribution of school supplies and materials remains a critical issue. Urban schools tend to get supplied first and rural and remote schools last. This syndrome is found in the delivery of most government services and prompted Richard Chambers, a leading rural sociologist, to call in 1997 for "the last first" as fundamental policy to support rural development. It is perhaps unlikely that central ministries of education, either nationally or in regions or districts, will provide isolated schools with computers, solar power, and communication dishes before they have provided the new panacea of information technology or e-learning to their urban schools. The gap between the poor and undereducated in rural areas and their urban counterparts is bound to increase.

Other strategies that have been employed with varying degrees of success include the Book Flood in Fiji, in which schools were given large numbers of storybooks, intended to attract students' attention and to expose them to a wide variety of subjects. The Book Flood was endorsed by the World Bank and has spread to other countries (reading enhances learning, no matter what is read). Inducement allowances have been used to attract and hold qualified teachers in isolated schools. In some countries a "bridging" or extra year of schooling is provided to help children from remote communities catch up. Indonesia has relied on nonformal education centers. In New Zealand and Papua New Guinea vernacular preschools, where reading and writing is taught before grade one, has enhanced the capacity of rural pupils to comprehend formal schooling and to excel in school. In some places, particularly in Central and South America, missionaries run private schools that are of a better quality than those provided by the government. More than 160 countries are struggling with issues related to developing rural education. Rarely do the policymakers strive for a comparative perspective or try to learn from each other. Therefore the policies employed are very diverse.

*See also:* INTERNATIONAL EDUCATION; INTERNATIONAL GAP IN TECHNOLOGY; POVERTY AND EDUCATION.

**BIBLIOGRAPHY**

CHAMBERS, ROBERT. 1983. *Rural Development: Putting the Last First.* London: Longman.

CHAMBERS, ROBERT. 1997. *Whose Reality Counts? Putting the First Last.* London: Intermediate Technology Publications.

COLCLOUGH, CHRISTOPHER, and LEWIN, KEITH. 1993. *Educating All the Children: Strategies for Primary Schooling in the South.* Oxford: Clarendon Press.

EDUCATION FOUNDATION. 2001. *Education Atlas of South Africa.* Johannesburg, South Africa: Education Foundation.

GIBSON, MARGARET, and WEEKS, SHELDON G. 1990. *Improving Education in the Western Province.* Waigani, Papua New Guinea: National Research Institute, Division of Educational Research.

LE ROUX, WILLEMIEN. 2000. *Torn Apart: San Children as Change Agents in a Process of Acculturation.* Shakawe, Botswana: Kuru Development Trust; Windhoek, Namibia: Working Group for Indigenous Minorities in Southern Africa.

LEVIN, HENRY M., and LOCKHEED, MARLAINE E. 1993. *Effective Schools in Developing Countries.* London: Falmer Press.

NYERERE, JULIUS. 1967. *Education for Self-Reliance.* Dar es Salaam, Tanzania: Government Printers.

REPUBLIC OF ZAMBIA. MINISTRY OF EDUCATION. 1996. *Educating Our Future: National Policy on Education.* Lusaka, Zambia: Zambia Educational Publishing.

SHELDON G. WEEKS

# S

## SANCHEZ, GEORGE I. (1906–1972)

Reformer and activist, George I. Sanchez is recognized for his contributions to educational equity, especially for Mexican-American children. Sanchez was born in Albuquerque, New Mexico, and attended schools in Arizona and New Mexico before graduation from high school in Albuquerque. He taught for eight years in rural schools while working on his bachelor's degree and taking weekend and summer courses at the University of New Mexico. After graduation Sanchez received a fellowship for graduate study from the General Education Board (GEB), a foundation funded by the Rockefellers, and the funding provided the means for him to receive his master's degree in education with specializations in educational psychology and Spanish, and his Ed.D. in educational administration from the University of California at Berkeley. His master's thesis concerned the inequity of using I.Q. tests developed for English-speaking children for evaluation of Spanish-speaking children.

### Career

The GEB provided the funding for his first position as director of the Division of Information and Statistics of the New Mexico State Department of Education (1931–1935). Sanchez's abilities were noticed by prestigious, national foundations. In 1935 the Julius Rosenwald Fund (founded by the owner of Sears Roebuck) asked Sanchez to conduct field studies concerning rural and Negro education in the south and in Mexico. The latter resulted in *Mexico: A Revolution by Education*, which remained the definitive source on education in Mexico for many years. Two years later Sanchez was invited to become a member of the Venezuelan Ministry of Education and to be responsible for organizing a normal school for secondary teachers. After serving as director of the Instititio Pedagogica Nacional from 1937 to 1938, he returned to New Mexico and to the renewal of a battle over school finance reform. Prior to leaving for Venezuela, he had served as president of the teachers association in New Mexico. In that capacity, he led the fight for the equalization of school finance through legislation. Sanchez had been told that he would be offered a tenured position at the University of New Mexico on his return, but after the school finance controversy, his politically powerful opponents blocked his appointment.

From 1938 to 1940 he surveyed Taos County, New Mexico, for the Carnegie Foundation (a survey that resulted in Sanchez's book, *Forgotten People: A Study of New Mexicans*) and taught at the University of New Mexico. *Forgotten People* brought about a public awareness of the severity of inequities for the school children of New Mexico. Sanchez pointed out that two-thirds of the other states had higher literacy ranking compared with New Mexico, with an illiterate population of 13.3 percent. He emphasized the lack of literature in rural schools, the low enrollment of Spanish-speaking children, the low expenditures per pupil, and the highest infant mortality rates in "counties where more than half of the population is Spanish-speaking" (Sanchez 1940, p. 29).

Sanchez's most productive years as an activist with national influence began after he came to Austin, Texas, in 1940 as a tenured, full professor at the University of Texas. His outspoken political opinions and actions exasperated many members of various boards of regents, but he never allowed himself to be pressured into denying his principles. Sanchez was hired as the first professor of Latin American studies and later served as chair of the History and Philosophy of Education Department.

In 1946 and 1947 Sanchez conducted a survey of Navajo education for the U.S. Department of the Interior. His findings, as presented in *The People: A Study of the Navajo,* pointed out the inequities of the education of Navajo children. Only about 25 percent of eligible children attended school, the schools were inadequate in materials and facilities, and most were located by traveling through roads that he described as gullies. He stated, "The Navajos are people—Americans worthy of a dignified, American way of life" (Mowry, p. 152).

After World War II Sanchez began a period of unceasing activism on behalf of equity for Mexican Americans, especially Mexican-American children in public education. In 1941 he was national president of the League of United Latin American Citizens (LULAC), and while he appreciated the contributions of LULAC, he saw a need for a more active approach to civil rights. The end of the war and return of veterans, the G.I. Bill, and Sanchez's foundation contacts all came together to assist him in his mission. Mexican-American men returned from World War II with a feeling that they should have equal rights in the country for which they risked their lives. Also, many had an opportunity for higher education not possible previously; many entered law school. Both undergraduates and law school students sought out Sanchez, and he later worked with them on court cases affecting the right of Mexican-American children to equity. His dedication to civil rights influenced many to become active in challenging discrimination in the courts. At this time Sanchez began to look for funding and court cases concerning equal rights. Throughout his career he was involved in causes that received support, moral and/or monetary, from Alianzo Hispano-Americana, the American G.I. Forum, the American Council of Spanish-Speaking People, American Civil Liberties Union, the Marshall Trust, and the Mexican-American Legal Defense and Education Fund. During the 1950s Sanchez received funding from the Marshall Trust to found an organization to work for equity for Mexican Americans. This organization, the American Council of Spanish-Speaking People, funded several court cases and provided encouragement and support for Mexican-American concerns, especially in the area of education.

## Contribution

The University of California at Berkeley recognized Sanchez in 1984 with a retrospective honoring him as the leader in laws affecting Mexican Americans. He was involved as advisor, expert witness, or investigator concerning legal issues throughout his life, and two cases are considered to be landmark cases. In *Delgado v. Gracy* (1948), a case that resulted in an agreed judgment, Sanchez and Gustavo Garcia, an attorney, were specifically given credit by the Texas State Board of Education for the formal policy adopted by the state board to oppose segregation of Mexican-American children in schools because of their Spanish surnames. The Delgado case set a precedent—the legality of separating and treating Mexican-American children as a class apart had been successfully challenged.

The other case, *Hernandez v. Texas* (1954), was the first U.S. Supreme Court case concerning Mexican-American rights and was decided unanimously in favor of the plaintiffs. Although the appeals concerned equity in jury selection, the final ruling could be applied to public education. Again the concern had been the treatment of Mexican Americans as a class apart. Garcia and Carlos Cadena were the lead attorneys, and Cadena gave credit to Sanchez for developing the theoretical basis for the brief—Sanchez's class apart theory—that it was illegal to discriminate and segregate based on Spanish surname. In numerous other cases Sanchez was called as an expert witness because of his research and publications on the misuse of I.Q. tests to place Mexican-American children. Besides his expert testimony, Sanchez's major contributions to legal cases were the following: (1) to advise attorneys to use the precedent of the class apart theory; (2) always to ask for one dollar in damages because opponents will rarely appeal since it would open the case back up for damages; and (3) to sue the members of the state board of education in each case because they usually will make a deal in order to have their names dropped. None of the cases in which he was involved was appealed.

As an individual Sanchez was a man of many interests. *Arithmetic in Maya* was written by him. His papers at the Benson Latin American Collection at the University of Texas contain his drawings of a computer—an unknown device for most people—and he corresponded with Walt Disney about making educational movies.

Professionally, Sanchez wrote books on education in Mexico, higher education in Mexico, education in Venezuela, and the education of New Mexicans and Navajos, as well as many journal articles. For many years he was on the editorial board of the *Nation's Schools.* He also wrote several textbooks.

National recognition was widespread. Sanchez served in the following capacities: member of John F. Kennedy's Committee of Fifty on New Frontier Policy in the Americas; National Advisory Committee for the Peace Corps; Latin American Consultant to the U.S. Office of Civil Defense as well as to U.S. Office of Indian Affairs; U.S. Office of Education on Migrants; U.S. Office of Interior; and Navajo Tribal Council.

After Sanchez's death in 1972 schools were named for him in Texas and California, as well as a room in the U.S. Office of Education. On May 2, 1995, the University of Texas at Austin named the College of Education after him. In life he was considered an all too vocal radical by university presidents and regents; in death a new, more enlightened leadership recognized him as a pioneer reformer.

*See also:* MULTICULTURAL EDUCATION; RACE, ETHNICITY, AND CULTURE, *subentry on* LATINO GROWTH.

#### BIBLIOGRAPHY

MOWRY, JAMES. 1977. "Study of the Educational Thought and Action of George I. Sanchez." Ph.D. diss., University of Texas at Austin.

SANCHEZ, GEORGE I. 1936. *Mexico: A Revolution by Education.* New York: Viking.

SANCHEZ, GEORGE I. 1940. *Forgotten People: A Study of New Mexicans.* Albuquerque: University of New Mexico Press.

SANCHEZ, GEORGE I. 1948. *The People: A Study of the Navajo.* Washington, DC: United States Indian Service.

SANCHEZ, GEORGE I. 1951. *Concerning Segregation of Spanish-Speaking Children in the Public Schools.* Austin, TX: Inter-American Occasional Papers.

TEVIS, MARTHA. 1994. "George I. Sanchez." In *Lives in Education: A Narrative of People and Ideas,* 2nd ed., ed. L. Glenn Smith, Joan K. Smith, et al. New York: St. Martin's Press.

WILEY, TOM. 1965. *Politics and Purse Strings in New Mexico.* Albuquerque: University of New Mexico Press.

MARTHA MAY TEVIS

# SCHEDULING

In 1994 the National Education Commission on Time and Learning found the issue of how time is spent in schools to be a matter of urgency. Likewise, the National Education Association reported that "across the nation in schools and districts engaged in transforming schools into more effective learning communities, the issue that has emerged as the most intense and the one that universally dominates discussion is time" (p. 9). To spend the "time budget" more wisely, schools use a variety of scheduling arrangements. Discussed here are the various types of schedules that schools use to make optimum use of the school day.

## Historical Background of Scheduling

In the early nineteenth century, teachers typically had a limited education and were expected to function well in all subject areas. Staff at all levels taught any subject at any time of the day. In the late 1800s, the *Carnegie unit*—comprised of approximately fifty-minute class periods in which a single subject is taught, and for which teachers specialize in particular subject areas—became the most frequently used scheduling format. J. Lloyd Trump's *An Image of the Future,* published in 1958, caused schools to experiment with ungraded instruction, long periods of independent study, and large group instruction. The plan failed, however, partly due to the large amount of unstructured, independent study time for students.

Other scheduling experiments have also failed. In the 1970s, the notion that flexibility in scheduling is beneficial to staff and students led to the Open School concept. Divisions between classrooms in elementary schools were eliminated and students were able to progress at their own speed, moving from one grade area to another. During the 1960s and 1970s, some schools modified the traditional seven-period day, breaking the day up into twenty-minute *modules* and calling the plan *modular flexible scheduling.* Neither plan took hold.

In the 1970s, with flexibility continuing to be a priority, *fluid block scheduling* became popular and successful. This scheduling pattern allots a block of two to three hours to teams of teachers from various subject areas, allowing teachers to schedule instruction according to student needs. Another flexible scheduling alternative that began in the late 1980s and continues in popularity is the *zero period schedule*. Designated courses begin an hour earlier than the regular school day, allowing some students to leave an hour earlier or enroll in an extra class.

The 1989 publication of *Turning Points,* by the Carnegie Council on Adolescent Development, brought major changes for middle-level schools. Recognizing that junior high schools were simply mirror images of high schools, the council recommended that schools be reconfigured to fit the developmental needs of young adolescents. Thus, various forms of block scheduling and interdisciplinary teaming took hold in middle schools, and later in high schools as well. With *block scheduling,* teachers are given longer periods of time—usually ninety minutes—to work with students. *Interdisciplinary teaming* is a popular arrangement where a group of teachers (usually four or five) works with 125 to 150 students, essentially creating a school within a school. Interdisciplinary units of study help students' understand the connections between subjects. Teaming is sometimes combined with block scheduling.

Throughout the history of school scheduling, the need for flexibility and the need for teachers to work cooperatively for the benefit of students are recurring themes. These themes impact educators' scheduling choices.

## Selecting a Schedule

Selecting an appropriate school schedule involves some fundamental assessments, including examining what teachers are doing and determining if classroom instruction is improving student achievement. When teachers make instruction optimally effective for students, it is appropriate to consider how use of time could further enhance learning—the schedule must support, not drive, the instructional program. As teachers become more innovative and experimental in their classroom activities, they adopt flexible and cooperative approaches that demand new organizational arrangements.

What students need is another consideration when choosing a schedule. For example, elementary and middle school students are restless, have short attention spans, and require frequent physical movement, and frequently changing settings allows for such movement. Elementary students need close relationships with adults, and thus need to remain in the care of one teacher, not five or six, during a school day. High school students need opportunities to explore more specialized areas of interest, and thus require a wide variety of courses from which to choose.

Other considerations can impact scheduling. Whether or not to group students by their ability levels is an issue on which parents and teachers do not always agree. If improving student behavior is a priority, reducing the number of times students change classes and interact in the halls is considered. Teachers' preferences for teaching assignments and planning periods, assigning enough lunch periods to accommodate students, arranging for televised classes, including courses that are popular (or eliminating outdated ones), and parents' attitudes about courses all impact scheduling decisions.

## Scheduling Models

Scheduling models are generally described in terms of the amount of time students spend in a specified classroom. The most frequently used scheduling models are (a) the traditional, self-contained classroom, (b) forty-five to fifty-minute class periods, (c) a variety of configurations of block scheduling, and (d) teaming.

**Self-contained classrooms.** Typically seen in elementary schools, self-contained classrooms are settings where a single teacher is in charge of instructing twenty to thirty students for the major portion of the day. The advantages of self-contained classrooms include strong student-teacher and student-to-student relationships; flexibility in time spent on subject areas; and buildings designed for self-contained classes. The cost of this arrangement is in the loss of high-quality instruction for some subject areas, and possibly in all subjects, if the teacher is not a master of instruction and discipline.

**Forty-five to fifty-minute class periods.** The traditional high school and middle school schedule, shown in Figure 1, is of fixed length and classes meet the same hour each day. Benefits include daily drill and practice for such subjects as mathematics; students miss only one period in each subject when they are absent; and schools are likely to be similar when

**FIGURE 1**

| Traditional seven-period day schedule for seventh and eighth grades | | | | | | | | | | | | |
|---|---|---|---|---|---|---|---|---|---|---|---|---|
| | **Math** | | **Science** | | **English** | | **Social Studies** | | **Reading** | | | **Electives** | |
| Period | 7th<br>Jones | 8th<br>Smith | 7th<br>Joe | 8th<br>Mims | 7th<br>Toms | 8th<br>Abott | 7th<br>Sole | 8th<br>Hughes | Dunbar | Tool | Typing | Art/Life<br>Skills | P.E./<br>Athletics |
| 1 | Seat<br>Count<br>Course<br>Number | | | | | | | | | | 1st<br>Term / 2nd<br>Term | Art | Athletics<br>Boys |
| 2 | | | | | | | | | | | | Art | P.E. |
| 3 | Planning<br>Period | | | | | | | | | | | Art | P.E. |
| 4 | | | | | | | | | | | | Life<br>Skills | P.E. |
| | Lunch | | | | | | | | | | | | |
| 5 | | | | | | | | | | | | Life<br>Skills | P.E. |
| 6 | | | | | | | | | | | | Life<br>Skills | P.E. |
| 7 | | | | | | | | | | | | Life<br>Skills | Athletics<br>Girls |

All periods are 45 minutes.

SOURCE: Schroth, Gwen. 1997. *Fundamentals of School Scheduling*. Lanham, MD: Scarecrow. Page 76. Reprinted with permission.

students transfer from one to another. The disadvantages are that periods are too short for extended teaching activities such as science labs; there is not enough time to form quality relationships; discipline problems occur during the frequent passing periods; teachers teach 150 or more students each day; and the class period, not the instruction, determines activity length.

**Block scheduling.** Of the many configurations possible under the umbrella of *block scheduling,* the *alternate day* block schedule—sometimes termed the *A/B block*—is the most popular (see Figure 2). Classes meet each day for ninety minutes. Four classes meet on A days, and four meet on B days, with days of the week alternating as A or B. Several combinations of forty-minute and longer periods are possible. For example, with the *fluid block schedule* three periods a day are ninety minutes in length and two are forty minutes long, allowing for such subjects as

mathematics to meet daily, while giving subjects such as science longer periods.

Some other forms of block scheduling are available but infrequently used. The *semester block schedule* allows students to attend just four classes for ninety minutes each day for an entire semester. The following semester students enroll in another four classes. The *75-30-75 plan,* proposed by Robert Canady and Michael Rettig, divides the school year into three blocks of time: two seventy-five-day terms and a thirty-day term. During each seventy-five-day term, the school day includes three 112-minute block classes and one forty-eight-minute period. The thirty-day term offers students the opportunity to study one core course intensively. The *trimester plan* divides the school year into three, rather than two, semesters, and combinations of forty-five-minute and ninety-minute periods are possible. A drawback to all such variations is coordination of schedules for transfer students.

**FIGURE 2**

**Alternate (A/B) day block schedule**

|              | A Day       | B Day       | A Day       | B Day       | A Day       |
| ------------ | ----------- | ----------- | ----------- | ----------- | ----------- |
| 8:30-10:00   | Period 1    | Period 5    | Period 1    | Period 5    | Period 1    |
| 10:10-11:40  | Period 2    | Period 6    | Period 2    | Period 6    | Period 2    |
| 11:40-12:20  | Lunch       |             |             |             |             |
| 12:20-1:50   | Period 3    | Period 7    | Period 3    | Period 7    | Period 3    |
| 2:00-3:30    | Period 4    | Period 8    | Period 4    | Period 8    | Period 4    |

All periods are 90 minutes.

SOURCE: Schroth, Gwen. 1997. *Fundamentals of School Scheduling.* Lanham, MD: Scarecrow. Page 83. Reprinted with permission.

Canady and Rettig designed the *parallel block schedule* for elementary and middle schools. To reduce class size for key subjects such as reading and mathematics, small groups are rotated out for special education and talented and gifted classes, as well as for computer labs. Advantages of all types of block scheduling arrangements are:

- The number of subjects students take yearly is increased
- Time is available for developing more meaningful relationships
- Daily homework is assigned for half as many classes
- Passing periods are reduced, which may decrease discipline problems
- Teachers have fewer students to instruct in one day
- Opportunities are available for instructional creativity and in-depth learning

Some disadvantages are:

- Some subjects require daily drill and practice
- New instructional methods are necessary to make full use of longer periods
- Staff, central office, parent, and community support must be sought
- An increased staff is necessary and costly

**Teaming.** For years, elementary school teachers have acknowledged the value of integrating instruction to blur the lines between subject areas and stress the links between fields of knowledge. A shift toward a more student-centered approach to educating middle school students became more prevalent with the publication of *Turning Points* in 1989. Consequently, interdisciplinary teams are formed and provide continuity for group membership and instruction, similar to what exists at the elementary level. When teaming, two or more teachers of two or more subjects share a common group of students. Students can be grouped and regrouped during the shared time period, depending on the activity. Interdisciplinary teaming requires more complex configurations because instruction is coordinated across subjects to offer a less fragmented and more relevant curriculum. Thematic units of instruction are the usual planning tools. The *flexibly blocked* team, sometimes termed the *team block schedule,* incorporates not only the sharing of a common set of students and the opportunity for a coordinated curriculum, but also the flexibility of long class periods, which provide optimum use of the instructional time. Advantages to teaming are:

- Teachers get to know students personally
- Studies report improvement in thinking and learning skills
- Stable friendships can develop
- Class time can be used flexibly
- Changes within the team do not interfere with other teams' plans, such as a scheduled field trip
- The team collectively assumes responsibility for each student's learning and meets with parents as a group

The disadvantages are:

- Ability grouping is more difficult
- Interpersonal problems are intensified
- An adjustment period is required for teachers
- Staff training on integrated instruction is necessary
- Support from central administration, parents, and community must be obtained
- Buildings are not designed for division of classrooms according to teams.

**Staff Development**

All types of schedules require staff training. For example, teachers need to be able to teach to a variety of learning styles, teach higher-order thinking skills, use problem-solving techniques, and use technology in the classroom. In order to vary instruction during the longer block-scheduled class periods, teachers should additionally be trained to move beyond lecture, drill, and practice and include cooperative learning, learning centers, inductive learning, the use of manipulatives, and student-conducted experiments. When teamed, teachers should understand interdisciplinary instruction and be able to address issues that arise when a small group of students and teachers interact intensely with one another. Training can include team building and teaching, consensus building, conflict resolution techniques, and interdisciplinary instruction.

Whatever the scheduling model, finding a schedule that works best for teachers and students while satisfying community needs is important. If instruction and student achievement drive choices, such satisfaction is more likely to be achieved.

*See also:* CARNEGIE UNITS; ELEMENTARY EDUCATION; INSTRUCTIONAL STRATEGIES; SCHOOL REFORM; SECONDARY EDUCATION; SOCIAL ORGANIZATION OF SCHOOLS; TEAM TEACHING.

### BIBLIOGRAPHY

CANADY, ROBERT LYNN, and FOGLIANI, A. ELAINE. 1989. "How to Cut Class Size." *The Executive Educator* 11(8):22–23.

CANADY, ROBERT LYNN, and RETTIG, MICHAEL D. 1992. "Restructuring Middle Level Schedules to Promote Equal Access." *Schools in the Middle* 1(4):20–26.

CANADY, ROBERT LYNN, and RETTIG, MICHAEL D. 1993. "Unlocking the Lockstep High School Schedule." *Phi Delta Kappan* 75(4):310–314.

CARNEGIE COUNCIL ON ADOLESCENT DEVELOPMENT. 1989. *Turning Points: Preparing American Youth for the 21st Century. The Report of the Task Force on Education of Young Adolescents.* New York: Carnegie Council on Adolescent Development.

FULLAN, MICHAEL G. 1990. "Staff Development, Innovation and Institutional Development." In *Changing School Culture through Staff Development* ed. Bruce Joyce. Alexandria, VA: Association for Supervision and Curriculum Development.

HACKMAN, DONALD D. 1995. "Ten Guidelines for Implementing Block Scheduling." *Educational Leadership,* 53(3):24–27.

JACOBS, HEIDI HAYES. 1989. *Interdisciplinary Curriculum: Design and Implementation.* Alexandria, VA: Association for Supervision and Curriculum Development.

KRUSE, CAROL A., and KRUSE, GARY D. 1995. "The Master Schedule and Learning: Improving the Quality of Education." *NASSP Bulletin* 79(571):1–8.

NATIONAL EDUCATION COMMISSION ON TIME AND LEARNING. 1994. *Prisoners of Time: Report of the National Education Commission on Time and Learning.* Washington, DC: Government Printing Office.

SCHROTH, GWEN. 1997. *Fundamentals of School Scheduling.* Lanham, MD: Scarecrow.

SLAVIN, ROBERT E. 1993. "Ability Grouping in the Middle Grades: Achievement Effects and Alternatives." *The Elementary School Journal* 93(5):535–552.

SPEAR, ROBERT C. 1992. "Middle Level Team Scheduling: Appropriate Grouping for Adolescents." *Schools in the Middle* 2(1):30–34.

TRUMP, J. LLOYD. 1958. "An Image of the Future in Improved Staff Utilization." *Bulletin of the National Association of Secondary School Principals* XLII:324–329.

GWEN SCHROTH

# SCHOOL-BASED DECISION-MAKING

Since the release in 1983 of the National Commission on Excellence in Education report *A Nation at Risk,* there has been widespread call for education reform. The reform efforts of the 1980s and 1990s focused on organizational, curricular, and instructional changes necessary to improve the quality of education. Almost without exception, national reform reports advocated decentralization and enhanced teacher involvement in decision-making as a means of fostering necessary changes within school.

*School-based decision-making* is a concept based on the fundamental principle that individuals who are affected by the decision, possess expertise regarding the decision, and are responsible for implementing the decision, should be involved in making the decision. This concept often is attached to the broader school-system reform efforts of decentralization and school-based management (SBM), where decision-making authority is shifted from the district to the local school level. Some educators use the terms *shared decision-making* and *school-based management* interchangeably; others see shared decision-making as a component of SBM or decentralization. In general, the goal of school-based decision-making is to "empower school staff by providing authority, flexibility, and resources to solve the educational problems particular to their schools" (David, p. 52).

## Key Elements

School-based decision-making rests on two well-established propositions:

1. The school is the primary decision-making unit; and its corollary; decisions should be made at the lowest possible level.

2. Change requires ownership that comes from the opportunity to participate in defining change and the flexibility to adapt it to individual circumstances; the corollary is that change does not result from externally imposed procedures. (David, p. 46)

These propositions recognize that those closest to the technical core in education systems, because of their access to information concerning students' diverse characteristics, needs, learning styles, and performance levels, are better positioned to make decisions about educational programs than those farther removed from the teaching and learning process. Thus, decisions concerning curricula, instructional technologies, and other school initiatives will be most effective and enduring when carried out by those who feel a sense of ownership and responsibility for those decisions.

For school-based decision-making to work, four key resources need to be present to develop the capacity to create high performance organizations:

1. *Knowledge and skills* in new instructional strategies; interpersonal, problem-solving, and decision skills for working together as a team; business knowledge for managing the organization, including budgeting and fiscal planning; and assessment strategies for analyzing, interpreting, and acting on school performance data.

2. *Information* about the performance of the organization, including student performance data, budgets, and demographic-trend data.

3. *Power and authority* to make decisions, especially in the areas of curriculum and instruction, staffing and personnel, and resource allocation and budgeting.

4. *Rewards* for high performance, including intrinsic and extrinsic rewards, such as salary adjustments, professional development opportunities, performance-based pay, group or team-based rewards, and public recognition for their accomplishments.

## Scope of Decision-Making

In general, three areas of decision-making can be school based: budget, personnel, and curriculum. Regarding school finances, under school-based decision-making models, schools receive either a lump-sum budget or some portion of the district budget from which they may make decisions regarding personnel, equipment, materials, supplies, and professional development. Although budget authority implies a new level of autonomy, because personnel expenditures account for approximately 85 percent of the district budget and other fixed costs cover an additional 5 to 10 percent, few discretionary dollars actually remain for school-level allocation. Therefore, staffing expenditures and decisions regarding staffing structures and assignments are key to schools making decisions that might substantively affect the school's operation and effectiveness.

In terms of personnel decisions, schools are afforded flexibility and the power to determine how best to staff their schools. Personnel decisions typically fall in two areas: determining staffing needs based on the school's mission and educational plan and selecting people to fill the positions. Schools are afforded the latitude to decide whether their personnel funds are best spent on teachers, instructional aides, specialists, or clerical support. Once determinations are made regarding staffing needs, schools are actively engaged in the selection of new school personnel.

In the third decision area, decisions regarding the curriculum and instructional strategies are determined at the school level within a framework of district or state goals, while attending to the school's unique mission and needs. School-level personnel draw on their professional expertise and localized knowledge in making decisions that affect the school's educational program and instructional system. School personnel monitor the effectiveness of their programs and their students' academic performance. Decisions pertaining to budgeting, staffing, and the instructional program are often restricted and controlled, however, by district policies regarding matters such as class size, tenure, hiring, firing, assignment, curriculum initiatives, textbooks, and assessment procedures.

## Decision-Making Structures

To operationalize school-based decision-making, structures at the school level need to be implemented to facilitate the involvement of key stakeholders in the decision-making process. Schools embracing shared decision-making typically develop councils consisting of representative stakeholders in the school, such as teachers, parents, support personnel, and administrators. The school's governance structure is supported by guidelines that specify representation, terms of membership, council size, meeting format, and delineated lines of authority. Frequently, site councils further disperse involvement through the use of subcommittees. Subcommittees allow greater numbers of teachers to participate in the formal decision-making process and reduce the overall burden of extended involvement of others.

In addition to decision-making governance councils, schools that embrace shared decision-making understand that reaching collective agreement and consensus around difficult decisions require extended discussions, off-site meetings, and collective planning. Thus, schools that engage in shared decision-making at an authentic level set aside time for teachers to meet and places for them to congregate and talk. In addition, school schedules are often redesigned to facilitate teacher interaction by structuring common planning periods.

## Effectiveness of School-Based Decision-Making

Although school-based decision-making is often the centerpiece of school reform, there remains little empirical evidence that relates it to improved school performance. Most of the evidence of effectiveness of decision involvement at the school level focuses on teachers and administrators. Studies exploring organizational variables have generally found positive relationships between decision involvement and organizational outcomes, such as organizational commitment, job satisfaction, and organizational change. In addition, studies have found that participation enhances communication among teachers and administrators, contributes to the quality of teachers' work lives, and assists in professionalizing teaching and democratizing schools. Other research on school-based decision-making has generally been descriptive, and yet a substantive body of research has not yet explored causative relationships between school empowerment and school improvement or student achievement. Nonetheless, the combined effects related to participative structures that are democratic and collaborative and focus mainly on issues of curriculum and instruction are likely to bring about change at the classroom level.

## Issues and Controversies

The successful implementation of school-based decision-making is affected by a number of organizational factors and institutional constraints, including (1) clarity of purpose and access to information; (2) power and authority relationships; (3) administrative support and the changing role of central office personnel; and (4) policies at the district, state, and federal levels. These issues taken singularly or collectively affect the long-term effectiveness of decentralizing decision-making at the school level.

**Clarity of purpose and access to information.** Schools that are active in decision-making have a vision statement that focuses their decision-making process on the technical core of schooling—teaching and learning. Determining the school's vision is a schoolwide effort affording the faculty the opportunity to understand the power of their commitment to decisions they make. Those involved in decision-making understand the necessity of using school-based and student-centered data to inform their decisions. In districts where data are limited or not disaggregated at the school level, the decision-making process is limited and curtailed to issues that hold less promise of impact on the school's educational program.

**Power and authority relationships.** Frequently, when decision-making authority is delegated, the degree of authority given to the site is often limited and ambiguous. In schools where there is confusion over decision-making authority, issues addressed at the school level tend to focus on secondary-level issues, such as school climate, scheduling, safety, and parent involvement, rather than on primary concerns, such as instructional programs and strategies, student achievement, and school performance. In order to focus on the primary issues affecting school success, decision-making authority in the areas of curriculum, staffing, and budgeting must be real and authentic.

**Administrative support and the role of central office personnel.** District-level support of school-based decision-making is critical to its success. Superintendents play instrumental roles in moving central offices from a directive function toward a service orientation and resource support network. This shift in roles from a bureaucratic orientation to a service organization is often difficult and misunderstood by those occupying various roles in the district office and in the schools.

**Policies at the district, state, and federal levels.** In a similar manner, decision-making latitude is often restricted at the school level by various state and federal policies or mandates. Under school-based decision-making, schools are encouraged to make decisions regarding the curriculum and supporting instructional strategies. These decisions should be made within a framework of district goals or the core curriculum required by the district or state. Yet schools are often limited by state mandates affecting their educational programs and are similarly restricted by compliance requirements related to federally funded programs within their school or district. Thus, these competing and often contradictory policies constrain school-based decision-making.

## Conclusion

School-based decision-making provides a framework for drawing on the expertise of individuals who are interested in and knowledgeable about matters that affect the successful performance of students. This process depends heavily on the district's leadership to define the parameters of decision-making, to define overarching goals, and to provide the information and professional development necessary to make effective, long-lasting decisions.

*See also:* DECENTRALIZATION AND EDUCATION; SCHOOL CLIMATE; SCHOOL REFORM.

### BIBLIOGRAPHY

CONLEY, SHARON C., and BACHARACH, SAMUEL B. 1990. "From School-Based Management to Participatory School-Site Management." *Phi Delta Kappan* 71:539–544.

DAVID, JANE L. 1989. "Synthesis of Research on School-Based Management." *Educational Leadership* 46(8):45–53.

DRURY, DAVID W. 1999. *Reinventing School-Based Management.* Washington, DC: National School Boards Association.

HESS, GORDON A. 1994. "Using School-Based Management to Restructure Schools." *Education and Urban Society* 26:203–219.

HILL, PAUL T., and BONAN, JOSEPHINE. 1991. *Decentralization and Accountability in Public Education.* Santa Monica, CA: RAND.

JOHNSON, MARGARET J., and PAJARES, FRANK. 1996. "When Shared Decision Making Works: A 3-Year Longitudinal Study." *American Educational Research Journal* 33:599–627.

NATIONAL COMMISSION ON EXCELLENCE IN EDUCATION. 1983. *A Nation at Risk: The Imperative for Educational Reform.* Washington, DC: U.S. Government Printing Office.

RICE, ELLEN MARIE, and SCHNEIDER, GAIL T. 1994. "A Decade of Teacher Empowerment: An Empirical Analysis of Teacher Involvement in Decision Making, 1980–1991." *Journal of Educational Administration* 32(1):43–58.

SMYLIE, MARK A.; LAZARUS, VIRGINIA.; and BROWNLEE-CONYERS, JEAN. 1996. "Instructional Outcomes of School-Based Participative Decision Making." *Educational Evaluation and Policy Analysis* 18:181–198.

WOHLSTETTER, PENELOPE, and ODDEN, ALLAN R. 1992. "Rethinking School-Based Management Policy and Research." *Educational Administration Quarterly* 16:268–286.

WOHLSTETTER, PENELOPE; SMYER, ROXANE; and MOHRMAN, SUSAN ALBERS. 1994. "New Boundaries for School-Based Management." *Educational Evaluation and Policy Analysis* 16:268–286.

GAIL T. SCHNEIDER
LINDA J. MACK

# SCHOOL BOARD RELATIONS

CONTROL OF THE SCHOOLS
Michael D. Usdan

RELATION OF SCHOOL BOARD TO THE COMMUNITY
Kenneth K. Wong
RELATION OF SCHOOL BOARD TO THE
SUPERINTENDENT
Thomas E. Glass

# CONTROL OF THE SCHOOLS

American public education is uniquely structured: Unlike most other nations that tend to have highly centralized national systems of education, the locus of educational decision-making in the United States has traditionally been local. Some 14,000 local school districts in fifty diverse state systems have had delegated to them much of the operational responsibility for public education. Legally, education is a responsibility of the states, which have historically given local districts broad discretionary latitude to operate their systems. The federal government, until the last decade or so of the twentieth century, has had little overt control over education, but has always had considerable influence as national programs have multiplied through the years.

Beginning in the 1990s, and to some extent before then, these traditional roles of the federal, state, and local governments have been changing. As in so many other policy areas of the American polity, the focus of decision-making in education is shifting from the local to the higher levels of government. Increasingly, educational problems are being discussed and resolved in state capitols and Washington, D.C. Citizens have recognized that the problems confronting the public schools cannot be detached from society's broader social, economic, and political concerns. There has been widespread concomitant acknowledgment that local property taxes cannot be the major source of support for schools and that local boards of education will be compelled to rely increasingly on state and federal governments for fiscal assistance. Thus, issues like inequities in school finance, racial and ethnic disparities in student achievement, the relationship of schools to economic growth and development, and related education problems require attention at the state and national levels.

Although many important issues are now debated and acted upon in state capitols and in Washington, D.C., it would be a mistake to underestimate the continuing influence of local school boards. School boards retain important powers that often are overlooked by education reformers who frequently ignore the district level—a vital, strategic cornerstone of the education governance structure.

Rightly or wrongly, local boards and the administrative staffs whom they employ are often regarded by reformers as part of the problem and not the solution to the complex issues confronting American education. As a result, local school boards and superintendents frequently have been unengaged in the ongoing education reform debate.

Indeed, other than a few studies, the relative strengths and weaknesses of the local governance structure have been remarkably ignored during a period of unprecedented public ferment and national interest in public education. But the school board, a unique grass roots representative institution with 97,000 individuals serving as members in approximately 14,000 local districts, persists as a crucial governance linchpin between the school and state levels.

Local school boards and the superintendents whom they employ do not necessarily have to be proactive, progressive, or creative to influence educational policy in very significant ways. Reformers must recognize that many boards and district administrators also influence and shape policy through their inaction. Indeed, as public polls reflect, in many school systems board members and administrators may be accurately reflecting and translating local values and goals in behaving in ways that do not aggressively push for education reform. In other words, in many communities there is basic acceptance of the status quo in schools; reformers, if they are to be successful in their laudable efforts to institutionalize change in the system, must be sensitive to the importance of such local values and goals. Critics will likely have to work with school boards as they appear to be permanent institutions and will continue in exercise considerable direct and indirect influence over the nation's decentralized and diffused educational system.

Local boards have enormous influence because they have the power to hire and fire the superintendent of schools, and have ultimate budgetary responsibilities and set the policy parameters for the district. Board members set the tone with regard to relationships with teachers, parents, and administrators as well as the community at large. If, for example, decentralization or restructuring (however defined) is to have any meaning, local school boards must support and perhaps prod their superintendents into delegating meaningful personnel and budgetary prerogatives to the building level.

Although it is extremely unlikely that the United States would create a fragmented governance structure with 14,000 local units if it could build the system de novo, the local board evidently appears to be too much a part of the fundamental political and educational tradition and culture to be structurally tampered with despite widespread apprehensions in the early twenty-first century about the effectiveness of schools and the pervasive and all too often justified criticism of school boards.

Education reformers can work more effectively within the existing structure to implement changes with the support of influential local officials; for example, district officials in their strategic position between state and building levels could serve as brokers or mediators. There are, for example, some definite contradictions between the "restructuring" movement with its emphasis on the importance of building level autonomy and the top-down regulatory nature of many late-twentieth-century state enactments that often have generated a numbing standardization in the educational process. Local boards and superintendents could be well-positioned intermediaries in efforts to reconcile these basic contradictions between top-down state regulations and bottom-up building level initiatives. Other steps could be taken to propel local boards more directly into the forefront of public discourse about education reform designed to increase student achievement. There is widespread civic ignorance about the roles and responsibilities of local boards and their strategic position in the education governance structure. Indeed, many of the new architects of educational policy from the political and business worlds could be given basic grounding in the rudiments of how schools are governed and organized.

More public attention should be focused upon issues such as the rapid turnover of local board members, the abysmally low voter turnout in local board elections, and the serious managerial, policy-setting, and operational problems that confront many local school officials. Educational reformers and the public at large must pay more attention to strengthening a vital institution that will continue to play an important role in shaping the nation's education future.

*See also:* NATIONAL SCHOOL BOARDS ASSOCIATION; SCHOOL BOARDS.

## BIBLIOGRAPHY

CARVER, JOHN. 2000. "Remaking Governance." *American School Board Journal* 187(3):100–108.

DANZBERGER, JACQUELINE; KIRST, MICHAEL; and USDAN, MICHAEL. 1992. *Governing Public Schools: New Times, New Requirements.* Washington, DC: The Institute for Educational Leadership.

DANZBERGER, JACQUELINE, and USDAN, MICHAEL. 2000. "The Role of School Boards in Standards-Based Reform." *Basic Education* 44(8).

GEMBERLING, KATHRYN W.; SMITH, CARL W; and VILLANI, JOSEPH S. 2000. *The Key Work of School Boards Guidebook.* Washington, DC: National School Boards Association.

### INTERNET RESOURCES

GOODMAN, RICHARD H., and ZIMMERMAN, WILLIAM G., JR. 2000. "Thinking Differently: Recommendations for 21st Century School Board/ Superintendent Leadership, Governance and Teamwork for High Student Achievement." <www.nesdec.org/Thinking_Differently.htm >.

INSTITUTE FOR EDUCATIONAL LEADERSHIP. 2001. "Leadership for Student Learning: Restructuring School District Leadership." <www.iel.org/ programs/21st/reports/district.pdf>.

MICHAEL D. USDAN

# RELATION OF SCHOOL BOARD TO THE COMMUNITY

American public schools are still primarily controlled by local school boards. There are fewer boards than in the past: In the early twenty-first century, 14,000 local school boards govern more than 90,000 schools; in the 1920s, there were 130,000 school boards. Although four out of five school boards are responsible for fewer than 3,000 students, the average size of each board has grown over the years. About a third of all boards are located in five states: California, Texas, Illinois, Nebraska, and New York. While 95 percent of the school boards are popularly elected, school boards in Chicago, Cleveland, Philadelphia, Boston, and several other cities are appointed by the mayor.

## Characteristics of School Boards

Autonomous school board control can be justified by several widely held views in the literature. First, the school board as an autonomous institution is embedded in strongly held public beliefs in democratic, nonpartisan control over public education. The public has traditionally equated local control with districtwide board authority in the constitutional-legal framework of educational governance. In contrasting private and public schools, John Chubb and Terry Moe characterized public school governance as "direct democratic control" (p. 2).

From an economic perspective, the presence of multiple school board systems resembles a quasi-market arrangement that can be cost-efficient to the consumers. States and localities with multiple suppliers of services promise a better fit between consumer-taxpayers' preferences and the level and quality of local services. As Charles Tiebout's (1956) classic work suggested, taxpayers make residential decisions that would maximize the benefits they expect to obtain from public services and minimize the level of taxes that they have to pay for those services. In particular, middle-class taxpayers who can afford to spend more on goods and services are keenly concerned about the quality of basic services, such as schools. As Albert Hirschman (1970) argued, they are more ready to exit when they perceive a decline in those municipal services that they value. Studies of district-level performance in metropolitan areas suggest that interdistrict competition can improve service quality. The out-migration of middle-class families to suburban school districts seems to provide the empirical support for this line of argument. Recent establishment of quasi-public boards that oversee charter schools also shows the increasing popularity of parental choice when the neighborhood schools are failing.

Yet a third view is based on functional consideration. Thomas Shannon, former executive director of the National School Boards Association, has argued that school boards serve several indispensable functions for the common good. They develop strategic plans, manage the operation of the system, comply with federal and state laws, evaluate educational programs, arbitrate complaints from citizens and employees, and represent the collective interests of the entire district. The boards also negotiate contracts with teachers unions and serve as managerial buffers between individual schools and state and federal agencies. In other words, local school boards make a "non-nationalized" educational system functional.

## Performance-Based Accountability

As the public increases its demands for performance-based accountability in public schools, the quality of school board governance is called into question. *Facing the Challenge: The Report of the Twentieth Century Fund Task Force on School Governance* by the Twentieth Century Fund observed in 1992 that school boards "are facing a serious crisis of legitimacy and relevance" (p. 1). According to a 1988 to 1990 survey by Jacqueline Danzberger and colleagues of school board members in 128 districts in 16 states, even school board members perceived themselves as least effective in "the core elements of governance—leadership, planning and goal setting, involving parents and the community, influence on others, policy oversight, board operations, and board development" (p. 56). For example, the survey showed that boards used inconsistent performance measures to evaluate their superintendents. Further, due to the Progressive tradition of taking politics out of schools, school boards are largely isolated from other lateral institutions (e.g., housing and health care agencies) that affect the well-being of children.

The decline in public confidence over school board leadership seems salient in urban districts. Based on a 1998 survey, the National School Boards Foundation found that "[t]here is a consistent, significant difference in perception between urban school board members and the urban public on a number of key issues" (p. 12). Although 67 percent of the urban board members rated schools in A and B categories, only 49 percent of the urban public did. Whereas three out of four board members rated the teachers as excellent and good, only 54 percent of the public agreed. The public seemed half as likely as the board members to agree that the schools were "doing a good job" in the following areas: preparing students for college, keeping violence and drugs out of schools, maintaining discipline among students, and teaching children who do not speak English. Subsequently, the National School Boards Foundation called upon urban leaders to sharpen the focus on student performance.

In light of these concerns, several reforms have been tried to improve accountability. One reform aims at promoting a sense of "ownership" among parents at the school site. While New York City and numerous urban districts experimented with some form of site-based governance in the 1960s, the most extensive decentralization occurred in Chicago when

1988 state legislation created local school councils in all the public schools in the city. Between 1989 and 1995, each of the 550 Chicago schools was primarily governed by an elected, parent-dominated local school council, whose authority included the selection of principal and the use of a substantial discretionary fund. However, community support for the local school council gradually declined. From 1989 to 1993, turnout among parents and community residents plunged by 68 percent, and fewer candidates signed up for local school council offices. As the reforms of the local school councils failed to turn around low performing schools, the legislature enacted another reform that enabled mayoral control over schools in 1995.

### Race and School Boards

A second type of reform is associated with racial succession in school boards. Many analysts observe that the predominantly white power structure seems less ready to respond to the minority and low-income constituency in urban schools. According to this view, a shift in racial control over governmental institutions would improve school quality and promote student performance. However, this conventional expectation is not empirically supported by a study in 2000 by Jeffrey Henig and colleagues of school reform in four African-American-led cities, namely Atlanta, Georgia; Baltimore, Maryland; Detroit, Michigan; and the District of Columbia. None of the cities were able to produce any measurable educational progress for minority students. The authors found that "racialized politics" has contributed to governance ineffectiveness in both direct and indirect ways. Particularly important is the intensity to which local stakeholders are affected by "fears, suspicions, expectations, loyalties, tactics, and habits related to race" (p. 7). Multiple facets of racialized politics are illuminated by the authors' careful analysis of interviews with hundreds of actors both outside and inside the formal governmental institutions, including generally influential people (e.g., city council members and business leaders), community advocates, and education specialists.

The four cities provide ample evidence on how racial concerns have constrained the collective behaviors of both black and white elites. For example, African-American community activists are reluctant to criticize African-American city officials because they want to preserve the reputation of black institutions in general. Likewise, white business elites tend to refrain from criticizing African-American-controlled school systems for fear that their actions are seen in racial terms. In other words, race "complicates" coalition building because it "continues to affect perceptions, calculations, loyalties, and concerns in ways that tug at the thread of collaboration and erode civic capacity to undertake meaningful and sustained reform" (p. 212). Interracial trust and confidence become so limited that civic capacity lacks a solid foundation.

### Integrated Governance

The third strand of reform is "integrated governance," where there is an integration of political accountability and educational performance standards at the systemwide level. In numerous urban districts, the mayor takes control over schools with an appointed school board and superintendent (for example, Chicago began such a system in 1995). In this regard, mayoral leadership in education occurs in a policy context where years of decentralized reform alone have not produced systemwide improvement in student performance in big city schools. Reform advocates who pushed for site-based strategies may have overestimated the capacity of the school community to raise academic standards. Decentralized reforms are directed at reallocating power between the systemwide authority and the schools within the public school system. However, decentralized initiatives often fail to take into full consideration powerful quasi-formal actors, such as the teacher union and other organized interests. Decisions made at the school site are constrained by collective bargaining agreements. In addition, decentralization may widen the resource gap between schools that have access to external capital (such as parental organizational skills and grants from foundations) and those that receive limited support from nongovernmental sources. In response to these concerns, "integrated governance" enables the mayor to rely on systemwide standards to hold schools and students accountable for their performance. Failing schools and students are subject to sanctions while they are given additional support.

### Measuring Performance

Efforts to improve school board accountability also present a challenge for developing a framework to measure performance of the school boards. Although student performance serves as a useful indicator of the overall performance of a school system, its aggregated character falls short of specifying the link between the functions of the school boards and school performance. In other words, there is a need to develop indicators of institutional effectiveness to assess the school boards. Toward this goal, Kenneth Wong and Mark Moulton attempted in 1998 to develop an institutional "report card" on various state and local actors, including the school board. Using survey responses from members of the broad policy community in Illinois, Wong and Moulton found that the school board and the central administration in Chicago have significantly improved their institutional rating following mayoral control.

In short, school boards are in transition. While many communities maintain the tradition of nonpartisan, popularly elected school boards, urban districts that are perceived as low performing are likely to attempt alternative governance. In the early twenty-first century, a greater number of urban school boards are likely to be appointed by mayors and/or challenged by charter schools. Thus, school boards, regardless of their student enrollment and region, will be driven by public concerns over accountability.

*See also:* EDUCATIONAL ACCOUNTABILITY; FAMILY, SCHOOL, AND COMMUNITY CONNECTIONS; SCHOOL BOARDS.

### BIBLIOGRAPHY

CHUBB, JOHN, and MOE, TERRY. 1990. *Politics, Markets and America's Schools.* Washington, DC: Brookings Institution.

DANZBERGER, JACQUELINE; KIRST, MICHAEL; and USDAN, MICHAEL. 1992. *Governing Public Schools: New Times, New Requirements.* Washington, DC: The Institute for Educational Leadership.

HENIG, JEFFREY; HULA, RICHARD; ORR, MARION; and PEDESCLEAUX, DESIREE. 1999. *The Color of School Reform: Race, Politics, and the Challenge of Urban Education.* Princeton, NJ: Princeton University Press.

HILL, PAUL. 1997. "Contracting in Public Education," In *New Schools for a New Century,* ed. Diane Ravitch and Joseph Viteritti. New Haven, CT: Yale University Press.

HIRSCHMAN, ALBERT. 1971. *Exit, Voice and Loyalty.* Cambridge, MA: Harvard University Press.

HOXBY, CAROLINE. 1998. "What Do America's 'Traditional' Forms of School Choice Teach Us about School Choice Reform?" *Economic Policy Review* 4(1):47–59.

NATIONAL SCHOOL BOARDS FOUNDATION. 1999. *Leadership Matters: Transforming Urban School Boards.* Alexandria, VA: National School Boards Foundation.

SHANNON, THOMAS. 1992. "Local Control and 'Organizacrats.'" In *School Boards: Changing Local Control,* ed. Patricia E. First and Herbert J. Walberg. Berkeley, CA: McCutchan.

TIEBOUT, CHARLES. 1956. "A Pure Theory of Local Expenditures." *Journal of Political Economy* 64:416–424.

TWENTIETH CENTURY FUND. 1992. *Facing the Challenge: The Report of the Twentieth Century Fund Task Force on School Governance.* New York: The Twentieth Century Fund.

WONG, KENNETH. 1999. *Funding Public Schools: Politics and Policy.* Lawrence: University Press of Kansas.

WONG, KENNETH. 2000. "Big Change Questions: Chicago School Reform: From Decentralization to Integrated Governance." *Journal of Educational Change* 1:97–105.

WONG, KENNETH. 2001. "Integrated Governance in Chicago and Birmingham (UK)." In *School Choice or Best Systems,* ed. Margaret C. Wang and Herbert J. Walberg. Mahwah, NJ: Erlbaum.

WONG, KENNETH, and JAIN, PUSHPAM. 1999. "Newspapers as Policy Actors in Urban School Systems: The Chicago Story." *Urban Affairs Review* 35(2):210–246.

WONG, KENNETH, and MOULTON, MARK. 1998. "Governance Report Cards: Accountability in the Chicago Public School System." *Education and Urban Society* 30:459–478.

KENNETH K. WONG

## RELATION OF SCHOOL BOARD TO THE SUPERINTENDENT

By providing a free public education for rich and poor, local school boards have nurtured and protected American democracy for more than a century. This American institution anchors a local governance model that is unique among the national systems of education throughout the world.

The organization of school districts and school boards has changed little in one hundred years. The new millennium finds about 14,320 school districts predominantly governed by elected layperson boards of five or seven members. The average school district enrolls 2,200 students and is located in a nonurban setting. Although the majority of Americans live in cities and suburbs, the majority of school districts are located in small towns and rural areas. There are nearly 80,000 school board members but only several hundred urban board members guide policy and management for half the nations' school children. Each decade a higher percentage of children attend schools in suburbs and the cities.

## School Board Members

Unfortunately, there is little available data describing demographics and characteristics of local school board members. It can be reasonably assumed from scattered data that about 60 percent of board members are men with a college education who work in white-collar positions. The number of women and minority board members appears to be increasing. It also seems that a minority of board members are parents of school-age children.

The role of local boards is characterized in the literature as the means by which community members can participate in setting educational policies affecting their children and the spending of local tax dollars. The local school board member role involves seeking out the opinions of the community and representing their educational interests through formulation of policy.

## School Board Service

Most members serve without pay in positions that require countless hours per week of listening to citizens, reading, and attending meetings. Until the 1960s, most authorities described a typical board members' motivation for serving as filling a community obligation. Boards were comprised of "main street" businessmen, professionals, and occasionally retired school administrators. These boards usually functioned without partisan politics, and seldom did members focus on single or controversial personal agendas.

Many boards in the early twenty-first century are comprised of members who are elected to represent specific interest groups, such as teachers or taxpayer groups. Or, they serve on the board with a single agenda interest, such as special education, bilingual education, school prayer, fixing a school program, or firing a coach or superintendent. Most

authorities agree school boards are considerably more politicized than in the past. Board members with political agendas sincerely believe their actions serve the schools and the public interest.

## The Superintendent

The most important action a school board takes is the selection of a superintendent. For the average school district this happens every six or seven years. For districts mired in conflict it might occur every two or three years. Superintendent tenure data suggests that districts with stable boards and communities tend to attract higher quality superintendents and keep them longer. Since a school district is almost a perfect reflection of its community, it is not surprising to find turmoil-ridden boards in communities beset by contentious issues, such as poverty, high unemployment, illiteracy, and racial tension.

The impression, established by media and journal articles, is that constant turmoil and struggle between boards and superintendents exist in all districts. Fewer than 1 percent of superintendents are terminated each year. A larger number, however, move on to other districts after acrimonious relations with the board or certain board members. The American Association of School Administrators study conducted every ten years gives a more realistic picture of the state of school board and superintendent relations. For decades superintendents have reported their annual evaluations given by boards to be "excellent" or "good." In about fifteen percent of the districts reported, however, the superintendent's evaluation does signal a problem in board relations.

The root of many conflicts between boards and superintendents is a "zone of acceptance." This is the zone in which the superintendent may operate and make decisions. Most boards directly and indirectly create the parameters of the zone. Often individual board members try to add to or delete from the actions a superintendent has been led to believe are in the zone. The result is conflict with the board or individual board members. In turn, superintendents generally create "zones of acceptance" within which other district administrators work. When the superintendent's "zone" is altered, sometimes the entire administrative structure of the district is changed.

## Boards and Superintendents: The Working Relationship

The relationship between board and superintendent begins prior to hiring. The superintendent search process for most districts is intensive and includes several visits to the district by each finalist. During these one- or two-day interviews, board members form an initial relationship with the future superintendent. This is probably not true if in-house candidates are being considered. Often one or more board members are not enthusiastic about a candidate later selected by the board majority. This may create a situation where the new superintendent must quickly "prove" himself or herself to the board member(s).

In many districts after initial hiring the superintendent enjoys a "honeymoon" period with the board. This is seldom more than six-months in duration, or until a serious problem arises with the superintendent's position or an action is opposed by one or more board members. During these first few months the superintendent and board are becoming acquainted with each others' views about district operations. This is a critical time for board and superintendent to establish parameters of decision-making. Perceptive boards set limits within which the superintendent may make unilateral decisions. The types of decisions that can be made by the board and those that are the responsibility of the superintendent should be clearly understood and respected by each party. By doing this many potential conflicts can be avoided between boards and superintendents. Well-functioning boards appear to have clear role definitions for the superintendent and themselves.

## Communication

Communication is the critical element of superintendent and board relations. Many superintendents spend very little time in direct communication with board members. Several national superintendent studies claim the average superintendent spends less than three hours per week in talking or meeting with board members. Not included in direct communication are written memos and letters from the superintendent to the board. Most likely a sizable percentage of the time superintendents do spend in board communication is with the board president.

A 2000 study of 175 of the nation's leading superintendents showed this group spent three times more effort in direct communication with board members. It was not uncommon for these superintendents to spend more than a full work day each week in talking with board members.

The lack of time spent with board members by some superintendents can be explained by a long-held negative view of boards and board members. Often educators view boards as "outsiders" possessing power to make unwise or arbitrary decisions affecting schools, students, and staff. Collective bargaining often hardens negative opinion about boards in the eyes of district staff.

An important piece of written communication is the "board package." In nearly every school district, prior to board meetings, a loose-leaf binder that contains information about each meeting agenda item is distributed by the superintendent's office. This board package can be voluminous, taking several hours of study time for board members. The content of the board package often serves to initiate communication between board members and the superintendent. A few superintendents take the initiative and personally call board members to ask if they have questions or concerns about the meeting agenda and the information included in the board package. Others wait for board members to call. The flow and type of superintendent and board communication varies from district to district, and is certainly being modified by the use of e-mail.

Some boards desire that the superintendent directly communicate with the board president (or chair), leaving to that board member the responsibility to inform other members. Most boards, however, wish to give each member the opportunity to directly communicate with the superintendent.

Communication problems arise when board members initiate communication directly with principals and staff without giving the superintendent prior notification. Some board members will go so far as to directly, or by insinuation, instruct a principal or staff member. This undercuts the superintendent's authority and creates confusion in the district. Teachers and administrators often interpret intrusion by board members to mean the superintendent lacks authority. The superintendent and other board members may take offense, and the result may be a severe strain on board and superintendent relations.

School problems of board members' children are sometimes a source of conflict between superintendents and individual board members. These personal conflicts can permanently damage working relationships. Despite restrictions on nepotism, in some states, board members have spouses or relatives working in the district. This can be the source of another serious personal conflict between the superintendent and board members. Lastly, some board members may possess direct or indirect business links with district vendors or competing vendors. Board business interests can create conflict with the superintendent and a legal problem for district.

Perhaps the most often encountered superintendent and board conflict area is the "special" interest of board members. Frequently, board members seek board office in order to see a specific objective enacted. This might be the termination of a coach or administrator, or even the superintendent. Or, the special interest might be to have the Ten Commandments posted in classrooms or open the school day with prayer. Superintendents (and other board members) are placed in a difficult position, as they might be required by law or procedure to withhold support of a given special interest. The problem is accentuated many times when the board member is allied with special interest groups in the community. A good example would be a board member who represents the interests of an antitax group. This board member may resist establishing a budget, setting a referendum for a new building, or negotiating with teachers. This type of resistance creates tension within the board, community, and with the superintendent.

Actually, the most serious board and superintendent conflict originates within the board itself. As boards become politicized, identifiable member coalitions emerge and clash with other board members. This is especially the case in large urban districts with boards divided by racial issues.

Conflict among board members often leads to each group trying to receive the superintendent's support for their position. In many conflicts there is little chance for the superintendent to remain neutral and efforts to do so result in alienation on the part of both groups. Internal board politics is a very serious problem in many districts, and there are usually no outside neutral parties available to mediate intraboard differences that are often disguised as superintendent and board conflict. Most likely a majority of superintendents leaving districts in midcontract do so because of intraboard conflict.

The outcome of board conflict, made public when the board votes on an issue, is usually a "split" board, meaning that consensus is very difficult to achieve. Generally, the public interprets the vote supporting a given proposition as reflecting the group of board members who support the superin-

tendent. Some superintendents attempt to insulate themselves from what they consider to be unfair board criticism or interference. A frequent strategy that is used is to create a citizens' advisory group for the superintendent comprised of leaders in the community. Superintendents believe this group can provide protection in the event of conflict with the board or act to stop intraboard squabbling. In addition many of the advisory group members are in a position to be future board candidates, giving the superintendent potential allies in these possible board members.

The superintendent's actions in the community can be a flashpoint for board conflict. Even though superintendents are prohibited from participation in board elections, conflict sometimes arises when board members perceive the superintendent's encouraging a community member to run for a board position. Some board members are also suspicious of a superintendent who serves as chief spokesperson for the district. They perceive this as diminishing their political stature with constituent groups.

## Putting Together a Superintendent/Board Relations Plan

Nearly all authorities indicate role conflict to be the leading cause of superintendent and board conflict. In order to reduce the likelihood of conflict it seems important that roles are clarified at the beginning of a superintendent's or a board's tenure. This is difficult to accomplish without a neutral third party facilitator and also because of increased board turnover in thousands of districts.

A potential source of assistance for board members and superintendents is in-service training offered to new board members by state school board associations. Districts that use a strategic planning process have a natural opportunity for the board and superintendent to mutually determine roles and responsibilities.

A majority of superintendents provide orientation sessions for new board members. This is another opportunity for the superintendent to clarify roles with at least one board member. Unfortunately, the politicization of boards has resulted in the increase of sensitive political issues, which makes superintendent and board relations very difficult. In a number of cases, superintendents never even have an opportunity to establish working relations with a board. More often board members are elected on a quasi-political platform of candidates who are sponsored by special interest groups. When this slate of candidates is elected, they immediately "buy out" the superintendent's contract in order to hire a person sharing their political views.

One problem contributing to a negative climate between superintendents and boards can usually be adjusted if not eliminated by the superintendent. This is the time required for board members to spend on district governance and activities. Many board members complain board membership is actually a second full-time job. This is nearly true in large urban districts with serious student achievement and political problems. Board time can be dramatically reduced by the superintendent and management team through careful examination of time demands placed on the board. The superintendent must know the board well enough to be able to screen out unnecessary paperwork and meetings. Needless hours of time can be eliminated if the board is willing to trust the superintendent and management team to perform this task.

Board members who give up family and even work time for board business often believe the superintendent and management team are foisting off decision-making and management responsibilities on the board. In districts where board members spend no more than five hours per week on board business, it is quite likely that superintendent and board relations function more effectively.

The relationship between a board and superintendent establishes a tone for the district environment. If the relationship is cooperative and harmonious district employees feel secure as roles are clarified, expectations are clear, and ambiguity does not cloud attempts to change and improve programs. Conflict between the superintendent and board creates tension inside the district and in the community. The situation discourages program innovation and reform, and deters constructive community involvement in the schools. It certainly can be fatal to any bond or tax rate referenda attempts. Unfortunately, many districts are not proactive in meeting the challenge of board and superintendent relations.

*See also:* SUPERINTENDENT OF LARGE-CITY SCHOOL SYSTEMS; SUPERINTENDENT OF SCHOOLS.

**BIBLIOGRAPHY**

AMUNDSEN, KRISTIN, et al. 1996. *Becoming a Better Board Member.* Alexandria, VA: National School Boards Association.

DANZBERGER, JACQUELINE; KIRST, MICHAEL; and USDAN, MICHAEL. 1992. *Governing Public Schools: New Times, New Requirements.* Washington, DC: Institute for Educational Leadership.

GLASS, THOMAS. 1992. *The Study of the American School Superintendency: America's Leaders in a Time of Reform.* Arlington, VA: American Association of School Administrators.

GLASS, THOMAS. 2001. *A Few Good Men and Women Need Apply: The Superintendent Applicant Crisis.* Denver, CO: Education Commission of the States.

GLASS, THOMAS; BJORK, LARS; and BRUNNER, CRYSS. 2000. *The Study of the American School Superintendency 2000: A Look at the Superintendent in the New Millennium.* Arlington, VA: American Association of School Administrators.

INSTITUTE FOR EDUCATIONAL LEADERSHIP. 1982. *School Boards: Strengthening Grass Roots Leadership.* Washington, DC: Institute for Educational Leadership.

KOWALSKI, THEODORE. 1999. *The School Superintendent: Theory, Practice and Cases.* Englewood Cliffs, NJ: Prentice-Hall.

MCCURDY, DAVID. 1992. *Superintendent and School Board Relations.* Arlington, VA: American Association of School Administrators.

ROGERS, JOY. 1992. *On Board: A Survival Guide for School Board Members.* Bloomington, IN: Phi Delta Kappa.

SMOLEY, EUGENE. 1999. *Effective School Boards: Improving Board Performance.* San Francisco: Jossey-Bass.

THOMAS E. GLASS

# SCHOOL BOARDS

DUTIES, RESPONSIBILITIES, DECISION-MAKING, AND LEGAL BASIS FOR LOCAL SCHOOL BOARD POWERS
Joseph Beckham
Barbara Klaymeier Wills
SELECTION AND EDUCATION OF MEMBERS
Kent M. Weeks

# DUTIES, RESPONSIBILITIES, DECISION-MAKING, AND LEGAL BASIS FOR LOCAL SCHOOL BOARD POWERS

Local school boards have been an integral feature of the U.S. public education system for nearly 100 years, and they are widely regarded as the principal democratic body capable of representing citizens in local education decisions. The formal institutional roles assigned to school boards, and the designated position board members play as representatives of the community, would lead one to believe that the school board has a decisive role in public education policy and school system administration. In the minds of many lay citizens, school boards have considerable influence over educational decisions and provide a key social and political connection to the schooling process.

Although research has affirmed the important role that local school boards played in implementing educational reforms such as student testing and graduation requirements, some critics have contended the traditional leadership and policymaking roles of local school boards have been compromised by bureaucratic intransigence, a tendency to micromanage school system operations, and divisiveness caused by special interest groups. While one researcher has suggested that lay control of schools is a myth, others have argued that the school board is essential to ensure the quality of public education services at the local level.

## Legal Basis for Local School Board Powers

The U.S. Constitution contains no mention of education. With the federal government limited to those powers either expressly stated or implied in the Constitution, the federal role in public education is secondary to that of the states. Power over public education is as essential an attribute of state sovereignty as that of the power to tax or to provide for the general welfare of the state's citizens. The state legislative mandate to provide for a system of public schools is found in the state constitution, usually in language requiring a "general," "uniform," "thorough," or "efficient" system of public schools.

Even though power officially resides with the states, concerns about efficiency and local involvement are addressed through the delegation of authority from the legislative branch to the local school board. Although the powers and duties of the local board vary by state jurisdiction, all fifty states except

Hawaii have a two-tiered governance structure and provide for local school districts governed by an elected or appointed board. States also govern through state boards of education, administer through state departments of education, and typically provide for an elected or appointed chief state school officer.

Sources of authority that influence the duties and responsibilities of the local school board include state and federal constitutions, legislative enactments, rules and regulations promulgated by the U.S. Department of Education and the state board of education, and legal interpretations by judges, attorneys general, and administrative agencies. A school board functions locally, within the confines of the state's delegation of power and the geographical boundaries of the district, but is a legal agency of the state and thus derives its power from the state's constitution, laws, and judicial decisions. By state legislative enactment, school boards are delegated power and authority to develop policies, rules, and regulations to control the operation of the schools, including system organization, school site location, school finance, equipment purchase, staffing, attendance, curriculum, extracurricular activities, and other functions essential to the day-to-day operation of schools within the district's boundaries. Boards may also be authorized by the state legislature to levy taxes, invest resources, initiate eminent domain proceedings, acquire land, and assume bonded indebtedness.

School boards are corporate bodies created for the purpose of implementing state legislative policy concerning public schools and locally administering the state's system of public education. Board members are state officers who act under color of state law when conducting the official business of the state. The exercise of the local board's authority must be predicated upon an express or implied delegation of authority from the legislature and must meet a test of reasonableness that avoids a judicial presumption of arbitrary or capricious action. Because the authority of the local board lies in its status as a corporate body created by the state legislature, an actual meeting of the board is an essential prerequisite to official action. Individual board members are not vested with powers outside their role as a member of the local school board, although the board is often vested with power to ratify the actions of its members, agents, or employees if the ratification vote occurs in an official board meeting and is documented in the official minutes of the board.

## State and Federal Reform Efforts

The states and the federal government increased their visibility in public education policy from the 1950s into the twenty-first century. The federal role in education was spurred with implementation of the National Defense Education Act of 1958 and the Elementary and Secondary Education Act of 1965. Federal antidiscrimination policy became a crosscutting social issue for public schools and school districts with the passage of the Civil Rights Act of 1964, Title IX of the Education Amendments of 1972, and the Rehabilitation Act of 1973. Federal entitlements to special education were initiated with the Education for All Handicapped Children Act of 1975. Whether in the form of categorical aid designed to meet targeted educational needs or in the form of block grants permitting states discretion in the allocation of funds, federal largess has been influential in shaping educational policy and shifting the locus of control over public schools.

At the same time that the state role in public education expanded to accommodate federal funding initiatives, demands for reform of public school finance systems were being heard in state and federal courts. The Texas school finance system survived a constitutional challenge in the 1973 case of *San Antonio Independent School District v. Rodriquez*, but judges in state courts showed less deference to the state legislature's authority to construct a school finance scheme and a concomitant willingness to interpret state constitutional provisions as a mandate providing for a system of public education. State courts in Kentucky, New Jersey, and Texas have been among those adopting an active role in the reform of school finance. With the possibility of litigation mounting in each state, the momentum for finance reform led state legislatures to embrace changes that centralized education governance and restricted the authority and influence of local school boards.

In 1954, prior to the decision in *Rodriquez*, the U.S. Supreme Court struck down racial segregation in the Kansas public school system in *Brown v. Board of Education of Topeka, Kansas.* The *Brown* decision was followed by a series of cases compelling local school district boards to desegregate public schools under consent decrees that were overseen by court-appointed special masters. As the Supreme Court expanded the desegregation mandate to address the pattern and practice of segregation in school districts throughout the United States, local school districts found their influence diminished and their actions scrutinized by federal courts intent on addressing a history of international segregative practices in America's public schools.

With the 1983 publication of *A Nation at Risk: The Imperative for Educational Reform,* by the National Commission on Excellence in Education, a dramatic escalation of national concern about public education led state and federal policymakers to advocate for quality and to require rigorous testing, higher graduation requirements, and more demanding academic standards. In a policy environment in which demands for scarce public resources were outstripping the revenue generated by the state's system of taxation, concern for state level accountability and efficient use of resources was magnified. The education reform movement considerably strengthened the power of the states in relation to the historic discretionary power that had been exercised by local school boards. Policies previously left to the discretion of local school boards were increasingly prescribed by the state.

Local school boards have been characterized as the largest losers in the reform efforts of the 1980s and 1990s. State legislatures have generated educational policies and regulations directed to academic standards, professional certification and preparation, and curriculum development. Bypassing local school boards in the haste to reform public education, additional legislation has emphasized choice as well as quality, and encouraged the development of charter schools with limited regulatory ties to the local school system, school-based management, vouchers, tax credits, and home-schooling options.

## Duties and Responsibilities

In most states, it is the local board that is charged with the responsibility to establish and maintain a basic organizational structure for the local school system, develop curriculum, meet federal and state mandates for public schools, appoint a superintendent and key members of the central office staff, adopt an annual budget, and create a climate that promotes educational excellence. Consequently, school boards initiate educational policies at the local level and have a responsibility for implementing a variety of state and federal policies. These boards provide important administrative oversight relative to the educational policies and programs they institute; play a central role in establishing systems and processes to ensure the school system's fiscal, programmatic, and outcome accountability; and undertake broad human resource functions that include making crucial decisions regarding the district's top-level leadership and key staff. Finally, school boards provide leadership for the local school system, adopting a unifying vision and mission, soliciting and balancing the participation and input of members of the community, and advocating on behalf of the educational needs of children at the local, state, and national levels.

Local school boards function as legislative, executive, and quasi-judicial agencies. They must develop, implement, and assess policy; institute sound employee relations; conduct open meetings; recognize and conform to the legal mandates imposed by state and federal laws; and govern within the limits of a delegation of state authority. Additionally, the board has an obligation to assess its successes and failures; inform the public of all deliberations and decisions; promote accountability; avoid abuse of power; enhance public understanding of its mission; conform to standards of ethical behavior; provide a framework for setting goals; and develop strategic plans for the accomplishment of those goals.

From the myriad tasks that have been delegated to school boards, or which have accrued over their history, three overlapping and often contradictory responsibilities can be distinguished. First, the board is a policymaking entity for the local school district. Second, the board is an administrative agency that must provide oversight for the operation of the local school system and is ultimately accountable for the system's operation. Third, the board is a democratically elected body that provides school system leadership and represents the interests of the community on public education issues.

**Policymaking.** The first responsibility of the local school board is to make policy for the sound operation of the school district. State statute law typically requires that the local school board approve the district's budget; develop long- and short-term goals; establish educational objectives, performance indicators, and pupil assessment systems; and approve curricular frameworks and standards for student achievement. In a rational planning model, board policies begin with the articulation of a shared vision and mission for the school district, followed by the establishment of key goals and strategic objectives. Comparing current outcomes with desired out-

comes and analyzing gaps between current outcomes and desired outcomes should then lead to the development and implementation of strategic plans for the accomplishment of key objectives. In reality, school boards often make policy under conditions in which competing demands and legal imperatives make systematic and rational planning difficult. As a result, board policies cover a vast array of school operations, and the policies may appear ambiguous or contradictory when viewed by those who are charged with the responsibility to implement the policy in practice.

The policy environment in which local school boards operate is complicated by a number of factors. Legal mandates based on state and federal legislation, judicial decisions, and negotiated union contracts may impose substantial constraints on the local board's policymaking authority. Board members may have conflicting and irreconcilable views on the appropriate means to achieve key objectives. Educators may insist that the board defer to the professional expertise of administrators and teachers on matters of educational policy. The degree of board turnover may affect policymaking capabilities because of a loss of institutional or collective memory essential to recall the purpose and intent of previous policies. In addition, the policymaking environment often involves urgent and immediate policy decisions inflamed by public controversy, influenced by local interest groups, and complicated by insufficient time to analyze the policy in light of system objectives.

**Administration.** Another major role of the school board is that of administrative agency. While local boards are discouraged from becoming involved in the day-to-day operation and administration of schools, demands for public accountability dictate some level of involvement in the administration of the school system. Public accountability requires that the board must, at a minimum, provide oversight, adopt standards, and assess progress toward the accomplishment of key district objectives. To some extent, the board's administrative functions require knowledge of the operational procedures and organizational structures instituted to accomplish board policies. This knowledge cannot be achieved without some degree of administrative oversight.

A regular criticism of local boards is the tendency of board members to confuse monitoring of key outcomes and executive performance with prescribing how to manage the components of the system. A study conducted in West Virginia found that school boards spent 3 percent of their time on policy development and as much as 54 percent of their time on administrative matters. A study of fifty-five randomly selected school boards indicated that financial and personnel issues were among the most frequent areas of decision-making, displacing deliberations on educational policy by a significant margin.

It is axiomatic that school boards should focus on policymaking and eschew micromanagement of the school system. One national report—*Facing the Challenge: The Report of the Twentieth Century Task Force on School Governance*—has proposed that school boards emphasize their role as policy boards instead of collective management committees, with the aim of establishing policies to enhance student academic progress. As a practical matter, many local boards assume time-consuming duties that are primarily administrative. For example, many local boards act as hearing agencies for employee and student grievances. This quasi-judicial role conflicts with the policymaking priorities of the board. It has been recommended that school districts delegate the responsibility to hear complaints and appeals from individual students or employees to administrative law judges or other qualified third parties.

The local school board's responsibility for district personnel is another illustration of the practical difficulty in separating policymaking and administrative functions. In an organization that is labor intensive and commits a substantial portion of its annual operating budget to salaries and benefits for its teachers, administrators, and support staff, the board's administrative responsibility for personnel is unavoidable. State law typically requires that school boards select a superintendent, adopt and implement personnel policies for staff, appraise school and employee performance, ratify individual and collective employee contract agreements, and serve as the final administrative agency in dismissal proceedings. Issues such as recruitment, selection, and retention of teachers; setting compensation levels; and developing contract provisions are recurring agenda items for local school boards.

**Leadership.** The local school board has a vital role in providing leadership for district schools, serving as a forum for citizen input relevant to public education, and inculcating the beliefs, behaviors, and symbolic representations that define the organizational culture of the school system. In this role, the board's responsibilities include adopting a unifying vision and mission, soliciting and balancing the participation and input of members of the community, and advocating on behalf of the educational needs of children at the local, state, and national levels. Consistent with this leadership responsibility, the local school board should emphasize the standard of continuous improvement for its own operations as well as that of the school system as a whole and undertake to evaluate its performance and improve upon that performance.

As a democratically elected body intended to represent the interests of the community on public education issues, the local school board is a symbol of local control of public education. By providing an accessible forum for discussion of education issues that affect local communities, school boards maintain a key component of their viability. Founded on the belief that citizens should play a dominant role in determining how children in a community are educated, local school boards have been described as a historic linchpin of American educational governance. In a diverse society with a multiplicity of cultures, the board has become the body in which all constituencies find expression, a role seen as crucial to sustaining participatory and representative government.

Though the local school board must provide leadership for the school system, the complexity, ambiguity, and uncertainty clouding the environment for public education in the United States makes assuming this role difficult. Education policymakers at the federal and state level; competing interest groups with substantial influence in the political process; and a multitude of stakeholders, including business organizations, parents' groups, taxpayers, labor organizations, and special-interest groups, complicate the policymaking process. As laypeople with limited experience, board members may hold outdated beliefs about best practices or be focused on a single issue that subsumes the broader responsibility for visionary leadership. Because elected school boards are especially sensitive to public criticism, board members may adopt a posture of reacting to these groups rather than taking a proactive role, resulting in crisis management and a tendency to consider issues on an ad hoc basis rather than in the context of defined goals and objectives.

## Decision-Making

A host of contemporary concerns present challenges to the local school board's pivotal role in the governance structure in American public education. These challenges include declining public confidence in public schools; limited financial and operational support; changing demographics; perceived drops in student achievement and performance; persistent student attrition or dropouts; reports of crime and violence in the school setting; and adversarial relationships with employee groups. At the same time that major challenges confront local boards, centralization of educational policymaking at the state level, initiated by the educational finance reforms of the second half of the twentieth century, when coupled with a heightened federal role in public education, has changed the locus of control over public schools and diminished local board powers.

Given the variety of policy considerations for school boards, the decision-making process of the board will vary depending upon the issues addressed, the parties involved, and the organizational interests, operational procedures, time constraints, and personal values of the decision makers. School boards are political organizations with members elected to serve a broad constituency. Decision-making in this environment is a highly political process in which coalition building, bargaining, competition, and adaptation are common. As with most organizations, it cannot be assumed that school board members are unified actors, and studies of school board decision-making show that individual role interests and social roles often serve as analytical constructs to explain decision-making processes. Local boards typically consist of members who possess divergent individual agendas and a limited set of mutually shared values or beliefs. Nevertheless, existing school board policies, extant procedures, and regularized customs and practices create and then enforce a unifying culture within the school board that is designed to maintain the status quo and has a relatively conservative perspective.

Board meetings follow the policies and procedures traditionally created to manage operations and are often characterized as ritualistic, systematic, and programmed. Although local boards are authorized by state law to adopt their own procedures, they are bound by law to follow those procedures once adopted. For example, procedural rules for establishing a quorum in order to take official action must be followed. A record of minutes of board meetings must be maintained in order that the board documents its deliberations and actions. Notice of meetings must conform to state sunshine laws, and business must be conducted in public, open meetings unless an exception to state law permits an executive session authorizing the board to deliberate in private.

The work of board members is seldom self-selected and is more likely to be defined for them by the superintendent, other professional educators, community leaders, interest groups, or state and federal actors. Despite the importance of policymaking, board members report that day-to-day responsibilities consume most of their time and complain that they seldom have time for reflection, brainstorming, and long-term planning. Despite concerns for educational equity and quality, boards more often address matters of financial accountability, which tends to enforce a role as steward of the public purse and a perspective of fiscal conservatism.

Models of decision-making emphasize inventing, developing, and analyzing possible solutions before selecting a particular course of action. Selecting a possible course of action is informed by the judgment of the decision maker, the analyses of the alternatives on a logical or systematic basis, and the political bargaining process. A major criticism of decision-making in the context of local school boards is that adequate alternative solutions are not always considered in the decision-making process prior to drafting policies. Educational policymaking is distinctive because of its lack of regular formal procedures for generating alternative proposals to those advanced by professional educators or school officials. School board members are often constrained by limits imposed by existing law and policy and become dependent on school district professionals and administrators for proposals and information. Some authorities contend that school boards perform the function of legitimating the policies of the school system in the larger community rather than representing the various segments of that community to the school system.

*See also:* EDUCATIONAL LEADERSHIP; NATIONAL SCHOOL BOARD ASSOCIATION; SCHOOL BOARD RELATIONS; SCHOOL FACILITIES.

**BIBLIOGRAPHY**

ALEXANDER, S. KERN, and ALEXANDER, DAVID. 2001. *American Public School Law,* 5th edition. Belmont, CA: Wadsworth.

*Brown v. Board of Education of Topeka, Kansas,* 347 U.S. 483 (1954).

CAROL, LILA N.; CUNNINGHAM, LUVERN L.; DANZBERGER, JACQUELINE; McCLOUD, BARBARA A.; KIRST, MICHAEL W.; and USDAN, MICHAEL D. 1986. *School Boards: Strengthening Grass Roots Leadership.* Washington, DC: Institute for Educational Leadership.

CHUBB, JOHN E., and MOE, TERRY M. 1990. *Politics, Markets, and America's Schools.* Washington, DC: Brookings Institute.

COUNCIL OF CHIEF STATE SCHOOL OFFICERS; EDUCATION COMMISSION OF THE STATES; NATIONAL ASSOCIATION OF STATE BOARDS OF EDUCATION; NATIONAL CONFERENCE OF STATE LEGISLATURES; and NATIONAL GOVERNORS ASSOCIATION. 2000. "The State Action for Education Leadership Project: State Policy and Practice Compendium." Washington, DC: Council of Chief State School Officers.

DANZBERGER, JACQUELINE; KIRST, MICHAEL W.; and USDAN, MICHAEL D. 1992. *Governing Public Schools: New Times, New Requirements.* Washington, DC: Institute for Educational Leadership.

DANZBERGER, JACQUELINE; KIRST, MICHAEL W.; and USDAN, MICHAEL D. 1993. *A Framework for Redefining the Role and Responsibilities of Local School Boards.* Washington, DC: Institute for Educational Leadership.

FINN, CHESTER. 1992. "Reinventing Local Control." In *School Boards: Changing Local Control,* ed. Patricia First and Herbert Walberg. Berkeley: McCutchan.

HERMAN, JERRY J., and HERMAN, JANICE L. 1999. *The Positive Development of Human Resources and School District Organizations.* Lancaster, PA: Technomic.

HESS, FREDERICK. 1999. *Spinning Wheels: The Politics of Urban School Reform.* Washington, DC: Brookings Institution.

KIRP, DAVID L., and JENSEN, DONALD N. 1986. *School Days, Rule Days: The Legalization and Regulation of Education.* Philadelphia: Falmer Press.

KIRST, MICHAEL W. 1984. *Who Controls Our Schools? American Values in Conflict.* New York: Freeman.

KIRST, MICHAEL W., ed. 1970. *The Politics of Education at the Local, State, and Federal Levels.* Berkeley: McCutchan.

KIRST, MICHAEL W., ed. 1972. *State, Schools, and Politics.* Lexington, MA: D.C. Heath.

LEITHWOOD, KENNETH, ed. 1995. *Effective School District Leadership: Transforming Politics into Education.* Albany: State University of New York Press.

LUTZ, FRANK W., and IANNACCONE, LAURENCE, eds. 1978. *Public Participation in Local School Districts.* Lexington, MA: Lexington Books.

MINZBERG, HENRY; RAISINGHANI, DURU; and THEORET, ANDRE. 1976. "The Structure of Unstructured Decision Processes." *Administrative Science Quarterly* 21:246–275.

NATIONAL COMMISSION ON EXCELLENCE IN EDUCATION. 1983. *A Nation at Risk: The Imperative for Educational Reform.* Washington, DC: U.S. Government Printing Office.

NATIONAL SCHOOL BOARD ASSOCIATION. 1987. *American School Boards: The Positive Power.* Alexandria, VA: National School Boards Association, Center for Federation Member Relations, State Legislation, and Public Policy.

POSTON, WILLIAM K., JR. 1994. *Making Governance Work: TQE for School Boards.* Thousand Oaks, CA: Corwin Press.

*San Antonio Independent School District v. Rodriquez,* 411 U.S. 1 (1973).

SIMON, HENRY. 1997. *Administrative Behavior: A Study of Decision-Making Processes in Administrative Organizations,* 4th edition. New York: Free Press.

TODRAS, ELLEN. 1993. *The Changing Role of School Boards.* Washington, DC: U.S. Department of Education, Office of Educational Research and Improvement.

TWENTIETH CENTURY FUND TASK FORCE. 1992. *Facing the Challenge: The Report of the Twentieth Century Fund Task Force on School Governance.* New York: Twentieth Century Fund.

TYACK, DAVID, and CUBAN, LARRY. 1995. *Tinkering toward Utopia: A Century of Public School Reform.* Cambridge, MA: Harvard University Press.

WILES, JON, and BONDI, JOSEPH. 1985. *The School Board Primer: A Guide for School Board Members.* Newton, MA: Allyn and Bacon.

WIRT, FREDERICK, and KIRST, MICHAEL. 2001. *The Political Dynamics of American Education,* 2nd edition. Berkeley: McCutchan.

WONG, KENNETH K. 1999. "Political Institutions and Educational Policy." In *Handbook of Educational Policy,* ed. Gregory J. Cizek. San Diego, CA: Academic Press.

ZEIGLER, HARMON, and JENNINGS, M. KENT. 1972. "Participation in Governance through Interest Groups." In *People and Politics in Urban Society,* ed. Harlan Hahn. Beverly Hills, CA: Sage.

JOSEPH BECKHAM
BARBARA KLAYMEIER WILLS

# SELECTION AND EDUCATION OF MEMBERS

Local control of public education, grounded in the federal constitution, is exercised through local school boards. Although they enjoy some autonomy, local school boards are the product of state legislatures with enumerated powers. The federal government, state legislature, and state boards of education also make policy decisions affecting local schools.

In 2000 about 95,000 school board members adopted policies for some 15,000 public school districts. Due to consolidations and other restructuring, the number of school districts has dramatically declined from 1940, when there were 117,000. The state of Hawaii has only one board of education for the entire state. From 1999 to 2000 public school districts educated about 47 million students in prekindergarten through grade 12 with about 3 million teachers, according to the National Center for Education Statistics.

## Elected Versus Appointed Members

Most states prefer to elect school board members: Citizens in school districts elect more than 94 percent of their school board members. Several states both elect and appoint members. There is an increasing trend to appoint and not elect superintendents.

The typical school board member is a college-educated homeowner, who lives in a suburb or small town, and serves a school system enrolling between 1,000 and 5,000 students. Many districts are larger or smaller and reflect a greater diversity in membership. In western states, school boards have a higher percentage of Hispanics than do boards in other parts of the country. In southern states, 16 percent of school board members are African American, the highest percentage in the country, according to the National School Boards Association.

## Advantages and Disadvantages of Selection Processes

Advocates of electing school board members argue that elected boards are more responsive to the public will. In addition, electing members increases public interest in the schools as it ensures that people have a direct voice in the selection of the school system's governing body. Elected school board members have greater independence and freedom to act in the best interests of the school system than do appointed board members. An elected board is in a better position to work closely and effectively with its superintendent and professional staff than an appointed board.

The proponents of appointing board members assert that the appointive method provides opportunity for greater selectivity in choosing board members, thus assuring capable board members with proper motives. Appointment of board members helps ensure harmonious working relationships between the school board and the local government. Appointing board members ensures board stability and continuity of service are better secured by the appointive method. The elective method encourages candidates for board office to develop issues for their public appeal or to make charges against incumbent board members or professional staff in order to secure votes, while appointed board members generate less community controversy. In order to depoliticize the process and to be proactive in candidate selection, some school districts work through a citizen advisory or caucus process in order to identify and seek out qualified school board candidates.

There is no definitive literature on whether elected or appointed school boards are more effective in improving student achievement. Furthermore, governance and organizational changes do not appear to improve classroom instruction.

## Geographic Selection

Most school board members are elected from single-member districts; however, some school board members are elected at large. It has been argued that single-member districts tend to create a more parochial school board member; however, at large elections a single-member district can generate legal challenges in states covered by the Voting Rights Act of 1965. Several lawsuits alleging minority dilution in the establishment of single member or at large elected board districts have been decided (*Reno v. Bossier Parish School Board* (1997), *Perez v. Pasadena Independent School District* (5th Cir. 1999), and *Valdespino v. Alamo Heights Independent School District* (5th Cir. 1999).

## Term and Turnover of Office

Most school board members serve terms of three to six years. Most boards have three to nine members; however, some are larger to accommodate large populations or to reflect interests of multiple constituencies. Although in most cases, term limits do not apply to board service, in the 1990s some advocates called for term limits for school board members, arguing that some school board members use their offices for political gain and promotion.

The national tenure for school board members is declining. According to a study by the National School Boards Association, the average term of a board member has dropped from five and a half years in 1982 to five years in 1992. School board members choose not to seek another term because of changing interests, frustrations with the job, and the demands of mounting an election campaign.

## State Takeovers

In the 1990s rising national concerns about the quality of public education led states to adopt laws providing for the takeover of school districts or, in some cases, individual schools. At the beginning of the twenty-first century, twenty-four states have enacted policies that allow them to take over a school district due to academic problems within the school district. These state policies provide for application of progressive sanctions on a school district, with the ultimate sanction being a takeover. State policies may also permit a takeover for reasons other than academic problems: these include fiscal mismanagement, inept administration, corrupt governance, and crumbling infrastructure within the school district. Through state law, policy, or court action, the state designates an entity to manage the school district for a certain amount of time.

The consequences for school board members vary. For example, state officials can relieve school board members and other high level administrators of their duties and appoint others to manage the school district in their place. Or, school board members and high level administrators might remain in place as an advisory group. In certain large cities, the mayor has governance authority. In cities such as Boston, Chicago, Cleveland, and Detroit, mayors, enabled by state legislation, have taken over the school systems and assumed the governance of them. Mayors either appoint the school board members or the superintendent or appoint the chief executive officer of the system.

The proponents of state takeovers argue that takeovers are a necessary extension of a state's constitutional responsibilities: They provide a good opportunity for state and local decision makers to combine resources and knowledge to improve children's learning and allow a competent executive staff to guide an uninterrupted and effective implementation of school improvement efforts. State takeovers also serve as a catalyst for creating the right environment for the community to address a school district's problems and allow for more radical, necessary changes in low-performing school districts. Finally, takeovers place school boards on notice that personal agendas, nepotism, and public bickering have severe consequences. Typically the new leadership uses achievement data collected from school districts and schools to bolster accountability efforts.

Opponents of this approach assert that state takeovers represent a thinly veiled attempt to reduce local control over schools and increase state authority over school districts. Takeovers imply that the problem lies with the community and it is up to the state to provide the solution; Thus, there is a false assumption that states have the ability to effectively run school districts. States may place poorly prepared state-selected officials in charge, who will not be able to produce meaningful change in the classroom, and will use narrow learning measures (i.e., standardized test scores) as the primary justification for takeover decisions. State takeovers often focus on cleaning up petty corruption and incompetent administration, and do not go to the root of the social problems that face disadvantaged students in urban school districts. Takeovers can foster negative connotations and impressions that hinder the self-esteem of school board members, administrators, teachers, students, and parents. Finally, takeovers encourage confrontation between state and local officials that slows the overhaul of management practices, drains resources from educational reforms, and reinforces community resentments.

## Continuing Education of Board Members

The educational background of school board members varies widely; some members have high school degrees or diplomas and others have doctorates. Formal education by itself does not adequately prepare school board members for their specific functions. Accordingly, many argue that school board training and education should be mandatory for all school board members.

In the 1970s board members attended a national convention, but relatively few attended systematic and targeted programs of continuing education. By 2001, however, more half of the states required mandatory training for school board members. Typically, the school board member must participate in some recognized form of continuing education for a specified number of hours per year. In a study conducted by Marilyn Grady and Bernita Krumm in 1996, it was determined that of forty-three states in the study, ten states had mandatory training for school board members and thirty-two had voluntary training. In some states, if members do not attend training they could lose their seat on the school board. Often they are compensated for attendance at these required continuing education programs. The programs are provided by state school boards association or other recognized school board agencies such as the National School Boards Association or the Council of Urban Boards of Education.

## Orientation

As part of school board training, new school board members need orientation. New board members join a board of existing members who are continuing their service and who have developed a culture and context for their decision-making process. It is important that new school board members understand substantive information on school programs and operations. Without pre-service or orientation programs, it will take at least two years of school board service before board members gain the background and confidence to perform effectively and confidently.

## Content of Education

The key topics offered in state training included education law, finance, and board-superintendent relations. Other topics included negotiations, curriculum management, labor relations, policy development, roles and responsibilities, leadership, legislation, community relations, strategic planning, and special education.

A significant new dimension to school board training is acquainting the school board members with research-based information. The data available to educators to support and assess educational programs is extensive. Many school board members are not accustomed to consulting research materials to inform their decisions. Solid information can also form the foundation for alternative solutions and provide the basis for choosing the best option.

In 2000 the National School Boards Association urged school boards to concentrate on raising student achievement by focusing on eight key areas: vision; standards; assessment; accountability; alignment; climate; collaborative relationships; and continuous improvement. This position undergirds the need for adequate school board training on issues of student expectations, achievement, testing, assessment, and accountability. A school board member also needs to be able to respond to questions from the press regarding achievement measures and the school board's assessment of its progress toward meeting its district's measurable goals.

One of the key challenges for school board education is not only to define its objectives and mission, but also to stay focused on these key issues. Even though many school boards attempt to concentrate on student performance and achievement, in some circumstances, boards might devote a minimum amount of their time to these critical issues. To forestall this, there must be a change in governance structure, culture, and agenda of boards so that they will remain focused on student achievement and performance.

Toward the end of the twentieth century, the role of local boards of education received scrutiny. Although most observers acknowledge that school boards have an important role in maintaining involvement of local citizens and in governing local schools, some confusion regarding the specific functions of boards persists.

In response to the changing demands on school boards, a National School Boards Association task force identified four core decision-making functions that are fundamental to a school system's accountability:

1. The establishment of a long-term vision for the school system.

2. The establishment and maintenance of a basic organizational structure for the school system, including employment of a superintendent, adoption of an annual budget, adoption of governance policies, and creation of a climate that promotes excellence.

3. The establishment of systems and processes to ensure accountability to the community, including fiscal accountability, accountability for programs and student outcomes, staff accountability, and collective bargaining.

4. Advocacy on behalf of children in public education at the community, state, and national levels.

## Training Activities

According to one study, the most common type of activities for training were annual conventions, orientations for new members, regional meetings, board president training sessions, and some summer and winter conferences. Other activities include the reading of appropriate literature, discussions of important issues, visiting schools, and board self-evaluations.

In order to encourage continuing education and training, state associations utilized awards for board members who completed extensive training. The more hours earned in a continuing education, the higher the award to the board member. Further, state school board associations select a "school board of the year" composed of members from the state who have demonstrated leadership including commitment to continuing education.

Superintendents play an important role in training of school board members. They can supply members with position papers, provide members with options and best practice research, conduct special briefing sessions on key issues, and model continuing improvement in the area of professional development.

School board education requires balancing issues of structure such as board–superintendent relations and education law with issues of student achievement and accountability that are part of the national agenda in the early twenty-first century.

*See also:* EDUCATIONAL LEADERSHIP; NATIONAL SCHOOL BOARD ASSOCIATION; SCHOOL BOARD RE-LATIONS; SUPERINTENDENT OF LARGE-CITY SCHOOL SYSTEMS; SUPERINTENDENT OF SCHOOLS.

### BIBLIOGRAPHY

DYKES, ARCHIE R. 1965. *School Board and Superintendent: Their Effective Working Relationships.* Danville, IL: Interstate.

EDUCATION COMMISSION OF THE STATES. 2001. "State Takeovers and Reconstitutions." Denver, CO: Education Commission of the States.

GEMBERLING, KATHERYN; SMITH, CARL W.; and VILLANI, JOSEPH S. 2000. *The Keywork of School Boards Guidebook.* Alexandria, VA: National School Boards Association.

GRADY, MARILYN, and KRUMM, BERNITA. 1998. "Learning to Serve: The State of School Board Member Training." *American School Board Journal* 185:36–43.

KIRST, MICHAEL, and BULKLEY, KATRINA. 2000. "'New, Improved' Mayors Take Over City Schools." *Phi Delta Kappan* 81:538–546.

MARLOWE, JOHN. 1997. "All on Board: Grooming Citizens for School Board Service." *American School Board Journal* 184:46.

MOREHOUSE, WILLIAM. 2001. "Training for My Board Colleagues? You Bet." *School Administrator* 58:68–70.

NATIONAL CENTER FOR EDUCATION STATISTICS. 2000. *Education and Statistics Quarterly.* Washington, DC: National Center for Education Statistics, Office of Educational Research and Improvement, U.S. Department of Education.

NATIONAL SCHOOL BOARDS ASSOCIATION. 1996. *Becoming a Better Board Member,* 2nd edition. Alexandria, VA: National School Boards Association.

NATIONAL SCHOOL BOARDS ASSOCIATION. 2000. *Resolutions, Beliefs and Policies, Constitution and Bylaws.* Alexandria: VA: National School Boards Association.

KENT M. WEEKS

# SCHOOL CLIMATE

Anyone who spends time in schools quickly discovers how one school can feel different from other schools. *School climate* is a general term that refers to the feel, atmosphere, tone, ideology, or milieu of a school. Just as individuals have personalities, so too do schools; a school climate may be thought of as the personality of a school.

The concept of *organizational climate* has a rich history in the social science literature. In the early 1960s George Sterns was one of the first psychologists who saw the analogy with individual personality and used the concept of organizational climate to study institutions of higher education. The use of the concept quickly spread to schools and business organizations, each with a somewhat different conceptual view of climate. Although there are a variety of conceptualizations, there is general agreement that organizational climate arises from routine organizational practices that are important to an organization's members, that it is defined by member perceptions, and that it influences members' attitudes and behavior. Thus, school climate is a relatively enduring character of a school that is experienced by its participants, that affects their actions, and that is based on the collective perceptions of behavior in the school.

## Measuring School Climate

Andrew Halpin and Don Croft's pioneering analysis, *The Organizational Climate of Schools,* has had a great impact on the study of school climate. They developed the Organizational Climate Description Questionnaire (OCDQ), a sixty-four-item Likert-scale questionnaire that is used to assess the teacher–teacher and teacher–administrator interactions found in elementary schools. Teachers and administrators are asked to describe the extent to which key behaviors occur, such as how frequently (rarely, sometimes, often, or very frequently) "The principal stays after school to help teachers finish their work," "The principal looks out for the personal welfare of teachers," and "The teachers accomplish their work with great vim, vigor, and pleasure." Thus, school climate is defined in terms of educators' perceptions of the leadership behavior of the principal and interactions among teachers. Patterns of principal and teacher behaviors are then arrayed along a rough continuum, ranging from *open* to *closed* school climates. An open school climate is one in which teacher and principal behavior is supportive, genuine, and engaged, whereas a closed climate is characterized by lack of authenticity, game playing, and disengaged behavior. There were a number of limitations to

early versions of the OCDQ. For example, it only measured the climate of elementary schools, and the validity of some of its subtests was questioned.

Subsequent revisions of the OCDQ have addressed these issues, and three new and simplified versions of the questionnaire have been formulated for use in elementary, middle, and secondary schools. The revised OCDQ was conceptualized using the same framework of open versus closed climates and behaviors. For example, open principal behavior in elementary schools is measured through items that describe supportive principal behavior that is neither directive nor restrictive, and open teacher behavior is that which is collegial, intimate, and committed to teaching and learning.

Another climate framework uses a health metaphor—school climate is measured in terms of healthy interpersonal dynamics. In the tradition of the OCDQ, the Organizational Health Inventory (OHI) is a set of descriptive statements that tap productive relationships in school. There are three versions of the OHI—elementary, middle, and secondary. This broad climate perspective examines the relationships between the school and environment, the leadership of the principal, relationships among teachers, and relationships between teachers and students. For example, the secondary version maps seven aspects of school climate:

1. *Institutional Integrity* is the extent to which the school is able to manage its constraints from the community

2. *Consideration* is principal behavior that is genuinely collegial, friendly, open, and caring toward the faculty

3. *Initiating Structure* is principal behavior that is oriented toward both tasks and achievements through clearly articulated work expectations and performance standards

4. *Principal Influence* describes the principal's ability to influence superiors

5. *Resource Support* is the ability of the principal to obtain classroom materials and supplies needed by teachers

6. *Morale* is the collective sense of friendliness, openness, and enthusiasm among members of the teaching staff

7. *Academic Emphasis* is the extent to which the teachers and students are committed to academic excellence

A pattern of high scores on these variables defines a healthy school climate. There are, of course, other measures of school climate, but the openness and health frameworks have generated the bulk of the systematic research on school climate.

## School Climate and Outcomes

Empirical evidence has linked school climate with achievement. Though school climate is often defined differently in various studies, the research evidence using the OCDQ and the OHI measures of climate is encouraging. Openness of school climate has been linked primarily to expressive characteristics in schools. For example, the more open the school climate, the more committed, loyal, and satisfied the teachers are. Similarly, the more open the climate of the school, the less alienated students tend to be. School climate, from the health perspective, has been positively related to school effectiveness. Most of the health variables correlate significantly with general subjective measures of effectiveness, and the variable of academic emphasis has consistently been related to student achievement in high schools, middle schools, and urban elementary schools. In fact, the relationships hold even controlling for the effects of socioeconomic status.

## Trends, Issues, and Controversies

School climate has become a global construct that researchers often use loosely to group together studies of school environment, learning environment, learning climate, sense of community, leadership, academic climate, and social climate. This broad application reveals both the strength and weakness of school climate study—it is a useful integrating concept on the one hand, but it also suffers from a lack of clear definition. Like so many other terms that are bandied about, the word *climate* threatens to become meaningless. Because its referents are so diverse, the word sometimes obscures, rather than creates, understanding. *School culture* is a related term that has been use to describe the work environment; in fact, climate and culture are often used interchangeably by some educators to refer to the distinctive workplace of a school. A useful distinction is that culture consists of shared values and assumptions, whereas climate is defined by shared perceptions of behavior.

In many studies, after a small number of "effective" and "ineffective" schools are identified, researchers catalog each school's organizational characteristics and attempt to find consistent differences between the two types of schools. Not surprisingly, the differences vary from study to study when such post hoc methods are used, and the list of effective school attributes grows as such studies accumulate. In addition, organizational characteristics are defined differently in each study, so that reviewers use general terms to summarize the characteristics of effective schools—terms such as *positive school climate* and *strong leadership,* which are often defined quite differently in various studies.

What is missing in much of the research on school climate is the theoretical linkage that explains these relationships. It is important, for example, not only to know that climate is related to student achievement, but also to ascertain why this is so. What are the generalizations and mechanisms that explain higher achievement? These are critical questions, and their answers will provide a deeper understanding of the dynamics of organizational life in schools and suggest more effective and lasting solutions to the problems of practice. Evidence is beginning to suggest, for example, that a school climate with open, healthy, and collegial professional interactions and strong academic emphasis empowers teachers and creates norms of collective efficacy that shape the normative environment of schools and influence teacher behavior. When teachers believe that they can organize and execute their teaching in ways that are successful in helping students learn, and when the school climate supports them, teachers plan more, accept personal responsibility for student performance, are not deterred by temporary setbacks, and act purposefully to enhance student learning. It is important to try to understand how specific school climate attributes influence critical teacher behaviors that improve teaching and learning in the classroom.

*See also:* PRINCIPAL, SCHOOL; SCHOOL-BASED DECISION-MAKING; SOCIAL ORGANIZATION OF SCHOOLS.

### BIBLIOGRAPHY

BANDURA, ALBERT. 1997. *Self-Efficacy: The Exercise of Control.* New York: Freeman.

BROOKOVER, WILBUR B., and COLLEAGUES. 1987. "Elementary School Social Climate and School Achievement." *American Educational Research Journal* 15:301–318.

Bossert, Steve T. 1988. "School Effects." In *Handbook of Research on Educational Administration,* ed. Norman J. Boyan. New York: Longman.

Goddard, Roger D.; Hoy, Wayne K.; and Woolfolk Hoy, Anita. 2000. "Collective Teacher Efficacy: Its Meaning, Measure, and Impact on Student Achievement." *American Educational Research Journal* 37:479–507.

Goddard, Roger D.; Sweetland, Scott R.; and Hoy, Wayne K. 2000. "Academic Emphasis of Urban Elementary Schools and Student Achievement in Reading and Mathematics: A Multi-Level Analysis." *Educational Administration Quarterly* 36:683–702.

Halpin, Andrew W., and Croft, Don B. 1963. *The Organizational Climate of Schools.* Chicago: Midwest Administration Center of the University of Chicago.

Hoy, Wayne K., and Miskel, Cecil G. 2001. *Educational Administration: Theory, Research, and Practice,* 6th edition. New York: McGraw-Hill.

Hoy, Wayne K., and Sabo, Dennis J. 1998. *Quality Middle Schools: Open and Healthy.* Thousand Oaks, CA: Corwin.

Hoy, Wayne K.; Tarter, C. John; and Kottkamp, Robert B. 1991. *Open Schools/Healthy Schools: Measuring Organizational Climate.* Beverly Hills, CA: Sage.

Sweetland, Scott R., and Hoy, Wayne K. 2000. "School Characteristics and Educational Outcomes: Toward an Organizational Model of Student Achievement in Middle Schools." *Educational Administration Quarterly* 36:703–729.

Wayne K. Hoy

# SCHOOL CURRICULUM

*See:* Curriculum, School.

# SCHOOL FACILITIES

OVERVIEW
Jeffery A. Lackney
MAINTENANCE AND MODERNIZATION OF
Lawrence O. Picus

## OVERVIEW

An effective school facility is responsive to the changing programs of educational delivery, and at a minimum should provide a physical environment that is comfortable, safe, secure, accessible, well illuminated, well ventilated, and aesthetically pleasing. The school facility consists of not only the physical structure and the variety of building systems, such as mechanical, plumbing, electrical and power, telecommunications, security, and fire suppression systems. The facility also includes furnishings, materials and supplies, equipment and information technology, as well as various aspects of the building grounds, namely, athletic fields, playgrounds, areas for outdoor learning, and vehicular access and parking.

The school facility is much more than a passive container of the educational process: it is, rather, an integral component of the conditions of learning. The layout and design of a facility contributes to the *place experience* of students, educators, and community members. Depending on the quality of its design and management, the facility can contribute to a sense of ownership, safety and security, personalization and control, privacy as well as sociality, and spaciousness or crowdedness. When planning, designing, or managing the school facility, these facets of place experience should, when possible, be taken into consideration.

### Constructing New Facilities

During strategic long-range educational planning, unmet facility space needs often emerge. The goal of educational planning is to develop, clarify, or review the educational mission, vision, philosophy, curriculum, and instructional delivery. Educational planning may involve a variety of school and community workshops and surveys to identify and clarify needs and sharpen the vision of the district. Long-range planning activities, such as demographic studies, financing options, site acquisitions, and community partnering opportunities are often initiated by the district administration as a response to the results of educational planning. An outcome of long-range planning is the development of a comprehensive capital improvement program to address unmet facility needs.

The district superintendent appoints a steering committee to oversee the details of the capital improvement program. The responsibility of the steering committee includes the selection of various consultants, the review of planning and design options, and the reporting of recommendations to the school board for a final decision. Depending on the needs of the district, one of the first tasks of the steering committee is to retain a variety of consultants. Educational and design consultants, financial consultants, bond counsels, investment bankers, and public relations consultants are retained to perform pre-referendum planning activities during which project scope, budget, financing, legal issues, and schedule are defined. Once project feasibility is established, a public referendum package is developed and presented to the taxpaying public through public hearings. Upon passage of the public referendum, more detailed facility planning of the school can begin.

An architect is often selected to assist in facility planning in cooperation with the educational planning consultant and in-house facility staff. The school board, as the owner, enters into a contract for services with the chosen architect. The architect, in turn, negotiates contracts with a variety of consultants, including interior designers, landscape architects, mechanical, electrical, and civil engineers, and land surveyors.

The facility planning process at its best involves an assessment of functional needs in light of the educational program developed during educational planning. There are several names for this process: Educators refer to the development of *educational specifications,* while architects refer to it as *facility programming.* Facility planning includes any or all of the following activities: feasibility studies, district master planning, site selection, needs assessment, and project cost analysis. Spatial requirements and relationships between various program elements are established. The outcome of the facility planning process is a public facility program, or educational specifications document, that outlines physical space requirements and adjacencies and special design criteria the school facility must meet.

The design phase of the process, which includes schematic design, design development, and construction documents and specifications, can last from six months to one year. Each step in the design process involves more detailed and specific information about the technical aspects of the building systems, components, and assemblies. The design process requires school board decisions and approval, with each phase offering more detailed descriptions of the scope, budget, and schedule. The products of this phase include sketches, drawings, models, and technical reports, which are shared with the school and community through public hearings, workshops, and other forms of public relations and

community involvement. Community participation during the earliest stages of the design phase can be as critical for stakeholder support as it was in the educational planning process.

There are several construction delivery methods available to the school district: competitive bidding, design/build, and construction management. Each state has evolved its own laws regulating the acceptable forms of construction project delivery. Competitive bidding is still the most common form of construction delivery. It allows contractors in each trade, such as general, mechanical, electrical, and plumbing, to compete for individual prime contracts and form separate contracts with the school district. In principle, it provides the most open and fair competition appropriate for a public sector project; however, project communication and coordination may ultimately affect schedule and budget. Design/build is most popular with private sector owners but is occasionally used in the public sector. Under a design/build contract, the owner contracts with one firm that completes both design and construction of the project under one contract. Cost and time savings are possible but often with a loss in quality of the product. Construction management is a service that often is established simultaneously with the hiring of the architect. A construction manager's responsibility is to act as project manager throughout the design and construction process, coordinating the project budget and schedule along the way. A fourth form of construction delivery is actually a comprehensive project management delivery service, which includes construction management but also extends from pre-referendum through occupancy and even facility management, offering one-stop shopping for facility development. Large school districts that have multiple projects often contract with project management services. Project management firms offer a wide array of financial, legal, and construction services promising economies of scale.

Following the competitive bidding process, the next phase of the school building process is that of bidding and negotiation. An *Invitation for Bids* is publicized to obtain bids from prime construction contractors. Most states require the school district to accept the lowest responsible and responsive bidder. However, the school district reserves the right to reject all bids. Once low bids are accepted, the school district, as owner, negotiates a contract with each prime contractor. The architect represents the owner in the construction phase, but the contract and legal relationship is between the school district, as owner, and each prime contractor. The construction of the school can last from twelve to eighteen months, depending on the project scope, material selections, lead times for shipment to the site, weather, unforeseen subsurface site conditions, and a variety of other factors. With the use of school buildings being tied to the school year schedule, project phasing is always an issue that needs to be addressed. Other factors that can escalate cost and slow the project are change orders to rectify unforeseen conditions or errors and omissions in the original construction documents. Once the architect is satisfied that the project is complete, a *Certificate of Substantial Completion* is issued and the owner can legally occupy the facility.

### Facility Management

While the planning, design, and construction of the school facility may take two to three years, the management of it will last the entire life cycle of the facility. At the beginning of the twenty-first century, the mean age of a school building in the United States as forty-two years, with 28 percent of school buildings built before 1950. Many of the building materials, furnishings, and equipment will not last half that long and will require constant upkeep, maintenance, and inevitable replacement to defer building obsolescence.

The costs of managing school facilities have historically received much less attention than facility planning. The percentage of the operating budget for the maintenance and management of school facilities has steadily decreased, creating a capital renewal crisis as a result of years of deferred maintenance at all levels of education.

Best practice requires that a comprehensive facility maintenance program be established and monitored by the school district. The maintenance program often includes several distinct programs, including deferred, preventive, repair/upkeep, and emergency maintenance. Responsibility for facility management is divided between the district office and the school site, with the principal being the primary administrator responsible for the day-to-day operation of the school, including custodial, food, and transportation services. Custodians are typically hired by the school district but managed by the principal. Custodial staff is generally responsible for cleaning the building; monitoring the mechanical,

electrical, and plumbing systems; and providing general maintenance of both building and grounds. District staff is responsible for long-term maintenance programs and the procurement of outsourced services for specialized maintenance projects.

Several environmental quality issues have emerged over the past few decades, such as classroom acoustics, indoor air quality, water quality, energy conservation, and abatement of asbestos, radon, and other hazardous materials. Many of these issues require the services of facility consultants hired through the district. Other issues for the building-level administrator include safety and security, vandalism and threats, and acts of violence and terrorism. All of these functions must be conducted within a constantly changing set of government mandates, such as energy deregulation, accessibility guidelines, codes, and other regulations and guidelines at the state and federal levels.

### Trends and Issues

Many communities recognize that in addition to school facilities being cost effective, they should be more learner-centered, developmentally and age appropriate, safe, comfortable, accessible, flexible, diverse, and equitable. By location of new facilities in residential neighborhoods and partnering with other community-based organizations, schools are becoming true community centers. In addition, schools are taking advantage of educational resources in the community, as well as partnering with museums, zoos, libraries, and other public institutions and local businesses.

Based on mounting evidence that smaller schools lead to improved social climate as well as better achievement, school leaders have begun to create smaller schools or have created schools within schools.

The design of safe schools increasingly recognizes the desirability of providing natural, unobtrusive surveillance mechanisms, rather than installing checkpoints and security guards. Smaller scaled school buildings allow for both natural surveillance and territorial ownership, where students and teachers are on familiar terms, thereby decreasing the possibility that any one student is overlooked.

The self-contained classroom can no longer provide the variety of learning settings necessary to successfully support project-based, real-world authentic learning. Research indicates that smaller class size is a factor contributing to improved achievement. Learning settings are being designed to support individualized, self-directed learning and small informal group learning, in addition to traditional large-group instruction. Rather than lining up classrooms along a long corridor, instructional areas are being organized around central cores of shared instructional support.

A trend in the provision of professional space for teachers has emerged as well. Teacher office space, including desk and storage, phone/fax, and information technologies, is seen as essential to the development of teachers as professionals.

Information technology is precipitating a variety of changes in the organizational and physical form of schools. With respect to instructional processes, technology is facilitating the movement toward project-based, self-directed learning and individualized instruction. As learning becomes increasingly virtual, web-based, and wireless, it still must physically take place somewhere. As information technology is becoming ubiquitous, more schools are decentralizing technology throughout the school building and across the community.

The trend toward *smart buildings,* or buildings that are designed and constructed to integrate the technologies of instruction, telecommunications, and building systems, will have increased responsiveness to occupant needs as well as the educational process.

Finally, because of the recognition that spending too much time in buildings can be detrimental not only to health but also to learning, school buildings will begin to connect more to the natural environment visually, aurally, and kinesthetically by including transitional indoor and outdoor learning spaces.

## Cost Considerations

Estimates of cost to repair and modernize school facilities nationwide continue to grow from the $112 billion estimated by the U.S. General Accounting Office (GAO) in their landmark 1995 report, to the National Center for Educational Statistics (NCES) estimate of $127 billion in 1999, to $268.2 billion estimated by the National Education Association in 2000.

The construction and operation of a school building involves a substantial expenditure of public funds. The investment for construction, however, represents only a fraction of the cost of operating a school over the life of the building. When life-cycle costs of operating a school are considered (including staff salaries and overhead costs, in addition to maintenance and operation of the facility), the initial cost of the school facility may be less than 10 to 15 percent of the life-cycle costs over a thirty-year period. Properly designing and constructing school buildings for the realities of management can often provide cost savings over time that could in turn provide additional funds for education. Operational costs for power and fuel, water and sewer, garbage disposal, leases and insurance, building maintenance, and custodial staff are important items in the annual budget, competing yearly for funds identified for educational delivery. Building life-cycle cost analysis is admittedly difficult for taxpayers and school boards to comprehend when available building funds are tight, but the rewards in effective facility management are potentially great.

*See also:* CLASS SIZE AND STUDENT LEARNING; FINANCIAL SUPPORT OF SCHOOLS; LIABILITY OF SCHOOL DISTRICTS AND SCHOOL PERSONNEL FOR NEGLIGENCE; RURAL EDUCATION; SCHOOL BOARDS; SCHOOL CLIMATE; YEAR-ROUND EDUCATION.

### BIBLIOGRAPHY

BITTLE, EDGAR H., ed. 1996. *Planning and Financing School Improvement and Construction Projects.* Topeka, KS: National Organization on Legal Problems in Education.

BRUBAKER, C. WILLIAM. 1998. *Planning and Designing Schools.* New York: McGraw Hill.

CASTALDI, BASIL. 1994. *Educational Facilities: Planning, Modernization and Management.* Boston: Allyn and Bacon.

CROWE, TIMOTHY. 2000. *Crime Prevention through Environmental Design: Applications of Architectural Design and Space Management Concepts.* National Crime Prevention Institute. Boston: Butterworth-Heinemann.

EARTHMAN, GLEN I. 2000. *Planning Educational Facilities for the Next Century.* Blacksburg: Virginia Polytechnic Institute and State University.

GRAVES, BEN E. 1993. *School Ways: The Planning and Design of America's Schools.* New York: McGraw Hill.

HOLCOMB, JOHN H. 1995. *A Guide to the Planning of Educational Facilities.* New York: University Press of America.

KOWALSKI, THEODORE J. 1989. *Planning and Managing School Facilities.* New York: Praeger.

LACKNEY, JEFFREY A. 2000. *Thirty-Three Educational Design Principles for Schools and Community Learning Centers.* Washington, DC: National Clearinghouse for Educational Facilities.

MACIHA, JOHN C. 2000. *Preventive Maintenance Guidelines for School Facilities.* Kingston, MA: RS Means.

MAGEE, GREGORY H. 1988. *Facilities Maintenance Management.* Kingston, MA: RS Means.

NATIONAL CENTER FOR EDUCATIONAL STATISTICS. 2000. *Condition of America's Public School Facilities: 1999.* Washington, DC: National Center for Educational Statistics.

SANOFF, HENRY. 1994. *School Design.* New York: Van Nostrand Reinhold.

U.S. GENERAL ACCOUNTING OFFICE. 1995. *School Facilities: Condition of America's Schools.* Washington, DC: U.S. General Accounting Office.

U.S. GENERAL ACCOUNTING OFFICE. 2000. *School Facilities: Construction Expenditures Have Grown Significantly in Recent Years.* Washington, DC: U.S. General Accounting Office.

JEFFERY A. LACKNEY

## MAINTENANCE AND MODERNIZATION OF

As public education in the United States entered the twenty-first century, educational leaders and policymakers were faced with increasing costs for the maintenance and modernization of educational facilities. Driven by two factors—a considerable backlog of deferred maintenance expenditures and needs, and the need to ensure that classrooms have adequate facilities to accommodate the growing use of technology—estimates of the costs for maintenance and modernization of school facilities have soared.

In a 2002 article, Philip E. Geiger stated that as of January 2002 it would cost between $112 and 150 billion to "bring the nation's schools up to good condition" (p. 43). The U.S. Department of Education (DoE) estimated that the cost would be $127 billion. Moreover, the DoE estimated that 30 percent of the country's schools needed extensive repairs and another 40 percent needed replacement of some major component. This suggests that at the beginning of the twenty-first century some 70 percent of schools across the United States were in need of major repairs.

In 2000 the National Education Association estimated that total school infrastructure needs—including technology—amounted to some $322 billion. This estimate included costs of new school construction, additions to existing buildings, renovation and retrofitting, deferred maintenance, and major improvements to school grounds, as well as the costs of technology.

Estimating the age of a school building is difficult because many schools have had additions or major remodeling at some point in their history, either to accommodate more students or to update and upgrade the facility. The DoE found that in 1999 the average age of public schools across the United States was forty years. Moreover, on average it had been eleven years since these schools had been renovated. The DoE estimated the functional age of each building and found that the average functional age of school buildings was sixteen years.

Schools in central cities tend to be older than those in other areas. Moreover, in such urban districts, it has often been somewhat longer since a major renovation has taken place. While the differences are relatively small, high minority population schools tend to be in older buildings as well. Many of these older schools need substantial repairs as well as upgrading to meet newer building codes and fire safety standards.

In addition, it is generally these older buildings that do not have sufficient capacity to meet the wiring demands of new technology. Frequently classrooms do not have enough electrical outlets to support more than one or two computers, and many remain without connections to the Internet, even via telephone modem connections. Wiring for schoolwide networks is also made difficult because older construction often has solid walls and no false ceilings where wires and networking cable can be installed. This adds yet more to the costs of modernization for technology.

### Maintenance

When faced with a revenue shortfall, most school districts strive to keep major funding reductions away from the classroom. One way to save money in the short term is to defer maintenance on school facilities. While this is often a useful tool for short-term savings, the deterioration in the condition of an improperly maintained building is very obvious and can often begin within a matter of a few years. Given the high cost of building new schools, this approach may be inappropriate in the long term. California, for example, has an estimated school infrastructure need of more than $22 billion, with another $10 billion or more needed for technology.

Much of this could be prevented if proper preventative maintenance procedures are implemented and used by school districts. Geiger provided a list of seven priorities school districts need to consider in developing a high-quality school maintenance program:

1. A commitment on the part of the board, the superintendent, and senior staff to facility maintenance.

2. Development of a comprehensive preventative maintenance program.

3. Adequate funding for both preventative maintenance and capital improvement.

4. A willingness to consider new ideas for construction and maintenance of facilities.

5. Continual search for new and different ways to pay for maintenance and construction needs.

6. Careful review of district goals and policies to make sure facility management receives appropriate levels of funding in the annual budget cycle.

7. A plan to link academic programs to facility needs.

In a 1999 article, Michael Zureich provided evidence of the success of adopting the fourth priority above, that of considering new ideas. Zureich described three schools where a coordinated design and building committee had led to better use of less expensive and easier-to-maintain construction materials, resulting in reduced construction costs and lower lifetime maintenance costs. He pointed out that it is important to consider the strength, reliability, and life of all construction materials and to plan for maintenance needs in the initial construction. Zureich suggested that schools using this process have reduced design, construction, and maintenance costs by between 18 and 25 percent.

## Modernization

In addition to maintaining existing school buildings, there is a continual need for modernization. This is a far broader need than the typical concern over creating an infrastructure for technology. Many schools built in the past do not provide adequate space resources for the way schools educate children in the early twenty-first century. Efforts to reduce class size across the nation along with growth in the number of students have placed a burden on school facilities and increased the demand for more classroom space. Moreover, teacher efforts to use classrooms in different ways to maximize learning often require additional square footage in each classroom. For example, in elementary schools, the traditional room full of tables has often been replaced by a room with desks on one side and a large carpet in another part of the room where students sit on the floor for certain activities. Some rooms have special corners for computers or for quiet reading activities. All of this requires additional space and reorganization of the classroom space.

In earlier periods, schools were built to meet the requirements of educational methods that are no longer in favor. Many schools built in the 1970s relied on the "open classroom" model where there were no walls between classrooms. As teaching moved away from this model, schools had to spend substantial sums of money to reconfigure their facilities.

Other more mundane changes are also an important part of a continuous modernization process. Installation of white boards to replace traditional chalk boards or changing wall surfaces to make it easier to hang displays and teaching aids can make a tremendous difference in the appearance of a classroom. Yet even these simple things can be expensive, and planning for such upgrades is important. Furthermore, as new schools are built with such features as work areas for teachers attached to clusters of classrooms, the school budget needs to provide adequate funds for work materials and equipment for teachers (such as computers, copiers, and telephones) and for reasonable replacement programs for these important tools.

## Technology

The growing use of technology—particularly computers—in instruction has placed a whole new set of demands on the construction, maintenance, and modernization of school facilities. Although technology in schools is a much broader concept than simply the use of computers, it is computers that are most frequently thought of in discussions of educational technology today. Schools face problems with acquiring adequate numbers of computers, replacing them on a regular and frequent basis, providing the electrical power to operate them in each classroom, and providing and maintaining the wiring infrastructure needed to keep them connected with the school and across the district and the community more generally.

Computers represent a new challenge to school budgeting processes as they have a life span of three to five years, somewhat longer than typical "current" expenditure plans and considerably shorter than the traditional capital funding models used by school districts. As a result, many districts have had difficulty in purchasing and keeping adequate numbers of up-to-date computers. Some have turned to lease programs; others rely on donations of computers—new and used. Other districts have simply not replaced old and obsolete computers in a timely fashion.

Even if a district has managed to develop a purchase plan to provide adequate computer systems for all its schools, there is still the problem of electrical wiring and connections between computers. Older schools simply do not have the capacity to handle the electrical and wiring needs of state-of-the-art computers. Funding for installation of the infrastructure may be available through the e-rate funding, a process whereby telecommunications firms contribute to a fund whose proceeds are distributed on a competitive basis to school districts for technology needs.

Once installed, there are also substantial costs to maintaining computer networks. Updating all of the routers and servers needed to keep the computers communicating as well as repair technicians to fix computers and related peripherals when they break down are essential to successful technology implementation. Funding for all of this needs to be a regular part of a district's budget.

## Sources of Funding

The maintenance and modernization needs of schools require both one-time and continuing sources of money, with maintenance and modernization requiring different approaches. Maintenance is probably best funded through budget allocations of current resources. This means that adequate funds need to be allocated each year to be sure that the investment a district has made in facilities is not lost because of premature deterioration of the buildings. Some districts in some states have had some success in getting community redevelopment agencies to provide a portion of the tax increment they receive to stimulate development for school facility needs. Often this money is used to supplement existing allocations for maintenance.

Modernization may require one-time funding options. Some of the alternatives available to school districts include:

- Bond Issues: By taking advantage of the tax-exempt status of school district bond issues, education agencies can often borrow funds for capital projects at relatively low interest rates. Bonds typically require voter approval and, depending on state law, may need to be accounted for in a separate budgetary and accounting fund. Nevertheless, they remain a powerful and relatively inexpensive way to fund facility needs.

- Special Local Option Sales Taxes: Allowed in some states, these are sales tax increments added to the state and local sales taxes already collected. While such taxes can be a reliable source of funds, local sales taxes may also inhibit development of commercial and retail centers in the district.

- Voter-Approved Levies or Sinking Funds: Some states allow school districts to levy special taxes for specific purposes such as technology. Others allow districts to levy taxes for a sinking fund, which collects the revenues and accumulates interest so that construction and/or modernization needs can be funded through the cash balance in the fund.

- State and Federal Funding: Special state and federal programs are sometimes available to fund improvements and construction. Individual state programs to help meet deferred maintenance needs are common, and the federal government has provided funding for school facilities through the Qualified Zone Academy Bond program. In each case these programs provide local school districts with funds for improving or building school facilities.

## Conclusion

Maintaining school facilities is important to providing high-quality education programs. More important, by investing in strong preventative maintenance programs, school facilities can continue to serve students for long periods of time. Modernization of school facilities has faced a number of new challenges in recent years with the advent of the personal computer. As new technologies are increasingly integrated into programs of instruction, the ability to adequately finance the acquisition of this equipment and to have the infrastructure in each school to support this technology is also important.

*See also:* FINANCIAL SUPPORT OF SCHOOLS; RURAL EDUCATION; SCHOOL BOARDS; TECHNOLOGY IN EDUCATION; URBAN EDUCATION.

**BIBLIOGRAPHY**

GEIGER, PHILIP E. 2002. "Deferred School Maintenance Creates National Crisis." *School Business Affairs* 68(1):43.

NATIONAL CENTER FOR EDUCATION STATISTICS. 2000. *Condition of America's Public School Facilities, 1999.* Washington, DC: U.S. Department of Education, National Center for Education Statistics.

NATIONAL EDUCATION ASSOCIATION. 2000. *Modernizing Our Schools: What Will It Cost?* Washington, DC: National Education Association.

ZUREICH, MICHAEL. 1999. "Yes, Reductions in School Construction Costs Are Possible." *CASBO Journal* 64(2):32–38.

LAWRENCE O. PICUS

# SCHOOL FOOD PROGRAMS

Food service programs have long been recognized as important components of education in the American schools. "You can't teach a hungry child" has been an accepted principle since the early years of the country, when children were expected to bring lunches from home to get them through the day. However, not all children were able to do so because of financial and other circumstances. In addition, the food brought from home was often lacking in nutritional quality and desirability, and the schools usually lacked the facilities to store milk and other perishable food products. At the same time, food supplies in this country have usually been abundant and, at least during recessionary periods, in excess of market demands.

Particularly during the 1930s, farmers faced extremely low prices and excess food supplies while people were literally starving. Children were perceived as being in critical need of food support. To solve both problems, the Congress passed Public Law 74-320, authorizing the U.S. Department of Agriculture (USDA) to purchase surplus agricultural commodities and distribute them to needy families and specifically to school lunch programs. At the same time, the Works Progress Administration (WPA), established in 1935, provided labor and trained supervisory personnel for staffing school lunch program on a national scale.

## Early Lunch Programs

Precedents for school lunch programs date back to the mid-nineteenth century in England and western Europe. In 1849, school canteens were established in France, and in 1866 the Destitute Diner Society was established in London. By the beginning of the twentieth century, most western European countries had national laws or extensive municipal legislation providing for school meals.

In 1853, the Children's Aid Society of New York served food to all children who attended its industrial schools, which later became public schools. Serving food became an inducement to children from the slums to attend school. In the economic downturn of 1893, the problem of hungry school children came to public attention. The conviction arose that children in a weak physical and mental state resulting from poverty learned little or nothing at school.

The Star Center Association began school food service in Philadelphia elementary schools in 1894. In 1909, the Philadelphia Board of Education took over all school food service in secondary schools, making Philadelphia the first large city to establish central food control. School lunch programs increased rapidly in the 1920s, as new knowledge of nutrition led to greater concern for the health of children. As a result, the purpose of school food service broadened from provision for the needy and undernourished to provision for all children who need food at school.

## The National School Lunch Program

During World War II, many U.S. draftees were found to be malnourished to such an extent that they were turned down for military service. The realization of this low nutritional state of the general population led to the passage of the National School Lunch Act (NSLA) in 1946, which established the National School Lunch Program (NSLP) in elementary and secondary schools. This landmark legislation, although amended many times, continues in force today, with its original objectives still in place. These objectives are "to safeguard the health and well-being of the Nation's children, and to encourage the domestic consumption of nutritious agricultural commodities and other food."

The NSLA provided annual appropriations to the USDA to purchase surplus foods and apportion them to state agencies, along with certain funds that were to be matched three-to-one with state funds or volunteer labor. Commodities and funds were provided to state educational agencies and to other nonprofit agencies participating in the program (private schools in about twenty-five states that could not transmit funds through their state educational agency). These agencies managed the lunch programs at the local level, and sometimes added state funds. They were provided with state operating expenses that covered part, but not all, of their own expenses, also on an apportionment basis. Apportionments after 1962 were made on the basis of state level of participation during the previous year and per capita state incomes relative to the U.S. total. Nonfood assistance for the purchase of food service equipment was also provided selectively in low-income areas by grants authorized by the Child Nutrition Act of 1966 (Pub. L. 89-642).

The Food and Nutrition Service of the USDA operates the NSLP at the national level, and the individual states must sign agreements to operate the program in accordance with the regulations to receive federal reimbursements for meals served. Normally, the state educational agency is responsible for operating the program at the state level. More than 97,700 public and nonprofit private schools and residential child-care institutions operated the program in fiscal year 2002. Among the important requirements for operating the program, NSLP meals served at the local level are required to meet nutritional standards specified in the NSLA. Those requirements originally were called the *Type A* lunch pattern (as opposed to *Type B*, which consisted only of milk). That term, while still in use locally in many places, was replaced in the 1970s with *USDA menu pattern*, which refers to service of specified portions of meat, milk, vegetables or fruits, and bread. The legislation recognized that federal support was only supplemental to total costs, and therefore it was expected that meals would be sold at cost to the chil-

dren that could afford to pay, while low-income children would receive their lunches free.

## More Recent Program Changes

Three key changes have been made in the funding and operations of the NSLP: (1) Public Law 91-248, enacted in 1971, specified that federal dollar appropriations apportioned to the states for the program's operation were to be replaced with a federal reimbursement entitlement of a certain number of cents in cash and another entitlement value of commodities for each meal served that meets requirements. Funds and commodities provided per meal are updated annually based on changes in prices of *food-away-from-home*, as measured by the Consumer Price Index (CPI). Thus, the program was transformed into an ongoing, performance-based federal obligation. (2) With the same legislation, the federal government assumed the obligation for the full cost of all meals served to needy children, with entitlements updated annually based on price changes reflected in the CPI. Eligibility for free or reduced-price meals was specified by law and measured in accordance with the Federal Income Poverty Guidelines. These guidelines are also updated each year, based on changes in the CPI. (3) In 1995, nutritional requirements were changed from specifying the service of specified portions of specified kinds of food to the requirement that nutritional meals needed to be provided (Pub. L. 103-448). These requirements are tied to the service of meals that meet one-third of the daily Recommended Dietary Allowances (RDAs), as specified by the Food and Nutrition Board of the National Research Council, which is part of the National Academy of Sciences, as well as the Dietary Guidelines for Americans.

Another change occurred in 1998 when Congress expanded the NSLP to include reimbursement for the service of snacks in after-school, educational, and enrichment programs to students up to eighteen years of age. Organized sports activities with limited eligibility of student participation do not qualify for support.

## NSLP Payment Rates

In school year 2001–2002, all qualified meals served, regardless of the income level of the students' parents, were reimbursed at 20 cents per meal. But if the meals were served in relatively low-income districts, these meals received an extra 2 cents reimbursement. The qualification of "low-income district" is measured by the percentage of free or reduced-price meals served in the district two years previously. If more than 60 percent of the meals served went to students qualifying for free or reduced-price meals, the district gets the extra 2 cents. If the number is less that 60 percent, they get only the basic reimbursement level.

For student meals served free to qualifying low-income students, an additional federal reimbursement of $1.89 was made, for a total, including the above 20 or 22 cents, of $2.09 or $2.11 per meal depending on whether the meals were served in low-income areas. Reduced-price meals were reimbursed at 40 cents per meal less than for free meals. In total, reduced-price meals were reimbursed at $1.69 or $1.71, depending on the income level of the location served.

The above rates were the same in each of the forty-eight contiguous states and the District of Columbia. Higher rates were paid for meals served in Alaska and Hawaii, in recognition of their higher costs. All meals served in Alaska in 2001–2002 received 32 or 34 cents reimbursement. Free meals received a total of $3.38 or $3.40, and reduced-price meals received a total of $2.98 or $3.00. In Hawaii, the rates were 23 or 25 cents for all meals, for a total of $2.44 or $2.46 for free meals and $2.04 or $2.06 for reduced-price meals, depending on the income criteria. Note that the 2-cent differential for income level of the district was the same as in the 48 states, and the 40-cent differential between free and reduced-price meals was maintained.

The above payment rates increase by law each year, as noted above. The average increase for school year 2001–2002 year was 2.85 percent, reflecting price increases over the previous year.

In addition to the above cash payments, schools also receive in-kind commodity support. They received an entitlement level of 15.5 cents worth of foods in 2001–2002 for all meals served. These foods are purchased and distributed to the states by the USDA. The types of foods purchased are determined in consultation with the states to be those preferred by program operators, based on feedback from children's preferences. In addition, a variable amount of bonus foods are provided when foods are in surplus from an agricultural supply perspective. The entitlement level of 15.5 cents increases each year based on wholesale food-price increases as measured by the Bureau of Labor Statistics.

### Free and Reduced-Price Lunches

Since 1971, free lunches have been available to all children from households with incomes below 100 percent (or more) of the Income Eligibility Guidelines, which were patterned after the Income Poverty Guidelines published by the Office of Management and Budget (OMB). In August 1981, the level of eligibility for free lunches was raised to 130 percent of the guidelines, and reduced-price meals were made available to all children from households with incomes between 130 percent and 185 percent of the Guidelines.

In school year 2001–2002, these guidelines provided free meals to students from four-person households with annual cash incomes (before taxes and other deductions) below $22,945 in the forty-eight contiguous states and the District of Columbia. Income levels varied by household size, and were about 25 percent higher in Alaska and 15 percent higher in Hawaii. Reduced-price meals were available to students from four-person households with incomes below $32,653 in the forty-eight states, with similar adjustments by household size and for Alaska and Hawaii. The numbers for 2001–2002 were raised by 3.52 percent from the previous year, based on CPI price changes measured by the Bureau of Labor Statistics.

In order to receive free or reduced-price lunches, a household must return applications sent home with students each Fall soon after school begins. Applications include household income levels, which are used to determine the income criteria given above. Every attempt is made to keep applications confidential, as well as the daily service to students of the free or reduced-price meals. Often, meal coupons are used for this purpose; they are purchased by those paying for their meals and provided free or at reduced price to qualifying students.

All meals are provided free to students in Puerto Rico and the Virgin Islands. Federal reimbursements are based on incomes of households with students, using the forty-eight-state eligibility levels as a benchmark.

### Nutrient Standards

Public Law 103-448, passed in November 1995, offered three alternative ways of meeting the new menu standards: (1) NuMenus, or Nutrient Standard Menu Planning (NSMP); (2) Assisted Nu-Menus, which provides outside assistance in conducting NSMP; and (3) Food-Based Menu Planning, which consists of a modified set of foods from the traditional USDA menu-planning system. A fourth menu planning system was authorized by the Healthy Meals for Children Act (Pub. L. 104-149), which was passed in May 1996. This system provides a further option that allows schools additional freedom in using various food-based menu planning systems, as long as they ended up meeting the basic nutrient standards.

Even though much flexibility is provided in menu planning, the nutrient-based requirements of Public Law 103-448 remain in effect. Once every five years, each school district is monitored by the state agency, and a week of menus is evaluated for conformance in meeting the nutrient standards. These standards consist of specified levels of energy (calories), fat and saturated fat, protein, calcium, iron, Vitamin A, and Vitamin C. The levels are specified as averages for kindergarten through sixth grade, and for seventh through twelfth grades.

### The School Breakfast Program

The School Breakfast Program (SBP) is a federal nonprofit entitlement program that operates independently of, but alongside, the NSLP. It began as a pilot program in 1966, authorized by the Child Nutrition Act of 1966, and was made permanent in 1975. The original purpose of the program was to primarily to provide breakfasts to elementary and secondary school children coming from poor economic areas, and to those traveling long distances to school. After becoming permanent, the program has been equally available to all eligible children. However, reimbursement rates favor those areas in severe need, which are those districts serving a relatively large share of meals at free or reduced prices.

The program is similarly administered at the federal level by the Food and Nutrition Service of the USDA, and usually at the state level by state education agencies. It is still not as broadly available as the NSLP, but operates nationally in 72,000 schools and institutions. All meals served under SBP must meet the recommendations of the Dietary Guidelines for Americans. In addition, they must provide one-fourth of the daily recommended levels of calories and RDAs for protein, calcium, iron, Vitamin A, and Vitamin C.

Any child at a school with an approved program may purchase breakfasts under the program, and those meeting NSLP requirements may also receive free or reduced-price breakfasts. However, the preponderance of those participating receive their meals free or at reduced prices, which reflects the original purposes of the program. As in the case of lunches, funds for SBP were initially allocated on a state-by-state basis, with a basic grant of $50,000 per state. The program was later turned into a federal entitlement, with meals reimbursed on the basis of the number of meals served.

Paid breakfasts were reimbursed by the federal government at 21 cents in school year 2001–2002, one cent more than for paid lunches served under NSLP. Free breakfasts received $1.15 and reduced-price breakfasts received 85 cents under the regular program. However, districts classified as in severe need received $1.37 for free breakfasts and $1.07 for reduced-price meals—two-thirds of the total breakfasts served usually meet this criterion. As in the case of lunches, Alaska and Hawaii receive higher reimbursement levels for all breakfasts served.

There have long been strong feelings that the breakfast program provides key nutritional benefits to schoolchildren, perhaps even greater than those provided by the lunch program. In part, these feelings reflect the fact that the lack of breakfast can adversely affect student performance until lunch is served at school. However, no known studies have established a firm basis for this conclusion. The 1992 School Nutrition Dietary Assessment Study found that the availability of a SBP at school did not increase the likelihood of a child eating breakfast. This 1992 study confirmed an earlier study of data from the 1980–1981 National Evaluation of School Nutrition Programs that had found the same result. However, a 1998 Mathematica Policy Research study showed that these conclusions depended heavily on the content definition of a breakfast. The 1992 study defined breakfast as eating any food containing at least fifty calories. The conclusion was that if a breakfast was defined to require the serving of more substantial nutrients, then the SBP would be found to be more useful. Partly for this reason, Congress, in 1998, funded a three-year evaluation of a pilot program in which all children would receive free breakfasts regardless of household income.

### The Special Milk Program

The Special Milk Program (SMP) provides federal reimbursements for milk (alone) served to children in nonprofit schools and child-care institutions that

**TABLE 1**

| Average daily participation in National School Lunch Program and School Breakfast Program | | | | | | | | |
| --- | --- | --- | --- | --- | --- | --- | --- |
| | National School Lunch Program | | | | School Breakfast Program | | | |
| | Free | Reduced | Paid | Total | Free | Reduced | Paid | Total |
| | millions of participants | | | | | | | |
| Fiscal year 1981 | 10.6 | 1.9 | 13.3 | 25.8 | 3.05 | 0.25 | 0.51 | 3.81 |
| Fiscal year 1991 | 10.3 | 1.8 | 12.1 | 24.2 | 3.61 | 0.25 | 0.58 | 4.44 |
| Fiscal year 2001 | 12.9 | 2.6 | 12.0 | 27.5 | 5.80 | 0.67 | 1.32 | 7.79 |
| SOURCE: Courtesy of author. | | | | | | | | |

do not participate in other federal food service programs. These would include schools without NSLP or SMP food service, as well as those with half-day kindergarten programs where children do not have access to the lunch or breakfast program. The SMP program has declined slightly in scope over time as the NSLP and SBP have expanded, but the SMP has remained a viable niche program. In 2000-2001, SMP milk was served in nearly 7,000 schools and residential child-care institutions, along with 1,100 summer camps and 500 nonresidential child-care institutions.

Those schools or institutions that participate in SMP offer milk on a paid or free basis using the same criteria of eligibility as under the NSLP. Reimbursements of paid milk are made on the basis of the number of half-pints of milk served. In 2001–2002, schools received 14.5 cents per half pint. But for free milk served, they are reimbursed at the net purchase price for the milk. Various kinds of milk—flavored or unflavored, low-fat or whole milk—are eligible to be served.

### After-School Care Program

The After-School Snack Program, which began in 1998, must operate under the school food authority that operates the NSLP. It must provide children with regularly scheduled educational or enrichment activities in an organized, structured, and supervised environment to be eligible for federal reimbursements. It also must be located in a geographic area served by a school in which 50 percent or more of the children enrolled are eligible for free or reduced-price school meals.

Reimbursement rates for 2001–2002 were 55 cents for free snacks, 27 cents for those at reduced price, and 5 cents for those paid. Rates were higher for Alaska and Hawaii, where free snacks were reimbursed at 93 cents and 67 cents, respectively.

### Participation and Costs of School Food Service

Table 1 shows the average daily participation, by payment categories, in the National School Lunch Program and School Breakfast Program for fiscal years 1981, 1991, and 2001. The data represent sums of monthly averages of participation reported by the states, averaged for the federal fiscal years for the months of October through May, plus September. Participation is defined as the number of meals per enrolled student, adjusted for absenteeism.

One can readily see that participation in the NSLP increased slightly between 1981 and 2001, and that the increase in participation is centered on free or reduced-price meal participants. Paid meal participation declined 10 percent. In terms of percentages, the reduced-price category increased the most (more than one-third) but it remained less than 10 percent of total participation. Paid lunch participation accounted for less than one-half (44 percent) of the total in 2001.

In contrast, the SBP increased quite substantially over the two decades. In fact, total participation doubled. This growth was no accident, for considerable attention was focused on growing the School Breakfast Program during this period. Free meals dominate the program, accounting for nearly three-fourths of the total in 2001. Reduced-price participants accounted for another 9 percent, leaving paid participants at 17 percent. SBP participation was small in 2001 in relation to the NSLP, at less than one-third the total number of participants.

Table 2 shows the federal costs of the NSLP and SMP, in millions of dollars, again for fiscal years 1981, 1991, and 2001. Total federal costs for the NSLP doubled over the two decades, with most of the increase in terms of cash payments. Commodity costs increased only slightly, and they included bonus commodities that had shrunk considerably,

**TABLE 2**

| Federal costs for National School Lunch Program and School Breakfast Program | | | | |
|---|---|---|---|---|
| | National School Lunch Program | | | School Breakfast Program |
| | Cash | Commodities | Total | Total |
| | millions of dollars | | | |
| Fiscal year 1981 | 2,381 | 895 | 3,276 | 332 |
| Fiscal year 1991 | 3,526 | 699 | 4,224 | 685 |
| Fiscal year 2001 | 5,605 | 963 | 6,468 | 1,445 |

SOURCE: Courtesy of author.

accounting for only $60 million in 2001, compared with $316 million in 1981. Entitlement commodities increased from $579 million to $802 million over this period. Federal SBP costs increased more than four times over the 20 years, reflecting increases in participation, as well as an increase in reimbursements per meal.

Not included in Table 2 are the costs of the SMP and a relatively small program that provides only commodities to some schools not participating in NSLP. The federal SMP cost $15.4 million in 2001, down from $19.8 million in 1981. During this period the number of half-pints of milk served declined from 177 million to 115 million in FY 2001. The commodity-only program cost $23.3 million in 2001, compared with $21.9 million a decade earlier.

The data in this section were obtained from unpublished sources from the Food and Nutrition Service of USDA (*Program Information Reports*). However, the primary data were published annually for 1981 through 1995 in the *School Food Service Research Review*.

## Related Food Programs

Child and adult care programs and summer food service programs supported by USDA reimbursements may operate in school locations. These programs are very substantial in many areas, but they are not included in this discussion because they are not directly supporting school educational programs.

*See also:* FEDERAL EDUCATIONAL ACTIVITIES; NUTRITION AND CHILDREN'S PHYSICAL HEALTH.

**BIBLIOGRAPHY**

ALMANZA, BARBARA, and HIEMSTRA, STEPHEN J. 1997. *School Meals Initiative: Implementation Manual for Indiana Schools.* West Lafayette, IN: RHIT Department, Purdue University.

BRYAN, MARY DE GARMO. 1971. "School Food Programs: Overview." In *The Encyclopedia of Education,* 1st edition. New York: Macmillan.

DEVANEY, BARBARA, and FRAKER, THOMAS. 1989. "Dietary Impacts of the School Breakfast Program." *American Journal of Agricultural Economics* 71(4):932–948.

GLEASON, PHILIP M. 1995. "Participation in the National School Lunch Program and the School Breakfast Program." *The American Journal of Clinical Nutrition* 61(1):2135–2205.

HIEMSTRA, STEPHEN J. 1995. "Summary of Trends." *School Food Service Research Review* 19(1):51–53.

HUNTER, ROBERT. 1994. *Poverty.* New York: Macmillan.

MATHEMATICA POLICY RESEARCH, INC. 1998. *Eating Breakfast: Effects of the School Breakfast Program.* Princeton, NJ: Mathematica Policy Research, Inc.

NATIONAL ACADEMY OF SCIENCES, NATIONAL RESEARCH COUNCIL. 1989. *Recommended Dietary Allowances,* 10th revised edition. Washington DC: National Academy Press.

PARGO, JOHN. 1906. *Underfed School Children: The Problem and the Remedy.* Chicago: C. H. Kerr.

TODHUNTER, E. NEIGE. 1968. "Approaches to Nutrition Education." *Journal of Nutrition Education,* prototype issue.

U.S. DEPARTMENT OF AGRICULTURE, FOOD AND NUTRITION SERVICE. 1996. *Healthy School Meals Training.* Alexandria, VA: USDA.

U.S. DEPARTMENT OF AGRICULTURE, and UNITED STATES DEPARTMENT OF HEALTH AND HUMAN SERVICES. 1995. *Dietary Guidelines for Americans,* 4th edition. Washington DC: DOA, DHHS.

**INTERNET RESOURCE**

FEDERAL REGISTER. 2002. "Child Nutrition." <www.fns.usda.gov/cnd>.

STEPHEN J. HIEMSTRA

# SCHOOL LIBRARIES

The modern school library media center has a professionally trained school library media specialist who manages a central collection of diverse learning resources to support a school's curriculum, meet individual students' needs and interests, and ensure that young people develop information literacy skills within the school's curriculum. This concept of a learning resource center is both a social development of the twentieth century and an evolution of information exchange.

## History

The ancient library in Alexandra, founded in the fourth century B.C.E., was a treasure trove of written manuscripts. Medieval libraries comprised collections of hand-copied, illuminated manuscripts that were typically created and maintained by monks and used by privileged classes; manuscripts were often as valuable as farms or houses. An early print format put into the hands of children and used for reading instruction from the fifteenth to the eighteenth century was the hornbook, typically a small wooden paddle with printed paper pasted on top and covered with translucent horn. By the seventeenth century the concept of books created specifically for young people was established with such works as the first picture book, *Orbis Sensualium Pictus* by Johann Amos Comenius in 1657. The invention of the printing press in 1455 promised young people greater access to printed materials, and philosophers like John Locke (1632–1704) and publishers like John Newbery (1713–1767) promoted materials that were both pleasurable and informative to young people. Yet, well into the twentieth century, books and other learning materials remained expensive and rare for most young people in the United States.

Although Benjamin Franklin envisioned a library in his academy (founded in 1740), widespread public recognition and support for school libraries did not develop until the nineteenth century when state legislatures (beginning in 1835 with New York) acknowledged the value of school library resources and began promoting their funding. By 1876, nineteen states appropriated funding for school libraries. Two factors, however, limited the overall success of these early efforts to support school libraries: the lack of library facilities for maintaining the developing collections within the schools and the lack of trained personnel for selecting, organizing, and cir-

culating the collections. The resources were often overseen in small classroom collections by individual teachers, who could not ensure students had access to materials throughout a school; who were not coordinated with other teachers to track library inventories; and who often took materials from one building to another as they changed teaching positions. Meanwhile, the public library movement was developing in the United States, and trained public librarians reached out to address public school needs. Their outreach efforts coincided with the founding in 1876 of the American Library Association (ALA), and at the close of the nineteenth century, the professional voice for school library services to young people often had a public library perspective.

The twentieth century was a tumultuous one in which school librarians continued to address the challenges of the nineteenth century and developed the vision for school library media programs in the twenty-first century. Setting the stage for changes to come was the dialogue in the early 1900s on such educational principles as the importance of intrinsic motivation, the creation of genuine learning experiences in a field setting or a learning laboratory, and the teacher as a guide not a taskmaster. Even in 1900, these were not new ideas, but the educator and philosopher John Dewey, with the 1899 publication of *School and Society,* envisioned a single concept of Progressive education, comprising these elements, in opposition to rote learning, inflexibility, conformity, and competition. Thus, challenges to nineteenth-century assumptions were an aspect of educational planning as school libraries began their twentieth century transformation that included such milestone events as:

**1900** Mary Kingsbury, librarian at Erasmus Hall High School in New York City, becomes the first professionally trained school librarian.

**1915** The School Libraries Section of ALA holds its first meeting.

**1918** The National Education Association (NEA) adopts Standard Library Organization and Equipment for Secondary Schools of Different Sizes. These first national standards define expectations that a professionally trained librarian should manage a centralized collection that included audiovisual resources.

**1920** ALA adopts the 1918 NEA standards.

**1925** The Department of Elementary Principals of the NEA and the School Librarians' Section of ALA develops the *Report of the Joint Committee on Elementary School Library Standards.* This first set of national library standards for elementary schools emphasizes the library's support of teaching and learning within a flexible schedule that ensures ready access for students and teachers.

**1945** ALA publishes *School Libraries for Today and Tomorrow, Functions and Standards,* the first national standards for both elementary and secondary school library programs. These standards link the quality of school library programs to qualitative and quantitative guidelines.

**1951** ALA adopts Standards for Accreditation, which moves the first professional degree in librarianship to the master's level.

**1951** The American Association of School Librarians (AASL) becomes a division within ALA.

**1958** The U.S. Congress passes the National Defense Education Act, which funds major development of school libraries in the 1960s.

**1960** AASL and the Department of Audiovisual Instruction (DAVI) of NEA publishes *Standards for School Library Programs,* national guidelines that address the integration of library skills into classroom work and provide a descriptive narrative with quantitative recommendations and detailed lists.

**1962** AASL receives the Knapp Demonstration Project, a $1.13 million grant supporting a five-year demonstration project of exemplary school libraries.

**1965** The U.S. Congress passes the Elementary and Secondary Education Act, which supports funding of library resources.

**1969** ALA and the DAVI of NEA publishs *Standards for School Media Programs,* national guidelines that unify the roles of librarians and audiovisual personnel under the terminology of library media program and library media specialist.

**1971** The DAVI of NEA becomes the Association for Educational Communications and Technology (AECT).

**1972** AASL begins publishing *School Library Media Quarterly,* the division's research journal.

**1975** AASL and AECT publish *Media Programs: District and School,* national guidelines that are the first to focus on district goals and responsibilities in the support of building-level library media programs.

**1988** AASL and AECT publish *Information Power: Guidelines for School Library Media Programs,* national guidelines that define the mission of the library media program to "ensure that students and staff are effective users of ideas and information" (1988, 1).

**1988** ALA becomes a specialty organization within the National Council on Accreditation of Teacher Education (NCATE).

**1988** The DeWitt Wallace—Reader's Digest Fund initiates Library Power, a 10-year, $40-million-grant project for the revitalization of school library media programs across the United States.

**1998** AASL and AECT publish *Information Power: Building Partnerships for Learning,* national guidelines that set forth AASL's information literacy standards for student learning.

Milestone markers for progress across the twentieth century are the eight sets of published national standards and guidelines.

### Goals and Purposes

Although school library media specialists collaboratively establish library media program goals relevant to the needs of individual schools, they are guided by a mission such as that articulated by the American Association of School Librarians (AASL) and Association for Educational Communications and Technology (AECT) "to ensure that students and staff are effective users of ideas and information" (1998, p. 6). The authors identify seven library media program goals through which the library media specialists support the mission by providing the following:

- Learning activities that foster in students the abilities to select, retrieve, analyze, evaluate, synthesize, create, and communicate "information in all formats and in all content areas of the curriculum"

- "Physical access to information"
- Learning experiences in "communications media and technology"
- Consultation with teachers in designing instruction
- Learning resources and activities that accommodate "differences in teaching and learning styles, methods, interests, and capacities"
- Access to a "full range of information beyond the school building"
- Learning resources "that represent diversity of experiences, opinions, and social and cultural perspectives and to support responsible citizenship in a democracy" (American Association of School Librarians and Association for Educational Communications and Technology 1998, pp. 6–7).

## Materials and Equipment

The materials and equipment in a library media program provide information that supports active, authentic learning, and thus ensures that young people develop the information literacy skills crucial to their success as students and as lifelong learners. Historically the primary source of information for an entire school was an on-site collection of diverse materials and equipment. However, technological changes have altered this traditional view by increasing the quantity of information, accentuating the need for strong literacy and technology skills, creating new formats and packages of information, and interconnecting worldwide information. Such developments have changed the nature of the local collection, now defined in terms of access to and delivery of information and learning resources within and beyond the school. The early-twenty-first century library media collection includes printed materials, realia (the "real thing," i.e., living, synthesized, or preserved animal, vegetable, or mineral objects in their natural state), hardware and software, online databases, production equipment, and adaptive resources for students and others with special needs.

Access to and delivery of information and learning resources has two dimensions: physical and intellectual. Physical access to library media resources is ensured when resources are usable from a central location that oversees circulation, distribution, organization, and classification for effective and efficient use, and managed according to policies that ensure flexible scheduling that supports focused and pro-

ductive use of learning resources. Intellectual access to information and learning resources requires that they are matched to individual needs and interests; that students and others can find, evaluate, and use them; and that they are supported by comprehensive reference services, including bibliographies and resource lists.

Physical and intellectual access is guided by principles of intellectual freedom, legal standards, and professional ethics. Intellectual freedom is essential for students to become critical thinkers and lifelong learners who can contribute productively and responsibly in a democratic society. Access guided by legal standards and professional ethics ensures confidentiality in the use of information, respect for intellectual property rights, and equity for all students, regardless of ability or cultural considerations.

## Personnel

Qualified school library media personnel are fundamental to successful programs that contribute to student learning, and a program's level of professional and support staffing is based upon a school's instructional program, services, facilities, and the quantity of students and teachers. Basic, building-level staffing for an effective program necessitates at least one certified or licensed school library media specialist per building. The library media specialist should hold a master's degree in librarianship from a program accredited by the American Librarian Association or a master's degree with a specialty in school library media from an educational institution accredited by the National Council for the Accreditation of Teacher Education. In addition to the minimum of one school library media specialist, each school program requires qualified clerical and technical support staff. The paraprofessional support staff are key to the library media specialist's ability to fulfill the position's professional roles. There is a distinction between a technician, who works with hardware and systems software, and a technologist, who integrates people, learning, and the tools of technology.

According to the American Association of School Librarians and the Association for Educational Communications and Technology, the library media specialist accomplishes the program's primary charge, to "ensure that students and staff are effective users of ideas and information" (1998, p. 6), by fulfilling four roles: teacher, instructional partner, information specialist, and program administrator.

The four roles focus on instilling nine student information literacy standards across the school's curriculum. According to those AASL/AECT standards, young people should be able to:

- Access "information efficiently and effectively"
- Evaluate "information critically and competently"
- Use "information accurately and creatively"
- Pursue "information related to personal interests"
- Appreciate "literature and other creative expressions of information"
- Strive "for excellence in information seeking and knowledge generation"
- Contribute "positively to the learning community" and recognize "the importance of information to a democratic society"
- Behave ethically "in regard to information and information technology"
- Participate "effectively in groups to pursue and generate information" (American Association of School Libraries and Association for Educational Communications and Technology 1998, pp. 9–43).

Library media specialists value information literacy as the foundation of lifelong learning, and they emphasize the process of learning rather than the accumulation of information. By collaborating with diverse individuals within and beyond the school, by building awareness of the program's contributions, and by applying and introducing instructional and informational technologies, library media specialists promote a clear vision for successful library media programming.

*See also:* ELEMENTARY EDUCATION, *subentries on* CURRENT TRENDS, HISTORY OF; SECONDARY EDUCATION, *subentries on* CURRENT TRENDS, HISTORY OF; TECHNOLOGY AND EDUCATION, *subentry on* SCHOOL.

### BIBLIOGRAPHY

AMERICAN ASSOCIATION OF SCHOOL LIBRARIANS and ASSOCIATION FOR EDUCATIONAL COMMUNICATIONS AND TECHNOLOGY. 1975. *Media Programs: District and School.* Chicago: American Library Association and Washington, DC: Association for Educational Communications and Technology.

AMERICAN ASSOCIATION OF SCHOOL LIBRARIANS and ASSOCIATION FOR EDUCATIONAL COMMUNICATIONS AND TECHNOLOGY. 1988. *Information Power: Guidelines for School Library Media Programs.* Chicago: American Library Association and Washington, DC: Association for Educational Communications and Technology.

AMERICAN ASSOCIATION OF SCHOOL LIBRARIANS and ASSOCIATION FOR EDUCATIONAL COMMUNICATIONS AND TECHNOLOGY. 1998. *Information Power: Building Partnerships for Learning.* Chicago: American Library Association and Washington, DC: Association for Educational Communications and Technology.

AMERICAN ASSOCIATION OF SCHOOL LIBRARIANS and DEPARTMENT OF AUDIOVISUAL INSTRUCTION OF THE NATIONAL EDUCATION ASSOCIATION. 1960. *Standards for School Library Programs.* Chicago: American Library Association.

AMERICAN ASSOCIATION OF SCHOOL LIBRARIANS and DEPARTMENT OF AUDIOVISUAL INSTRUCTION OF THE NATIONAL EDUCATION ASSOCIATION. 1969. *Standards for School Media Programs.* Chicago: American Library Association.

AMERICAN LIBRARY ASSOCIATION. 1945. *School Libraries for Today and Tomorrow.* Chicago: American Library Association.

HAYCOCK, KEN, ed. 1999. *Foundations for Effective School Library Media Programs.* Englewood, CO: Libraries Unlimited.

LATROBE, KATHY HOWARD, ed. 1998. *The Emerging School Library Media Center: Historical Issues and Perspectives.* Englewood, CO: Libraries Unlimited.

NATIONAL EDUCATION ASSOCIATION and NORTH CENTRAL ASSOCIATION OF COLLEGES AND SECONDARY SCHOOLS. 1920. *Standard Library Organization and Equipment for Secondary Schools of Different Sizes.* Chicago: American Library Association.

NATIONAL EDUCATION ASSOCIATION and NORTH CENTRAL ASSOCIATION OF COLLEGES AND SECONDARY SCHOOLS. 1925. *Elementary School Library Standards.* Chicago: American Library Association.

WOOLLS, BLANCHE. 1998. *The School Library Media Manager,* 2nd edition. Englewood, CO: Libraries Unlimited.

KATHY HOWARD LATROBE

# SCHOOL-LINKED SERVICES

TYPES OF SERVICES AND ORGANIZATIONAL FORMS
  Robert L. Crowson
OUTCOMES
  Sidney L. Gardner

## TYPES OF SERVICES AND ORGANIZATIONAL FORMS

There has been a rapid expansion of coordinated-services efforts throughout the United States since the late 1980s. Solid historical roots can be found in the Progressive era of the early twentieth century, as well as some of the Great Society interventions of the 1960s. However, the aggressive development of a system of coordinated services for children and families in need received its major impetus in the late 1980s in reports of some service-needs conferencing, the results of some early experimentation, and in reports of the conditions of children and families in poverty. Two of the most influential documents were *The Conditions of Children in California* (1989) by Michael Kirst and *Joining Forces* (1989) by Janet Levy and Carol Copple.

The spread of children's services programs, from the late 1980s on, was so rapid that by 1993 one of its foremost advocates, Sharon Lynn Kagan, was claiming that efforts were "blossoming across the country from Maine to California" (Kagan and Neville, p. 78). Such "blossoming" had already received a solid boost from state legislation in New Jersey (1988), Kentucky (1990), and California (1991); with each establishing statewide family services programs.

In 1993 in the *American Journal of Education,* Robert Crowson published the first in a series of co-authored inquiries into issues surrounding the administration and organization of school-based services. Drawing on the available reports, handbooks, evaluations, and case studies of the time, it was observed that an array of institutional realities presented a difficult, uphill climb for service coordination. Among the problematic elements were matters of professional control and turf; organizational disincentives to collaboration; legal and budgetary dilemmas; communications and confidentiality barriers; questions of governance and managerial support; and reconceptualizations of professional or organizational roles.

Through the 1990s additional reports and analyses continued to document the deep administrative problems encountered by those attempting to coordinate services. A substantial blow to the movement in the United States occurred in 1994 when the Pew Charitable Trust announced the termination of its then sizeable support of school-linked family centers. The Trust's decision came on the heels of some weak evaluation results.

Just a year later, an assessment by Julie White and Gary Wehlage of the New Futures initiative, then funded by the Annie E. Casey Foundation, added fuel to the no-effects fire. Among the most damaging of the findings was the observation that the outreach programs were invariably of the from-the-top-down variety, and that they ignored family and community expressions of service needs, depending instead upon professionally identified definitions of client need.

However, none of this bad press stopped, or even slowed, the movement. The notion of coordinated services has continued to increase in popularity into the twenty-first century. In a 1997 survey of school-based and school-linked initiatives across some forty states, Mary Driscoll, William Boyd, and Crowson found a particularly heavy emphasis nationwide upon programs in parenting education, family support and advocacy, and family health services. A surprising finding was that nearly a third of the programs surveyed in 1997 reported efforts in employment-related services for families, a feature not highlighted in the existing literature on service integration. Perhaps the greatest growth, however, continues to be in the specialized area of health services. Indeed, another survey in late 2000 reported a more than ten-fold increase during the 1990s in the number of school-based health clinics in operation across the United States.

### Current Directions in Service Provision

Amid its continuing growth, a conception of the central problem behind much of the services effort has undergone a bit of change. The talk of a dangerously fragmented delivery system, and of the need for a heavy emphasis upon the coordination of children's and family services, has declined. Coordination, it has been discovered, is exceptionally hard to do. Instead, in the United States, there has been a reduced focus upon interagency cooperation and a greater emphasis upon the provision of an array of services, coordinated or not.

There has also been less attention paid to school-centered programs of family assistance. Instead, efforts have gone toward the development of a much greater variety of forms and strategies for outreach, including neighborhood organization–led programs, communities-of-faith efforts, private-sector interventions, and many more school-linked, rather than school-based, programs. Finally, activity in the services movement has been directed toward efforts that bridge pedagogically between schools and families and communities—particularly with programs of after-school activities and after-school tutoring, youth development and assistance programs, summer schooling, arts and music education, and day care.

This changed direction is finding roots in a sense of the ecology of community development activities, as opposed to programs of family assistance. Although interest continues in interagency partnering, the focus has increasingly been on community action rather than the delivery of professional services to a poverty-area clientele.

Lizbeth Schorr, nationally known advocate for children and youth, has argued in favor of this new paradigm, claiming that the added delivery of professional services by themselves falls far short of the full scope of efforts needed to strengthen families and improve learning opportunities in low-income neighborhoods. As Schorr puts it, people increasingly recognize that educational success necessitates a key place for the school "at the table where community reform is being organized" (p. 291).

There have been a number intellectual shifts of consequence in the movement toward a community development approach to family assistance. First, the concept of social capital has grown in importance and application. Much influenced by the work of James Coleman, social capital has, over time, become central to the rationale underlying coordinated services. The claim is that critical cultural resources and supports, as well as so-called hard resources through direct assistance, are passed from institutions to families in full-services programming.

Second, without denying the power and importance of services to children and families, the altered ecological paradigm foresees a much larger program of economic outreach beyond professional, interagency partnering. A services agenda may be necessary but not sufficient—especially in deep-poverty circumstances with major infrastructure needs in housing quality, employment opportunities, recreational outlets, law enforcement, and other areas. Matters of public and private investment, entrepreneurialism, regeneration, rebuilding, resourcefulness, incentives creation, market forces, and assisting self-help efforts can all join in creating a climate of assistance that goes far beyond the narrow scope of activity captured in a purely services agenda.

## New Issues in the Organization of Services

The coordinated-services movement encountered many well-documented difficulties in the ability of cooperating partners to share information, deal with turf issues, retain and reorient participating professionals, mingle resources, merge or blend disciplinary perspectives, and involve the neighborhood clientele. In comparison, however, the newer community ecology approach is by no means without its own set of organizational issues.

As an initial issue, there has been a central question regarding basic assumptions of "approach" in assistance to families. The community development idea assumes that market forces can be effectively introduced to low-income communities—that enterprise and investment, incentives and subsidies, employment and empowerment, and rebuilding and repair can begin a transformation process that trickles down to produce much-improved opportunities for families and their children, and reformed and better-performing schools. In contrast, the earlier and narrower services approach has strong Progressive era roots in efforts to *protect* poor families from the ravages of the market. Healthy homes and neighborhoods, and what was thought to be "good" for families and children, were to be provided by a well-trained cadre of informed and committed persons as a hedge against the horrors of sweatshop industrialism. A residue of distrust against the market forces characterizes much of human-services professionalism.

A second unresolved organizational issue involves questions of ownership. To be sure, ownership emerged as a constraint in school-based programming—ranging from turf protection to determining just what is involved in partnering and who's in charge administratively. With its much broader scope of linkages and collaborations, with less focusing upon a from-the-school-outward delivery of services, and with overtones of community development and empowerment (as well as assistance), the new ecological paradigm is far from clear on just what, or whose, property rights are to be attended to. Foundations, banks, businesses, and schools may initiate community development activities, but the paradigm calls for a quick shift to grassroots ownership. Institutional controls may well be operative, but the paradigm calls for a full recognition of the controlling forces present in the very culture of each community.

As a key organizational issue, consider that school-based services have typically been backed by the best professional practices and undertaken by highly trained (and usually certified) service providers. Under such a structure, agency services will look much the same whatever the community. But, with lessened professional ownership, local values and some clashes around basic premises can easily introduce into best-practice professionalism some extremely strange elements of local accommodation. Professionals are put to a test around just how much ownership they are comfortable in giving up.

## Implications and Conclusions

In brief recapitulation, the emerging context surrounding service provision in the United States finds less activity than earlier in school-centered programs of generalized assistance to families, and somewhat more interest today in direct pedagogical services to children. Additionally, there is a movement away from fairly narrow services agendas and toward a larger arena of community development activity, as well as a decided movement toward initiatives working up from the community rather than trickling down from professional and academic sources.

Increasingly, community-based organizations, rather than schools, are displaying an initiative in offering an array of after-school services (e.g., after-school child care, youth development programs, tutoring, successful parenting classes). These neighborhood organizations typically cover the institutional waterfront, and include local churches, city parks departments and libraries, Boys and Girls Clubs, YMCAs and YWCAs, community organizers, and banks or local for-profit organizations.

As community institutions have displayed a greater level of initiative, a larger and broader paradigm around interagency partnering has been emerging as well. A definition of the problem has proceeded from community responsiveness, through children's and family services, to cooperation in the regeneration of the community itself. By no means, however, is there less regard than before for the local school. Indeed, an added embeddedness of the school in the culture of its community, and a leadership role for the school as part of an overall community of support for families and children, are both very much a part of the revised agenda.

There are implications in the new scenario for the organization of administrative activities. One administrative implication is the need for rethinking some key mental models of school leadership. A longtime part of the lore of school principalship has been a balancing act in the school-community relationship, usually referred to as *bridging and buffering*. School administrators have been taught to walk the tightrope of bridging to the community while simultaneously buffering the organization and its professionals from undue intrusion by the community.

The result, a number of scholars claim, has been the maintenance over the years of a sizeable gap between schools and their communities. This has created a call for a new role that replaces bridging and buffering with a more outreach-oriented exercise of *civic capacity*. School administrators who exercise civic capacity reach out actively from their schools to help build or develop their respective communities.

A related implication is the need to clarify just what it means to partner in linkages with other community groups. Seymour Sarason and Elizabeth Lorentz argue that partnering in the early twenty-first century requires much more than just a bit of collaboration. It means meaningful boundary crossing—where there is resource exchange, a true network approach to shared objectives, and much more selflessness (or less ownership) than is typical of most interagency relationships. This is the type of partnership activity that was called for by White and Wehlage in 1995. Community services, they argued at that time, should be judged less by their success in providing resources and services and more by their success in reshaping the priorities and practices of schools toward a closer understanding of, and partnership with, the family and the neighborhood.

*See also:* DENTAL HEALTH AND CHILDREN; FAMILY SUPPORT SERVICES; HEALTH SERVICES, *subentry on* SCHOOL.

### BIBLIOGRAPHY

BEHRMAN, RICHARD E., ed. 1999. "When School Is Out." *The Future of Children* 9(2):4–20.

CHASKIN, ROBERT J.; CHIPENDA-DANSOKHO, SELMA; and RICHARDS, CARLA J. 1999. *The Neighborhood and Family Initiatives: Entering the Final Phase.* Chicago: University of Chicago, Chapin Hall Center for Children.

CIBULKA, JAMES, and KRITEK, WILLIAM, eds. 1996. *Coordination Among Schools, Families, and Communities: Prospects for Educational Reform.* Albany: State University of New York Press.

COHEN, DONALD L. 1994. "Demise of PEW Project Offers Lessons to Funders." *Education Week* 15(32):1, 8–9.

COLEMAN, JAMES. 1988. "Social Capital and the Creation of Human Capital." *American Journal of Sociology* 94:S95–S120.

COLEMAN, JAMES. 1990. *Foundations of Social Theory.* Cambridge, MA: Belknap.

CROWSON, ROBERT L., and BOYD, WILLIAM L. 1993. "Coordinated Services for Children: Designing Arks for Storms and Seas Unknown." *American Journal of Education* 101(2):140–179.

DEAL, TERRENCE E., and PETERSON, KENT D. 1994. *The Leadership Paradox: Balancing Logic and Artistry in Schools.* San Francisco: Jossey-Bass.

DRISCOLL, MARY E.; BOYD, WILLIAM L.; and CROWSON, ROBERT L. 1997. "Collaborative Services Initiatives: A Report of a National Survey of Programs." In *Coordination, Cooperation, Collaboration: What We Know About School-Linked Services,* ed. Geneva D. Haertel and Margaret C. Wang. Philadelphia: Temple University Center for Research in Human Development and Education.

DRISCOLL, MARY E., and KERCHNER, CHARLES T. 1999. "The Implications of Social Capital for Schools, Communities, and Cities." In *Handbook of Research on Educational Administration,* 2nd edition, ed. Joseph Murphy and Karen S. Louis. San Francisco: Jossey-Bass.

GOLDRING, ELLEN B., and HAUSMAN, CHARLES. 2001. "Civic Capacity and School Principals: The Missing Links for Community Development." In *Community Development and School Reform,* ed. Robert L. Crowson. Oxford: Elsevier Science.

HANSON, E. MARK. 1981. *Educational Administration and Organizational Behavior.* Boston: Allyn and Bacon.

HAVEMAN, ROBERT, and WOLFE, BARBARA. 1994. *Succeeding Generations: On the Effects of Investments in Children.* New York: Russell Sage Foundation.

"Health Clinics in Schools Are Taking on a Bigger Role in Many States." 2000. *Wall Street Journal* November 9, p. 1.

JACOBSON, LINDA. 2000. "New Event Making Case for Better After-School Options." *Education Week* 20(6):7.

KAGAN, SHARON L., and NEVILLE, PETER R. 1993. *Integrating Services for Children and Families: Understanding the Past to Shape the Future.* New Haven, CT: Yale University Press.

KIRST, MICHAEL, ed. 1989. *The Conditions of Children in California.* Berkeley: Policy Analysis for California Education.

LAWSON, HAL, and HOOPER-BRIAR, KATHARINE. 1997. *Connecting the Dots: Progress Toward the Integration of School Reform, School-Linked Services, Parent Involvement and Community Schools.* Oxford, OH: The Danforth Foundation and Miami University, Institute for Educational Renewal.

LEVY, JANET, and COPPLE, CAROL. 1989. *Joining Forces: A Report from the First Year.* Alexandria, VA: National Association of State Boards of Education.

LITTELL, JULIA, and WYNN, JOAN. 1989. *The Availability and Use of Community Resources for Young Adolescents in an Inner-City and a Suburban Community.* Chicago: University of Chicago, Chapin Hall Center for Children.

OGAWA, RODNEY T. 1994. "The Institutional Sources of Education Reform: The Case of School-Based Management." *American Educational Research Journal* 31:519–548.

OGAWA, RODNEY T., and WHITE, PAULA A. 1994. "School-Based Management: An Overview." In *School-Based Management: Organizing for High Performance,* ed. Susan A. Mohrman and Priscilla Wohlstetter. San Francisco: Jossey-Bass.

SARASON, SEYMOUR B., and LORENTZ, ELIZABETH M. 1998. *Crossing Boundaries: Collaboration, Coordination, and the Redefinition of Resources.* San Francisco: Jossey-Bass.

SCHORR, LIZBETH B. 1997. *Common Purposes: Strengthening Families and Neighborhoods to Rebuild America.* New York: Anchor Books.

SKOCPOL, THEDA. 1992. *Protecting Soldiers and Mothers.* Cambridge, MA: Harvard University Press.

SMREKAR, CLAIRE E. 1996. *The Impact of School Choice and Community.* Albany: State University of New York Press.

SMREKAR, CLAIRE E., and MAWHINNEY, HAMML B. 1999. "Integrated Services: Challenges in Linking Schools, Families, and Communities." In *Handbook of Research on Educational Administration,* 2nd edition, ed. Joseph Murphy and Karen S. Louis. San Francisco: Jossey-Bass.

SMYLIE, MARK A.; CROWSON, ROBERT L.; CHOU, VICTORIA; and LEVIN, REBECCA. 1994. "The Principal and Community-School Connections in Chicago's Radical Reform." *Educational Administration Quarterly* 30(3):342–364.

STONE, REBECCA, ed. 1996. *Core Issues in Comprehensive Community-Building Initiatives.* Chicago: University of Chicago, Chapin Hall Center for Children.

WEHLAGE, GARY G.; RUTTER, ROBERT A.; SMITH, GREGORY A.; LESKO, NANCY; and FERNANDEZ, RICARDO R. 1989. *Reducing the Risk: Schools as Communities of Support.* London: Falmer Press.

WHITE, JULIE, and WEHLAGE, GARY G. 1995. "Community Collaboration: If It Is Such a Good Idea, Why Is It So Hard to Do?" *Educational Evaluation and Policy Analysis* 17(1):23–38.

ROBERT L. CROWSON

## OUTCOMES

School-linked services are health and family services that are provided to students in one or more schools through a variety of linkages. Services may be located at or near a school (e.g., a mobile medical van, a family resource center housed in a modular classroom), provided after school to some students, or students may be referred to services provided by an external agency made available based on an agreement between the school and the provider agency. Appropriate measures to assess the effectiveness of these services differ depending on the form of school-linked services being reviewed.

*School-linked services* is a label that overlaps with earlier phrases that describe school-connected efforts to connect students with community resources they need to perform in the classroom and to address problems that may impair their learning. *Community schools, school-based clinics, full-service schools, learning supports,* and *family resource centers* located at schools are all labels used currently as well as in earlier eras. The emphasis upon linkage is usually intended to signal that services may not be physically located at schools, but are intended to be connected with schools through a variety of administrative and policy agreements among schools and other agencies.

School-linked services are in addition to those health and social services provided by school staff, including psychologists, counselors, social workers, school nurses, and others. Within the broad field of noneducational learning supports, some policy advocates and practitioners have emphasized the need for better connections among the staff already working for schools, while others have emphasized the relatively small number of these professionals compared to the number of students with noneducational problems that affect their learning. That number may be as high as one-third of all students in some schools who are affected by poor health and other factors, including:

- dental, physical, vision, and other health problems;
- inadequate or no health insurance coverage;
- family stress due to substance abuse, low income, family violence, or behavior by the students themselves that involves high-risk sexual activity, substance abuse, or criminal activity and gang involvement.

The need to tap outside agencies that are funded to work with youth is the basis for the argument that school-linked services are a critical supplement to what the school systems' own professionals can accomplish in addressing these problems.

### Measuring Effectiveness—Which Outcomes?

A question that arises early in the discussions between school and agency over school-linked services is what standards and measures should be used in assessing the effectiveness of these services. Are they to be assessed based on their impact on the core mission of the school—academic performance by students—or are there other, noneducational measures of the impact of school-linked services on students?

Each party to this discussion has a different starting point. Schools naturally begin the dialog stressing the academic outcomes for which they are held accountable, while other agencies with a greater concern for health, family services, and youth development measure what school-linked services do for students and their parents. The negotiations about goals and outcomes among the sponsoring agencies and schools turn on the relative importance of classroom performance compared with interventions aimed at the external causes of classroom achievement gaps.

School-agency-community partnerships eventually need to move toward agreement on the specifics of the outcomes and indicators to be used as fair measures of progress. Three types of outcomes typically emerge from these discussions, each moving out in a wider circle from a core of education-only outcomes and indicators.

For school-based outcomes, the triad of achievement measured by test scores, attendance, and school completion/graduation rates constitutes the standard that most schools would take seriously as basic measures of school-linked services. Some schools would add the number of suspensions and classroom behavior as measured by disciplinary incidents as indicators of effectiveness. These are the core outcomes for most schools.

In the next circle of outcomes, beyond the classroom, the outcomes are still related to academic achievement, but are no longer restricted to what happens in the classroom. These outcomes include parent involvement, help with homework, reading to primary-age children, and parent engagement with teachers in responding to behavior problems in the classroom.

The third circle consists of those outcomes that are further out into the arenas of community building and youth development, and may include such things as schools' success in attracting community volunteers, children's health coverage in the immediate neighborhood, and the effects of early childhood programs that aim at school readiness goals.

These three circles of outcomes, marked by their increasing distance from academic achievement, set

up a further distinction between tightly-linked learning supports, in which the objectives of school-linked services are closely connected with academic achievement and are stronger than in those looser-linked systems in which noneducational goals are given standing independent of their impact on classroom achievement. Experience suggests that the choice of which system is most appropriate should emerge from each district's negotiations with its partners, rather than being mandated by external funders. In a district with weak leadership or strained relations with its surrounding community, academic achievement may be all the partnership can handle. But in a district that has built credibility with its neighbors, parents, and nearby agencies, the wider circles of outcomes may be exactly the right way to take advantage of that history of good relationships.

At the same time, evaluation of school-linked services models in multiple sites underscores the importance of a close fit between what is being measured and what resources are devoted to achieving. To use educational outcomes to measure an after-school program that primarily focuses upon health and recreation goals, rather than academic activities, is not an appropriate use of outcomes. Improved family functioning is unlikely to result from tutoring models and using family functioning scales to measure the effects of such programs is not a good allocation of evaluation resources.

Two other sets of distinctions are also important to keep in mind when evaluating the outcomes of school-linked services.

1. Between short-term and longer-range outcomes, that is, between those outcomes that are markers of movement in the right direction, such as student attendance improvements, and those which are long-term positive results, such as college entrance/completion or mastery of key vocational skills.

2. Between measures of negative behavior—suspensions and expulsions—and measures of positive development. In working with youth, in particular, it is important not to overemphasize those measures that connote negative behavior, as they convey a message that youth are being monitored only for their mistakes. Emphasizing positive accomplishments in developing outcomes provides better feedback to students.

## What Is Known About Outcomes?

A recent compilation of evaluation results from forty-nine different community school models was developed by Joy Dryfoos for the Community Schools Coalition, an organization based at the Institute for Educational Leadership. In forty-six of these reports, positive effects were noted. Thirty-six programs reported academic gains, nineteen reported improvements in attendance, eleven reported a reduction in suspensions, eleven reported reductions in high-risk behaviors, twelve reported increases in parent involvement, and six reported safer communities as a result of the initiative. Another compilation, developed by the UCLA School Mental Health Project, provides information on outcomes from a sample of almost 200 programs. These outcomes were organized into six basic areas that addressed barriers to learning and enhance healthy development: (1) enhancing classroom-based efforts to enable learning, (2) providing prescribed student and family assistance, (3) responding to and preventing crises, (4) supporting transitions, (5) increasing home involvement in schooling, and (6) outreaching for greater community involvement and support—including use of volunteers.

The challenges facing evaluation of these initiatives should not be underestimated. Such evaluations seek to separate the effects of programs that were deliberately designed to combine different interventions, aimed at highly disparate student populations that are hard to compare with students not receiving the interventions, and taking place in complex, partially open systems that include large bureaucracies, complex funding streams, and strongly held professional and community values. These evaluation problems correspond closely to those encountered in evaluating comprehensive community initiatives, which have been the subject of several reports by the Aspen Institute Roundtable on Comprehensive Community Initiatives.

## Enduring Importance

School-linked services are a continuing effort to respond to educational challenges that arise in the wider community, reminding us that children are in school only 9 percent of the time from birth to adulthood at age eighteen. As schools come under increasing pressure for academic outcomes through discussion of statewide and national testing standards, it is important to recognize that the test scores and academic performance of some children are significantly affected by problems that arise outside the schools and that cannot be addressed by schools alone. It is crucial that that school-linked services are evaluated as broadly as possible in their impacts on academic outcomes as well as their effects in addressing the underlying problems that some students bring to school.

*See also:* Dental Health and Children; Family Support Services; Health Services, *subentry on* School.

### BIBLIOGRAPHY

Adler, Louise, and Gardner, Sidney. 1994. *The Politics of Linking Schools and Social Services.* London: Falmer.

Connell, James, et al., eds. 1995. *New Approaches to Evaluating Comprehensive Community Initiatives, Vol. 1: Concepts, Methods, and Contexts.* Washington, DC: The Aspen Institute.

Dryfoos, Joy. 1994. *Full-Service Schools: A Revolution in Health, Mental Health, and Social Services for Children, Youth, and Families.* San Francisco, CA: Jossey-Bass.

Dryfoos, Joy. 2000. *Evaluation of Community Schools: An Early Look.* Washington, DC: Coalition for Community Schools.

Lodge, Rachel. 1996. *California's Healthy Start: Strong Families, Strong Communities for Student Success.* Davis, CA: Healthy Start Field Office, University of California.

Melaville, Athelia, and The Institute for Educational Leadership. 1998. *Learning Together: The Developing Field of School-Community Initiatives.* Flint, MI: Mott Foundation

### INTERNET RESOURCE

Adelman, Howard, and Taylor, Linda. 2001. "A Sampling of Outcome Findings from Interventions Relevant to Addressing Barriers to Learning." UCLA School Mental Health Program. <http://smhp.ucla.edu>.

Sidney L. Gardner

# SCHOOL PRINCIPAL

*See:* Principal, School.

# SCHOOL PSYCHOLOGIST

*See:* PSYCHOLOGIST, SCHOOL.

# SCHOOL READINESS

School readiness refers to the extent to which a child exhibits the behaviors, skills, and knowledge necessary to be successful in elementary school. These can be grouped into four categories: social and emotional development, oral language development and pre-reading skills, oral mathematics development and pre-mathematics skills, and general knowledge. Because individual schools vary in the timing with which they introduce academically demanding reading and mathematics instruction in kindergarten and first grade, the skills and habits recommended below are only approximate goals, to be attained to the greatest extent possible during the preschool and kindergarten years.

## Social and Emotional Development

To be ready for school, the child must develop the social and emotional maturity to participate appropriately and learn from classroom activities. This requires adequate nutrition and health. It also requires that any hearing or speech deficits have been reduced to the greatest extent possible. Physical maturity may also be important and may be interrelated with social and emotional development. For example, the child must be able to care for her own toileting needs without supervision. Other self-help behaviors that must be developed include the ability to locate and care for personal belongings, to feed oneself independently, to get on and off the school bus with minimal supervision, to avoid obvious dangers, to put on and remove outer clothing within a reasonable length of time, to recognize problems and try strategies for solving them, and to communicate one's own needs and wants.

Beyond self-help, the child must also show appropriate group-oriented social behavior and classroom conduct. He must separate from parents and accept school personnel. The student must learn appropriate means for expressing emotions and feelings and properly play the role of an individual within the group. This includes showing respect for others and their property, playing cooperatively, and sharing and taking turns. The student must initiate and maintain peer interactions, and do so without aggression, while defending himself as needed. The student should be able to play both independently and with the group. When required, he should imitate peer actions, such as lining up and waiting appropriately. The student should be willing to try something new. The student should follow classroom rules, including voice control. He must respond to warning words (e.g., "No," "Stop") and modify his behavior when given verbal feedback.

Finally, the child must have sufficient maturity to successfully engage in task-related behaviors. This includes finding the materials needed for a task, holding and manipulating the materials, and doing so without disrupting other students. The student must be able to stay in her "own space" during the activity, work on the activity for an appropriate amount of time (e.g., fifteen minutes) with minimal cues and supervision by teachers, and complete the task on time and at a satisfactory performance level. If help is needed, the student should ask peers or the teacher for assistance in an appropriate manner (e.g., raising her hand). She should also replace materials, "clean up" the workspace, and follow classroom routines in the transition to the next activity.

In sum, to be socially and emotionally ready for classroom participation and learning, the child must be able to learn classroom routines and comply appropriately with teacher instructions. The child must maintain appropriate focus on the group's activity, learn from the activity, make choices, and generalize the knowledge gained to future activities.

## Oral Language and Pre-Reading Skills

The child's understanding and production of oral language is the principal mechanism by which she communicates with others. To be ready for school, the child must be sufficiently skilled in both receptive and expressive language, and in verbal reasoning. In this regard, it is helpful if the child speaks Standard English, including the use of Standard English grammar. Vocabulary knowledge is also important. The child's transition to schooling is facilitated by already being familiar with the words and concepts employed by the teacher. In addition, such vocabulary knowledge can be critically important in learning to read. The size of a child's vocabulary on entering school has been shown to be one of the key predictors of the ease with which the child learns to read.

A rich oral language environment in the home and/or preschool provides the best preparation for schooling. This includes extensive conversation with adults, in which the child uses language to answer questions and discuss issues. The parent should interact with the child in a way that assists the child to develop reasoning skills and to understand and express more complex ideas.

By being read to and engaging in other print activities, such as playing with magnetic letters, puzzles, games, and so on, the child should have developed a variety of "concepts about print." These include the purpose of reading, the structure of written text, how stories work, what a word is, how words are composed of letters, and what spaces signify. The child should be able to show the front cover of a storybook and open it to start reading. He should know that one goes from left to right and top to bottom when reading English text. He should be able to identify a few words by sight. He should already have had some practice identifying and writing the letters of the alphabet. This practice, along with related activities in drawing and coloring, should be developing the child's fine motor skills to prepare for more systematic and demanding writing exercises.

A particularly important aspect of the child's oral language skill is her *phonemic awareness.* This is the ability to consciously pick out and manipulate from spoken words the smallest sound chunks that make up those words. These chunks are called *phonemes.* Learning to consciously pick these out of the sound stream of spoken language is a form of "ear training" that is very useful for the child's first major task in school—learning to read. This is because phonemic awareness involves identifying the spoken sound units that correspond to the letters or letter groups in written words. This helps the child to understand the "alphabetic principle"—that any combination of written letters can be "sounded out" and may represent a word that has meaning in the child's oral vocabulary. That is, groups of letters written together constitute a "code" that can be "decoded" by sounding out and listening for meaning. Another aspect of this principle is the idea that spoken words are composed of sounds that can be represented by letters, which can be written down to "encode" the spoken language into its written form. Thus, reading involves going from written to spoken words, whereas spelling involves going from spoken to written words (or at least to the letters required to write the words). The two together illustrate the one-to-one correspondence between spoken and written language.

Because speech is heard naturally as a continuous stream of sound, and short words and syllables are heard as one sound, children must be taught how to segment these sound chunks. For example, children and adults hear the word *mat* as a whole, even though it is made up of three phonemes. Teaching phonemic awareness to preschool children begins with the ability to hear and reproduce rhymes and alliteration, as in nursery rhymes. It then moves on to the ability to do oddity tasks (which first sound is different in the oral words *big, hill,* and *bit*?; which last sound is different in *ball, pop,* and *mop*?; or which middle sound is different in words such as *pin, fun,* and *sit*?). This skill may also be practiced by asking the child to repeat the first or last sound in a series of words spoken by the teacher or parent. It may help to prolong beginning sounds when pronouncing them for the child—for example, "ssssat" or "mmmmat."

With kindergarten-age children, one can begin to teach the ability to orally blend separate sounds (what word do the sounds /m/, /a/, and /t/ make?). This is a key skill that will be needed when the child first tries to read by sounding out words. A related ability is phonemic segmentation—skill at breaking a spoken word into its separate sounds. Instruction can begin by having the child tap out the separate phonemes, progressing to having the child actually reproduce the separate sounds after the instructor has said the word (for example, *mat* becomes /m/, /a/, /t/).

Oral vocabulary knowledge and phonemic awareness ability have already been discussed as keys to success in the most important first-grade task—learning to read. Other keys include knowing the names of the letters and the sounds they are associated with. Children should be able to identify most letters of the alphabet upon request and to indicate what sound the letter makes. They should be able to write the letters on request. Kindergartners also can begin to write some easy words. At this point they should begin to fully understand the alphabetic principle underlying the language, that letters combine to make words and that words, properly pronounced, carry meaning.

## Oral Mathematics and Pre-Mathematics Skills

To be ready for first-grade mathematics, preschool and/or kindergarten children need skill, knowledge, and experience with mathematical ways of thinking and performing. It is helpful if children have been involved in games and activities in which they sort and classify objects by size, shape, and function. They should be given practice recognizing sets of objects and identifying items that belong and do not belong in a given set.

Children should learn to use concepts such as "the same as," "more than," "less than," "most," and "least." They should know the first ten or twenty numbers, being able to recite them and use them to count objects. They should recognize these numbers when they are written down and should be able to write them upon request. They should be able to orally respond to simple adding and subtracting tasks. They should understand simple geometric shapes and be able to copy them and answer simple questions about them. (What are their names? Which are alike? Which are different? In what ways?) They should be able to copy more complex geometric figures, such as a star or parallelogram, and be able to answer questions about them. They should know the parts of a whole and be able to identify half of a region, object, or set of objects.

In sum, to succeed in first-grade mathematics students should have as much experience as possible with numbers, counting, and simple geometric concepts. They should be able to count at least to ten, and perhaps to twenty or thirty, both forward and backward. They should be able to identify written numbers and to write down the first ten numbers on request. They should be able to apply this knowledge to simple counting problems. They should know the symbols "+" and "−" and be able to do simple addition and subtraction problems, as well as play games involving pattern recognition and strategic choices. The student should be prepared for first-grade work in both computation and problem solving. She should also be able to copy and identify simple geometric figures (square, triangle, and circle) and discuss their properties.

### General Knowledge

To be ready to be successful at school, children need sufficient general knowledge to orient them properly within the school and the world at large, and to correctly respond to teacher requests. They should be able to tell their full name and age and be learning to write these. They should be able to identify the colors by name. They should know the names of their parents and the city or town where they live. They should be able to draw simple pictures, such as of people, animals, and places.

Children should know that objects have properties, such as length, weight, and capacity. They should have played hands-on games involving counting, comparing, sorting, and ordering objects. They should recognize pennies, nickels, dimes, and quarters. They should have some experience with measurement, using a ruler, a scale, and a thermometer. They should be able to orient themselves in time: morning, afternoon, tomorrow. They should be able to tell time to the hour using a clock face. They should know the days of the week and the months of the year. They should know their left and right hands and be able to explain such contrasts as top/bottom, on/under, and in front/behind.

### Summary

To be ready to be successful in kindergarten and/or first grade, a child must demonstrate adequate social and emotional maturity, oral language and pre-reading skills, oral mathematics and pre-mathematics skills, and general knowledge. Where maturity is concerned, the child must have adequate self-help skills. He must also show appropriate group-oriented social behavior and classroom conduct, including the ability to successfully engage in task-related behaviors. Regarding oral language and pre-reading skills, the child must be skilled in both receptive and expressive language and in verbal reasoning. He should be familiar with "concepts about print" and be developing phonemic awareness (the ability to hear and manipulate the separate sounds in spoken language). For oral mathematics and pre-mathematics skills, the child should be able to understand and use simple arithmetic and geometric concepts. Where general knowledge is concerned, the child needs sufficient command of information to be properly oriented within the school and to correctly respond to teacher requests. When these behaviors and skills are in place, the child is ready to take his place as a member of the learning community in the classroom and the school.

*See also:* EARLY CHILDHOOD EDUCATION; READING, *subentry on* BEGINNING READING.

### BIBLIOGRAPHY

ADAMS, MARILYN. 1990. *Beginning to Read.* Cambridge, MA: MIT Press.

BARR, REBECCA; KAMIL, MICHAEL L.; MOSENTHAL, PETER; and PEARSON, P. DAVID, eds. 1996.

*Handbook of Reading Research,* Vol. II. Mahwah, NJ: Erlbaum.

HIRSCH, ERIC D., and HOLDREN, JOHN, eds. 1996. *What Your Kindergartner Needs to Know: Preparing Your Child for a Lifetime of Learning.* New York: Delta.

SNOW, CATHERINE; BURNS, M. SUSAN; and GRIFFIN, PEG, eds. 1998. *Preventing Reading Difficulties in Young Children.* Washington, DC: National Academy Press.

STEUART, WATSON T., and GRESHAM, FRANK M., eds. 1998. *Handbook of Child Behavior Therapy.* New York: Plenum.

GEORGE FARKAS

## SCHOOL RECORDS AND REPORTS

*See:* RECORDS AND REPORTS, SCHOOL.

## SCHOOL REFORM

Two decades of school reform came to a close at the end of the twentieth century. These efforts, led by E. D. Hirsch and Ted Sizer, began in the early 1980s and continued through the 1990s, leading to the development of programs such as Success for All. These programs were aimed at developing comprehensive school reform models. The New American Schools Development Corporation supported many of these models.

This massive education reform effort set out to achieve educational goals never before attempted in the United States. Two major premises drove these ambitious goals. The first premise was that nearly everyone in the United States deserved, was capable of, and should be required to receive academic instruction through high school regardless of race, economic status, or post–high school plans. Second, academic standards needed to be raised considerably for all students. These driving premises were a result of the nation's leaders coming to an understanding that education, the economy, and a sustainable democracy are deeply intertwined in a postindustrial society.

The impetus for these two decades of reform took place in the 1980s, but it was a result of the major challenges facing education in the years before. In these years the nation's education system realized a major decline in enrollment. The 1970s marked the baby boom's departure from the schools and schools all over the country faced a sharp decline in enrollment. Along with this came a growing disengagement with education. As fewer and fewer residents had children in school, communities became less interested in schools and began resenting funding them through property taxes. This, along with other economic factors, brought on a major property-tax revolt in the late 1970s.

The school system was further challenged by social revolution. Teacher unions, the disabled, students with limited English proficiency (LEP), minorities, and women began to demand fair treatment in schools. Teacher unions in the late 1960s became increasingly active, organizing strikes regularly. Congress and the judiciary became more involved in protecting school-age citizens from discrimination with resolutions such as the Rehabilitation Act of 1973, the Education for All Handicapped Children Act of 1975, and the 1974 Supreme Court decision *Lau v. Nichols.*

Perhaps the most important of all the discrimination decisions was *Brown v. Board of Education* (1954) which demanded that public schools be racially desegregated. In order to desegregate schools busing was mandated. This practice caused major upheaval. As minorities entered traditionally segregated schools looking for stable learning environments, they found themselves amid great chaos and violence. The result of the efforts mainly led to "white flight" from public education to private schools.

Concurrent efforts to make education a place of equal opportunity for all led to a de-emphasis on teaching and learning. Schools across the nation became increasingly bureaucratic as the nation became more litigious. School employees were often more concerned with enforcing and maintaining order and the new regulations than with teaching their students. It was said educators became more concerned with "dodging lawsuits than with the quality instruction in their schools, and they made the broadening of education opportunities rather than the quality of education the priority in much of public schooling" (Toch, p. 7).

As American public education was deteriorating rapidly in the late 1960s and early 1970s, it began to draw the attention of critics who published many reports detailing the problems in schools and calling for widespread reform. In 1966 James S. Coleman released a study reporting that socioeconomic status was the primary determinant in academic achievement. In other words, schools, teachers, and money had little bearing on the level of academic achievement that a student could reach. Another leading sociologist, Christopher Jencks, reaffirmed Coleman's study by stating that academic achievement was more an indicator of the student's characteristics than of the school input.

Despite more and more public attention to the education crisis, the federal role was still limited. Not until 1979, after a major lobbying effort by the National Education Association (NEA), which later became the largest teacher union in the country, was the U.S. Department of Education created by the Carter administration.

With a cabinet-level education office the problems in education drew more and more public attention. Newspapers reported major declines in students' scores on the SAT and the National Assessment of Educational Progress (NAEP). The National Science Foundation also reported that academic standards were declining in the nation's schools. This news was alarming when compared to the high standards that the United States' economic competitors required of their students. By the early 1980s business leaders, the government, and the general public had decided that public education in the United States was in "parlous trouble" (National Commission on Excellence in Education).

### A Nation at Risk

Major economic problems in the 1980s magnified the public's disenchantment with public education. More and more people began to connect the downturn in the economy to the poor system of education in the United States. Under the direction of President Ronald Reagan, the Department of Education faced sharp criticism and calls for its abolition from the president's own political party. Reagan had appointed Terrel H. Bell to the department as Secretary of Education despite the skepticism of the Republican Party, who considered Bell too moderate. The new secretary of education was sympathetic to the department and was reluctant to entertain efforts to abolish the new cabinet office.

In response to claims that he was too soft on the problems in education, Bell proposed the creation of a independent presidential commission to investigate the state of education in the United States in a fair and balanced manner. Reagan, who saw little value in presidential commissions, turned down Bell's proposal. As a result, in 1981 Bell commissioned his own cabinet-level panel, to be called the National Commission on Excellence in Education (NCEE), to review education. The eighteen-member panel was composed of representatives from a wide spectrum of political perspectives. The panel produced the report *A Nation at Risk: The Imperative for Education Reform,* which stands as perhaps the most important document in the late twentieth century's history of education reform. *A Nation at Risk* became the impetus for two decades of standards-based reform. Ironically, once the report's themes became known at the White House, Reagan adopted the report as his own.

The seminal report came in the form of an open letter to the American people and President Reagan in April 1983. The report was a serious indictment of education in the United States. It stated, "Our nation is at risk. . . . If an unfriendly foreign power had attempted to impose on America the mediocre education performance that exists today, we might well have viewed it as an act of war" (p. 5). Despite acknowledging some gains in education, the report overall displayed a severely negative portrait of American education. Even though Bell's commission was pessimistic it maintained that if their strict recommendations were followed, they could reverse the declines and restore excellence in education.

*A Nation at Risk* made five recommendations for attaining excellence in education. The recommendations were: (1) that "five new basics" be added to the curriculum of America's schools. The basics included four years of English, three years of mathematics, three years of science, three years of social studies, and half a year of computer science in high school; (2) that more rigorous and measurable standards be adopted; (3) that the school year be extended in order to make more time for learning the "New Basics"; (4) that the teaching be improved with enhanced preparation and professionalization; (5) that accountability be added to education.

*A Nation at Risk* shocked the country. The report galvanized the public to demand action to restore education in the United States. The report was followed by a series of other critical reports on education from organizations such as the Committee for Economic Development and the Education Commission of the States. While no other report had the impact that *A Nation at Risk* did, the accumulation of the reports created the impetus for the start of two decades of education reform. The nation needed to regain its competitiveness among its economic rivals globally.

The calls to arms energized the nation's governors. Education reform became one of the most politically popular agendas for governors regardless of political leanings. The South became the hotbed for education reform led by governors. Progressively minded governors such as Lamar Alexander of Tennessee, William Clinton of Arkansas, James Hunt of North Carolina, and Richard Riley of South Carolina accepted the challenge of reforming education in their states and in turn led the country. The president, who even before *A Nation at Risk* wanted to return the responsibility of education to the states, embraced the new energy of the governors.

Leadership from the nation's "education governors" inserted itself into the National Governors' Association (NGA), which released its own report on the state of education. The NGA report reaffirmed the NCEE notion that without reforming education the nation would not continue to be economically competitive on a global level. This theme was especially provocative for the nation's business leaders, who began to call for improvement in the schools. Business leaders became a strong force in the reform movement and influenced political leaders to allocate more resources to education.

Education reform desperately needed the support of an unlikely ally—the president. Reagan had been opposed to a major federal role in education, had attempted to dismantle the Department of Education, and even denied the creation of the presidential commission, eventually established at the cabinet level by Secretary Bell, that wrote *A Nation at Risk*. After this report, however, Reagan realized the importance of the growing reform movement and began to champion school reform.

Reagan took *A Nation at Risk* on the road for eleven weeks after its release to announce his new emphasis on education. The president's leadership was essential in elevating the movement to the highest level. Reagan was able to use his control of the media to make education reform the highest national priority.

## Reform in Action

With new levels of publicity, recommendations at hand, and ambitious governors, education reform activity was high. In fact some real improvement was taking place. High school curricula broadened and became more focused on academics. High school graduation requirements increased, modeled after the NCEE recommendation, in opposition to old ideas that proposed that intellectual/academic education was not for everyone. Reformers, especially business leaders, recognized that a new postindustrial economy needed skilled workers with higher-order thinking skills. No longer was an uneducated worker needed to stand in an assembly line. Employers demanded workers who could think.

With the reform movement's success in establishing more rigorous intellectual content in American education, students returned to the public schools. Enrollment surged and course work in the academic subjects became standard for almost every student. Students graduated with evidence of solid backgrounds in mathematics, science, history, and foreign languages on their transcripts. Many students even took Advanced Placement tests for college. As a result of the new emphasis of academic subject matter and higher rates of enrollment more teachers prepared with strong content were required. Unfortunately, there were not enough teachers with the content knowledge to meet the demand. Teachers were underprepared and their teaching methods were inadequate. As a result, curricular reform for most students came in name only; most students did not receive real academic training due to the lack of infrastructure to support it.

In addition, watered-down courses began to pop up in the school curricula across the country. In essence a new sequence of courses was created. Students could spend most of their high-school careers without being exposed to academic subject matter in depth. Critics began to note that American education was "an inch deep and a mile wide" for most students. Many students migrated to the easier tracks and many were forced into a shallow education experience. Despite advances in curricular reform, the majority of students felt few real learning gains. At the same time, with the new emphasis on academics, vocational education was fighting to stay alive in schools.

Still the education reforms were mostly undercut by the lack of teachers with the essential content knowledge to teach students adequately and accommodate the growing enrollment in academic courses. Teachers were being assigned to subjects in which they had no training or experience, just to satisfy the new curricular requirements. Tracking persisted and became more problematic as students in the lower tracks received instruction more often from the least-qualified teachers.

This led to a movement that spawned many initiatives promoting the professionalization of teaching, although the NEA often attacked the movement. Despite much work done to improve teaching and to improve the profession, it remained "business as usual" for most teachers. The NEA preserved the status quo.

## Better Teachers, Greater Goals, and More Accountability

In response to the Carnegie Forum on Education report, *A Nation Prepared: Teachers for the Twenty-First Century*, the focus on the teaching profession was magnified. The Carnegie task force responded to *A Nation at Risk* by proposing solutions to improve the teaching profession. The report called for the formation of the National Board for Professional Teaching Standards and later national board certification for exemplary teachers.

With the reform movement well underway in 1987, there was a call by the U.S. Secretary of Education William Bennett for accountability. The significant amount of money and effort spent to reform education required results. Business leaders and state lawmakers led the way in demanding evidence of change in education. The National Governors Association also began demanding greater accountability from the schools.

The nation's governors had played a large role in education reform since the announcement of *A Nation at Risk*. Their leadership became most prominent in September 1989 when President George H. W. Bush convened them in Charlottesville, Virginia, for an education summit.

The nation had already come to grips with the fact that improvement in education needed to be measurable if all the attention and resources were going to be recognized as worthwhile. In order to be able to recognize educational progress goals had to be established. President Bush and the governors made a commitment to establish measurable goals for education reform that they named America 2000.

They agreed on a process for developing the goals at the education summit that would involve teachers, parents, local administrators, school board members, elected officials, business and labor communities, and the public at large. Their charge was to establish a common mission for improving education for all.

The goals the panel finally agreed upon and released early in 1990 were:

- By the year 2000, all children will start school ready to learn.
- By the year 2000, the high school graduation rate will increase to at least 90 percent.
- By the year 2000, all students will leave grades four, eight, and twelve having demonstrated competency over challenging subject matter including English, mathematics, science, foreign languages, civics and government, economics, arts, history, and geography. Every school in America will ensure that all students learn to use their minds well, so they may be prepared for responsible citizenship, further learning, and productive employment in our nation's modern economy.
- By the year 2000, the nation's teaching force will have access to programs for the continued improvement of their professional skills and the opportunity to acquire the knowledge and skills needed to instruct and prepare all American students for the next century.
- By the year 2000, U.S. students will be the first in the world in mathematics and science achievement.
- By the year 2000, every adult American will be literate and will possess the knowledge and skills necessary to compete in a global economy and exercise the rights and responsibilities of citizenship.

The governors and the president accepted responsibility for achieving these measurable goals. The conclusion of their declaration stated that "as elected chief executives, we expect to be held accountable for progress in meeting the new national goals, and we expect to hold others accountable as well. . . . The time for rhetoric is past; the time for performance is now."

## Striving to Achieve Measurable Goals

In response to growing talk of creating academic standards Congress established the National Council on Education Standards and Testing (NCEST) in June 1991. The council was formed to explore establishing national education standards and to assess progress in reaching these standards. In 1992 NCEST released its report recommending that voluntary national standards be created. This report, combined with statements from the National Council of Teachers of Mathematics (NCTM) and the National Research Council, propelled the creation of rigorous academic standards that would establish the appropriate content for learning grade by grade. It was hoped that the depth and breadth of knowledge would be increased for all students.

In March 1994 President Clinton signed into law the Goals 2000: Educate America Act. Goals 2000 encompassed the goals established at the Charlottesville education summit as well as two additional goals that stated:

- By the year 2000, every school in the United States will be free of drugs, violence, and the unauthorized presence of firearms and alcohol and will offer a disciplined environment conducive to learning.
- By the year 2000, every school will promote partnerships that will increase parental involvement and participation in promoting the social, emotional, and academic growth of children.

The Goals 2000: Educate America Act also established the National Education Standards and Improvement Council (NESIC), which had the responsibility to review and certify voluntary state and national education standards that were being developed. The NCEST and NESIC faced severe opposition, however, from those who raised the specter of federal involvement in education.

Despite opposition to national standards, efforts to develop state standards and assessments continued. The chief executive officer of IBM, Louis Gerstner, and Governor Tommy Thompson of Wisconsin convened the nation's top business leaders, governors, and the White House and Department of Education elite in Palisades, New York, for the 1996 National Education Summit. The summit was a reaction to the declining progress in education reform after Goals 2000.

The participants in the summit continued the work started in Charlottesville. In fact, the summit pushed for a sustained and more directed effort in establishing academic standards and assessments. Participants recognized that some opponents criticized standards as too much federal involvement in education, but noted that state standards were essential for improving education for all. Writing and measuring standards was not enough for the summit participants, however. They recognized that a commitment to helping students achieve the standards was essential. Another outcome of the summit was the call for an independent clearinghouse, free of ties to any federal agency, that would provide information to help the coordinate states' efforts to establish standards and assessments.

In 1997 in a landmark report, *What Matters Most: Teaching for America's Future,* the National Commission on Teaching and America's Future once again established that teachers were critical to improving student achievement. The report challenged the nation to install high quality teachers in every classroom in America by 2006.

## Options for Parents and Students

Throughout this period of reform many suggested school choice as a solution to improving education. School choice can mean several different things. Some of the models are districtwide, or intradistrict, which allow parents to choose from schools within their own district; statewide, or interdistrict, in which students can choose from the entire state's public schools; and perhaps the most controversial, private-school choice, which permits parents to send their children to private schools using public funds.

Although controversial, school choice has been a significant contributor to education reform. Perhaps the most salient examples took place in Wisconsin and Ohio. Since the early 1990s the city of Milwaukee has engaged in an experiment in private-school choice. Milwaukee offers vouchers for children to attend private schools, including religious schools. Although the program has come up against lawsuits, the courts have upheld the practice in Wisconsin. In November 1998, the U.S. Supreme Court declined to take up a case against Milwaukee that claimed that the program led to racial segregation in Milwaukee schools. The U.S. District Court in Ohio questioned the Cleveland school-choice program because 98 percent of the students leaving public schools were migrating to religious schools, raising the issue of separation of church and state. In June 2002 the U.S. Supreme Court overturned the lower court ruling and upheld the use of public money for religious school tuition.

The court decisions have helped proponents of school reform who claim that a free-market approach to education will improve the schools. In addition, the movement has also gained some victories as more and more analysis of data shows some success in educating children though school choice. Studies from Harvard University and Princeton University suggest that children participating in school-choice programs are at least performing as well as their counterparts in traditional public schools and the Harvard study even suggests that privatization might make schools more efficient.

## Staying the Course

The contemporary standards movement that resulted from *A Nation at Risk* continues; in fact the message remains that the nation must "stay the course." In 1999 another national education summit was convened and it reasserted that the standards movement was the most prudent way to improve education for all. In addition, the participants demanded that action be taken to ensure that all students achieve the rigorous standards that had been set.

Yet the United States continues to be "a nation at risk." Business leaders, government officials, educators, and the public at large are heeding the Third International Mathematics and Science Study (TIMSS) warning that the United States ranks in the middle of the pack of its global economic competitors in student achievement. Continued focus on raising standards, improving teachers to help students achieve the standards, and holding all stakeholders (parents, teachers, and the business community) accountable for the education of the nation's future leaders is essential.

President George W. Bush continues to follow the direction of Secretary Bell's National Commission for Excellence in Education. President Bush's proposal for education calls for higher standards, annual measurement and accountability, more parental choice, and greater flexibility in federal funding. Perhaps the most significant part of Bush's proposal is the annual assessment of student achievement from grades three through eight to determine the value added by each school year and increase accountability.

*See also:* CURRICULUM, SCHOOL; EDUCATION REFORM; ELEMENTARY EDUCATION, *subentry on* CURRENT TRENDS; MAGNET SCHOOLS; NATIONAL BOARD FOR PROFESSIONAL TESTING STANDARDS; NO CHILD LEFT BEHIND ACT, 2001; PAIDEIA PROGRAM; SCHOOL-BASED DECISION-MAKING; SECONDARY EDUCATION, *subentry on* CURRENT TRENDS; STANDARDS MOVEMENT IN AMERICAN EDUCATION.

### BIBLIOGRAPHY

NATIONAL COUNCIL FOR EXCELLENCE IN EDUCATION. 1983. *A Nation at Risk.* Washington, DC: U.S. Department of Education.

TOCH, THOMAS. 1991. *In the Name of Excellence.* New York: Oxford University Press.

VINOVSKIS, MARIS A. 1999. *The Road to Charlottesville.* Washington, DC: National Education Goals Panel.

### INTERNET RESOURCES

ACHIEVE. 1999. "1999 National Education Summit." <www.achieve.org>.

EAKIN, SYBIL. 1996. "Forum: National Education Summit." *Technos Quarterly* 5(2): <www.technos.net/tq_05/2eakin.htm>.

CHRISTOPHER T. CROSS
M. RENÉ ISLAS

# SCHWAB, JOSEPH (1909–1988)

University of Chicago professor of education and natural sciences, Joseph Schwab was the originator of *The Practical,* a program for educational improvements based on curriculum deliberations.

## Education and Career

Joseph Jackson Schwab was born in Columbus, Mississippi, where he attended a private elementary school. After the sixth grade, Schwab entered the public schools, where he discovered science. As Schwab was virtually alone among his classmates in this interest, the principal of the high school, a former science teacher, encouraged his creative license by giving him free reign in the school laboratory. Schwab became fascinated with the poisonous snakes and other animals kept there, and delighted in setting off homemade gunpowder by pounding it with an ax. He finished high school in three years, and in 1924, at the age of fifteen, he set off for the University of Chicago, where he was to remain for almost fifty years, receiving degrees in English literature

(Ph.B), zoology (S.M.), and genetics (Ph.D). Schwab was also a Visiting Fellow at the Center for the Study of Democratic Institutions.

Since the late 1930s Schwab has had an important impact on educational research and practice, conceptualizing and instigating reform at all levels of schooling. His early work through the 1940s was part of Robert Hutchins's efforts to create an undergraduate curriculum of general education at Chicago. Schwab taught practically every course in the College of the University of Chicago, developed classroom discussion as a viable alternative to lecture, worked on integrating the humanities and natural sciences, and won the award for excellence in teaching twice, the first to do so. In 1942 he began writing comprehensive examinations for the biological sciences, and by 1947 had become chairman of the natural sciences staff.

## Scholarly Work

In the 1950s and 1960s, as the "Hutchins College" period ended, Schwab turned his attention to wider pursuits. From 1959 to 1961 he was chairman of the Committee on Teacher Preparation for the Biological Sciences Curriculum Study, he coauthored the Curriculum's *Biology Teacher's Handbook,* and edited the first editions of its textbooks. He helped found *The Journal of General Education,* and consulted on *The Great Books of the Western World.* He also worked in Jewish education as chairman of the Academic Board of the Melton Research Center at the Jewish Theological Seminary of America.

In *College Curriculum and Student Protest* (1969) Schwab diagnosed student turmoil as symptomatic of failures in schooling. He prescribed curricular changes and teaching devices that were based on liberal arts, which could actively engage students in their education. Arguing against undergraduate education as a body of rote methods or rhetoric of conclusions, he explored the liberal arts as resources for students to find their own questions for texts or problems so they could become their own critics. Most importantly, he showed how the disintegrating college communities could be restored and renewed.

Schwab is best remembered for the last and most comprehensive of his critiques of education, focused on curriculum making. His invited address in 1969 at the annual meeting of the American Educational Research Association challenged the field of curriculum research, which had become moribund because of inveterate unexamined reliance on direct application of theories, especially from the social sciences. Schwab believed that any given theory was necessarily incomplete in terms of its subject and oversimplified the complexities of problematic situations. His proposal that the field must identify and solve its own practical problems continues to energize curricular debate.

## The Practical

*The Practical* requires that five bodies of disciplines and experience be represented in a collaborative group that undertakes the task of curriculum revision. Schwab called four of these the "commonplaces" of educational thinking, which require representatives of the affected learners, teachers, subject matters, and (sociocultural) milieux. The fifth is that of the curriculum specialist, who must work with the other representatives to ensure that the commonplaces are properly coordinated, because changes in any one will have consequences for the others. Unbalanced deliberations, either dominated by a single commonplace or omitting some, lead to successive "bandwagon" curricula, each based on an exclusive theory (e.g., of child development, teacher needs, subject matter innovation, or social change). Schwab designed a set of eclectic arts to join theories across disciplines so that scholarly and research materials could be shaped into teachable curricula. He developed another set of practical arts for the problem-posing and problem-solving activities required by the unsatisfactory curricular situation.

As the members of the curriculum group discover and develop their capacities in an actual deliberation, they turn the commonplaces into "particular places," by perceiving details in the "pinch" of their problem. The process is incremental, local, and ongoing. Institutions need gradual, coherent improvements, not destruction. They must discover their own problems and resources, without dictation by centralized authorities. Ongoing deliberations change a problematic situation into a situation of problems discerned and solutions undertaken and evaluated. The deliberative process develops in a spiral rather than a serial progression as the deliberators discover what solutions can run with which problems, what problems or solutions can be combined with other problems and solutions, and how the effects of solutions can have unintended consequences that create further problems and opportunities.

From 1969 to 1986 Schwab produced six articles (the last two unpublished) on the various dimensions of the *The Practical,* the first three of which are included in a compilation by Ian Westbury and Neil J. Wilkoff. *Practical 1* gives his basic critique in terms of flights from the curriculum field. *Practical 2* demonstrates the proper use of the eclectic arts on theories through an imagined course in educational psychology. *Practical 3* focuses on the constitution and functions of the curriculum group. *Practical 4* gives special attention to the institutional role of the curriculum specialist as chairperson of the group. *Practical 5* and *Practical 6* describe the eclectic arts for development and use of commonplaces that can map pluralistic views of subject matter, using literature and psychology as examples.

### Legacy

As a scholar and teacher Schwab pulled together such wide experience in the five bodies of disciplines necessary for curriculum development that he became a genuine polymath in education. He was quick to trace positions to unexpected consequences. Expressed in a down-to-earth no-nonsense rhetoric, this made him a formidable and provocative presence in public forums and the classroom.

Schwab's concern for education as a deliberative activity connects him to John Dewey and American Pragmatism. His respect for the formulations and proper uses of theories connects him to the Aristotelian distinction between theoretical, practical, and productive activities. Internationally, educational practitioners in the European Didaktik tradition, especially in Germany and Norway, have recognized the *The Practical.*

Overall, Schwab's continuing effect is that of Socratic gadfly whose stinging critiques have stimulated education by pointing out chronic deficiencies and indicating new directions for inquiry and action. The recurring nature of educational problems makes much of his work, such as that on defining and testing objectives, still applicable.

*See also:* CURRICULUM, SCHOOL; EDUCATIONAL REFORM, *subentries on* OVERVIEW, REPORTS OF HISTORICAL SIGNIFICANCE; UNIVERSITY OF CHICAGO.

### BIBLIOGRAPHY

PEREIRA, PETER. 1984. "Deliberation and the Arts of Perception." *Journal of Curriculum Studies* 16(4):347–366.

REID, WILLIAM A. 1999. *Curriculum as Institution and Practice: Essays in the Deliberative Tradition.* Mahwah, NJ: Erlbaum.

SCHWAB, JOSEPH J. 1969. *College Curriculum and Student Protest.* Chicago: University of Chicago Press.

SCHWAB, JOSEPH J. 1976–1977. Transcriptions of Seminars Taught at the Institute for Research on Teaching at Michigan State University. Archived at the Museum of Education, University of South Carolina.

SCHWAB, JOSEPH J. 1983. "The Practical 4: Something for Curriculum Professors to Do." *Curriculum Inquiry* 13(3): 239–265.

SCHWAB, JOSEPH J., and ROBY, THOMAS W., IV. 1986. "The Practicals 5 and 6: Finding and Using Commonplaces in Literature and Psychology." Archived at the Museum of Education, University of South Carolina.

SHULMAN, LEE S. 1991. "Joseph Jackson Schwab." *Remembering the University of Chicago,* ed. Edward Shils. Chicago: University of Chicago Press.

TYLER, RALPH W. 1984. "Personal Reflections on The Practical 4." *Curriculum Inquiry* 14(1):97–102.

WESTBURY, IAN, and WILKOFF, NEIL J., eds. 1978. *Joseph J. Schwab, Science, Liberal Education, and Curriculum: Selected Essays* [includes "Practicals 1–3"]. Chicago: University of Chicago Press.

THOMAS W. ROBY IV

# SCIENCE EDUCATION

OVERVIEW
  Robert E. Yager
PREPARATION OF TEACHERS
  Robert E. Yager

## OVERVIEW

Science has become an important component in the K–12 curriculum in American schools—but less so than reading and mathematics. At the end of the twentieth century reading and mathematics received more attention, government support, and focus for testing. It was assumed that reading and mathematics must be mastered first and that these skills were essential before the study of science and social studies. Science is often not taught daily in elementary schools, does not receive major attention in middle schools, and is often organized around disciplines that emphasize college preparation in high schools.

## The Role of Science and Technology Education

As the twentieth century ended, it was clear that science and technology played significant roles in the lives of all people, including future employment and careers, the formulation of societal decisions, general problem solving and reasoning, and the increase of economic productivity. There is consensus that science and technology are central to living, working, leisure, international competitiveness, and resolution of personal and societal problems. Few would eliminate science from the curriculum and yet few would advance it as a curriculum organizer. The basic skills that characterize science and technology remain unknown for most.

As the twenty-first century emerges, many nations around the world are arguing for the merger of science and technology in K–12 schools. Unfortunately many are resisting such a merger, mostly because technology (e.g., manual training, industrial arts, vocational training) is often not seen as an area of study for college-bound students. Further, such courses are rarely parts of collegiate programs for preparing new teachers. Few see the ties between science and technology, whereas they often see ties between science and mathematics. Karen F. Zuga, writing in the 1996 book *Science/Technology/Society as Reform in Science Education,* outlined the reasons and rationale for and the problems with such a rejoining of science and technology. A brief review of what each entails is important.

Although science is often defined as the information found in textbooks for K–12 and college courses or the content outlined in state frameworks and standards, such definitions omit most essential features of science. Instead, they concentrate wholly on the products of science. Most agree with the facets of science proposed by George G. Simpson in a 1963 article published in the journal *Science.* These are:

1. Asking questions about the natural universe, that is, being curious about the objects and events in nature.

2. Trying to answer one's own questions, that is, proposing possible explanations.

3. Designing experiments to determine the validity of the explanations offered.

4. Collecting evidence from observations of nature, mathematical calculations, and, whenever possible, experiments that could be carried out to establish the validity of the original explanations.

5. Communicating evidence to others, who must agree with the interpretation of evidence in order for the explanation to become accepted by the broader community (of scientists).

Technology is defined as focusing on the human-made world—unlike science, which focuses on the natural world. Technology takes nature as it is understood and uses the information to produce effects and products that benefit humankind. Examples include such devices as lightbulbs, refrigerators, automobiles, airplanes, nuclear reactors, and manufactured products of all sorts. The procedures for technology are much the same as they are for science. Scientists seek to determine the ways of nature; they have to take what they find. Technologists, on the other hand, know what they want when they begin to manipulate nature (using the ideas, laws, and procedures of science) to get the desired products.

Interestingly, the study of technology has always been seen as more interesting and useful than the study of science alone. Further, the public has often been more aware of and supportive of technological advances than those of basic science.

Science (along with technology) in the school curriculum has assumed a central role in producing scientifically (and technologically) literate persons. Since 1980 the National Science Teachers Association (NSTA) has identified such literacy to be the major goal of science instruction. The organization also described what literacy would entail. Its *NSTA Handbook, 1999–2000* defined a scientifically literate person as one who can:

• Engage in responsible personal and civic actions after weighing the possible consequences of alternative options

• Defend decisions and actions using rational arguments based on evidence

• Display curiosity and appreciation of the natural and human-made worlds

- Apply skepticism, careful methods, logical reasoning, and creativity in investigating the observable universe
- Remain open to new evidence and realize the tentativeness of scientific/technological knowledge
- Consider the political, economic, moral, and ethical aspects of science and technology as they relate to personal and global issues

Whatever schools can do to produce graduates who have such skills defines the role for science education in schools. The curriculum is the structure provided to accomplish such goals. The 1996 National Science Education Standards set out just four goals, namely, the production of students who:

- Experience the richness and excitement of knowing about and understanding the natural world
- Use appropriate scientific processes and principles in making personal decisions
- Engage intelligently in public discourse and debate about matters of scientific and technological concern
- Increase their economic productivity through the use of the knowledge, understanding, and skills of the scientifically literate person in their fields

## History of Science Courses in American Schools

Early American public schools did not include science as a basic feature. The purpose of the early school was to promote literacy—defined to include only reading and numeracy. The first high schools primarily existed to prepare students for the clergy or law. Typical science courses were elective and included such technology courses as navigation, surveying, and agriculture. Not until the turn of the twentieth century did the current science program begin to form.

Physics began to be offered as a high school course in the late 1800s. It became even more common when Harvard University required it for admission in 1893; Harvard also required chemistry ten years later. Physics and chemistry were soon identified as college preparatory courses as other universities followed Harvard's lead in requiring both for college entrance. Biology, the third high school course, was not identified until the 1920s—resulting from the merger of such common courses as botany, physiology, anatomy, and zoology.

Traditionally the high school curriculum has consisted of physics in grade twelve, chemistry in grade eleven, and biology in grade ten. Often schools have moved to second-level courses in each of these three disciplines; at times these advanced courses are titled *Advanced Placement* and can be counted toward college degrees if scores on national tests are high enough to satisfy colleges. This focus on school science as preparation for college has been a hindrance to the casting of science courses as ways to promote science and technology literacy.

Science below the high school level (grade ten) has a varied history. Science classes at this level became more common in the middle of the twentieth century with the creation of junior high schools—often grades seven, eight, and nine. In many instances the science curriculum was similar to the high school curriculum except that science was usually termed *general science,* with blocks for each course coming from biology, chemistry, physics, and earth science. There have been attempts to unify and to integrate science in these middle grades. With the emergence of substantial national financial support for curriculum and teacher professional development, however, the major effort in the 1960s was to create life, physical, and earth science courses for the junior high schools. During the 1970s and 1980s, middle schools were created with ninth grade returning to high schools (grades nine through twelve) and sixth grade becoming a part of the middle schools. As the National Science Education Standards emerged in 1996, the middle grades were defined as grades five through eight.

Middle school philosophy calls for teams of teachers (from all facets of the curriculum) to work with a given set of middle school students and to unify and relate all study for those students. Project 2061, formulated in the late twentieth century, is a reform project that ties the curriculum together, especially science, mathematics, technology, and social studies.

Elementary school science was rarely found until the middle years of the twentieth century. Although there were textbooks and courses listed in the offerings, science frequently did not get taught. This was because teachers placed reading and mathematics first, they often lacked preparation in science, and there was no generally accepted way of measuring science learning across grade levels.

During the 1960s and 1970s several national curriculum projects were funded, developed, and offered across the K–12 years. This continued into the twenty-first century, with many programs that provide ways to meet the visions of the National Science Education Standards supported by the National Science Foundation. Unfortunately not many of these ideas are in typical textbooks offered by the major publishers, who, understandably, are more interested in sales and offering what teachers, schools, and parents want. These textbooks are often quite different from what reform leaders and cognitive science researchers envision for an ideal science curriculum.

## Comparing Science Education Requirements around the World

Reformers in most industrial nations across the world advocate similar school reforms of science with new goals, procedures, materials, and assessment. The United Nations Educational, Scientific and Cultural Organization (UNESCO) has initiated a reform effort for the twenty-first century that is targeted for developing nations and relates science to technology. Many educational teachers across the world call openly for a science curriculum that is responsive to personal needs, societal problems, and attentive to technological as well as scientific literacy. New attention to assessment and evaluation has arisen from the Third International Mathematics and Science Study.

Elementary school science is similar the world over with the focus being hands-on and minds-on activities that are not discipline-based. Often middle schools have science programs that frequently focus on problems. In the United States some of the major science programs include Event-Based Science and Science Education for Public Understanding Program. Similar programs exist elsewhere, especially in the United Kingdom, Israel, the Netherlands, and Australia, and in other European countries.

Although the goals for high school science are the same in most countries, the traditional discipline-based courses (biology, chemistry, and physics) in the United States are typical yearlong courses for grades ten, eleven, and twelve. Most other countries organize the secondary curriculum to respect discipline divisions, but spread the courses over a five- or six-year sequence. They do not delay physics and chemistry to grade eleven or twelve or place biology solely in grade ten.

The interest in international comparisons has never been greater. There is great concern that test-

ing and learning is based on little other than students' ability to recite definitions and/or to solve mathematical problems given to them. Cognitive science research indicates that most of the brightest science students can do little more than to repeat what they have been told or what they read, or to duplicate procedures they have been directed to follow. Educators now want more evidence that students can use information and skills in new situations. Such performance is demanded to assure scientific and technological literacy.

## Trends, Issues, and Controversies

Science education is evolving once again—as it has since the emergence of public schools in the United States—to a focus on mastering basic concepts and skills that can be used in new situations. Yet, in order to truly accomplish this, contexts need to be established first. Concepts and process skills are desirable end points. But if real learning is to occur, concepts and skills cannot be approached directly and used as organizers for courses and instruction. Without the proper background, students do not understand and are rarely able to use the information and skills that are taught. This explains why science lacks popularity and why most students stop their study of science as soon as they are permitted to do so. Little is gained by simply requiring more for a longer period of time.

Another trend is the open inclusion of technology with the study of science. Contrasting the two can help develop an awareness of the history, philosophy, and sociology of both. Since more students are interested in technology than in science, including technology within science education can provide a vehicle for getting students more involved with basic science. Instead of authorities proclaiming science as important and useful, students discover that for themselves as they develop and use new technologies.

Taking statements of goals seriously is another trend. Goals can and should provide the framework for the curriculum, indicate the instruction selected, and provide form and structure for evaluating successes and failures. Each of these critical factors provides a basis for doing science in education.

The involvement of more people and organizations in the process of educating youth is another important trend. Responsibility for setting science goals, choosing instructional strategies, determining curriculum structure, and defining assessment efforts must rest with teachers as well as with students. Outside agencies—administrators, state departments of education, national governments, professional societies, and the public—all must be involved and are integral to the plan to improve science education.

Major issues include how to evaluate and enlarge goals, how to change instruction, how to move assessment from testing for memory and repetition (copying) of procedures to making these constructs and skills a part of the mental frameworks of the students. When does real learning pass from mimicry to understanding and personal use?

Engaging student minds requires changes that are essential to current reform efforts. According to Vito Perrone, such engagement is accomplished when:

1. Students help to define the content—often by asking questions.
2. Students have time to wonder and to find interesting pursuits.
3. Topics often have strange features that evoke questions.
4. Teachers encourage and request different views and forms of expression.
5. The richest activities are invented by teachers and students.
6. Students create original and public products that enable them to be experts.
7. Students take some actions as a result of their study and their learning.
8. Students sense that the results of their work are not predetermined or fully predictable.

Can science teachers really become major players in cross-disciplinary efforts in schools? Can they embrace technology as a form of science and/or an entry point to it? Can they refrain from telling students what they want them to do and to remember (for tests)? According to the National Research Council's 1998 book *Every Child a Scientist*, Carl Sagan argued that "every student starts out as a scientist." Students are full of questions, ready to suggest possible answers to their questions. Unfortunately, however, most lose this curiosity as they progress through their science studies. In typical schools they rarely design their own experiments, get their own results, and use the results for any purpose. They do not see or practice science in any full sense.

Major controversies remain. But why should this not be so? Science is an activity where there are changes, differences of opinions, differences in designing good experiments or making calculations, and differences in collecting evidence and convincing others of the validity and accuracy of the evidence offered.

Certainly most educators remain committed to the model of relying on the science found in textbooks, state curriculum frameworks, and standards documents. They are committed in spite of the research evidence that highlights the advantages of new approaches to learning and new ways of measuring learning and understanding. Humans tend to resist change—even when they know it will occur. It is sad that science educators do not lead in the attack on the unchanging curriculum and lack of attention and use of the new information on how humans learn.

*See also:* CURRICULUM, SCHOOL; ELEMENTARY EDUCATION, *subentries on* CURRENT TRENDS, HISTORY OF; NATIONAL SCIENCE TEACHERS ASSOCIATION; SCIENCE EDUCATION, *subentry on* PREPARATION OF TEACHERS; SCIENCE LEARNING; SECONDARY EDUCATION, *subentries on* CURRENT TRENDS, HISTORY OF; TECHNOLOGY IN EDUCATION, *subentry on* SCHOOL.

**BIBLIOGRAPHY**

CHAMPAGNE, AUDREY B., and KLOPFER, LEO E. 1984. "Research in Science Education: The Cognitive Psychology Perspective." In *Research within Reach: Science Education,* ed. David Holdzkom and Pamela B. Lutz. Charleston, WV: Appalachia Educational Laboratory, Research and Development Interpretation Service.

*Event-Based Science Project.* 1999. White Plains, NY: Dale Seymour.

NATIONAL RESEARCH COUNCIL. 1996. *National Science Education Standards.* Washington, DC: National Academy Press.

NATIONAL RESEARCH COUNCIL. 1998. *Every Child a Scientist: Achieving Scientific Literacy for All.* Washington, DC: National Academy Press.

NATIONAL RESEARCH COUNCIL. 1999. *How People Learn: Brain, Mind, Experience, and School.* Washington, DC: National Academy Press.

NATIONAL SCIENCE TEACHERS ASSOCIATION. 2000. *National Science Teachers Association (NSTA) Handbook, 1999–2000.* Arlington, VA: National Science Teachers Association.

PERRONE, VITO. 1994. "How to Engage Students in Learning." *Educational Leadership* 51(5):11–13.

RESNICK, LAUREN B. 1987. "Learning in School and Out." *Educational Researcher* 16(9):13–20.

RUTHERFORD, F. JAMES, and AHLGREN, ANDREW. 1990. *Science for All Americans: A Project 2061 Report on Literacy Goals in Science, Mathematics, and Technology.* New York: Oxford University Press.

*Science Education for Public Understanding Program (SEPUP).* 1998. Ronkonkoma, NY: Lab-Aids.

SIMPSON, GEORGE G. 1963. "Biology and the Nature of Science." *Science* 139(3550):81–88.

UNITED NATIONS EDUCATIONAL, SCIENTIFIC AND CULTURAL ORGANIZATION. 1986. *Summary Report of Science, Technology, and Mathematics Education Worldwide.* Paris: United Nations Educational, Scientific and Cultural Organization.

U.S. NATIONAL RESEARCH CENTER FOR TIMSS. 1996. *A Splintered Vision: An Investigation of U.S. Science and Mathematics Education.* Dordrecht, Netherlands: Kluwer.

ZUGA, KAREN F. 1996. "STS Promotes the Rejoining of Technology and Science." In *Science/Technology/Society as Reform in Science Education,* ed. Robert E. Yager. Albany: State University of New York Press.

INTERNET RESOURCE

LESSONLAB. 2000. "TIMSS-R." <www.lessonlab.com/timss-r/>.

ROBERT E. YAGER

# PREPARATION OF TEACHERS

Programs for preparing science teachers in the United States are numerous—numbering about 1,250. These programs vary considerably, though most require a major in one discipline of science and a strong supporting area. The professional sequence varies greatly with smaller programs unable to maintain a faculty with expertise in science education per se. The programs generally consist of half the credits in science, a quarter in education, and a quarter in liberal arts requirements. In the 1990s the quantity of preparation in science and in science education increased—often making it difficult to complete programs as part of a four-year bachelor's degree program. Fifth-year programs that include more time spent in schools with direct experience with students are becoming the norm.

## Historical Background

Early in the 1800s science teachers typically had no formal preparation; often they were laypersons teaching such courses as navigation, surveying, and agriculture in the first high schools. By 1870, with the emergence of the first teacher training colleges, some science teachers completed formal study of science in colleges. Qualifications for specific teaching, however, varied considerably across the United States.

In the early 1890s Harvard University required completion of a high school course in physics for admission. This spurred the beginning of the science curriculum in American schools. Ten years later Harvard added chemistry to its requirements for admission. Many other colleges and universities followed suit. High school science classes became gatekeeper courses for college admission—a situation that turned out to be a continuing problem for science in schools and for the preparation of science teachers.

By the end of World War II, the place of science in school programs had attained universal acceptance. Teacher education programs were standardized to include science methods courses and student teaching after a year of introduction to education and educational psychology courses. School programs were to provide functional science experiences, that is, skills and knowledge that students could use. Faculty at preparatory institutions became the chief proponents for a useful science program for students.

Science education changed in the 1950s as leaders and the general public demanded improvements to match the Soviet successes in space. National spending for improving school science programs and the preparation of science teachers were made a priority in the National Science Foundation (NSF). Scientists were called to provide leadership in the reform of school programs and the development of better-prepared teachers.

In the 1970s these national efforts to improve school programs and teacher education, including the goals for science teaching, were reassessed. The public had become disillusioned with the expendi-

2164 SCIENCE EDUCATION: PREPARATION OF TEACHERS

tures for science teacher enhancement and curriculum development projects. The NSF Project Synthesis effort established four new goals: science for meeting personal needs, science for resolving current societal issues, science for assisting with career choices, and science for preparing for further study.

In this climate the NSF established a new program to influence science teacher education directly. Called the Undergraduate Pre-Service Science Teacher Education Program (UPSTEP), its premises included the following:

1. Effective preservice programs integrate science and education and often require five years.

2. Science faculties are important ingredients in program planning, teaching, and program administration.

3. The preparation of an effective science teacher involves more than providing a student with up-to-date content and some generalized teaching skills.

4. Effective programs involve master teachers, school and community leaders, and faculty members.

5. Teacher education can be evaluated and used to improve existing programs.

6. Effective programs should include advances in computer technology, educational psychology, philosophy, sociology, and history of science.

### Current Structure and Organization

Most of the 1,250 institutions that prepare science teachers start with the assumption that an undergraduate major in one of the sciences is a must. Many teacher education programs merely require science courses (typically about one-half of a degree program) and increase the number of methods courses and associated practica (experiences in schools) prior to student teaching. Many institutions moved to a five-year program and/or the completion of a master's degree before licensure.

In the 1990s the U.S. Department of Education funded studies, known as Salish I and Salish II, to discern the condition of preservice teacher education programs in the United States. Salish I was a three-year study of programs and graduates from ten different universities across the United States. The study's major findings included the following:

1. During their initial years of teaching, most new science teachers use little of what teacher education programs promote.

2. Few teacher education programs are using what is known about science as envisioned by the National Science Education Standards.

3. The courses comprising teacher education programs are unrelated to each other.

4. There are few ties between preservice and in-service efforts.

5. Support for teacher education reforms has been largely unrecognized and underfunded.

Salish II involved fifteen new universities, which agreed to alter some aspects of their teacher education programs and to use research instruments from Salish I to determine the effectiveness of the changes. Major findings from Salish II were as follows:

1. Significant changes in teacher education majors can be made during a single year, when part of a collaborative research project.

2. There is strength in the diversity of institutions and faculty involved with science teacher education.

3. Science instruction at colleges must change if real improvement is to occur in schools.

4. Collaboration in terms of experimentation and interpretation of results is extremely powerful.

### In-Service and Staff Development Programs

A persistent problem has been the lack of articulation between pre- and in-service science teacher education. NSF support for in-service teacher education from 1960 to 1975 focused on updating science preparation in an attempt to narrow the gap. In fact, NSF efforts often tended to deepen the problem. The NSF assumed that science teachers needed only more and better science backgrounds and the NSF model was simply one of giving teachers current science information, which they were to transmit directly to their students. What was needed was a set of intellectual tools with which teachers could evaluate the instruction they provided.

According to David Holdzkom and Pamela B. Lutz, authors of the 1984 book *Research within Reach: Science Education*, effective science teachers must have a broader view of science and of education. They need to be in tune with the basic goals of science education in K–12 settings and be prepared to deal with all students in efforts to meet such objectives. H. Harty and Larry G. Enochs, in a 1985 article in the journal *School Science and Mathematics*, offered an excellent analysis of the form in-service programs should take, contending that such programs should:

- Have a well-defined, organized, and responsible governing mechanism
- Involve teachers in needs-assessment, planning, designing, and implementing processes
- Provide diverse, flexible offerings that address current concerns of the practitioner and that can be used readily in the classroom
- Include an evaluation plan of the individual components of the program and their effect in the classroom.

The content versus process debate continues and is counterproductive at best. Science cannot be characterized by either content (products produced by scientists) or process (behaviors that bring scientists to new understandings). Effective teacher education programs cannot be developed if science preparation focuses on content mastery and the education component focuses on process. Teachers must learn to use both the skills and processes of science to develop new knowledge of both science and teaching. They need to use the research concerning learning, such as the National Research Council's 1999 book *How People Learn*.

In the late 1990s NSF initiated new programs designed to improve in-service teachers—and later preservice teachers as well. These systemic projects were funded at approximately $10 million each in about twenty-five states. Later urban, rural, and local systemic projects were conceptualized and funded. Teacher education programs involving several college/university situations were also funded to relate in-service efforts directly to the preparatory programs. These collaborations often tied institutions together in order to share expertise, faculty, and program features.

## Major Trends, Issues, and Controversies

Major trends in science teacher education include:

- Extending the pedagogical facet of the program over two calendar years with extensive school practica provided as places to try new ideas
- Replacing four-year bachelor's programs with five-year master of arts in education programs
- Using the National Science Education Standards for visions of goals for all students, effective teaching strategies, content and curricula features, assessment strategies, and staff development

- The extensive collaborating of all stakeholders (administrators, parents, community leaders, and all teachers across the curriculum) for reform efforts
- Broadening the view of science to include the human-made world (technology) as well as natural science, science for meeting present and societal challenges, a focus on inquiry as content and skills that characterize science, and the history/philosophy/sociology of science.

Some of the major unresolved controversies include:

- Limiting the number of institutions preparing science teachers
- Teaching teachers, over a five-year program, in the same manner that they should teach
- Using the four goals for school science to prepare teachers to internalize the National Science Education Standards, including experiencing science as: an investigation of natural phenomena, a means for making sound personal decisions, an aid in public discussion and debate of current issues, and a means of increasing economic productivity.

Optimism for even greater successes with meeting the goal of scientific literacy for all is a central focus for science teacher education. Certainly the new Centers for Learning and Teaching that NSF began funding in 2000 are designed to help. By definition they combine preservice and in-service science education—making the two seamlessly connected. They require a common research base while also assuring that a major effort of the center will be to extend that research base. They must design and implement new doctorate programs to prepare future leaders. The history of science education is replete with identification of current problems, new ideas for their resolution, major national funding (since 1960), and then almost immediate abandonment after initial trials are not successful. The current challenge facing science teacher education is whether there is adequate national commitment, determination, and know-how to realize the visions elaborated in current reform documents.

*See also:* NATIONAL SCIENCE TEACHERS ASSOCIATION; SCIENCE EDUCATION, *subentry on* OVERVIEW; SCIENCE LEARNING.

**BIBLIOGRAPHY**

BROCKWAY, CAROLYN. 1989. "The Status of Science Teacher Education in Iowa, 1988." Ph.D. diss., University of Iowa.

HARMS, NORRIS C., and YAGER, ROBERT E. 1981. *What Research Says to the Science Teacher.* Washington, DC: National Science Teachers Association.

HARTY, H., and ENOCHS, LARRY G. 1985. "Toward Reshaping the Inservice Education of Science Teachers." *School Science and Mathematics* 85:125–135.

HOLDZKOM, DAVID, and LUTZ, PAMELA B., eds. 1984. *Research within Reach: Science Education.* Charleston, WV: Appalachia Educational Laboratory, Research and Development Interpretation Service.

LANIER, JUDITH, and LITTLE, JUDITH WARREN. 1986. "Research on Teacher Education." In *Handbook of Research on Teaching,* 3rd edition, ed. M. C. Wittrock. New York: Macmillan.

NATIONAL EDUCATION ASSOCIATION. EDUCATIONAL POLICIES COMMISSION. 1944. *Education for All American Youth.* Washington, DC: National Education Association and American Association of School Administrators.

NATIONAL EDUCATION ASSOCIATION. EDUCATIONAL POLICIES COMMISSION. 1952. *Education for All American Youth: A Further Look.* Washington, DC: National Education Association and American Association of School Administrators.

NATIONAL RESEARCH COUNCIL. 1996. *National Science Education Standards.* Washington, DC: National Academy Press.

NATIONAL RESEARCH COUNCIL. 1999. *How People Learn: Brain, Mind, Experience, and School.* Washington, DC: National Academy Press.

PENICK, JOHN E., ed. 1987. *Focus on Excellence: Preservice Elementary Teacher Education in Science.* Washington, DC: National Science Teachers Association.

ROBINSON, JANET B., and YAGER, ROBERT E. 1998. *Translating and Using Research for Improving Teacher Education in Science and Mathematics* (SALISH II). Iowa City: University of Iowa, Science Education Center.

SALISH RESEARCH CONSORTIUM. 1997. *Secondary Science and Mathematics Teacher Preparation Programs: Influences on New Teachers and Their Students: Final Report of the Salish I Research Project* (SALISH I). Iowa City: University of Iowa, Science Education Center.

YAGER, ROBERT E. 1980. *Status Study of Graduate Science Education in the United States, 1960–1980.* Washington, DC: National Science Foundation.

YAGER, ROBERT E. 2000. "A Vision for What Science Education Should Be Like for the First Twenty-Five Years of a New Millennium." *School Science and Mathematics* 100:327–341.

YAGER, ROBERT E.; LUNETTA, VINCENT N.; and PENICK, JOHN E. 1980. *The Iowa–UPSTEP Program: Final Report.* Iowa City: University of Iowa, Science Education Center.

YAGER, ROBERT E., and PENICK, JOHN E. 1990. "Science Teacher Education." In *Handbook of Research on Teacher Education,* ed. W. Robert Houston. New York: Macmillan.

ROBERT E. YAGER

# SCIENCE LEARNING

## EXPLANATION AND ARGUMENTATION

The K–12 U.S. science education standards, now published state by state, without exception cite competence in scientific investigation as an important curriculum goal from the early grades on. Students, it is claimed, should be able to formulate a question, design an investigation, analyze data, and draw conclusions. Reference to such skills in fact appears in discussions of curriculum objectives extending well beyond the discipline of science. The following description, for example, comes not from science education literature but from a description of language arts goals specified by the National Council of Teachers of English (NCTE): "Students conduct research on issues and interests by generating ideas and questions, and by posing problems. They gather, evaluate, and synthesize data from a variety of sources . . . to communicate their discoveries in ways that suit their purpose and audience" (NCTE and International Reading Association website).

It is important that the cognitive skills involved in such activities be defined in a clear and rigorous enough way to make it possible to specify how they develop and how this development is best supported educationally. At the same time, to make the case that scientific thinking is a critical educational objective, it must be defined more broadly than "what professional scientists do." Scientific thinking is essential to science but not specific to it.

But are not children naturally inquisitive, it may be asked, observant and sensitive to the intricacies of the world around them and eager to discover more? Do inquiry skills really need to be developed? The image of the inquisitive preschool child, eager and energetic in her exploration of a world full of surprises, is a compelling one. But the image fades as the child grows older, most often becoming unrecognizable by middle childhood and certainly by adolescence. What happens to the "natural" inquisitiveness of early childhood? The answer is that it needs to be channeled into the development of the cognitive skills that make for effective inquiry. More needs to be done than keeping alive a "natural curiosity." The natural curiosity that infants and children show about the world around them needs to be enriched and directed by the tools of scientific thought.

## Coordination of Theories and Evidence

One way to conceptualize these scientific thinking skills is as skills in the coordination of theories and evidence. Even very young children construct theories to help them make sense of the world, and they revise these theories in the face of new evidence. But they do so without awareness. Scientific thinking, in contrast, involves the *intentional* coordination of theories with new evidence. Another way to define scientific thinking, then, is as *intentional knowledge seeking*. Scientific thinkers intentionally seek evidence that will bear on their theories. Defined in this way, the developmental origins of scientific thinking lie in awareness of knowledge states as generating

from human minds. Awareness of the possibility of false belief is thus a prerequisite to scientific thinking. If knowledge states are fallible, one's own knowledge may warrant revision in the face of new evidence.

Regarded in this way, scientific thinking is more closely aligned with argument than with experiment and needs to be distinguished from *scientific understanding* (of any particular content). Scientific thinking is something one does, whereas scientific understanding is something one has. When conditions are favorable, the process of scientific thinking may lead to scientific understanding as its product. Indeed, it is the desire for scientific understanding—for explanation—that drives the process of scientific thinking. Enhanced understandings of scientific phenomena are certainly a goal of science education. But it is the capacity to advance these understandings that is reflected in scientific thinking.

Scientific thinking requires that evidence be represented in its own right, distinct from the theory, and that the implications of the evidence for the theory be contemplated. Although older children, adolescents, and even adults continue to have trouble in this respect, young children are especially insensitive to the distinction between theory and evidence when they are asked to justify simple knowledge claims.

Note that the outcome of the theory-evidence coordination process remains open. It is not necessary that the theory be revised in light of the evidence, nor certainly that theory be ignored in favor of evidence, which is a misunderstanding of what is meant by theory-evidence coordination. The criterion is only that the evidence be represented in its own right and its implications for the theory contemplated. Skilled scientific thinking always entails the coordination of theories and evidence, but coordination cannot occur unless the two are encoded and represented as distinguishable entities.

The following six criteria for genuine scientific thinking as a process (in contrast to scientific understanding as a knowledge state) can be stipulated:

1. One's existing understanding (theory) is represented as an object of cognition.

2. An intention exists to examine and potentially advance this understanding.

3. The theory's possible falsehood and susceptibility to revision is recognized.

4. Evidence as a source of potential support (or nonsupport) for a theory is recognized.

5. Evidence is encoded and represented distinct from the theory.

6. Implications of the evidence for the theory are identified (relations between the two are constructed).

## The Epistemology of Scientific Learning

There is more to scientific thinking that needs to develop, however, than a set of procedures or strategies for coordinating theories with evidence. As hinted earlier, at its core this development is epistemological in nature, having to do with how one understands the nature of knowledge and knowing. An until recently largely neglected literature on the development of epistemological understanding shows a progression from an absolutist belief in knowledge as certain and disagreements resolvable by recourse to fact, to the multiplist's equation of knowledge with subjective opinion. Only at a final, evaluativist level is uncertainty acknowledged without foregoing the potential for evaluation of claims in a framework of alternatives and evidence.

If facts can be readily ascertained with certainty, as the absolutist understands, or if all claims are equally valid, as the multiplist understands, scientific inquiry has little purpose. There is little incentive to expend the intellectual effort it entails. Epistemological understanding thus informs intellectual values and hence influences the meta-level *disposition* (as opposed to the competence) to engage in scientific thinking.

Similarly, a strategic meta-level that manages strategy selection can be proposed. This meta-strategic level entails explicit awareness of not so much *what* to do as *why* to do it—the understanding of why one strategy is the most effective strategy to achieve one's goals and why others are inferior. It is this meta-strategic understanding that governs whether an appropriate inquiry or inference strategy is actually applied when the occasion calls for it.

The phases of scientific thinking themselves—inquiry, analysis, inference, and argument—require that the process of theory-evidence coordination become explicit and intentional, in contrast to the implicit theory revision that occurs without awareness as young children's understandings come into contact with new evidence. Despite its popularity in educational circles, once one looks below the surface of inquiry learning, it is less than obvious what cognitive processes are entailed. Research suggests that

children lack a mental model of multivariable causality that most inquiry learning assumes. They are not consistent over time in their causal attributions, attributing an outcome first to one factor and later to another, and infrequently do they see two factors as combining additively (much less interactively) to produce an outcome. A mature mental model of causality in which effects combine additively to produce an outcome is critical to adoption of the task goal of identifying effects of individual factors and to the use of the controlled comparison strategy (which has been the focus of research on scientific reasoning) to achieve that goal. If a single (not necessarily consistent) factor is responsible for any outcome (as reflected in the inferential reasoning of many young adolescents), what need is there to worry about controlling for the effects of other factors?

If it is this total structure (including meta-strategic, meta-cognitive, and epistemological understanding, as well as values) that needs to develop, where do educators start? They probably need to begin at multiple entry points. Opportunities should be plentiful for the frequent and regular exercise of skills of inquiry, analysis, inference, and argument, thereby enabling these skills to be practiced, elaborated, consolidated, and perfected. At the same time, meta-level awareness and understanding of skills should be promoted by helping students to reflect on what and particularly *how* they know and what they are doing as they acquire new knowledge. The two endeavors reinforce one another: understanding informs practice and practice enhances understanding.

## The Social Context

Equally critical is the social context in which all of this needs to take place, the often neglected dispositional side of knowing. Educators want children to become skilled scientific thinkers because they believe that these skills will equip them for productive adult lives. But it is not enough that these adults believe it. If children are to invest the sustained effort that is required to develop and practice intellectual skills, they too must believe that learning and knowing are worthwhile. These values and beliefs can develop only through sustained participation in what Ann Brown in 1997 called a "community of learners." Here, scientific thinking skills stand the best chance of developing because they are needed and practiced and socially valued.

Returning scientific thinking to its real-life social context is one approach to strengthening the meta-level components of scientific thinking. When students find themselves having to justify claims and strategies to one another, normally implicit meta-level cognitive processes become externalized, making them more available. Social scaffolding (supporting), then, may assist less able collaborators to monitor and manage strategic operations in a way that they cannot yet do alone. A number of authors have addressed scientific thinking as a form of discourse. This is of course the richest and most authentic context in which to examine scientific thinking, as long as the mistake is not made of regarding these discourse forms as exclusive to science. Scientific discourse asks, most importantly, "How do you know?" or "What is the support for your statement?" When children participate in discourse that poses these questions, they acquire the skills and values that lead them to pose the same questions to themselves. Although central to science, this critical development extends far beyond the borders of traditional scientific disciplines.

*See also:* DISCOURSE, *subentries on* CLASSROOM DISCOURSE, COGNITIVE PERSPECTIVE; LEARNING, *subentries on* CONCEPTUAL CHANGE, KNOWLEDGE ACQUISITION, REPRESENTATION, AND ORGANIZATION; READING, *subentry on* CONTENT AREAS; SCIENCE EDUCATION.

### BIBLIOGRAPHY

BROWN, ANN. 1997. "Transforming Schools into Communities of Thinking and Learning about Serious Matters." *American Psychologist* 52:399–413.

HATANO, GIYOO, and INAGAKI, KAYOKO. 1991. "Sharing Cognition through Collective Comprehension Activity." In *Perspectives on Socially Shared Cognition,* ed. Lauren Resnick, John Levine, and Stephanie Teasley. Washington, DC: American Psychological Association.

HERRENKOHL, LESLIE, and GUERRA, MARION. 1998. "Participant Structures, Scientific Discourse, and Student Engagement in Fourth Grade." *Cognition and Instruction* 16:431–473.

KUHN, DEANNA. 1989. "Children and Adults as Intuitive Scientists." *Psychological Review* 96:674–689.

KUHN, DEANNA. 1993. "Science as Argument: Implications for Teaching and Learning Scientific Thinking." *Science Education* 77:319–337.

KUHN, DEANNA; AMSEL, ERIC; and O'LOUGHLIN, MICHAEL. 1988. *The Development of Scientific Thinking Skills.* Orlando, FL: Academic Press.

KUHN, DEANNA; BLACK, JOHN; KESELMAN, ALLA; and KAPLAN, DANIELLE. 2000. "The Development of Cognitive Skills That Support Inquiry Learning." *Cognition and Instruction* 18:495–523.

KUHN, DEANNA, and PEARSALL, SUSAN. 2000. "Developmental Origins of Scientific Thinking." *Journal of Cognition and Development* 1:113–129.

LEHRER, RICHARD; SCHAUBLE, LEONA; and PETROSINO, ANTHONY. 2001. "Reconsidering the Role of Experiment in Science Education." In *Designing for Science: Implications from Everyday, Classroom, and Professional Settings,* ed. Kevin Crowley, Christian Schunn, and Takishi Okadapp. Mahwah, NJ: Erlbaum.

OLSON, DAVID, and ASTINGTON, JANET. 1993. "Thinking about Thinking: Learning How to Take Statements and Hold Beliefs." *Educational Psychologist* 28:7–23.

PERNER, JOSEF. 1991. *Understanding the Representational Mind.* Cambridge, MA: MIT Press.

WELLMAN, HENRY. 1988. "First Steps in the Child's Theorizing about the Mind." In *Developing Theories of Mind,* ed. Janet Astington, Paul Harris, and David Olson. Cambridge, Eng.: Cambridge University Press.

### INTERNET RESOURCE

NATIONAL COUNCIL OF TEACHERS OF ENGLISH and INTERNATIONAL READING ASSOCIATION. 1996. *Standards for the English Language Arts.* Urbana, IL: National Council of Teachers of English; Newark, DE: International Reading Association.

DEANNA KUHN
DAVID DEAN JR.

# KNOWLEDGE ORGANIZATION AND UNDERSTANDING

Educational research is frequently construed as focusing on how teachers should teach. However, before this question is addressed, it is important to ask what should be taught. One might ask if the problem of what to teach is really a problem. Why not just ask scientists or rely on existing textbooks? There are good reasons a serious inquiry cannot be sidestepped, however. A fundamental realization of cognitive science is that almost all of the competence of experts is tacit. Careful studies of what scientists actually do show a vast repertoire of invisible (to them) processes and structures. Furthermore, textbooks are at best secondary sources, and they are much more likely idiosyncratic products of a complex social history than trustworthy sources for the essence of science. Progress is being made, even if cognitive science (including history, philosophy, and sociology of science) has not definitively identified the essence of scientific knowledge.

### Target Areas

The essence of "what to teach" can be divided into five target areas: content, process, meta-content and process, representational competence, and discourse and membership.

**Content.** *Content* concerns science concepts that students need to acquire. Content is of two different types: (1) central, difficult to learn ideas; and (2) concepts that are more peripheral and more amenable to straightforward instruction. Starting in the late 1970s, a huge literature emerged delineating certain misconceptions. The idea behind studying misconceptions is that difficult-to-acquire concepts are difficult not only (if at all) because of any intrinsic complexity, but because they are incompatible with well-developed and entrenched prior ideas. *Conceptual change* describes learning that involves substantial recrafting of prior ideas. While learning science concepts might, in principle, be difficult for many reasons, the preponderance of research suggests that conceptual change is a major factor. Conceptual change has been implicated in learning about force and motion, optics, electricity, heat and temperature, evolution, particulate theory of matter, and other topics.

Probably the most robust result of conceptual change research is that such change is not difficult for simple or accidental reasons, such as bad instruction. Instead, even the best instructional strategies require time and effort on the part of both students and teachers. This has major implications for selecting targets of instruction. Most notably, at the start of the twenty-first century, especially in the United

States, curricula are dramatically overly ambitious in terms of coverage. If students are to understand any science deeply, then choices must be made about the things that are to be taught. Study of cross-national science instruction has come to a similar conclusion. The U.S. science curriculum seems to be lacking in comparison to the best science instruction in the world because it is too shallow; it has been called "a mile wide and an inch deep."

Another result of conceptual change research is that calculation does not seem to be strongly tied to conceptual change. Students can often calculate without understanding, and numerical exercises do not often promote conceptual change. Quantitative reasoning is a hallmark of scientific thought, yet its centrality to deep understanding is questionable.

Conceptual change researchers have suggested several promising instructional techniques. One notable suggestion is that the curriculum needs pedagogically specific *intermediate models* that abandon a direct aim at scientifically complete and correct ideas. Instead of trying to jump a wide stream directly, metaphorically speaking, one may need to hop to rocks midstream, and then to the far shore. While teaching intermediate ideas—which are prone to be described as "wrong" or "incomplete"—may be counterintuitive, the scientific rationale is sound, and results are encouraging.

Conceptual change research is developing a new and refined vocabulary for various types of knowledge and knowledge system organizations, such as concepts, theories, mental models, ontologies, and various forms of intuitive, inarticulate knowledge. Identifying which of these are central instructional targets helps to define curriculum, plausible instructional techniques, and assessments.

**Process.** The process of *doing* science is the traditional complement to content. For example, introspection of scientists and textbook descriptions of what scientists do led to the introduction of the *scientific method* as part of science instruction. Scientists supposedly (a) define problems carefully; (b) generate hypotheses; (c) design experiments to select among hypotheses; and (d) carry out those experiments to determine results. This sort of instructional goal has generally been discredited by cognitive and other researchers. It seems quite likely that no general skills exist for "defining problems carefully" or "generating hypotheses." Instead, these are knowledge-intensive activities that require knowing many specific things about the particular domain that is being investigated. This is an important cognitive principle, which may be called the *virtual knowledge problem,* meaning that naming a process does not entail a particular body of knowledge. Instead, the process might require different knowledge in different circumstances, hence it may not name a coherent instructional target.

Other formulations of process skills in science (e.g., careful observation) seem certain to suffer from the virtual knowledge problem. Even if a general skill is real, rather than virtual, it is often very weak and overwhelmed by domain-specific knowledge. Mathematical problem-solving research has found similar results.

Jean Piaget (1896–1980) began an important line of thinking about science process. However, his assumptions about broad changes in logic and reasoning (e.g., younger students can think only concretely) have proved generally unsupportable. Young students, given proper support, can engage in remarkably abstract and cogent scientific study. More specific skills from Piagetian studies, such as *proportional reasoning* (reasoning in ratios), and *controlling variables* (understanding that experiments that change many things at once are difficult to evaluate), have proven more productive, although their importance is uncertain.

An important trend in the late 1990s was to regard many process issues as matters of effective frameworks for action, rather than matters of knowledge or skills. For example, many educational researchers embed instruction in an *inquiry cycle,* where students formulate ideas, test them, and then iteratively refine them. However, the consequences of such activities may be robust content learning and epistemological sophistication, rather than learning science process. A concern for frameworks for action also reflects the realization that students' taking fuller responsibility for authentic activities has many advantages over exercising isolated skills. This parallels the well-supported result that remediation by practicing isolated skills fails to produce transferable, long-term improvement.

**Meta-content and process.** Starting about 1990 research focused increasingly on students' conceptions of knowledge, or, more specifically, scientific knowledge. Students have naive assumptions about the nature of knowledge, in somewhat the same way that they have naive conceptions about the content of

science. Students may believe (falsely) that their own sense of what is sensible is irrelevant to science—they must be told everything that is true and should not expect to figure anything out on their own. Students may also believe (falsely) that knowledge of science is embodied in small, simple chunks (e.g., sentences or equations) that can be memorized and do not form a larger fabric. Researchers refer to this knowledge as *student epistemologies* (theories of knowledge).

Unlike most versions of science process, it appears in theory and practice that improving student epistemologies also improves science-content learning. However, the precise nature of student epistemologies is unsettled. Some researchers hold closely to epistemological ideas that characterize professional science, such as: "Scientific knowledge is contingent and always subject to revision." Others focus on general qualities of knowledge, like simplicity or modularity (as in the example beliefs stated above). Still others teach schemes abstracted from the history of science (e.g., evaluating the plausibility and productivity of competing theories) as part of inquiry-based science instruction.

**Representational competence.** A comparative newcomer to the repertoire of potential knowledge goals is *representational competence.* Representation competence entails knowing: How do representations (like pictures, graphs, or algebra) work? What are qualities of good representations? and How does one design effective, new, scientific representations? Older conceptions of representational competence were restricted to a narrower, less creative base, such as being able to generate and interpret a few standard representations. Promising characteristics of this new conception of representational competence are (a) students appear to have strong and productive intuitive ideas to build on; (b) concern for it parallels the broader move toward more authentic frames for action, rather than a focus on isolated skills; and (c) the rapid computerization of science evidently requires a more flexible representational competence than previously. This may entail interpreting dynamic, three-dimensional data displays or adjusting and interpreting color-coded visualizations.

**Discourse and membership.** Among the instructional trends in science learning is an increased reliance on social, rather than individual, methods, such as whole-class or small-group discussion. The parallel theoretical move is the realization that science is, in essence, a social process. Ways of speaking and interacting, and one's feeling of affiliation to various groups (*membership*), are not only means to an end, but are, in fact, vital to scientific competence. Adherents to this view often hold apprenticeship to be a fundamental model for learning and instruction.

Viewed *instrumentally* (only as a means to another goal—developing robust conceptual or procedural competence), considerations of discourse and membership are particularly appropriate for understanding difficulties encountered by cultural or linguistic minorities. If one does not speak or have values aligned with privileged modes in schools, one will be at a disadvantage. On the other hand, interpreted *essentially* (i.e., particular discourse patterns are goals in themselves, the essence of science), study of discourse and membership suggests a radical shift in current instructional goals.

## Implications

The potential practical impact of research on science learning goals is obvious and immense. The very things students should understand and be able to do are at stake. On the other hand, science is slow and arduous, and although research is progressing, definitive answers are not at hand.

An important social process to determine science-learning goals is to engage multiple stakeholders, particularly disciplinary scientists and teachers, and to establish common standards. While this approach has advantages, a review of existing standards suggests areas of concern.

**Definition and learnability.** Standards rely on common-sense meanings of *understanding* and *knowing*. Cognitive research suggests that there are many different ways of knowing; appropriate means of instruction (memorizing, discussing, experiencing) and assessment (verbal answers, competence in extended inquiry) depend strongly on which is involved. Standards do not systematically distinguish easy-to-accomplish goals from deep conceptual change. Not calibrating how much time it takes to master particular items perpetuates a failing *mile-wide and inch-deep* curriculum. Limited empirical testing of the feasibility of standards does not screen out virtual knowledge.

**Focus.** Current standards only minimally reflect topics that have emerged from cognitive research. Representational competence and student epistemologies are almost absent. Furthermore, interme-

diate models and goals tend to be screened out because they are unfamiliar to both disciplinary scientists and teachers. Lack of consideration of discourse and membership may perpetuate marginalization of cultural or linguistic minority students.

**Sequence.** Bad theories of sequencing, or no theory at all, prevent students from encountering ideas as early as they might—and they do not build optimally. For example, as previously mentioned, characterizing young science students' thinking as *concrete* seems to have inappropriately limited instruction.

**Coherence.** Long lists of goals (the bread and butter of most standards) encourage piecemeal instruction, which is at odds with a fundamental shift in thinking about learning, which is that coherent frames for activity almost always enhance learning—compared to rehearsing isolated facts or skills. A common strategy in standards for providing coherence via *broad themes* is likely to lead to the virtual knowledge problem.

Pitting standards against scientific research suggests a false dichotomy. Both are appropriate. However, bringing standards and the standards-producing process into better alignment with research will provide a great opportunity for advancement.

*See also:* LEARNING, *subentry on* CONCEPTUAL CHANGE; READING, *subentry on* CONTENT AREAS; SCIENCE EDUCATION.

### BIBLIOGRAPHY

BROWN, ANN L., and CAMPIONE, JOSEPH C. 1986. "Psychological Theory and the Study of Learning Disabilities." *American Psychologist* 41:1059–1068.

BROWN, DAVID E., and CLEMENT, JOHN. 1989. "Overcoming Misconceptions Via Analogical Reasoning: Abstract Transfer Versus Explanatory Model Construction." *Instructional Science* 18:237–261.

CALIFORNIA STATE BOARD OF EDUCATION. 2000. *Science Content Standards for California Public Schools, Kindergarten through Grade Twelve.* Sacramento: State of California Department of Education.

COBB, PAUL; WOOD, TERRY; and YACKEL, ERNAL. 1993. "Discourse, Mathematical Thinking, and

Classroom Practice." In *Education and Mind: Institutional, Social and Developmental Processes,* ed. Norris Minick, Ellice Forman, and Addison Stone. New York: Oxford University Press.

Confrey, Jere. 1990. "A Review of the Research On Student Conceptions in Mathematics, Science, and Programming." In *Review of Research in Education 16,* ed. Courtney Cazden. Washington, DC: American Educational Research Association.

diSessa, Andrea A. 1996. "What Do 'Just Plain Folk' Know About Physics?" In *The Handbook of Education and Human Development: New Models of Learning, Teaching, and Schooling,* ed. David R. Olson and Nancy Torrance. Oxford: Blackwell.

diSessa, Andrea A., and Minstrell, Jim. 1998. "Cultivating Conceptual Change with Benchmark Lessons." In *Thinking Practices in Mathematics and Science Learning,* ed. James G. Greeno and Shelly V. Goldman. Mahwah, NJ: Erlbaum.

diSessa, Andrea A., and Sherin, Bruce. 1998. "What Changes in Conceptual Change?" *International Journal of Science Education* 20:1155–1191.

diSessa, Andrea A., and Sherin, Bruce. 2000. "Meta-Representation: An Introduction." *Journal of Mathematical Behavior* 19(4):385–398.

Friedman, Jeff, and diSessa, Andrea A. 1999. "What Should Students Know About Technology? The Case of Scientific Visualization." *International Journal of Technology and Science Education* 9(3):175–196.

Greeno, James G.; Benke, Gertraud; Engle, Randi A.; Lachapelle, Cathy; and Wiebe, Muffie. 1998. "Considering Conceptual Growth as Change in Discourse Practices." In *Proceedings of the Twentieth Annual Conference of the Cognitive Science Society,* ed. M. Ann Gernsbacher and Sharon J. Derry. Mahwah, NJ: Erlbaum.

Hofer, Barbara K., and Pintrich, Paul R., eds. 2002. *Personal Epistemology: The Psychology of Beliefs about Knowledge and Knowing.* Mahwah, NJ: Erlbaum.

Larkin, Jill; McDermott, John; Simon, Herbert; and Simon, Dorthea. 1980. "Expert and Novice Performance in Solving Physics Problems." *Science* 208:1335–1342.

Metz, Kathleen. 1995. "Reassessment of Developmental Constraints on Children's Science Instruction." *Review of Educational Research* 65(2):93–127.

Schmidt, William H.; McKnight, Curtis; and Raizen, Senta. 1997. *A Splintered Vision: An Investigation of U.S. Science and Mathematics Education.* Dordrecht, Netherlands: Kluwer.

Schoenfeld, Alan. 1985. *Mathematical Problem Solving.* Orlando, FL: Academic Press.

White, Barbara Y. 1993. "Intermediate Causal Models: A Missing Link for Successful Science Education?" In *Advances in Instructional Psychology,* ed. Robert Glaser. Mahwah, NJ: Erlbaum.

**INTERNET RESOURCES**

American Association for the Advancement of Science. "Project 2061: Science for All Americans Online." 2001. <www.project2061.org/tools/sfaaol/sfaatoc.htm>.

National Research Council. 2001. "National Science Education Standards." <http://books.nap.edu/html/nses/pdf/index.html>.

Andrea A. diSessa

# STANDARDS

The release in 1983 of *A Nation At Risk: The Imperative for Educational Reform* is a reasonable place to begin consideration of the standards movement in science education in the United States in the later twentieth and early twenty-first centuries. This document, prepared by the National Commission on Excellence in Education (NCEE), was a response to "the widespread public perception that something is seriously remiss in our educational system" (p. 1). The document contained sentiments that became slogans of the standards movement. Science education for all is foreshadowed: "All, regardless of race or class or economic status, are entitled to a chance and to the tools for developing their individual powers of mind and spirit to the utmost" (p. 4). Recommendations focused on content, standards and expectations, time, teaching and leadership, and fiscal support. Science content was defined as "(a) the concepts, laws and processes of the physical and biological sciences; (b) the methods of scientific inquiry and reasoning; (c) the application of science knowledge to everyday life; and (d) the social and environmental implications of scientific and technological development" (p. 25).

The science education community both anticipated and responded to this report with numerous efforts. The American Association for the Advancement of Science (AAAS) initiated Project 2061, which began by defining scientific literacy for all high school graduates. The National Science Teachers Association (NSTA) began its Scope, Sequence, and Coordination Project and ultimately, in 1992, published *Scope, Sequence, and Coordination: The Content Core.* Professional organizations and curriculum development corporations began to produce curriculum materials that emphasized hands-on science, another slogan of the period.

## Mathematics Standards and National Education Goals

In 1989 two events occurred that would influence the development of national science education standards. The National Council of Teachers of Mathematics (NCTM) released *Curriculum and Evaluation Standards for School Mathematics.* The term *standards* assumed new prominence in education reform.

Also in 1989 the National Governors Association met with then U.S. President George H. W. Bush at an education summit. They endorsed six national education goals, which were articulated as America 2000 under the Bush administration and were enacted as the Goals 2000: Educate America Act in 1994, during the administration of Bill Clinton. Two of the national goals made specific reference to improving the knowledge and skills of students in science:

> Goal 3: Student Achievement and Citizenship. By the year 2000, American students will leave grades four, eight and twelve having demonstrated competency in challenging subject matter, including English, mathematics, science, history and geography; andGoal 4: Science and Mathematics. By the year 2000, U.S. students will be first in the world in science and mathematics achievement. (Malcom, p. 4)

The National Council on Education Standards and Testing, instituted by the U.S. Congress, referred explicitly to the mathematics standards when they recommended in 1992 that standards for school subjects were a desirable and feasible vehicle for meeting the national education goals. This council noted that the mathematics standards had been developed by a professional society that included mathematicians and teachers. Further, the standards had been subjected to cycles of public review and feedback that encouraged consensus building about what students should know and be able to do. Development by a professional society and public review became two requirements as federal agencies began awarding grants to develop high, voluntary, national standards in school subjects including science.

While there was public consensus that educational standards were good and useful, there was no consensus on what standards were. Examining ordinary dictionaries, two apparently contradictory meanings are found. A standard is an object used as an emblem, symbol, and rallying point for a leader, people, or movement; standards are banners. A standard also is an established basis or rule of comparison used to measure quality or value; standards are bars. Further, three types of standards were identified: content standards, performance standards, and delivery standards. Shirley Malcom, in a 1993 report of the National Education Goals Panel, defined content standards as what students should know and be able to do and performance standards as specifying how good is good enough. Diane Ravitch, in the 1995 book *National Standards in American Education: A Citizen's Guide,* defined delivery standards, later called opportunity-to-learn standards, as conditions for schooling under which content and performance standards would be attained.

## Two Key Documents: NSES and *Benchmarks*

When the U.S. Department of Education (DoE) began to deliberate about which association to consider to develop national education standards for science, two were immediately apparent: AAAS and NSTA. Each had reasons to assume leadership in the enterprise. Project 2061 was well underway at AAAS and in 1989 had produced *Science for All Americans,* which was having an impact on thinking and practice in curriculum and instruction in science. Work had begun on *Benchmarks for Science Literacy,* which parsed what students at different grade levels needed to understand if they were to attain science literacy by grade twelve. Alternatively, NSTA is the largest organization of science teachers in the country and is analogous to NCTM.

In spring 1991 the president of NSTA, supported by the unanimous vote of the board, asked the president of the National Academy of Sciences (NAS) with its operating arm, the National Research Council (NRC), to coordinate the development of national science education standards. The DoE encouraged NAS/NRC, a prestigious organization, to draw on expertise and experience from both AAAS and NSTA. Subsequently, by the early twenty-first century, two works were acknowledged at the national level as setting education standards for science: *National Science Education Standards* (NSES), which was produced by NRC in 1996; and *Benchmarks for Science Literacy,* which was published in 1993 by AAAS and is one product of Project 2061. A 1997 analysis of the science content in NSES and *Benchmarks* conducted by Project 2061 revealed that, although organized differently, there is greater than 90 percent overlap in what the two documents claim all students should understand and should be able to do.

NSES describes science content as fundamental and included as a standard if it: represents a central event or phenomena in the natural world; represents a central scientific idea and organizing principle; has rich explanatory power; guides fruitful investigations; applies to situations and contexts common to everyday experience; can be linked to meaningful learning experiences; and is developmentally appropriate for students at the grade levels specified. In NSES, the science content begins with the unifying concepts and process standard: systems, order, and organization; evidence, models, and explanations; change, constancy, and measurement; evolution and equilibrium; and form and function. These are not sorted by grade level but are applicable in some form to all students and all science disciplines. The other science content standards in NSES are displayed in Table 1. An array of the fundamental ideas in science that constitute the standards illustrates three points. The ideas build on one another from grade level to grade level. The ideas increase in complexity and abstractness across grade levels. There is an increase in the number of ideas across grade levels.

At the standard statement level the knowledge and abilities of students about inquiry and about technological design are similar for all students. Across grade levels, the ideas with which inquiry and design interact are increasingly complex and sophisticated. The increased complexity and sophistication of inquiry and design are captured in the guide to

the standards. For example, grade K–4 students are to "Ask a question about objects, organisms and events in the environment" (NRC, p. 122). Grade 5–8 students are to "Identify questions that can be answered through scientific investigations" (p. 145), while grade 9–12 students are to "Identify questions and concepts that guide scientific investigations" (p. 175).

The NSES went beyond the charge from DoE and developed standards for teaching and assessment, recognizing that change in content is not sufficient to produce change in teaching and learning. Further, NSES produced professional development standards, which focus on initial and continuing education of teachers; program standards, which focus on changes for schools and school districts; and system standards, which focus on changes in the entire educational system. *Benchmarks* extended science content to mathematics and to human society.

## Implementation

Although science education standards have been generally well received, their implementation has been difficult and uneven. Returning to an emphasis on local control in education, some states chose to keep the frameworks they had in place prior to 1989, some adopted the NSES or *Benchmarks,* others adapted either NSES or *Benchmarks,* while still others created their own state science standards. By 2000 most instructional materials claimed to be standards based. An analysis of many of them in 2001 by Project 2061, however, indicated that few actually are. Some of the questions that plague those implementing standards include: What is inquiry? What does it mean to understand a science idea? and Are the indicated grade levels appropriate? To answer these and other questions and to extend the influence and implementation of the NSES, the NRC has held numerous conferences and published more than fifteen documents addressed to teachers, parents, policymakers, and curriculum and assessment developers. *Benchmarks* is only one in a series of materials available or planned by Project 2061 to promote science literacy. The *Atlas of Science Literacy,* published by AAAS in 2001, graphically presents how the understanding of important science ideas is developed by students over time. Project 2061 also has developed a number of online tools such as *Blueprints for Reform,* which was published by AAAS in 2001, and conducts meetings and workshops for various stakeholders in science education.

**TABLE 1**

### Science content standards in *National Science Education Standards*

| Grades K–4 | Grades 6–8 | Grades 9–12 |
| --- | --- | --- |
| **Science as inquiry** | | |
| Abilities to do scientific inquiry | Abilities to do scientific inquiry | Abilities to do scientific inquiry |
| Understanding about scientific inquiry | Understanding about scientific inquiry | Understanding about scientific inquiry |
| **Physical science** | | |
| Properties of objects and materials | Properties and changes of properties in matter | Structure of atoms |
| Position and motion of objects | Motions and forces | Structure and properties of matter |
| Light, heat, electricity, and magnetism | Transfer of energy | Chemical reactions |
| | | Motions and forces |
| | | Conservation of energy and increase in disorder |
| | | Interactions of energy and matter |
| **Life science** | | |
| Characteristics of organisms | Structure and function in living systems | The cell |
| Life cycles of organisms | Reproduction and heredity | Molecular basis of heredity |
| Organisms and environments | Regulation and behavior | Biological evolution |
| | Populations and ecosystems | Interdependence of organisms |
| | Diversity and adaptations of organisms | Matter, energy, and organization in living systems |
| | | Behavior of organisms |
| **Earth and space science** | | |
| Properties of Earth materials | Structure of the Earth systems | Energy in the Earth system |
| Objects in the sky | Earth's history | Geochemical cycles |
| Changes in Earth and sky | Earth in the solar system | Origin and evolution of the Earth system |
| | | Origin and evolution of the universe |
| **Science and technology** | | |
| Abilities to distinguish between natural objects and objects produced by humans | Abilities of technological design | Abilities of technological design |
| Abilities of technological design | Understanding about science and technology | Understanding about science and technology |
| Understanding about science and technology | | |
| **Science in personal and social perspectives** | | |
| Personal health | Personal health | Personal and community health |
| Characteristics and changes in populations | Populations, resources, and environments | Population growth |
| Types of resources | Natural hazards | Natural resources |
| Changes in the environment | Risk and benefit | Environmental quality |
| Science and technology in local challenges | Science and technology in society | Natural and human-induced hazards |
| | | Science and technology in local, national, and global challenges |
| **History and nature of science** | | |
| Science as a human endeavor | Science as a human endeavor | Science as a human endeavor |
| | Nature of science | Nature of scientific knowledge |
| | History of science | Historical perspectives |

SOURCE: Based on National Research Council. 1996. *National Science Education Standards.* Washington, DC: National Academy Press.

### Other Standards Documents

The picture of education standards in science would be incomplete without mentioning the *Standards for Technological Literacy* released by the International Technology Education Association in 2000. Also, in 1989 the National Board for Professional Teaching Standards produced standards for experienced science teachers, while the Interstate New Teacher Assessment and Support Consortium published *Standards in Science for New Teachers: A Resource for State Dialogue* in 2001. There are also standards for programs that educate science teachers and for instructors in such programs.

At the beginning of the twenty-first century, standards are seen alternatively as vision or hurdle, as influential or intrusive, as realistic or impractical.

Beyond question, however, they have become an integral part of the science education enterprise.

*See also:* NATIONAL BOARD FOR PROFESSIONAL TEACHING STANDARDS; SCIENCE EDUCATION; SCIENCE LEARNING, *subentry on* KNOWLEDGE ORGANIZATION AND UNDERSTANDING; STANDARDS FOR STUDENT LEARNING; STANDARDS MOVEMENT IN AMERICAN EDUCATION.

## BIBLIOGRAPHY

AMERICAN ASSOCIATION FOR THE ADVANCEMENT OF SCIENCE. 1993. *Benchmarks for Science Literacy.* New York: Oxford University Press.

AMERICAN ASSOCIATION FOR THE ADVANCEMENT OF SCIENCE. 1997. *Resources for Science Literacy: Professional Development.* New York: Oxford University Press.

AMERICAN ASSOCIATION FOR THE ADVANCEMENT OF SCIENCE and NATIONAL SCIENCE TEACHERS ASSOCIATION. 2001. *Atlas of Science Literacy.* Washington, DC: American Association for the Advancement of Science and National Science Teachers Association.

ASSOCIATION FOR THE EDUCATION OF TEACHERS OF SCIENCE. 1997. "Professional Knowledge Standards for Science Teacher Educators." *AETS Newsletter* 31(3) (suppl.):1–6.

GILBERT, STEVEN. 1997. "Status Report on Certification and Accreditation in Science Education." *AETS Newsletter* 31(3):6–10.

*Goals 2000: Educate America Act of 1994.* U.S. Public Law 103-227. *U.S. Code.* Vol. 20, secs. 5801 et seq.

INTERNATIONAL TECHNOLOGY EDUCATION ASSOCIATION. 2000. *Standards for Technological Literacy.* Reston, VA: International Technology Education Association.

INTERSTATE NEW TEACHER ASSESSMENT AND SUPPORT CONSORTIUM. 2001. *Standards in Science for New Teachers: A Resource for State Dialogue.* Washington, DC: Interstate New Teacher Assessment and Support Consortium.

MALCOM, SHIRLEY. 1993. *Promises to Keep: Creating High Standards for American Students.* Washington, DC: U.S. Government Printing Office.

NATIONAL BOARD FOR PROFESSIONAL TEACHING STANDARDS. 1989. *Toward High and Rigorous Standards for the Teaching Profession.* Detroit, MI: National Board for Professional Teaching Standards.

NATIONAL COMMISSION ON EXCELLENCE IN EDUCATION. 1983. *A Nation at Risk: The Imperative for Educational Reform.* Washington, DC: U.S. Government Printing Office.

NATIONAL COUNCIL OF TEACHERS OF MATHEMATICS. 1989. *Curriculum and Evaluation Standards for School Mathematics.* Reston, VA: National Council of Teachers of Mathematics.

NATIONAL COUNCIL ON EDUCATION STANDARDS AND TESTING. 1992. *Raising Standards for American Education.* Washington, DC: U.S. Government Printing Office.

NATIONAL RESEARCH COUNCIL. 1996. *National Science Education Standards.* Washington, DC: National Academy Press.

NATIONAL SCIENCE TEACHERS ASSOCIATION. 1992. *Scope, Sequence, and Coordination: The Content Core: A Guide to Curriculum Designers.* Washington, DC: National Science Teachers Association.

RAVITCH, DIANE. 1995. *National Standards in American Education: A Citizen's Guide.* Washington, DC: Brookings Institution.

RUTHERFORD, F. JAMES, and AHLGREN, ANDREW. 1989. *Science for All Americans: A Project 2061 Report on Literacy Goals in Science, Mathematics, and Technology.* New York: Oxford University Press.

### INTERNET RESOURCES

AMERICAN ASSOCIATION FOR THE ADVANCEMENT OF SCIENCE. 2001. *Blueprints for Reform.* <www.project2061.org/tools/bluepol/blpframe.htm>.

AMERICAN ASSOCIATION FOR THE ADVANCEMENT OF SCIENCE. 2001. *Textbook Analysis.* <www.project2061.org/newsinfo/research/textbook/default.htm>.

ANGELO COLLINS

# TOOLS

Research on the use of technology to support science learning reveals promise to improve learning and potential pitfalls. Technology offers promise for increasing science inquiry and is a major component of science education reforms and standards. In inquiry activities, students intentionally address challenging science questions by engaging in complex, sustained, reflective reasoning to design solutions, test ideas, revise solutions, critique ideas, and collaborate with others.

The focus here is on technologies including scientific visualizations, statistical modeling, real time data collection, dynamic modeling software, and collaborative environments that support inquiry practices. This discussion highlights uses of technology that are integrated into an inquiry-based, science curriculum and often delivered using a learning environment, to help students engage in substantial scientific reasoning. Technology research seeks applications that help students develop a coherent understanding of science rather than fragmented ideas, and that set students on a path toward lifelong learning.

Many researchers and software designers have identified pitfalls of technology use. Often technology distracts learners with glitzy animations or colorful photographs that not only do not connect to the ideas that students hold, but also reinforce perceptions of science as inaccessible, irrelevant to personal concerns, or inscrutable. Internet sites and software designed to transmit information can deter students from viewing scientific sources critically. Applications like word processors or spreadsheets designed for business may require valuable classroom time to learn yet not contribute to understanding of science. Software designers are just beginning to develop robust applications that contribute to students' understanding by capitalizing on both late twentieth-century research on learning and iterative design studies conducted in settings where learning takes place.

Consistent with the rapid change in educational technologies, this article presents criteria for selecting promising technological tools that are synthesized from research on effective uses of technology and describes applications that exemplify these criteria and have supporting empirical research to demonstrate effectiveness in the classroom. The purposes is to seek benefits in terms of student learning gains, student engagement in scientific practice, or teacher professional development using a range of methodologies, and the criteria are based on reviews of studies featuring general comparisons, studies based on iterative design, and case studies of student learning.

## Engaging Students in Scientific Inquiry Activities

Technological resources can help students in inquiry activities, such as researching a complex question, building explanations, testing ideas, and refining understanding of the world. Applications that support modeling phenomena, visualizing, or collecting data also support inquiry. Emphasized are highlight modeling and simulation, visualization, and real time data collection.

**Modeling and simulation environments.** Modeling and simulation environments allow students to perform "what if" experiments or simulate experiments that would be difficult, impossible or dangerous to perform using real-world materials. Learners typically manipulate computer-based objects to see how they react under different conditions. Models represent complex scientific situations like an ecosystem or the world of Newtonian physics. Students construct or manipulate models to make conjectures, test ideas, and explore rules underlying scientific phenomena. Modeling and simulation environments generally fall within two types, either content based or open ended.

The software program Interactive Physics is an example of a content-based modeling environment. Interaction Physics provides a simulation environment and libraries of simulations for physics curricula. This program allows students to conduct controlled, simulated experiments without costs in time and materials. Students readily repeat experiments, change values of variables, and explore parameters of experiments. Students interact with their simulations in real time, and display measurements graphically in a variety of ways. Research demonstrates that students improve their physics understanding when interacting with modeling tools.

Open-ended, simplified modeling environments include Model-It, which is based on a more complex precursor, STELLA (Structural Thinking Experimental Learning Laboratory with Animation). Using Model-It, students can readily construct qualitative and quantitative models. Students define objects and factors within a system and build relationships between factors. Students "run" their models and monitor changes by viewing indicators or graphs. The design and use of Model-It in high school and middle school science classrooms is the focus of research at the University of Michigan. Model-It supports learners by allowing students to use personally meaningful images, providing information in qualitative, quantitative and graphical form, and prompting students for explanations. Case studies show that students use several higher order cognitive tasks when creating models with Model-It, including identifying causal relationships and elaborating upon explanations. Students learn the scientific content that forms the basis of their models as well as ideas related to the nature of science, including purposes of modeling.

**Visualization software.** Visualization software provides students with access to scientific visualizations such as molecular models or geographic information systems. For example, WorldWatcher uses scientific visualization software and historical data to help students recognize patterns in weather data by translating numerical data, such as temperature, to a palette of colors and displaying results on a world map. The software allows students to annotate data, make predictions, and perform sophisticated analysis by overlaying data sets. A Global Warming Project, an eight-to-ten-week unit intended for students in grades seven to ten, involves teams of students advising world leaders on issues countries may face due to global warming. The WorldWatcher formative classroom research reveals the challenges that students face in interpreting complex data and suggests ways to reduce complexity to support inquiry.

**Real-time data collection software.** An important technological support for science learning connects sensors to a computer, calculator, or handheld Personal Digital Assistant (like a PalmPilot or Visor), and allows students to record real-time data about their environment. Common probes include temperature, voltage, and motion sensors. Researchers have studied the use of probes in computer-based labs and microcomputer-based labs, showing how real-time graphing helps students understand complex scientific phenomena. The use of probes in an inquiry environment assists student in distinguishing between important scientific concepts, such as heat and temperature.

## Complex Science Content and Integrated Understanding

Technology can help students make sense of standards-based complex topics and provide a window on science in the making to illustrate science inquiry. To enable students to gather, organize, and display information, technology can combine visualization, modeling, and real-time data collection with a full curriculum. Ideally science instruction encourages

students to build a more coherent understanding of science and to apply ideas from one domain to the next. Processed applications such as simulations depend on the curriculum and the teacher to emphasize connections. Whole curricula can support integrated understanding when well designed and complemented by a thoughtful teacher.

For example, Constructing Physics Understanding (CPU), a National Science Foundation-funded project, encourages robust physics understanding by connecting laboratory and computer-based materials to elicit students' ideas, guide students to modify ideas, and help students apply target ideas to new situations by using simulations.

The Virtual High School (VHS) allows teachers in a consortium to use online materials and collaborative tools to create specialty NetCourses online for students at other schools that belong to the consortium. VHS offers a wide range of courses, but science selections include ethnobotany, evolutionary genetics, paleontology, astronomy, and bioethics. VHS research helps teachers redesign courses and enhance inquiry by supporting inquiry-based teaching online.

## Supporting Peer Learning

Research shows benefits when students productively specialize and tutor their peers. To support peer learning, software offers some group and individual activities, specifies how groups should work together, and accommodates the contributions of individuals to the group.

For example, software can support geographically separated students in sharing quantitative and qualitative data that are location dependent and/or time-sensitive, including weather, astronomical, or water quality data. Synchronized collaborative programs provide the tools and curricula to organize students over large distances. Synchronized collaborative programs range from days to weeks to a semester, and work best when several classrooms use them simultaneously and share findings. The programs use communication technologies including e-mail and discussion forums to coordinate activity and discussion. For example, in One Sky Many Voices students serve as "resident experts" and communicate with other sites to compare local environments. Participation encourages scientific discussion and debate, asking questions, and presenting evidence to students in distant classrooms.

Several programs use software, including electronic probes to facilitate group data collection and analysis. For example, the Global Learning and Observations to Benefit the Environment (GLOBE) project has three major goals: "to enhance the environmental awareness of individuals throughout the world; to contribute to scientific understanding of the earth; and to help all students reach higher levels of achievement in science and mathematics" (GLOBE Teacher's Guide, Program Overview). Through GLOBE, elementary to high school students around the world investigate earth science, including atmosphere, hydrosphere, land use, and soil. Scientists and students partner to collect and use data to gain a better understanding of global environmental processes. Providing online tools and materials, GLOBE uses high quality satellite photos and graphical representations of temperature, climate, and land use data. Students add findings to the Student Data Archive and use an Internet-based forum called GLOBEMail to communicate with schools and scientists. GLOBE is effective in improving student achievement in key mathematics, science, and geography skills. Students and teachers also report more interest and awareness of environmental issues and believe their data contributes to scientific research.

## Recognizing Relevant Experiences, Diverse Contributions to Science, and Autonomy

Effective instruction should connect students' complex and varied ideas from prior observation and instruction, and introduce new scientific ideas. Technology can help students make connections, test their ideas against normative ones, and sort out varied perspectives on a topic.

To promote independent inquiry, technology-enhanced environments can prompt students to reflect on their progress and critique solutions proposed by others. Effective software should invite diverse students to engage in science by providing a variety of ways to learn (discussion, projects, reading, designing, debating), and by using students' views and experiences as a springboard to further learning. Software can support students in refining ideas, developing interest in new scientific topics, and carrying out sustained, complex projects.

In the early twenty-first century, learning environments are emerging to meet this challenging criteria. Computer-based learning environments combine curricula, classroom activities, and assessments into packages designed to improve teacher effectiveness and to provide cognitive and social supports for students who are conducting inquiry projects. Learning environments incorporate results of cognitive research including hint giving, prompts for reflection, and connections to online discussions. They free teachers to tutor individuals, identify common theories, and monitor progress.

The Web-based Integrated Science Environment (WISE), a browser-based application, offers a library of middle school and high school activities that enable students to critique real-world "evidence" from the Internet, compare scientific arguments, and design solutions to scientific problems. WISE projects offer inquiry activities that are personally relevant to students. These activities present multifaceted, interdisciplinary scientific issues, introduce scientific methodology, and encourage students to gain lifelong learning skills, including the ability to critique websites and support conclusions with appropriate evidence. The WISE technology provides an organizational structure helping students to reflect upon their learning, take notes, sort evidence, and discuss arguments online with peers. Many WISE projects involve hands-on data collection, online modeling of observations, or design activities. WISE provides scientific evidence, differing points of view, and visualizations (e.g., images, diagrams, animations or models). Students perform all work collaboratively, and are assessed in terms of their notes, arguments, models, and designs. WISE draws upon extensive cognitive and educational research, summarized by Marcia Linn and Sherry Hsi, to explore how computer technology can guide and support students' understanding.

## Benefits

There is widespread agreement that students benefit from learning with and about technology in science. Nevertheless, effective incorporation of information technologies into the curriculum has been controversial, difficult, and demanding. Finding ideal uses of technology in science instruction remains an active research area, and the technology itself is a "moving target," as new projects emerge on a regular basis. The recommendations in this entry capture current practices and research findings, and require regular revision as new tools and new research results become available. The best gift science teachers can give this generation of students is to offer them courses and tools that enable them to become lifelong science learners and to add new technological resources regularly to their repertoire.

*See also:* MATHEMATICS LEARNING, *subentry on* LEARNING TOOLS; PEER RELATIONS AND LEARNING; READING, *subentry on* CONTENT AREAS; SCIENCE EDUCATION; SCIENCE LEARNING *subentry on* STANDARDS; TECHNOLOGY EDUCATION; TECHNOLOGY IN EDUCATION, *subentry on* CURRENT TRENDS.

**BIBLIOGRAPHY**

AMERICAN ASSOCIATION FOR THE ADVANCEMENT OF SCIENCE. 1993. *Benchmarks for Science Literacy: Project 2061.* New York: Oxford University Press.

BRANSFORD, JOHN D.; BROWN, ANN L.; and COCKING, RODNEY R., eds. 1999. *How People Learn: Brain, Mind, Experience, and School.* Washington, DC: National Academy Press.

BROWN, ANN L., and CAMPIONE, JOSEPH C. 1990. "Communities of Learning and Thinking, or a Context by any Other Name." *Developmental Perspectives on Teaching and Learning Thinking Skills,* ed. Deanna Kuhn. Basel, NY: Karger.

BROWN, MATTHEW, and EDELSON, DANIEL C. 1999. "A Lab by Any Other Name: Integrating Traditional Labs and Computer Supported Collaborative Science Investigations." In *Proceedings of Computer-Supported Collaborative Learning 1999,* ed. Christopher M. Hoadley. Palo Alto, CA: Stanford University.

COMMITTEE ON INFORMATION TECHNOLOGY LITERACY. 1999. *Being Fluent with Information Technology.* Washington, DC: National Research Council.

EDELSON, DANIEL. C.; GORDIN, DOUGLAS N.; and PEA, ROY D. 1999. "Addressing the Challenges of Inquiry-Based Learning through Technology and Curriculum Design." *Journal of the Learning Sciences* 8(3/4):391–450.

ESPINOZA, CARLOS; DOVE, TRACEY; ZUCKER, ANDREW A.; and KOZMA, ROBERT B. 1999. *An Evaluation of the Virtual High School after Two Years of Operation.* Menlo Park, CA: SRI International.

JACKSON, SHARI L.; STRATFORD, STEVEN J.; KRAJCIK, JOSEPH S.; and SOLOWAY, ELLIOT. 1996. "Making Dynamic Modeling Accessible to Pre-College Science Students." *Interactive Learning Environments* 4(3):233–237.

LINN, MARICA C., and HSI, SHERRY. 2000. *Computers, Teachers, Peers: Science Learning Partners.* Mahwah, NJ: Erlbaum.

MEANS, BARBARA. 1994. *Technology and Education Reform: The Reality behind the Promise.* San Francisco: Jossey-Bass.

MOKROS, JANICE R., and TINKER, ROBERT F. 1987. "The Impact of Micro-Computer-Based Labs on Children's Ability to Interpret Graphs." *Journal of Research in Science Teaching* 24(4):369–383.

NATIONAL RESEARCH COUNCIL. 1996. *National Science Education Standards.* Washington, DC: National Academy Press.

SONGER, NANCY B. 1996. "Exploring Learning Opportunities in Coordinated Network-Enhanced Classrooms: A Case of Kids as Global Scientists." *The Journal of the Learning Sciences* 5:297–327.

SPITULNIK, MICHELE W. 1998. "Construction of Technological Artifacts and Teaching Strategies to Promote Flexible Scientific Understanding." Ph.D diss., University of Michigan.

WHITE, BARBARA Y., and FREDERIKSEN, JOHN R. 1998. "Inquiry, Modeling, and Metacognition: Making Science Accessible to All Students." *Cognition and Instruction* 16(1):3–118.

MICHELE SPITULNIK
MARCIA LINN

# SEA GRANT PROGRAM

The sea is an integral part of American heritage. Historically, marine commerce, seafood products, and the productivity of coastal communities have been essential to the U.S. economy. However, the marine sciences did not enjoy a prominent role in the early development of the country's science enterprise. This began to change during the post-*Sputnik* years, spurred by U.S. President John F. Kennedy's statement in 1961 that "knowledge and understanding of the oceans promise to assume greater importance in the future." By 1963 the Federal Council for Science and Technology published a long-range plan for oceanography that marked a greater federal commitment to the field.

Unlike the ocean sciences, engineering and agricultural research flourished during the late nineteenth century and throughout the twentieth century. This was made possible by the land-grant program, perhaps America's greatest contribution to university education. The Morrill Act, in 1862, and subsequent legislation established in every state a unique university-based, federally funded system that combined programs of research and education—and the extension of that knowledge to practical application. The land grant experiment has been an enormously successful model for federal-state partnerships.

The land grant concept provided the model that Athelstan Spilhaus, then a dean at the University of Minnesota, referred to in September 1963 when he remarked, "Why do we not do what wise men have done for the better cultivation of the land a century ago, why not have Sea Grant Colleges?" Thus originated the idea of a National Sea Grant College Program. Given the importance placed on the oceans during the 1960s, the Spilhaus concept rapidly became reality. With support from the academic community, led by Spilhaus and John Knauss, then dean of the University of Rhode Island's Graduate School of Oceanography, the Sea Grant idea attracted the attention of Congress. Under the leadership of Senator Claiborne Pell of Rhode Island and Congressman Paul G. Rogers of Florida, the National Sea Grant College and Program Act (Pub. L. 89-688) was signed into law by President Lyndon Johnson on October 15, 1966.

The fledgling Sea Grant Program was initially housed at the National Science Foundation, and the first grants were awarded in 1968. With the formation of the National Oceanic and Atmospheric Administration (NOAA), Sea Grant was moved to that agency in the early 1970s. By 1974 grants had been made to twenty-three institutional programs in coastal and Great Lakes states.

## Operating Concepts

The National Sea Grant College Program operates under authorization of the Sea Grant Act, which is consistent in concept and intent with the original 1966 law. Sea Grant grew out of a desire to achieve preeminence in oceanography and to support education and research in the marine sciences. The current version of the act explicitly states that the objective is to "increase understanding, utilization, and conservation of the Nation's ocean, coastal and Great Lakes resources by providing assistance to promote a strong educational base, responsive re-

search and training activities, and broad and prompt dissemination of knowledge and techniques, assessment, development, and multi-disciplinary approaches to environmental problems." Sea Grant's mission is to engage the nation's research universities in management-critical issues relating to coastal and ocean resources. The mechanism used is federal sponsorship of grants to universities for education, research, and information transfer to users through an extension service.

Eligibility, qualifications, and responsibilities for sea grant programs are set forth in the act and the Federal Register (Vol. 44, No. 244). A sea-grant program is a university-based program administered by an academic institution or consortia. Responsibility for designation of sea-grant colleges rests with the U.S. Secretary of Commerce. Sea-grant colleges receive funds through federal grants that require matching funds from nonfederal sources at 50 percent of the federal portion. Special provisions in the act also allow NOAA to make grants to sea-grant institutions by "passing through" funds from other federal agencies on a nonmatching basis.

## Magnitude and Scope

In 2001 Sea Grant managed about $100 million in funds annually from federal and matching sources. Approximately 75 percent of those funds are invested in grants for the core operations of the thirty designated sea grant institutional programs. Most of the remainder is distributed through a national competitive process open to all programs. Each of these institutions is responsible for developing an integrated program for addressing management-critical issues important to the state, region, and nation. This is done through merit-reviewed research, education, and outreach projects. Emphasis is placed on engaging users and stakeholders, including federal, state, and local agencies.

Sea Grant programs draw upon academic talent not only at the sponsoring institution but also through a wider network of more than three hundred participating universities. Annually, more than 800 individual projects are funded, 300 extension specialists engaged, and about 500 graduate fellowships supported nationally. In the three-year period between 1997 and 1999, more than 2,500 journal articles and publications were produced. Overall, about 60 percent of available funds are expended on merit-based research, 27 percent on outreach, and 5 percent on precollege training programs.

Sea Grant programs focus on three broad portfolios: economic leadership, coastal ecosystem health and public safety, and education and human resources. A broad range of multidisciplinary topics are addressed, including aquaculture, aquatic nuisance species, coastal community development, estuarine research, fisheries habitats and management, coastal hazards, marine biotechnology, marine engineering, seafood safety, and water quality. Educational efforts involve targeting K–12 teachers and their students, mentoring college and graduate students conducting research projects, and transferring useful technology to coastal residents and businesses.

While Sea Grant has yet to gain the stature and resources its founders envisioned, it has been a highly productive investment of public funds and has made significant contributions through its science, education, and extension programs. With the enormous growth in, and the economic importance of, the nation's coasts and associated habitats, the demand for Sea Grant's services continues to increase dramatically.

Athelstan Spilhaus's brainchild promises to increase its contributions to building the United States' capacity to manage its coastal resources in the future. The establishment of a Sea Grant Program in Korea portends an international dimension as well.

## BIBLIOGRAPHY

MILOY, JOHN. 1983. *Creating the College of the Sea: The Origin of the Sea Grant Program.* College Station: Texas A&M University Sea Grant Program.

NATIONAL RESEARCH COUNCIL. 1994. *A Review of NOAA National Sea Grant College Program.* Washington, DC: National Academy Press.

NATIONAL SEA GRANT EXTENSION REVIEW PANEL. 2000. *A Mandate to Engage Coastal Users.* Corvallis: Oregon Sea Grant.

OMELCZENKO, VICTOR, ed. 2000. *National Sea Grant College Program Biennial Report 1998–1999.* Silver Spring, MD: National Oceanic and Atmospheric Administration.

RYAN, PAUL R., ed. 1988. "Sea Grant Education, Research, Advisory Services." *Oceanus: The International Magazine of Marine Science and Policy* 31(3). Woods Hole, MA: Woods Hole Oceanographic Institution.

SEA GRANT ASSOCIATION. 1985. *Sea Grant: Past, Present and Future (Twentieth Year Commemorative Anniversary).* Narragansett: University of Rhode Island.

SEA GRANT ASSOCIATION. 1993. *The National Sea Grant College Program 1987–1992.* Seattle: Washington Sea Grant Program.

## INTERNET RESOURCE

BAIRD, RONALD C. 2001. "Toward New Paradigms in Coastal Resource Management: Sea Grant as International Role Model." Oceanology International Americas. <www.oiamericas.com/conference/program.htm>.

RONALD C. BAIRD

# SECONDARY EDUCATION

HISTORY OF
  Susan L. Mintz
CURRENT TRENDS
  Gerald N. Tirozzi
INTERNATIONAL ISSUES
  Donald B. Holsinger

## HISTORY OF

In the mid- to late nineteenth century, the United States became the first country to open secondary education to the general public. In the early twenty-first century, secondary education follows a common elementary school experience, typically beginning at age twelve and continuing through age seventeen or eighteen. Elementary education deals with the rudimentary skills of reading, writing, and computation, as well as social goals deemed important by curriculum developers. Secondary education, however, extends beyond the elementary curriculum and addresses a combination of the personal, intellectual, vocational, and social needs of adolescents in society. Educators and policymakers have engaged in ongoing debate over what should be included in the secondary curriculum. In fact, the emphases of the secondary curriculum have shifted according to local and national goals; the historical, philosophical, and intellectual context; and societal beliefs about the role of youth in society, as well as other factors.

## The Beginnings of Secondary Education

Public secondary schools began to proliferate throughout the United States in the mid- to late nineteenth century. Before then, private endeavors provided a variety of educational experiences. Throughout the seventeenth and eighteenth centuries, private academies and tutors prepared wealthy boys for college. Academies, controlled by an independent board, required tuition and were distinguished from one another by regional and local needs. As a result, the curriculum and religious orientation were not the same at each school. The college preparatory curriculum was classical in nature, focusing on Greek and Latin. Boston Latin Grammar School epitomizes an example of such an academy. Opened in 1635 with some public funding and control, Boston Latin was designed to give boys from elite families the education they needed in order to attend college and take their place in society.

As the merchant and craftsmen class grew, private academies began to cater to the sons of the middle class in order to prepare these young men to succeed in commerce. These academies, called English academies, offered classes in modern languages, literature, mathematics, natural science, history, and geography, rather than Latin and Greek. Both English and Latin academies offered admission through examination. The differences in these academy curricula foreshadowed what would become the continuing debate over what should constitute the secondary curriculum—a question that has been addressed throughout the history of American high schools.

## The First Public High Schools

The first public high school opened in Boston in 1821. What became known as English High School was established as an alternative to private academies that offered a college preparatory curriculum. Boys who passed the entrance examination participated in a three-year English curriculum. High schools became more common in Massachusetts after an 1827 law required towns to provide a free public high school. Other early high schools could be found across the United States, although the biggest growth came in urban areas. Many early high schools did not admit girls and minorities. Boston opened a High School for Girls in 1826 that closed within two years. It was not until Boston Girls High and Normal School opened in 1857 that young women had the opportunity to attend a public secondary school. In the late eighteenth and nineteenth century, it was not uncommon for urban schools to include a *normal* curriculum at the secondary level. Normal schools trained young women to teach in local elementary schools.

## Growth of Public High Schools

The public high school movement gained momentum following the Civil War (1861–1865). Only 300 high schools existed in the United States prior to the war; by 1900 there were more than 6,000 high schools annually graduating 6 percent of American seventeen-year-olds. Public high schools, however, had their detractors as well as supporters. Advocates argued that high schools completed the public school system, could attract businesses by providing competent labor, and increased the value of land. Opponents viewed the taxes that supported high schools as a burden. In many cases, families could not afford to send their children to school. Family economic stability was needed for high school attendance, and some families did not have this luxury. In other cases, families might choose to send their children to private schools and not get the direct benefit of the public high school. The tax question was resolved in 1872 when the Michigan Supreme Court (in what became known as the Kalamazoo Case) heard arguments for and against using taxes for secondary schools. The ruling favored tax support of public high schools, which subsequently became common practice throughout the United States.

## Curriculum Standardization

As the number of public high schools grew, the variety among curricula increased. No standards existed concerning curriculum or organization. Curriculum decisions made by local school boards hampered the links between colleges and high schools. Entrance to college was usually determined by examinations that had specific, individual requirements, making it difficult to anticipate the necessary preparation. To provide more standardization in the curriculum and help untangle the college admission process, the National Education Association sponsored the Committee of Ten in 1892. Ten influential educators, mostly from colleges and universities, debated the appropriate role of secondary schools. The report of this committee examined a central question in the ongoing curriculum debate—what constitutes a good secondary education?

The Committee of Ten recommended a rigorous academic curriculum for all students, regardless of their future plans, and elucidated the pursuit of knowledge and training of the intellect as the mission of secondary schools. High schools held the responsibility for designing courses of study that focused on the nine core subjects: Latin, Greek, English, modern languages, mathematics, sciences, natural history, history (including economics and government), and geography. College admission would follow for interested students who successfully completed this course of study. But the desire to attend college was not the only reason to partake of these classes. The committee argued that in order for students to be educated, college bound or not, an academic curriculum was necessary. Criticisms of the report abounded. Many academicians believed that there was too little rigor; others commented that the courses were too impractical.

Curriculum standardization was not the only approach to articulating the secondary school–college divide. As noted, in the late nineteenth century admission to most colleges was determined by an entrance examination. High school and state educators wanted to use a diploma admission requirement rather than have to prepare students for the wide range of college admissions tests. The University of Michigan began diploma admission as early as 1871, but this practice did not become common until accreditation became popular.

The New England Association of Schools and Colleges was founded in 1885 and is the oldest of the six regional accrediting agencies servicing the United States in the early twenty-first century. These accreditation agencies helped to cement the distinctions between colleges and universities and standardize the evaluation of high school programs. Accreditation continues to be voluntary and involves parents, teachers, students, and community members. A school self-study that is based on regional standards and is tied to state standards is the basis of the accreditation evaluation. In another regulatory push, the College Entrance Examination Board came into existence in 1899 with the goal of providing uniform examinations for college admission.

The Carnegie unit also played a role in the standardization of high schools in the early part of the twentieth century. Again, the issue was how to report high school experiences to colleges. The Carnegie Foundation for the Advancement of Teaching, a nonprofit corporation founded in 1906, developed the Carnegie unit as a measure of the amount of time a student had studied a subject. One Carnegie unit was equivalent to 120 hours of contact time, and fourteen units was established as the minimum for an academic high school course of study.

## Curriculum Differentiation

Early in the twentieth century the population of secondary schools increased dramatically. In 1910, 8.8 percent of seventeen-year-olds were in high school; by 1930 this figure rose to almost 30 percent. Progressive educators took note of both this increase and that many of the students in secondary schools would not be attending college. They believed schools needed to expand the rigorous academic curriculum to include more practical subjects and in this way create more equitable schools. Rather than focusing solely on intellectual training, high schools began to emphasize social and vocational skills that prepared students for later life. Social skills were necessary to assimilate the large wave of immigrants and to promote democratic ideals so that new Americans could function in society.

The term *curriculum differentiation* means different courses of study for different students. The comprehensive high school attempts to meet the needs of a variety of students in one location. Curriculum differentiation was championed in another National Education Association report, the *Cardinal Principles of Education*. This report, released in 1918 and authored by the NEA's Committee on the Reorganization of Secondary Education, did not emphasize intellectual skills or the standard school subjects. Rather, the committee recommended that secondary education focus on health, the command of fundamental processes, worthy home membership, vocation, citizenship, worthy use of leisure time, and ethical character. As high school education became universal, comprehensive high schools, the committee argued, should meet the needs of the widely diverse student population. These needs could be met through varied curriculum options relevant to the lives of current students. Guidance departments would help students make appropriate selections from the available choices by determining the students' strengths and weaknesses. IQ tests would be used to determine student placement. The committee emphasized that offering a wide variety of relevant choices for students was the only way universal secondary education could provide equal educational opportunity and allow all students to succeed.

Using the high school curriculum to solve social problems was compatible with the relevant curriculum choices in the Cardinal Principles. This trend has continued in high schools as seen in the substance abuse programs, family life education, and driver's education courses at the beginning of the twenty-first century.

## Secondary School Structures

The development of secondary schools led to a number of different structural arrangements. During the late nineteenth and early twentieth centuries the prevalent pattern was eight years of graded elementary school followed by four years of high school. The first junior high schools, grades seven through nine, were established in California and Ohio around 1910. This organization allowed for greater flexibility in the curriculum and slowly assimilated students into the world of high school subjects, classes, and teaching styles. The junior high school pattern typically includes six years of elementary school, three years of junior high school, and three years of senior high school. There were more than 7,000 junior high schools by the 1960s.

Middle schools evolved in the 1960s with a new pattern—five years of elementary, three years of middle school, and four years of high school. Middle schools were designed to meet the intellectual, social, and physical needs of young adolescents rather than to help these students get ready for high school. The structural and curricular changes in middle schools included advisories (long-term student groups that meet with one faculty member over a period of time), team planning and teaching, exploratory classes, and adequate health and physical education classes. Middle schools are currently the predominant mode of organization in grades six through eight.

## Minorities in Public High Schools

The idea of a public high school education had taken hold in the white, middle-class population by the late 1800s. High schools were mostly coeducational and, in fact, girls made up the majority of the high school population by the late 1800s. The education of blacks and Native Americans, however, took a different turn. During Reconstruction education was aimed at helping African Americans adjust to the prevailing political and social norms. The separate but equal doctrine elucidated in the U.S. Supreme Court case *Plessy v. Ferguson* in 1896 severely cur-

tailed the development of black high schools, yet the perennial high school curriculum debate was also relevant to the education of African Americans. The educators W. E. B. Du Bois and Booker T. Washington disagreed about the course that black education should take. Du Bois believed in an academic curriculum allowing talented students to excel, a curriculum promoting intellectual life, whereas Washington favored industrial and agricultural training, a curriculum promoting the worthiness of hard work.

This debate, centering on how African-American youth should be educated in high school, was a moot point for many years because most localities, particularly in the South, did not provide public high schools for blacks. In an 1899 decision (*Cummings v. School Board of Richmond County, Georgia*), the Supreme Court decided that school boards were not required to provide public secondary education for African Americans. This decision restrained the evolution of black secondary education. Only a few black public high schools managed to struggle into existence. In general, these high schools focused on a college preparatory curriculum. Nevertheless, once the population of African-American youth in urban areas increased, local officials, and later northern philanthropists, promoted black secondary schools focusing on industrial education. Many believed that this curriculum would train students for the kinds of employment then available. Black leaders, however, often argued for a curriculum that would prepare students for college, not work.

In *Brown v. Board of Education of Topeka, Kansas*, the Supreme Court unanimously struck down the *Plessy v. Ferguson* separate but equal ruling, arguing that the separation of children in public schools by race violates the Fourteenth Amendment. This 1954 ruling sent shock waves through the state of Kansas and several other states that had segregated school systems. The *Brown* decision did not solve all of the problems associated with black education. Desegregation did not come easily, and only a year later the Supreme Court needed to create procedures for school boards to integrate schools "with deliberate speed." In 1957 federal troops had to be called into Little Rock, Arkansas, so that nine black students could attend the previously all-white Central High School. Although high school graduation rates for African-American students have improved since the *Brown* decision, the historic exclusion of black youth from secondary schools continues to be reflected in the discrepancies in the dropout rates and standardized test scores of white and black adolescents.

The Bureau of Indian Affairs (BIA) in Washington, D.C., was in charge of the education of American Indian youth and developed an official policy of detribalization. Many Native Americans were sent away from their families to boarding schools to be immersed in white culture and values. For example, the curriculum of the Carlisle Indian Industrial School, established in 1879 and closed in 1918, was designed with the intention of transforming Native American children by focusing on the vocational skills that Booker T. Washington was promoting for the education of African Americans. After the U.S. government granted citizenship to Native Americans following World War I (1914–1918), local schools replaced boarding schools.

In the early twenty-first century, Native American schools on reservations are still controlled by the BIA, and Native American students are the least successful students in the public school system. Poverty, low attendance rates, and the lack of exposure to a rigorous academic curriculum directly contribute to high failure rates among Native American students. Almost 50 percent of Native American students drop out of high school, and only 17 percent continue on to college.

### Education and the Economy

The economy directly influenced secondary schools from the time such schools were created. Access to transportation and family economic stability influenced high school enrollment rates, but as jobs required more education, a higher number of students stayed in high school. In the late 1920s youth unemployment emerged as a contentious political and social issue. Politicians and educators wanted students to remain in high school in order to reduce increased delinquency, crime, and political radicalization. With millions of youth unemployed during the Great Depression of the 1930s, every attempt was made to keep more students in school. At the same time, budgets were reduced, putting a major strain on most schools. During the 1920s and 1930s the school curriculum became more custodial in nature in order to meet the immediate needs of youth. Consequently, emphasis shifted from academic courses to consumer-oriented classes, and life skills were emphasized.

In the 1940s and 1950s the common form of secondary education was a comprehensive high school with differentiated curriculum tracks. During World War II (1939–1945), enrollment in secondary schools dipped, but the curricular trends of making courses relevant to the lives of students continued to be important. In 1944 the Educational Policies Commission released Education for All American Youth, a report calling for a highly practical curriculum similar to that described in the Cardinal Principles. Many feared that the economic difficulties that occurred before the war would continue after the war, so the push continued to keep students in school. American youth would not be competing for jobs with returning servicemen.

The economy continued to influence educational decisions in the 1950s, 1960s, and 1970s, but clearly played a central role in the 1980s. A Nation at Risk, a report from the National Commission on Excellence in Education, published in 1983, directly tied the quality of American schooling to the strength and position of the American economy in the global marketplace. Alarmed by the economic advances made by Japan and other countries, the commission argued that schools in the United States were declining, which presented an immediate threat to the country's well-being and economic strength.

### Education and the National Defense

The cold war of the 1950s and 1960s brought further challenges to the schools. Many people called for strengthening academics in secondary schools by removing the popular but less rigorous life-adjustment classes. The launching of Sputnik by the Soviet Union in 1957 instigated loud cries for educational reform. As a result, the National Defense Education Act that was passed in 1958 provided financial aid to states for the improvement of the teaching of science, mathematics, and foreign languages.

As a result of the cold war, the debate over the public high school curriculum shifted to how the educational system could ensure the survival of the United States and its democratic ideals. Many asserted that American youth could be protected from the ideas of communism and fascism through universal secondary education that emphasized equality of educational opportunity. A central question emerged: Is educational opportunity best served through curriculum differentiation and good guidance services or through a rigorous academic curriculum? The educator James B. Conant studied American high schools and concluded that the solution was universal enrollment in a comprehensive high school that met the needs of all students by providing the opportunity to succeed. He noted that the comprehensive high school also allowed for student interaction among academic tracks, which facilitated the development of the social skills that are necessary in productive citizens. Conant also suggested that authorities strengthen the differentiation in secondary schools with an increased focus on the gifted. He believed talented students must be exposed to advanced classes in mathematics and science. To this end, there were a number of curricular reform efforts that found their way into secondary schools, several sponsored by the National Science Foundation. Most of these reforms failed because the science and mathematics programs were designed by academicians who paid little attention to the day-to-day realities of schools.

## Standards

The argument between high academic standards and life skills as the central focus of the American high school curriculum continued in the last three decades of the twentieth century. This debate also occurred internationally. Great Britain readjusted its system of examinations that put eleven-year-olds into specific secondary schools and replaced it with comprehensive schools similar to those in the United States. *A Nation at Risk* galvanized the United States into forming higher academic standards. Great Britain did the same with a national curriculum instituted in 1988.

The recommendations from the report *A Nation at Risk* were similar to those discussed by the Committee of Ten a century before. The report called for higher graduation requirements, including rigorous academic study for all students regardless of whether they were college bound. Curricular tracking, the report stated, had led to mediocrity. In response, the standards movement was born. By the end of the twentieth century, forty-nine of the fifty states had adopted academic standards based on the work of national organizations in the major subject areas. States began to hold students, teachers, and schools accountable to these standards through examinations. The reauthorization of the national Elementary and Secondary Education Act, known as the No Child Left Behind Act of 2001, reconfirmed this push for accountability by requiring states to develop annual testing programs for students in grades three through eight in reading and mathematics. School districts must be able to show that all students reach proficiency or will be subject to corrective procedures.

## Secondary Education Elsewhere

Many other countries have been faced with similar issues to the United States in terms of secondary education. Discussions about the purpose of secondary schools and the content and focus of the curriculum occur throughout the world. In some countries, vocational and technical programs run parallel to upper secondary education. For example, the Russian Federation and other former Soviet nations provide an eight-year general education program and then funnel qualified students to academic, vocational, or technical schools. At seventeen or eighteen, students are selected for higher education. Only 20 percent of graduates from secondary schools continue to college, whereas in the United States more than 60 percent of high school graduates go on to college.

Several European countries are also invested in secondary school curriculum reform with a stress on national standards. Throughout most of Europe, secondary education is compulsory up to the eighth grade. A large increase in secondary enrollment in the mid-twentieth century led schools to attempt to craft curricula that balanced cognitive, affective, and psychomotor needs of a diverse student population. The European nations also offered secondary options that include comprehensive high schools, parallel schools, and full- or part-time programs. Vocational education programs tend to lag behind general education programs in most countries.

The Republic of China also has a nine-year compulsory education program. The National Ministry of China controls the school curriculum, although there is diversity in secondary school options. Forty-five percent of Chinese secondary students attend the general secondary schools that are the gateway to higher education. Unlike the United States and many European countries, China does not have comprehensive secondary schools. There are vocational schools, teacher-training schools, and craftsmen schools, along with the general academic high schools. Examinations are used to categorize students into the appropriate educational track. After their junior year, secondary school students must pass an examination to go to the next level. The national higher education examination is given only once per year and is highly competitive.

## Trends in Secondary Education

Secondary school reform represents a vitally important topic. In the early twenty-first century, the major goal is helping all students reach high academic standards. This has yielded a number of innovative programs that attempt to balance students' personal and academic needs. Effective curricula include core learning in discrete academic subjects, increased foreign languages, interdisciplinary courses, and alternative assessment approaches. The foundational skills of reading and writing are garnering more attention at the secondary level in all content area classes.

Along with high standards, public schools must meet the needs of all students and provide an appropriate education for students with many diverse needs. Inclusion of students with disabilities requires schools to rethink the way classes are tracked and how services are provided to students who have difficulty in the school environment. Coteaching arrangements, which allow subject area specialists to work with trained special educators in the same classroom, constitute one approach to meeting diverse needs.

Some research indicates that smaller high schools are better settings for meeting adolescent needs and helping students reach their full academic potential. In an attempt to break down large comprehensive high schools, a number of options are being tried. Small school alternatives include schools-within-schools and parallel schools sharing the same physical space with distinct missions and programs. Some large high schools separate students by grade level into separate wings.

Flexible scheduling is used so that students and teachers can have enough time for a variety of instructional strategies and more personalized interactions. Block scheduling, one form of flexible scheduling, has increased class time. These larger blocks allow teachers to use a variety of teaching strategies and provide time for differentiating instruction to meet specific student needs. In addition to academic gains, evidence shows a decrease in behavior problems when block scheduling is used.

Crime and violence in secondary schools garner extensive media attention. Many schools are attempting to circumvent alienated youth through social and emotional intelligence programs, organizational structures, and increased surveillance.

Where schooling takes place is also changing. In some areas, state-supported academies for gifted students have been established. Charter schools attempt to meet the needs of a diverse group of students by forming a specific vision and plan outside of the ordinary. Technology may also play a role in the place and mode of secondary instruction as distance learning becomes more popular. Secondary schools continue to experiment with a variety of ways to meet the social, intellectual, personal, and vocational needs of students.

*See also:* CURRICULUM, SCHOOL; INTERNATIONAL BACCALAUREATE DIPLOMA; MIDDLE SCHOOLS; SCHOOL FACILITIES; SUMMER SCHOOL; YEAR-ROUND EDUCATION.

### BIBLIOGRAPHY

ANDERSON, JAMES D. 1988. *The Education of Blacks in the South, 1860–1935.* Chapel Hill: University of North Carolina Press.

ANGUS, DAVID L., and MIREL, JEFFREY E. 1988. *The Failed Promise of the American High School, 1890–1995.* New York: Teachers College Press.

FENSKE, NEIL R. 1997. *A History of American Public High Schools, 1890–1990: Through the Eyes of Principals.* Lewiston, NY: Edwin Mellen Press.

GEORGE, PAUL S.; McEWIN, C. KENNETH; and JENKINS, JOHN M. 2000. *The Exemplary High School.* Fort Worth, TX: Harcourt College.

KALLEN, DENIS. 1997. *Secondary Education in Europe: Problems and Prospects.* Strasbourg, Germany: Council of Europe Publishing.

MARSH, DAVID D., and CODDING, JUDY B. 1999. *The New American High School.* Thousand Oaks, CA: Corwin Press.

RAVITCH, DIANE. 2000. *Left Back: A Century of Failed School Reforms.* New York: Simon and Schuster.

URBAN, WAYNE J., and WAGONER, JENNINGS L. 2000. *American Education: A History,* 2nd edition. Boston: McGraw-Hill.

WATKINS, WILLIAM H.; LEWIS, JAMES H.; and CHOU, VICTORIA. 2001. *Race and Education: The Roles of History and Society in Educating African-American Students.* Boston: Allyn and Bacon.

### INTERNET RESOURCES

NATIONAL CENTER FOR EDUCATION STATISTICS. 2001. "Digest of Educational Statistics." <nces.ed.gov/pubs2001/digest>.

REYHNER, JON. 1989. "Changes in American Indian Education: A Historical Retrospective for Educators in the United States." ERIC Clearinghouse on Rural Education and Small Schools. <www.ed.gov/databases/ERIC_Digests/ed314228.html>.

SUSAN L. MINTZ

# CURRENT TRENDS

The term *secondary school* refers to the levels of schooling that follow elementary school and conclude with high school graduation. Typically, these include middle schools or junior high schools, the most common configuration of which is grades six through eight, and high schools, the most common configuration of which is grades nine through twelve. The 1983 release of the National Commission on Excellence in Education document *A Nation at Risk* focused national attention on the need for school reform. This reform movement took clearer shape in the late 1980s and early 1990s with the introduction, by the first Bush administration, of America 2000, a list of goals for U.S. education to be achieved by 2000. America 2000 was later refined and renamed Goals 2000 by the Clinton administration. So began the standards movement, which evolved throughout the 1990s and was ultimately codified by President George W. Bush and the 107th Congress in the No Child Left Behind Act of 2001. This act sharpened the teeth of the standards movement with accountability measures in the form of "high-stakes" standardized tests that all students must take at various points in their education. It is against this backdrop of the standards, assessment, and accountability movements that secondary schools craft their reform efforts.

## Standards

By the late 1990s nearly every state had developed standards for student achievement in most content areas. Greatest attention has been focused on "core" subjects, typically English/language arts, mathematics, science, and social studies, but "elective" courses—foreign languages, music, and visual arts, for instance—have standards as well that drive the curriculum and instruction in those subject areas. The quantity and quality of content standards vary widely from state to state, though many content-area professional organizations have developed their own

national standards to provide a benchmark for rigor and appropriateness of content-area standards. Many see the standards movement as the great contemporary revolution in U.S. education: No longer is middle level or high school credit granted solely on the basis of attendance. In theory, students would not be promoted or graduated until the standards were achieved.

## Assessment

To assess standards achievement, most states had begun to develop standardized tests by the start of the twenty-first century. These efforts were spurred by the No Child Left Behind Act, which requires states to test every student periodically in certain secondary content areas. Like the standards themselves, the quality of assessments varies widely from state to state, and the implementation of mandatory standardized assessments has introduced several dilemmas and controversies:

- How do schools accommodate students with special needs and English language learners in the administration and reporting of test scores? These students are not exempt from tests, and principals and teachers struggle to find the most equitable way to honor their needs while not violating the integrity of the testing process and the value of the final results.

- Do standardized tests truly address the content standards? Many standards speak to higher-order thinking skills, and educators disagree on the capacity of paper-and-pencil multiple-choice tests—where one answer and only one answer is correct—to adequately gauge problem solving and critical thinking.

- How will test scores be used? Ideally, tests will provide a wealth of data that informs the instructional program of individual students and schools. Questions remain about the capacity of the assessment instruments to provide these data and about the professional capacity of school personnel to interpret the data for instructional decision-making.

## Accountability

With standards and tests in place, most states have begun to implement or develop plans to implement accountability measures for performance on standardized tests. In most cases, students who do not achieve a required score on certain tests—usually in the core subjects of English/language arts, mathematics, science, and social studies, though some states include foreign language and other elective courses—will not be promoted to the next grade. The accountability issue casts a brighter light on the above questions and introduces other issues:

- Retention versus promotion. Educators do not agree on the placement of a student who does not achieve a required score on standardized tests. Advocates of both student retention and student "social" promotion speak with the backing of practice and research, and the argument remains unsettled in education circles.

- Teaching to the test. With principals' and teachers' jobs on the line, many educators perceive a temptation to focus on test-taking skills and test preparation rather than to teach the curriculum the mastery of which the test is intended to assess. This controversy speaks to the perception of the quality of the assessment instruments many states use. If the tests were genuinely aligned with the standards, many educators believe, teaching to the test would not be an issue.

Many states also report each school's aggregate scores and encourage low-performing schools to develop improvement plans. School accountability was codified in the No Child Left Behind Act, which calls for schools to demonstrate "adequate yearly progress," as determined by disaggregated test scores in mathematics, reading, and science. Schools that fail to show adequate yearly progress must take required steps to improve, or they will eventually be subject to corrective procedures.

National, state, and local education reforms have produced many positive changes, but in middle level and high schools, reform is still lagging. Although secondary student achievement has increased in some subjects for some groups, progress has been spottier and success more elusive than at the elementary level. The nation still has a way to go to ensure that all students are graduated from high school with the knowledge and skills to compete in a global economy—a challenge that will become even greater as enrollments swell.

Powerful recommendations for transforming secondary schools have come from the National Association of Secondary School Principals, in their 1996 groundbreaking report on the twenty-first-century U.S. high school, titled *Breaking Ranks: Changing an American Institution*; the Carnegie

Foundation in their 1989 and 2000 *Turning Points* reports on middle-level reform; and other groups. But the renaissance has not yet happened. The majority of high schools "seem to be caught in a time warp," noted U.S. Secretary of Education Richard Riley in his 1999 back-to-school address, which he devoted entirely to high school reform.

The problem is not a lack of understanding about what needs to be done. Across the country, secondary schools are demonstrating what a difference it makes when effective strategies are combined with strong commitment and adequate resources. But, regrettably, secondary school improvement has not been a high priority of the U.S. Congress or the states. Secondary schools are far less likely than elementary schools to receive funds under the Title I program, the largest source of federal K–12 aid. Seventy-seven percent of Title I funds go to the elementary level. When secondary schools are funded, they receive smaller Title I allocations per low-income pupil than elementary schools. Several members of Congress have introduced or endorsed legislation to meet the urgent educational and infrastructure needs of secondary schools.

States have raised student performance standards and are revising secondary curriculum and instruction. The public also supports school improvement: 71 percent of respondents to the 1999 Phi Delta Kappa/Gallup Poll felt that reforming the existing public school system, rather than finding an alternative system, should be the priority for education. Yet, the legislation dedicates disproportionate attention to elementary education at the expense of secondary education. Policymakers often choose to target resources on the early years to promote child development and address learning problems before they become too severe. But early intervention does not necessarily "inoculate" children from later difficulties, and many students need continuing services to cope with the more demanding middle and high school curricula and to avoid falling further behind.

### Trends That Inform a Reform Initiative for Secondary Schools

Trends in achievement, demographics, leadership, and funding are among the major reasons secondary schools require additional attention and support.

**Graduation rates.** To succeed in the workplace, further education, and adult life, all students should obtain at least a high school diploma and have a solid base of knowledge and skills. The percentage of young people completing high school rose during the 1970s and early 1980s and has hovered around 86 percent since then. But too many students—more than 380,000 students in grades ten through twelve—continue to drop out each year. As states raise their requirements for graduation, the challenge of keeping students in school and educating them to high levels will become more daunting.

**Achievement.** The average scores of secondary school students on the National Assessment of Educational Progress (NAEP)—the only national measure of trends in student achievement—increased in science and mathematics during the 1990s but showed mixed results or declines in reading and writing. To assess how much academic growth students made between elementary school and the end of middle school, the Educational Testing Service (ETS) analyzed average gains in students' NAEP scores between the fourth and eighth grades. By this measure, ETS concluded, academic growth from the mid-1970s to the late 1990s was flat in science, reading, and writing and went down in mathematics. Regardless of whether one views the NAEP data with optimism or concern, it seems clear that further improvements in student achievement are necessary.

**International comparisons.** In the 1999 Third International Mathematics and Science Study, which compared achievement in more than twenty nations, U.S. secondary students performed at lower levels for their grades than U.S. elementary students and were outperformed by students from a number of other countries. In science, U.S. fourth graders scored in the very top tier of nations and U.S. eighth graders achieved above the international average, but U.S. twelfth graders performed below the international average. In mathematics, U.S. fourth graders achieved above the international average, whereas U.S. eighth graders performed below average and U.S. twelfth graders scored among the lowest tier of nations.

**The baby boom echo.** Between 1999 and 2009, U.S. secondary school enrollments were expected to grow by 9 percent, or about 1.3 million students. Minority students and children from different language backgrounds will constitute a greater share of enrollments. The nation will need many more well-trained teachers to educate this diverse and growing population.

**Inadequate facilities.** A 1999 report by the Campaign to Rebuild America's Schools revealed that about 14 million children attend severely dilapidated public schools with leaky roofs, inferior heating, broken plumbing, and other threats to health and safety. Schools in many communities are overcrowded, a problem that will worsen with rising enrollments. The nation will need a projected 6,000 new schools to keep pace with a decade of enrollment growth; this will require substantial resources, as well as creative approaches for using existing facilities.

**Teacher needs.** Federal and state actions during the 1990s to strengthen teacher supply and quality are promising. But it will take more concerted and continuing efforts to fill the demand for well-prepared teachers in secondary schools, where shortages of teachers for particular disciplines are serious and where teachers must be prepared to teach advanced courses, integrate technology, and inspire young people to do their best. More than the supply of new teachers, research shows that teacher retention remains a critical issue in schools, as many teachers leave within their first five years on the job. The problem is exacerbated in secondary schools by the problem of out-of-field teaching—which is most pronounced in urban and rural areas. Again, with the passage of the No Child Left Behind Act, which calls for a "highly qualified teacher" in every classroom, there is a renewed focus on providing all teachers, new and veteran, the support and professional development they need to do their jobs well, as well as salaries commensurate with the value of their work.

**Leadership shortages.** Urban, suburban, and rural districts in every region of the country are experiencing shortages of qualified candidates for principals' jobs, yet this issue has met with near silence. While the responsibilities of the principalship have escalated considerably, there has been no comparable increase in incentives (not the least of which is a commensurate salary) to attract highly qualified candidates. Few school districts have structured recruitment or training programs to find the best candidates or groom their own, or to encourage minorities and women to enter leadership positions. Promising candidates are dissuaded from applying for principals' positions by such factors as mounting job stresses, inadequate school funding, and reluctance to give up their tenure as teachers.

**Secondary school programs.** Federal programs of special importance to secondary schools are significantly underfunded. These include: the Carl D. Perkins Vocational and Technical Education Act of 1998, which prepares students for the workforce by integrating academic and technical education; the Individuals with Disabilities Education Act Amendments of 1997, which requires school districts to provide a free and appropriate education to children with disabilities up through age twenty-one, but which covers only a small portion of the costs; and the GEAR UP program (Gaining Early Awareness and Readiness for Undergraduate Programs), which encourages disadvantaged middle school students to prepare for college.

## Elements of Secondary School Reform

Secondary schools throughout the country are achieving positive results through a combination of research-based strategies, committed teachers and leaders, and sufficient resources. National support and momentum could expand these successful efforts into many more schools. Research and practice have shown the following elements to be especially important: academic rigor, individualized attention, and leadership development.

**Academic rigor.** All secondary school students, whether headed for the workforce or postsecondary education, should be held to high expectations and take a challenging academic course of study. The rigor of the academic course work that a student takes in high school is a better predictor than test scores, grade point average, or class rank of whether that student will be graduated from college. This correlation is even stronger for African-American and Latino students and is very significant for low-income students. Taking courses such as algebra and geometry in middle school is an essential step, because it prepares students for the higher-level mathematics courses that correlate highly with college success. Unfortunately, some high schools do not offer advanced courses in mathematics, science, and foreign languages.

**Individualized attention.** To achieve in academic courses, many students will need varied instructional strategies, a different pace, extra help with reading, or intensive interventions, such as tutoring or after-school or summer programs. Students also do better when teachers and other adults take a close, personal interest in their academic progress, but these kinds of connections can be hard to forge in large secondary schools. Educators in some districts are developing individual plans for students, organizing big schools into smaller academic houses, or using other strategies to create more personalized learning environments.

**Leadership development.** Effective schools research has long recognized that well-trained, capable leaders are the individuals best situated to spur school-wide reform. Although the role of the teacher is essential, an excellent leader can bring about improvements on a wider scale and in a shorter time than is possible with teacher-by-teacher implementation. Yet the needs of principals have been somewhat neglected. Secondary school reform must include support for administrators' professional development as an ongoing, integral part of their responsibilities. In addition, current postsecondary education and training programs should be audited to determine how effectively they are training future principals.

## Making an Investment: A Secondary Schools Achievement Act

The United States must step up its investment in middle and high schools to ensure that all such schools are high achieving, housed in adequate facilities, and staffed and led by well-qualified educators. Toward this end, the National Association of Secondary School Principals (NASSP) has proposed federal legislation with the following two critical components.

First, the NASSP has advocated a "Secondary Schools Achievement Act" to help secondary schools implement or expand promising reforms. This act would provide federal support:

- To ensure that all middle schools offer algebra and some geometry instruction
- To increase attention to reading instruction from the early grades through high school
- To make Advanced Placement, international baccalaureate, foreign language, and other advanced courses available in all high schools and expand opportunities for students to take them
- For technology integration and training
- To create an individualized development plan for all students who are having difficulty in core subject areas
- For intensive and sustained professional development for each principal and teacher
- To improve and modernize facilities and infrastructure
- To improve evaluation systems so that states can measure the results of these new initiatives

All elements of this plan should be funded to ensure that all secondary school students truly meet high standards.

Second, the NASSP has contended that federal legislation to improve secondary schools must include a major national effort to train a sufficient cadre of qualified school principals for the next century. As a nation, the need for leadership development programs for business leaders has been recognized, and the nation has long supported a network of service academies to train outstanding young men and women for military leadership. Preparing the leaders who will guide the educational development of the nation's children should be just as high a priority. The United States needs to do all it can to develop strong, effective leaders who will give vision, focus, and direction to the nation's schools. Qualified leaders will set the course for meeting the challenges of the new century, and their needs must not be overlooked.

## Conclusion

Secondary school reform remains an unfulfilled promise with an incomplete agenda. If all schools are going to improve and if all children are going to reach high standards, the "missing link" must be filled in: National and state leaders must focus attention and support on the secondary level. It is time to stop neglecting the institutions that have played such a formative role in U.S. history and individual citizens' lives.

*See also:* ASSESSMENT, *subentry on* NATIONAL ASSESSMENT OF EDUCATIONAL PROGRESS; CURRICULUM, SCHOOL; EDUCATIONAL LEADERSHIP; MIDDLE SCHOOLS; NATIONAL ASSOCIATION OF SECONDARY SCHOOL PRINCIPALS; STANDARDS MOVEMENT IN AMERICAN EDUCATION; SCHOOL REFORM; SECONDARY EDUCATION, *subentry on* HISTORY OF.

### BIBLIOGRAPHY

ADELMAN, CLIFFORD. 1999. *Answers in the Tool Box: Academic Intensity, Attendance Patterns, and Bachelor's Degree Attainment.* Washington, DC: U.S. Department of Education.

EDUCATIONAL TESTING SERVICE. 1998. *Growth in School: Achievement Gains from the Fourth to the Eighth Grade.* Princeton, NJ: Educational Testing Service Policy Information Center.

JACKSON, ANTHONY, and DAVIS, GAYLE. 2000. *Turning Points 2000: Educating Adolescents in the Twenty-First Century.* New York: Teachers College Press.

KAUFMAN, PHILLIP; KLEIN, STEVE; and FRASE, MARY. 1999. "Dropout Rates in the United States, 1997." Washington, DC: U.S. Department of Education, Office of Educational Research and Improvement, National Center for Education Statistics.

NATIONAL ASSESSMENT OF EDUCATIONAL PROGRESS. 1998. *NAEP 1996 Trends in Academic Progress.* Washington, DC: National Assessment of Educational Progress.

NATIONAL ASSOCIATION OF SECONDARY SCHOOL PRINCIPALS. 1996. *Breaking Ranks: Changing an American Institution.* Reston, VA: National Association of Secondary School Principals.

NATIONAL ASSOCIATION OF SECONDARY SCHOOL PRINCIPALS and NATIONAL ASSOCIATION OF ELEMENTARY SCHOOL PRINCIPALS. 1998. "Is There a Shortage of Qualified Candidates for Openings in the Principalship? An Exploratory Study." Reston, VA: National Association of Secondary School Principals; Alexandria, VA: National Association of Elementary School Principals.

NATIONAL CENTER FOR EDUCATION STATISTICS. 1998. *Pursuing Excellence: A Study of U.S. Twelfth-Grade Mathematics and Science Achievement in International Context.* Washington, DC: U.S. Department of Education, Office of Educational Research and Improvement, National Center for Education Statistics.

NATIONAL COMMISSION ON EXCELLENCE IN EDUCATION. 1983. *A Nation at Risk: The Imperative for Educational Reform.* Washington, DC: U.S. Government Printing Office.

NATIONAL EDUCATION ASSOCIATION. 1999. *Modern Schools, Better Learning: The Campaign to Rebuild America's Schools.* Washington, DC: National Education Association.

ROSE, LOWELL C., and GALLUP, ALEC M. 1999. "The 31st Annual Phi Delta Kappa/Gallup Poll of the Public's Attitudes toward the Public Schools." *Phi Delta Kappan* 81:41–56.

U.S. DEPARTMENT OF EDUCATION. 1999. *The Baby Boom Echo: No End in Sight.* Washington, DC: U.S. Department of Education.

U.S. DEPARTMENT OF EDUCATION. 1999. *Targeting Schools: Study of Title I Allocations within School*

*Districts.* Washington, DC: U.S. Department of Education.

GERALD N. TIROZZI

## INTERNATIONAL ISSUES

Secondary education has increasingly become a central policy concern of developing countries, particularly among those that have made rapid progress in universalizing primary education and among those in which the demographic trend has shifted in favor of adolescents. The majority of countries in Latin America and the Caribbean, East Asia, and the Middle East, as well as some African countries, are grappling with the questions of how to provide skills and knowledge that enable adolescents to move to tertiary education and how to ensure a smooth transition to work for students whose education will end with secondary schooling.

Secondary education also addresses problems unique in human development. Without requisite education to guide their development, not only would young people be ill prepared for tertiary education or for the workplace, but they would also be susceptible to juvenile delinquency and teen pregnancy, thereby exacting a high social cost. Hence the challenge for secondary education is enormous. It represents an unfinished agenda that all countries will face as they develop.

### Secondary Education in Europe and the United States

In Europe, higher education, including secondary education, began with training in religion and philosophy. Its purpose was to prepare leaders—especially religious leaders—and its curriculum reflected this purpose. As time passed, general topics for more applied professions were added as part of secondary and higher education curricula, and the curriculum was broadened accordingly. As these general topics were gradually added to the curriculum, they remained philosophical or theoretical in orientation. They were not studied as systems of empirical data, and proofs and validation of knowledge were theoretical rather than experimental.

The earliest secondary schools were based on Renaissance models, with the role of Latin and Greek being paramount. In 1599 the Jesuits implemented the first clear and complete specification of subjects and content as part of the Counterreforma-

tion. This curriculum was called the *Ration Studiorum* (plan of studies), and it was initially implemented at the University of Salamanca in Spain. These early European secondary schools were almost exclusively for males, focusing on intellectual training in its narrow sense and preparation for leadership roles in all sectors of social and economic life.

The Enlightenment of the eighteenth century and the Industrial Revolution of the late eighteenth and early nineteenth centuries brought a new emphasis on scientific and technology studies and on empirical studies in general. Moreover, formal government involvement in secondary education grew, with concomitant involvement in curriculum. The first public high school in the United States was established in Boston in 1821.

From the nineteenth century to World War II, the curriculum at the secondary level began to encompass more subjects and became more specific, detailing the content to be covered and the time allotted for doing so. During this period, emphasis on philosophy, divinity, classical languages, and ancient history began to wane and was replaced with modern languages and literature, modern history, and scientific and technological subjects. At this time, most governments decided to educate a broader segment of their secondary-school-age population and included females for the first time. Secondary education became less elitist and more universal and its curriculum more inclusive, or diverse. Although the curriculum was dominated by the needs of the socially and economically privileged rather than by the needs of the masses, there began, nevertheless, an irreversible process of change that acknowledged a growing diversity of student backgrounds and postsecondary options.

### A Broader and More Universal Curriculum

In the two decades before World War II, the influence of John Dewey and the Progressive movement, though targeted at the primary education level, had a major influence on secondary-level education. The progressives helped increase curricular emphasis on the practicality and social usefulness of schooling and on "learning by doing." Moreover, separate lower and junior secondary schools were established to cater to the growing number of students entering the secondary level.

The trend to broaden the curriculum began earliest and went farthest in the United States. In the twentieth century, it was responsible for introducing many new practical and vocational subjects. In the second half of the century, courses in driver education, family living, consumer economics, and mathematics for everyday life appeared for the first time. As students with a greater range of abilities, interests, and motivation entered the secondary level, "streaming" and "homogeneous grouping" became more prevalent. Academic secondary schools became more comprehensive and diversified. Courses and even course sequences in such vocational areas as graphic design, hair care and styling, automotive repair, carpentry and machine shop, and home economics began to appear. The launching of *Sputnik* by the Soviet Union in 1957 was a powerful impetus behind the increase in the amount of scientific topics taught in the Western secondary curriculum, the rigor with which they were taught, and the care taken in their organization and presentation.

In general, the trend in the post–World War II period has been to divide students into streams, to make a single comprehensive secondary school serve a wider variety of interests and abilities, to provide access to a wide range of higher education through alternative curricula, and to broaden the secondary curriculum to include more subjects. Great Britain is a partial exception to this trend, as students tend to study only three subjects for their A-level examinations.

## Secondary Education in Developing Countries

Colonial powers in the eighteenth, nineteenth, and early twentieth centuries educated only a very small portion of colonized peoples, and they educated this portion only at a basic level. In general, their interest was to produce complacent workers. Little education was necessary for this purpose; indeed, education could be seen as antithetical to it. Colonial policy for those few individuals educated beyond the primary school tended to emphasize the production of middle-level clerical and administrative personnel. Hence, the curriculum stressed correct language, arithmetic and accounting abilities, and an adequate fund of general knowledge—as distinct from scientific, aesthetic, or vocational subjects. Great importance was placed on the authority of the teacher and of the spoken and written word.

The independence of colonial countries in the two decades after World War II brought a near universal recognition of the importance of education at all levels for a greatly increased proportion of local populations. After independence, former colonial countries kept old colonial curriculums for a surprisingly long time—indeed, some have been maintained intact into the early twenty-first century.

## Some Problems of Definition

The secondary subsector presents some problems of definition in the sense that it falls between primary and tertiary levels and there is no universal agreement as to where primary ends and tertiary begins. The duration of (or the number of grades covered in) secondary education varies from three years in El Salvador to eight years in such countries as Yugoslavia and Kuwait. Similarly, when secondary education begins is highly variable (ranging from grade five to grade nine). The usual duration, however, is grades seven to twelve.

Most countries (the Latin American and Caribbean region is an exception) divide the secondary level of education into a first or lower segment and a second or higher segment. These may be denoted by different names, with a particularly varied set of names for the lower segment: middle, intermediate, lower secondary, junior high, upper elementary, and so on. In different countries these labels may encompass different grades, student ages, curriculum, and objectives, and may be related to the educational levels above and below them in a variety of ways. The higher or upper secondary level is usually labeled simply in these terms or may be called senior high school in areas influenced by American nomenclature. It is also sometimes referred to as the pre-university level.

There is a worldwide trend to establish the concept of *basic education,* which is understood to mean a minimum standard of schooling for everyone in a given society. This is frequently done by adding to the primary grades the first part of the secondary cycle (typically called the lower or junior secondary cycle). The combination of primary and lower secondary grades then becomes "basic education," which is usually administered separately from secondary education.

An additional complexity of the secondary subsector is the wide range of types of educational institutions falling under this heading. Attempts to define types by organization, curricular emphasis, or outcome objectives almost always reveal substantial overlap among categories. Exceptions to any classification, including this one, are plentiful. The most common classification includes three overlapping types: (1) general/academic schools, (2) vocational and technical schools, and (3) diversified or comprehensive schools, which are multipurpose institutions that try to combine under one roof the objectives of an academic course of study and one or more vocational fields.

It is clear that these three broad categories of secondary schools are arranged along a continuum of specialization in their dominant instructional objectives. At one end the schools are single-purpose institutions with an intensely academic curriculum. At the other end they are similarly specialized but with a vocational/technical curriculum. Secondary schools lying in the middle of the continuum are multipurpose institutions combining elements of both ends of the spectrum into their instructional program.

Stated outcomes and long-term social objectives of the different types of secondary schools often overlap. Almost all statements of the goals or objectives of all types of secondary education include items such as preparing students for the world of work and making students smoothly functioning members of society.

## Differentiating National Curricula as a Response to Increased Coverage

While a traditional academic curriculum may be appropriate for upper level secondary education in a developing country with a relatively low upper secondary school enrollment ratio (for example, 20%), the path toward very much higher enrollment ratios (in excess of 50%) will require much greater curriculum diversity to meet the differing educational needs of different groups. It may well be that vocational education does not have a significant role here; but if not vocational schooling, then what other forms of secondary schooling (either existing or to be developed) would be appropriate? Indeed, for many lower secondary education completers, nonschooling programs, such as apprenticeship, may be more appropriate than continued secondary schooling at the upper level.

The key ideas in secondary education practice can be divided into three categories: organization and subject content, vocationalization, and control. These categories overlap and several ideas could be placed logically in more than one category. Developing countries and development agency projects have dealt with most of these ideas at one time or another.

**Organization and subject content.** A single nationally set curriculum consistently delivered is a successful educational procedure at the primary level. Where flexibility and student choice are present there is widespread consensus that this should begin after primary school, although whether or not flexibility should begin in lower secondary, where it exists, is still debated. The decision as to whether a curriculum should prepare specialist or generalist knowledge and skills is often decided on the basis of whether a particular level is seen as preparatory or terminal. The trend appears to be one in which the mandated curriculum of the lower secondary grades, or their equivalent by whatever name, is a linear extrapolation of primary school.

Primary schools are almost always general-purpose institutions with considerable social and political consensus surrounding their mission, which is, simply put, to prepare all children for competent adulthood by giving them basic literacy and numeracy skills and, in many countries, an explicit set of moral values. The situation at the secondary level is vastly more complex. Nevertheless, a growing number of countries, often for political and economic reasons rather than pedagogical, put together in a single, all-purpose school, students from different backgrounds, with different needs, abilities, and interests. The question most often asked by policymakers is: Do the financial economies and the social integration hoped for by this "comprehensive" arrangement outweigh the problems created by attempting to handle such diversity in a single place?

In the majority of poor countries there appears to exist growing recognition that science education is an important element in the national primary and secondary curricula. This is due to both the now commonly recognized relationship between quality research and development in science and technology and stable economic growth, and also the need to begin to prepare students more effectively for future scientific and technological employment. Agriculture, health, nutrition, population control, environmental management, and industrial development are a few of the areas that benefit directly from a wider understanding of science and technology.

Science education is therefore in a position of privilege and peril. It is privileged because decision makers recognize the relationship between good science and economic development. In many developing countries this recognition has resulted in additional support for science education. Moreover, in the majority of poor countries there appears to exist growing recognition that science education is an important element in the national secondary curriculum. "Science for all" is a frequently voiced rallying cry. At the same time, science education is imperiled by: (1) unrealistic expectations for quick results, (2) improper and inadequate teacher training, (3) a lifeless, exam-driven curriculum, and (4) expensive and outdated reliance on traditional classroom methods and laboratory equipment.

**Vocationalization of the secondary curriculum.** The issue of education for all versus elite preparation is more than simply a question of coverage. Most countries have based their education curricula on the needs of their elites rather than on the needs of their masses. Yet as coverage expands, the questions of vocational relevance and quality invariably arise. This is so because the single-purpose elite preparation that characterized the curriculum when enrollments were small is not suitable for the needs of the diverse majority.

The debate over the desired degree of vocationalization of the school curriculum is shifting grounds as the nature of the market for schooled labor changes. This debate is worldwide and intense. At the heart of the new debate is a redefinition of the school courses that are vocationally relevant. Science, mathematics, and English, all traditionally viewed as academic in the sense of college preparatory, are increasingly demanded for their vocational relevance. The case for a "new vocational curriculum" can be stated in these terms. At the close of World War II, people in industrialized countries expected to have a single career throughout their productive lifetime. Moreover, skills useful at the start of their careers were expected to remain so throughout their job tenure with only minimal retraining and updating required. Under these conditions specific job-skills training was valued for its immediate and long-term relevance to occupational requirements. But the workplace changed. Jobs were lost from heavy industry and agriculture to service and high-technology sectors. Even the remaining agriculture, equipment repair, and manufacturing jobs began to require higher levels of communication (reading and writing) and mathematics abilities. Market changes have seen massive redeployment of workers across sectors. Lifetime job security in a single sector gave way to needs for a flexibly trained and rapidly redeployable labor force, and with these changes came a redefinition of certain fundamental education requirements. Suddenly the general curriculum was vocationally relevant for a much larger share of the school-age population, including those not college bound.

**Control.** Who should control the structure and content of curriculum? Politicians? University professors? Teachers? Parent associations? When teachers are in control, the curriculum tends to emphasize individual needs and classroom realities. Teacher control can imply highly trained teachers, a condition difficult to meet in developing countries. When university professors are in control, the latest knowledge may be included but it is often academic—meaning abstract and overloaded with content—which is usually too difficult for the students at the grade level indicated. When politicians are in control, the needs of nationalism and social and economic development may be served, but factors relevant to successful learning may be ignored.

*See also:* CURRICULUM, INTERNATIONAL; INTERNATIONAL ASSESSMENTS; VOCATIONAL AND TECHNICAL EDUCATION, *subentry on* INTERNATIONAL CONTEXT.

### BIBLIOGRAPHY

BRAY, MARK. 1985. "High School Selection in Less Developed Countries and the Quest for Equity: Conflicting Objectives and Opposing Pressures." *Comparative Education Review* 29:216–231.

CAILLODS, FRANÇOISE; GOTTELMANN-DURET, GARIELE; and LEWIN, KEITH. 1997. *Science Education and Development: Planning and Policy Issues at Secondary Level.* Paris: United Nations Educational, Scientific and Cultural Organization.

FULLER, BRUCE, and HOLSINGER, DONALD B. 1993. "Secondary Education in Developing Countries: Issues Review." Washington, DC: World Bank, Education and Social Policy Department.

HOLSINGER, DONALD B. 2000. *Positioning Secondary-School Education in Developing Countries: Expansion and Curriculum.* Paris: International Institute for Educational Planning.

PSACHAROPOULOS, GEORGE, and LOXLEY, WILLIAM. 1985. *Diversified Secondary Education and Development.* Baltimore: Johns Hopkins University Press.

DONALD B. HOLSINGER

# SEGREGATION, LEGAL ASPECTS

Segregation in education is a systemic practice or policy of establishing and maintaining racially separate educational facilities, services, and activities. Historically, racial segregation in education includes assigning African-American and white students to separate school facilities because of race, and assigning only African-American teachers, staff, and administrators to schools established for African-American students while assigning only white teachers, staff, and administrators to schools established for white students. Racial segregation also involves the use of separate buses for African-American and white students and racially separate extracurricular activities, such as athletic programs. Segregation in education also includes widespread discrimination in the educational process against groups other than African Americans, such as Asian Americans, Native Americans, and Hispanics. The practice of segregation in education involves all levels of the educational process: elementary, secondary, undergraduate, graduate, and professional schools.

The American legal system has played a major role in the creation, maintenance, and elimination of segregation in public education. In the American legal system the courts generally are responsible for the interpretation of laws, and major court decisions constitute a framework of reference for discussion of the legal aspects of segregation in education. There are fifty-one legal systems in the United States: one for each of the fifty states and a separate federal legal system created by the Constitution of the United States. Although each state legal system has some responsibility for resolving legal issues about segregation in education, it is the federal legal system, and particularly the Supreme Court of the United States, that has the major role in deciding legal issues involving segregation in public education.

Any meaningful discussion of the legal aspects of segregation in education inevitably centers on the national commitment to equality that has been read into the Constitution of the United States. America did not formally commit itself to equality until after the Civil War when it abolished slavery in the Thirteenth Amendment (1865), provided individuals equal protection of the law in the Fourteenth Amendment (1868), and guaranteed individuals the right to vote in the Fifteenth Amendment (1870). An important provision of the Constitution that embraces the national commitment to equality is the Fourteenth Amendment which provides that "[n]o State shall . . . deny any persons within its jurisdiction the equal protection of the laws." A primary reason for the national commitment to equality is to eliminate racial discrimination against African-Americans in all aspects of governmental (or public) activities. Congress has a role in implementing the equality policy and carries out this role when it enacts laws, including laws to eliminate segregation in education. In the final analysis the federal courts, and particularly the Supreme Court, have final authority to interpret the meaning of equality. Over time the federal courts have adopted different meanings of equality.

## History

No provision in the Constitution of the United States requires governments to provide an education for any person. Rather the equal protection clause of the Fourteenth Amendment requires only that if a state provides public education it must make it available to all of its individuals without regards to race. All states provide a system of public education at all levels: elementary, secondary, and college-level. Racial segregation in education in the United States has its genesis in the institution of slavery. The dominant social philosophy during slavery was that African Americans were inferior to whites. The Supreme Court legalized slavery's social philosophy in 1857 in *Dred Scott v. Sanford.* The Court held, in *Dred Scott,* that even emancipated African Americans who had been free for many years were to be "regarded as beings of an inferior order" who were "altogether unfit to associate with the white race," and were "so far inferior that they [had] no rights which the white man was bound to respect." Laws prohibited education of slaves prior to the abolition of slavery in slave-holding states.

In some nonslave-holding states, public schools were desegregated when they first appeared in the United States, but eventually some African-American parents took steps to set up privately funded separate schools for their children because of their dissatisfaction with the quality of education their children received in racially integrated schools. Later, some of these African-Americans students sought admission to publicly funded schools, but public school committees instead set up racially separate schools for them.

As early as 1849 a Massachusetts state court, in *Roberts v. City of Boston,* upheld the segregation of African-American and white students in public schools. The plaintiff in *Roberts* was a five-year-old African-American student who challenged the Boston, Massachusetts, school committee's refusal to admit her to an all-white primary school. Rejecting the plaintiff's argument that segregation of students in public schools because of race violated the state's constitutional mandate of equality, the court held that the school committee's decision represented a reasonable and nondiscriminatory exercise of its power. The court held also that if racial segregation generated feelings of prejudice in black students, then law probably could not change those feelings. Roberts was one of the first cases to adopt the separate-but-equal theory of equality. The separate-but-equal theory of equality, like the *Dred Scott* philosophy, was motivated by racism; thus it did not make it lawful for school boards to establish racially segregated schools. The Supreme Court relied on the *Roberts* case in its 1986 decision in *Plessy v. Ferguson* to hold that racial segregation of African Americans and whites was lawful and therefore did not violate the equality policy in the federal constitution. A few state courts rejected the *Roberts* case's separate-but-equal doctrine by holding that racially segregated schools violate the rights of African-American students to equality.

Almost immediately after the Civil War and the adoption of the Thirteenth Amendment, southern states enacted laws called "black codes." These codes were enacted to try to retain as much as possible the *Dred Scott* philosophy by codifying almost every aspect of the lives of former slaves, including circumstances under which they could be educated. Legally mandated racial segregation was not confined to public schools, nor was it confined to the south. Many border and northern states maintained some form of segregation, including public schools, until the end of World War II.

## From *Plessy* to *Brown*

In *Plessy v. Ferguson,* the Supreme Court held that a Louisiana law requiring racial segregation of passengers in railway coaches was not prohibited by the equal protection clause of the Fourteenth Amendment. The Louisiana law required "separate railway carriages for the white and colored races" on all passenger railways within Louisiana. In upholding the Louisiana law, the Court legally sanctioned the sepa-

rate-but-equal theory of equality. The separate-but-equal doctrine holds that the equality does not require racial integration if a state provides separate accommodations or services for blacks that are equal to those provided to whites. The *Roberts* decision, rather than its subsequent repeal by the Massachusetts legislature, was a major legal precedent on which the Supreme Court relied in its *Plessy* decision. In *Cumming v. Richmond Board of Education,* the Court suggested that the constitutionality of segregation in the field of education had not yet been decided. But in *Gong Lum v. Rice,* decided in 1927, the Court relied upon both the *Plessy* and *Roberts* cases to reject a claim by a Chinese-American student who claimed that she had been denied equal protection because she had been assigned to a public school for African-American students. Despite the ambivalence in the Supreme Court cases on whether the *Plessy* separate-but-equal theory of equality applied to public education, the courts, including the Supreme Court, accepted the view that the *Plessy* case stated a legal rule that applied equally to public education (*Briggs v. Elliot*).

The separate-but-equal theory of equality provided the legal foundations for racial segregation in education (and all other state supported activities) until the Supreme Court decided the landmark case of *Brown v. Board of Education* (*Brown I*) in 1954. *Brown I* was the result of a litigation strategy that relied upon a series of test cases to try to convince the Supreme Court to reject the separate-but-equal theory of equality. In a series of "equalization" cases before *Brown I,* major civil rights organizations claimed that state-funded graduate and professional schools for African Americans, although racially "separate," did not provide African-American students an education opportunity "equal" to educational opportunities available to white students in schools reserved for whites. Thurgood Marshall, who later became the first African-American justice of the Supreme Court, played a major role in the legal campaign to overturn the separate-but-equal doctrine. *Brown I* involved legal challenges to segregated elementary and secondary public schools in Kansas, South Carolina, Delaware, Maryland, and the District of Columbia.

The Supreme Court rejected the separate-but-equal doctrine in *Brown I.* The legal issue in *Brown I* was whether state-supported racial segregation in public elementary and secondary schools was lawful under the equal protection clause of the federal constitution even though the physical facilities and other tangible factors may be equal. In specifically addressing this issue, the Court held that "[i]n the field of public education the doctrine of 'separate but equal' has no place" because "[s]eparate educational facilities are inherently unequal." The Court, in *Brown I,* left undecided the issue of what states had to do to eliminate racially segregated schools, but it addressed that issue about year later in *Brown II.* In *Brown II,* the Court ordered lower federal courts to require school authorities to "make a prompt and reasonable start toward full compliance" with *Brown I,* and to admit students to public schools on a "racially nondiscriminatory basis with all deliberate speed."

### From *Brown* to *Freeman*

The southern states engaged in massive resistance to the *Brown* decisions. "Massive resistance" is a term that was coined in the era after *Brown* to describe southern states' efforts to evade and avoid the legal mandate of *Brown I.* Massive resistance took many forms. Some southern communities, for example, closed their schools rather than allow African-American and white students to attend the same schools. President Dwight D. Eisenhower had to use the National Guard to help integrate white schools in Arkansas. Other school districts adopted "pupil placement" plans, "minority to majority" transfer plans, or "freedom of choice" schemes, all of which were adopted to avoid compliance with *Brown I;* and most of these tactics succeeded in maintaining racially segregated state-supported school systems for more than a decade. The various massive resistance schemes required African-Americans parents and students to initiate legal action against many school districts in an effort to compel compliance with *Brown I.*

The massive resistance to *Brown I* produced minimal desegregation of schools by the time the Court decided *Green v. School Board of New Kent County* in 1968. In *Green,* the Court held, for the first time, that *Brown I* imposed an affirmative obligation on school districts to convert segregated, dual-school school systems to unitary school systems in which racial discrimination would be eliminated "root and branch." A unitary school system is one that has fully complied with the mandate of *Brown I. Green* also enunciated at least six criteria that lower federal courts should consider in determining whether a school system has achieved a unitary sta-

tus. Those criteria focus on student assignments, faculty assignments, staff assignments, transportation (busing), extracurricular activities, and school facilities. A year later, the Court, in *Alexander v. Holmes County Board of Education,* held that the *Brown II* "'deliberate speed' for desegregation is no longer constitutionally permissible." The federal courts have developed a substantial body of case law on remedies to determine whether dual school systems are progressing toward a unitary, nonsegregated system. These remedies include busing, magnet schools, and the location of new schools in geographical areas to maximize racial integration.

In school desegregation litigation, the Supreme Court has made an important distinction between de jure and de facto racial discrimination. De jure segregation is intentional racial discrimination that is affirmatively required by state law, custom, or usage. De facto segregation is racial separateness that occurs without the sanction of law. *Brown I* generally is inapplicable to de facto segregation. There has been no effort by the Supreme Court to address the constitutionality of de facto segregation since 1973 when the Supreme Court refused in *Keyes v. School District No. 1* to abandon the distinction between de jure and de facto segregation.

During the years following World War II, there developed an exodus of white families who relocated to suburbia. This exodus has been described as "white flight." In the school desegregation cases, white flight is the mass migration of whites from urban communities to suburban communities to avoid enrolling their children in racially integrated inner-city schools. One of the results of white flight has been that African Americans and other persons of color have largely populated many inner cities. As a result, there are many school districts throughout the United States with a significant number of schools with no or very little racial integration.

Many school districts have been under the supervision of federal courts since 1954 when the Court decided *Brown I.* The Supreme Court has held that federal supervision of school desegregation programs was intended to be a temporary measure, and not to operate in perpetuity. Local control of education comes from the Constitution. The power to control education has not been delegated to the federal government; rather it is the responsibility of the various states. In several cases, the Supreme Court has provided illustrations of circumstances under which school boards should be released from federal courts supervision of desegregation orders. In *Board of Education of Oklahoma City Public Schools v. Dowel,* the Court held that a formerly segregated school districts may be released from court-ordered busing as long as all "practicable" steps to eliminate the vestiges of past de jure segregation have been taken. In *Freeman v. Pits,* the Court made clear that racial isolation of schools brought on by white flight that was not the fault of school districts is not subject to the mandate of *Brown I* and its progeny. In *Freeman,* the Court held that federal courts are justified in relinquishing supervision over school districts subject to desegregation in piecemeal fashion before full compliance with the *Green* criteria has been achieved. And in *Missouri v. Jenkins,* the Court held that a lower federal district court funding order, which relied upon creating and maintaining "desegregative attractiveness" in order to deal with white flight, was outside of the authority of the federal courts under *Brown I.*

### Segregation in Higher Education

The Supreme Court has held that the rule it announced in *Brown I* is applicable to segregation in higher education, but made a distinction between the obligation of states to remedy segregation in higher education and elementary and secondary education. In *United States v. Fordice,* the Court addressed the issue whether, under *Brown I,* states that have engaged in de jure discrimination in higher education are obligated to take steps beyond adopting race-neutral admission policies to desegregate these educational institutions. In response to this question, the Court held that states have an affirmative legal obligation to remedy the remnants of prior de jure segregation. The standard the Court adopted for higher education was that states have an obligation to eliminate all policies and practices that continue to have a discriminatory effect and that are traceable to the prior de jure system.

### Sex-Based Segregated Schools

*United States v. Virginia* is an important Supreme Court case involving sex discrimination in higher education. The case involved the Virginia Military Institute (VMI), an educational institution established by Virginia. VMI excluded females because of their gender. The Court held that the equal protection clause of the Fourteenth amendment applies to sex segregation, but applied a different standard than is applicable to race discrimination. The legal rule for determining the legality of publicly supported separate schools based on gender is a more differential standard than the legal rule that is applied to racially segregated schools. Even under the differential standard used in sex discrimination cases, the Supreme Court held that VMI's policy of excluding women because of their gender was unconstitutional under the equal protection clause.

*See also:* AFFIRMATIVE ACTION COMPLIANCE IN HIGHER EDUCATION; RACE, ETHNICITY, AND CULTURE, *subentries on* CULTURAL EXPECTATIONS AND STUDENT LEARNING, RACIAL AND ETHNIC MINORITY STUDENTS IN HIGHER EDUCATION; SINGLE-SEX INSTITUTIONS; SUPREME COURT OF THE UNITED STATES AND EDUCATION.

### BIBLIOGRAPHY

BROWN, S. CHRISTOPHER, II. 1999. *The Quest to Define Collegiate Desegregation.* Westport, CT: Bergin and Garvey.

FAIRFAX, LISA. 1999. "The Silent Resurrection of Plessy: The Supreme Court's Acquiescence in the Resegregation of America's Schools." *Temple Political and Civil Rights Law Review* 9:1–57.

KLUGER, RICHARD. 1976. *Simple Justice: The History of* Brown v. Board of Education *and Black America's Struggle for Equality.* New York: Knopf.

WARE, LELAND B. 2001. "Setting the Stage for Brown: The Development and Implementation of the NAACP's School Desegregation Campaign, 1930–1950." *Mercer Law Review* 52:631–673.

WILLIAMS, JUAN. 1987. *Eyes on the Prize: America's Civil Rights Years: 1954–1965.* New York: Viking.

ROBERT BELTON

# SELF-EFFICACY AND SELF-CONCEPT

*See:* AFFECT AND EMOTIONAL DEVELOPMENT.

# SERVICE LEARNING

SCHOOL
  Richard J. Kraft
HIGHER EDUCATION
  Janet Eyler

# SCHOOL

While the origins of the service-learning movement can be found in volunteerism, community service, citizenship training, character education, youth service, and experiential learning, it is safe to say that the words *service learning* have come into common usage only since the 1980s in the United States, and even later internationally. The Commission on National and Community Service (1993) provides perhaps the most widely accepted definition, and includes the following components.

- the need for active participation
- thoughtful organization
- the meeting of actual community needs
- collaboration between school and community
- integration with the students' academic curriculum
- structured time for reflection
- opportunities to use newly acquired skills in real-life situations
- extension of learning beyond the classroom
- the fostering a sense of caring for others

The typology in Table 1 is based on Robert Sigmon's work that differentiates the types of service learning based on the emphasis given the service or learning in a given program. Although experts in the movement would like to limit it to the fourth type, in which service and learning are given equal weight, the reality varies greatly in schools and colleges implementing programs.

## Involvement of Students

The most comprehensive attempt at discovering the extent of community service and service-learning programs in the schools was conducted by the National Center for Education Statistics (NCES) of the U.S. Department of Education (1999). According to that survey, more than 64 percent of all public schools and 83 percent of all public high schools organized some form of community service for their students. The percentage of high schools involved in some form of community service rose from 27 percent in 1984 to 83 percent in 1999. Nearly a third of the schools and half of the public high schools provide service-learning programs in which service is linked to the curriculum. This translates into 14,063,000 students involved in community service with 57 percent of those students involved in some

**TABLE 1**

| Emphases of service-learning programs | |
| --- | --- |
| service-LEARNING | Learning goals primary; service outcomes secondary |
| SERVICE-learning | Service outcomes primary; learning goals secondary |
| service learning | Service and learning goals separate |
| SERVICE-LEARNING | Service and learning goals of equal weight; each enhances the other for all participants |

SOURCE: Based on Sigmon, Robert. 1996. "The Problem of Definition in Service-Learning." In *The Journey to Service-Learning,* ed. Robert Sigmon et al. Washington, DC: Council of Independent Colleges.

form of service learning. Due in large part to the influence of the national Campus Compact, an association of college presidents, and the student led Campus Outreach Opportunity League (COOL), community service and service learning can now be found on a large majority of college campuses throughout the United States, involving thousands of classes in all disciplines, and hundreds of thousands of postsecondary students.

The NCES survey found that students in grades eleven and twelve were more likely to be involved in some type of community service or service learning than younger students, girls more likely than boys, and white students more likely than black or Hispanic students. The survey also found that community service is positively correlated to parents' highest level of education and to ethnicity (white), but that these factors were inversely correlated to service learning. It appears from the data that schools with larger numbers of black and Hispanic young people are more likely to require and arrange service-learning programs than is true for schools that are predominantly white. Given the historical commitments of many religious groups to volunteerism and service, it is not surprising that the survey found that 72 percent of students in private schools report participation in community service, compared to 50 percent in public schools.

## As a Requirement for Graduation

The issue of requiring community service for graduation or service learning as a course requirement is a contentious one that has led to more than one lawsuit in the United States. Proponents claim that service learning is a pedagogical tool to enhance student learning, while opponents claim it is a form of "mandatory volunteerism." Given the separation of the schools from their communities and the traditional academic nature of most schooling, it is likely that this will continue to be an issue in the future. There appears, however, to be strong community support for service learning. A Roper Starch survey (2000) found that while 61 percent of Americans were unfamiliar with the term *service learning*, over 90 percent endorse the concept when it is explained to them. Americans see it is a teaching strategy that will help students transform their academic learning into success after graduation.

## Effect on Student Participants

Most research on the effects of service-learning programs at both the K–12 and higher education levels has only been conducted in the 1990s, and thus there are few, if any, long-term follow up studies. Janet Eyler, Dwight Giles, and Charlene Gray state that the effects of service learning on students can be divided into personal, social, learning outcomes, and career development. On a personal level it appears to have a positive effect on students' personal efficacy, personal identity, spiritual growth, moral development, interpersonal development, the ability to work well with others, leadership, and communication skills. Lillian Stephens found that students involved in service-learning programs appear to have reduced levels of alienation and behavioral problems, while Allan Melchior found them less likely to engage in behaviors that lead to pregnancy or arrest. Melchior and other researchers have also found a greater acceptance of cultural diversity by service-learning students.

Learning outcomes research indicates that service-learning has a positive impact on students' academic learning, improves their ability to apply what they have learned in the "real world," may positively affect academic learning as measured by grades or GPA, and impacts such academic outcomes as demonstrated complexity of understanding, problem analysis, critical thinking, and cognitive development. Daniel Weiler and colleagues found that students in more than half of the high quality service-learning schools studied showed moderate to strong positive gains on student achievement tests in language arts or reading, engagement in school, sense of accomplishment, and homework completion. Other researchers have found an association of service learning with higher scores on state basic skills tests and with higher grades. According to Frank

O'Bannon school attendance appears to be positively correlated with schools sponsoring service-learning programs.

Service-learning programs have recently been linked to the School-to-Work/Career programs in many districts and schools. Career and communication skills, career exploration awareness, and knowledge were increased through service-learning programs, according to Thomas Berkas. This connection to the world of work has been an important factor in increasing support for the movement on the part of legislators, school board members, the business community, and the non-profit sector.

There are literally thousands of adaptations across the curriculum of service learning as practiced in the schools and colleges of the United States. The most widely used service-learning activity is peer and cross-age tutoring, with positive effects found on both the tutor and the tutee. Children, young people, and college students also find environmentally related activities in hundreds of schools and colleges, with water monitoring programs in streams, rivers, and lakes by biology and chemistry classes, tree-planting programs for biology and science classes, and thousands of recycling programs. Many language programs have students teaching English in exchange for learning Spanish or another language from native speakers. Students in social studies and the social sciences explore issues of race, culture, and class through joint projects with persons of other cultural groups and through working at homeless shelters and soup kitchens. Medical, dental, business, and law students conduct free clinics for persons unable to afford assistance, while engineering students design technological assistance for persons with disabilities. The adaptations of service learning are only limited by the creativity of its practitioners, and there are numerous books available on its theory, practice, and evaluation.

## The Voice of the Client

An important critique of the movement is made by those who believe that it is too focused on doing things to people, rather than with them, that it emphasizes the value and benefit to the service provider, while all too often ignoring those served, and that it thus perpetuates societal injustices. Given the growing body of research on the positive effects of service learning on the provider and near complete lack of research on positive or negative effects on "clients," such a critique is warranted. The voices of recipients are too often missing in the current service-learning literature. Service and giving must go beyond meeting the short-term needs of recipients, and move towards the removal of societal barriers that keep too many on the margins of American society. As the movement matures and goes beyond its "evangelistic" phase, it is rapidly deepening its intellectual and philosophical roots, and looking more into root causes of societal inequalities and injustice. It is also moving beyond the words service provider and service recipient or client and into the use of term partners in service.

## Future Directions

Service learning appears to have the potential to be an important contributor to bringing about a more just and caring society. It has also been called the "Trojan Horse" of school reform, and has become a mechanism which many schools and colleges are using to bring the school and community closer together and to provide a more active learning environment for students. Government and business are increasingly looking to service-learning as a promising mechanism for preparing children and young people for citizenship and the world of work.

*See also:* COMMUNITY EDUCATION; ELEMENTARY EDUCATION, *subentry on* CURRENT TRENDS; EXPERIENTIAL EDUCATION; SECONDARY EDUCATION, *subentry on* CURRENT TRENDS; VOLUNTEER WORK.

### BIBLIOGRAPHY

BERKAS, THOMAS. 1997. *Strategic Review of the W. K. Kellogg Foundation's Service-Learning Projects, 1990–1996.* Battle Creek, MI: Kellogg Foundation.

COMMISSION ON NATIONAL AND COMMUNITY SERVICE. 1993. *What Can You Do for Your Country.* Washington, DC: Government Printing Office.

EYLER, JANET; GILES, DWIGHT; and GRAY, CHARLENE. 1999. *At a Glance: What We Know about the Effects of Service-Learning on Students, Faculty, Institutions and Community, 1993–1999.* Nashville, TN: Vanderbilt University.

KRAFT, RICHARD. 1996. "Service Learning: An Introduction to Its Theory, Practice, and Effects." *Education and Urban Society* 28(2):131–159.

MELCHIOR, ALLAN. 1999. *Summary Report: National Evaluation of Learn and Serve America.* Waltham, MA: Center for Human Resources, Brandeis University.

O'BANNON, FRANK. 1999. "Service-Learning Benefits Our Schools." *State Education Leader* 17:3.

ROPER STARCH WORLDWIDE, INC. 2000. *Public Attitudes Toward Education and Service Learning.* Washington, DC: Academy for Education Development and the Learning in Deed Initiative.

SIGMON, ROBERT. 1996. "The Problem of Definition in Service-Learning." In *The Journey to Service-Learning,* ed. Robert Sigmon et al. Washington, DC: Council of Independent Colleges.

STEPHENS, LILLIAN. 1995. *The Complete Guide to Learning through Community Service: Grades K–9.* Boston: Allyn and Bacon.

U.S. DEPARTMENT OF EDUCATION. 2000. *Youth Service-Learning and Community Service among 6th through 12th-Grade Students in the United States: 1996 and 1999.* Washington, DC: National Center for Education Statistics.

WEILER, DANIEL; LAGOY, AMY; CRANE, ERIC; and ROVNER, ABBY. 1998. *An Evaluation of K–12 Service-Learning in California: Phase II Final Report.* Emeryville, CA: RPP International with the Search Institute.

RICHARD J. KRAFT

## HIGHER EDUCATION

Service learning in higher education is an experiential learning pedagogy that balances the needs of student and community members involved, links the service and learning through reflective processes, and if skillfully managed leads to positive student personal, social or citizenship, career, and intellectual development.

### Programs

The central claim of service learning is that both the quality of student learning and the quality of service to the community are enhanced when the two are combined. Although there are literally dozens of definitions of the term, the characteristics identified in the 1990 National and Community Service Act are central to most of them; this act describes service learning as an instructional method that accomplishes the following objectives.

- Students learn and develop through active participation in thoughtfully organized service experiences that meet actual community needs and that are coordinated in collaboration with the school and the community.

• Student's academic curriculum provides structured time for a student to think, talk, or write about what the student did and saw during the actual service activity.

• Students are given opportunities to use newly acquired skills and knowledge in real-life situations in their own communities.

• Enhancement of what is taught in school is accomplished by extending student learning beyond the classroom and into the community and fostering of the development of a sense of caring for others.

While most service-learning programs are part of the school or college curriculum, cocurricular programs in which there are intentional goals for student learning and in which efforts are made to assist students in reflecting on their experience also qualify. The term, however, is also commonly applied to a variety of activities that do not meet these standards. Perhaps because of the growing popularity of community service for young people and because *service learning* sounds more important than *volunteerism,* the term is often applied to volunteer programs where there is very little formal attempt to facilitate learning through reflection. Service learning is also sometimes confused with traditional field-based instructional programs such as clinical experiences for those studying to be nurses, social workers, teachers, or other human services professionals. In an attempt to sort out the many programs that involve students in the community and draw a distinction between service learning and related activities like volunteer service and internships, Andrew Furco (1996) has suggested an approach to assigning programs to categories along two dimensions: the balance between goals (i.e., of service or learning) and the primary intended beneficiary (service recipients or students).

Service-learning programs are designed to equally benefit both the provider and recipient of service and to focus on both the quality of the service and the learning. This is most often accomplished when the service learning is part of an academic course. It is easier to achieve this balance if service is a required part of the class, and all students participate in projects where the service is closely tied to the subject matter goals for the course. For example, a course on program evaluation in which students develop an evaluation plan for a local nonprofit agency program is easily designed to benefit both students and the agency. Discussion and analysis of the class service project can serve as a central part of the course. Other examples of tight subject matter/ service links include the following: (1) courses in women's studies where students work with victims of domestic violence; (2) Spanish courses where students assist new immigrants in learning to negotiate the community; (3) sociology classes where students conduct needs-assessment activities for a mayor's office that is considering new services for the homeless; or (4) a botany class where students classify and remove invasive non-native species from a park.

Many service-learning classes do not integrate the service program into the regular course of study, but make service an option for extra credit or a substitute for a research paper or other assignment; some provide an additional course credit for those choosing that option. Unless the professor plans carefully to incorporate the service work of these students into class discussion and activities, and plans for continuous individual reflection activities for students choosing service, these classes often fail to maximize either the service or the learning. Without reflective integration with the substance of the course, add-on service options become simply classes plus volunteerism. Since some resistance to service learning comes from people who feel that providing course credit for volunteerism is inappropriate, it is important to draw a distinction between volunteerism and service-learning experience, which has an academic focus and yields measurable learning outcomes. And it is important to reserve the label *service learning* for experiences in which intentional efforts are made to link the two through discussion, assignments or other forms of reflective activity.

Of course, students may also learn from volunteer service and community service programs. These are valuable experiences for students and may contribute to their personal development and commitment to active involvement in the community. The primary focus is on service, not learning, and the primary intended beneficiaries are the service recipients, not the students. Some students who have a naturally reflective bent may be motivated to explore questions that arise from their service, but the programs themselves provide little or no challenge to make that happen. Many colleges and universities have volunteer service centers that develop opportunities for students to serve, and hundreds of thousands of hours of community service are donated each year by these students.

A popular program is the Alternative Spring Break (ASB) where college students travel in student-led teams to international and domestic sites to undertake a week of community service. Break Away, founded in 1991 at Vanderbilt University, is the national organization that provides technical assistance to college and university ASB programs; they estimate that in the spring of 2001, 30,000 American college students spent their spring break in an organized service project. College community service programs like ASB do often devote some attention to providing guidance to programs leaders on how to develop reflection sessions for students, and occasionally such programs become service-learning opportunities by being integrated into an academic course or what has been called a curriculum-based alternative break. Most of these programs are probably best placed in the community service rather than service learning category.

Field-based study, clinical practice, and internships all provide useful service to communities, but have as their primary purpose student learning. Student teachers spend time in the classroom to master instructional skills. Student nurses may spend time in clinics giving vaccinations, conducting well baby examinations to master nursing skills. Many students spend a semester in a business internship to develop skills and contacts necessary to move their career forward. All these students also provide a service, but the intended beneficiary of such programs is the student, who develops professional skills.

## Benefits of Service Learning in Higher Education

Service learning is a form of experiential learning and is built on the assumption that learning occurs through active engagement and application of academic subject matter to real world problems and vice versa. Many of its founders were followers of John Dewey who believed that for an experience to be educative, it needed to engage students in significant worthwhile activity that leads to curiosity and sustained inquiry. Service learning is thought to enhance learning partly because students become highly motivated to learn when they work with people in the community and see how their efforts can make a difference. Cognitive psychologists are discovering that learning that is absorbed and can be transferred to new settings is best developed through repeated engagement in complex realistic situations.) Community projects used in service-learning programs offer this opportunity.

The dramatic increase in interest in service learning in higher education in the late 1980s and into the twenty-first century may have occurred because it is an approach to learning that seems to answer many criticisms of higher education. The experiential, interdisciplinary, and community-based nature of service learning addresses criticisms that American colleges and universities have created compartmentalized, sterile bodies of knowledge that students have difficulty integrating or applying in their lives in the community. It is also responsive to concerns that the academy is divorced from society and has abdicated its traditional role of service and community citizenship. Concern with these issues led both college leaders and the federal government to create institutions to support development of community service and service-learning programs.

Service learning was first identified as a type of instruction in the mid-1960s but has become visible and grown dramatically since the founding of Campus Compact in the mid-1980s. Campus Compact is a national coalition with more than 750 colleges and universities as members that has provided visibility and support for the development of community service and service-learning programs on campuses.

The goals participating faculty have identified as most important include promoting active engaged learning, developing citizenship skills and responsibility, developing critical thinking capabilities, addressing campus responsibility to community, taking social action, providing opportunities for career development, exposing students to diversity, and promoting moral and religious development.

Service-learning classes are most likely to be in education or the social sciences but there are many examples of courses being developed in the sciences, engineering, the humanities and business as well. The passage of the National and Community Service Act in 1990 and the National and Community Service Trust Act in 1993 and the subsequent creation of the Corporation for National Service provided additional resources to train faculty, support startup costs for new programs, and provide an infrastructure to disseminate information on best practices for these programs.

## Impact of Service Learning on Students

An analysis of research conducted by Eyler, Giles, Stenson, and Gray during the 1990s identified more than 100 higher education studies completed during this period that provide considerable support for the power of service learning. While most of this research has involved evaluation studies or programs in single institutions, there have been several that were national in scope. Most have focused on student outcomes with a lesser number exploring institutional or community impact.

These studies provide evidence of growing presence of service learning on campuses, student endorsement of this pedagogy, and of general satisfaction of community agencies with student contributions. Studies of student impact have consistently shown small but significant effects on personal and social or citizenship development; evidence of academic or cognitive impact is less consistent.

Given the very wide range of experiences labeled *service learning*, it is not surprising that the quality of the program also makes a difference in its impact on students. High quality community placements, in which students are challenged, have opportunities to interact with members of the community and engage in interesting work lead to positive outcomes. Other measures of quality include the quantity and quality of reflective activity (such as discussion and written analysis of the service), application (i.e., the degree to which the service and course of study are related), the duration and intensity of the experience, diversity (i.e., the opportunity to interact with people from different ethnic, racial, or social groups), and community voice (i.e., participation of the community partners in shaping the nature of the service). Some of what is known about the effects of service learning on students including effects of quality is summarized below.

**Students like service learning.** Service learning is popular with college students. Students report that they have good community experiences, they learn more, and are more interested and motivated to work hard in these classes than in their traditional classes. Not surprisingly, service learning that includes strong community placements and is well integrated into coursework through reflection and application is more highly regarded than experiences of lower quality.

**Stronger connections to college or university.** College students tend to do better academically and graduate when they are engaged in college social and academic life, and when they have close personal ties to faculty members. There is evidence that students who are active in community service during college are more likely to persist to graduation, but this has not yet been established for academic service learning. There is a growing body of evidence however, that suggests that service learning contributes to engagement with college life and satisfaction with the college experience. Students who participate in service learning report closer ties to faculty than those who do not. Closeness to faculty and the amount of time spent in interaction with faculty members are also affected by the quality of the service-learning experience. Courses that involve strong community placements and include a lot of discussion about the service experience and its relationship to the course of study are more likely to build close relationships with faculty members. Service learning can be a powerful tool for creating conditions that enhance college impact on students.

**Personal development.** The college years are an important time for the development of personal identity and the skills needed to function effectively in social groups. Service learning has long been valued because the personal connection students make with diverse others in the community is thought to contribute to personal development, motivation to learn, and commitment to do something about social problems. The research suggests that both community service and service learning lead to increased personal confidence and sense of efficacy; students develop a stronger sense of personal identity, and increased cultural understanding and empathy. Some students report that service learning also leads to their spiritual development. There is also evidence that participation in service learning increases interpersonal and leadership skills.

The quality of service learning may enhance the impact of service on personal development. The two most important factors for increasing personal outcomes are the quality of the placement itself and the degree to which the service is relevant to the subject matter being studied. When students have the chance to work with people from different ethnic groups than their own, they are also likely to show an increase in cultural understanding, identity development, and spiritual growth.

**Career development.** Students who participate in service learning report a greater confidence in their choice of major and in their career choice. They also indicate that they feel better prepared for work than do their peers who do not participate. Alumni also report that their community service during college has increased the likelihood of incorporating service into their career development.

**Academic or cognitive development.** Students who are engaged in community service during college are likely to get higher grades than those who are not. Faculty and students who participate in service learning report that students learn more from the experience than they do in traditional classes, but research on the impact of service learning on achievement as measured by grades is mixed. Some experimental studies have shown that service-learning students achieve at a higher level; others show no real difference on these traditional academic measures.

Grades might not be the best measure of the intellectual impact of service learning, however, because they are often not based on the outcomes-measures that service learning is best designed to affect. Studies that have analyzed student essays before and after service or that have used taped and transcribed problem-solving interviews have shown that highly reflective service learning, especially when the problems assessed and the service are closely related, has a positive impact on the quality of student understanding of complicated social problems. Similar in-depth analysis of changes in student thinking over the course of a semester shows increases in cognitive development (i.e., the ability of students to use critical thinking to analyze issues that don't have clear answers).

**Citizenship and social responsibility.** Advocates for service learning are convinced that it improves the quality of the college or university's citizenship within its community and that it also helps students develop the skills and commitments necessary for effective community engagement. Participation in service learning increases the sense of social responsibility felt by students and their commitment to community service. It also enhances their sense of engagement in their community and their confidence that community members can solve problems. Many studies show students active in service learning report that they intend to participate in future service. Growing evidence in studies of alumni shows that these students are in fact more likely to become actively engaged in their community after graduation.

Values and commitment—for example, the belief that one ought to and will become involved in the community—is not sufficient, however, for effective citizenship. In fact all outcomes of service learning summarized previously contribute to effectiveness. Confidence that one can make a difference, personal efficacy, knowing how to work with others on community tasks, understanding complex social issues, and having the critical thinking skills to make good decisions all form part of the contribution of service learning to preparing students for active citizenship. Students who have had service-learning experiences are more likely to feel that they ought to participate in their communities, know how to participate, and understand issues so that they can participate in intelligent ways.

*See also:* CIVICS AND CITIZENSHIP EDUCATION; COMMUNITY EDUCATION; MULTICULTURALISM IN HIGHER EDUCATION; SERVICE LEARNING, *subentry on* SCHOOL; VOLUNTEER WORK.

**BIBLIOGRAPHY**

BOYER, ERNEST L. 1994. "Creating the New American College." *Chronicle of Higher Education* 67:A48.

BRANSFORD, JOHN. D., and SCHWARTZ, DANIEL L. 1999. "Rethinking Transfer: A Simple Proposal with Multiple Implications." *Review of Research in Education* 24:61–100.

DEWEY, JOHN. 1938. *Experience and Education.* New York: Collier.

EHRLICH, THOMAS. 1997. "Civic Learning: Democracy and Education Revisited."*Educational Record* 78(3,4):56-75.

EYLER, JANET, and GILES, DWIGHT E., JR. 1999. *Where's the Learning in Service-Learning?* San Francisco: Jossey-Bass.

EYLER, JANET; GILES, DWIGHT E., JR.; STENSON, C.; and GRAY, CHARLENE J. 2001. *At a Glance: Summary and Annotated Bibliography of Recent Service-Learning Research in Higher Education,* 2nd edition. Minneapolis, MN: Learn and Serve America National Service-Learning Clearinghouse.

FURCO, ANDREW. 1996. "Service-Learning: A Balanced Approach to Experiential Education." In *Expanding Boundaries: Service and Learning* 1(1):2–6.

GRAY, MARIANNE J., et al. 1998. *Coupling Service and Learning in Higher Education: The Final Re-*

*port of the Evaluation of the Learn and Serve America, Higher Education Program.* San Francisco: Rand.

RESNICK, LAUREN B. 1987. "The 1987 Presidential Address: Learning in School and Out." *Educational Researcher* 16(9):13–20.

SCHÖN, DONALD A. 1995. "Knowing in Action: The New Scholarship Requires a New Epistemology." *Change* 27(6):27–34.

WUTZDORFF, ALAN, and GILES, DWIGHT E., JR. 1997. "Service-Learning in Higher Education." In *Service Learning, Ninety Sixth Yearbook of the National Society for the Study of Education,* Part 1, ed. Joan Schine. Chicago: University of Chicago Press. 105–177.

JANET EYLER

# SEVERE AND MULTIPLE DISABILITIES, EDUCATION OF INDIVIDUALS WITH

Individuals with severe disabilities and multiple disabilities are highly diverse in both their abilities and disabilities. What they share is a capacity to learn and a lifelong need for support.

## Definition and Types of Severe and Multiple Disabilities

Persons with *severe disabilities* are: "individuals of all ages who require extensive ongoing support in more than one major life activity in order to participate in integrated community settings and to enjoy a quality of life that is available to citizens with fewer or no disabilities" (TASH, p. 19). Mental retardation is regarded as a characteristic common to those with severe disabilities. Most severely disabled individuals are limited in their ability to communicate, though these skills can become functional with appropriate intervention. In addition, these individuals often have medical conditions or physical limitations that affect their movement, vision, or hearing.

Persons with *multiple disabilities* have a combination of two or more serious disabilities (e.g., cognitive, movement, sensory), such as mental retardation with cerebral palsy. The U.S. federal government definition includes those who have more than one impairment, "the combination of which causes such severe educational needs that they cannot be accommodated in special education programs solely for one of the impairments" (Code of Federal Regulations, 1999, Vol. 34 Sec. 300.7, [c][7]). (Dual sensory impairment, or deaf-blindness, is defined as a separate disability group.) Multiple disabilities have interactional, rather than additive, effects, making instruction and learning complex.

In 1996 Fred Orelove and Dick Sobsey defined this group as individuals with mental retardation who require extensive or pervasive supports and who also possess one or more significant motor or sensory impairments and/or special health care needs. These physical and medical problems result in the presence of two or more of the following characteristics: restriction of movement, skeletal deformities, sensory disorders, seizure disorders, lung and breathing control, or other medical problems related to these characteristics, such as skin breakdown or bladder infections.

The two groups overlap somewhat in definition. *Multiple disabilities,* depending upon the definition used, may or may not include mental retardation as one disability, while *severe disabilities* requires mental retardation but does not require an additional disability. Some movement disabilities are associated with mental retardation; for example, 60 to 70 percent of those with cerebral palsy have some degree of mental retardation. However, a child with cerebral palsy who does not meet the cognitive requirements of mental retardation might fit the federal definition of multiple disabilities, due to having movement and communication disabilities, but not the definition of severe disabilities. Most individuals who have multiple disabilities also fit the criteria for severe disabilities, while not all with severe disabilities have multiple disabilities.

The primary measures used to diagnose these individuals are individual intelligence tests and tests of adaptive behavior. Early assessment of movement limitations, muscle tone and flexibility, seizure activity, breathing control, sucking and swallowing, vision and hearing, and genetic makeup are also, and prenatal assessment of genetic material or physical identification of deformities via sonograms may be conducted. Accurate psychological testing of these individuals is challenging due to their frequent limitations in controlled movement, vision, hearing, communication, or cooperative behavior. Thus, interviews with family members and educators regarding the person's adaptive behavior skills (i.e., communication, self-care, home living, social skills, community use, self-direction, health and safely, functional academics, leisure, and work) may be more informative and reliable than a norm-based IQ or achievement score.

Definitions of this highly variable group with both severe and multiple disabilities are less precise than some other disability groups, making an estimate of their prevalence difficult. Prevalence ranges from less than .25 percent to .50 percent of the population; and is considered relatively uniform across socioeconomic classes.

Persons with severe and multiple disabilities may carry a variety of diagnostic labels, including: (1) severe or profound levels of mental retardation (IQ scores below 40); (2) mental retardation that requires extensive or pervasive supports for an extended time; (3) autism, childhood disintegrative disorder, or Rett syndrome (several types of autism spectrum disorders); and (4) various genetic disorders accompanied by extensive mental retardation (e.g., Tay-Sachs disease, untreated phenylketonuria, tuberous sclerosis, Lesch-Nyhan syndrome). Individuals with several autism spectrum disorders, by definition, have significant developmental delays in communication and social interaction, and may exhibit extensive limitations in many adaptive skills. Thus, their disability may be extensive enough to fit the definition for mental retardation and severe disabilities, though this is not true for all persons identified with autism (e.g., Asperger's syndrome).

## A Brief History of Education of People with Disabilities

In the United States individuals with severe and multiple disabilities are legally entitled to education and other support services; however, these groups do not have the same rights in much of the world. Those with severe and multiple disabilities are identified early in life by their noticeable delays in development or by their physical abnormalities. Many require medical interventions not available until recently; thus, earlier in history (and still today in less-developed countries), many with severe disabilities did not live long. Historically, in many cultures, the presence of severe physical abnormalities at birth has been associated with stigma and shame. Current technology has enabled interventions that extend both the length and quality of life of these persons.

Historical reports of individuals with severe and multiple disabilities who survived indicate that they were subjected to the same poor treatment experienced by persons with milder forms of mental retardation. They suffered greatly prior to the 1700s; but from 1700 to the late 1800s there was an optimistic period, due to education methods that were "discovered" by Jean-Marc-Gaspard Itard (1775–1838) and Edouard Seguin (1812–1880) in France and spread to other Western countries. This period was followed by disillusionment with the nonuniform results of these education practices. From the late 1800s through the 1960s there was widespread building of institutions to house these individuals, and then, starting in the 1970s, the institutional population in the United States was gradually reduced, due primarily to a reduction in admissions. Many former residents were relocated to smaller community-based settings, while others remained in their own homes with services and supports provided to their families. Of those now remaining in state institutions, persons over forty who have profound mental retardation and multiple disabilities dominate the population.

## Implications of Educational Legislation

Legislation in the early 1970s addressed the right to education and other habilitation services for all individuals with disabilities. In 1975 the Education for All Handicapped Children Act (known since 1990 as the Individuals with Disabilities Education Act, or IDEA) formed the legal basis for public education for all children, including those with severe and multiple disabilities. IDEA added requirements that are especially valuable for these individuals, including: (1) early intervention starting at birth or whenever a disability is suspected; (2) related services such as physical, occupation, and speech and language therapy, including augmentative and alternative communication (AAC) methods; (3) the requirement for a plan and services to facilitate transition to work and adulthood; and (4) a value placed on inclusion in general education with nondisabled peers. Most states provide services to these students until age twenty-two or beyond, focusing upon functional skill development.

Prior to the 1975 law mandating public education for all children, students with severe and multiple disabilities, if educated, received services in institutions or settings operated by parent groups or state mental health departments. When laws enacted in the mid-1970s required publicly funded special education, most schools established programs for these students but continued to isolate them from their nondisabled peers in separate buildings or self-contained classrooms in elementary schools. Currently in many states, the "least restrictive environment" for most of these students is the age-appropriate school setting alongside nondisabled peers, though not necessarily in the general education classroom. Currently, a majority of these students are served in separate classrooms for most of the school day.

Since 1975 U.S. courts have defined specific portions of special education law. For those with severe and multiple disabilities, several legal battles have resulted in: (1) summer educational programs being required in many states to lessen or prevent skill regression; (2) interventions that enable students to stay at school (e.g., providing catheterization for those unable to urinate voluntarily); (3) related services and technology to assist with movement, positioning, speech, and alternate forms of communication; (4) the mandate to educate all students with disabilities, and not limit services based on an assessment of educational potential; and (5) the provision of regular opportunities for interaction with nondisabled peers and inclusion in general education classrooms—or justification for not providing these opportunities. While all states are required to provide a free and appropriate education for these students, there are many differences in how localities implement the law and thus in the actual quality of educational services for these students.

## Educating Students with Severe and Multiple Disabilities

When compared to their peers, most students with severe and multiple disabilities learn more slowly, forget more readily, and experience problems generalizing skills from situation to situation. These characteristics are best addressed when educators follow accepted practices. First, the public education of these students must start early and continue at some level throughout life. Second, all students typically need speech and language intervention, while many others will need physical and occupational therapy. Students with sensory impairments may need interpreters and mobility trainers, while some with medical needs may require nursing services or supervision. Third, because the educational teams of students are often large, close collaboration between

members is essential if their expertise is to result in improved student functioning. The benefits of integrating therapy into natural activities is widely accepted over the traditional practice of isolated, or pull-out, therapy.

Fourth, curriculum for these students tends to be functional in nature, reflecting skills needed in everyday life across domestic, leisure, school, community, and vocational domains. Students are taught to make choices, communicate in functional ways (which may include AAC methods such as signing, use of pictures, etc.), develop useful skills that reduce their dependence on others, and learn social skills suited to their chronological age. Fifth, when skills are taught in multiple, normalized settings, generalization problems are lessened. Thus, communication and social skills are most effectively taught in the context of interactions with typical classmates, while job and community skills are best taught during community-based instruction.

## Trends and Controversies

Several important trends, some considered controversial because they advocate the inclusion of these students in general education with the necessary supports, reflect improvements in the lives of these students. First, through advancements in medicine and technology these individuals not only experience longer lives, but also have better options in mobility, communication, sensory augmentation, and other areas. Second, starting in the 1960s, there has been gradual improvement in societal attitudes toward people with significant disabilities. This has led to legal protections, special education, community living alternatives, supported employment, and an increase in relevant supports. Third, with the Timothy W. decision (*Timothy W. v. Rochester, New Hampshire, School District,* 1989), "free and appropriate education for all" was reaffirmed, schools were required to keep current with best practices for educating those with significant disabilities, and the procedure of selecting who can and cannot learn was declared illegal.

The current trend to include individuals with severe or multiple disabilities in classrooms and community activities with their nondisabled peers has been particularly controversial. Special education placement data show gradual growth of students with disabilities who are placed in a general education setting, but much slower growth for students with severe and multiple disabilities. Schools have complained that they are not able to include these students or provide the necessary supports and services to achieve a meaningful education for all involved. Some general education teachers have communicated an unwillingness to have these students in their classrooms, even with support, and they also may lack the required skills necessary to teach these children in a general education classroom. However, there are numerous examples of schools meaningfully including these students in ways that promote social and educational participation, as well as evidence to support the benefits of inclusion for both students with severe disabilities and typical classmates. More research, the dissemination of information on inclusion, and improvements in teacher training are needed.

*See also:* ADAPTED PHYSICAL EDUCATION; ASSISTIVE TECHNOLOGY; AUTISM, EDUCATION OF INDIVIDUALS WITH; COUNCIL FOR EXCEPTIONAL CHILDREN; MENTAL RETARDATION, EDUCATION OF INDIVIDUALS WITH; PHYSICAL DISABILITIES, EDUCATION OF INDIVIDUALS WITH; SPECIAL EDUCATION; SPEECH AND LANGUAGE IMPAIRMENT, EDUCATION OF INDIVIDUALS WITH.

**BIBLIOGRAPHY**

ANDERSON, LYNDA L., et al. 1998. "State Institutions: Thirty Years of Depopulation and Closure." *Mental Retardation* 36:431–443.

BATSHAW, MARK L. 1997. *Children with Disabilities,* 4th edition. Baltimore: Brookes.

BEST, SHERWOOD. 2001. "Definitions, Supports, Issues, and Services in Schools and Communities." In *Teaching Individuals with Physical, Health, or Multiple Disabilities,* ed. June L. Bigge, Sherwood J. Best, and Katheryn W. Heller. Upper Saddle River, NJ: Merrill/Prentice-Hall.

DYKENS, ELISABETH M.; HODAPP, ROBERT M.; and FINUCANE, BRENDA M. 2000. *Genetics and Mental Retardation Syndromes.* Baltimore: Brookes.

*Education for All Handicapped Children Act of 1975.* U.S. Public Law 94-142. *U.S. Code.* Vol. 20, secs. 1401 et seq.

*Individuals with Disabilities Education Act of 1997.* U.S. Public Law 105-17. *U.S. Code.* Vol. 20, secs. 1400 et seq.

LORD, CATHERINE, and RISI, SUSAN. 2000. "Diagnosis of Autism Spectrum Disorders in Young Children." In *Autism Spectrum Disorders: A Transactional Developmental Perspective,* ed. Amy M. Wetherby and Barry M. Prizant. Baltimore: Brookes.

ORELOVE, FRED P., and SOBSEY, DICK. 1996. *Educating Children with Multiple Disabilities: A Transdisciplinary Approach,* 3rd edition. Baltimore: Brookes.

SNELL, MARTHA E., and BROWN, FREDDA, eds. 2000. *Instruction of Students with Severe Disabilities,* 5th edition. Upper Saddle River, NJ: Merrill/Prentice-Hall.

TASH (THE ASSOCIATION FOR PERSONS WITH SEVERE HANDICAPS). 1991. "Definition of the People TASH Serves." In *Critical Issues in the Lives of People with Severe Disabilities,* ed. Luanna H. Meyer, Charles A. Peck, and Lou Brown. Baltimore: Brookes.

TRENT, JAMES W., JR. 1994. *Inventing the Feeble Mind: A History of Mental Retardation in the United States.* Berkeley: University of California Press.

MARTHA E. SNELL

# SEXUALITY EDUCATION

At the turn of the twenty-first century the rate of sexual intercourse among U.S. teenagers has declined; teen contraception rates, particularly condom use, have increased; and, as a result, teen birthrates declined during most of the 1990s.

Support for sexuality education also seems to be at an all-time high. A poll jointly conducted in 1999 by the Sexuality Information and Education Council of the United States (SIECUS) and Advocates for Youth showed that 93 percent of adults supported teaching sexuality education in high school and 84 percent supported teaching sexuality education in middle school/junior high school. And although most Americans believe abstinence should be a topic in sexuality education, the poll indicates that they reject abstinence-only-until-marriage education that denies young people information about contraception and condoms. The poll and subsequent focus groups demonstrate that many American parents do not see a conflict between providing information about abstinence and providing information about contraception in sexuality education programs. For these parents, it is not a matter of either/or—they want both.

## The Basics of Sexuality Education

Human sexuality encompasses the sexual knowledge, beliefs, attitudes, values, and behaviors of individuals. Its various dimensions include the anatomy, physiology, and biochemistry of the sexual response system; identity, orientation, roles, and personality; and thoughts, feelings, and relationships. The expression of sexuality is influenced by ethical, spiritual, cultural, and moral concerns.

Sexuality education is a lifelong process that begins at birth. Parents, family, peers, partners, schools, religion, and the media influence the messages people receive about sexuality at all stages of life. These messages can be conflicting, incomplete, and inaccurate. SIECUS, along with many other national organizations, believes that all people have the right to comprehensive sexuality education that addresses the biological, sociocultural, psychological, and spiritual dimensions of sexuality from the cognitive domain (information); the affective domain (feelings, values, and attitudes); and the behavioral domain (communication, decision-making, and other relevant personal skills).

Comprehensive school-based sexuality education that is appropriate to students' age, developmental level, and cultural background should be an important part of the education program at every grade. A comprehensive sexuality education program will respect the diversity of values and beliefs represented in the community and will complement and augment the sexuality education children receive from their families, religious and community groups, and health care professionals.

SIECUS's *Guidelines for Comprehensive Sexuality Education: Kindergarten–Twelfth Grade* provide an organizational framework for the knowledge of human sexuality and family living within four development levels. The *Guidelines* are organized into six key concepts that represent the most general knowledge and encompass the components of the broad definition of sexuality. These six key concepts are human development, relationships, personal skills, sexual behavior, sexual health, and society and culture. Each key concept has associated life behaviors, topics, subconcepts, and age-appropriate developmental messages.

The primary goal of sexuality education is the promotion of sexual health. In 1975 the World Health Organization defined sexual health as "the integration of the physical, emotional, intellectual, and social aspects of sexual being in ways that are positively enriching, and that enhance personality, communication, and love. . . . Every person has a right to receive sexual information and to consider accepting sexual relationships for pleasure as well as for procreation."

There is public and professional consensus about what is sexually unhealthy for teenagers. Professionals, politicians, and parents across the political spectrum share a deep concern about unplanned adolescent pregnancy; out-of-wedlock childbearing; sexually transmitted diseases, including HIV/AIDS; sexual abuse; date rape; and the potential negative emotional consequences of premature sexual behaviors.

There is, however, little public, professional, or political consensus about what is sexually healthy for teenagers. The public debate about adolescent sexuality has often focused on which sexual behaviors are appropriate for adolescents and has ignored the complex dimensions of sexuality.

Becoming a sexually healthy adult is a key developmental task of adolescence. Achieving sexual health requires the integration of psychological, physical, societal, cultural, educational, economic, and spiritual factors. Sexual health encompasses sexual development and reproductive health, and such characteristics as the ability to develop and maintain meaningful interpersonal relationships; appreciate one's own body; interact with both genders in respectful and appropriate ways; and express affection, love, and intimacy in ways consistent with one's own values.

Adults can encourage adolescent sexual health by providing accurate information and education about sexuality, fostering responsible decision-making skills, offering young people support and guidance to explore and affirm their own values, and modeling healthy sexual attitudes and behaviors. Society can enhance adolescent sexual health by providing access to: comprehensive sexuality education; affordable, sensitive, and confidential reproductive health care services; and education and employment opportunities.

Most scholars and activists argue that adolescents should be encouraged to delay sexual behaviors until they are ready physically, cognitively, and emotionally for mature sexual relationships and their consequences. This support should include education about intimacy; sexual limit setting; resisting social, media, peer, and partner pressure; the benefits of abstinence from intercourse; and the prevention of pregnancy and sexually transmitted diseases.

## Ongoing Challenges

In spite of recent declines, the birthrates among African-American and Hispanic young women aged fifteen to nineteen are still significantly higher than the overall birthrate in this age group. The rates of intercourse, pregnancy, and sexually transmitted diseases (STDs) are still much higher in the United States than in other industrialized countries.

Adults, whether they agree with young people's actions or not, cannot ignore the fact that millions of America's teenagers are engaging in a range of sexual behaviors. From a public-health perspective, some of these behaviors are less risky in terms of pregnancy or sexually transmitted disease transmission, whereas others carry greater risks. Because of these realities, *all* young people in the United States need the information, skills, and access to services to make and carry out informed, responsible decisions about their sexuality—both at the present time in their lives and in the future.

Americans hold both confused and contradictory attitudes about sexuality. While being generally relaxed enough to participate in sexual behaviors, Americans are not accepting enough of these behaviors to avoid guilt or shame. And Americans often have no commitment to pregnancy and disease prevention. This cultural confusion about sexuality is especially profound considering that adults must deal not only with their own sexuality-related issues but also with adolescent sexuality and sexual behaviors.

In American society, many adults do not model sexual health for young people. In fact, teenagers often behave more responsibly than adults. For example, 75 percent of unintended pregnancies in the United States occur to adult women. Never-married teens use birth control more consistently than never-married young adults in their twenties, and adolescents are much more likely to use condoms than older couples. Nearly all sexually transmitted HIV infection among both female and male teens and 60 percent of all teen births are the result of sexual intercourse with adult males.

Discussions about adolescent sexuality and sexuality education often revolve around adults' per-

ceptions of how "things should be" rather than a realistic understanding or appreciation of the dynamics of adolescents' lives. Adolescence is the time when young people develop the knowledge, attitudes, and skills that become the foundation for their healthy adulthood. Recognizing that nearly all Americans eventually become sexually active, an effective sexuality education program would ensure that young people have the information and skills they need to make responsible decisions about their sexuality—whether they make those decisions as adolescents or adults.

## Supporting Parents in Their Roles as Sexuality Educators

Parents and families play a major role in ensuring adolescent sexual health. Parents are the primary sexuality educators of their children. They educate both by what they say (and do not say) as well as by how they behave. Research indicates that young people who are able to talk to their parents about sexuality often behave more responsibly.

With open communication, young people are more likely to turn to their parents for help and support. Some parents have difficulty communicating with their children about sexuality, particularly because many of *their* parents also had difficulty with this issue. In order to overcome this difficulty, the education community can provide parents with information about sexuality and show them how to provide this education and information to their children. Educational programs may also provide parents with the help and encouragement they need to express their values about sexuality to their children and to provide accurate, honest, and developmentally appropriate sexuality information.

Parents and other trusted adult family members play an important role in encouraging and supporting adolescent sexual health. Parents and adults can assure that young people have access to accurate information and education about sexuality issues through direct communication and by providing books, pamphlets, and videos. Parents and other adults need to foster responsible sexual decision-making skills and need to model healthy sexual attitudes and responsible behaviors in their own lives.

## Training Teachers

Comprehensive sexuality education is an important component of formal schooling. Yet often teachers do not have the skills, knowledge, or inclination to teach such courses. Few have received training in sexuality education, and even fewer have received certification as sexuality educators. A 1995 SIECUS study revealed that the nation's elementary and secondary school teachers are not adequately prepared at the pre-service level to provide sexuality education, including the teaching of HIV prevention, to their students. Because sexuality issues touch on so many developmental issues relating to children and youth, SIECUS has, since 1965, urged that all pre-kindergarten through twelfth grade pre-service teachers receive at least one course in human sexuality.

Research shows that one of the characteristics that effective sexuality education programs share is that they are taught by teachers and leaders who believe in the program and are trained to deliver it. Trained teachers can complement the education provided by families as well as that provided by religious and community groups. Yet studies reveal that teachers do not feel adequately trained to teach sexuality education. Teachers report concern about their ability to teach personal skills, about their knowledge of HIV/AIDS, and about their knowledge of STDs. Most of those teaching sexuality education report receiving their training in short workshops or seminars.

Training for teachers on how to teach sexuality education is critical to the success of programs and to the health of American children. Teachers responsible for sexuality education must receive specialized training in human sexuality that includes basic information on sexuality topics and a special focus on the philosophy and methodology of teaching sexuality education. Teachers should, ideally, receive this training as pre-service teachers in academic courses or programs in schools of higher education that provide them with time-intensive and rich training. This training can be complemented by extensive in-service courses, continuing education classes, or intensive seminars.

Few states have either training or certification requirements for teachers who deliver sexuality or HIV-prevention lessons. Although the vast majority of states require or recommend teaching about sexuality or HIV/AIDS, a 1995 study found that only twelve states, the District of Columbia, and Puerto Rico required any licensure for teachers of sexuality education and only twelve states and the District of Columbia required licensure for teachers of HIV-prevention education. Only six states and Puerto Rico required teacher training for sexuality educators, and nine states, the District of Columbia, and Puerto Rico required training for teachers of HIV-prevention education. States should develop requirements that integrate expertise in the methodology and pedagogy of sexuality education into existing health education licensure requirements. Current licensing and accreditation bodies should also integrate these criteria into their requirements for health educators.

## Building Support Networks for Sexuality Education

A wide range of organizations support comprehensive sexuality education—including those representing health care professionals, businesses, the media, and faith communities—and are willing to advocate on its behalf. On the national level, the National Coalition to Support Sexuality Education includes more than 130 national organizations that support comprehensive sexuality education such as the American Association of School Administrators, the American Medical Association, the National School Boards Association, the National Association of School Psychologists, the National Education Association Health Information Network, the Religious Institute for Sexual Morality, Justice, and Healing, and the United States Conference of Mayors. Many of these organizations have affiliates at the state and community levels.

Education professionals can also become actively involved in supporting sexuality education programs in their communities. Professionals have an important role to play as outspoken advocates by writing letters to editors, voting in school board elections, writing supportive letters to teachers and administrators, and serving on community advisory committees. This involvement will help assure that young people have access to effective programs.

## Reaching People outside of School

While an important component of efforts toward ensuring a sexually healthy society focuses on sexuality education in schools, these efforts need to be broadened beyond schools. Out-of-school adolescents are more likely to report having had sexual intercourse and to having had four or more sexual partners.

One of the challenges for the education and health community is to develop innovative, accessible approaches that meet the sexual health needs of adolescents who are not in school. Community-based organizations, youth-serving agencies, health agencies, families, and faith communities often have contact with young people who may not be engaged in school, and these entities can be important sources of sexuality information and programming. Agencies need to be encouraged and supported in their efforts to work together to establish and strengthen partnerships for ensuring the sexual health of all young people, particularly those at most risk.

In addition, the Internet and other technologies are making sexuality information more accessible for many young people, both inside school and out. Many Internet sites provide age-appropriate, unbiased sexuality information for teens.

## Conclusion

The debate continues in the United States over the focus and content of sexuality education programs. The prevailing political climate makes it difficult for people to publicly advocate for much beyond abstinence for young people. In spite of this there is much parental and scientific support for a more comprehensive approach to sexuality education. The challenge for the education community is to ensure that school policies and programming provide *all* young people with the information, services, and support they need to grow up to become sexually healthy adults.

*See also:* HEALTH EDUCATION, SCHOOL; RISK BEHAVIORS, *subentries on* HIV/AIDS AND ITS IMPACT ON ADOLESCENTS, SEXUAL ACTIVITY AMONG TEENS AND TEEN PREGNANCY TRENDS, SEXUALLY TRANSMITTED DISEASES, TEEN PREGNANCY.

### BIBLIOGRAPHY

ADVOCATES FOR YOUTH. 1999. *European Approaches to Adolescent Sexual Behavior and Responsibility.* Washington, DC: Advocates for Youth.

ALAN GUTTMACHER INSTITUTE. 1990. *Preventing Pregnancy, Protecting Health.* New York: Alan Guttmacher Institute.

BALLARD, DANIEL; WHITE, D.; and GLASCOFF, M. 1990. "AIDS/HIV Education for Pre-service Elementary School Teachers." *Journal of School Health* 60:262–265.

BROWN, SARAH S., and EISENBERG, LEON, eds. 1995. *The Best Intentions.* Washington, DC: National Academy Press.

CENTERS FOR DISEASE CONTROL AND PREVENTION. 1992. "Health Risk Behaviors among Adolescents Who Do and Do Not Attend School—United States, 1992." *Morbidity and Mortality Weekly Report* 43(8):129–132.

COUNCIL OF ECONOMIC ADVISERS. 2000. *Teens and Their Parents in the Twenty-First Century: An Examination of Trends in Teen Behavior and the Role of Parental Involvement.* Washington, DC: Council of Economic Advisers.

FOREST, JACQUELINE DARROCH, and SILVERMAN, JANE. 1989. "What Public School Teachers Teach about Preventing Pregnancy, AIDS, and Sexually Transmitted Diseases." *Family Planning Perspectives* 21(2):65–72.

HAFFNER, DEBRA W., and WAGONER, JAMES. 1999. "Vast Majority of Americans Support Sexuality Education." *SIECUS Report* 27(6):22–23.

INSTITUTE OF MEDICINE. COMMITTEE ON PREVENTION AND CONTROL OF SEXUALLY TRANSMITTED DISEASES. 1997. *The Hidden Epidemic: Confronting Sexually Transmitted Diseases.* Washington, DC: National Academy Press.

KANN, LAURA; KINCHEN, STEVEN A.; WILLIAMS, BARBARA I.; ROSS, JAMES G.; LOWRY, RICHARD; GRUNBAUM, JO ANNE; BLUMSON, PAMELA S.; COLLINS, JANET L.; KOLBE, LLOYD J.; and STATE AND LOCAL YRBSS COORDINATORS. 2000. "Youth Risk Behavior Surveillance—United States, 1999." *Morbidity and Mortality Weekly Report Surveillance Summaries* 49(SS-5):1–94.

KIRBY, DOUGLAS. 2001. *Emerging Answers: Research Findings on Programs to Reduce Teen Pregnancy.* Washington, DC: National Campaign to Prevent Teen Pregnancy.

LEVENSON-GINGISS, P., and HAMILTON, R. 1989. "Teacher Perspectives after Implementing a Human Sexuality Education Program." *Journal of School Health* 59:427–431.

MALES, MIKE A. 1996. *The Scapegoat Generation.* Monroe, ME: Common Courage Press.

NATIONAL COMMISSION ON ADOLESCENT SEXUAL HEALTH. 1995. *Facing Facts: Sexual Health for America's Adolescents.* New York: Sexuality Information and Education Council of the United States.

RODRIGUEZ, MONICA; YOUNG, REBECCA; RENFRO, STACIE; ASENCIO, MARYSOL; and HAFFNER, DEBRA W. 1995/1996. "Teaching Our Teachers to Teach: A SIECUS Study on Training and Preparation for HIV/AIDS Prevention and Sexuality Education." *SIECUS Report* 25(2):15–23.

SEXUALITY INFORMATION AND EDUCATION COUNCIL OF THE UNITED STATES. 1995. *SIECUS Position Statements on Sexuality Issues.* New York: Sexuality Information and Education Council of the United States.

SEXUALITY INFORMATION AND EDUCATION COUNCIL OF THE UNITED STATES. 1995. *SIECUS Review of State Education Agency HIV/AIDS Prevention and Sexuality Education Programs.* New York: Sexuality Information and Education Council of the United States.

SEXUALITY INFORMATION AND EDUCATION COUNCIL OF THE UNITED STATES. 1996. *Guidelines for Comprehensive Sexuality Education: Kindergarten–Twelfth Grade.* New York: Sexuality Information and Education Council of the United States.

*Temporary Assistance to Needy Families Act of 1996.* U.S. Public Law 104-193. *U.S. Code.*

VENTURA, STEPHANIE J.; MATHEWS, T. J.; and CURTIN, SALLY C. 1999. "Declines in Teenage Birthrates, 1991–1998: Update of National and State Trends." *National Vital Statistics Reports* 47(26):1–9.

WHITAKER, DANIEL J.; MILLER, KIM S.; MAY, DAVID C.; and LEVIN, MARTIN L. 1999. "Teenage Partners' Communication about Sexual Risk and Condom Use: The Importance of Parent-Teenager Discussions." *Family Planning Perspectives* 31(3):117–121.

MONICA RODRIGUEZ

# SEXUAL ORIENTATION

Because adolescence is a time of transition from childhood into adulthood, adolescents are "journey people"—neither adults nor children, but traveling somewhere in between. Their identities on all levels are dynamic and convoluted. They are changing rapidly and often unevenly on physical, emotional, intellectual, moral, and spiritual levels.

The sexual identity of an adolescent is also being formed, and it cuts across all categories of human development. Sexual orientation, or the primary direction of one's romantic, relational, and psychological desires, is in flux for many adolescents. Sexual orientation and the personal, communal, societal, and educational issues surrounding it are instrumental in the lives of all adolescents, especially those who find themselves experiencing attractions to those of the same sex or in the case of transgendered youth, those who are unable or unwilling to adhere to traditional gender roles (behavior that is traditionally understood to be associated with women or men).

While the inclusion of transgendered issues in the lesbian, gay, and bisexual movement is controversial to some, gender and sexual orientation intersect in inseparable ways. For example, many students are harassed in school because they are *perceived* to be lesbian or gay, not because they actually are lesbian or gay. Some individuals do not or cannot adhere to traditional gender roles in the way they look, dress, behave, or speak—for example, when a boy has many feminine mannerisms, or when a girl appears traditionally masculine in dress or behavior. A fear of being labeled gay or lesbian based on gender assumptions can affect students in many different ways, as when boys are reticent to participate in school choir or when girls become ambivalent about academic achievement. Therefore, this discussion of sexual orientation includes transgender issues. Also included are those who are questioning their sexual orientation or gender identity.

## The Problem with Definition

It is important to note that the desire to measure, define, and keep statistics on sexual orientation and gender is a relatively new phenomenon in human history. The terms homosexual, heterosexual, and transgender did not exist until early in the twentieth century with the advent of modern psychology. In ancient times, same sex erotic behaviors and romantic love for those of the same sex existed as part of normal and everyday life. Some researchers and theorists believe that society has created categories for sexual orientation and gender to control sexual behavior and to create a catalogue of sexual deviancies. Society's need to classify sexual orientation and gender and attitudes toward people who are lesbian, gay, bisexual, transgendered, or questioning (i.e. sexual minorities) reflect society's assumptions about what is normal and who is welcomed and excluded. Educators should approach the labeling and classifying of sexual orientation of adolescents with great caution due to its potential for exclusion. James Brundage asserts that people are continuing to live with codes of sexual conduct established in Medieval Europe, and he calls for new reflections on an understanding of people as sexual beings in modern times. Living in a world, however, of what Thomas Popkewitz calls "population reasoning" that seeks to define children as members of groups with certain characteristics requires that people, however hesitantly, must acquiesce.

## Sexual Orientation Hesitantly Defined

When a compass is moved, the needle fluctuates for a bit before settling on true north. Similarly, a significant number of adolescents will find themselves confused about their sexual orientation and gender before settling into their sexual identity. Many will engage in sexual behaviors with others of the same sex. For most, these behaviors are experimental as young people make their way to a heterosexual orientation. But, for others, the attractions to those of the same sex remain consistent as they continue to personally develop and become more experienced in relationships. Many psychologists theorize that one's sexual orientation is found on a continuum, that no person is 100 percent heterosexual or homosexual, and that some are right in between. Research is suggesting that gender identity can also be understood along a continuum.

Sexual orientation is also understood to be more than just genital-sexual behaviors and includes emotional preference as well as intensity of spiritual connection with another person. Those who fall on the continuum closer to being attracted to those of the opposite sex, which accounts for the majority, are commonly known as straight or heterosexual. Those in the middle (studies show this to be anywhere from 2% to 5%) are considered bisexual. When a person is physically, emotionally, and spiritually attracted primarily to members of the same sex, they are considered to be lesbian, if female, and gay, if male. Studies show these numbers to be anywhere from 5 percent to 10 percent of the general population.

It is difficult to design studies that accurately reveal the proportion of straight and sexual minorities in the adolescent population. Even if a survey is anonymous, those with minority orientations may be denying their attractions to themselves as well as others because of the societal expectation that the only acceptable and normal orientation is heterosexual (i.e. *heteronormativity*). Some adolescents may have sexual attractions to either gender but would not categorize themselves in the same way as the survey instrument would. Others may know that they are members of a sexual minority, but because sexual orientation is invisible, many force themselves to live as heterosexuals, thus feeling one way on the inside, but living another way on the outside.

## The Impact of Invisibility and the Sense of Self

Although evidence shows that more and more individuals are *coming out* (divulging one's sexual orientation to others), minority adolescents are especially susceptible to the tendency of keeping their orientation invisible and silent. Instead, they choose to emulate their straight peers. This contradiction between a minority adolescent's developing internal sense of sexual identity and external actions and words exacts a great toll on their emotional and spiritual well-being. This disintegration (lack of ability to integrate invisible identity with visible identity) of the adolescent plays itself out through a higher than average rate of drug and alcohol abuse, depression, misbehavior, and suicide rate among sexual minority adolescents. Some reports show that up to one-third of teen suicides are committed by sexual minority youth. Spiritually, many adolescents find themselves alienated from their faith communities (either internally, externally, or both) and their family's spiritual traditions. Where do sexual minority youth develop a sense of needing to keep their identities invisible? How do they come to understand the world as a place that is hostile to their sexual desires?

## Sexual Socialization of Adolescents

Heterosexual people often have difficulty understanding the trials of sexual minority individuals. Since the majority of people in the world are heterosexual (including the parents of most minority youth), most persons in the mainstream culture spend little time reflecting on their sexual orientation. However, if one were to imagine what it would be like to be a young person beginning to develop an internal sense of a minority sexual identity, one could quickly notice how modern society is hostile to and nonrepresentative of minority sexual orientations. The comments family members and friends make when sexual orientation issues are discussed, television shows, popular songs, books, movies, billboards, magazines, the content of laws and policies, and people's assumptions and expectations all teach children from a very early age that it is best to be heterosexual.

Debbie Epstein and Richard Johnson's work in elementary schools shows that heteronormative sexual roles are rehearsed and reinforced both in the classroom and on the playground. Children play games that celebrate heterosexual pairings, read stories with exclusively straight characters, absorb assumptions about people based on gender behaviors, and are asked questions by teachers and classmates that assume a future heterosexual orientation. In short, from the first day of kindergarten, sexual minority youth are sexually socialized to think and feel in a straight way. When these youth reach adolescence and discover that they cannot fulfill the prepared sexual script, school becomes a place that both explicitly and subtly makes them feel abnormal and deviant.

### High Schools and Sexual Minority Adolescents

Citing a Massachusetts Governor's Task Force report, the Gay Lesbian Straight Education Network (GLSEN) reports that about two-thirds of sexual minority students said they have been verbally, physically, or sexually harassed at school. GLSEN seeks to make schools safer through education about orientation issues. It also provides logistical support for teachers, administrators, and students who want to help make their schools more welcoming to and accepting of sexual minority students. In some schools, lesbian, gay, bisexual, transgender, and questioning students, as well as their straight peers, meet (often in groups called Gay/Straight Alliances or GSAs) to discuss the problems faced by sexual minority students and share ideas about how to cultivate a tolerant atmosphere. The 1984 Federal Equal Access Act permits the formation of such groups anywhere that student clubs of any kind exist. This law, originally heavily promoted by conservative Christian groups to allow students to organize religious clubs in public secondary schools, applies only to public school settings where the administration has been found to have established a policy of making their facilities available to after-school groups. Sexual minority students in smaller or conservative communities are often more isolated, since the topic rarely, if ever, becomes part of the public discourse of the school. Advocates say the presence of GSAs makes sexual minority students feel safer. Opponents argue that GSAs encourage impressionable teens to experiment with homosexuality and a lifestyle that leads to un-

happiness and death. Often, religious language is evoked to explain why homosexuality is unfavorable.

Even if sexual minority students are ready to talk about their sexual orientation (and many are not and just continue pretending to be like their straight peers), the level of support from and comfort level of the adults in the school can vary widely. Even counselors and social workers are often not prepared to discuss issues of sexual orientation with adolescents. Sometimes faculty who want to teach about the contributions of sexual minority individuals throughout history or want to support students individually are prevented from doing so by administrators and school boards. Parental pressure and perceived public opinion often keep school leaders from supporting sexual minority youth. In other places, however, teachers and staff display "safe zone" symbols (a symbol designed as a sign of support to students) and feel comfortable talking about sexual orientation as it comes up in classroom conversation or individual conversations with students.

### The Controversy and Conclusion

In terms of attitudes and actions towards sexual minority issues and students, there is little uniformity across American schools. The majority of schools, however, are not dealing with the issues, and minority students continue to suffer in silence and denial of their own sexual orientation.

The sexual orientation issue in education is at the intersection of societal sexual, psychological, and religious norms with the school. While the legal system tends to defend the rights of lesbian, gay, bisexual, transgender, and questioning students to be free from harassment and to start GSAs, it has not held schools accountable for proactively creating more welcoming and supportive environments for sexual minority youth.

Ultimately, administrators, school boards, and citizens decide on the curriculum and policies of the school. Though the American Psychological Association (APA) removed homosexuality from their list of mental disorders in the 1970s, many still do not consider a minority sexual orientation to be normal or acceptable. Some religious groups such as Focus on the Family contend that adolescents can be converted to heterosexuality using a process known as reparative therapy. While mainstream psychological (e.g., the APA) and religious groups reject such therapies (e.g., see *2000 Religious Declaration of Sexuali-*

ty, *Morality, Justice, and Healing,* written by the Sexuality Information and Education Council of the United States), their level of support for open discourse and action in schools varies widely. The school is simply the crossroads of a much wider societal debate. Sexual minority adolescents challenge educators to think about the tension between pleasing majority publics and serving all students. The presence of minority adolescents can encourage reflection, conversation, and changes in policy and practices that many educators are not ready for and yet which sexual minority adolescents cannot survive without.

*See also:* GAY AND LESBIAN STUDIES.

## BIBLIOGRAPHY

BOSWELL, JOHN. 1980. *Christianity, Social Tolerance, and Homosexuality.* Chicago: University of Chicago Press.

BRUNDAGE, JAMES A. 1987. *Law, Sex, and Christian Society in Medieval Europe.* Chicago: University of Chicago Press.

EPSTEIN, DEBBIE, and JOHNSON, RICHARD. 1998. *Schooling Sexualities.* Bristol, PA: Open University Press.

FOUCAULT, MICHEL. 1978. *The History of Sexuality: An Introduction.* Vol. 1. New York: Random House.

GIBSON, PAUL. 1989. "Gay Male and Lesbian Youth Suicide." Report of the Secretary's Task Force on Youth Suicide. Washington, DC: U.S. Department of Health and Human Services.

JAGOSE, ANNAMARIE. 1996. *Queer Theory: An Introduction.* New York: New York University Press.

MARTINO, WILLIAM. 2000. "Policing Masculinities: Investigating the Role of Homophobia and Heteronormativity in the Lives of Adolescent School Boys." *Journal of Men's Studies* 8(2):213–236.

MOLLENKOTT, VIRGINIA. 2000. *Omnigender: A Transreligious Approach.* Cleveland, OH: Pilgrim Press.

POPKEWITZ, THOMAS S. 1998. *Struggling for the Soul: The Politics of Schooling and the Construction of the Teacher.* New York: Teachers College Press.

RATHUS, SPENCER A.; NEVID, JEFFREY S.; and FICHNER-RATHUS, LOIS. 1997. *Human Sexuality in a World of Diversity.* Needham Heights, MA: Allyn and Bacon.

RUBENSTEIN, WILLIAM. 1997. *Cases and Materials on Sexual Orientation and the Law,* 2nd edition. St. Paul, MN: West Publishing.

SEARS, JAMES. 1992. *Sexuality and the Curriculum: The Politics and Practice of Sexuality Education.* New York: Teachers College Press.

STORMS, MICHAEL D. 1980. "Theories of Sexual Orientation." *Journal of Personality and Social Psychology* 38:783–792.

### INTERNET RESOURCES

GAY LESBIAN STRAIGHT EDUCATION NETWORK (GLSEN). 2000. <www.glsen.org>.

INTERSEX SOCIETY OF NORTH AMERICA (ISNA). 2000. *Frequently Asked Questions.* <www.isna.org/faq/index.html>.

SEXUALITY INFORMATION AND EDUCATION COUNCIL OF THE UNITED STATES. 2000. <www.siecus.org>.

DONALD J. FRAYND
COLLEEN A. CAPPER

# SHANKER, ALBERT (1928–1997)

President of the American Federation of Teachers (AFT), the nation's second largest teachers' union, Albert Shanker was born in New York City in 1928 to Russian working-class immigrant parents. He grew up during the depression on the Lower East Side of New York, his father a newspaper deliveryman, his mother a sewing machine operator. Shanker was reared in a union home where, he said, "Unions were just below God" (Swerdlow and Weiner Internet site). When he began school, he spoke no English and endured beatings and anti-Semitic taunts in his mostly non-Jewish neighborhood.

Shanker excelled academically. After completing high school he earned a bachelor's degree in philosophy from the University of Illinois, Champaign-Urbana, and, in 1949, entered the Ph.D. program at Columbia University. Having completed all requirements but a dissertation, Shanker began teaching elementary and junior high school mathematics in New York City in 1952.

He left teaching in 1959 to become a full-time organizer for the Teachers Guild, New York City's

AFT affiliate. The guild was just one of 106 small New York City teacher organizations. Founded in 1917 with John Dewey as a charter member, the guild was the only New York City teacher organization to support collective bargaining, in which teachers elect a single organization to represent them in contract negotiations with their employer. In 1960 the Teachers Guild merged with New York City's High School Teachers Association to form the United Federation of Teachers. Shanker was elected president in 1964.

In the early 1960s Shanker helped New York City teachers gain collective bargaining rights and achieve the first contract in any major city in the United States. A supporter of the civil rights movement (Shanker marched in nearly every major demonstration in the country), his tenure as UFT president was partially defined by the Oceanhill-Brownsville events of 1968.

The city had divided the school district into multiple subdistricts, each with a community-based governing board. Oceanhill-Brownsville was a predominantly African-American district staffed by a largely white, largely Jewish teaching population. In 1968 the district superintendent, Rhody McCoy, removed the white teachers from the black community schools and Shanker called a strike. Before matters were settled (the teachers were returned to their jobs), there would be three strikes, all illegal under New York State's collective bargaining law, and Shanker would spend fifteen days in jail. Even when the issue seemed to be put to rest, critics continued to label Shanker a racist.

Shanker was concerned that Oceanhill-Brownsville would label him for life. He wanted educators and New Yorkers in general to better understand his principles and ideas, even if they did not always agree with him. Unable to get op-ed pieces placed in New York newspapers, he bought a paid ad in the December 13, 1970 edition of the Sunday *New York Times.* That ad would become his "Where We Stand" column, a weekly opportunity for Shanker to put forth his ideas about education, the union, and social and political issues to a large public audience. He would write the column for twenty-seven years.

Shanker continued to gather supporters and critics. Under his leadership, the New York City teacher union grew into a large and politically powerful organization, which in 1975 pulled New York

City back from the brink of bankruptcy when Shanker placed teacher pension funds in city bonds. Although he was approached to run for mayor (he declined), there were those who believed he wielded too much power. In Woody Allen's 1973 movie, *Sleeper,* Allen's character, frozen, awakens in the year 2173 and is asked how civilization was destroyed. "A man named Al Shanker got the bomb," he replies.

In 1974 Shanker became president of the American Federation of Teachers (AFT), a post to which he was re-elected every two years until his death. He remained president of the AFT and UFT for twelve years, relinquishing the UFT presidency in 1986.

When Shanker became AFT president, the organization was relatively small, particularly in comparison to its national rival, the National Education Association (NEA). The AFT, founded in Chicago in the early 1900s, was a union, a member of the AFL-CIO, and an adherent to trade union principles. Shanker had an unshakable faith in unionism, but in the early 1980s, he would set the AFT on a different, and unexpected, path.

In 1983 the National Commission on Excellence in Education released its landmark education reform report, *A Nation at Risk.* Shanker expected that this report, like its predecessors, would not support teachers and the AFT would need to oppose it. On reading the report, Shanker concluded that it provided an opportunity for his union to begin to tackle many important issues. A supporter of pubic schools, Shanker was nonetheless realistic about the problems, particularly unacceptably low levels of student achievement.

Shanker used the 1983 report as a springboard to change the conversation about and within his union and to catapult him to a prominent role in the education reform debate. He acknowledged his members' nervousness about new directions in July 1985 when he told a large AFT gathering in Washington, DC, "It's dangerous to let a lot of ideas out of the bag, some of which may be wrong. But there's something more dangerous and that's not having any new ideas at all at a time when the world is closing in on you."

Shanker had many ideas. In 1985 he called for the creation of the National Board for Professional Teaching Standards. In 1988 he publicly made a case for charter schools. Throughout the 1980s and 1990s, Shanker was a vocal advocate for high academic standards for all students, accountability for results (and consequences for failure to achieve them), peer review (in which teachers judge the quality of their colleagues' work), and minimum competency testing of new teachers. He told his members, "It is as much your duty to preserve public education as it is to negotiate a good contract." He argued that preserving public schools meant improving them.

During Shanker's AFT tenure, the American labor movement continued to shrink in size, but the AFT grew to an organization of more than a million members, including teachers, teacher aides, health care workers, and public employees, the last two categories of which Shanker added to the AFT's rolls during his presidency.

A focus on professional issues—improved academic standards for students and improved teacher quality—became hallmarks of the union under Shanker's leadership. He never abandoned collective bargaining, continuing to believe that the system was essential to secure basic rights and employment conditions for teachers. He broadened the interests of the union and in so doing, reshaped the organization. By the time of his death, attendance at the AFT's semiannual professional issues conference (called the QuEST conference for Quality Educational Standards in Teaching) outstripped attendance at AFT policymaking conventions.

Shanker was called a radical, a liberal, and a conservative—sometimes all at the same time. Never afraid of a controversial view or an unorthodox idea, Shanker would take a position and then, if someone or something convinced him otherwise, would just as quickly reverse course. Shanker's counsel was sought by Republicans and Democrats alike, and by presidents Jimmy Carter, Ronald Reagan, and Bill Clinton. A member of the AFL-CIO Executive Committee, Shanker was founding president of Education International, a worldwide federation of teacher unions.

Although Shanker accomplished much of his agenda, he was never able to secure a merger between the AFT and NEA. Shanker argued that the dollars that the two teacher unions were spending on internecine organizational warfare could be better spent fighting the enemies of public education.

When he died of bladder cancer at age sixty-nine in 1997, the president of the NEA, Bob Chase summed it up: "American public education has . . . lost one of its most eloquent and effective

advocates. A true leader, Al Shanker was always one bold step ahead of us all."

*See also:* AMERICAN FEDERATION OF TEACHERS; TEACHER UNIONS.

**BIBLIOGRAPHY**

AMERICAN FEDERATION OF TEACHERS. 1997. "The Power of Ideas: Al in His Own Words." *The American Educator,* Special Issue. Washington, DC: American Federation of Teachers.

WOO, ELAINE. 1996. "Al Shanker's Last Stand." *Los Angeles Times Magazine,* December 1.

**INTERNET RESOURCES**

CHASE, ROBERT. "Statement from Bob Chase, President of the National Education Association, on the Death of Albert Shanker, President of the American Federation of Teachers." <www.nea.org/nr/st970222.html>.

SWEDLOW, MARIAN, and WEINER, ADAM. "Al Shanker, Image and Reality." <www.igc.apc.org/solidarity/shank69.txt>.

JULIA E. KOPPICH

# SHELDON, EDWARD (1823–1897)

Edward Austin Sheldon was instrumental in bringing object training to the United States. As president of the Oswego Training School in Oswego, New York, from 1861 until his death, Sheldon worked to fulfill his commitment to make education accessible to all children, both in practice through free schools and in theory through a Pestalozzian teaching style.

Born in Perry Center in Genesee County, New York, Edward Sheldon grew up on the family farm. After completing a college-preparatory course of education, Sheldon fulfilled family expectations by leaving home at age twenty-one for Hamilton College in Clinton, New York. Sheldon originally intended to pursue a law career but a bout with pleurisy in his second year at Hamilton forced him to take a leave of absence, during which he returned to the family farm and dabbled in horticulture. His interest in this field—coupled with his fond memories of life on the farm—inspired him to leave college in 1847, after his junior year, to invest with a partner in a nursery in Oswego, New York. Within a year, financial mismanagement by Sheldon's partner caused the nursery to fail. However, struck by the poverty he observed in Oswego, Sheldon already was immersed in his new life: spearheading and organizing an educational system in Oswego that would serve all children.

Sheldon solicited the support of a committee of prominent community members to open the Orphan and Free School in Oswego in 1848. Although it was not his intention to take charge of the "ragged school," at least one of the most influential backers of the committee said she would pull her support without Sheldon as the teacher. Thus, Sheldon reluctantly began his short stint as a teacher. He reflected, "Nothing could ever have been farther from my thoughts than the idea of teaching school; nothing for which I considered myself so poorly adapted" (Barnes, p. 78). Sheldon struggled through this stressful year, teaching upwards of one hundred pupils at a time and witnessing the depraved conditions in which they lived when he visited their homes on Saturdays. The high point of the year was his marriage in May 1849, to Frances A. B. Stiles, whose own educational attainment enabled her to serve as a helpful partner for forty-six years as Sheldon worked to realize his vision of an educational system to serve all children. Their five children kept the Sheldon household busy.

Financial support for the school waned, and after one year Sheldon accepted a position at a private school in Oswego. But, for Sheldon, the idea of a unified educational system to serve all children lingered. After a brief time at the private school and one year as superintendent of public schools in Syracuse, New York, Sheldon returned to Oswego in 1853 and settled into his life work of reforming education, especially instruction. As secretary of the board of education (essentially, superintendent) in Oswego, Sheldon reorganized the Oswego public schools into a unified system, enacting such reforms as assigning students to schools and grades according to age and requiring all teachers to pass certification exams.

By the mid-1850s the Oswego schools were flourishing, serving as exemplars for education reformers, and Sheldon became well known in education circles. He soon realized, however, that this smooth-running system was "a machine found wanting" because the instructional methods "lacked vitality," and intensified his study of educational reforms in other school systems (Barnes, p. 116). In 1859 Sheldon was inspired to invest three hundred dollars in materials from the Home and Colonial Institute of London, in the hopes of duplicating the innovative practices he observed in classrooms in Toronto, Canada. There, teachers based lessons not on recitation and memorization, but on pictures, charts, and other objects, a teaching technique credited to Swiss educator, Johann Pestalozzi (1746–1827). Many people saw shades of Pestalozzi himself in Sheldon's life and work—both loved children, worked for the benefit of the poor, and maintained the courage of their convictions in reforming education. Pestalozzi developed object training out of necessity; he used field trips and actual objects as teaching tools because his students were poor and his school was inadequately funded. This active learning style was child-centered and engaged total sensory learning. Pestalozzi's belief in nurturing the natural and orderly development of the mind struck Sheldon so strongly that "he became a Pestalozzian overnight" (Snyder, p. 231).

Following his enlightening exposure to Pestalozzianism, Sheldon began, in his capacity as secretary of the board of education, to prepare teachers in this systematic objective style of teaching. He was soon frustrated, however, as he found that these teachers left for better-paying jobs in other districts. Recognizing the demand for teachers who were familiar with object training, he convinced the school board to establish a teacher training school and sought to find an appropriate teacher for the school. Because the method of teaching he had been emulating was based on the Home and Colonial Institute of London, he hired Pestalozzian expert Margaret E. M. Jones of the institute for the inaugural year of the Oswego Training School. Classes began in 1861 and Sheldon was a regular attendee during Jones's tenure. In 1865 New York made Sheldon's institution its second state-supported normal school. In 1869 Sheldon resigned as secretary of the board of education to devote himself full-time to the Oswego State Normal and Training School, which gained national attention for what rapidly became known as the *Oswego method* of object training. Sheldon remained as president of the school until his death in 1897.

The impact of the Oswego (Normal) Training School cannot be overstated. Teachers trained at Oswego fanned out across the country, beginning a revolution in classroom instruction. The majority of Oswego's early graduates taught in elementary and even normal schools outside of the state of New

York, often in the growing pioneer West. An Oswego graduate, Sheldon's daughter Mary followed in her father's footsteps; she became a professor of history at Stanford University and was well-known for her work in developing historical teaching methods. Mary and other Oswego-trained teachers helped to transform not only the subject matter and the methods of formal education, but also the spirit of education. Sheldon's graduates took his object-training vision across the country and around the world. Oswego State Normal and Training School became synonymous with object training; many normal schools taught the Oswego method for years to come.

*See also:* PESTALOZZI, JOHANN; TEACHER EDUCATION, *subentry on* HISTORICAL OVERVIEW.

### BIBLIOGRAPHY

BARNES, MARY SHELDON, ed. 1911. *The Autobiography of Edward Austin Sheldon.* New York: Ives-Butler.

HOLLIS, ANDREW PHILLIP. 1898. *The Contribution of the Oswego Normal School to Educational Progress in the United States.* Boston: Heath.

ROGERS, DOROTHY. 1961. *Oswego: Fountainhead of Teacher Education.* New York: Appleton-Century-Crofts.

SNYDER, CHARLES M. 1968. *Oswego: From Buckskin to Bustles.* Port Washington, NY: Friedman.

### INTERNET RESOURCE

OSWEGO COLLEGE, NEW YORK. "College History." <www.oswego.edu/library/archives/CollegeHistory.html>.

CHRISTINE E. WOLFE
CHRISTINE A. OGREN

# SINGLE-SEX INSTITUTIONS

At the beginning of the twenty-first century there are only two men's colleges in the United States—Wabash College in Indiana and Deep Springs in California, although there are approximately eighty women's colleges. For all intents and purposes, men's colleges seem to have outlived their function, although women's colleges continue to offer women students a worthwhile postsecondary option. Following a brief history of single-sex education for men and women, this entry explores the characteristics of women's colleges and the outcomes associated with attending these colleges. Given the small numbers of men's colleges, similar research has not been conducted on these institutions.

## Historical Contribution

Single-sex colleges and universities have a long and storied history in American higher education. The original colleges in the United States, including Harvard (1636), William and Mary (1693), Yale College (1716), and the College of New Jersey at Princeton (1746), were founded to educate men only. During this era, formal educational options for women were nonexistent. It was widely believed that women were intellectually inferior to men and that educating women might lead to health problems. Because higher education in the colonial period was aimed at preparing men for the clergy and for leadership, there was no real impetus to provide higher education for women.

In the early 1800s several seminaries for women only were founded to provide girls with a liberal education, equivalent to a high school education. Graduates of these seminaries were prepared to be mothers, wives, and teachers. Women's seminaries were not immediately classified as colleges, although schools such as that founded by Emma Willard (established in 1821) modeled their curriculum, in large part, after that offered at the most prestigious men's colleges of the day. Other women-only institutions, such as those founded by Catherine Beecher and Mary Lyon, became prototypes for modern women's colleges.

There are several women-only institutions that claim to be the first "college." Georgia Female College was chartered by the state legislature in 1836; its curriculum, however, was more similar to a high school than a college. In 1853 Mary Sharp College in Tennessee was founded; its curriculum looked very similar to the four-year degree program offered at the men's colleges. Similarly, Elmira Female College in New York, chartered in 1855, offered a true collegiate course. In the early days of women's access to higher education, single-sex institutions were the norm for both men and women. By 1860 there were approximately 100 women's colleges in existence, about half of which offered a collegiate-level curriculum. Approximately 67 percent of the existing colleges and universities at this time were for men only.

By 1850 several institutions, including Oberlin, began experimenting with coeducation. The passage of the Morrill Land Grant Act after the Civil War led to the creation of land-grant institutions, all of which were coeducational. The original colonial colleges continued to operate for men only. By 1870 there were 582 colleges in the United States, of which 343 were for men only, 70 were for women only, and 169 were coeducational. By 1890 the number of men's colleges reached its peak—400 institutions. At this time, there were 465 coeducational colleges and 217 women's colleges. The bulk of the single-sex institutions for both men and women were founded in the South and Northeast. In the Midwest and West, coeducation was the norm during this era. The women's colleges in the South were widely perceived as "finishing schools" and were not taken seriously by many in higher education.

After the Civil War, the women's colleges of the Northeast, especially the Seven Sisters (Barnard, Bryn Mawr, Mount Holyoke, Smith, Wellesley, Vassar, and Radcliffe), wished to demonstrate that women were as capable of achieving advanced education as were men. These institutions replicated the classical curriculum of the most elite men's colleges also located in the Northeast. Indeed, compared to other educational options for women through normal schools and coeducational institutions, the curriculum at these women's colleges focused on liberal education rather than on pre-professional programs. These women's colleges not only replicated the curriculum of the men's colleges, they also required students to meet the admission standards of the men's schools. This created enrollment problems, as few women had the necessary background in Greek and Latin. Finding qualified faculty willing to teach at these women's colleges was also a significant problem in the early days. One solution to these dilemmas was the founding of *coordinate colleges,* institutions that shared the faculty and curriculum of men's colleges but operated as separate institutions. These coordinate colleges, including Radcliffe, Pembroke, and Barnard, were considered women's colleges because the male and female students did not take classes together and because the institutions had different administrators. The Seven Sisters served as an enduring model of high-quality education for women.

Between 1890 and 1910 enrollment at women's colleges increased by 348 percent, while the gain of female students at coeducational colleges was 438 percent. Over a similar period, male student attendance in college increased by 214 percent. By the turn of the century, coeducation had become the norm for both men and women, although the most elite institutions in the country continued to be available only to men. Among the arguments in favor of coeducation were that separate education was economically wasteful, that women were equal to men and should therefore be educated together, that single-sex institutions were unnatural, and that coeducation would be helpful in taming the spirits of young men. By 1920 women students represented 47 percent of the student body in colleges and universities. Indeed, the 1920s were a high point in women's education, and in many cases women outnumbered men in colleges. During this era, 74 percent of the colleges and universities were coeducational and the vast majority of women in higher education attended these institutions. Women's colleges, however, continued to attract sufficient numbers of students.

The 1930s through 1950s were marked by a return to a more traditional view about the role of women in society, a view that emphasized women in the home and family. In the 1950s there were 228 men's colleges, 267 women's colleges, and 1,313 coeducational institutions. Indeed, by 1950 the percentage of women in higher education dropped to a low of 30 percent, and enrollment at many of the single-sex institutions—both men's and women's colleges—began to decline precipitously.

The 1960s and 1970s saw a more pronounced shift away from single-sex institutions toward coeducation. During this period, the most prestigious exclusively male colleges and universities began to admit women and many women's colleges also became coeducational. Many of the women's colleges that decided not to admit men closed due to financial exigency during this period. Indeed, many small, private liberal arts colleges, both coeducational and single-sex, closed during this era. To many, the replacement of single-sex education with coeducation was seen as part of women's attainment of parity with men. In fact, many believe that the shift away from single-sex institutions to coeducational ones served both sexes better. Some argued that if one believed that women should attend women's colleges, it somehow implied that women are different or inferior to men. Others argued that women who attend single-sex institutions do not learn to deal with men and are therefore less ready to compete and function in the "real world." As a result, the number of men's colleges declined to only two institutions while the number of women's colleges declined to fewer than eighty institutions. The women's colleges that survived the decline in the 1970s transformed themselves from women's colleges to "colleges for women." The difference between a women's college and a college for women is subtle; but essentially, in order to survive, women's colleges rededicated themselves and their missions to serve women and their unique needs. As colleges for women, these institutions were more purposeful in regard to the needs of their women students as opposed to operating in the same manner as a coeducational institution without the men. The Women's College Coalition, founded in 1972, was created to support these institutions and to increase the visibility and acceptability of women's colleges.

## Characteristics of Contemporary Women's Colleges

Women's colleges educate fewer than 1 percent of all women attending postsecondary institutions and award 1 percent of all degrees conferred—25,000 degrees in 1998. Estimates are that fewer than 5 percent of college-going high school seniors will even apply to attend a women's college. Women's colleges tend to be small, ranging in size from 94 full-time students to 5,000 full-time students. Although all women's colleges are private institutions, more than half of the existing women's colleges have a religious affiliation, most often with the Roman Catholic Church (33%). In terms of geographic location, almost half of the women's colleges are located in the northeastern United States, while 33 percent are located in the South. There are three women's colleges in California, and the rest are scattered around the country.

Although the most selective women's colleges, those known as the Seven Sisters, receive the most attention in the media and in the research literature, women's colleges represent a diverse array of institutions. The Seven Sisters are the oldest, most selective, and most well endowed of the women's colleges, although two of the sisters, Vassar and Radcliffe, are no longer women's colleges. There are also two historically black four-year women's colleges, and six two-year women's colleges. In addition, seventeen

women's colleges grant master's degrees, while forty-seven grant bachelor's degrees. Women's colleges range in selectivity from very selective to nonselective. From a resource perspective, the women's colleges also vary greatly—from those with healthy endowments (including the Seven Sisters) to those institutions that are entirely dependent on tuition revenue to cover operating expenses.

Though women's colleges do not represent a single mold, they do share some common traits. For example, they serve women of color and nontraditional-aged women in higher proportions than comparable coeducational institutions. The explanation for this is twofold. First, serving women, in all their diversity, is a major component of the mission of many women's colleges. Second, in order for the existing women's colleges to survive with their original missions still intact, many had to be creative in attracting and retaining women students. As fewer than 5 percent of high school women will even consider applying to a women's college, this means that many women's colleges have had to focus their attention on attracting older women, part-time students, and transfer students. Women's colleges are also more likely than their coeducational counterparts to grant undergraduate degrees to women in the more male-dominated fields as compared to similar coeducational institutions.

## Contemporary Importance of Women's Colleges

The contemporary importance of women's colleges outweighs their number and size. A wide array of research projects, using both quantitative and qualitative data, have demonstrated that women's colleges are among the most accessible and promoting environments wherein women are taken seriously and ultimately experience success. Specifically, research suggests that women's colleges have a direct, positive impact on their students. Compared to women at coeducational institutions, for example, students at women's colleges are more satisfied with their overall college experience, are more likely to major in nontraditional fields, and express higher levels of self-esteem and leadership skills. Researchers have also found that students who have attended women's colleges are more likely than their coeducational counterparts to graduate, to have high expectations of themselves, to attend graduate school, and to be successful in their adult lives.

There are some critics who have questioned the results of individual studies, especially those studies

2228 SKINNER, B. F.

that focus on the impact of attending a women's college on career and postgraduate outcomes. These critics focus on those studies that use institutions rather than individuals as the unit of analysis and the fact that the studies cannot adequately control for individual student background characteristics. In addition, some critics suggest that the relative success of graduates of women's college may be a dated phenomenon. In other words, when women students began to have access to prestigious men's colleges did claims about women's colleges remain true? This question assumes that the success of women's colleges is because the "best" women students couldn't attend the "best" schools in the country. It also assumes that studies of women's colleges focus on the most elite of these institutions. A third critique about the research on women's colleges is that it fails to account for the self-selection of students. In other words, some suggest that women who choose to attend women's colleges are predestined to be successful and that one cannot credit the institutions at all for the outcomes produced.

Proponents of women's colleges counter such critiques by examining the literature on women's colleges in its totality rather than looking at one study at a time. They contend that research is most powerful when conclusions are drawn from a wide variety of studies using different methods, sources of data, and time periods. In reviewing the literature the majority of studies on women's colleges, including those that control for both institutional and individual characteristics of students, come to the same conclusion. As such, although it is impossible to randomly assign students to attend either a women's college or coeducational college, advocates of women-only institutions maintain that the self-selection argument appears specious. According to these researchers, it is not only dated studies that make claim to the outcomes associated with women's colleges, as studies using contemporary college attendees also come to the same conclusions. Given the totality of the research on women's colleges, proponents conclude that despite differences between methodologies and approach, the extent of overlap, the consistency, and the corroboration in the research findings are so great as to warrant the conclusion that a woman attending an all-women's college, compared with her coeducational counterpart, is more likely to achieve positive outcomes, such as having higher educational aspirations, at-

taining a graduate degree, entering a sex-atypical career, and achieving prominence in her field.

*See also:* HIGHER EDUCATION IN THE UNITED STATES, *subentries on* HISTORICAL DEVELOPMENT, SYSTEM.

HARWARTH, IRENE; MALINE, MINDI; and DEBRA, ELIZABETH. 1997. *Women's Colleges in the United States: History, Issues, and Challenges.* Washington, DC: U.S. Government Printing Office.

PASCARELLA, ERNEST T., and TERENZINI, PATRICK T. 1991. *How College Affects Students: Findings and Insights from Twenty Years of Research.* San Francisco: Jossey-Bass.

RUDOLPH, FREDERICK. 1962. *The American College and University: A History.* Athens: University of Georgia Press.

SOLOMON, BARBARA. 1985. *In the Company of Educated Women: A History of Women and Higher Education in America.* New Haven, CT: Yale University Press.

TIDBALL, ELIZABETH; SMITH, DARYL; TIDBALL, CHARLES; and WOLF-WENDEL, LISA. 1999. *Taking Women Seriously: Lessons and Legacies for Higher Education from Women's Colleges.* Phoenix, AZ: ACE/Oryx Press.

LISA WOLF-WENDEL

# SKINNER, B. F. (1904–1990)

Burrhus Frederick Skinner pioneered the science of behavioral analysis and positive reinforcement as an educational tool. Skinner grew up in Susquehanna, Pennsylvania, a small railroad town thirty miles from the New York state line. His father was an ambitious lawyer for the Erie railroad; his mother, a civic-minded woman that continually reminded Frederick to be aware of "what other people think." Despite his mother's strictures, young Skinner enjoyed his Susquehanna boyhood, roamed the countryside, built ingenious gadgets, and did well in school. In 1922 he was valedictorian of his high school class, having gained a reputation for debating intellectual matters with his teachers. That year he enrolled in Hamilton College, just outside Utica,

New York, where he spent a miserable first year as he lacked athletic ability and connections with Hamilton alumni. In his second year, however, he entered a social circle at Hamilton that appreciated intellectual and artistic life. He began writing short stories; one was praised by poet Robert Frost.

Graduating in 1926, Skinner, against the advice of his parents, decided to spend the next year becoming a writer. He moved into their house in Scranton where his father had taken a position as general counsel for a coal company. It was Skinner's "dark year" as he discovered he had "nothing to say" as a writer. But he was drawn toward behavioral psychology, having read philosopher Bertram Russell's favorable review of John B. Watson's *Behaviorism* (1928). After a short fling with bohemian life in Greenwich Village, Skinner enrolled in graduate school at Harvard University in the psychology department.

## Behavioral Analysis

Skinner, however, was not attracted to psychology at Harvard so much as to the physiology of Professor William Crozier, a student of German physiologist Jacque Loeb. Loeb and Crozier insisted that real science depended on controlling experimental results rather than mere observation of the phenomena being studied. For Skinner the foundation of behavioral analysis became the control of experimental variables. By 1930 he had devised an apparatus to control a specific behavior of a rat. Starting with a runway resembling a rat maze, Skinner gradually fashioned a box with a lever that delivered a food pellet when the rat pushed it. He also invented the *cumulative recorder,* a kymograph-like device that marked a paper every time the rat pressed the lever. He allowed the rat (only one to a box) to be fed a pellet only after it pressed a certain number of times, a behavior control known as *schedules of reinforcement.* He was able to shape lever-pressing behavior so that every time a rat was put on a particular schedule of reinforcement the rate of lever pressing remained constant. The measured behavior was as regular as a pulse beat and marked the beginning of the science of behavioral analysis.

Skinner took great pains to distinguish his science from the stimulus-response conditioning of Ivan Pavlov. The latter conditioned surgically altered dogs. He measured the increase in saliva flow (the response) when a bell was rung (the stimulus) before feeding. Skinner, on the other hand, always used intact organisms (either rats or pigeons), and was only concerned with lever-pressing behavior, never glandular secretion. He acknowledged Pavlov's pioneering work in reinforcement and conditioning but insisted that the science of behavioral analysis involved *operant conditioning.* By 1933 he admitted that there were a multitude of rat behaviors that were not conditioned in what became known as the *Skinner Box.* The rat ran about, stood on hind legs, sniffed, and so forth. But the operation (operant) of lever-pushing was controlled by the schedule of reinforcement—not immediately by the food itself but by the sound of the magazine as it dropped the pellet. Hence although stimulus and response could not always be identified, let alone controlled, the operant or behavior of lever-pressing could be. The rat was not conditioned, only one class of rat behavior was.

*The Behavior of Organisms* (1938) clearly established operant behavioral analysis as a new science. Had he only been exclusively concerned with the behavior of rats and pigeons, Skinner would have already secured a significant place in the history of science. But he became a social inventor whose creations (both mechanical and literary) made him one of the most controversial scientists of the twentieth century. *The Behavior of Organisms* announced Skinner's vision for the future of behavioral analysis: "The importance of a science of behavior derives largely from the possibility of an extension to human affairs" (pp. 441-42). Ultimately this extension would impact American education.

## Social Service

Upon leaving Harvard in 1936 (he received his doctorate in 1933 but continued as a junior fellow) Skinner married Yvonne (Eve) Blue after accepting a position at the University of Minnesota. There he began to transfer operant science to social service. During World War II Skinner and a team of students developed a guidance system for bomb-carrying missiles. A pigeon was conditioned through positive reinforcement to peck the aiming device. But the army deemed "Project Pigeon" unfeasible for wartime use. Disappointed but not discouraged, Skinner moved more directly into a career as a social inventor. He turned his attention to building a *baby-tender,* later trademarked the *aircrib,* for his youngest daughter, Deborah.

The contraption was a carefully designed enclosed space, thermostatically controlled to allow the infant to move freely without constraining clothes.

The child could be removed from the baby-tender at any time. It also freed the mother from constant vigilance over the baby because the infant was much more secure than in a conventional crib. Skinner did not do operant experiments on Deborah in the baby-tender; rather, it was designed to improve the quality of life for both mother and child. After an article in *Life* magazine, the baby-tender was immediately criticized as another Skinner Box, one that imprisoned the child and destroyed the intimate mother-child relationship. For the first time Skinner's fascination with social invention had thrust him into national limelight and controversy.

Thereafter Skinner became evermore controversial as he moved aggressively into the possibilities for using operant science to build a better world. *Walden Two* (1948) envisioned a planned environment that shaped the behaviors of a community using operant techniques of positive reinforcement. Community cooperation and welfare were seemingly naturally conditioned and destructive competition disappeared. The novel met fierce critical commentary as many Americans thought it a grotesque distortion of Henry David Thoreau's *Walden*. Nonetheless by the late 1960s the book became a best-seller and several actual communities were established modeled after the fictional *Walden Two*.

## Educational Reform

Leaving the University of Minnesota in 1945, Skinner spent three years at Indiana University before returning to Harvard in 1948. In November 1953 he visited a Cambridge school where Deborah was a student and was appalled by the mathematics instruction. Students were given problems to solve while the teacher walked up and down the aisles, helping some but ignoring others. Some students finished quickly and fidgeted; others struggled. Graded papers were returned days later. Skinner thought there must be a better way and immediately fashioned a crude teaching machine by cutting up manila folders. The manila folder effort evolved into a slider machine used mostly for arithmetic and spelling. Math problems, for example, were printed on cards that students placed in the machine. The right answer caused a light to appear in a hole in the card. Later he made a device that allowed students to compose answers to questions on a tape that emerged from the machine. Later still, students could compose answers on cardboard disks. A lever was moved that covered the student's answer with

a Plexiglas plate—an innovation that prevented altering the answer and also revealed the correct one. Students mostly answered correctly because questions were designed sequentially from simple to complex. This "programmed instruction" was engineered with positive reinforcement coming from correctly answering the questions. With few mistakes the student progressed rapidly toward mastering arithmetic and spelling. Hence, learning behaviors were shaped by immediate positive reinforcement.

Skinner did not invent the first teaching machine and gave full credit to Sidney Pressey of Ohio State University who had developed a revolving drum device in 1926. Pressey's machine allowed students to press one of four buttons that revealed the correct or incorrect answer—in effect a multiple choice test. Skinner's machines, however, facilitated programmed instruction designed as sequential positive reinforcement. The teaching machine simply transferred immediate positive reinforcement to the mastery of subject matter. One teacher could not possibly immediately reinforce twenty or thirty students in a classroom. What was needed in American education was a technology that incorporated operant conditioning to shaping the learning behavior of each individual student. Skinner assembled a group of former students and colleagues to produce programmed instruction across of full spectrum of subject matter. He convinced companies such as IBM and Rheem to develop prototype teaching machines that could be mass produced. He hoped for a revolution in American education that he described in *Technology of Teaching* (1968).

But the companies refused to aggressively market the machines and educational leaders, most notably former Harvard President James Bryant Conant, though initially enthusiastic, lost interest. IBM and Rheem could make more money on safer investments, while Conant believed the machines and programmed instruction had not proved their viability to educational experts in each subject area. Then, too, the fears of school administrators and teachers over losing control of a traditionally structured classroom, and perhaps also their jobs, dampened enthusiasm for the teaching machine and programmed instruction. The failure of his teaching machine to become as common as automobiles and televisions was Skinner's most bitter disappointment as a social inventor. He fervently believed that the survival of American culture depended upon a revolution in education. With population growth threatening to overwhelm the ability of people to avoid catastrophic wars and ecological disasters, only a technology of teaching incorporating behavioral science could properly educate a citizenry capable of effectively coping with an enveloping ominous world.

*Beyond Freedom and Dignity* (1971) was Skinner's last and most controversial social statement. He attacked what he believed were the fictions of individual freedom and autonomous man. Every person was under the control of his or her evolutionary, cultural, and immediate operant or behavioral contingencies. What was needed was not only a frank admission of this reality, but the application of the science of behavioral analysis to social problems—most importantly to the obvious failure of U.S. schools. But the critics and the public read the word *beyond* in the book title as *in place of* and were enraged. Skinner made the cover of *Time* with the inscription, "B. F. Skinner Says We Can't Afford Freedom." He was bewildered by the firestorm of criticism and spent his remaining years answering critics and defending behavioral analysis. He never quite understood the historical entrenchment of treasured American values such as freedom and autonomy. Nonetheless, the alternative road for American schools that Skinner, a great and provocative thinker-inventor, devised remains an important contribution to the field of education.

*See also:* DEVELOPMENTAL THEORY, *subentry on* HISTORICAL OVERVIEW; HARVARD UNIVERSITY; LEARNING THEORY, *subentry on* HISTORICAL OVERVIEW; PRESSEY, SIDNEY L.

### BIBLIOGRAPHY

BJORK, DANIEL. 1993. *B. F. Skinner: A Life.* New York: Basic Books.

SKINNER, B. F. 1935. "The Generic Nature of the Concepts of Stimulus and Response." *Journal of General Psychology* 9:40–45.

SKINNER, B. F. 1938. *The Behavior of Organisms: An Experimental Analysis.* New York: Appleton-Century-Crofts.

SKINNER, B. F. 1948. *Walden Two.* New York: Macmillan.

SKINNER, B. F. 1958. "Teaching Machines." *Science* 129: 969–977.

SKINNER, B. F. 1968. *The Technology of Teaching.* New York: Appleton-Century-Crofts.

SKINNER, B. F. 1971. *Beyond Freedom and Dignity.* New York: Knopf.

SMITH, LAURENCE D., and WOODWARD, WILLIAM R., eds. 1996. *B. F. Skinner and Behaviorism in American Culture.* Bethlehem, PA: Lehigh University Press.

DANIEL BJORK

# SLEEP AND CHILDREN'S PHYSICAL HEALTH

Sleep is not a passive extravagance that people allow themselves to indulge in. On the contrary, sleep is a highly regulated, active state of being that engages many aspects of one's physiology in a complex manner. It is essential to life. While the purpose of sleep remains a complicated mystery, depriving one's self of sleep has serious consequences for one's health and waking functions. Nevertheless, sleep continues to be encroached upon by daily activities. Of particular concern are accounts of inadequate sleep and daytime sleepiness among school-age children and adolescents, and the potential impact these conditions may have on development and learning.

### Biological Factors That Affect Sleep

Sleepiness refers to the tendency for a waking person to fall asleep. This tendency may be strong or weak, and is determined by both *homeostatic* and *circadian* influences. Homeostatic determinants include the amount of time since a child last slept and the amount of *sleep debt* (i.e., previously poor or inadequate sleep over one or more nights) that the child is carrying. Sleep debts can only be paid back with sleep, and increasing homeostatic pressure to sleep cannot, ultimately, be denied. The circadian system influences daytime sleepiness through *clock-dependent alerting.* Clock-dependent altering refers to the function of people's circadian system to promote wakefulness at certain times of their biological clock—namely, at the beginning and just before the end of their biological "day"—thereby helping them wake from sleep in the morning and stay awake in the latter part of the day when homeostatic pressure increases. Clock-dependent alerting is lowest in the early afternoon, which helps to explain why an adolescent or young adult may find it easier to fall asleep in the early afternoon than in the early evening.

While sleepiness is primarily determined by homeostatic and circadian influences, environmental and time-of-day factors influence the immediate effects of sleepiness on daytime functioning. Arousing elements of one's external environment and/or internal state can temporarily *mask* sleep tendency. Someone out late at a nightclub after working all day has an increased tendency to fall asleep, but this can be masked temporarily by arousing environmental elements (e.g., music), the physical exercise of dancing, and possibly by consuming psychostimulants, such as caffeinated beverages, nicotine, or certain illicit drugs. But sleepiness that is masked is not diminished and could quickly be *unmasked* after leaving the nightclub. Depending on the time of night and the amount of homeostatic pressure, the person could experience *microsleeps* during the drive home. Microsleeps are brief, involuntary sleep attacks of a second or more that can occur outside of awareness. They are more likely to occur when excessive sleepiness is unmasked at a time of low clock-dependent alerting, such as during one's biological "night."

Daytime sleep tendency also appears to be affected by age or, more specifically, pubertal development. Mary Carskadon and colleagues examined sleep and sleepiness in children studied annually from age ten to age sixteen or seventeen. Study participants were allowed a sleep opportunity (i.e., bedtime to risetime) of ten hours per night at each assessment, and daytime sleep tendency was measured the following day using the Multiple Sleep Latency Test (MSLT), a series of objective tests measuring the time it takes to fall asleep under optimal "nap" conditions. Results across years showed virtually no change in the average amount of sleep (9.2 hours) recorded from bedtime to risetime. Thus, the need for sleep at night did not appear to decrease across puberty. However, when children reached midpuberty their midday sleep tendency on the MSLT appeared to increase relative to their prepubertal levels, even though participants were sleeping the same amount at night. These results demonstrate that pubertal development is associated with an increase in daytime sleepiness, suggesting that postpubertal adolescents may actually need *more sleep* to maximize daytime alertness.

## Societal Factors

For the average middle and high school student, getting 9.2 hours of sleep or more on school nights may seem impossible and not worth the sacrifices required to maintain such a schedule. This is not surprising. The twenty-four-hour society of the United States makes ever-increasing demands on the time available for studying, working, and exercising, and offers ever-increasing opportunities for socializing and recreating. As a result, students are easily drawn into a pattern of pursuing daily activities at the expense of a good night's sleep.

In addition, role models for marginalizing the importance of sleep are plentiful. Physicians, lawyers, stockbrokers, and even political operatives are portrayed on television as heroically pushing their physical limits and rising above their lack of sleep. Closer to home, parents often fail to convince children to "do as I say not as I do" with regard to obtaining a good night's sleep, as they often allow their own commitments to encroach on sleep. Thus, from the beginning of primary school to the end of secondary school the average amount of time students spend sleeping on school nights gradually diminishes at the rate of one hour every three years, mostly through postponing bedtime. By the end of high school students average just over seven hours of sleep each school night, close to the adult work-night average of just under seven hours. These trends in school-night sleep time have been described in industrialized countries around the world.

While societal and familial factors influence these trends, at least one biological process may also be involved. As children move through puberty they often begin to prefer activities occurring later in the day. This shift toward evening preference may be expressed biologically as a shift in the timing of the body's readiness for sleep and wake, also referred to as *circadian timing of sleep phase*. A shift toward evening preference accompanied by a biological tendency to delay sleep phase may make it easier for adolescents to stay up later. Sleeping later in the morning would offset this tendency and allow students to be more consistent in the sleep they obtain on school nights, but this conflicts with trends for the average school day, which usually starts and ends earlier as children move from primary to middle to secondary school.

The direct consequence of these social, behavioral, and biological trends is that older children and adolescents often do not obtain enough sleep on school nights to optimize daytime alertness and, they therefore carry a burgeoning sleep debt into the weekend. The typical solution is to wake up later on weekends. In adolescence, weekend sleep amounts average approximately nine hours per night, which might allow students to "pay back" the sleep debt accumulated across the week—if that debt was not so large. Given the amount of sleep determined to optimize alertness (approximately nine hours) and the fact that school-night sleep amounts average below 7.5 hours for adolescents, the average adolescent accumulates seven or more hours of sleep debt per school week. In addition to failing to pay back the sleep debt, going to bed later and sleeping substantially later in the morning on weekends can possibly exacerbate evening preference and delay the circadian timing of sleep phase, thus making sleep less likely to occur at a student's normal bedtime on Sunday.

### Effects of Insufficient Sleep

The consequences of insufficient sleep and chronic daytime sleepiness in the lives of school-age children and adolescents are difficult to characterize at this time due to the limited number of scientific studies with this age range. Available data suggests that behavior, health, learning, and mood are likely to be impaired by excessive sleepiness among pediatric groups, but causal connections have not been proven and any relation between amount of sleep loss and amount of subsequent impairment (a dose-response relationship), has yet to be described.

**Behavior.** Children who show increased sleepiness or who have a disorder that compromises the quality and/or quantity of sleep appear to be at greater risk for daytime behavioral problems. Decreased behavioral difficulties have been associated with successful treatment of sleep disorders.

**Health.** Correlations have been shown between poor quantity and/or quality of sleep and the following: increased days sick from school, increased physical complaints, risk for accidents or injuries, and adoption of health-risk behaviors such as increased consumption of alcohol, nicotine, and caffeine. Of particular note for older adolescents, drivers age twenty-five or younger were shown to be responsible for a majority of fall-asleep automobile crashes in one region of the country.

**Performance and learning.** Tests of cognitive performance administered to students with sleep disorders or to healthy students experimentally sleep-restricted have generally failed to produce consistent results, but data suggest that students process infor-

mation and react more slowly following inadequate sleep, and may be more prone to errors with so-called higher cognitive functions that involve abstract problem solving, creativity, or rule-governed behavior. Survey studies consistently demonstrate that students with later school-night bedtimes, more irregular bedtimes, less sleep on school nights, sleep problems, and increased complaints of daytime sleepiness have lower academic achievement than children with earlier, more regular bedtimes, more sleep, no sleep problems, and fewer complaints of sleepiness. Improved performance and academic achievement have been reported following treatment for sleep disorders.

**Mood.** Preliminary results from experimental and correlational studies provide consistent support for an association between inadequate quantity and quality of sleep among children and diminished happiness and/or increased depressed mood.

In conclusion, there is a need to learn more about the life-enhancing benefits of increasing sleep and the high cost of failing to protect it among children and adolescents. Determining the optimal quantity and timing of nocturnal sleep is likely to vary among individuals but existing trends suggest that many students should consider expanding school-night sleep opportunities, especially in the second decade. Students need to be more consistent with bedtimes and risetimes on school and nonschool nights to avoid confusing the biological clock. Students also need to avoid caffeinated beverages and nicotine, as these substances can mask sleepiness and lead to difficulty falling asleep if taken later in the day. A brief afternoon nap is a much healthier alternative. Parents need to work with their children to create sleep-friendly family routines that make it easier for children (and adults) to protect sleep. Finally, more work is needed in communities to create sleep-friendly school schedules and work guidelines for minors, and to raise awareness about the risks associated with drowsy driving.

*See also:* HEALTH AND EDUCATION; OUT-OF-SCHOOL INFLUENCES AND ACADEMIC SUCCESS; PARENTING.

### BIBLIOGRAPHY

CARSKADON, MARY A. 1982. "The Second Decade." In *Sleeping and Waking Disorders: Indications and Techniques,* ed. Christian Guilleminault. Menlo Park, CA: Addison-Wesley.

CARSKADON, MARY A. 1999. "When Worlds Collide: Adolescent Need for Sleep Versus Societal Demands." *Phi Delta Kappan* 80:348–353.

CARSKADON, MARY A., ed. 2002. *Adolescent Sleep Patterns: Biological, Sociological, and Psychological Influences.* Cambridge, Eng.: Cambridge University Press.

DAHL, RONALD E. "The Consequences of Insufficient Sleep for Adolescents: Links Between Sleep and Emotional Regulation." *Phi Delta Kappan* 80:354–359.

GRAHAM, MARY G., ed. 2000. *Sleep Needs, Patterns, and Difficulties of Adolescents: Summary of a Workshop.* Forum on Adolescence, Board on Children, Youth, and Families, National Research Council, Institute of Medicine. Washington, DC: National Academy Press.

SADEH, AVI; GRUBER, REUT; and RAVIV, AMIRAM. 2002. "Sleep, Neurobehavioral Functioning, and Behavior Problems in School-Age Children." *Child Development* 73:405–417.

SADEH, AVI; RAVIV, AMIRAM; and GRUBER, REUT. 2000. "Sleep Patterns and Sleep Disruptions in School-Age Children." *Developmental Psychology* 36:291–301.

VALENT, FRANCESCA; BRUSAFERRO, SILVIO; and BARBONE, FABIO. 2001. "A Case-Crossover Study of Sleep and Childhood Injury." *Pediatrics* 107(2):E23.

WOLFSON, AMY R., and CARSKADON, MARY A. 1998. "Sleep Schedules and Daytime Functioning in Adolescents." *Child Development* 69:875–887.

GAHAN FALLONE

# SMALL GROUP INSTRUCTION

*See:* INSTRUCTIONAL STRATEGIES.

# SMALL NATIONS

In purely numerical terms, the world is a world of small nations. More than half the globe's sovereign states have populations of less than 5 million, and about fifty have populations below 1.5 million. Some of these states are islands, some are archipelagos, and some are enclaves. The states are scattered in all parts of the world, but with concentrations in the Caribbean and South Pacific.

In 1985 the Commonwealth Secretariat convened a seminal meeting on education in small nations. Its report stated the following:

> The style of educational development . . . is too frequently modeled on what is appropriate and fashionable in large states. Small countries are not simply a scaled-down version of large countries. They have an ecology of their own. We believe there is a cluster of factors which suggest particular strategies in the smaller states of the world. (quoted in Bray, p. 9)

The majority of small nations are members of the Commonwealth, therefore, this statement set the agenda for a major program of work by the Commonwealth Secretariat. Other work since the mid-1980s has also made a major contribution to conceptual understanding and practical strategies.

## Definitions

*Small* is of course a relative concept. Singapore may feel small in comparison with China, India, and Indonesia, but might feel large compared with Fiji. Likewise, Fiji might feel small compared with Papua New Guinea, but might feel large compared with Tuvalu, Tonga, and Vanuatu.

Most of the literature recognizes that relative distinctions are important, but nevertheless uses absolute indicators. Population is usually the main criterion, though common alternative or supplementary indicators are area and size of economy. One common cutoff point in the literature is a population size of 1.5 million. However, this cutoff point is entirely arbitrary, and it is often more appropriate to examine issues along a continuum of size.

It is also necessary to consider the term *nation*. The usual starting point is an entity with sovereign autonomy. However, many nonsovereign but self-governing territories have attributes that resemble those of their sovereign counterparts. Thus to some extent the literature on education in small nations may embrace such entities as Montserrat (a colony of the United Kingdom), Macau (a special administrative region of the People's Republic of China), and Guam (an unincorporated territory of the United States).

## Problems Faced by Small Nations

Among the problems common to small nations, three deserve specific attention: economic vulnerability, isolation, and high costs of administration. These problems have implications for education as well as for other domains.

On the economic side, most small nations are dependent on international forces over which they have almost no control. Some small countries have become wealthy from tourism or tax-free trading, but these activities are sensitive to international exchange rates and the economies of other countries. Also, few small nations have sufficiently convenient geographic positions to enable them to earn money in this way. Many are also highly dependent on cash crops, and are unable to diversify. Economic fluctuations can create crises for educational budgets. Also, dependence on external forces may require small nations to match their education systems to those of larger countries.

Many small nations, particularly island ones, also suffer from isolation. This may be geographic, political, and/or cultural. The people of Seychelles, for example, suffer from geographic isolation because they are 1,500 kilometers from any other country. It is costly to import and export goods, and it is expensive both to send local people abroad and to bring specialists from outside.

Small nations are also generally unable to achieve the economies of scale of their larger counterparts, for the machinery of government requires a basic number of administrators whatever the population size. Every country needs a head of state, for example, whether the person serves a large or a small population, and similar points may be made at all other administrative levels. Costs may be lowered if one person does two jobs, but this only reduces the problem and does not remove it. Personnel in ministries of education must be much more multifunctional than their counterparts in larger states.

## Benefits Gained by Small Nations

On the other side of the coin are various benefits gained by small nations. Particularly worth highlighting are national identity, transparency, sensitivity to administrative changes, and interpersonal relations.

One of the greatest benefits for small nations arises from the fact that they are countries, even if they are small ones. The 8,000 people of Tuvalu, for example, receive more prominence than comparable groups of 8,000 in the suburbs of Los Angeles, Calcutta, or Mexico City. Likewise the island of Domi-

nica receives much more prominence than islands of similar size off the coasts of Canada, Scotland, or Chile. Even if the individual votes of small state governments do not carry so much weight in some international forums as do the votes of large state governments, the small governments do at least have votes. Partly because of national visibility, small nations generally have much higher levels of per capita foreign aid than do medium-sized and large states.

Small nations may also benefit from transparency, because it is often easier to identify and diagnose problems. Moreover, once bottlenecks have been identified, it may be relatively easy to remedy them. Particularly in compact states, communications are usually good. It may be possible, for example, to call a meeting of all primary school principals—a task that would be impossible in a large country. Also, individual officers can have a big impact on the system. The education systems of small nations may be much more sensitive to reform initiatives.

Allied to these points are features of interpersonal relations. In countries with small populations, daily life is usually more personal than in those with large populations. Of course, this may cut both ways, for interpersonal relations can cause considerable difficulties. However, knowledge of other people's backgrounds and personalities can greatly facilitate the processes of planning and coordination.

## The Range of Provision

Many small nations, including prosperous ones, encounter limits in the range of education which they can provide for their citizens. For example, the smallest of the small cannot operate universities; and the states that do operate universities can only have institutions with a restricted range of specialties.

The responses to these limits vary. Some small nations simply send their students abroad. Others group together to form regional universities. Particularly striking are the University of the West Indies, which was founded by fifteen member states in 1948, and the University of the South Pacific, which was founded by eleven member states in 1968. Other countries form partnerships with external institutions for particular courses and/or for distance education.

Each of these strategies has merits and problems. Sending students abroad and/or making arrangements with external institutions often makes more economic sense than trying to do everything domestically. Such arrangements also give planners flexibility to choose from a wide range of countries and institutions. However, external institutions are often perceived to be less relevant to local needs, and national pride often requires at least some domestic higher education provision. Regional institutions may be a compromise, but often suffer severe political strains.

## Small Is Complex

An officer in the Ministry of Education of Maldives has pointed out the following:

> Educational planning in small countries is sometimes thought to be less of a challenge than in large countries. The experience in Maldives and in other small countries indicates otherwise. . . . Small but complex societies have their unique problems in the planning and management of education. These include remoteness and isolation of small communities, no economies of scale, greater transparency, closely knit social organizations, heavy dependence on external assistance, and critical shortage of essential manpower. (quoted in Bray, p. 112)

Many planners in other small nations would echo these points. Planners have to find careful balances between the demands of small-state nationalism and the realities of economics and international dependence. The nature of the balances naturally varies in different situations; but the growing literature on this topic has shown a considerable range of tools that can be deployed.

In some ways, new technologies have reduced the challenges faced by small nations. The Internet, for example, has reduced the problems arising from the lack of specialist libraries in small nations by providing access to a variety of information electronically. The Internet also facilitates distance learning, and allows personnel in small nations to gain specialist assistance without going abroad.

At the same time, the new technologies and other forces have increased the challenges for small nations. Small nations have become more fully integrated into a globalized world, which has intensified questions of identity on the periphery of decision making. These factors have had major implications for curricula, examination systems, and even media of instruction.

Small nations should not be treated as merely scaled-down versions of larger countries. They have distinctive characteristics and ecologies of their own, which must be taken into consideration during analysis and planning of education systems.

**See also:** DECISION-MAKING IN DEVELOPING NATIONS, APPLYING ECONOMIC ANALYSIS TO; EDUCATION DEVELOPMENT PROJECTS.

### BIBLIOGRAPHY

ATCHOARENA, DAVID. 1993. *Educational Strategies for Small Island States.* Fundamentals of Educational Planning 44. Paris: UNESCO International Institute for Educational Planning.

BACCHUS, KAZIM, and BROCK, COLIN, eds. 1993. *The Challenge of Scale: Educational Development in the Small Nations of the Commonwealth.* London: The Commonwealth Secretariat.

BALDACCHINO, GODFREY, and BRAY, MARK, eds. 2001. "Human Resource Strategies for Small Nations." *International Journal of Educational Development* 21(3):231–244.

BRAY, MARK. 1992. *Educational Planning in Small Countries.* Paris: UNESCO.

BRAY, MARK, and PACKER, STEVE. 1993. *Education in Small Nations: Concepts, Challenges and Strategies.* Oxford: Pergamon Press.

BRAY, MARK, and STEWARD, LUCY, eds. 1998. *Examination Systems in Small Nations: Comparative Perspectives on Policies, Models and Operations.* London: The Commonwealth Secretariat.

CROSSLEY, MICHAEL, and HOLMES, KEITH. 1999. *Educational Development in the Small Nations of the Commonwealth: Retrospect and Prospect.* London: The Commonwealth Secretariat.

"Education in Small Nations." 1991. Special issue. *Prospects: Quarterly Review of Education* 21(4).

LILLIS, KEVIN M. 1993. *Policy, Planning and Management of Education in Small Nations.* Paris: UNESCO International Institute for Educational Planning.

MARK BRAY

# SMITH, DAVID EUGENE (1860–1944)

Professor of mathematics at Teachers College, Columbia University, David Eugene Smith is considered one of the founders of the field of mathematics education. Smith was born in Cortland, New York, to Abram P. Smith, attorney and surrogate judge, and Mary Elizabeth Bronson, who taught her young son Latin and Greek. Smith studied at Syracuse University, earning a B.Ph. (1881), M.Ph. (1884), and Ph.D. (1887) with a concentration in aesthetics and the history of fine arts.

In 1881 Smith began to practice law in his father's office, but welcomed a chance opportunity in 1884 to teach mathematics at the local normal school, where he had studied as a boy, embarking upon what would become a forty-two-year career in academia. He left Cortland Normal School in 1891 to head the mathematics department at Michigan State Normal School (later Eastern Michigan University) in Ypsilanti. From 1898 to 1901 Smith served as principal of Brockport (New York) Normal School. In 1901 he accepted the chair in mathematics at Teachers College, Columbia University, where he remained until his retirement in 1926.

During the 1890s and early 1900s, as enrollments in American high schools increased, national committees convened to examine education recommended curricular reform. For mathematics, the curriculum was to decrease emphasis on rule-based learning and "mental discipline" and move toward a more inductive approach, with practical applications that would better prepare students for college. To be effective, this approach would require teachers well-prepared in mathematics and knowledgeable in its instruction.

Smith was a leader in developing programs that combined the study of mathematics and teaching. At Michigan State Normal School he offered one of the earliest courses in methods for teaching algebra and geometry in secondary school. He also offered a course in the history of mathematics—unique at the time—that examined how the subject developed and how it had been taught in the past. Smith's interest in history continued throughout his career, and he made it a hallmark of his programs. In 1900 Smith published *The Teaching of Elementary Mathematics,* a handbook for teachers that would become a seminal work in the field of mathematics education.

At Teachers College Smith developed graduate programs for secondary and postsecondary teachers that included a two-year or three-year sequence of course work in the history of mathematics. In 1906, two of Smith's students were awarded the first American doctorates in mathematics education. All Smith's programs, whether undergraduate or graduate, shared three distinguishing characteristics: They encouraged teachers to take an active role in determining the mathematics curriculum and classroom pedagogy, to gain a historical perspective on teaching their subject, and to consider international viewpoints on education.

From 1908 to 1912 Smith took to the international stage, seeking to establish mathematics education as a field worthy of special study, separate from mathematics or general education alone. He conceived of the International Commission on the Teaching of Mathematics (ICTM), convinced the eminent mathematician Felix Klein to accept the presidency of the commission, and was primarily responsible for the organization of an extensive network of national committees that prepared detailed reports on mathematics instruction in their respective countries. The American commission, with Smith as chair, identified its country's greatest need as the improved preparation of teachers. With the 1912 presentation of the series of ICTM reports to the International Congress of Mathematicians and the decade-long support of Eliakim Hastings Moore, Jacob William Albert Young, and George Myers at the University of Chicago, mathematics education emerged as a distinct field of study. Smith served as ICTM vice president (1908–1920) and later as president (1928–1932).

Smith's concern for history grew out of long-cultivated interests. From boyhood, Smith enjoyed travel and became an avid collector. When he began to teach mathematics, he turned his attention to mathematical artifacts. By the time Smith donated his collection to Columbia in the 1930s, he had gathered more than 3,000 portraits and autographed letters of famous mathematicians, and approximately 300 rare astronomical instruments and ancient counting devices.

Smith enjoyed collecting not only for himself, he also delighted in sharing his broad knowledge and insight with others. Beginning in 1901, Smith advised George A. Plimpton, head of the New York office of the publishing house Ginn and Company, on acquisitions for his mathematical textbook collection. By 1908, Plimpton had assembled the most complete library of arithmetics printed before 1601. Since Plimpton generously permitted Smith's graduate students access to his collection, they had the rare opportunity to study valuable primary sources. To make the collection more widely known, Smith prepared a richly illustrated catalogue, *Rara Arithmetica* (1908).

As a highly regarded historian of mathematics, Smith contributed numerous books, articles, translations of and commentaries on the subject, most notably his two-volume *History of Mathematics* (1923, 1925). In 1924 Smith joined with others to found the History of Science Society, and, subsequently, served as its president (1927). In 1932 he founded the journal *Scripta Mathematica* with Jekuthiel Ginsburg. Smith also took on the role of mathematics editor for a number of encyclopedias, including *Cyclopedia of Education* (1911–1913) and *Encyclopedia Britannica* (1927).

Smith made other significant contributions to the professional mathematics community. From 1902 to 1920 he served as librarian of the American Mathematical Society (AMS) and associate editor of its *Bulletin*. He became a charter member of the Mathematical Association of America (MAA) when it was organized in 1916, served as associate editor for its publication, *The American Mathematical Monthly,* and was elected president for the term 1920 to 1921.

A significant portion of Smith's writings dealt with issues relating to the newly developing field of mathematics education. *The Teaching of Arithmetic* appeared in 1909, followed by *The Teaching of Geometry* in 1911. These works were complemented by Smith's prodigious production of textbooks, often in collaboration with others. Smith-Wentworth textbooks in arithmetic, algebra, and geometry were dominant during the 1910s. Smith also helped to organize associations for mathematics teachers. In 1903, together with Thomas Fiske, a Columbia mathematics professor who had founded AMS in 1888, Smith convened an organizational meeting for the Association of Teachers of Mathematics in the Middle States and Maryland and was elected its first president.

Major national committees concerned with educational reform invited Smith to join their ranks. The National Committee of Fifteen on the Geometry Syllabus, appointed by the National Educational Association, included Smith as a member. It issued its report in 1911. In 1920 the MAA appointed Smith to the National Committee on Mathematical Requirements, which issued its influential report in 1923.

Smith combined his interests in teaching, mathematics, history, travel, and collecting to support the development of new programs to prepare mathematics teachers for the nation's schools. His vision, efforts, and accomplishments left a rich legacy to mathematics education, a field of study he pioneered in the early twentieth century.

*See also:* MATHEMATICS EDUCATION, PREPARATION OF TEACHERS; PROGRESSIVE EDUCATION.

### BIBLIOGRAPHY

DONOGHUE, EILEEN F. 1998. "In Search of Mathematical Treasures: David Eugene Smith and George Arthur Plimpton." *Historia Mathematica* 25:359–365.

DONOGHUE, EILEEN F. 2001. "Mathematics Education in the United States: Origins of the Field and the Development of Early Graduate Programs." In *One Field, Many Paths: U. S. Doctoral Programs in Mathematics Education,* ed. Robert E. Reys and Jeremy Kilpatrick. Washington, DC: American Mathematical Society/Mathematical Association of America.

SMITH, DAVID EUGENE. 1900. *The Teaching of Elementary Mathematics. Teachers' Professional Library,* ed. Nicholas Murray Butler. New York: Macmillan.

SMITH, DAVID EUGENE. 1908. *Rara Arithmetica.* Boston: Ginn.

SMITH, DAVID EUGENE. 1912. *Report of the American Commissioners of the International Commission on the Teaching of Mathematics.* Washington, DC: Government Printing Office.

SMITH, DAVID EUGENE. 1923, 1925. *History of Mathematics,* 2 vols. Boston: Ginn.

EILEEN F. DONOGHUE

# SMITHSONIAN INSTITUTION, EDUCATION PROGRAMS

The Smithsonian Institution, an independent trust instrumentality of the United States, is a center for research dedicated to public education, national service, and scholarship in the arts, science, and history. Its collections hold more than 140 million artifacts and specimens. The Smithsonian was established in

1846 with funds bequeathed to the United States by James Smithson, a British scientist. This bequest to establish in Washington, D.C., an institution for the increase and diffusion of knowledge is responsible for establishing the world's largest museum complex. The U.S. Congress provided that the institution be administered by a board of regents—consisting of the vice president of the United States, the chief justice of the Supreme Court, three congressmen, three senators, and six private citizens chosen by Congress—and a secretary.

The Smithsonian is composed of sixteen museums and galleries, the National Zoological Park, and research facilities in the United States and abroad. Nine Smithsonian museums are located on the National Mall between the Washington Monument and the Capitol. Five other museums and the zoo are elsewhere in Washington, D.C.; the Cooper-Hewitt National Design Museum and the National Museum of the American Indian Heye Center are in New York City. Smithsonian education programs in these facilities demonstrate how museums can be powerful learning environments. Smithsonian research and outreach units also provide significant educational programming. These units include the Smithsonian Astrophysical Observatory in Cambridge, Massachusetts; the Smithsonian Tropical Research Institute in Panama; the National Science Resource Center; the Smithsonian Center for Education and Museum Studies; and The Smithsonian Associates (TSA). More information on Smithsonian museums, research, and outreach units can be found at the institution's website.

The Smithsonian is committed to serving as the most extensive provider of authoritative experiences that connect the American people to their history and their cultural and scientific heritages. A major objective of the institution is to bring Smithsonian education resources to the nation through a comprehensive education program that focuses on the kindergarten through college student population, teachers at all levels, and lifelong learners. A wide variety of educational offerings take place every day and many evenings throughout the institution to meet this objective. These include formal programs for elementary and secondary students both in the galleries of Smithsonian museums and over the World Wide Web; internships and fellowships open to qualified undergraduate, graduate, and postgraduate students; and programming for the general public, in the galleries during the day and in evening

and weekend courses, lectures, and study tours. Smithsonian staff members teach courses at nearby institutions and around the country, conduct seminars and lectures, and act as supervisors and mentors for undergraduate and graduate students and visiting associates. Each year the breadth and scope of Smithsonian education programs has an impact on millions of students and learners of all ages.

## Elementary and Secondary Education Programs

Each Smithsonian museum, research, and outreach unit has an education department with responsibility for planning and implementing programs for students. These programs are interactive and encourage students to use analytical and deductive reasoning skills as they experience exhibitions, demonstrations, and other activities. All museums offer previsit materials such as activity sheets, museum guides, and teachers' guides that provide hands-on lessons for use in the classroom and at home. The museums also offer curriculum packets developed by classroom educators working with museum curators and scientists, which provide multidisciplinary activities. Teaching materials include reproductions of objects, specimens, or artwork; lesson plans with examples of student work; resource lists; and reference information. The Smithsonian Early Enrichment Center introduces preschool-age children to the arts and sciences through objects and exhibits in Smithsonian museums. The center has developed a comprehensive, theoretical framework regarding museum-based education for the youngest audience of museum visitors and communicates these concepts in training seminars for teachers around the country.

More than 6.5 million school children visit the institution each year. Smithsonian education is not, however, limited by physical space or geographic location. The institution is working to dramatically enlarge its audiences and its degrees of engagement with the public throughout the country. Millions more students nationwide can access a wealth of on-line resources made available by all Smithsonian units and can attend the many programs and exhibitions that the Smithsonian's Office of National Programs sponsors in local museums and schools across the country. Smithsonian museums create comprehensive educational websites with activities for families, teachers, and students. Many of these sites offer interdisciplinary lesson plans that emphasize inquiry-based learning with primary sources and museum collections. Provided are photographs of objects, guidelines for working with them, and links to other online resources. The Smithsonian's central education website lists standards in science, U.S. history, world history, and visual arts, and it identifies specific collections and online resources from Smithsonian museums that can be used to help address those standards. Initiatives from the Office of National Programs include traveling exhibitions, Scholar in the School programs, teacher development programs, and affiliations with other museums throughout the United States.

## Higher Education Programs

The Smithsonian Institution offers a variety of internship and fellowship programs for undergraduate, graduate, and postgraduate students. An internship at the Smithsonian Institution is a prearranged, structured learning experience scheduled within a specific time frame. The experience must be relevant to the intern's academic and professional goals and to research and museum activities of the institution. An internship is performed under the direct supervision of Smithsonian staff. Internships are arranged by contacting the appropriate internship coordinator at a Smithsonian museum, office, or research institute, or through the Internship Central Referral Service offered by the Smithsonian Center for Education and Museum Studies. Stipends are available to qualified students for several of the institution's internship programs.

Pre- and postdoctoral fellowships at the Smithsonian Institution provide students and scholars with opportunities to pursue independent research projects in association with members of the Smithsonian professional research staff. The Office of Fellowships has the central management and administrative responsibility for the institution's programs of research grants, fellowships, and other scholarly appointments. One of its primary objectives is the facilitation of the Smithsonian's scholarly interactions with students and scholars at universities, museums, and other research institutions around the world. The office administers institution-wide research support programs, and encourages and assists other Smithsonian museums, research institutes, and research offices in the development of additional fellowships and visiting appointments. Applicants are evaluated on their academic standing, scholarly qualifications, experiences, the quality of the research project or study

proposed, and its suitability to Smithsonian collections, facilities, and programs. Stipends and additional allowances are available for most appointments. Scholars and students with outside sources of funding are also encouraged to use the institution's resources and facilities. The Office of Fellowships can facilitate visiting appointments in such cases provided that the investigator obtains approval from the staff member with whom he or she would consult.

## Professional Development

The Smithsonian works with teachers in the Washington, D.C., metropolitan area and throughout the nation. Through special events, for-credit courses, and long-term partnerships, teachers discover innovative ways to meet their teaching objectives using museum resources. These programs support local and national standards and many are approved for in-service credit or recertification points in the District of Columbia, Maryland, and Virginia. The institution also collaborates or partners with various educational, professional, and service organizations, such as the College Board, the International Literacy Network, the National Writers Project, and the U.S. Department of Education to establish models that demonstrate how the use of museum resources and research methodologies can strengthen teaching and instruction at the elementary, secondary, and college level. The Smithsonian is also a leader in providing professional development opportunities for museum professionals in the United States and abroad. The institution sponsors an annual series of training programs in collections care, museum management, and education topics in Washington, D.C., and in museums around the country.

## Family and Continuing Education Programs

Lifelong learning takes many shapes at the Smithsonian. Visitors, whether individuals or with family and friends, can participate in educational programming on most weekends at every Smithsonian museum and, in the summer, at special evening events at the institution's international art museums. The Center for Folklife and Cultural Heritage organizes the annual Smithsonian Folklife Festival on the National Mall each summer, featuring demonstrations, storytelling, and narrative sessions for discussing cultural issues. The Smithsonian Associates (TSA) offers programming for lifelong learners that highlights and complements the work done across the

Smithsonian. TSA's Resident Associate program offers more than 120 programs each month in the Washington D.C., area and also provides educational and cultural programs to audiences outside the Washington, D.C., area, through the Scholar in the School and Smithsonian Voices of Discovery programs, and the Study Tour program, which organizes more than 300 trips each year to locations around the world.

**INTERNET RESOURCE**

Smithsonian Institution. 2002. <www.si.edu.>.

Bruce C. Craig

## SMOKING

*See:* Family Composition and Circumstance, *subentry on* Alcohol, Tobacco, and Other Drugs; Risk Behaviors, *subentry on* Smoking and Its Effect on Children's Health.

## SNEDDEN, DAVID (1868–1951)

One of the most prominent educators of the Progressive era, David Samuel Snedden was probably the most articulate advocate of *social efficiency*—a term popularized by Benjamin Kidd in *Social Evolution* (1894) and taken up by Snedden for his approach to design an educational program that reconciled the demands of industrial society with the capabilities and interests of children.

Born on a farm in Kavilah, California, and educated by his mother, Snedden attended St. Vincent's College in Los Angeles, taking the B.A. (1890) and the M.A (1892). He received his second B.A. from Stanford University (1897) and another M.A. (1901) degree from Teachers College, Columbia University. For ten years he served as teacher, principal, and superintendent at California's schools, then he taught as assistant professor at Stanford (1901–1905), and as adjunct professor at Teachers College, Columbia University (1905–1909). In his dissertation, "Administration and Educational Work of American Juvenile Reform Schools" (1907), he presented the practical and useful education of reform schools as a model for the improvement of the public school system. With Samuel T. Dutton, he coauthored the

first school administration textbook, *The Administration of Public Education in the United States* (1908), in which he pled for a legislative reform that safeguarded the democratic rights of the people, but took school government from politicians, placing it in the hands of experts.

From 1909 to 1916 Snedden served as the first State Commissioner of Education in Massachusetts with Charles A. Prosser as deputy for vocational education and Clarence Kingsley as assistant for secondary education. In 1906, the Massachusetts (Douglas) Commission on Industrial and Technical Education had found that the public schools—including manual training and household arts—did not furnish the skills and industrial intelligence that "students needed to participate effectively in industry and life." As adherent of Herbert Spencer and Edward A. Ross, Snedden shared the commission's view that the American school system was "unefficient" and "undemocratic" since it answered the needs of the small band of theoretically inclined students bound for college, but neglected the interests of the great majority of practically minded youth, who in the United States—contrary to "autocratic" Germany—had no chance of preparing themselves early and thoroughly for their life's work. To deliver industry, commerce, and agriculture the skilled and intelligent workers they needed, Snedden advocated the spread of the project method of teaching and the expansion of the common school system by establishing, besides the traditional high schools for "officers," new vocational schools for the "rank and file." In fact, he institutionalized a wide range of specialized schools and courses in Massachusetts, which taught the skills and techniques of specific callings and reflected their students' intellectual capabilities, vocational interests, and future careers. Like Charles Prosser and Georg Kerschensteiner, Snedden propagated part-time and full-time industrial education and practical project work nationwide as means to secure, through differentiation and learning by doing, equality of opportunity for the individual and economic and social progress for the community.

During his second term at Teachers College as professor of educational sociology (1916–1935) Snedden elaborated his concept of social efficiency and applied it to curriculum construction, civic education, and character building. In *Sociological Determination of Objectives in Education* (1921), Snedden argued that production, as the ability to do, and consumption, as the ability to appreciate, were the two main components of adult life; but to make the liberal and vocational elements of life effectively teachable, social life had to be divided by empirical analysis into thousands of minute objectives, called "peths," which were to be organized into "strands" and the more complex "performance practices." Here, Snedden adopted the concept of scientific management originally developed by Frederick W. Taylor for the raise of industrial productivity, and transferred to school and teaching by Franklin Bobbitt. Like Bobbitt and W. W. Charters, Snedden believed that scientific curriculum-making took school education out of the stone age into the industrial present. It supplied teachers with lists and catalogs enumerating in detail the abilities, attitudes, habits, and forms of knowledge that would increase their students' social efficiency and would help them to survive and advance in the struggle of life. His book *Educational Sociology* (1922) became a standard in the field; it promoted the idea that each subject—history as well as Latin and mathematics—had to meet the test of social usefulness and that the efficient society resembled a winning "team group" with above-average people as leaders and the rest as followers: each group was trained for its specific role and fulfilled its proper function. Like all Progressive educators, Snedden opposed the traditional ways of abstract, unreal, and bookish instruction; at the same time, he criticized his colleagues for an overemphasis on growth, creativity, and self-realization. His debates with John Dewey, Boyd H. Bode, and H. Gordon Hullfish about liberal education, democracy, and social predestination demonstrate his belief in the value of specific instruction, expert knowledge, and scientific inquiry.

*See also:* VOCATIONAL AND TECHNICAL EDUCATION, *subentry on* HISTORY OF.

### BIBLIOGRAPHY

BODE, BOYD H. 1927. *Modern Educational Theories.* New York: Macmillan.

DROST, WALTER H. 1967. *David Snedden and Education for Social Efficiency.* Madison: University of Wisconsin Press.

HULLFISH, H. GORDON. 1924. "Looking Backward with Snedden." *Educational Review* 67(February).

KLIEBARD, HERBERT M. 1986. *The Struggle for the American Curriculum, 1893–1958.* New York: Routledge and Kegan Paul.

SNEDDEN, DAVID. 1907. *Administration and Educational Work of American Juvenile Reform Schools.* New York: Teachers College, Columbia University.

SNEDDEN, DAVID. 1910. *The Problem of Vocational Education.* Boston: Houghton Mifflin.

SNEDDEN, DAVID. 1913. *Problems of Educational Readjustment.* Boston: Houghton Mifflin.

SNEDDEN, DAVID. 1920. *Vocational Education.* New York: Macmillan.

SNEDDEN, DAVID. 1921. *Sociological Determination of Objectives in Education.* Philadelphia: Lippincott.

SNEDDEN, DAVID. 1922. *Civic Education: Sociological Foundations and Courses.* New York: World Book Company.

SNEDDEN, DAVID. 1922. *Educational Sociology.* New York: Century.

SNEDDEN, DAVID, and DUTTON, SAMUEL T. 1908. *The Administration of Public Education in the United States.* New York: Macmillan.

WIRTH, ARTHUR G. 1972. *Education in the Technological Society: The Vocational-Liberal Studies Controversy in the Early Twentieth Century.* Scranton, PA: Intext.

MICHAEL KNOLL

# SOCIAL CAPITAL AND EDUCATION

Social capital refers to the intangible resources embedded within interpersonal relationships or social institutions. Social capital can exist in three major forms: as obligations and expectations, as information channels, and as social norms. Obligations and expectations can be conceived of as a "credit slip" that people hold, and that can be cashed when necessary. Information channels provide appropriate information as an important basis for action. Social norms provide the criteria for rewarding or sanctioning individual actions.

In the context of education, social capital in the forms of parental expectations, obligations, and social networks that exist within the family, school, and community are important for student success. These variations in academic success can be attributed to parents' expectations and obligations for educating their children; to the network and connections between families whom the school serves; to the disciplinary and academic climate at school; and to the cultural norms and values that promote student efforts. The concept of social capital is a useful theoretical construct for explaining the disparities in students' educational performance among different nations.

In the 1980s James Coleman developed the concept of social capital to conceptualize social patterns and processes that contribute to the ethnic disparities of student achievement. He argued that the educational expectation, norms, and obligations that exist within a family or a community are important social capital that can influence the level of parental involvement and investment, which in turn affect academic success.

At the family level, parents' cultural capital and financial capital become available to the child only if the social connection between the child and the parents is sufficiently strong. Youths from single-parent families or with larger numbers of siblings are more likely to drop out of high school because of the eroded social capital associated with the nontraditional family structure. As new structures of the household in modern society become more prevalent, many linkages and activities that provided social capital for the next generation are no longer present, and their absence may be detrimental to children's learning.

At the institutional level, disciplinary climate and academic norms established by the school community and the mutual trust between home and school are major forms of social capital. These forms of social capital are found to contribute to student learning outcomes in East Asian countries such as Singapore, Korea, and Hong Kong. They have been shown to have a significant impact, not only on creating a learning and caring school climate, but also on improving the quality of schooling and reducing inequality of learning outcomes between social-class groups.

In summation, the concept of *social capital* is a useful tool for understanding differences among student learning outcomes. Nations with high stocks of social capital are more likely to produce students with better academic performance than nations with low stocks. However, studies by Pamela Paxton, and Michael Woolcock and Deepa Narayan, have noted

that high levels of social capital could restrict individual growth and societal development. Further analysis is needed to identify the potential negative impact of high social capital.

*See also:* COMMUNITY EDUCATION; FAMILY, SCHOOL, AND COMMUNITY CONNECTIONS; PARENTAL INVOLVEMENT IN EDUCATION; SOCIAL COHESION AND EDUCATION.

**BIBLIOGRAPHY**

COLEMAN, JAMES S. 1988. "Social Capital in the Creation of Human Capital." *American Journal of Sociology* 94 (supplement):95–120.

HO, SUI CHU. 2000. "The Nature and Impact of Social Capital in Three Asian Education Systems: Singapore, Korea, and Hong Kong." *International Journal of Educational Policy: Research and Practices* 1(2):171–189.

HO, SUI CHU, and WILLMS, J. DOUGLAS. 1996. "Effects of Parental Involvement on Eighth-Grade Achievement." *Sociology of Education* 69(2):126–141.

PAXTON, PAMELA. 1999. "Is Social Capital Declining in the United States? A Multiple Indicator Assessment." *American Journal of Education* 105(1):88–127.

SAMPSON, ROBERT J.; MORENOFF, JEFFREY D.; and EARLS, FELTON. 1999. "Beyond Social Capital: Spatial Dynamics of Collective Efficacy for Children." *American Sociological Review* 64:633–660.

STEVENSON, HAROLD W., and STIGLER, JAMES W. 1992. *The Learning Gap: Why Our Schools Are Failing and What We Can Learn from Japanese and Chinese Education.* New York: Simon and Schuster.

WOOLCOCK, MICHAEL, and NARAYAN, DEEPA. 2000. "Social Capital: Implications for Development Theory, Research, and Policy." *The World Bank Research Observer* 15(2):225–249.

SUI CHU ESTHER HO

# SOCIAL COHESION AND EDUCATION

Social cohesion is said to be high when nearly all members of a society voluntarily "play by the rules of the game," and when tolerance for differences is demonstrated in the day-to-day interactions across social groups within that society. But how does social cohesion occur?

## Background: Social Cohesion and Development

One principal lesson of history is so obvious that it is sometimes ignored. Economic development is made possible through human cooperation. Cooperation offers the possibility for individuals and nations to accumulate or maximize economic gains that have resulted from creative enterprise and the trade that that enterprise engenders. Because of the complexities of measurement, this branch of economics, institutional economics, is not the most well known, but basically concerns the study of these mechanisms for human cooperation and how they work.

Two elements seem to make cooperation possible. First are the institutional rules that guide all types of organizations. Second are the stabilizing traditions within the organizations themselves.

Institutional rules include codes for public conduct, norms for private behavior, manifest statutes, common law, and contracts among individuals and organizations. An organization consists of groups of individuals bound together for a common purpose. Stabilizing traditions within each organization differ from one another. There are many types of organizations, but, in general, they can be reduced to four basic categories: (1) political organizations (the honesty and transparency of courts, legislatures, and the executive branches of government); (2) social organizations (shared moral principles of church groups and voluntary associations); (3) economic organizations (the quality of corporate governance, the adherence to legal procedures when acquiring and promoting employees); and (4) educational organizations, schools, and universities).

Each type of organization makes its own contribution to social cohesion. Political organizations arrange the debate and establish the means for public policy. Economic organizations arrange entrepreneurial endeavors and generate income. Social organizations sponsor altruistic endeavors that bind people to moral norms. A discussion follows regarding the social function of schools and why nations invest in schools.

## Social Functions of Education

Some, such as Robert Bates, suggest that the inability of societies to develop low-cost and effective self-regulating mechanisms for enforcement of social contracts prevents economic development.

**The social contract.** The concept of a social contract is broader than a legal contract. A social contract includes for instance, a willingness to pay taxes and fulfill other public obligations; it may include the willingness to participate in public affairs, maintain cleanliness of one's property, act responsibly, or be a good citizen. In instances where a society's general philosophy, such as racial tolerance for one's fellow citizens, conflicts with one's private opinion, the social contract of racial tolerance is expected to take precedence, particularly in public forums. Countries that lack economic development are often associated with an environment in which contracts are not enforceable by any mechanism, and most certainly are not self-regulating.

People are more likely to adhere to social contracts under certain conditions. They are more likely to adhere to contracts when they do not consider each other as cultural "strangers"; that is, when they have more understanding of each other as people, as citizens of the same country or as citizens of a "similar" country where it is believed that the same norms and expectations govern social contracts. People are more likely to adhere to social contracts when they have a greater understanding of the reasons for those contracts, and are more knowledgeable about the sanctions that may be expected in the event of non-compliance. The most common mechanism for achieving compliance is through the state, particularly through the state's authority to sanction. But states can become tyrannical. In a tyranny, those who run the state may force compliance in their own interest at the expense of the rest of society. The challenge then is to achieve compliance without tyranny.

The most effective check against tyranny is a public consensus on the definition of tyranny; on the rights of those who believe they are the objects of tyranny; and on the obligations and responsibilities of those who use coercive power. Such a consensus makes it more difficult for tyranny to occur because it can be more easily identified and controlled. How can this public consensus come about, and more importantly, how can it be passed to the young?

**The mechanisms of education's social functions.** Education should contribute to social cohesion in four ways. First, schools ought to teach the rules of the game: those that govern interpersonal and political action. They consist of the social and legal principles underpinning good citizenship, obligations of political leaders, behavior expected of citizens, and consequences for not adhering to these principles. Schools can also facilitate a student's appreciation for the complexity of issues related to historical and global current events and, in so doing, may increase the likelihood that a student will see a point of view other than his or her own. By teaching the rules of the game in this manner, schools foster tolerance and lay the groundwork for voluntary behavior consistent with social norms.

Second, schools are also expected to provide an experience roughly consistent with those citizenship principles, in effect, decreasing the "distance" between individuals of different origins. The educational experience derives from a wide variety of activities, whether in the classroom, the hallway, schoolyard, playing field, or bus. The degree to which a school may do this well depends on its ability to design the formal curriculum, its culture, and the social capital of its surrounding community. The purpose for providing experiences that are consistent with the principles of citizenship is clear. Both formal and informal social contracts require elements of trust among strangers—to the extent that the socialization of citizens from different social origins allows them to acknowledge and respect each other; that is, decreasing the "distance." If the educational task is done effectively, this allows political institutions to adjudicate differences and economic institutions to operate efficiently.

Third, school systems are expected to provide an equality of opportunity for all students. If the public perceives that the school system is biased and unfair, then the trust that citizens place in various other public institutions is compromised. For instance, the willingness of adults to play by the rules of the game may be compromised if fairness in the system appears suspect.

Fourth, public schools are expected to incorporate the interests and objectives of many different groups and at the same time attempt to provide a common underpinning for citizenship. Often there are disagreements over the balance between these objectives. These disagreements must be adjudicated. Adjudication can be accomplished through many mechanisms—public school boards, professional councils, parent-teacher associations. The

success of a school system is based in part on its ability to garner public support and consensus, and hence its ability to adjudicate differences over educational objectives.

Adjudication is not an easy task. Schools vary in the manner by which different groups' interests are accommodated. This is particularly the case when teaching local history. Some teachers avoid areas where problems are likely; some address sensitive areas more fully; others proactively seek out opinions and views to ensure that consensus is reached over what and how to teach. Schools differ also in the success of these efforts. For example, while it is true that the Alamo constitutes an important juncture for Texas and U.S. history, it is also true that motives—on both sides—were multiple and conflicting. And while it is true that civil rights in the American South can be characterized as a struggle for minority inclusion, it is also true that courage on that issue could be found among whites as well as minorities. This ingredient of education's contribution to social cohesion concerns the degree to which schools help students understand and weigh alternative explanations and incorporate the lessons of multiple points of view without losing a common moral rudder.

These four mechanisms constitute the manner by which education might contribute to social cohesion. But given that education is but one of four categories of social organizations that can make a social cohesion contribution, the degree to which education makes a larger or lesser contribution than political, social, or economic institutions has not been calculated. What is known is that social cohesion itself is quite important for the future stability of nations, and the more research available to quantify the constructive mechanisms necessary to effect it, the more likely it is that citizens can live in a harmonious environment.

## Education and Social Cohesion in the U.S. Context

Thomas Jefferson first argued for a literate citizenry in America's fledgling democracy: democracies require that citizens understand political institutions and evaluate the claims of politicians—capacities that would protect the democracy from various forms of demagoguery. By the mid-nineteenth century, however, the role of education had expanded. As immigrants began arriving from non-Protestant countries, educator Horace Mann's advocacy for the common school was one among several efforts to build a system of public schools that could create one nation from many peoples—peoples who differed not only in class origins, but also in their ethnic and racial origins, and religious commitments.

In the early twenty-first century, however, the foundations for social cohesion have shifted. Well into the twentieth century, Americans understood social cohesion as the outcome of assimilating peoples of diverse religions, ethnicities, and social groups into a nation with common values and language. That perception has changed. The use of Spanish by both presidential candidates in the year 2000 campaign confirms a new understanding of social cohesion—taking shape since the 1970s—that fosters accommodation, not simply assimilation, of diverse groups. The number of Hispanic and Asian persons in this nation has, according to the most recent U.S. Census, increased by more than 50 percent. Diversity in ethnicity and religion is pervasive in small towns as well as large urban areas. Social cohesion must be built among these increasingly diverse populations: a cohesion that constitutes a pervasive commitment to voluntary compliance to broadly constituted social norms and to active tolerance for differences among social groups.

Paradoxically, American concern with the apparent breakdown of social cohesion is not a simple extension of the growing diversity. Rather, the focus of concern and debate is within schools that on the surface have considerable racial and social homogeneity, but reveal many social fractures that presumably lead to antisocial behavior. Although national statistics show school violence has decreased, its distribution and causes appear different; namely, more suburban and rural incidents occur that are unrelated to gang activity. School violence in Colorado, California, and Arkansas, to name a few states, led to considerable debate in the media regarding the relative effects of school organization, American culture, and parenting practices on the behavior of adolescents. In the early twenty-first century, lawmakers in Colorado, Washington, and Oregon have legislation pending that would require each school district to have a policy directed at student bullying. Similar legislation has already passed in Georgia, New Hampshire, Arkansas, and Delaware. Some states require mediation, others give new powers to schools to discipline students.

Yet antisocial behavior, such as bullying, is not new. It is an ancient phenomenon, and it provided a classic character in much of children's literature. What has changed, though, is the institutional charter accorded to schools in the United States. The discretion in 1932, for instance, that Willard Waller's teachers had to inculcate roles and responsibilities of citizenship has been greatly attenuated by court decisions and the often-adversarial role assumed by parents as documented by Gerald Grant in 1988. The links between community and school have been weakened through different catchment areas for schools and dual-income families. Even the framework for providing welfare benefits has affected how families can be involved in their children's schooling. Other scholars emphasize (usually with different rank orderings) weak parenting skills, fractured school cultures, anomic communities, technological access to hate-group propaganda (such as the Internet), and easy access to weapons. Yet, the level of social cohesion in schools is not manifest simply by presence or absence of antisocial behavior, it is also manifest in positive actions of civility, reflecting trust and tolerance across social groupings of students.

Social cohesion is a desired outcome of schooling, but its significance extends beyond that. Social cohesion can also affect the academic achievement vulnerable students—those whose commitment to schooling is weak and is further compromised by schools with weak social cohesion.

Educators and commentators have argued that schools contribute more to the well-being of children and the larger society than academic achievement, yet the introduction of massive systems of accountability have diminished the value of other contributions. This work will create a measure of social cohesion outcomes, and therefore may broaden the discussion over the contributions of schooling, allowing the national debate, for the first time, to include the other important outcomes, which the public expects from its education system.

International analyses of citizenship in emerging democracies provide a greater appreciation of the role of schooling in building social cohesion. A growing consensus has emerged globally on the nature of the civics education curriculum. With many new nations aspiring to become stable democracies, the varying conditions that challenge social cohesion are more apparent. Thus, the educational contribution to social cohesion and the measure of social cohesion performance must be culturally specific to the challenge at hand. In the United States, heterogeneity, geographic mobility, and impersonal social relations present relatively unique challenges to social cohesion.

## New Challenges

In the early twenty-first century school systems face social cohesion challenges that have little historical precedent. Expectations for what students should know and be able to do are not determined simply by economic needs, but also by what it takes to perform the responsibilities of citizenship adequately. Participating in political discourse in the eighteenth century did not require as much understanding of science or statistics. In the twenty-first century citizens need to make judgments about issues with strong statistical underpinnings—the evaluation of competing claims over health and the environmental risk, the use of genetically altered foods, choice of sexual behavior. In essence the citizenship standards for literacy and numeracy have risen.

Also, the foundations for social cohesion have shifted. Well into the twentieth century, social cohesion was understood to be the outcome of assimilating peoples of diverse religions, ethnicities, and social groups into a nation with a common language and values. That has changed. A new understanding of social cohesion fosters accommodation, not simply assimilation. It often requires compromise and redefinition of the "typical citizen" from many sides, including by the majority as well as minority population.

In some parts of the world, challenges to social cohesion are not a simple extension of growing social diversity. Street violence in Rio de Janeiro, corruption in public service in Asia, the provision of social services by drug lords in South America and by mafia figures in Italy and Russia, the egocentric consumerism among suburban youth—these trends pose problems of a different sort. In these instances, the task of the public schools is much broader than forging ethnic harmony.

The twenty-first-century challenge of education in eastern and central Europe and the former Soviet Union might be analogous to that faced by education in Europe and North America in the early nineteenth and twentieth centuries. New nations must be forged, at peace within themselves and tolerant of their often divergent neighbors. But so far the record of success is mixed.

In fact school systems are neutral as to the direction of their influence. They are like a sharp tool—a knife or a saw. School systems can fashion views, which lead to social cohesion, or they can do the opposite. In the case of Sri Lanka, pedagogical materials as early as the 1950s led to the opposite situation. The dominant historical image portrayed in textbooks was that of a glorious but embattled Sinhalese nation repeatedly having to defend itself and its Buddhist traditions against the ravages of Tamil invaders. Tamils were portrayed as historical enemies. National heroes were chosen whose reputations included having vanquished Tamils in ethnic-based wars. Segregated in their own schools, Tamil textbooks emphasized historical figures whose reputations included accommodation and compromise with the Sinhalese. In neither the Tamil nor the Sinhalese texts were there positive illustrations drawn from the other ethnic group. There were few attempts to teach about the contribution of Tamil kings to Buddhist tradition, or the links between Sinhalese kingdoms and Buddhist centers in India. Language texts were largely monocultural with few positive references to other ethnic groups.

Because texts were culturally inflammatory and because there was no effective effort to balance the prejudice stemming from outside the classroom with more positive experiences, the Sri Lankan schools can be said to have achieved the opposite of the intention of good public systems. Instead of laying a foundation for national cooperation and harmony, they helped lay the intellectual foundations for social conflict and civil war.

The former Yugoslavia provides a more recent illustration. Here is a 1994 civics textbook intended for twelve-year-olds in Bosnia:

> Horrible crimes committed against the non-Serb population of Bosnia and Herzegovina by Serb-Montenegrin aggressors and domestic chetniks were aimed at creating an ethnically cleansed area where exclusively Serb people would live. In order to carry out this monstrous idea of theirs, they planned to kill or expel hundreds of thousands of Bosniaks and Croats . . . . The criminals began to carry out their plans in the most ferocious way. Horror swept through villages and cities . . . . Looting, raping, and slaughters . . . screams and outcries of the people being exposed to such horrendous plights . . . Europe and the rest of the world did nothing to prevent the criminals from ravaging and slaughtering

innocent people. (Bosnia and Herzegovina, Ministry of Education, Science and Culture, 1994)

Whether the events occurred or not is an issue separate from whether the text is appropriate. The public school experience is intended to mold desired behavior of future citizens; therefore citizens of all different groups must feel comfortable about the content. If one group is uncomfortable then the school system has abrogated its public function. This is an example of where that abrogation of public responsibility occurred.

The lessons could hardly be clearer. Many organizations have taken an interest in the problems of social studies and civics education out of professional concern about the possible implications of interethnic and national tension. These organizations include the United Nations Development Programme (UNDP), United Nations Educational, Scientific and Cultural Organization (UNESCO), the European Union, the Council of Europe, United Nations Children's Fund (UNICEF), the Soros Foundations, and many others.

So sensitive have been the threats to peace and stability that military organizations have developed a new concern over education on the premise that interethnic tensions expressed through education could well constitute a risk to peace in the region. The Organization for Security and Cooperation in Europe (OSCE) for instance, established a High Commissioner on National Minorities, based in The Hague. The High Commissioner has already issued recommendations pertaining to the education of the Greek minority population in Albania, the Albanian population in Macedonia; the Slovak population in Hungary, the Hungarian population in Slovakia, and the Hungarian population in Romania. In 1996, the High Commissioner requested assistance from the Foundation on Inter-Ethnic Relations to work on a possible set of guidelines governing the education rights of national minorities. After considerable discussion and consultation, these guidelines, known as The Hague Recommendations, were published in 1997 and can be added to the many other international conventions and regulations that attempt to identify and to protect the educational rights of children and various subpopulations. These include the Polish Minorities Treaty of 1919; the UN Universal Declaration of Human Rights in 1948; the UNESCO Convention against Discrimination in Education in 1960; the UN Declaration on the Rights of the Child

in 1959; the subsequent UN Convention on the Rights of the Child in 1989; the European Convention on Human Rights and Fundamental Freedoms in 1950; the Council of Europe's Framework Convention for the Protection of National Minorities in 1995; the UN Declaration on the Rights of Persons Belonging to National or Ethnic, Religious and Linguistic Minorities in 1992; the Council of Europe Charter on Regional or Minority Languages in 1992; the UNESCO Declaration on Race and Racial Prejudice in 1978; the Copenhagen Declaration of the Conference of the Human Dimension in 1990; and the UN Universal Declaration of the Rights of Indigenous Peoples in 1993.

In general these covenants and conventions pertain to the problems of populations that may be subjected to discrimination and prejudice. They concern the right to be educated in one's native tongue, the right of fair access to more selective training in higher and vocational education, freedom from discrimination, cultural bias, and the like. Although these issues are indeed important, effectively they address only one-half of the problem.

The other half of the problem pertains to the rights of the majority or the rights of the national community. Their educational interests are no less compelling: the Kazakhs in Kazakhstan; the Latvians in Latvia; the Romanians in Romania, and so forth. What protects the national community from extremist versions of history as portrayed by curricula designed by minority populations? What are the rights of the national community for having a sense of compromise and historical dignity ascribed to their national culture by minority populations in their own country? What protection does the national community have against the possibility that a minority community within the same country may encourage loyalty to another nation where their ethnic group is more numerous? The problem of civics education has multiple sources, and therefore must involve multiple solutions. Not all solutions can be incorporated under the auspices of the "rights of minorities." None of these conventions address this other side of the equation.

**Final Thoughts**

Although the notion of public schooling was established in seventeenth century, it is not true to suggest that the educational challenge in modern era is analogous. The fledgling nation-states of the seventeenth century required social cohesion, but they often used a central authoritarian system to achieve it. The techniques of nation-building in Africa, Latin America, and eastern Europe and the former Soviet Union today are not uniform, but for the most part they have emerged from an era of extreme authoritarianism into one more tolerant of divergence and local opinion. This complicates matters considerably. Not only are nations in the early twenty-first century faced with achieving cohesion, they are faced with the difficulties of achieving it, for better or worse, through widespread participation in the rules of engagement and flexibility as to its direction.

*See also:* CIVICS AND CITIZENSHIP EDUCATION; INTERNATIONAL ASSESSMENTS; MORAL EDUCATION; SOCIAL ORGANIZATION OF SCHOOLS; VIOLENCE, CHILDREN'S EXPOSURE TO.

## BIBLIOGRAPHY

ALMOND, GABRIEL ABRAHAM, and VERBA, SIDNEY. 1963. *The Civic Culture.* Princeton, NJ: Princeton University Press.

ALMOND, GABRIEL ABRAHAM, and VERBA, SIDNEY. 1965. *The Civic Culture: Political Attitudes and Democracy in Five Nations, an Analytic Study.* Princeton, NJ: Princeton University Press.

ALMOND, GABRIEL ABRAHAM, and VERBA, SIDNEY. 1989. *The Civic Culture Revisited.* Princeton, NJ: Princeton University Press.

BATES, ROBERT H. 1989. *Beyond the Miracle of the Market: The Potential Economy of Agrarian Development in Kenya.* Cambridge, Eng.: Cambridge University Press.

BOSNIA AND HERZEGOVINA, MINISTRY OF EDUCATION, CULTURE AND SPORTS. 1994. *Poznavanje Prirodei Drustva* (Nature and society). Sarajevo: Bosnia and Herzegovina, Ministry of Education, Culture and Sports.

BRYK, ANTHONY S. 1988. "Musings on the Moral Life of Schools." *American Journal of Education* 96(2):256–290.

BRYK, ANTHONY S.; LEE, VALERIE E.; and HOLLAND, PETER BLAKELEY. 1993. *Catholic Schools and the Common Good.* Cambridge, MA: Harvard University Press.

BYANI, C., et al. 1994. *Education Rights and Minorities.* London: Minority Rights Group.

COLEMAN, JAMES S. 1987. "Families and Schools." *Education Researcher* 16(6):32–38.

COLEMAN, JAMES S. 1988. "Social Capital in the Creation of Human Capital." *American Journal of Sociology* 94:S95–S120.

COMER, JAMES P. 1996. *Rallying the Whole Village.* New York: Teachers College Press, Columbia University.

DREEBEN, ROBERT. 1968. *On What Is Learned in School.* Reading, MA: Addison-Wesley.

ECKERT, PENELOPE. 1989. *Jocks and Burnouts: Social Categories and Identity in the High School.* New York: Teachers College Press, Columbia University.

EGGERTSSON, THRÁINN. 1990. *Economic Behavior and Institutions.* Cambridge, Eng.: Cambridge University Press.

FINN, CHESTER E., JR.; RAVITCH, DIANE; and FANCHER, ROBERT T. 1984. *Against Mediocrity.* New York: Holmes and Meier.

FOGELMAN, KEN, and EDWARDS, JANET. 1997. *Education for Citizenship: A Pedagogic Dossier.* Strasbourg, France: Council of Europe.

GIDDENS, ANTHONY. 2000. *Runaway World: How Globalization is Reshaping Our Lives.* New York: Routledge.

GRANT, GERALD. 1988. *The World We Created at Hamilton High.* Cambridge, MA: Harvard University Press.

HEYNEMAN, STEPHEN P. 2000. "From the Party/State to Multi-Ethnic Democracy: Education and Social Cohesion in the Europe and Central Asia Region." *Educational Evaluation and Policy Analysis* 22(2):173–191.

HEYNEMAN, STEPHEN P., and TODORIC-BEBIC, SANJA. 2000. "A Renewed Sense of Purpose of Schooling: Education and Social Cohesion in Africa, Latin America, Asia and Europe and Central Asia." *Prospects* 30(2):145–166.

LIPSET, SEYMOUR MARTIN. 1959. "Some Social Requisites of Democracy: Economic Development and Political Legitimacy." *American Political Science Review* 53:69–105.

MAYNES, MARY JO. 1985. *Schooling in Western Europe: A Social History.* Albany: State University of New York Press.

MEYER, JOHN W. 1970. "The Charter: Conditions of Diffuse Socialization in Schools." In *Social Processes and Social Structure,* ed. W. Richard Scott. New York: Holt Rinehart and Winston.

MITTER, WOLFGANG. 1996. "Democracy and Education in Central and Eastern Europe." In *Can De-*

*mocracy be Taught?* ed. Andrew Oldenquist. Bloomington, IN: Phi Delta Kappa Educational Foundation.

NISSAN, ELIZABETH. 1996. *Sri Lanka: A Bitter Harvest.* London: Minority Rights Group.

NORTH, DOUGLASS C. 1990. *Institutions, Institutional Change, and Economic Performance.* Cambridge, Eng.: Cambridge University Press.

OAKES, JEANNIE. 1995. "More Than Meets the Eye: Links between Tracking and the Culture of Schools." In *Beyond Tracking: Finding Success in Inclusive Schools,* ed. Harbison Pool and Jane A. Page. Bloomington, IN: Phi Delta Kappa Educational Foundation.

OGBU, JOHN. 1974. "Social Stratification and the Socialization of Competence." *Anthropology Educational Quarterly* 10(1):3–20.

OLSON, MANCUR. 1965. *The Logic of Collective Action: Public Goods and the Theory of Groups.* Cambridge, MA: Harvard University Press.

OLSON, MANCUR. 1977. "The Treatment of Externalities in National Income Statistics." In *Public Economics and the Quality of Life,* ed. Lowdon Wingo and Alan Evans. Baltimore: Johns Hopkins University Press.

OLSON, MANCUR. 1982. *The Rise and Decline of Nations: Economic Growth, Stagflation and Social Rigidities.* New Haven, CT: Yale University Press.

PACKER, JOHN. 1996. "On the Content of Minority Rights." In *Do We Need Minority Rights? Conceptual Issues,* ed. Juha Raikka. The Hague, The Netherlands: Martinus, Nijhoff.

POWELL, ARTHUR. G.; FARRAR, ELEANOR; and COHEN, DAVID K. 1985. *The Shopping Mall High School.* Boston: Houghton-Mifflin.

SHADRIKOV, VLADIMIR. 1993. "Ethnic Cultural and National Requirements in the Education Policy of the Former Soviet Union." In *Nationalism in Education,* ed. Klaus Schleicher. New York: Lang.

TORNEY-PURTA, JUDITH. 1995. "Psychological Theory as a Basis for Political Socialization Research." *Perspectives on Political Science* 24:23–33.

TORNEY-PURTA, JUDITH, and SCHWILLE, JOHN. 1986. "Civic Values Learned in School: Policy and Practice in Industrialized Nations." *Comparative Education Review* 30:30–49.

TORNEY-PURTA, JUDITH; LEHMANN, RAINER; OSWALD, HANS; and SCHULZ, WOLFRAM. 2001. *Citizenship and Education in Twenty-Eight Countries: Civic Knowledge and Engagement at Age 14.* Amsterdam, The Netherlands: International Association for the Evaluation of Educational Achievement.

WALLER, WILLARD WALTER. 1932. *The Sociology of Teaching.* New York: Wiley.

WEHLAGE, GARY G.; RUTTER, ROBERT A.; SMITH, GREGORY A.; LESKO, NANCY; and FERNANDEZ, RICARDO R. 1989. *Reducing the Risk: Schools as Communities of Support.* New York: Falmer.

STEPHEN P. HEYNEMAN

# SOCIAL FRATERNITIES AND SORORITIES

The American college Greek-letter societies, consisting of fraternities and sororities, remain a popular form of association for students on college campuses in the early twenty-first century. Known as the oldest form of student self-governance in the American system of higher education and called perhaps the clearest example of a student subculture, fraternities and sororities have been a force on college campuses since 1825. The fraternity or sorority ideal cherishes and embraces all of the characteristics of a campus subculture: residential proximity through the chapter house, transmission of norms and values to the membership in a concrete and systematic way, a history of longevity, and social control for conformity. Artifacts, symbols, rituals, and shared assumptions and beliefs add significantly to the shared initiatives of scholarship, leadership development, service to others, and fellowship among members.

## History

The American fraternity traces its genesis to the emergence of literary societies in the late eighteenth century. Debating and literary societies, whose names evoked memories of ancient Greece, emerged as purveyors of forensics, but their main contribution was that they were primary social clubs contrasting with the bleak campus dormitories. The elaborate lounges and private libraries they maintained outstripped those operated by colleges. As quickly as the literary societies filled the curriculum

SOCIAL FRATERNITIES AND SORORITIES **2251**

vacuum of the early college student, the fraternity emerged to fill the social needs of the more independent college students.

The need for a distinct counterpart for women became evident early on college campuses, especially in women's colleges. For many years, societies for young women bearing Greek and classical names were common at women's colleges and academies and were organized similar to fraternities. The first fraternity for women was Alpha Delta Pi, founded as the Adelphean Society in 1851. Sororities were chartered as women's fraternities because no better word existed. In 1882 Gamma Phi Beta was the first to be named a sorority.

From the beginning, the norms and values of fraternities were independent of the college environment. Since the founding of Kappa Alpha at Union College (in Schenectady, New York) in 1825 as the oldest secret brotherhood of a social nature, fraternities developed with different personalities and histories on each campus. The trappings of an idealized ancient Greece were added to those of Freemasonry to create secret societies dedicated to bringing together young men who were seeking conviviality. Members historically met weekly in a student dormitory room or rented facility for social and intellectual fellowship. To fight the monotony of mid-nineteenth-century colleges, fraternities institutionalized various escapes of a social nature.

In the 1890s the chapter-owned house became a reality and gave a physical presence to the fraternity movement. Supported by prosperous and influential fraternity alumni, the chapter house relieved the need for housing on many campuses. The popular German university model of detachment from the student replaced the English model of providing room and board. Colleges and universities began to shape college life rather than oppose it, and the institutions reluctantly began accepting the fraternity system.

As more and more fraternities occupied their own houses, their interest shifted from intellectual issues to that of running and sustaining a chapter house. The chapter house had great influence upon fraternity chapters. The increasing prominence of the chapter house in the 1920s illustrates the power of this social movement on most colleges and universities. The total number of fraternity houses in the nation increased from 774 in 1920 to 1,874 in 1929, and the subculture was strengthened at state universities, where half of the students belonged to a fraternity by 1930.

To keep the chapter house full, current members instituted a recruiting method to secure new groups or classes of new members. New students were "rushed" or recruited to become new initiates, commonly called "pledges." Once affiliated, the new pledges were soon put to work doing menial chores and running errands for upperclassmen. This was the beginning of the most troubling and reviled custom, hazing. Old-fashioned hazing generally was punishment for household jobs not done; it was left to later generations to introduce road trips, asinine public stunts and practical jokes, and forms of psychological and physical discomfort.

After surviving the Great Depression and World War II, fraternities returned to campuses in full and more diverse force. As American higher education became more democratic, the fraternity movement confronted the discriminatory nature of its membership polices. Slowly, Greek organizations began to admit members more reflective of the college-attending population. Fraternities and sororities saw great growth during the time between World War II and the Vietnam War. The war in Vietnam and the cultural changes that followed had a negative effect on fraternities. Their traditional and historic loyalty to the college was in direct contrast to social movements of the time. As in the past, fraternity and sorority membership rebounded. During the period between 1977 and 1991 students joined at a greater rate than at any time in the system's history.

The name of fraternities and sororities is usually composed of two or three Greek letters, such as Sigma Pi, Delta Zeta, or Phi Kappa Theta. These letters represent a motto, known only to the members, that briefly states the aims and purposes of the organization. The affiliated branches of the Greek organizations at other colleges are called chapters; they are organized by states or regions and often are designated by a Greek letter, such as Zeta Chapter of Sigma Pi. These chapters are organized under the banner of the national or international organization and are governed through an assembly of delegates and managed through a central office. Incipient chapters are called colonies until they reach full chapter status on new campuses. Almost all Greek organizations publish a journal and maintain close contact with alumni. Many have their own educational foundations.

## Characteristics of Fraternities and Sororities

Fraternity and sorority leaders prefer to use the term *general fraternity* when describing what are commonly called "social" fraternities. General fraternities and sororities can best described by the umbrella group or coordinating association to which they belong. These organizations are the National Interfraternity Conference (NIC), which represents sixty-six men's groups, and the National Panhellenic Conference (NPC), which represents twenty-six women's groups. There still remain many local fraternities and sororities on college campuses that boast of long traditions and have never affiliated nationally. Professional, recognition, and honor societies that use Greek names are organized separately and can include general fraternity members.

It is estimated that more than 10 percent of all college students are members of a Greek-letter society. After hitting a record of more than 400,000 undergraduates in 1990, fraternity membership in the year 2000 in sixty-six national fraternities was estimated at 370,000 and is slowly increasing. In the early twenty-first century, there are more than 5,500 chapters on 800 campuses throughout the United States and Canada. National data suggests that women's sororities are healthy, with membership in the twenty-six national sororities exceeding 300,000 and the size of the average chapter on the increase. There are 2,913 chapters on more than 630 college and university campuses. Membership in local fraternities and sororities adds significantly to this total, and there are more than 10 million alumni members of Greek-letter societies.

Men's general college fraternities are mutually exclusive, self-perpetuating groups, which provide organized social life for their members in colleges and universities as a contributing aspect of their educational experience. They draw their members from the undergraduate student body. Women's general college sororities are primary groups of women at colleges and universities, which, in addition to their individual purposes, are committed to cooperation with college administrators to maintain high social and academic standards and do not limit their membership to any one academic field. Both fraternities and sororities provide unusually rich out-of-class learning and personal development opportunities for undergraduates.

Fraternities and sororities offer an organized and varied schedule of activities, including intramural sports, community service projects, dances, formals, and parties. The NIC and NPC make convincing arguments that Greek organizations benefit the sponsoring campus, stipulating that students who affiliate with a fraternity are more likely to remain in school and that alumni affiliated with a fraternity make significantly higher donations to the school. There is strong research to back up these claims. Affiliating with a fraternity or sorority enhances the development of mature interpersonal relationships, facilitates the development of leadership skills, teaches teamwork, fosters interchange of ideas, promotes values clarification, and can facilitate the development of sense of autonomy and personal identity. On isolated campuses, Greek organizations may provide the only social life.

Underlying the whole experience is the ritual that is exclusive to each fraternity or sorority. While often incorrectly associated with illegal and immoral hazing activities, a fraternity or sorority ritual is the solemn and historic rationale for an organization's existence. The ritual is often presented to new members during a serious churchlike ceremony where new members learn the underlying meaning of their respective organizations. Because of the esoteric nature of most Greek-letter societies, usually only members attend these ceremonies. The conflict between these stated ideals and the behavior of undergraduate members on campuses have caused confusion and lack of support for the fraternity system. From the 1980s into the twenty-first century, both constructive and destructive relationships have brought mixed results for fraternities on a number of campuses.

## Reforms and Renewal

Many college administrators have sought to limit the role fraternities play within the social life and have taken a hard stand against illegal hazing and the use of alcohol among Greek members. Sororities have escaped most of the criticism because of their more adamant commitment to scholarship and service, stronger alumni intervention, and encouragement of campus oversight. A variety of concerns have been raised about fraternities, including that they encourage narrow social and academic experiences for members, have restrictive membership policies, practice hazing, discriminate on the basis of sex, perpetuate stereotypes about women, and wield too much power over social life. Also, there are allegations that racism, violence, and discrimination still exist. Most unfortunately, alcohol- and hazing-related deaths have occurred at fraternity events.

Reforms of the Greek system on college campuses, especially concerning fraternities, range from the complete abolition of fraternities and sororities to investing new personnel and increased resources into improving and enhancing Greek life. Attempts to make fraternities and sororities coeducational have not been successful, and even the U.S. Congress has expressed the belief that colleges should not act to prevent students from exercising their freedom of association, especially off-campus and on their own time. Some colleges have allowed fraternities to remain as approved student organizations but have forced them to separate from and close the chapter house.

Fraternity and sorority administrators agree that the abuse of alcohol is a contributing factor to hazing and is usually the cause of other destructive Greek problems. They have joined college and university trustees and administrators in taking a strong stand against hazing outrages. National fraternities and sororities are spending thousands of dollars educating and developing alternative programs. Hazing is one of the biggest problems facing fraternities and some sororities, who in the past never considered mistreating their pledges. Now every fraternity and sorority has stringent prohibitions against the practice. Members have been expelled and chapters have been closed when charges have been substantiated. Most states have antihazing legislation, and some make it a felony to practice dangerous or degrading activities against pledges or members.

For Greek organizations, especially fraternities, to survive and prosper, undergraduates must take the bans on hazing and alcohol excesses to heart. National officers and students continue to clash over efforts to transform fraternity culture, and many resist any changes that threaten the social aspects of Greek life that originally attracted students to affiliate. At the same time, much has been accomplished. Sororities are addressing eating disorders, such as anorexia and bulimia, and several fraternities have devised pledging programs that emphasize academic development, leadership, and community service while de-emphasizing hazing and alcohol.

Altering Greek life obligates colleges to provide attractive alternatives for housing, dining, and social functions. Many campuses are increasing Greek life budgets and taking an active role in supporting Greek life and the cultural changes that are necessary to strengthen the experience. Fraternities and sororities, quintessentially American student organizations, remain a positive social option for college and university students in the early twenty-first century.

*See also:* ADJUSTMENT TO COLLEGE; COLLEGE AND ITS EFFECT ON STUDENTS; COLLEGE EXTRACURRICULAR ACTIVITIES; COLLEGE STUDENT RETENTION; DRUG AND ALCOHOL ABUSE, *subentry on* COLLEGE.

### BIBLIOGRAPHY

ASTIN, ALEXANDER W. 1977. *Four Critical Years.* San Francisco: Jossey-Bass.

ASTON, JACK L., and MARCHESANI, ROBERT F., eds. 1991. *Baird's Manual of American College Fraternities,* 20th edition. Indianapolis, IN: Baird's Manual Foundation.

HOROWITZ, HELEN L. 1987. *Campus Life: Undergraduate Cultures from the End of the Eighteenth Century to the Present.* Chicago: University of Chicago Press.

NATIONAL PANHELLENIC CONFERENCE. 2000. *Annual Report.* Indianapolis, IN: National Panhellenic Conference.

NUWER, HANK. 1990. *Broken Pledges: The Deadly Rite of Hazing.* Atlanta, GA: Longstreet Press.

RUDOLPH, FREDERICK. 1962. *The American College and University: A History.* New York: Knopf.

MICHAEL A. GRANDILLO

# SOCIAL MOBILITY OF UNDERPRIVILEGED GROUPS

*See:* INTERNATIONAL ISSUES OF SOCIAL MOBILITY OF UNDERPRIVILEGED GROUPS.

# SOCIAL ORGANIZATION OF SCHOOLS

Understanding contemporary schools requires examining their purposes, evolution, structure, and political dynamics. Ordinary ideas of how schools operate are clouded by a number of misconceptions and assumptions. People often think that schools only teach skills and content, such as reading, writing, and math; or history, English, and social studies. They also think about extracurricular activities, such as football, proms, and childhood peer groups. When visualizing schools, people think of buildings like the elementary, secondary, or tertiary ones they attended. Further, given how politicians talk about their "education agendas," people assume that most control and funding of schools comes from the state or national government. However, schools do much more than just teach content, and encompass more than individual buildings. Regardless of their size or complexity, schools fulfill a wide range of overt and less obvious functions.

Schools are embedded within districts established by communities to provide both educational and extracurricular activities for young people and a center for social, political, and cultural community events. Moreover, in the United States, schools are preeminently local, not national. They are controlled by locally elected officials and their appointed superintendents, and are largely funded by local property taxes. Thus, what is described here is only typical of schools and districts in the United States, where pressures for *democratic localism* conduce to an almost radical decentralization—at least compared to schools in other countries.

## American Public Schools in Context

In most other countries, a national ministry or office controls curricula, instructional methods, teacher qualifications and salaries, and individual school budgets. In the United States, however, the Constitution specifies that education must be provided by the individual states, which in turn have delegated responsibility for schooling to local communities. While funding for and control over schools in other countries is often shared by the national government and the established church, the U.S. Constitution mandates a marked separation between secular and religious affairs—a mandate with which public schools comply. While strong systems of parochial schools exist in some communities—particularly ones with large Catholic populations—and while private schools, semi-private charter schools, and home-schooling have become increasingly popular, these enroll only a small minority of U.S. children.

Local control—a response to both constitutional silence and to deep-seated cultural aversion in the United States to centralization—is one of the most unique characteristics of American public schools. Nowhere else are public schools so explicitly run by locally elected school boards. This means that those most active in educational affairs are often business and professional persons, since they are more likely than working and middle-class individuals to have the time and money to run for elected office. The United States also differs from other countries in that more than half of all revenue for schools comes from the local community. The federal government, in fact, contributes only about 7 percent of all educational revenues, and only for specific programs such as school lunches; vocational training; impact aid to districts located on military bases or Indian reservations, which generate no property taxes; entitlement programs to educate disabled and language minority students; and compensatory educational programs for children in economically disadvantaged communities. These patterns of governance and funding make U.S. schools extremely vulnerable to influences from interest groups, taxpayers (particularly property owners), upper- and middle-class residents, and business interests.

Schools and school districts must be understood and analyzed on many academic and organizational levels and in terms of often conflicting demands for their services. Contradictions of goals, purposes, control, and functioning complicate a clear understanding of how schools, broadly defined, really work—in general, and in different communities. Differences in demographic characteristics; economic resource bases; proximity to urban centers; specific constituencies such as labor unions, religious groups, and industries; and historical factors make each school district, and each school within districts, unique.

## The Purposes of Schooling

Schools have multiple purposes, and each of these purposes has its own constituency or advocacy group, and each affects the goals and organization of schools. Since the goals of advocacy groups may contradict one another, schools face important dilemmas that can complicate their organizational structure and goals. As will become clear, schools are called upon to provide solutions to a variety of social problems, including poverty, disability, and illness of students, and the fraying of civic culture.

**Academic competencies: basic skills or college preparatory?** American society asks schools simultaneously to provide job training for children who will not go to college and college preparatory training for those who will. Historically, these two types of training were provided in separate institutions. Public schools initially were established in the mid-nineteenth century to provide primary school training in reading, writing, computation, and, sometimes, citizenship to the children of poor and working-class families who could not, or would not, educate their children themselves. Public elementary schools supplanted earlier programs of apprenticeship, in which poor and working-class children were apprenticed out to learn a trade, and the masters they worked for were required to teach them basic literacy skills.

Children of the wealthy learned their "three R's" at home from parents, governesses, or tutors, while secondary academic schooling was provided by private academies with a classical liberal arts and college preparatory curriculum program—and was usually limited to males. Maintaining public elementary training for the lower classes and private secondary academic training for the wealthy reinforced the social class structure, even though private academies offered scholarships to some deserving and needy children. This system gave working-class children sufficient literacy for citizenship and the labor market, and provided advantaged children the academic training, cultural knowledge, and contacts needed to assume positions of leadership in society. The comprehensive public high school that evolved to eliminate this dichotomy has not resolved the tension between these two types of schooling.

David P. Resnick and Lauren B. Resnick (1985) argue that by the beginning of the twentieth century the labor market demanded higher levels of literacy and numeracy for greater numbers of people. However, private academies were too expensive for the masses and insufficient in number to fulfill an increased demand for more schooling. It was for this reason that the American comprehensive high school developed—to provide free secondary education to all children. This "poor man's academy" was lauded by labor unions and business people because it provided a terminal vocational education for working people, but it was not enthusiastically received by families and communities desirous of distinguishing their children academically, occupationally, and socially from those in vocational training. The result has been an uneasy—and often invidious—system of *streaming,* or *tracking,* in which the same school offers vocational, and often remedial, training; a terminal general education; and an elite college prep program. Since each stream

often serves quite different groups of children, the effect is to house separate institutions within the same building.

**Citizenship: for diversity or uniformity?** American schools are asked to inculcate in children the attitudes, values, and habits needed for good citizenship because, since the family is suited best for developing individual personality, institutions such as schools must provide the overall civic training needed to create allegiance to a uniform set of cultural values and to the society's political system. This purpose is unambiguous in a homogenous society, but difficult in the polyglot, multicultural United States. Initially, public elementary schools were given the task of *Americanizing* or assimilating immigrant children to the English language, a northwestern European cultural heritage, and the desirable habits of industry, hygiene, thrift, and obedience to the laws.

As *moral* or *civic* education evolved into *social studies* in high schools, its focus changed somewhat to emphasize studies of the American government and economic system and appropriate ways for citizens to vote and participate in legitimate political activity. The overall purpose, however, remains: To create a culturally uniform, English-speaking, and law-abiding citizenry—an increasingly problematic task as the United States has become more culturally, linguistically, religiously, and ethnically diverse. Schools in the early twenty-first century must serve children with mental, physical, and emotional disabilities; children who do not speak or write English; children whose parents are nontraditional, absent, poor, working so many jobs that they cannot participate in their children's education, or who are themselves disabled, not working, non–English speaking, and poorly educated. Ensuring academic success for such children has required the establishment of a variety of support services, including bus transportation, meals at school, health screenings, counseling, medical care, language training, sex and drivers' education, and free clothing. This *support service* sector has added many more levels of organization to schools.

Some ethnic groups resist being assimilated to what they perceive to be a white, western European, Christian, middle-class culture, arguing that schools should equally celebrate their own origins, experiences, and heritage. These goals pose a dilemma: Do schools continue to promote assimilation to a uniform version of American life, or do they promote diversity and multiculturalism? If diversity is to be promoted, how is it to be done? What impact would it have on school structures, curricula, and instruction? Parents of ethnic and language minority children and parents of disabled children form one of the strongest and most vocal advocacy groups in the educational system. Their claims are backed up by constitutional guarantees for "equal protection" and "equal access" under the law. These federal guarantees, however, are left to the individual states and local communities to enforce. These claims, and the services they require, complicate the goals of schools and add yet more departments and staff members to them.

**Schools as centers for social life.** Academic instruction aside, friendship groups and the social activities they participate in are a significant aspect of school life for children. In part, schools must teach children to maintain healthy social relationships. They also have created a wide range of extracurricular activities to motivate students who otherwise underachieve academically. School activities such as drama, music, and competitive athletics also entertain the entire community, while adding departments and sometimes diverting resources from instruction. Athletics in particular is a significant consumer of school space, time, money, and staff energy.

## Defining Organizations and Bureaucracies

Schools are usually described as organizations or bureaucracies. These terms have technical meanings that often conflict with popular understandings. Social scientists define *organizations* as social structures that (a) possess a distinct set of goals agreed upon by their members, (b) operate under uniform rules and stable patterns of interaction, (c) are governed by a system of authority, (d) recruit members and resources to implement their purposes, and (e) maintain autonomy in decision-making.

Bureaucracies, or complex organizations, have goals and operations large and complex enough to require a staff division of labor or specialization, and to create rational and standardized sets of procedures for employees to do their work. These procedures include standards—such as job descriptions—for carrying out specific tasks or occupying specific positions. Authority and decision making in bureaucracies is hierarchical, governed with each staff member held accountable to those in higher positions. Superiors hold their positions because they have demonstrated that they are competent to do so. Bureaucracies resemble a typical hierarchical organi-

zational chart, and most businesses, government agencies, social services agencies and schools are bureaucratized.

**Unrealistic assumptions: schools as bureaucratic hierarchies.** The bureaucratic model assumes clearcut and unambiguous goals and authority structures, consistent systems of accountability, operations based on exercise of professional judgment and rational logic, clear and fair operating rules, and the capacity to generate sufficient resources to carry out necessary tasks. If a superior gives orders, it is assumed the subordinate will follow them or risk sanctions. If funds are needed to operate, they can be generated and controlled. While these assumptions may well characterize most businesses, they do not typify schools. This is problematic, since the business people who often are key players on schools boards may have difficulty discerning differences between how schools and the businesses with which they are more familiar operate. This causes strain between expectations for, and assumptions about, what schools should do and what they can actually deliver.

In addition, American culture values businesslike models more over diffuse structures such as those in schools—so much so that many systems in schools, including supervisory patterns, age-grading, fifty-minute periods, systems of accountability, and ergonomic desks, all derive from the Scientific Management movement of the 1920s. This movement, which revolutionized industrial practice, was enthusiastically applied to educational institutions as well.

## Organization and Funding of Schools and Districts

School districts generally encompass the elementary grades, which include kindergarten through grades 5 or 6; middle (grades 6 through 8) or junior high schools (grades 7 through 9), and high schools (grades 9 or 10 through 12). Some districts also include preschools and a two-year community college. Elementary schools are relatively small (300 to 1,000 students) and located in relatively homogenous neighborhoods. Middle schools and junior high schools are larger, and usually include the enrollments of several elementary schools. High schools are larger still; many communities have only one.

Schools also group within grade levels by ability for ease of instruction. Most elementary classrooms divide children into high-, middle-, and low-ability groups for basic subjects such as reading and math. Tracking begins in middle school or high school as students are grouped by ability and occupational destinations into college preparatory, general, and vocational curricula. These tracks tend to divide the academically able students from those who are not. Because vocational training does not prepare students for college (and vice versa), it becomes more and more difficult to change tracks as a student progresses further in school. Thus, early tracking has serious consequences for children, as small initial differences in skills learned are magnified with each successive year.

Instructional functions are carried out in the individual school buildings, each of which is administered by a principal. Middle schools and high schools also have several assistant principals and secretarial staff. The central office, under the leadership of the appointed superintendent, provides overall supervision of the individual schools, coordination of all instructional and support services, and staff development for teachers and administrators. The central office also houses offices for school board members; legal, personnel, and financial departments—and departments for research, evaluation, testing, and accountability; grants development; and enumeration and monitoring of student attendance. Central office staff are geographically located at some distance from individual schools, which can make close surveillance of activities in them difficult.

**The structure of schools.** Schools are divided into levels according to the age of students. Elementary teachers generally teach all subjects to one group of students in the same classroom year-round. They usually are assisted by resource teachers for disabled and language minority children, and, where resources allow, by special teachers for instruction in physical education, art, music, and computers. Middle schools and junior high schools are departmentalized or specialized—teachers teach only in their areas of specialization, and students move periodically from room to room for each content area. In the sixth and seventh grade, students may be grouped so they attend classes together with the same four or five teachers; however, by eighth or ninth grade, the *high school model* prevails. Here, students are scheduled according to the availability of the classes they choose to take. In middle and high schools, teachers are departmentalized by subject area—such as English, French, Spanish, biology, business practice, social studies, mathematics, and physical education.

Larger schools can offer more subjects, and they have more departments. Large size, then, can be an advantage, but it creates social costs in terms of alienation and isolation for students and teachers, who cannot know all their classmates or students. Although team teaching and sharing classrooms exists; these innovative practices are rare. Most teachers teach by themselves; only elementary school teachers and teachers with severely handicapped children generally have aides. This isolation can impede collegiality, opportunities for teachers to learn from each other, and their capacity to organize; however, the *autonomy of the closed door,* as Dan Lortie calls it, also serves to insulate teachers from excessive supervision by their principals.

**Coupling and control.** Patterns of what Lortie calls *variable zoning* ensure that overall control is fragmented in schools. Individual offices or personnel in schools have jurisdiction only over specific activities. Teachers control delivery of instruction, though the type of instruction and assessment may be imposed upon them by principals, the central office, or state mandates. Teachers also control management and discipline of students and how time is organized within the class period or day. School-level administrators handle overall coordination; disbursing the budget; assigning and scheduling teachers and students to classes; hiring and firing building staff; maintaining relationships with other schools, the central office, parents, and the wider community; and providing an overall instructional and managerial vision for school operation.

Within buildings, principals seldom can supervise the day-to-day activities of teachers; likewise, teachers' choices of materials and activities are limited by priorities established by the principal, central office, and community. Central office staff are responsible for carrying out the dictates of the school board, mediated by professional judgments about the best way to educate children and operate schools. They oversee overall planning, staff development, administration, public relations, fundraising and financial planning, hiring, accountability, and research and evaluation, and they coordinate all service and support activities.

Dispersion of physical units within school districts, as well as the discreteness of individual classrooms, also fragments control because it creates, according to Karl E. Weick, *loose coupling,* or difficulty in assuring that directives from supervisors are carried out by subordinates. Neither school boards, nor superintendents, nor principals can assume that orders given will always be carried out as desired. Some scholars, such as John W. Meyer and Brian Rowan describe American schools as "decoupled," while Cora Marrett (1990) argues that inner-city schools actually are "uncoupled"—following no upper-level directives at all. This poses dilemmas for educators. Fairness and the need for teachers to build on what children have learned previously requires that all children at each grade level be provided the same quality, type, and quantity of instruction. However, despite the responsibility of principals and central office staff for enforcing some degree of uniformity in instructional practice and policy, individual neighborhoods can exercise considerable leverage to distinguish the instruction their children receive from that in other neighborhoods. Further, individual districts can resist policies mandated by states or the federal government. Some mandates, such as desegregation of schools and services to students with disabilities and language minority students, have been ignored by states and districts for decades.

Even when districts try to implement specific policies regarding instruction, individual teachers can avoid compliance by simply neglecting to follow guidelines unless they are observed by supervisors. Further, in transferring some aspects of decision-making authority to school principals, some popular organizational reforms, such as shared decision-making and site-based management, can complicate district attempts to institute overall reform, since principals in *site-based* districts argue that they alone have responsibility in their buildings. Nevertheless, current reforms, which include state-mandated accountability systems, require schools to meet uniform academic standards for test performance or face consequences such as loss of funds and accreditation, or wholesale firing of administrators and staff.

**Budgets and funding.** Looseness in organizational structure is paralleled by looseness in budgeting and fund-raising. The public often fails to understand why schools cannot simply buy the materials and teachers they need. However, school budgets are based on school board priorities and superintendent decisions. Since individual principals usually receive their allotment of funds, and even the individual categories of expenditure, yearly, the degree of control exercised over expenditures at the building level may be very small. District level constraints also exist. The majority of school district revenues come from local real-estate taxes. Although a few communities have given their school boards—within limits—the authority to establish tax rates, rates usually are controlled by voters, who periodically must approve requests both for school tax levies and the bond issues used for major capital expenditures such as construction of new buildings. Districts that experience emergencies—such as a sudden influx of needy immigrant students, destruction of a building by fire or its sudden obsolescence because of new earthquake codes, or radical increases in enrollment because of explosive population growth in the community— cannot quickly raise funds to meet their needs. School personnel and their supporters cannot compel, they can only argue persuasively for, additional funds. Further, they must await the usual political cycle to request increased funds from the voters, who can vent their displeasure over taxes in general by disapproving the only taxes they directly control.

Similarly, districts have little control over revenue received from state foundational funds, called *ADA* because they are calculated on the *average daily attendance* of all students in the district. States raise educational funds from a variety of sources, including gasoline taxes, lotteries, and sales taxes. They give each district a certain amount for each child enrolled in mid-October; these funds are intended to "equalize" educational provisions across districts. However ADA is the same for children in all communities. Since communities vary widely in the value of their real property, and since they are not limited in the amount—above foundational funding—they can generate locally, wide inequities exist in educational services. Not only can rich communities generate more money than poor ones, their residents pay fewer taxes, proportionately, than those in poor communities with decaying housing and little industry. Poor communities often struggle to cover the cost of minimal educational services.

Politicians, including school board officials, often are elected on the basis of promises to reform or redirect educational policies and practices. In fact, their ability to do so is severely curtailed by their inability to affect already established budgets and revenues. Over the years, few attempts to change the local nature of school funding have been successful. States that have tried *equalization*—giving a larger share of foundational funding to poor districts and correspondingly less to rich ones—have met strong opposition from well-funded communities reluctant to lose their privileged economic position. Federal funds cannot make up the difference, as they are earmarked for specific programs and constitute only a minuscule proportion of overall educational cost.

## Reform Issues: Recurring Problems and Proposed Solutions

While parents usually say that they are satisfied with the schools their own children attend, their support has been dropping since 1983. A significant segment of the public in the United States has always been dissatisfied with the education system. This is understandable, given that many segments of the population hold expectations for schools that either cannot be met or are contradictory. David Berliner and Bruce Biddle also suggest that the declining confidence in American schooling is a crisis "manufactured" by political conservatives to usher in the privatization of public schools.

Typical solutions proposed for real or imagined school failure often involve instituting changes in the organizational structure and patterns of control in schools and districts. Reforms proposed since the 1970s are discussed below. These reforms have attempted to improve student performance by changing power balances in schools and districts; raising standards; increasing assessment; creating smaller organizational units; changing on-the-job training for teachers; increasing local control of schools; giving public-education funds to parents, semi-private, and private schools; and devolving more autonomy to teachers and principals.

**Decentralizing pathological bureaucracies.** Believing that "bigger is better," Americans consolidated their school districts, reducing the total number of school districts by more than 80 percent from 1930 to the 1970s. Consolidation created larger funding bases and greater variety in course and curriculum offerings, but it also required districts to provide transportation for students who could no longer walk to nearby schools, weakened immediate neighborhood and community control of schools, and increased bureaucratization of educational administration.

However, by the 1970s, public disaffection with district size; excessive diversion of revenue to administration at the expense of instruction; lack of re-

sponsiveness to the needs of local neighborhoods, particularly minority communities; and, at times, administrative mismanagement and corruption led to the decentralization movement. Decentralization created subdistricts within larger ones. The superintendent's office retained overall coordination and fund-raising responsibility, but many other functions were delegated to subdistrict offices. Decentralization reformed "pathological" school bureaucracies unable to reduce corruption and operate effectively and made schools more responsive to immediate communities.

**Localism: giving control to schools and communities.** While decentralization dismantled and reduced the authority of central school-district administrations, localism went further. Three approaches dominated: site-based management, shared decision-making, and creating school-based school boards. All of these approaches weakened the central administration's ability to direct and coordinate overall district policy. Site-based management devolves decision-making powers in specific areas such as curriculum, hiring and firing of teachers, instructional methods, and even disbursement of budgets to school principals. They, in turn, can make all such decisions themselves, or engage teachers, staff, and sometimes parents in shared decision-making. School Improvement Teams (SIT teams) consisting of parents and teachers are popular; their responsibilities can include everything from fund-raising and volunteer services to actual policy decisions. While parents often participate enthusiastically, recruiting effective parent groups that include working-class and minority parents can be difficult. Shared decision-making not only dilutes the power of the principal, but can cause work overload for teachers, who argue that they do not have time to both teach and run the school.

*A Nation at Risk:* **assessment and standards.** While decentralization and localism addressed school responsiveness to constituencies, it did not affect student achievement. In the early 1980s conservative political forces commissioned *A Nation at Risk: The Imperative for Educational Reform* (1983), a report calling for improving school quality by raising standards. The authors of this report argued that higher expectations for students would produce greater achievement. In response, states and districts increased the number of courses needed for graduation from high school, instituted state-wide and district-level basic skills and content area standardized tests to measure pupil achievement, and raised the test scores students needed to pass from one grade to the next. While these changes did little to change overall school organization, they did dilute district, school, and teacher control over what was taught, since teachers were forced to teach to the tests for their students to do well.

**Improving instructional quality: testing teachers.** The second attack on educational quality addressed the competence of teachers. The argument was that simply raising standards for students would not improve performance if teachers could not provide instruction commensurate with the level of the tests. In response, national and state-level minimum competency tests were created for beginning and experienced teachers. While the reforms initially required firing teachers who could not pass these tests, in practice, the passing levels for the tests were rather low. Many opportunities for remediation were offered, and few teachers were either found to be so poorly prepared that they could not pass. The testing programs did remove some district control over who could be hired and retained. Testing programs also took a heavy toll on teacher and student morale.

**Privatization.** In the 1990s disaffection with schools led to innovations in school funding and control, including privatization, charter schools, and vouchers. *Privatization* involves turning over to for-profit or nonprofit corporations and groups the operation of individual schools or districts deemed to be failures because of the low achievement of their students. These corporations receive funds from districts or the state that are normally allocated to those students enrolled in the privatized school or district; and the corporation then promises to do a better job than the public schools of educating children.

*Charter schools,* while still public, are run by parent or secular nonprofit special interest groups. Often using facilities owned by the public school district, they too are allocated ADA and local funds for the pupils they can enroll. Both privatization and chartering exempt the schools from a number of regulations—including the requirement that the schools serve all students (including language minority, poorly performing, and handicapped students) and specific guidelines regarding teacher qualifications, student teacher ratios, curricula and assessment. This effectively dilutes district and state capacity both to control what occurs in schools and to create consistent and coordinated educational policies and practices.

*Vouchers,* perhaps the most popular fiscal reform, involve giving to parents a sum equivalent to the local funds that would be expended for their child's education, and allowing them to use those funds to enroll the child wherever they wish, including private or parochial schools. Vouchers are popular with conservatives, who seek to dilute the influence of public schools by diverting public funds to private schools, which more often are attended by wealthier persons. By contrast, politicians of the left support strengthening the public schools to promote equality of educational opportunity for all children.

**Open enrollment.** Larger school districts historically have been divided into *zones* for attendance— students attended the school to which they were *zoned,* usually the one closest to their home. However, as parents have grown dissatisfied with the education offered at neighborhood schools, they have looked to enroll them in other schools—often those with special programs—within their district. Open enrollment policies dismantle attendance zones, allowing children to attend anywhere they choose, given available space or specific qualifications established by the receiving schools. They also disrupt patterns of school-level budgetary control, because funds earmarked for open-enrolling students go with them to the receiving schools, impoverishing the sending schools.

## Conclusions

Schools are asked to assume a myriad of responsibilities quite separate from simply teaching social and academic skills. Each of these has transformed organizational structures and patterns of control and funding in schools. The question remains whether public schools, with their original mission of educating children of all backgrounds, will survive; or whether the public schools, like those in many countries, will become the last resort for disadvantaged and poor children while more affluent segments of the population send their children to private institutions.

*See also:* GIFTED AND TALENTED EDUCATION; PUBLIC SCHOOL BUDGETING, ACCOUNTING, AND AUDITING; SCHOOL-BASED DECISION-MAKING; SCHOOL CLIMATE; SCHOOL REFORM; STANDARDS MOVEMENT IN AMERICAN EDUCATION; STUDENT ACTIVITIES; SUPERVISION OF INSTRUCTION; TEACHER EVALUATION.

## BIBLIOGRAPHY

BERLINER, DAVID C., and BIDDLE, BRUCE J. 1995. *The Manufactured C: Myths, Fraud and the Attack on America's Public Schools.* Reading, MA: Addison-Wesley.

BOURDIEU, PIERRE, and PASSERON, JEAN-CLAUDE. 1977. *Reproduction in Education, Society, and Culture.* London: Sage.

CALLAHAN, RAYMOND. 1962. *Education and the Cult of Efficiency.* Chicago: University of Chicago Press.

CORWIN, RONALD G. 1965. *Sociology of Education.* New York: Appleton.

CUBAN, LARRY. 1993. *How Teachers Taught: Constancy and Change in American Classrooms: 1880–1900,* 2nd edition. New York: Teachers College Press.

DEMARRAIS, KATHLEEN, and LeCOMPTE, MARGARET D. 1999. *The Way Schools Work: A Sociological Analysis of Education,* 3rd edition. White Plains, NY: Longman.

DEWEY, JOHN. 1916. *Democracy in Education.* New York: Macmillan.

DURKHEIM, ÉMILE. 1930. *Moral Education.* New York: Basic Books.

DWORKIN, ANTHONY GARY. 1987. *Teacher Burnout in the Public Schools: Structural Causes and Consequences for Children.* Albany: State University of New York Press.

DWORKIN, ANTHONY GARY. 1997. "Coping with Reform: The Intermix of Teacher Morale, Teacher Burnout, and Teacher Accountability." In *International Handbook of Teachers and Teaching,* Volume I, ed. Bruce J. Biddle, Terence L. Good, and Ivor F. Goodson. Dordrecht, The Netherlands: Kluwer Academic Publishers.

DWORKIN, ANTHONY GARY. 2001. "Perspectives on Teacher Burnout and School Reform." *International Educational Journal* 2(2):1–10.

DWORKIN, ANTHONY GARY, and TOWNSEND, MERRILL. 1994. "Teacher Burnout in the Face of Reform: Some Caveats in Breaking the Mold." In *Investing in U.S. Schools: Directions for Educational Policy,* ed. Barry A. Jones and Kathleen M. Borman. Norwood, NJ: Ablex.

GOULDNER, ALVIN W. 1959. "Organizational Analysis." In *Sociology Today,* ed. Robert K. Merton, Leonard Broom, and Leonard S. Cottrel, Jr. New York: Basic Books.

HESS, G. ALFRED. 1991. *School Restructuring, Chicago Style.* Newbury Park, CA: Corwin Press.

KATZ, MICHAEL B. 1971. *Class, Bureaucracy and the Schools.* New York: Praeger.

LORTIE, DAN. 1969. "The Balance of Control and Autonomy in Elementary School Teaching." In *The Semi-Professions and their Organization: Teachers, Nurses, Social Workers,* ed. Amitai Etzioni. New York: The Free Press.

LORTIE, DAN. 1975. *School Teacher: A Sociological Study.* Chicago: University of Chicago Press.

MARRETT, CORA B. 1990. "The Changing Composition of Schools: Implications for Social Organization." In *Change in Societal Organizations,* ed. Maureen T. Hallinan, David M. Klein, and Jennifer Glass. New York: Plenum.

MEYER, JOHN W., and ROWAN, BRIAN. 1978. *Environments and Organizations.* San Francisco: Jossey-Bass.

NATIONAL COMMISSION ON EXCELLENCE IN EDUCATION. 1983. *A Nation At Risk: The Imperative for Educational Reform.* Washington, DC: U.S. Government Printing Office.

OAKES, JEANNIE. 1985. *Keeping Track: How Schools Structure Inequality.* New Haven, CT: Yale University Press.

RESNICK, DAVID P., and RESNICK, LAUREN B. 1985. "Standards, Curriculum, and Performance: A Historical and Comparative Perspective." *Educational Researcher* 14:5–20.

ROGERS, DAVID. 1968. *110 Livingston Street: Politics and Bureaucracy in the New York City Schools.* New York: Random House.

SHEPARD, LORRIE, and KREITZER, AAMELIA. 1987. "The Texas Teachers' Test." *Educational Researcher* August–September:21–23.

SPRING, JOEL H. 1986. *The American School: 1642–1985.* New York: Longman.

TROW, MARTIN. 1967. "The Second Transformation of American Secondary Education." *International Journal of Comparative Sociology* 2:144–166.

WEICK, KARL E. 1976. "Educational Organizations As Loosely Coupled Systems." *Administrative Science Quarterly* 21:1–19.

MARGARET D. LeCOMPTE
ANTHONY GARY DWORKIN

# SOCIAL PROMOTION

Social promotion is the most common name for the policy of promoting students to the next grade level despite poor achievement at their current grade level. It is motivated by a desire to protect the social adjustment and school motivation of struggling students, as well as a belief that these students will get more from exposure to new content at the next grade than they would from repeating their current grade.

## In Comparison to Grade Retention

Social promotion is usually studied and discussed in comparison to its opposite: grade retention. A grade retention policy calls for requiring students who have failed to achieve satisfactorily to repeat their current grade the following year, instead of moving on to the next grade. This policy is motivated by the belief that an extra year in the grade will give struggling students an opportunity to master content that they failed to master the first year, and consequently leave them better prepared to succeed in higher grades in the future. Those who favor grade retention policies also tend to believe that it is important for schools to maintain high standards, and that social promotion policies fail to do this and instead send students the message that little is expected of them.

Grade retention and social promotion occur because many students fail to achieve at desired levels. If assessed using norm-referenced tests that yield grade-level equivalence scores, almost half of all students necessarily will score "below grade level" (although with considerable variation across schools and districts). More students will pass the criterion-referenced minimum competency tests used by many states, but even here, significant percentages of students will fail to meet standards. This forces schools to choose between socially promoting these students and retaining them in the grade for another year.

Retention in grade is common, with about a third of all students retained at least once before high school. Students retained in a grade are more likely than other students to be small in stature or youngest in the grade, to be from lower socioeconomic status or minority backgrounds, to have parents with lower educational attainment, to be boys rather than girls, and to have moved or been absent frequently. Presumably these same generalizations also would

be true of socially promoted students, simply because these categories of students are represented more heavily among low achievers. It is not possible to collect social promotion statistics the way it is possible to collect grade retention statistics because school districts usually do not distinguish in their records between regular promotions and social promotions.

At any given time, both grade retention and social promotion have their adherents, probably because each policy is based on an appealing rationale. Attitudes toward the two policies tend to flow in cycles, with first one and then the other gaining ascendancy for a decade or so, and the same essential arguments repeated on both sides. Grade retention was ascendant in the 1990s and early 2000s, with U.S. Presidents Bill Clinton and George W. Bush, many state governors, and many state- and district-level policymakers calling for eliminating social promotion as part of their plan for reforming schools. These policymakers tend to believe that unless poorly achieving students are faced with the prospect of flunking and being forced to repeat the grade, they will have little incentive to apply themselves to their studies. Most teachers also favor grade retention as a potential option for occasional use, especially in the early grades. Teachers tend to view it less as a motivational stick with which to threaten underachieving students, however, than as a way to enable them to catch up and begin to achieve more successfully. Barring information to the contrary, it is reasonable to believe that the threat of grade retention might motivate students who do not apply themselves to invest more effort in their studies, and that an extra year to catch up might benefit students whose low achievement is due to limited maturity or readiness.

However, a great deal of information to the contrary exists. Research comparing retained students with similar students who were socially promoted repeatedly shows that most students do not catch up when held back; that even if they do better at first, they fall behind again in later grades; that they are more likely to become alienated from school and eventually drop out; and that these findings hold just as much for kindergarten and first-grade students held back because they were presumed to lack maturity or readiness as they do for older students. By itself, retention provides either no achievement advantage or only short-lived advantages relative to social promotion, and it imposes costs on the retained students, their teachers, and the school system.

What typically happens is that administrators announce a "no social promotions" policy with a great deal of fanfare, then over the next couple of years call attention to any data that appear to suggest that the policy is working. Later, however, when it becomes clear that too many students are being retained (some repeatedly) and the administrators are confronted with angry parents, frustrated teachers, upset students, and rising costs, they quietly begin to back off by lowering standards (i.e., the test scores that will be required to earn promotion to the next grade) and by exempting certain categories of students from the policy (e.g., those who are learning English as their second language or have been assigned a special education diagnosis). Eventually they or the administrators who succeed them quietly drop the policy (without, of course, admitting that all of the problems that it created could have been foreseen if attention had been paid to the relevant research literature).

## Advantages and Disadvantages

Costs to the retained students include the shame and embarrassment of being held back and the separation from age mates in the short run, as well as alienation from schooling as an institution and a much greater propensity to drop out prior to graduation in the longer run. Costs to teachers include increases in the student motivation and classroom management challenges that are involved in teaching classes that include a significant number of retained students, as well as the problems that ensue in junior high and high school when physically more mature older students are in the same classes with less developed younger students. For school districts, there are costs in both expense (grade retentions translate into higher class sizes and related logistical problems) and effort (increased administrative responsibilities for establishing and maintaining mechanisms to implement grade retention policies and for defending them when students or their families challenge them).

Occasionally, research, such as that of C. Thomas Holmes in 1989, appears to suggest that grade retention is helpful, at least to some students. Usually these data are confined to short-term findings that the retained students showed higher achievement during the year that they repeated the grade than they had the year before. Longitudinal data, howev-

er, typically show that grade retention is not helpful. For example, in 1995 Karl Alexander and colleagues reported findings from Baltimore indicating that retainees did somewhat better after retention than they had before (although with diminishing advantage over time) and even displayed positive attitudes toward self and school. This study was frequently cited by proponents of grade retention as evidence that newer studies were beginning to show a different pattern of findings from the conventional wisdom. However, an update six years later indicated that the earlier reported advantages to grade retention had washed out and that the retained students proved to be much more likely to drop out of school than the socially promoted students. Reports from Chicago, another district that had made a high-profile commitment to grade retention policies, also indicated that initially mixed findings had turned negative within three years, according to Melissa Roderick and colleagues in 2000. More generally, a meta-analysis that focused on studies published between 1990 and 1999 once again proved unfavorable to grade retention, refuting the claim that newer studies were showing a different pattern of findings.

In 1989 Holmes completed a meta-analyses of sixty-three comparisons of grade retention with social promotion. He reported that fifty-four of the sixty-three studies yielded overall negative effects for grade retention but nine showed positive effects. The latter studies involved suburban settings and middle-class families, and usually not retention alone but also efforts by the school to identify struggling students early, involve the parents, and provide special assistance such as placement in classes with low student-teacher ratios. Even so, the advances made by the retained students during their repetition year tended to diminish over time.

## Different Perspectives

In 1998 Richard Rothstein put social promotion, grade retention, and related issues into perspective by noting that the dilemma of what to do with students who don't progress "normally" is endemic to compulsory education. As long as all students are required to stay in school until they reach a certain age (e.g., sixteen), the decision on what to do with those who are less advanced will remain. Research throughout the twentieth century repeatedly indicated that, on the whole, age is a better grouping principle than academic achievement.

Researchers and reviewers who have focused on grade retention and social promotion typically conclude that neither policy is an effective treatment for unsatisfactory achievement, but if one must choose between them, social promotion is preferable. This is because grade retention imposes too many social and motivational costs, and students appear to get more out of a year spent in the next grade than they do out of a year spent repeating a grade, even though they are likely to continue to achieve less successfully than their classmates. However, social promotion does not help low achievers to begin to catch up with their age peers. Therefore, better than either social promotion or grade retention are policies that mobilize schools to identify struggling students early and provide them with special forms of assistance that might allow them to achieve more satisfactorily (placement in smaller classes, provision of tutoring or other special assistance, enrollment in after-school or summer school programs, and so on). Organizations such as the International Reading Association and the National Association of School Psychologists have published policy statements advocating this approach to students who are not achieving satisfactorily. Some ideas about intervention alternatives to both grade retention and social promotion mentioned by McCay (2001) and U.S. Department of Education (1999) include setting clear performance standards at key grades, emphasizing early childhood literacy, providing high-quality curriculum and instruction and professional development, reducing class sizes in the primary grades, keeping students and teachers together for more than one year, and using effective student grouping practices.

*See also:* ELEMENTARY EDUCATION, *subentry on* CURRENT TRENDS; NONGRADED SCHOOLS; SECONDARY EDUCATION, *subentry on* CURRENT TRENDS.

## BIBLIOGRAPHY

ALEXANDER, KARL; ENTWISLE, DORIS; and DAUBER, SUSAN. 1995. *On the Success of Failure: A Reassessment of the Effects of Retention in the Primary Grades.* New York: Cambridge University Press.

ALEXANDER, KARL; ENTWISLE, DORIS; DAUBER, SUSAN; and KABBANI, NADER. 2001. "Drop Out in Relation to Grade Retention: An Accounting from the Beginning School Study." *CEIC Review* 10(5):3–4, 12, 21.

HOLMES, C. THOMAS. 1989. "Grade Level Retention Effects: A Meta-Analysis of Research Studies." In *Flunking Grades: Research and Policies on Retention,* ed. Lorrie Shepard and Mary Lee Smith. London: Falmer.

JIMERSON, SHANE. 2001. "Meta-Analysis of the Effects of Grade Retention: 1990–1999." *CEIC Review* 10(5):7–8, 21.

MANTZICOPOULOS, PANAYOTA, and MORRISON, DELMONT. 1992. "Kindergarten Retention: Academic and Behavioral Outcomes through the End of Second Grade." *American Educational Research Journal* 29:192–198.

McCAY, ELIZABETH, ed. 2001. Moving beyond Retention and Social Promotion. Bloomington, IN: Phi Delta Kappa International.

OWINGS, WILLIAM, and MAGLIARO, SUSAN. 1998. "Grade Retention: A History of Failure." *Educational Leadership* 56(1):86–88.

REYNOLDS, ARTHUR. 1992. "Grade Retention and School Adjustment: An Exploratory Analysis." *Educational Evaluation and Policy Analysis* 14:101–121.

REYNOLDS, ARTHUR, and WOLFE, BARBARA. 1999. "Special Education and School Achievement: An Exploratory Analysis with a Center-City Sample." *Educational Evaluation and Policy Analysis* 21:249–269.

RODERICK, MELISSA. 1994. "Grade Retention and School Drop Out: Investigating the Association." *American Educational Research Journal* 31:729–759.

RODERICK, MELISSA; NAGAOKA, JENNY; BACON, JEN; and EASTON, JOHN. 2000. *Update: Ending Social Promotion: Passing, Retention, and Achievement Trends among Promoted and Retained Students: 1995–1999.* Chicago: Consortium on Chicago School Research.

ROTHSTEIN, RICHARD. 1998. "Where Is Lake Woebegone, Anyway? The Controversy surrounding Social Promotion." Phi Delta Kappan 80:195–198.

SHEPARD, LORRIE, and SMITH, MARY LEE, eds. 1989. *Flunking Grades: Research and Policies on Retention.* London: Falmer.

TANNER, C. KENNETH, and COMBS, F. EDWARD. 1993. "Student Retention Policy: The Gap between Research and Practice." *Journal of Research in Childhood Education* 8:69–75.

THOMPSON, CHARLES, and CUNNINGHAM, ELIZABETH. 2000. *Retention and Social Promotion: Research and Implications for Policy.* New York: ERIC Clearinghouse on Urban Education, Teachers College, Columbia University.

TOMCHIN, ELLEN, and IMPARA, JAMES. 1992. "Unraveling Teachers' Beliefs about Grade Retention." *American Educational Research Journal* 29:199–223.

U.S. DEPARTMENT OF EDUCATION. 1999. *Taking Responsibility for Ending Social Promotion.* Washington, DC: U.S. Department of Education.

JERE BROPHY

# SOCIAL STUDIES EDUCATION

OVERVIEW
Michael J. Berson
Bárbara C. Cruz
James A. Duplass
J. Howard Johnston
PREPARATION OF TEACHERS
Susan A. Adler

## OVERVIEW

The contemporary social studies curriculum has its roots in the Progressive education movement of the early twentieth century. With its emphasis on the nature of the individual learner and on the process of learning itself, the movement challenged the assumptions of subject-centered curricula. Until this time, the social studies curriculum was composed of discrete subject areas, with a primary emphasis on history. To a slightly lesser degree, geography and civics were also featured, completing the triumvirate.

There were indications that change was coming when the 1893 *Report of the Committee of Ten on Secondary School Studies* advocated an interdisciplinary approach in the social studies. By 1916 the National Education Association (NEA)'s Committee on the Social Studies was urging that an interdisciplinary course of instruction be created based on the social sciences. When the NEA 1916 report established *social studies* as the name of the content area, it presented the scope and sequence that is still in use at the start of the twenty-first century. Social studies received further support when the 1918 *Cardinal Principles of Secondary Education* called for the unified study of subject areas heretofore taught in isolation. This course, called social studies, would have as its main goal the cultivation of good citizens.

The emphasis on citizenship development was understandable. At the time, because of increased immigration from non-English speaking countries, educators were given the task of teaching English and "the American way of life" in addition to their content areas. As World War I raged in Europe, social studies courses were viewed as a means of developing patriotism among the new foreign-born citizens.

Indeed, citizenship education was one of the main missions of the National Council for the Social Studies (NCSS) when it was formed in 1921. What began as a service organization intending to close the gap between social scientists and secondary school teachers soon advanced an integrated study of the social studies and a broader conception of social studies education.

### The Role of Social Studies in the Curriculum of U.S. Schools

The terms *social studies education* and *social science education* are often used interchangeably and are, at times, a source of confusion. *Social studies* is the preferred term in part because it is more inclusive. Although *social science* typically refers only to academic disciplines such as anthropology, sociology, psychology, geography, economics, and political science, the term *social studies* includes the aforementioned social sciences as well as humanities disciplines like history, American studies, and philosophy.

At the elementary grade level, social studies is typically organized and taught in an integrative and interdisciplinary fashion, but by the high-school-level social studies teaching and learning are organized by courses in the academic disciplines. At all levels, however, the goals of social studies have been characterized by Peter Martorella (1985) as: (1) transmission of the cultural heritage; (2) methods of inquiry; (3) reflective inquiry; (4) informed social criticism; and (5) personal development. Personal development has traditionally received the greatest emphasis at the elementary level; at the high school level, methods of inquiry have received more emphasis. As phrased in the curriculum guidelines released by the NCSS (1979), "the basic goal of social studies education is to prepare young people to be humane, rational, participating citizens in a world that is becoming increasingly interdependent" (p. 262).

**Elementary social studies.** In the early 1940s, Paul Hanna articulated the Expanding Communities approach as the vehicle in elementary education by which teachers could best present social studies knowledge. For the most part, Hanna's model has been characterized as organizing the content as a series of concentric circles starting with the self at the center and progressing to the family, school, neighborhood, until reaching the international community. It also provided a thematic approach to the content: protecting and conserving; creating, governing, producing resources, transporting, expressing, educating, recreating, and communicating. The content approach still dominates elementary education, but the thematic approach has largely disappeared.

Eric D. Hirsch's (1987) concept of *core knowledge* has gained some footing as an alternative to the Hanna model. Hirsch proposes a core of information that every American should know. The core knowledge approach relies heavily on world (some would characterize this as primarily European) and U.S. history and culture, democratic ideology, geography, and literature that amplify the human experience; the content is organized to introduce students to subject matter at all grades but at different degrees of intensity.

**Secondary social studies.** The 1960s brought significant changes to the middle school and high school curricula with the introduction of the elective system. Courses in subjects like anthropology, economics, sociology, and psychology were added to a curriculum that had formally been primarily limited to world history, world geography, government, and U.S. history. Advanced Placement courses were also introduced.

In 1994 NCSS published *Expectations of Excellence: Curriculum Standards for Social Studies.* Citing the need to promote civic ideals and principles for life in the twenty-first century, the standards consisted of ten interdisciplinary thematic strands as a guide for developing social studies curriculum.

### The National Council for the Social Studies

The National Council for the Social Studies was founded in 1921, and is the largest organization in the United States to focus exclusively on social studies education. Historically, the organization was established as a coordinating entity and clearinghouse. It evolved at a time when social studies was immersed in disagreement on scope and sequence. Dissent ensued among teacher educators and content specialists, and certification requirements in the social studies were nonexistent. The founders, comprised of professors from Teachers College at Columbia University, envisioned NCSS as the unifying organization that could merge the social studies disciplines with education.

At the start of the twenty-first century NCSS plays a leadership role in promoting an integrated study of the social studies and offers support and services to its members. The membership includes K–12 teachers, curriculum specialists, content supervisors, college and university faculty, students, and education leaders in the social studies. The organization has members in all fifty states, the District of Columbia, and numerous foreign countries. It draws on multidisciplinary studies and emphasizes a civic-based approach.

The council has articulated a framework to foster academic and civic competence by integrating national standards across disciplines. These NCSS standards are published in *Expectations of Excellence: Curriculum Standards for Social Studies,* and serve as a guide for decision-making by social studies educators. They have integrated approaches from the social sciences, behavioral sciences, and humanities to aid in structuring a comprehensive and effective social studies program. Ten themes are highlighted in the framework, which include culture; people, places and environments; individuals, groups, and institutions; production, distribution, and consumption; global connections; time, continuity, and change; individual development and identity; power, authority, and governance; science, technology, and society; and civic ideals and practices. The council also has developed position statements to guide the profession on critical areas of education, such as ability grouping, character education, ethics, information literacy, multicultural and global education, religion, and testing.

### Teaching Social Studies in Other Countries

The term *social studies* appears in the literature and the names of professional associations and organizations, academic institutions, and curriculum projects and centers throughout the world. Its meaning, however, is as varied as the contexts in which it appears, and may have little to do with the way content is organized or delivered. Three types of content organization predominate.

Social studies in its most interdisciplinary form combines the integrated study of humanities and the social sciences. This integrated focus appears in relatively few nations, such as the United States and Canada, where both instructional materials and curriculum objectives focus on interdisciplinary learning. In other nations, the mandate for such a system is somewhat more direct. Australia's Adelaide Declaration (DETYA) calls upon schools to prepare students to "exercise judgment and responsibility in matters of morality, ethics and social justice, and the capacity to make sense of their world, to think about how things got to be the way they are" and to "be active and informed citizens" committed to democratic principles and ideals. Recent changes in Japanese national educational policy and law require all students to study integrated courses such as "Human Beings and Industrial Society." The Constitution of the Republic of China (Taiwan) requires education for citizenship that "shall aim at the development among the citizens of the national spirit, the spirit of self-government, national morality, good physique, scientific knowledge and the ability to earn a living" (Article 158). And, while no "social studies" course is mandated per se, the South African Ministry of Education requires that the "values of human rights, civic responsibility and respect for the environment [be] infused throughout the curriculum."

The more common use of the term *social studies* is as an organizing term for the social science disciplines in faculties, schools, and professional interest groups. In Ghana, for example, social studies faculties in the local secondary schools and university are composed of historians, anthropologists, sociologists, and other social scientists. Similar organizations are found in Zimbabwe, New Zealand, the Czech Republic, the United Kingdom, Hong Kong, and other nations throughout Asia and Europe.

The organizational patterns noted above exist in a minority of nations in the world community. The large majority of educational institutions, including schools, universities, ministries of education and culture, and local educational agencies organize the social studies into separate, distinct disciplines: history, economics, anthropology, political science, and other traditional social sciences. Indeed, the university entrance examinations or secondary school exit exams in nations such as the United Kingdom, France, Germany, Saudi Arabia, Indonesia, and Russia, for example, focus on specific social science disciplines, notably history and geography. Even in nations with emerging integrated curriculum standards such as Japan and the Republic of China, however, examination programs tend to follow traditional social science academic disciplines.

## Issues and Controversies

Since its very inception, social studies education has weathered a number of controversies and challenges. The core idea of an integrated field of study has been under scrutiny since its earliest days. The field's eclectic nature not only draws on a wide range of disciplines, but also attracts continuing debate and conflict.

One of the most publicized controversies in the United States was triggered by the curriculum "Man: A Course of Study" (MACOS) during the 1960s. Developed with a National Science Foundation grant, the mixed media curriculum was designed to stimulate the learner's curiosity, promote scientific literacy, and help children learn to think like social scientists. Almost immediately, the program was at the center of a backlash from the "Back to Basics Movement." Central to the MACOS controversy was its focus on inquiry and discovery rather than content. Among other things, critics charged that students were not developing basic skills, that the curriculum promoted cultural relativism, and that it was a threat to democracy. Not surprisingly, the curriculum was eventually phased out.

Conflicts regarding new teaching and learning strategies still abound. For example, role-playing and simulations, guided imagery, cooperative learning, and technology-based learning have all received their share of criticism and opposition.

The content of the social studies curriculum has also been the source of debate and disagreement. When the National Center for History in the Schools published *National Standards for World History: Exploring Paths to the Present* in 1994, some educators charged that the standards were too inclusive; others claimed that certain groups were omitted altogether. Other controversies center on the plausibility of a national curriculum and the ongoing development of state-level standards, mandates, and high-stakes testing.

Debates surrounding culture continue in the teaching of history, geography, ethnic studies, and multicultural education. While many educators support a cultural relativist position, many others argue that "the mission of public schools is to instill in children our shared, not our separate, cultures" (Ravitch, p. 8). These "culture wars" (as termed by Nash, Crabtree, and Dunn) have resulted in a rich, intellectual, and academic debate that will hopefully illuminate the field. Global education and international studies have also been criticized for their emphases on issues and events outside the United States' borders. Critics charge that global studies advance cultural relativism, minimize patriotism, and emphasize skills at the expense of content. Advocates point out, however, that national borders are becoming less relevant in the face of technology, international politics, and environmental issues.

### The Future Role of Technology in the Social Studies

Technology has gained prominence as a tool within the social studies with the potential to enhance current pedagogic practice. Although an increasing body of research suggests that technology can improve academic achievement, changes in social studies instruction based on these findings have been tempered by the following: (1) questions about the efficiency and effectiveness of computer technology applications in the classroom; (2) the role of teacher education institutions and school settings in facilitating or hindering computer-based activities; (3) the unrealized potential of technology; and (4) the overlooked consequences of technological development on children and youth with regard to their social functioning, interpersonal interactions, and global understanding. Various technologies such as Internet and web-based resources, hypermedia, data instruments, digital video, and tele-collaborative teaching represent emerging resources implemented in social studies instruction.

Technology, however, is more than just a tool of instruction, and these resources have effects on the political, social, and economic functioning of American society. Technology's impact on society is exemplified in the phenomenon of the digital divide that separates those who are information rich through their access to telecommunications, computers, and the Internet from the information and technologically poor. Within the social studies educators focus on the differential impact of privileged access to these resources in the early stages of development and consider the potential ongoing conse-

quences of this separation of haves and have-nots on economic success, civic influence, and personal advancement.

Social studies education will continue to evolve as it is affected by events and trends in the United States and abroad. These include the globalization of the media and the economy, advancements in technology, shifts in schools and school demographics, teacher accreditation standards, student testing mandates, changes in the American family, and swings of the political pendulum. These forces will certainly impact ideological perspectives and influence the direction of the social studies in the future.

*See also:* CIVICS AND CITIZENSHIP EDUCATION; CURRICULUM, SCHOOL; ELEMENTARY EDUCATION, *subentries on* CURRENT TRENDS, HISTORY OF; GEOGRAPHY, TEACHING OF; HISTORY, *subentry on* TEACHING OF; NATIONAL COUNCIL FOR THE SOCIAL STUDIES; SECONDARY EDUCATION, *subentries on* CURRENT TRENDS, HISTORY OF; TECHNOLOGY IN EDUCATION, *subentry on* SCHOOL.

### BIBLIOGRAPHY

BERSON, MICHAEL J. 2000. "Rethinking Research and Pedagogy in the Social Studies: The Creation of Caring Connections through Technology and Advocacy." *Theory and Research in Social Education* 28(1):121–131.

BERSON, MICHAEL J.; LEE, JOHN K.; and STUCKART, DANIEL W. 2001. "Promise and Practice of Computer Technologies in the Social Studies: A Critical Analysis." In *Critical Issues in Social Studies Research for the Twenty-First Century,* ed. William B. Stanley. Greenwich, CT: Information Age.

DEPARTMENT OF EDUCATION, TRAINING, AND YOUTH AFFAIRS. 1999. *The Adelaide Declaration on National Goals for Schooling in the Twenty-First Century.* Canberra: Government of Australia, Department of Education, Training and Youth Affairs.

HANNA, PAUL R. 1965. *Design for a Social Studies Program. Focus on the Social Studies.* Washington, DC: National Education Association, Department of Elementary School Principals.

HIRSCH, ERIC DONALD. 1987. *Cultural Literacy: What Every American Needs To Know.* New York: Houghton Mifflin.

Martorella, Peter H. 1985. *Elementary Social Studies: Developing Reflective, Competent, and Concerned Citizens.* Boston: Little, Brown.

Merryfield, Merry M. 1997. "Infusing Global Perspectives Into the Social Studies Curriculum" in *The Social Studies Curriculum,* ed. E. Wayne Ross. Albany: State University of New York Press.

Nash, Gary B.; Crabtree, Charlotte; and Dunn, Ross E. 1997. *History on Trial: Culture Wars and the Teaching of the Past.* New York: Knopf.

National Center for History in the Schools. 1994. *National Standards for World History: Exploring Paths to the Present.* Los Angeles: National Center for History in the Schools.

National Council for the Social Studies. 1979. "Revision of the NCSS Social Studies Curriculum Guidelines." *Social Education* 43:261–278.

National Council for the Social Studies. 1994. *Expectations of Excellence: Curriculum Standards for Social Studies.* Washington, DC: National Council for the Social Studies.

National Education Association of the United States. 1916. *Addresses and Proceedings of the Annual Meeting.* Washington, DC: National Education Association of the United States.

National Education Association of the United States. 1918. *Cardinal Principles of Secondary Education.* Washington, DC: Government Printing Office.

National Education Association of the United States. 1969. *Report of the Committee of Ten on Secondary School Studies* (1893). New York: Arno Press.

Nelson, Murray R. 1996. *Directionless from Birth.* ERIC Document Reproduction Service No. ED391706.

Ravitch, Diane. 1991. *A Culture in Common. Educational Leadership.* 49(4):8–11.

The Republic of China (Taiwan). 1997. *Constitution of the Republic of China. Article 158* Republic of China (Taiwan).

Social Sciences Curriculum Program. 1968. *Man: A Course of Study.* Washington, DC: Curriculum Development Associates.

Thornton, Stephen J. 1996. "NCSS: The Early Years." In *NCSS in Retrospect,* ed. Orzo Luke Davis, Jr. Washington, DC: National Council for the Social Studies.

**INTERNET RESOURCES**

Ministry of Education, Culture, Sports, Science and Technology (MEXT). 2000. "What is an Integrated Course?" Tokyo: Government of Japan, Ministry of Education. <www.mext.go.jp/english/shotou/index.htm>.

South Africa Ministry of Education. 2000. "Report of the Curriculum 2005 Review Committee." <http://education.pwv.gov.za/Policies%20and%20Reports/2000_Reports/2005/chisolm_2005.htm>.

Michael J. Berson
Bárbara C. Cruz
James A. Duplass
J. Howard Johnston

## PREPARATION OF TEACHERS

The development of the education of social studies teachers mirrors, in large part, the history and changes of teacher education generally. Social studies teacher preparation has moved from teachers' institutes and normal schools begun in the nineteenth century to teacher colleges and university-based teacher preparation in the twentieth century. But the education of social studies teachers has also had to take into account the unique definitions and issues connected to the teaching of social studies.

### Defining Social Studies

Social studies is remembered by many who have gone through schools in the United States as a series of names, dates, and state capitals. In fact, both the definition and content of the field have been a matter of controversy since the early twentieth century. Social studies can be seen both as an umbrella term for a broad field of studies encompassing history and the social sciences and as an integrated field of study in its own right. But whatever the definition, the objectives of social studies education are highly contested. Values such as patriotism, an appreciation of free enterprise, respect for diverse cultures and nations, and knowledge of the structures and functions of American government are each seen by some group as the major goal of social studies teaching. The National Council for the Social Studies (NCSS) defines the field as "the integrated study of the social sciences and humanities to promote civic competence" (NCSS webiste). Because the NCSS standards for the education of social studies teachers (1997) are widely accepted by teacher preparation programs, the goal of enabling learners to acquire knowledge, skills, and dispositions necessary to citizen participation helps to provide a focus for both the social studies curriculum and the preparation of social studies teachers.

## Structure and Organization

What most distinguishes the preparation of social studies teachers from the preparation of other secondary and middle school teachers are the course requirements in their teaching content field and the special methods course. There is a good deal of variation of requirements across the fifty states. Since social studies is an interdisciplinary field, a major concern regarding content requirements is that of depth versus breadth across the various disciplines. How much content knowledge in each of the disciplines making up social studies is enough? How can prospective social studies teachers be prepared both broadly and deeply in all the areas they are expected to teach? In some programs, pre-service teachers major in social studies and take a broad array of courses across history and the social sciences. In other programs, they major in one field and take one or more courses in each of the other social studies disciplines. In some states teachers are certified in "social studies," while in others they may receive certification in a particular discipline such as history or geography.

The social studies methods class is the cornerstone of the professional course work taken by prospective social studies teachers. In this course teachers are expected to learn how to transform content into curriculum and to select and implement appropriate teaching strategies. Through the social studies methods course, combined with related field experiences, pre-service social studies teachers must learn ways to bridge the gap between the experiences of learners and content knowledge. However, although the methods course is a key component of the pre-service education of social studies teachers, there is not general agreement on a number of issues concerning this course: What should be the depth versus breadth of methods taught? How much emphasis should be given in this class to the needs of diverse learners? How much time should be spent preparing pre-service teachers to work with state-mandated assessments? What emphasis should be placed in the methods course on developing a sufficient background in the social science disciplines?

The question of subject field content is complemented by the related ontological question, often dealt with in the social studies methods class: What is the nature of knowledge? How teachers conceive of knowledge determines, to a large extent, how they will teach. Is knowledge transmitted by experts or is it constructed by each learner? In teaching methods classes, pre-service teachers may be asked to consider whether history, for example, is largely basic facts of what happened, a method of inquiry, or broad concepts and ideas that enable learners to understand today's world. Generally, the answers teachers develop to these questions are based on the beliefs and expectations pre-service teachers bring to the teacher education program. They bring their already developed conceptions of the content as well as what it means to teach and they make sense of their teacher education experience through the screen of these preconceived ideas. For this reason, the study of pre-service teachers' perspectives and the influences on forming and changing these perspectives has been an important focus for research.

The issues raised by a consideration of the social studies methods class are confounded by the fact that in some programs the instructor of that course may not be a specialist in social studies; indeed, that individual may not be well acquainted with the field itself. Thus questions about the nature and goals of the field may be dealt with only superficially or not at all.

## In-Service and Staff Development

Professional development occurs in both formal and informal ways. Informally, students, the school culture, collegial interactions, administrative interaction, and support all work in powerful ways to shape the development of teachers. Formal mechanisms explicitly aimed at guiding teacher development are in place as well. Increasingly, schools and school districts have begun to create and implement teacher induction programs. These programs are intended to provide support for beginning teachers as they deal with day-to-day challenges. Often, a beginning teacher is paired with an experienced teacher who serves as an advisor, guide, and sounding board. The goal of teacher induction programs is to both assist and retain novice teachers and revitalize mentor teachers. But little is known about the making of effective mentors and mentor programs.

Another professional development opportunity routinely provided by school districts is the school-

or district-developed in-service program. Once again, there is no common program model. Such programs may be one-day presentations or yearlong sustained efforts. They may be built around the idea of teachers working together to improve their teaching or they may rely on outside experts who make an occasional appearance. Teachers may see these programs as meeting their needs or as completely irrelevant.

There is the expectation, in many states and school districts, that teachers will continue to do graduate work in their teaching field or in professional education. While teachers in such programs are expected to find useful ways to apply what they learn to their teaching practice, there is generally little support in the classroom for these efforts. Some teachers find that membership in professional associations, such as the National Council for the Social Studies, is a meaningful form of professional development. Reading journals, attending conferences and workshops, and working with other teachers in one's own field are important benefits of getting involved with professional associations. However, not all schools and school districts are supportive of teacher involvement in professional associations. Districts often expect membership in professional associations to be at the teacher's own cost and on the teacher's own time. Some districts will discourage teachers from taking time from their teaching to attend professional association meetings and conferences, while others support such efforts as a form of professional renewal.

Certification by the National Board for Professional Teaching Standards is a challenging form of professional development voluntarily undertaken by experienced teachers. National board certification in social studies, as in other fields, is based on a demonstration of a teacher's practice as measured against high and rigorous standards. Yet, states and school districts differ in the support they give to teachers seeking board certification and in the ways in which they recognize those who achieve certification through this rigorous process.

## Major Trends and Issues

Important trends in the education of social studies teachers are similar to those in teacher education as a whole, but they are often manifest in distinct ways. The growing interest in accountability for both teachers and students, for example, is a major issue in the early twenty-first century. The work of teaching and teacher education has come to focus increasingly on helping students to meet state standards. In addition, many states require teachers to pass some form of content knowledge test to receive certification. In social studies, both student content standards and teacher testing may be highly political rather than professional. Decisions about what knowledge should be taught are often very controversial. Decision-making often involves politicians, content experts with divergent points of view, and the general public, as well as professional educators. Consensus among and within various groups may be difficult to attain; those with the most powerful voices often become the decision-makers.

Another challenge for teaching and teacher education is the appropriate use of technology both in teacher education programs and in K–12 classrooms. Research suggests that social studies preservice teacher motivation is increased by online dialogue, facilitated (but not controlled) by the instructor. Additional research suggests great potential for improved learning of social studies through the use of technology, such as using the Library of Congress website to bring primary sources into the classroom. However, at the start of the twenty-first century, teacher educators are only beginning to use technology in sophisticated ways in their own teaching and only just developing ways to prepare teachers for high-power uses of technology.

Teacher education faces the challenge of preparing teachers to effectively teach culturally and linguistically diverse students. In social studies, issues of diversity go to the heart of the field. The concept of citizenship on which social studies is based must be a dynamic one that considers the many different cultural and national identities of learners. It must also take into account that citizenship in an interdependent world must have a global, as well as a national, component. Making the social studies curriculum meaningful and significant for learners and for society remains the greatest challenge of social studies teaching and teacher education.

*See also:* ELEMENTARY EDUCATION, *subentry on* PREPARATION OF TEACHERS; TEACHER EDUCATION.

### BIBLIOGRAPHY

ADLER, SUSAN A. 1991. "The Education of Social Studies Teachers." In *Handbook of Research on Social Studies Teaching and Learning,* ed. James Shaver, 210–221. New York: Macmillan.

ARMENTO, BEVERLY. 1996. "The Professional Development of Social Studies Educators." In *Handbook of Research on Teacher Education*, 2nd edition, ed. John Sikula, 485–502. New York: Macmillan.

BANKS, JAMES A., and PARKER, WALTER C. 1990. "Social Studies Teacher Education." In *Handbook of Research on Teacher Education*, ed. W. Robert Houston, 674–686. New York: Macmillan.

BANKS, JAMES A. 2001. "Citizenship Education and Diversity: Implications for Teacher Education." *Journal of Teacher Education* 52(1):5–16.

ENGLE, SHIRLEY H., and OCHOA, ANNA A. 1988. *Education for Democratic Citizenship: Decision Making in the Social Studies.* New York: Teachers College Press.

GRIFFIN, GARY A. 1999. "Changes in Teacher Education: Looking to the Future." In *The Education of Teachers: Ninety-Eighth Yearbook of the National Society for the Study of Education*, ed. Gary A. Griffin. Chicago: University of Chicago Press.

MASON, CHERYL L., and BERSON, MICHAEL. 2000. "Computer Mediated Instruction in Elementary Social Studies Methods: An Examination of Students' Perceptions and Perspectives." *Theory and Research in Social Education* 28(4):527–545.

NATIONAL COUNCIL FOR THE SOCIAL STUDIES. 1997. *Expectations of Excellence: Curriculum Standards for Social Studies.* Washington, DC: National Council for the Social Studies.

NATIONAL COUNCIL FOR THE SOCIAL STUDIES. 1997. *National Standards for Social Studies Teachers.* Washington, DC: National Council for the Social Studies.

ROSS, E. WAYNE, ed. 1994. *Teachers as Curriculum Theorizers: Reflective Practice in Social Studies.* Washington, DC: National Council for the Social Studies.

THORNTON, STEPHEN J. 2001. "Educating the Educators: Rethinking Subject Matter and Methods." *Theory into Practice* 40(1):72–78.

PARKER, WALTER C.; NINOMIYA, AKIRA; and COGAN, JOHN. 1999. "Educating World Citizens: Toward Multinational Curriculum Development." *American Educational Research Journal* 36(2):117–145.

WILSON, SUZANNE M., and McDIARMID, G. WILLIAMSON. 1996. "Something Old, Something New: What Do Social Studies Teachers Need To Know?" In *The Teacher Educator's Handbook: Building a Knowledge Base for the Preparation of Teachers*, ed. Frank Murray. San Francisco: Jossey-Bass.

### INTERNET RESOURCE

BICKFORD, ADAM, and HAMMER, BARBARA. 2000. "MINTs Project Evaluation Report." Office of Social and Economic Data Analysis, University of Missouri System. <http://emints.more.net>.

SUSAN A. ADLER

# SOUTH ASIA

Writing about education in South Asian region means writing about one-fourth of the world's population. South Asia comprises seven contiguous countries: Bangladesh, Bhutan, India, Maldives, Nepal, Pakistan, and Sri Lanka. The region is geographically knit together and is homogenous in terms of sociocultural, political, historical, economic, and educational factors. The people of this area are heirs to a heritage of common culture and civilization steeped in history. At the beginning of the twenty-first century, however, it is one of the most backward regions of the world, both educationally and economically. It is the poorest region economically in the world, with an average per capita income of about US$350. Most of the countries in the region rank fairly poorly in terms of the human development index, a crude summary statistic of development compiled by the United Nations Development Program (UNDP). All the countries of the region, except Sri Lanka, are classified as *low human development* countries.

This is a historically rich region, with one of the most ancient civilizations of the world. The ancient scriptures associated with the region placed education and knowledge on a high pedestal, regarding it as the most important treasure one could have. Even in the early twenty-first century, many in the region value education very highly. Some of these countries were once very rich, industrially advanced, and materially prosperous. "The fame of their wealth earned for this region the appellation of the 'gorgeous East,' and inspired the quest which led to the discovery of the New World and created the preconditions for the Industrial Revolution in Europe" (Huq, p. 5). The countries of the region, except for Nepal and Bhutan, experienced various short and long phases of colonial rule and became independent in the middle of the twentieth century. The devastating colonial impact can be noted on the development of education in the region. The long colonial rule uprooted the *beautiful tree* in the undivided India and transformed an advanced intermediate society of India into an illiterate society, besides converting it into a raw material appendage on the economic front.

At the start of the twenty-first century, with the exception of Sri Lanka, South Asia is one of the most backward regions of the world in terms of educational development. The region has been described as "the poorest region," "the most illiterate region," "the least gender-sensitive region," and "the region with the highest human deprivation" (Haq and Haq 1997, pp. 2–3). It has emerged as an "anti-education society in the midst of a pro-education Asian culture" (Haq and Haq 1998, p. 42). In sheer numbers, the South Asian subcontinent poses the most serious challenges in education: nearly half the adult illiterates of the world live in the subcontinent, the rate of participation in schooling is low, and the quality of education is poor.

## Education Development after Independence

The importance of education is increasingly realized by every nation in the region. The human investment revolution in economic thought initiated by Theodore Schultz in an address to the American Economic Association had its own impact on public policy regarding educational development. The critical role of education in social, economic, and political development—as a means of development as well as a measure of development—is widely recognized. As a result, there has been an education explosion during the second half the twentieth century in most developing countries. Countries in the South Asian region also experienced an explosion in the number of people attending school. Between 1950 and 1997, enrollments in schools in South Asia increased sixfold, from 44 million to 262 million. The total teaching staff increased from 1.4 million to 7.2 million during this period. Enrollment ratios increased from 20 percent (net) in 1960 to 52 percent (gross) in 2000. (Gross enrollment ratios refer to the total enrollments as a proportion of the relevant age group population, while net enrollment ratio refers to en-

**TABLE 1**

**Educational progress in South Asia**

| Rate of illiteracy (%) | 1960 | 2000 |
|---|---|---|
| | 72.0 | 45.8 |
| **Net enrollment ratios (%)** | **1960** | **1997*** |
| Primary | 45.0 | 95.4 |
| Secondary | 19.2 | 45.3 |
| Higher | 1.9 | 7.2 |
| All levels | 20.4 | 52.0 |
| **Enrollments (in millions)** | **1950** | **2000** |
| Primary | 38.2 | 157.7 |
| Secondary | 4.7 | 94.6 |
| Higher | 0.6 | 9.3 |
| All levels | 43.5 | 261.6 |
| **Number of teachers (in millions)** | | |
| Primary | 1.1 | 3.5 |
| Secondary | 0.2 | 3.2 |
| Higher | 0.03 | 0.6 |
| All levels | 1.4 | 7.2 |

*Gross enrollment ratio

SOURCE: Based on United Nations Educational, Scientific and Cultural Organization. 1969; 1999. *Statistical Yearbook.* Paris: United Nations Educational, Scientific and Cultural Organization.

rollment in the relevant age group as a proportion of the population of the relevant age group.) The rate of adult illiteracy declined from 72 percent in 1960 to 46 percent in 2000 (see Table 1). These are no mean achievements, given the poor economic conditions of the newly independent countries of the region and their high rates of population growth.

Along with quantitative progress, however, the education system in the several countries of the region is characterized by conspicuous failures on many fronts. While the rate of illiteracy has decreased, the number of adult illiterates increased from 299 million in 1970 to 429 million in 2000, and the current adult illiteracy rate is quite high. Adult literacy campaigns—an important strategy adopted by the South Asian countries to improve literacy rates—have not met with great success. Sixty percent of the adults in Nepal and Bangladesh, and about 55 percent in Pakistan and Bhutan, are illiterate (see Table 2). Further, a large majority of the literate population have had little more than primary education, and very few have gone on to higher education institutions. For example, only 7 percent of adults age twenty-five and older in India have graduated from postsecondary institutions; the corresponding

**TABLE 2**

### Literacy in South Asia, 1999

| | Adult (15+) literacy (percent) | Youth (15–24) literacy (percent) | Number illiterate* (in millions) |
|---|---|---|---|
| Bangladesh | 40.8 | 50.2 | 49.6 |
| Bhutan | 47.3 | N/A | 0.6 |
| Nepal | 40.4 | 58.5 | 8.3 |
| Pakistan | 45.0 | 62.7 | 51.7 |
| India | 56.5 | 71.8 | 299.3 |
| Sri Lanka | 91.4 | 96.7 | 1.2 |
| Maldives | 96.2 | 99.1 | 6.0 |

*estimate (2000); N/A: not available

SOURCE: Based on United Nations Development Program. 2001. *Human Developnment Report*. New York: Oxford University Press; United Nations Educational, Scientific and Cultural Organization. 1999. *Statistical Yearbook*. Paris: United Nations Educational, Scientific and Cultural Organization.

figure is 2.5 percent in Pakistan; 1.1 percent in Sri Lanka; and 0.6 percent in Nepal. About 50 million children in the primary-school age group were estimated to be out of school in 1995.

As of 2001, the gross enrollment ratio in primary education in the region as a whole was impressive (about 95%). But this is only the gross enrollment ratio. The net enrollment ratio in Pakistan, for example, was only 49 percent in 2001. Universal primary education is still a distant dream for many countries in the region, except for Sri Lanka and Maldives (see Table 3). Similarly, though the number of teachers has increased at all levels, the pace of growth has not kept up with the increase in enrollments. According to the latest statistics available, the number of pupils per teacher in primary schools is as high as fifty-nine in Bangladesh, forty-nine in Pakistan, and forty-eight in India—and the situation has worsened in many countries over the years. The situation is similar in terms of internal efficiency in primary education, as measured by rates of survival of children in school (the converse of dropout rates) and promotion rates.

Dropout and repetition rates are also high. In fact, the completion rates in primary education in South Asia are the lowest in the world. Quality of education, reflected in levels of achievement of children in primary schools, has been found to be unsatisfactory in several countries of the region. The regional, social, and economic inequalities that are a glaring feature of the societies of South Asia are re-

flected in the education systems, with the poor and socially backward areas suffering a severe degree of exclusion from education. In addition to religious and cultural prejudices, gender prejudices are also strong, keeping girls out of schools.

Enrollment ratios in secondary and higher education are also low in South Asia compared to many other regions of the world. Many countries in South Asia (e.g., India, Pakistan, Sri Lanka) have emphasized vocational training in their secondary education plans, but have not succeeded. As Mahbub ul Haq and Khadija Haq have estimated, barely 1.5 percent of the enrollments in secondary education in South Asia were enrolled in vocational programs in the early 1990s, compared to six times that level in East Asia and fifteen times that level in Latin America. Secondary education has failed to provide any job-relevant skills, and as a result has served only as a transitory phase toward higher education and is not viable terminal level of education in these nations. In addition, gender disparities in secondary education are the largest in the world.

It is felt by some that higher education has expanded too fast in South Asian countries. Acute unemployment rates among the educated and high rates of emigration to the West are cited as testifying to this phenomenon. But higher education is, in fact, very much restricted in South Asia. Higher education is practically nonexistent in Maldives and Bhutan, and barely 3 percent of the relevant population is enrolled in higher education in Pakistan—with 4 percent enrollment in Bangladesh, 5 percent in Sri Lanka and Nepal, and 7 percent in India (see Table 4). This is in sharp contrast to most economically advanced countries, where the enrollment ratio is generally above 20 percent. Additionally, all South Asian countries compare very poorly with countries in East Asia, Latin America, and many other areas of the world with respect to scientific and technical manpower.

While the region as a whole is educationally backward, there are one or two important exceptions. In terms of numbers, India has one of the largest education systems in the world—its student population exceeds the total population of some of the countries of the world. This, however, does not place India ahead of others in educational development. While India could build the third largest reservoir of scientific and technical manpower in the world, this was found to inadequate to meet the challenges of growth in the rapidly globalizing and competitive world.

Sri Lanka and the tiny Maldives are far ahead of other countries in the region in literacy and basic education. More than 90 percent of the population in these two countries is literate. Basic education is nearly universal and enrollment ratios in secondary education are high, although Maldives does not have any higher education institution.

The problems of dropouts and grade repetition are also not so important in Sri Lanka as in other countries. With its emphasis on school education, Sri Lanka could improve the level of human development, as measured by the human development index, but it still continues to be economically backward. However, internal civil war and political unrest have had a serious adverse impact on educational development in Sri Lanka.

One of the important factors responsible for the unsatisfactory development of education in the region is the low level of public investment in education. The present levels of public investment in education in South Asia have been found to be of the lowest order, even less than those in sub-Saharan Africa. For instance, Bangladesh invested 2.2 percent of its gross national product (GNP) in education between 1995 and 1997 (the corresponding investment during this period was 2.7 percent in Pakistan; and 3.2 percent in Nepal and India). It is only in the relatively rich country of Maldives that the proportion is reasonably high (6.4 percent). As a proportion of the total government expenditure, education receives a small portion in countries like Bhutan and Pakistan (see Table 5). Particularly during the 1990s, after economic reform policies were introduced, public expenditures on education decreased—not only in relative proportions but also in absolute total and per student amounts—in real prices and sometimes even in nominal prices. In addition, political instability and the compulsion to allocate substantial resources for defense and internal security have also constrained India, Pakistan, Sri Lanka, Nepal, and Bangladesh in raising their levels of spending on education.

Though sound finances are not a sufficient condition for educational development, they are a critically necessary condition for development. For instance, high historical investments made in education helped Sri Lanka march ahead of others in literacy and school education. Education systems in

**TABLE 3**

**Progress in primary education in South Asia in the 1990s**

|  | Gross enrollment ratio (percent) | | Net enrollment ratio (percent) | |
|---|---|---|---|---|
|  | 1990–1991 | 1998 | 1990–1991 | 1998 |
| Bangladesh | 75.6 | 96.5 | 60.5 | 82.0 |
| Bhutan | 67.0 | 72.0 | 67.5** | 69.6+ |
| India | 100.1 | 90.3 | N/A | 71.1 |
| Maldives | 125.5* | 123.4 | 90.1 | 92.7 |
| Nepal | 106.0 | 122.1 | 67.5** | 69.6+ |
| Pakistan | 64.0 | 83.6 | N/A | 49.2 |
| Sri Lanka | 112.0 | 101.8 | 89.0 | 94.9 |

*1996; **1995; +1997; N/A: not available

SOURCE: Based on Tilak, Jandhyala B. G. 2000. *Education for All in South and West Asia: A Decade After Jomtien: An Assessment.* New Delhi, India: United Nations Educational, Scientific and Cultural Organization/South and West Asia Regional Technical Advisory Group.

most countries of the region are starved of scarce financial resources. A low level of economic development is generally believed to be the reason for a low level of public investment, but that is not necessarily true. With political and social will, some relatively poor societies could spend more on education than some relatively rich economies, even in South Asia.

**Recent Policies and Approaches**

Most countries of South Asia have recognized the vital role of education and the need to accord high priority to education in development efforts, and they have begun paying serious attention to education—particularly to basic education—as a part of the global program of Education for All (EFA). Several strategies have been adopted, some of which are not necessarily sound, and many of which are controversial. Along with strengthening formal schools with increased levels of physical and human infrastructure facilities (in India, for example, where a national program of improvement in school infrastructure on a massive scale was launched in 1986), all the countries in the region also place undue emphasis on nonformal education for universalizing basic education. Though started with good intentions, nonformal education is favored by the educational planners in the region primarily due to its low cost. It is also cheap in quality, however, with poor physical infrastructure facilities, inadequately trained teachers, and inadequate teaching and learning material. As a result, it did not take off well. Fur-

**TABLE 4**

### Gross enrollment ratios in secondary and higher education in South Asia, by percentage

|  | Year | Secondary | Higher | All levels* |
|---|---|---|---|---|
| Bangladesh | 1990 | 19 | 4 | 35 |
| India | 1996 | 49 | 7 | 55 |
| Maldives | 1997 | 69 | – | – |
| Nepal | 1996 | 42 | 5 | 59 |
| Pakistan | 1991 | 26 | 3 | 34 |
| Sri Lanka | 1995 | 75 | 5 | 67 |

*includes primary level

SOURCE: Based on United Nations Educational, Scientific and Cultural Organization. 1999. *Statistical Yearbook.* Paris: United Nations Educational, Scientific and Cultural Organization.

ther, no links exist between nonformal and formal education, and the graduates of nonformal education often tend to relapse back into educational poverty.

Effective compulsory basic education is still nonexistent in many countries of the region. Efforts to promulgate compulsory education laws have only recently been initiated in Sri Lanka, and India. However, even if enacted, such laws will not necessarily provide free education. Families incur huge expenditures in acquiring even basic education for their children, both in terms of payments to school and the cost of other necessary expenditures, such as for books, uniforms, and transportation. The high cost of schooling incurred by families is an important factor constraining the participation of the poor in schooling.

Decentralization has been regarded as "the key to improvement in education in South Asia" (Haq and Haq 1998, p. 82). Decentralization has become an important issue not only in large countries such as India and Pakistan, but also in relatively small countries like Nepal. Many responsibilities of schooling are being decentralized to the local level. The mechanisms envisaged would not only increase the role of local bodies, but would also ensure an increased level of participation by local communities. As a corollary to all this, however, it is feared that the role of the central government and of provincial governments may get minimized.

Private education is another important issue of concern, particularly in postprimary education. Though private education is not a new phenomenon in South Asia, public policies only recently began fa-

voring the rapid growth of private schools. Along with private education, public policies are also being formulated for improved mechanisms of cost recovery in education. This will be accomplished through the introduction or increase of fees in schools, as well as through various efforts of mobilization of nongovernmental resources. These measures are advocated not only because resources are scarce, but also because it is believed that they can improve the efficiency of the school system. However, according to some, the effects of such measures on equity may be very serious—not only on the education system but also on the society at large.

Given the scarcity of domestic resources, almost all the countries in the region have resorted to international aid for education, particularly since the World Conference on Education for All was held in Jomtien, Thailand, in 1990. While this has relaxed the constraints on resources to some extent, it has also led to an increased level of donor dependency, with every new educational program being dependent upon international aid. In addition, public policies are affected, as aid from some international organizations comes with severe policy conditions attached. On the whole, international aid for basic education has been increasing in South Asian countries, though positive and sustainable effects of this aid on educational development have yet to be noted.

One of the unintended effects of Education for All and an increased emphasis on basic education has been the neglect of secondary and higher education. While concentrating their efforts on EFA, countries in South Asia tend to ignore secondary and higher education altogether, based on the presumption that EFA goals could be realized only at the cost of growth of secondary and higher education. Therefore, public resources and policy initiatives have primarily been confined to basic education and adult literacy. This may lead to serious imbalances in the development of education, causing irreparable damage to secondary and higher education. Some countries, such as Sri Lanka and India, have already realized, with the rapid expansion of primary education, the need to expand secondary education. Further, these nations realize that higher education is not only important for economic growth and development, but also that quality higher education is important if these societies are to succeed in an increasingly globalized world.

## Conclusion

The present education system in South Asia is marked by low access; poor quality and low standards; gender, social, and economic inequities; and low levels of public investment. The region is caught "in a vicious circle of low enrollment, low levels of literacy, low levels of educated labor force, lower rates of economic growth, and lower levels of living" (Tilak 2001, p. 233). The low level of educational development in South Asia has constrained "the immediate potential for human resource led development," and it has also "stunted the future prospects for rapid human development in the region" (Haq and Haq 1998, p. 34). Some countries have realized the importance of education and taken several new policy initiatives, but not all of these initiatives are necessarily conducive for the development of sustainable education systems of high quality. The most important factors responsible for the poor education status of South Asian countries are the lack of political commitment to education and the lack social will to exert pressures on the political elite. Political activism is completely lacking, though social will is slowly being built, providing a ray of hope for the betterment of education in South Asia.

*See also:* DECENTRALIZATION AND EDUCATION; EAST ASIA AND THE PACIFIC; EASTERN EUROPE AND CENTRAL ASIA; GENDER ISSUES, INTERNATIONAL; INTERNATIONAL EDUCATION.

### BIBLIOGRAPHY

BASU, APARNA. 1972. *Essays in the History of Indian Education.* Delhi, India: Concept.

DHARMPAL. 1983. *The Beautiful Tree: Indigenous Indian Education in the Eighteenth Century.* Delhi, India: Biblia Implex.

DRÈZE, JEAN, and AMARTYA SEN, eds. 1997 *Indian Development: Selected Regional Perspectives.* Delhi, India: Oxford University Press.

HAQ, MAHBUB UL, and HAQ, KHADIJA. 1997. *Human Development in South Asia.* Karachi, Pakistan: Oxford University Press.

HAQ, MAHBUB UL, and HAQ, KHADIJA. 1998. *Human Development in South Asia: The Education Challenge.* Karachi, Pakistan: Oxford University Press.

HUQ, MUHAMMAD SHAMSUL. 1965. *Education and Development Strategy in South and Southeast Asia.* Honolulu, HI: East-West Center.

SCHULTZ, THEODORE W. 1961. "Investment in Human Capital." *American Economic Review* 51(1):1–17.

TILAK, JANDHYALA B. G. 1988. *Educational Finances in South Asia.* Nagoya, Japan: United Nations Centre for Regional Development.

TILAK, JANDHYALA B. G. 1994. *Education for Development in Asia.* New Delhi, India: Sage Publications.

TILAK, JANDHYALA B. G. 2000. *Education for All in South and West Asia: A Decade After Jomtien: An Assessment.* New Delhi, India: United Nations Educational, Scientific and Cultural Organization/South and West Asia Regional Technical Advisory Group.

TILAK, JANDHYALA B. G. 2001. "Education and Development: Lessons from Asian Experience." *Indian Social Science Review* 3(2):219–66.

UNITED NATIONS DEVELOPMENT PROGRAM. 2001. *Human Development Report.* New York: Oxford University Press.

UNITED NATIONS EDUCATIONAL, SCIENTIFIC AND CULTURAL ORGANIZATION (UNESCO). 1969; 1999. *Statistical Yearbook.* Paris: United Nations Educational, Scientific and Cultural Organization.

JANDHYALA B. G. TILAK

**TABLE 5**

### Public spending on education in South Asia

| | Percentage of GNP | | Percentage of total government expenditure | |
|---|---|---|---|---|
| | 1960 | 1995–1997 | 1965 | 1995–1997 |
| Bangladesh | 0.6 | 2.2 | 13.6[+] | 13.8 |
| Bhutan | 3.6[**] | 4.1 | 14.0 | 7.0 |
| Nepal | 0.5 | 3.2 | 8.2 | 13.5 |
| Pakistan | 1.1 | 2.7 | 7.4 | 7.1 |
| India | 2.3 | 3.2 | 17.5 | 11.6 |
| Sri Lanka | 2.3 | 3.4 | 11.7[*] | 8.9 |
| Maldives | 2.3[*] | 6.4 | 8.5[++] | 10.5 |

[*]1970; [**] 1974; [+]1975; [++]1985–1987

SOURCE: Based on Tilak, Jandhyala B. G. 1988. *Educational Finances in South Asia.* Nagoya, Japan: United Nations Centre for Regional Development; United Nations Development Program. 2001. *Human Development Report.* New York: Oxford University Press.

# SPECIAL EDUCATION

## HISTORY OF

Special education, as its name suggests, is a specialized branch of education. Claiming lineage to such persons as Jean-Marc-Gaspard Itard (1775–1838), the physician who "tamed" the "wild boy of Aveyron," and Anne Sullivan Macy (1866–1936), the teacher who "worked miracles" with Helen Keller, special educators teach those students who have physical, cognitive, language, learning, sensory, and/or emotional abilities that deviate from those of the general population. Special educators provide instruction specifically tailored to meet individualized needs, making education available to students who otherwise would have limited access to education. In 2001, special education in the United States was serving over five million students.

Although federally mandated special education is relatively new in the United States, students with disabilities have been present in every era and in every society. Historical records have consistently documented the most severe disabilities—those that transcend task and setting. Itard's description of the wild boy of Aveyron documents a variety of behaviors consistent with both mental retardation and behavioral disorders. Nineteenth-century reports of deviant behavior describe conditions that could easily be interpreted as severe mental retardation, autism, or schizophrenia. Milder forms of disability became apparent only after the advent of universal public education. When literacy became a goal for all children, teachers began observing disabilities specific to task and setting—that is, less severe disabilities. After decades of research and legislation, special education now provides services to students with varying degrees and forms of disabilities, including mental retardation, emotional disturbance, learning disabilities, speech-language (communication) disabilities, impaired hearing and deafness, low vision and blindness, autism, traumatic brain injury, other health impairments, and severe and multiple disabilities.

### Development of the Field of Special Education

At its inception in the early nineteenth century, leaders of social change set out to cure many ills of society. Physicians and clergy, including Itard, Edouard O. Seguin (1812–1880), Samuel Gridley Howe (1801–1876), and Thomas Hopkins Gallaudet (1787–1851), wanted to ameliorate the neglectful, often abusive treatment of individuals with disabilities. A rich literature describes the treatment provided to individuals with disabilities in the 1800s: They were often confined in jails and almshouses without decent food, clothing, personal hygiene, and exercise. During much of the nineteenth century, and early in the twentieth, professionals believed individuals with disabilities were best treated in residential facilities in rural environments. Advocates of these institutions argued that environmental conditions such as urban poverty and vices induced behavioral problems. Reformers such as Dorothea Dix (1802–1887) prevailed upon state governments to provide funds for bigger and more specialized institutions. These facilities focused more on a particular disability, such as mental retardation, then known as "feeble-mindedness" or "idiocy"; mental illness, then labeled "insanity" or "madness"; sensory impairment such as deafness or blindness; and behavioral disorders such as criminality and juvenile delinquency. Children who were judged to be delinquent or aggressive, but not insane, were sent to *houses of refuge* or *reform schools,* whereas children and adults judged to be "mad" were admitted to psychiatric hospitals. Dix and her followers believed that institutionalization of individuals with disabilities would end their abuse (confinement without treatment in jails and poorhouses) and provide effective treatment. Moral treatment was the dominant approach of the early nineteenth century in psychiatric hospitals, the aim being cure. Moral treatment employed methods analogous to today's occupational therapy, systematic instruction, and positive reinforcement. Evidence suggests this approach was humane and effective in some cases, but the treatment was generally abandoned by the late nineteenth century, due largely to the failure of moral therapists to train others in their techniques and the rise of the belief that mental illness was always a result of brain disease.

By the end of the nineteenth century, pessimism about cure and emphasis on physiological causes led to a change in orientation that would later bring about the "warehouse-like" institutions that have become a symbol for abuse and neglect of society's most vulnerable citizens. The practice of moral treatment was replaced by the belief that most disabilities were incurable. This led to keeping individuals with disabilities in institutions both for their own protection and for the betterment of society. Although the transformation took many years, by the end of the nineteenth century the size of institutions had increased so dramatically that the goal of rehabilitation was no longer possible. Institutions became instruments for permanent segregation. Many special education professionals became critics of institutions. Howe, one of the first to argue for institutions for people with disabilities, began advocating *placing out* residents into families. Unfortunately this practice became a logistical and pragmatic problem before it could become a viable alternative to institutionalization.

At the close of the nineteenth century, state governments established juvenile courts and social welfare programs, including foster homes, for children and adolescents. The child study movement became prominent in the early twentieth century. Using the approach pioneered by G. Stanley Hall (1844–1924; considered the founder of child psychology), researchers attempted to study child development scientifically in relation to education and in so doing established a place for psychology within public schools. In 1931, the Bradley Home, the first psychiatric hospital for children in the United States, was established in East Providence, Rhode Island. The treatment offered in this hospital, as well as most of the other hospitals of the early twentieth century, was psychodynamic. Psychodynamic ideas fanned interest in the diagnosis and classification of disabilities. In 1951 the first institution for research on exceptional children opened at the University of Illinois and began what was to become the newest focus of the field of special education: the *slow learner* and, eventually, what we know today as learning disability.

## The Development of Special Education in Institutions and Schools

Although Itard failed to normalize Victor, the wild boy of Averyon, he did produce dramatic changes in Victor's behavior through education. Modern special education practices can be traced to Itard, and his work marks the beginning of widespread attempts to instruct students with disabilities. In 1817 the first special education school in the United States, the American Asylum for the Education and Instruction of the Deaf and Dumb (now called the American School for the Deaf), was established in Hartford, Connecticut, by Gallaudet. By the middle of the nineteenth century, special educational programs were being provided in many asylums. Education was a prominent part of moral therapy. By the close of the nineteenth century, special classes within regular public schools had been launched in major cities. These special classes were initially established for immigrant students who were not proficient in English and students who had mild mental retardation or behavioral disorders. Descriptions of these children included terms such as *steamer children, backward, truant,* and *incorrigible.* Procedures for identifying "defectives" were included in the World's Fair of 1904. By the 1920s special classes for students judged unsuitable for regular classes had become common in major cities.

In 1840 Rhode Island passed a law mandating compulsory education for children, but not all states had compulsory education until 1918. With compulsory schooling and the swelling tide of anti-institution sentiment in the twentieth century, many children with disabilities were moved out of institutional settings and into public schools. However, by the mid-twentieth century children with disabilities were still often excluded from public schools and kept at home if not institutionalized. In order to respond to the new population of students with special needs entering schools, school officials created still more special classes in public schools.

The number of special classes and complementary support services (assistance given to teachers in managing behavior and learning problems) increased dramatically after World War II. During the early 1900s there was also an increased attention to mental health and a consequent interest in establishing child guidance clinics. By 1930 child guidance clinics and counseling services were relatively common features of major cities, and by 1950 special education had become an identifiable part of urban public education in nearly every school district. By 1960 special educators were instructing their students in a continuum of settings that included hospital schools for those with the most severe disabilities, specialized day schools for students with severe disabilities who were able to live at home, and special classes in regular public schools for students whose disabilities could be managed in small groups. During this period special educators also began to take on the role of consultant, assisting other teachers in instructing students with disabilities. Thus, by 1970 the field of special education was offering a variety of educational placements to students with varying disabilities and needs; however, public schools were not yet required to educate all students regardless of their disabilities.

During the middle decades of the twentieth century, instruction of children with disabilities often was based on process training—which involves attempts to improve children's academic performance by teaching them cognitive or motor processes, such as perceptual-motor skills, visual memory, auditory memory, or auditory-vocal processing. These are ancient ideas that found twentieth-century proponents. Process training enthusiasts taught children various perceptual skills (e.g., identifying different sounds or objects by touch) or perceptual motor skills (e.g., balancing) with the notion that fluency in these skills would generalize to reading, writing, arithmetic, and other basic academic tasks. After many years of research, however, such training was shown not to be effective in improving academic skills. Many of these same ideas were recycled in the late twentieth century as *learning styles, multiple intelligences,* and other notions that the underlying process of learning varies with gender, ethnicity, or other physiological differences. None of these theories has found much support in reliable research, although direct instruction, mnemonic (memory) devices, and a few other instructional strategies have been supported reliably by research.

## The History of Legislation in Special Education

Although many contend that special education was born with the passage of the Education for All Handicapped Children Act (EAHCA) in 1975, it is clear that special educators were beginning to respond to the needs of children with disabilities in public schools nearly a century earlier. It is also clear that EAHCA did not spring from a vacuum. This landmark law naturally evolved from events in both special education and the larger society and came about in large part due to the work of grass roots organizations composed of both parents and professionals. These groups dated back to the 1870s, when the American Association of Instructors of the Blind and the American Association on Mental Deficiency (the latter is now the American Association on Mental Retardation) were formed. In 1922 the Council for Exceptional Children, now the major professional organization of special educators, was organized. In the 1930s and 1940s parent groups began to band together on a national level. These groups worked to make changes in their own communities and, consequently, set the stage for changes on a national level. Two of the most influential parent advocacy groups were the National Association for Retarded Citizens (now ARC/USA), organized in 1950, and the Association for Children with Learning Disabilities, organized in 1963.

Throughout the first half of the twentieth century, advocacy groups were securing local ordinances that would protect and serve individuals with disabilities in their communities. For example, in 1930, in Peoria, Illinois, the first *white cane ordinance* gave individuals with blindness the right-of-way when crossing the street. By mid-century all states had legislation providing for education of students with disabilities. However, legislation was still noncompulsory. In the late 1950s federal money was allocated for educating children with disabilities and for the training of special educators. Thus the federal government became formally involved in research and in training special education professionals, but limited its involvement to these functions until the 1970s. In 1971, this support was reinforced and extended to the state level when the Pennsylvania Association for Retarded Children (PARC) filed a class action suit against their Commonwealth. This suit, resolved by consent agreement, specified that all children age six through twenty-one were to be provided free public education in the *least restrictive alternative* (LRA, which would later become the *least restrictive environment* [LRE] clause in EAHCA). In 1973 the Rehabilitation Act prohibited discriminatory practices in programs receiving federal financial assistance but imposed no affirmative obligations with respect to special education.

In 1975 the legal action begun under the Kennedy and Johnson administrations resulted in EAHCA, which was signed into law by President Gerald Ford. EAHCA reached full implementation in 1977 and required school districts to provide free and appropriate education to all of their students with disabilities. In return for federal funding, each state was to ensure that students with disabilities received nondiscriminatory testing, evaluation, and placement; the right to due process; education in the least restrictive environment; and a free and appropriate education. The centerpiece of this public law (known since 1990 as the Individuals with Disabilities Education Act, or IDEA) was, and is, a free appropriate public education (FAPE). To ensure FAPE, the law mandated that each student receiving special education receive an Individualized Education Program (IEP). Under EAHCA, students with identified disabilities were to receive FAPE and an IEP that included relevant instructional goals and objectives, specifications as to length of school year, determination of the most appropriate educational placement, and descriptions of criteria to be used in evaluation and measurement. The IEP was designed to ensure that all students with disabilities received educational programs specific to their "unique" needs. Thus, the education of students with disabilities became federally controlled. In the 1982 case of *Board of Education of the Hendrick Hudson Central School District v. Rowley,* the U.S. Supreme Court clarified the level of services to be afforded students with special needs and ruled that special education services need only provide some "educational benefit" to students—public schools were not required to maximize the educational progress of students with disabilities. In so doing the Supreme Court further defined what was meant by a free and appropriate education. In 1990 EAHCA was amended to include a change to person-first language, replacing the term *handicapped student* with *student with disabilities.* The 1990 amendments also added new classification categories for students with autism and traumatic brain injury and transition plans within IEPs for students age fourteen or older. In 1997, IDEA was reauthorized under President Clinton and amended to require the inclusion of students with disabilities in statewide and districtwide assessments, measurable IEP goals and objectives, and functional behavioral assessment and behavior intervention plans for students with emotional or behavioral needs. Because IDEA is amended and reauthorized every few years, it is impossible to predict the future of this law. It is possible that it will be repealed or altered dramatically by a future Congress. The special education story, both past and future, can be written in many different ways.

## Trends in Special Education

Researchers have conceptualized the history of special education in stages that highlight the various trends that the field has experienced. Although some of these conceptualizations focus on changes involving instructional interventions for students with disabilities, others focus on the place of interventions. The focus on placement reflects the controversy in which the field of special education has found itself throughout history. Samuel G. Howe was one of the first to assert—in the nineteenth century—that instructional settings had inherent qualities that alone insured effective interventions. Belief in the essential curative powers of place spurred the late nineteenth century crusade for bigger and better institutions, as well as the mid-twentieth-century movement for deinstitutionalization. Exclusive focus on the importance of place distracted many professionals and prevented them from recognizing that dramatic changes in philosophy were accompanying the movement for deinstitutionalization. In the late nineteenth century, social Darwinism replaced environmentalism as the primary causal explanation for those individuals with abilities who deviated from those of the general population, opening the door to the eugenics movement of the early twentieth century, and leading to the segregation and sterilization of individuals with mental retardation. At the beginning of the twentieth century, the debate had suddenly shifted from *whether* the disadvantaged should be helped to *where* these individuals should be served. As the institutionalization versus deinstitutionalization debate raged, many individuals were given custodial treatment, which is contrary to the mission of special education.

Almost a century after the placement debate began, special educators still focused on the importance of place. Many were calling upon the field to create not one perfect setting for the delivery of services, but a continuum of placement options that would address the needs of all students with disabilities. The civil rights movement had reconceptualized special education as a case of access of minorities to the educational privileges of the majority, and the least restrictive environment clause of EAHCA/IDEA prompted advocates for people with disabilities to call for *mainstreaming*—the return of students with disabilities to the regular classroom whenever and wherever possible. In the 1980s the Regular Education Initiative (REI) was an attempt to return responsibility for the education of students with disabilities to neighborhood schools and regular classroom teachers. In the 1990s the full inclusion movement called for educating all students with disabilities in the regular classroom with a single, unified and responsive education system. Advocates for full inclusion, following in the footsteps of Howe, argued for appropriate instruction in a single, ubiquitous place, contrary to the mandate of IDEA.

## Controversial Issues in Special Education

Special education has been the target of criticism throughout history. Some of the criticism has been justified, some unjustified. Some criticisms brought to light ineffective practices, such as the inefficacy and inhumanity of relegating all persons with disabilities to institutions. Other criticisms were distractions with disastrous repercussions, such as the singular focus on the importance of place while ignoring other inappropriate practices. The beginning of the twenty-first century found new criticisms being launched at special education. Some argue that the use of diagnostic labels is potentially stigmatizing to students, others that minority students are overrepresented in some disability categories, and still others that education of students with disabilities in special classes and schools, even pulling students out for instruction in resource classes, is akin to race-based segregation. Some of these criticisms may expose ineffective practices, others may only distract educators from the effort of finding and implementing effective instructional practices. Professionals must develop the ability to learn from history and differentiate between unimportant criticisms and those with merit.

One valid criticism repeatedly launched against special education involves the implementation of ineffective educational interventions. Although great concern about the *where* of instruction was expressed in the 1980s and 1990s, little attention was given to the *what* of instruction. Throughout the twentieth century the field of special education repeatedly adopted instructional strategies of questionable efficacy—interventions that have little to no empirical basis. Additionally, special educators have adopted, with "bandwagon" fervor, many practices that have been proven ineffective and have thereby repeated the mistakes of history. If special education is to progress, professionals will need to address and remedy the instructional practices used with students with disabilities.

Special education has also been validly criticized for the way in which students with disabilities are identified. In the early nineteenth century, physicians and educators had difficulty making reliable distinctions between different disability categories. In fact, the categories of mental retardation and behavioral disorders are inseparably intertwined. Many of the disability categories overlap to the extent that it is hard to differentiate one from the other. Additionally, some of the categories—learning disabilities and behavioral disorders, for example—are defined by the exclusion of other contributing disabilities. Thus, at the beginning of the twenty-first century, much work remains on the identification of students with disabilities.

Perhaps the largest, most pervasive issue in special education is its relationship to general education. The relationship of special to general education has been controversial since the beginning of universal public schooling. However, in the late twentieth and early twenty-first centuries, the question of whether special education should retain a separate identity or be fused with general education such that it has no separate identity (e.g., budget, personnel) was made prominent by proponents of a radical restructuring of special education. Proponents of radical restructuring and fusion argue that such integration is necessary to provide appropriate education for all students regardless of their disabilities and without stigma or discrimination. In their view, special education suffers primarily from structural problems, and the integration of two separate systems will result in a flexible, supple, responsive single system that will meet the needs of all students without "separating out" any. All teachers, according to this line of thinking, should be prepared to teach all students, including those with special needs.

Opponents of radical restructuring argue that special education's problems are primarily the lack of implementation of best practices, not structural. Moreover, they suggest, special education will not survive to serve the special needs of exceptional students if it loses its identity, including special budget allocations and personnel preparation. It is not feasible nor is it desirable, they contend, to prepare all teachers to teach all children; special training is required to teach students who are educationally exceptional. Arguments about the structure of education (special and general), who (if anyone) should receive special treatment, how they should be taught, and where special services should be provided are perpetual issues in special education. These issues will likely continue to be debated throughout the twenty-first century.

In the late twentieth and early twenty-first centuries, another issue became the basis for conceptual or theoretical bases for special education practices. Postmodern and antiscientific philosophies have been put forward in both general and special education. These ideas have been challenged by others who have noted the importance of the scientific method in discriminating among ideas and assertions. Likely, postmodern ideas and attempts to apply them to or refute them will be perpetual.

More than two hundred years after Itard began his work on the education of the wild boy of Aveyron, special educators are being asked to make decisions concerning such issues as placement and delivery of services. The inclusion debate, although important, has the potential to distract the field of special education away from issues of greater import—issues such as the efficacy of intervention and the accurate identification of students with disabilities. If special educators are to avoid the mistakes of the past, they will need to make future decisions based upon reliable data, evaluating the efficacy of differing options. Since the inception of what is now known as IDEA, significant progress has been made in applying scientific research to the problems of special education. In the twenty-first century, special education need not remain a field of good intentions, but can fully employ the scientific child-study techniques begun in the late eighteenth century to provide free and appropriate educations to all children with disabilities.

*See also:* ADAPTED PHYSICAL EDUCATION; ASSISTIVE TECHNOLOGY; ATTENTION DEFICIT HYPERACTIVITY DISORDER; COUNCIL FOR EXCEPTIONAL CHILDREN; EMOTIONALLY DISTURBED, EDUCATION OF; HEARING IMPAIRMENT; LEARNING DISABILITIES, EDUCATION OF INDIVIDUALS WITH; MENTAL RETARDATION, EDUCATION OF INDIVIDUALS WITH; SEVERE AND MULTIPLE DISABILITIES, EDUCATION OF INDIVIDUALS WITH; SPECIAL EDUCATION, *subentry on* CURRENT TRENDS; SPEECH AND LANGUAGE IMPAIRMENT, EDUCATION OF INDIVIDUALS WITH; VISUAL IMPAIRMENTS, EDUCATION OF INDIVIDUALS WITH.

## BIBLIOGRAPHY

BATEMAN, BARBARA D. 1994. "Who, How, and Where: Special Education's Issues in Perpetuity." *The Journal of Special Education* 27:509–520.

BATEMAN, BARBARA D., and LINDEN, MARY A. 1998. *Better IEPs: How to Develop Legally Correct and Educationally Useful Programs,* 3rd edition. Longmont, CO: Sopris West.

BOCKOVEN, J. SANBOURNE. 1956. "Moral Treatment in American Psychiatry." *Journal of Nervous and Mental Disease* 124:167–194, 292–321.

BOCKOVEN, J. SANBOURNE. 1972. *Moral Treatment in Community Mental Health.* New York: Springer.

CROCKETT, JEAN B., and KAUFFMAN, JAMES M. 1999. *The Least Restrictive Environment: Its Origins and Interpretations in Special Education.* Mahwah, NJ: Erlbaum.

DENO, EVELYN. 1970. "Special Education as Developmental Capital." *Exceptional Children* 37:229–237.

DORN, SHERMAN; FUCHS, DOUGLAS; and FUCHS, LYNN S. 1996. "A Historical Perspective on Special Education Reform." *Theory into Practice* 35:12–19.

FUCHS, DOUG, and FUCHS, LYNN S. 1994. "Inclusive Schools Movement and the Radicalization of Special Education Reform." *Exceptional Children* 60:294–309.

GALLAGHER, DEBORAH J. 1998. "The Scientific Knowledge Base of Special Education: Do We Know What We Think We Know?" *Exceptional Children* 64:493–502.

GARTNER, ALAN, and LIPSKY, DOROTHY K. 1987. "Beyond Special Education: Toward a Quality System for All Students." *Harvard Educational Review* 57:367–395.

HALLAHAN, DANIEL P., and KAUFFMAN, JAMES M. 2000. *Exceptional Learners: Introduction to Special Education,* 8th edition. Boston: Allyn and Bacon.

HOCKENBURY, JILL C.; KAUFFMAN, JAMES M.; and HALLAHAN, DANIEL P. 1999–2000. "What's Right About Special Education." *Exceptionality* 8:3–11.

KAUFFMAN, JAMES M. 1981. "Historical Trends and Contemporary Issues in Special Education in the United States." In *Handbook of Special Education,* ed. James M. Kauffman and Daniel P. Hallahan. Englewood Cliffs, NJ: Prentice-Hall.

KAUFFMAN, JAMES M. 1989. "The Regular Education Initiative as Reagan-Bush Education Policy: A Trickle-Down Theory of Education of the Hard-to-Teach." *Journal of Special Education* 23:256–278.

KAUFFMAN, JAMES M. 1993. "How We Might Achieve the Radical Reform of Special Education." *Exceptional Children* 60:6–16.

KAUFFMAN, JAMES M. 1999–2000. "The Special Education Story: Obituary, Accident Report, Conversion Experience, Reincarnation, or None of the Above?" *Exceptionality* 8(1):61–71.

KAUFFMAN, JAMES M. 2001. *Characteristics of Emotional and Behavioral Disorders of Children and Youth,* 7th edition. Englewood Cliffs, NJ: Prentice-Hall.

KAUFFMAN, JAMES M., and HALLAHAN, DANIEL P., eds. 1995. *The Illusion of Full Inclusion: A Comprehensive Critique of a Current Special Education Bandwagon.* Austin, TX: PRO-ED.

KAUFFMAN, JAMES M., and SMUCKER, KAREN. 1995. "The Legacies of Placement: A Brief History of Placement Options and Issues with Commentary on Their Evolution." In *Issues in Educational Placement: Students with Emotional and Behavioral Disorders,* ed. James. M. Kauffman, John W. Lloyd, Daniel P. Hallahan, and Terry A. Astuto. Hillsdale, NJ: Erlbaum.

KOERTGE, NORETTA, ed. 1998. *A House Built on Sand: Exposing Postmodernist Myths About Science.* New York: Oxford University Press.

LLOYD, JOHN W.; FORNESS, STEVEN R.; and KAVALE, KENNETH A. 1998. "Some Methods Are More Effective Than Others." *Intervention in School and Clinic* 33:195–200.

LLOYD, JOHN W.; REPP, ALAN C.; and SINGH, NIRBHAY N., eds. 1991. *The Regular Education Initiative: Alternative Perspectives on Concepts, Issues, and Methods.* Dekalb, IL: Sycamore.

MACMILLAN, DONALD L., and HENDRICK, IRWING G. 1993. "Evolution and Legacies." In *Integrating General and Special Education,* ed. J. I. Goodlad and T. C. Lovitt. Columbus, OH: Merrill/Macmillan.

MANN, LESTER. 1979. *On the Trail of Process: A Historical Perspective on Cognitive Processes and Their Training.* New York: Grune and Stratton.

MOSTERT, MARK P., and CROCKETT, JEAN C. 1999–2000. "Reclaiming the History of Special Education for More Effective Practice." *Exceptionality* 8:133–143.

PETERS, MICHAEL, ed. 1995. *Education and the Postmodern Condition.* Westport, CT: Bergin and Garvey.

SASSO, GARY M. 2001. "The Retreat from Inquiry and Knowledge in Special Education." *Journal of Special Education* 34:178–193.

SKRTIC, THOMAS M., and SAILOR, WAYNE. 1996. "School-Linked Services Integration: Crisis and Opportunity in the Transition to Postmodern Society." *Remedial and Special Education* 17:271–283.

SMITH, J. DAVID, ed. 1998. "The History of Special Education: Essays Honoring the Bicentennial of the Work of Jean Itard." *Remedial and Special Education* 19(4).

STAINBACK, WILLIAM, and STAINBACK, SUSAN. 1991. "A Rational for Integration and Restructuring: A Synopsis" In *The Regular Education Initiative: Alternative Perspectives on Concepts, Issues, and Models,* ed. John. W. Lloyd, Nirbhay N. Singh, and Alan C. Repp. Sycamore, IL: Sycamore.

WIEDERHOLT, J. LEE. 1974. "Historical Perspectives on the Education of the Learning Disabled." In *The Second Review of Special Education,* ed. Lester Mann and David. A. Sabatino. Philadelphia: JSE Press.

WINZER, MARGARET A. 1993. *History of Special Education from Isolation to Integration.* Washington, DC: Gallaudet University Press.

YELL, MITCHELL L.; ROGERS, DAVID; and ROGERS, ELISABETH L. 1998. "The Legal History of Special Education: What a Long, Strange Trip It's Been!" *Remedial and Special Education* 19:219–228.

DEVERY R. MOCK
JENNIFER J. JAKUBECY
JAMES M. KAUFFMAN

## CURRENT TRENDS

The adage "there are two sides to every story" applies to special education. In the early years of special education, there was one clearly defined goal—an appropriate education for students with disabilities. Parents, professionals, and students with disabilities rallied together to attain this right. Having secured this goal, the allies splintered into numerous advocacy groups, each fighting for different issues in special education. Issues such as school reform, full inclusion, standards assessment, and disability classification can be viewed not only from at least two perspectives, but from many variations or degrees of each.

## Special Education in the Context of School Reform

School reform has been a buzzword since the early 1980s, but special education was not often included in discussions of reform until about the turn of the twentieth century. In the early years of the twenty-first century, two of the most prominent school reform agendas having significant effects on special education were standards-based education and school choice.

**Standards-based education.** Standards-based reforms aim to improve school performance and use accountability systems to enforce the standards. Historically, schools have not included students with disabilities in accountability systems. By amending the Individuals with Disabilities Education Act (IDEA) in 1997, the federal government mandated that students with disabilities be included in district and state assessments. Local schools can face severe sanctions for inadequate test scores, including loss of accreditation and funding. Schools thus resist including lower scores that may bring down a school's average. Opponents argue that including students with disabilities on standards-based assessments creates an overemphasis on academic skills, when vocational or functional skills might better prepare the student for postsecondary school options other than higher education. Proponents believe that inclusion of students with disabilities on high-stakes tests increases school accountability and ensures access for students with disabilities to the general curriculum.

**School-choice reform.** School-choice reform focuses on the freedom of students to choose from a variety of alternatives to general public education. One trend is charter schools, which are publicly funded but follow a charter constructed by the school rather than by local government. Another form of school choice allows students to choose any public school within their designated district or cross district lines to attend another school. Choice may also involve magnet schools that offer special programs or con-

centrations, such as science and technology or performing arts. Open enrollment allows students to attend any public school in the state. Vouchers provide students with a designated amount of money to spend in any way on education, including private schools or home schooling. Other school choice alternatives are second-chance options (students may enter an alternative school or program) and workplace training (students learn a skilled trade through an apprenticeship).

School choice affects special education when restrictions are placed on entry into particular schools. For example, should a student with mental retardation be allowed to attend a science and technology magnet school? Should a student with severe emotional and behavioral disabilities be allowed to attend a charter school emphasizing visual and performing arts? If not, then school choice might be said to be an exclusionary and elitist system in which students with disabilities are denied an equal education.

School-choice proponents argue that no single educational program works for all students, thus it benefits children, including students with disabilities, to be able to choose the school that best meets their needs. Also, school choice provides options for students who might otherwise drop out of the public system and helps address issues such as racial and socioeconomic balance in schools.

## Placement

The debate about *where* a student with disabilities is best served is one of the most volatile issues in special education. The controversy is whether full inclusion or a continuum of alternative placements is better.

**Full inclusion.** In full inclusion, all students—regardless of disability, health needs, academic ability, service needs, and, often, preference of parent or student—are educated full-time in a general education class in their neighborhood school (the school they would attend had they no disability). In this model, the child receives special education support services in the general education classroom. Full inclusion requires either a team-teaching approach or consultation of the regular classroom teacher with a special educator. In team teaching, a classroom will have both a general education teacher and a special education teacher equally sharing the responsibility to teach the whole class. In consultation, a special education teacher works with many general education teachers, meeting with them and answering questions as needed or on a regular schedule.

Proponents of full inclusion believe that pulling a child out of the classroom to provide special education services or placing the child in a self-contained classroom or special school is inherently unequal and inferior and, therefore, immoral. They also argue that both the student with disabilities and his or her peers benefit from full inclusion, an argument that often places greater emphasis on social interaction than academic achievement.

**Full continuum of placements.** Proponents of a full continuum of alternative placements, required by IDEA, note that since 1975 the law has mandated a continuum of placements including placement: (1) full-time in a general education classroom; (2) part-time in a special education resource room; (3) full-time in a special education self-contained classroom; (4) in a separate special education school; (5) at a residential facility; and (6) homebound or in a hospital. They agree that full-time placement in general education is appropriate for some students, but not for every student with disabilities. Proponents argue that in accordance with IDEA each student should be assessed and placed individually. Many students with disabilities commonly need a more structured and clearly defined environment, either academically or behaviorally, than a general education classroom can provide. Also, students with severe emotional or behavioral disabilities can infringe on other students' education in a general education classroom by either monopolizing a teacher's attention or by placing peers and teachers in physical danger. While believing that students should be educated in the least restrictive environment with nondisabled peers to the maximum extent appropriate, proponents of the continuum also believe that it is immoral and illegal to place every student in the exact same placement regardless of individual needs.

### The Name Game

Controversies surrounding labels and categories of disabilities are a major concern to parents and professionals. One issue is whether students should be labeled at all. Proponents of labels such as *learning disabled, deaf,* or *autistic* believe that these labels provide a common ground for professionals, researchers, and parents to discuss practices and share knowledge about particular disabilities. Labels help teachers and administrators prepare for and provide a student with an appropriate education. Schools can better manage their budgets if they can quantify and describe the students needing additional funds and services.

Opponents of labels argue that labels permanently stigmatize the student. They believe that teachers and administrators lower their expectations of a labeled student, creating a vicious cycle in which the student is given fewer and fewer challenges and falls further behind grade level.

An extension of the labeling issue is categorical versus noncategorical labeling. Categorical labeling specifies a disability based on categories in IDEA. Noncategorical labeling tags a student as disabled or developmentally delayed without specifying the precise disability. Nondescript labels can provide educators and parents additional time to observe and evaluate the child before making a decision on disability type. Though this can help avoid mislabeling, the benefits of categorical labeling are lost.

### Disability Classifications

Some disabilities can be measured and defined objectively, and thus are easily identifiable. If a child is classified as blind, there is usually agreement about what blindness means and whether the child qualifies for special education or other services. However, many disabilities are not easy to identify and label. Judgmental categories such as learning disability, mental retardation, emotional disturbance, autism, and giftedness require professional judgment and subjective analysis. Severe and multiple disabilities, though often easier to identify, also create controversies because judgment is required to distinguish the level of disability (mild, moderate, or severe).

**Learning disability.** The majority of students categorically labeled have learning disabilities (LD). This is ironic because LD is one of the most difficult disabilities to define. Some individuals believe that LD is simply a social construct for those students who have not had adequate instruction. Another concern is that the IDEA definition describes what LD is not, rather than what it is, leaving localities with the task of finding a workable definition. Most localities define LD using a discrepancy between the student's actual achievement and the student's presumed ability or IQ. The problem is that not all localities use the same discrepancy standard or the same tests to measure achievement and ability and discrepancy scores have inherent limitations.

**Mental retardation.** Mental retardation (MR) is identified by below average intellectual ability and poor adaptive behavior that is pervasive in all areas of life. Intellectual ability and adaptive behavior can both be ambiguous, as different tests yield different intelligence quotients and assessment of adaptive behavior requires subjective judgment. A disproportionately large number of children from minority populations and low socioeconomic status are identified as having mental retardation, giving rise to the argument that identification of mental retardation is biased (too many African-American and Latino students and too many poor students are identified, but too few children of Asian descent are identified).

**Emotional disturbance.** Emotional disturbance refers to severe and protracted difficulties in relationships with other people. Controversies abound regarding who should be included in the category of emotional disturbance (ED). IDEA excludes from ED students who are socially maladjusted but not emotionally disturbed, but it does not define social maladjustment. Confounding the problem is another clause describing ED as "an inability to build or maintain satisfactory relationships with peers and teachers," which can be interpreted to mean social maladjustment. Thus the language of the law seems self-contradictory. Another issue in ED is disagreement on the actual number of students with this disorder. Many estimates based on prevalence studies range from 6 to 25 percent of the student population, but less that 1 percent of the school population has been identified as having ED for special education purposes.

**Autism.** Autism is a pervasive developmental disability affecting approximately one in 500 children. Its onset is noted before the age of three years. Professionals find it hard to agree on a definition. One of the main controversies in definition involves the closely related syndromes of Asperger's and Pervasive Developmental Disorder (PDD). There is great confusion and disagreement as to whether these are separate disabilities or different levels of severity of autism. Causes as well as the best treatments are also disputed for each.

**Attention deficit disorder and attention deficit hyperactivity disorder.** Attention deficit disorder (ADD) and attention deficit hyperactivity disorder (ADHD) have always been controversial. One reason for this is that the characteristics of ADD/ADHD, including careless mistakes on school work, forgetting daily activities, fidgeting with hands or feet, or talking excessively, can describe an average child. What makes a diagnosis of ADD/ADHD difficult is determining whether these characteristics are beyond normal for the student's age and have become a disability. In fact, some professionals argue that ADD/ADHD does not exist and that the label is used haphazardly on students who simply exhibit inappropriate behavior and a lack of discipline. Furthermore, IDEA does not acknowledge ADD/ADHD as a separate category but includes it under "other health impaired" (OHI). There is also a growing concern that too many children are being medicated for ADD/ADHD.

**Gifts and talents.** Gifts and talents are the opposite of disabilities, but some, if not all, of the same issues discussed previously apply (e.g., stigma of identification, judgment in assessment). Opponents of special programs for gifted and talented students argue that separating them from their nongifted classmates is elitist and that *all* students should be exposed to a superior, highly challenging education. A disproportionately high number of Caucasian and Asian students are identified as gifted, while a disproportionately low number of African-American and Hispanic students are found eligible for gifted programs. Proponents of special education for gifted students believe that these students need a special curriculum. Gifted students who are asked to work below their ability level or tutor their less gifted peers become bored and lose motivation. Identifying gifted students is also difficult because there is not one universally accepted definition, nor is gifted a category acknowledged under IDEA. The decision to provide gifted education and to determine what qualifies a student as gifted is often a local responsibility.

**Severe and multiple disabilities.** Compared to other conditions, there is less uncertainty in the identification of students with severe and multiple disabilities (SMD). Increased numbers of children identified as having SMD, however, is a fairly new trend in special education. Advances in medicine and technology are helping more children than ever before survive serious medical emergencies and severe injuries. This increase has spurred changes in special education and has placed new demands on personnel and the physical environment. These children often need assistive and medical technology in the classroom, as well as personnel knowledgeable about this equipment. Some of these students need continuous support from a classroom assistant, especially when included in general education.

## Trends in the Classroom

Three trends in special education have especially significant influence on the classroom environment: (1) early intervention and prevention, (2) technology, and (3) transition plans.

**Early intervention and prevention.** Early intervention and prevention of disabilities are not new ideas, but they have experienced increasing emphasis. Schools are realizing that early intervention and prevention not only benefit children in the long run but save money as well by reducing the later need for costly services. Two significant issues are the appropriate role for the family of the child and whether the intervention should be child-centered or teacher-directed. In addition, obstacles to early intervention and prevention are still being addressed.

**Technology.** Technology permeates our society with increasing intensity and reaches into classrooms. It helps students overcome limitations previously placed on them by a disability. Computer programs allow keyboarding and navigation of the Internet by eye movements. Cochlear implants allow deaf students to hear, and new prosthetics (artificial body parts) provide greater mobility and participation in education and society.

**Transition.** The 1997 amendments to IDEA added two mandates related to transition from one school setting to another or from school to work. The first amendment requires transition-planning conferences for children exiting early intervention programs, the second is a statement of needed services for the transition from high school to higher education or work in the Individualized Education Plan (IEP) for students age fourteen or older. Other forms of transition planning, such as from middle school to high school or from a self-contained or restrictive environment to a less restrictive environment, are also becoming common.

## Special Education Teachers

There is a critical teacher shortage in special education in all areas of licensure. Reasons include a shortage of people going through teacher training programs in special education and entering the field, and alarmingly high exit rates for special education teachers. For example, in the *20th Annual Report to Congress on the Implementation of the IDEA* (1998),

statistics from 1993–1994 show that the total demand for special education teachers was 335,000, yet there were only 18,250 special education degree graduates, covering a mere 5.4 percent of the demand. Because of this gross need, alternative licensure programs have evolved: army personnel are being trained for a second career in teaching and drastically intensified and accelerated summer programs are replacing four-year licensure programs. While these programs can help place more teachers in the classroom, some professionals question the quality of both the teacher education programs and the newly licensed teachers. Also, some districts fill special education positions with teachers having either no prior education experience or with only general education experience and provide provisional or conditional licensure to these newly hired teachers. Due to these difficulties, teacher retention has also become a critical issue.

Debate also exists over categorical or noncategorical licensure. Proponents of categorical licensure argue that each disability category is substantially different from others and that teachers should be highly specialized in that area. Proponents of noncategorical licensure argue that teachers should be prepared to teach all children and should have the expertise to address differing abilities and disabilities.

A closely related issue is a trend in higher education to merge the special education teacher program into the general education program, doing away with special education altogether. The arguments for and against this teacher education structure are similar to those for categorical versus noncategorical licensure.

## Funding Issues

Funding issues and controversies beset all areas of education, including special education. Because special education requires services above those specified in the general education curriculum, additional funding is critical. When IDEA was first enacted in 1975, the federal government acknowledged this additional need by promising to supplement 40 percent of the excess costs incurred in implementing the act's mandates. Unfortunately, the federal government has never come close to fulfilling this promise. Over the years, however, there has been a greater effort to provide these funds to the states.

Other issues persist at the local level. One common controversy stems from a belief that because the law requires special education services, these programs are funded first, utilizing the money that would otherwise be spent on general education. Another disputed issue is program consolidation—the blending of categorical programs such as special education, English as a second language, or other separately funded programs. Proponents believe that by pooling resources, all children can benefit and can be educated more effectively. Opponents of program consolidation believe it will diminish both the rights of children in these programs as well as the quality of special services provided.

## Conclusion

These controversies and issues, although the most widespread and disputed issues facing special education, represent only a small fraction of the numerous issues permeating special education today. School reform, labeling and classification, inclusion, teacher shortage, and special education funding can often be seen in the headlines of newspapers nationwide. Even though every story has two sides, more work is needed to ensure that every student's story will have a happy ending.

*See also:* ADAPTED PHYSICAL EDUCATION; ASSISTIVE TECHNOLOGY; ATTENTION DEFICIT HYPERACTIVITY DISORDER; COUNCIL FOR EXCEPTIONAL CHILDREN; EMOTIONALLY DISTURBED, EDUCATION OF; HEARING IMPAIRMENT; LEARNING DISABILITIES, EDUCATION OF INDIVIDUALS WITH; MENTAL RETARDATION, EDUCATION OF INDIVIDUALS WITH; SCHOOL REFORM; SPECIAL EDUCATION, *subentry on* HISTORY OF; SPEECH AND LANGUAGE IMPAIRMENT, EDUCATION OF INDIVIDUALS WITH; VISUAL IMPAIRMENTS, EDUCATION OF INDIVIDUALS WITH.

### BIBLIOGRAPHY

BATEMAN, BARBARA D., and LINDEN, MARY A. 1998. *Better IEPs: How to Develop Legally Correct and Educationally Useful Programs,* 3rd edition. Longmont, CO: Sopris West.

CROCKETT, JEAN B., and KAUFFMAN, JAMES M. 1999. *The Least Restrictive Environment: Its Origins and Interpretations in Special Education.* Mahwah, NJ: Erlbaum.

GERSTEN, RUSSELL; SCHILLER, ELLEN P.; and VAUGHN, SHARON, eds. 2000. *Contemporary Special Education Research: Syntheses of the Knowledge Base on Critical Instructional Issues.* Mahwah, NJ: Erlbaum.

HALLAHAN, DANIEL P., and KAUFFMAN, JAMES M. 2000. *Exceptional Learners: Introduction to Special Education,* 8th edition. Boston: Allyn and Bacon.

HALLAHAN, DANIEL P.; KAUFFMAN, JAMES M.; and LLOYD, JOHN W. 1999. *Introduction to Learning Disabilities,* 2nd edition. Boston: Allyn and Bacon.

HALLAHAN, DANIEL P., and KEOGH, BARBARA K., eds. 2001. *Research and Global Perspectives in Learning Disabilities: Essays in Honor of William M. Cruickshank.* Mahwah, NJ: Erlbaum.

HOCKENBURY, JILL C.; KAUFFMAN, JAMES M.; and HALLAHAN, DANIEL P. 1999–2000. "What's Right About Special Education." *Exceptionality* 8(1):3–11.

KAUFFMAN, JAMES M. 1999. "Commentary: Today's Special Education and Its Messages for Tomorrow." *The Journal of Special Education* 32:244–254.

KAUFFMAN, JAMES M. 1999. "How We Prevent the Prevention of Emotional and Behavioral Disorders." *Exceptional Children* 65:448–468.

KAUFFMAN, JAMES M. 2001. *Characteristics of Emotional and Behavioral Disorders of Children and Youth,* 7th edition. Upper Saddle River, NJ: Prentice-Hall.

KAUFFMAN, JAMES M., and HALLAHAN, DANIEL P. 1993. "Toward a Comprehensive Delivery System for Special Education." In *Integrating General and Special Education,* ed. John I. Goodlad and Thomas C. Lovitt. Columbus, OH: Merrill/Macmillan.

KAUFFMAN, JAMES M., and HALLAHAN, DANIEL P., eds. 1995. *The Illusion of Full Inclusion: A Comprehensive Critique of a Current Special Education Bandwagon.* Austin, TX: PRO-ED.

KAUFFMAN, JAMES M.; LLOYD, JOHN W.; HALLAHAN, DANIEL P.; and ASTUTO, TERRY A., eds. 1995. *Issues in Educational Placement: Students with Emotional and Behavioral Disorders.* Hillsdale, NJ: Erlbaum.

LLOYD, JOHN W.; HALLAHAN, DANIEL P.; KAUFFMAN, JAMES M.; and KELLER, CLAY E. 1998. "Academic Problems." In *Practice of Child Therapy,* 3rd edition, ed. Thomas R. Kratochwill and Richard J. Morris. Boston: Allyn and Bacon.

LLOYD, JOHN W.; KAMEENUI, EDWARD J.; and CHARD, DAVID, eds. 1997. *Issues in Educating*

*Students with Disabilities.* Mahwah, NJ: Erlbaum.

MASTROPIERI, MARGO A., and SCRUGGS, THOMAS E. 2000. *The Inclusive Classroom: Strategies for Effective Instruction.* Upper Saddle River, NJ: Merrill.

YELL, MITCHELL L. 1998. *The Law and Special Education.* Upper Saddle River, NJ: Prentice-Hall.

YSSELDYKE, JAMES E.; ALGOZZINE, BOB; and THURLOW, MARTHA L. 2000. *Critical Issues in Special Education,* 3rd edition. Boston: Houghton Mifflin.

JENNIFER J. JAKUBECY
DEVERY R. MOCK
JAMES M. KAUFFMAN

## PREPARATION OF TEACHERS

Special education is a complex enterprise. Students are classified by disability categories and placed in settings that range from classrooms and resource rooms to self-contained classes and separate schools. Special education teacher education also is complex. Teachers are prepared in specialized programs and often licensed to teach students with a particular disability. Licensure structures are complex and vary dramatically from state to state. Furthermore, how students with disabilities are served in schools has changed dramatically since the early 1980s, with implications for teachers' roles and teacher preparation.

### Special Education Students and Teachers

According to the U.S. Department of Education (DoE), in 1998–1999 about 5.7 million school-aged children were provided special education in the United States. Schools employed about 360,000 special education teachers, 90 percent of whom were fully qualified. Teacher preparation is also a substantial enterprise. The approximately 800 special education programs in the United States awarded more than 22,000 bachelor's and master's degrees in 1996–1997. Although such productivity would seem sufficient to address demand, many master's recipients are practicing teachers, and many newly graduated teachers decline to enter the work force.

The federal government has played an influential role in special education teacher education. Through the Individuals with Disabilities Education Act (IDEA), the DoE has invested tens of millions of dollars annually on the preparation of special education teachers. The department has leveraged these funds to promote program development, most notably in early childhood and secondary special education. The government also has taken an active role in support of programs for teachers of students with low-incidence disabilities—severe disabilities and visual and hearing impairments, to name a few. In many states, the number of students with low-incidence disabilities is so small as to make teacher preparation costly and inefficient. For example, only thirty programs nationally prepare teachers in the area of visual impairments, and sixteen states have no programs for teachers of the hearing impaired. Because it is inefficient for individual states to prepare teachers in low-incidence areas, by the early twenty-first century the DoE had come to consider program support a federal responsibility.

### History of Special Education Teacher Education

The development of special education was bolstered in 1975 by the passage of the Education for All Handicapped Children Act (EAHCA), which was amended in 1997 by the IDEA. With the emergence and diversification of special education services in schools came demand for specially trained teachers and programs to prepare them. Although special education teacher education programs existed before the passage of the EAHCA, its passage spurred growth. By the beginning of the twenty-first century, 871 colleges and universities in the United States prepared teachers in at least one special education field.

In spite of its complexity and distinctive character, special education teacher education has evolved in the same way that general teacher education has evolved. Once guided by causal models that related precisely defined teacher actions to specific student outcomes, teacher educators' conceptions of teaching and learning have broadened to include teacher thinking and decision-making. This shift is most evident in the Interstate New Teacher Assessment and Support Consortium (INTASC) standards for beginning teachers, which use general education practice as the foundation for special education practice, and the realignment of the Council for Exceptional Children's professional standards with those provided by INTASC.

**Issues in Special Education Teacher Education**

For decades, the overriding issue in special education teacher education has been the shortage of fully qualified practitioners. The IDEA requires that students with disabilities be provided a free and appropriate public education (FAPE), a promise that presumes a qualified teacher in every special education classroom. In 1998–1999, 10 percent of special education teachers were not fully qualified for their work. These 36,511 teachers worked with more than 570,000 students, who arguably may have been denied FAPE.

Shortages also are related to licensure area, geographical location, and diversity of the work force. Perhaps more invidious than overall shortages or variability in licensure areas are shortages of teachers in urban and rural areas—or, perhaps more precisely, in low-income schools in cities and rural areas. Also critical is the shortage of culturally and linguistically diverse (CLD) special education teachers, an issue that has plagued the general teacher work force as well. It is especially important in special education because of overrepresentation of CLD students, particularly African Americans, on special education rosters.

High attrition rates in special education contribute significantly to chronic teacher shortages. Some researchers have argued that attrition is the primary reason for continued shortages, particularly in high poverty schools. Attrition from special education classrooms is consistently higher than in general education. Analyses of the 1993–1994 Schools and Staffing Survey data suggest that, in a given year, more teachers leave the special education work force than enter. Consequently, the number of teachers entering the field each year is never sufficient to replace the demand for teachers created by attrition and growth, creating a chronic need for new teachers. In large-scale studies conducted since the early 1990s, researchers have identified specific teacher and workplace characteristics that contribute to attrition. Less experienced special education teachers are a greater attrition risk than more experienced counterparts, and unlicensed teachers are more likely to leave the classroom than their licensed counterparts. Moreover, studies of teacher induction indicate that high-quality programs may increase beginning teachers' intentions to remain in special education.

The chronic undersupply of teachers has spawned alternative special education training programs, many of which attempt to tap nontraditional pools of teacher candidates, such as retired military personnel and midlife career changers. Although many of these programs are quite rigorous in terms of the courses and field experiences required, not all are. Research on special education alternative programs has shown graduates of some programs to be capable teachers, often as competent and motivated as graduates of traditional programs. Moreover, their competence is associated with the length and intensity of their training. Longer and more rigorous programs have been shown to prepare better teachers than shortcut programs.

Amid concerns for preparing greater numbers of teachers are increasing pressures to improve their competence. Inclusion advocates believe that separate preparation of special and general education teachers does little to help teachers develop the knowledge and skills necessary for implementing inclusive classroom practices. Thus, there has been an increasing movement toward the unified preparation of classroom and special education teachers—at least those special education teachers who work with students with mild disabilities. Although some type of collaborative program was present at nearly 200 institutions by the beginning of the twenty-first century, critics worry that preparation for the distinctive work that special education teachers perform will be lost through unification.

Finally, researchers and teacher educators are concerned about the persistent gap between what is known about effective classroom practices and what teachers actually do. In special education, significant advances in behavior management, technology applications, and teaching reading have brought this issue into the spotlight. Both novice and practicing teachers are more likely to rely on traditional practices, perhaps learned through observation in K–12 education. Although the professional literature has provided substantial information about how best to help teachers improve their practice, state policymakers are reluctant to support professional development adequately. Moreover, there is limited research in general education and no research in special education delineating the characteristics of preparation programs that enable novice teachers to master and apply research-based practices in the classroom.

## Conclusions

Shortages of special education teachers have proven intractable, in spite of the substantial capacity for preparing teachers in the United States and a sustained federal investment in it. Solutions have been sought through studies of attrition, in which factors influencing teachers' decisions to leave the field have been identified, and in programs to attract nontraditional teacher candidates. Special education teacher education faces two additional challenges: preparing classroom teachers for the work they do with students with disabilities and bridging the research-to-practice gap for novice and veteran teachers. Although improving workplace conditions, establishing high-quality teacher induction programs, and providing effective professional development may ameliorate attrition and help resolve teacher shortages, the gap between what is known about supporting teachers professionally and what is done in the public schools persists. There is much to learn about effective practices in the initial preparation of teachers. In spite of these challenges, the special education teacher education enterprise annually produces more than 20,000 bachelor's and master's degree graduates and has sustained a fully qualified work force of more than 300,000 teachers—remarkable accomplishments in and of themselves.

*See also:* SPECIAL EDUCATION, *subentries on* CURRENT TRENDS, HISTORY OF; TEACHER EDUCATION.

### BIBLIOGRAPHY

BLANTON, LINDA P.; GRIFFIN, CYNTHIA C.; WINN, JUDITH A.; and PUGACH, MARLEEN C., eds. 1997. *Teacher Education in Transition: Collaborative Programs to Prepare General and Special Education.* Denver, CO: Love Publishing.

BOE, ERLING E.; BOBBITT, SHARON A.; COOK, LYNNE H.; WHITENER, SUMMER D.; and WEBER, ANITA L. 1997. "Why Didst Thou Go? Predictors of Retention, Transfer, and Attrition of Special and General Education Teachers from a National Perspective." *Journal of Special Education* 30:390–411.

BOE, ERLING E.; COOK, LYNNE H.; BOBBITT, SHARON A.; and TERHANIAN, GEORGE. 1998. "The Shortage of Fully Certified Teachers in Special and General Education." *Teacher Education and Special Education* 21:1–21.

BROWNELL, MARY T.; ROSS, DORENE R.; COLON, ELAYNE; and McCALLUM, CYNTHIA. 2001. "Teacher Education Practices in Special Education: How Do They Compare to Exemplary General Education Teacher Education Practices?" Gainesville: University of Florida, Center on Personnel Studies in Special Education.

GERSTEN, RUSSELL; VAUGHN, SHARON; DESHLER, DON; and SCHILLER, ELLEN. 1997. "What We Know about Using Research Findings: Implications for Improving Special Education Practice." *Journal of Learning Disabilities* 30:466–476.

HIRSCH, ERIC; KOPPICH, JULIA E.; and KNAPP, MICHAEL S. 2001. "Revisiting What States Are Doing to Improve the Quality of Teaching: An Update on Patterns and Trends." Seattle: University of Washington, Center for the Study of Teaching and Policy.

INGERSOLL, RICHARD M. 1999. "Teacher Turnover, Teacher Shortages, and the Organization of Schools: A CTP Working Paper." Seattle: University of Washington, Center for the Study of Teaching and Policy.

MILLER, M. DAVID; BROWNELL, MARY T.; and SMITH, STEPHEN W. 1999. "Factors that Predict Teachers Staying in, Leaving, or Transferring from the Special Education Classroom." *Exceptional Children* 65:201–218.

ROSENBERG, MICHAEL S., and SINDELAR, PAUL T. 2001. "The Proliferation of Alternative Routes to Certification in Special Education: A Critical Review of the Literature." Arlington, VA: Council for Exceptional Children, National Clearinghouse for Professions in Special Education.

SINDELAR, PAUL T.; BROWNELL, MARY T.; CORREA, VIVIAN; McLESKEY, JAMES; BISHOP, ANNE; SMITH, DEBORAH; TYLER, NAOMI; and WALDRON, NANCY. 2001. "The Center on Personnel Studies in Special Education: Assessing the Quality of Preservice Teacher Preparation." Paper presented at the annual meeting of the Teacher Education Division of the Council for Exceptional Children, St. Petersburg, FL.

STROSNIDER, ROBERTA; CRUTCHFIELD, MARGARET; and PASCHALL, ALBERT. 2000. "Dual, Blended, or Integrated Teacher Preparation Programs: Who, What, When, Where, and Why?" In *Unified Teacher Preparation Programs for General and Special Educators,* ed. Lee Sherry and Fred Spooner. St. Petersburg: Florida Comprehensive System of Personnel Development.

U.S. Department of Education. 2000. *Twenty-Second Annual Report to Congress on the Implementation of the Individuals with Disabilities Education Act, 2000.* Washington, DC: U.S. Department of Education.

Whitaker, Susan D. 2000. "Mentoring Beginning Special Education Teachers and the Relationship to Attrition." *Exceptional Children* 66:546–566.

Wideen, Marvin; Mayer-Smith, Jolie; and Moon, Barbara. 1998. "A Critical Analysis of the Research on Learning to Teach: Making the Case for an Ecological Perspective on Inquiry." *Review of Educational Research* 68:130–178.

Paul T. Sindelar
Mary T. Brownell

# INTERNATIONAL CONTEXT

A goal of the United Nations is to make education available for all the world's students, including those who are disabled and have special needs. Doing so, however, raises many questions:

- What children need special education?
- What is the nature of education for children with disabilities?
- What philosophies form the basis for education for children with special needs and their families?

Access to education for students with special education needs is a global phenomenon. The underlying assumptions, educational strategies, and authorization of legislation governing special education differ across nations, and are inextricably linked to local context, societal values, and beliefs about pedagogy and disability.

## Education Philosophies

Three major philosophies have governed how a nation identifies and educates children with special needs. Historically, the medical model is the most widespread and has been used in both diagnosis and educational treatment of children with disabilities. Children receive a medical diagnosis based on psychological and physical impairments across selected domains and both strengths and weakness are identified for education and training. Children with similar diagnoses and functional levels are grouped together for instructional purposes. Standardized testing is often used to provide a diagnostic name for a disability. According to Thomas Oakland and Sherman Hu, the accuracy of diagnoses is questionable as standardized tests are often not suitably normed, and reliability and validity estimates are often not available, making international comparisons difficult.

In the environmental model, disabilities are experienced as a function of the interaction between the person and the environment. Environments can be defined in terms of psychological and social environments as well as physical environments. Environmental impediments include architectural barriers, lack of assistive technology, and/or limited transportation. Instructional techniques and learning opportunities can be structured to compensate for environmental deficiencies to ensure that children learn and achieve skills of adaptive living. The role of the environment has been recognized in a World Health Organization classification scheme for individuals with disabilities.

The inclusion model incorporates aspects of the environmental model and views children as having a right to education with and alongside their nondisabled peers. Schools are organized to ensure that each student, disabled or nondisabled, receives age-appropriate, individualized attention, accommodations, and supports to provide access to the general education curriculum. Assistive technology often facilitates inclusive schooling practice for both teacher and student.

## Classification

Attempts to make meaningful international comparisons among students and the instructional supports and programs for children with disabilities are exceedingly difficult, given the differing definitions and eligibility criteria. For example, the Organisation for Economic Co-operation and Development (OECD) reports a range between 1 percent to 35 percent of the primary and lower secondary education population across twenty developed nations receiving special needs additional resources, including special teachers, assistive technology, classroom adaptations, and specialized teaching materials. Additional resources are typically provided to a higher proportion of males than females (averaging 63% to 37%, respectively).

The OECD also investigated how nations addressed the needs of students requiring support in the general-education curriculum and expanded their indicators designed to compare the proportions of students with disabilities, learning difficulties, and social and economic disadvantages. Three categories emerged. Category A refers to students who have diagnosed disabilities about which there is substantial international agreement (e.g., blind/partially sighted, deaf/hard of hearing, autism, cognitive disabilities, or multiple disabilities). Category B is an intermediary classification and refers to students who have difficulty learning and are not easily categorized in either Category A or C. Category C refers to students who have difficulty learning because of socioeconomic, cultural, and/or linguistic factors.

The OECD reported striking differences in educational placement for students with special education needs. Some nations serve virtually no disabled students in special segregated schools (e.g., Italy), while others serve more than two-thirds in segregated schools (e.g., Finland, France, Greece, and the Netherlands). Despite the increasing inclusion of students with disabilities (Category A) in the mainstream of general education, inclusion is an issue that continues to be debated.

## Approaches

Cecil R. Reynolds and Elaine Fletcher-Janzen provide brief descriptions of existing special education approaches that are available for more than thirty nations or regions of the world. More detailed information, data and case studies are also available for nineteen developed nations in the OECD's 1995 report *Integrating Students with Special Needs into Mainstream Schools.* Another collection of comparative studies by Kas Mazurek and Margaret A. Winzer includes nations with limited special education (South Africa, Papua New Guinea, Senegal, and the West Bank and Gaza Strip), emerging special education (Nigeria, Iran, Brazil, Indonesia, Egypt, Pakistan, China, India, and Uruguay), segregated special education (Japan, Taiwan, Russia, Czechoslovakia, and Hong Kong), approaching integration (Israel, Poland, Australia, and Canada), and integrated special education (Scandinavia, New Zealand, the United States, and England and Wales).

An examination of special education philosophies and approaches reveals the following:

- Special education often consists of national and local governmental involvement in funding and service provision that is supplemented by the work of nongovernmental service organizations. Oversight of these programs by governments varies widely.

- The medical model is the predominant philosophy in developing countries and in many developed countries. Environmental and inclusive models are emerging and are in varying stages of planning and implementation, primarily in the western developed nations.

- There are no coordinating international agencies monitoring global progress in special education, but the United Nations Educational, Scientific and Cultural Organization (UNESCO) and the United Nations Children's Fund (UNICEF) have developed teacher education materials in an effort to broaden the "Education for All" initiative to include children with disabilities.

- International funding sources for education (e.g., World Bank, Inter-American Development Bank, etc.), are proposing more inclusive approaches to special needs education.

- All nations recognize a need for improved teacher education, particularly in teaching children with special needs in regular classrooms.

- Nations with great needs for special education, usually the developing countries, are attempting to develop family or village-centered programs called *community-based special education.* These programs have been shown to be successful.

- A movement toward school-university partnerships shows promise in grounding teacher preparation in the practice of schooling.

Educating children with special needs is a humanitarian effort that is both a science and an art in some nations and an act of charity in others. In every nation, education for all has social, economic, and moral benefits.

This article was written by two of the authors (Jaeger and Smith) in their private capacity. No official support or endorsement by the U.S. Department of Education is intended or should be inferred.

*See also:* INTERNATIONAL DEVELOPMENT AGENCIES AND EDUCATION; SPECIAL EDUCATION, *subentries on* CURRENT TRENDS, HISTORY OF, PREPARATION OF TEACHERS.

## BIBLIOGRAPHY

LYNCH, JAMES. 1994. *Provision for Children with Special Educational Needs in the Asia Region.* World Bank Technical Paper Number 261, Asia Technical Series. Washington, DC: The World Bank.

MAZUREK, KAS, and WINZER, MARGRET A. 1994. *Comparative Studies in Special Education.* Washington, DC: Gallaudet University Press.

OAKLAND, THOMAS, and HU, SHERMAN. 1994. "International Perspectives on Tests Used with Children and Youth." *Journal of School Psychology* 31:501–517.

ORGANISATION FOR ECONOMIC CO-OPERATION AND DEVELOPMENT. 1995. *Integrating Students with Special Needs into Mainstream Schools.* Paris: Organisation for Economic Co-operation and Development.

ORGANISATION FOR ECONOMIC CO-OPERATION AND DEVELOPMENT. 2000. *Education at a Glance; OECD Indicators.* Paris: Organisation for Economic Co-operation and Development.

REYNOLDS, CECIL R., and FLETCHER-JANZEN, ELAINE. 2000. *Encyclopedia of Special Education,* 2nd edition. New York: Wiley.

## INTERNET RESOURCES

UNESCO, SPECIAL EDUCATION, DIVISION OF BASIC EDUCATION. 1994. "The Salamanca Statement and Framework for Action on Special Needs Education. World Conference on Special Needs Education: Access and Quality." Salamanca, Spain, 7–10 June 1994. <www.unesco.org/education/educprog/sne/salamanc/index.htm>.

WORLD HEALTH ORGANIZATION. 2001. "ICIDH-2: International Classification of Functioning, Disability and Health." Geneva. <www.who.int/icidh>.

PAUL ACKERMAN
ROBERT JAEGER
ANNE SMITH

# SPEECH AND LANGUAGE IMPAIRMENT, EDUCATION OF INDIVIDUALS WITH

Communication skills are the foundation of academic and social performance. The ability to participate in active and interactive communication with peers and adults in the educational setting is essential for student success in school. Problems with speech or language development can lead to difficulties learning to listen, speak, read, or write. As a result, children with communication disorders may perform at a poor or insufficient academic level, struggle with reading, have difficulty understanding and expressing language, misunderstand social cues, avoid attending school, show poor judgment, or have difficulty with tests. Speech and language services can help children become effective communicators, problem solvers, and decision makers, allowing them to benefit from a more successful and satisfying educational experience as well as improved peer relationships.

## The History of Speech and Language Services

Since their inception in the early twentieth century, speech and language services in the schools have undergone profound fundamental changes in scope and focus. Initially, *speech correctionists, speech specialists,* or *speech teachers* worked primarily with elementary school children who had mild to moderate speech impairments in the areas of articulation, fluency, and voice. Children with more severe disabilities were placed in private schools or institutions, or were not provided services at all. That is no longer the case, however, due to a number of social, political, and professional influences.

During the 1960s a number of state and federal laws were passed addressing the responsibility of public schools to provide an education to children with disabilities. Although a vast number of children with disabilities remained unidentified or inadequately educated according to Taylor, these laws served as the foundation, both legally and philosophically, for legislation passed in the 1970s that brought about profound and widespread changes in the responsibility that schools must accept in educating children with disabilities.

The Rehabilitation Act of 1973 was civil rights legislation that prohibited discrimination on the basis of disability in public or private programs and activities receiving federal financial assistance, including public education. This was followed in 1975 by the Education for All Handicapped Children Act (Pub. L. 94-142), requiring that all children with disabilities have available to them a free appropriate public education that emphasizes special education and related services designed to meet their unique needs. The act was amended in 1986 to ensure services for children from birth through age two, and to place that responsibility with public agencies. This expansion of special education services was accompanied by the Regular Education Initiative calling for a partnership between general and special education to eliminate barriers between disabled and non-disabled children.

In 1990 the act was reauthorized once again, this time as the Individuals with Disabilities Education Act (IDEA), with a renewed focus on free appropriate public education in the least restrictive environment. In the same year, the Americans with Disabilities Act was passed, mandating reasonable accommodations for disabilities across all public and private settings, including private and public schools.

The IDEA Amendments of 1997 (IDEA 1997) is designed to retain the basic rights and protections that have been in the law since 1975 while strengthening the focus on improving results for children with disabilities. The primary focus of IDEA 1997 is to establish an educational process that promotes meaningful access to the general curriculum for each student with a disability.

While landmark legislative initiatives were being enacted during the 1970s, an equally significant shift occurred in the professional domain with the expansion of scholarship in all language-related fields. This stimulated increased attention to disordered language as well as normal language acquisition, with a concomitant shift in the relative proportion of students receiving special services in the schools for language problems, as differentiated from speech problems. At the same time, there was an increase in awareness of the central role that language plays in academic achievement. The expanding learning disability movement had a significant impact on language services in schools, as a large proportion of services to students with learning disabilities focused on strengthening language skills. This was typically viewed as being within the purview of the speech-language clinician who was based in the school.

During the 1990s there was an increased awareness of the relationship between language and literacy (i.e., reading and writing). Language problems are both a cause and a consequence of literacy problems in children and adolescents. Spoken and written language have a reciprocal relationship—each builds on the other to result in general language and literacy

competence, starting early and continuing through childhood into adulthood. Because of this, speech-language clinicians play important roles in ensuring that children gain access to appropriate instruction in reading, writing, and spelling. These roles include early identification and assessment, intervention, and development of literacy programs.

U.S. demographics have undergone rapid changes since the 1970s. It is now estimated that nearly one of every three Americans is African American, Hispanic, Asian American or Native American. In addition, according to the American Speech-Hearing Association's 1999 study, the limited-English-proficient population is the fastest growing population in America. This increase has resulted in a student population that is culturally and linguistically more diverse than ever before, and requires attention to such issues as nonbiased assessment and intervention considerations related to this diverse population.

Changes in the medical arena have also affected our nation's demographics. Medical advancements have led to more children surviving neonatal and early childhood traumas and illnesses, yet those who survive are often physically or medically challenged. Additionally, with health-care reform, many patients are released earlier from hospitals or rehabilitation centers; those who are school age may enter or re-enter public schools requiring intensive speech-language services.

**Programs in the Twenty-First Century**

More than 1 million children receive services for speech or language disorders in public schools as of 2001, representing a 10.5 percent increase from the previous decade. In fact, speech-language intervention is the most common service provided for school children with disabilities. Caseloads include a wide range of disorders such as learning disabilities, autism, attention deficit disorder, stuttering, hearing loss, traumatic brain injury, specific language impairment, and cerebral palsy. Some children are medically fragile, have rare syndromes, or experience feeding and swallowing difficulties. In addition, children with speech or language disorders represent many racial and ethnic groups. The focus of intervention may include any or several components of speaking, listening, reading, or writing—language, voice, fluency, articulation, and/or swallowing.

Speech-language services are provided in the schools by approximately 35,000 speech-language clinicians. The credentials required of these professionals vary across states. These credentials may be teacher permits, teaching certificates, teacher licenses, or clinical service credentials. Also, credentials required for schools may differ from a state license that is required to practice speech-language pathology in nonschool settings. In addition, many school-based speech-language clinicians choose to obtain the certificate of clinical competence granted by the American Speech-Language-Hearing Association. Some states allow the use of speech-language pathology assistants under the supervision of fully qualified speech-language clinicians.

School-based clinicians have a range of roles and responsibilities. Although the majority of their time is spent providing direct intervention services to children, they must also conduct screenings and diagnostic evaluations, write reports and documentation, plan and prepare sessions, meet and/or consult with teachers and parents, and conduct classroom observations of students. The scope of their responsibilities includes prevention of communication disorders as well as assessment and intervention.

Speech and language services involve cooperative efforts with others, including parents, audiologists, psychologists, social workers, special education teachers, classroom teachers, guidance counselors, physicians, dentists, and nurses. Speech-language clinicians work with teams to provide comprehensive language and speech assessments, and to develop and implement intervention plans. Intervention services may be provided in individual or small group sessions, in classrooms, in teams with teachers, or in a consultative model with teachers and parents. To be effective, communication goals should be educationally relevant, that is, integrated with academic and social activities. The ultimate outcome is to help children overcome their disabilities, achieve pride and self-esteem, participate fully in major life activities, and find meaningful roles in their lives.

*See also:* HEARING IMPAIRMENT, *subentries on* SCHOOL PROGRAMS, TEACHING METHODS; LANGUAGE AND EDUCATION; SPECIAL EDUCATION, *subentry on* CURRENT TRENDS.

## BIBLIOGRAPHY

AMERICAN SPEECH-LANGUAGE-HEARING ASSOCIATION. 1999. *Guidelines for the Roles and Respon-* *sibilities of the School-Based Speech-Language Pathologist.* Rockville, MD: American Speech-Language-Hearing Association.

AMERICAN SPEECH-LANGUAGE-HEARING ASSOCIATION. 2000a. *2000 Omnibus Survey Caseload Report: SLP.* Rockville, MD: American Speech-Language-Hearing Association.

AMERICAN SPEECH-LANGUAGE-HEARING ASSOCIATION. 2000b. *2000 Schools Survey Executive Summary.* Rockville, MD: American Speech-Language-Hearing Association.

AMERICAN SPEECH-LANGUAGE-HEARING ASSOCIATION. 2000c. *IDEA and Your Caseload: A Template for Eligibility and Dismissal Criteria for Students Ages 3 to 21.* Rockville, MD: American Speech-Language-Hearing Association.

COUNCIL FOR EXCEPTIONAL CHILDREN. 2000. *Developing Educationally Relevant IEPs: A Technical Assistance Document for Speech-Language Pathologists.* Reston, VA: Council for Exceptional Children.

MOORE-BROWN, BARBARA J., and MONTGOMERY, JUDY K. 2001. *Making a Difference for America's Children: Speech-Language Pathologists in Public Schools.* Eau Claire, WI: Thinking Publications.

TAYLOR, JOYCE S. 1992. *Speech-Language Pathology Services in the Schools,* 2nd edition. Needham Heights, MA: Allyn and Bacon.

U.S. DEPARTMENT OF EDUCATION. 2000. *Twenty-Second Annual Report to Congress on the Implementation of the Individuals with Disabilities Education Act.* Washington, DC: U.S. Government Printing Office.

KATHLEEN WHITMIRE
ERIN SPINELLO
ROSEANNE CLAUSEN

# SPEECH AND THEATER EDUCATION

Speech communication education in the secondary schools is of critical importance in preparing students for their roles in a global society. Since the early 1970s, employers and college admissions personnel have identified speaking, listening, and critical thinking as skills and knowledge crucial to success. These three skills are the basis for most oral communication or speech classes in the schools. Despite the increased emphasis on speech communication education on the part of academics and employers, most elementary schools do not offer speech communication classes, and many secondary schools do not offer a full complement of classes in speech communication. On the other hand, many schools offer at least some opportunities for students to gain speaking, listening, and critical thinking experiences. In a 2002 publication, Sherwyn Morreale, associate director of the National Communication Association (NCA), wrote, "The need for communication education in grades K–12 is a crucial national concern that cannot and should not be ignored. Competence in oral communication—speaking, listening, and media literacy—is prerequisite to students' personal and academic success in life" (p. v).

Speech communication focuses on how people use messages to generate meaning within and across various contexts, cultures, channels, and media. Teachers in the field of speech communication promote the effective and ethical practice of human communication. The National Education Goals Panel set forth six broad targets for educational improvements, which became part of the Goals 2000: Educate America Act of 1994. One of the objectives within the goals identified communication as an important knowledge and skill base for every American.

## Functions

The functions of secondary school speech communication education are based on the premise that such instruction should provide for the need of all students—those who are deficient, those who are gifted, and those who are normal in basic oral communication abilities.

The needs of the student who has a speech defect cannot be ignored. Students who stutter, have a cleft palate, or have a severe hearing disorder cry out for special speech instruction. U.S. Census Bureau data from 1997 indicated that 2,270,000 people aged fifteen years and over had "difficulty with speech" (493,000 of those had severe problems). Another 7,966,000 had "difficulty hearing conversation," with 832,000 noted as having severe problems. Most school districts have access to specially educated speech and hearing therapists. The school therapist in the early twenty-first century is expected to have knowledge of the cultural and genetic aspects of speech and language development; the physical

bases of speech, hearing, and language; the principles used in diagnosing speech, hearing, and language disorders; and the methods of treating disorders of speech, hearing, and language. Thus, such remedial instruction is considered outside the province of the classroom teaching of speech.

Speech communication education also seeks to provide learning experiences for students with special interests and abilities in speech. The needs of gifted students are often met by cocurricular activities. Forensics contests, intrascholastic and interscholastic debate, school theatrical productions, radio and television clubs, and school variety programs are established parts of the secondary school curriculum through speech courses. Such courses are often electives and are available only in schools where the speech teacher's time, interests, and education make them available.

Speech communication educators urge an emphasis on programs that provide the best education for the greatest number. As justification for their claim that speech instruction should be a required part of the secondary school curriculum for all students, speech educators note that oral communication is an extraordinarily pervasive element of social life. In a 1980 article, Larry Barker and colleagues reported that college students spend from 42 to 53 percent of their time in listening and 30 to 32 percent of their time in speaking, and only 11 to 14 percent in writing and 15 to 17 percent of their time in reading. Earlier research suggested similar and even higher percentages of speaking and listening for K–12 students. And Robert Bohlken suggested in 1999 that all students are expected to listen 50 percent of the time despite few opportunities for listening instruction. Because of the importance of oral communication in social relations, systematic instruction for all students in the nature, principles, and skills of oral communication is considered the primary objective of contemporary secondary speech education.

## Incidence of Speech Instruction

Some states have mandated speech communication education. Texas students are required to take a course that covers communication fundamentals, speaking, and listening. California, Maryland, and North Carolina have passed legislation mandating oral communication. In addition, the National Council of Teachers of Mathematics and the National Council for Accreditation of Teacher Education have published guidelines and standards that include oral communication. The National Council of Teachers of English (NCTE)/International Reading Association (IRA) *Standards for the English Language Arts* include attention to oral literacy and communication skills. Standard 4 states, "Students adjust their use of spoken, written, and visual language (e.g., conventions, style, vocabulary) to communicate effectively with a variety of audiences and for different purposes" (NCTE/IRA, p. 33).

While these guidelines are given, speech communication educators feel that all students need to receive systematic and in-depth direct instruction in speech communication in specifically designated courses. For example, English teachers may use one formal speaking event such as an oral book report or a formal oral report as the sole measure of a student's speaking competence. Listening instruction is often only a request for students to "listen carefully"; at best, it may involve an activity where students must follow directions or summarize a story. While group work is common in classrooms, there is little instruction on how and why groups work.

Because of the need to provide speech communication instruction and the paucity of such courses in the schools, the National Communication Association developed a series of publications to address the issue of what to teach. *The Speaking, Listening, and Media Literacy Standards and Competency Statements for K–12 Education* provides a list of twenty standards for what should be taught in elementary and secondary schools in the United States. Each standard has a list of competencies addressing knowledge, behavior, and attitudes. While this list of standards and competencies is not intended to be prescriptive, it offers a beginning point for teachers, school districts, and states who want to know what professionals at all levels in the speech communication discipline deem "what K–12 students need to know and be able to do."

## Nature of Instruction

The field of speech communication consists of a rich amalgam of studies having to do with the act and art of oral communication. In university speech departments there are courses of study in rhetoric and public address; interpersonal, group, organizational, political, intercultural, and nonverbal communication; listening; speech science; theater, oral interpretation, or performance studies; and radio, television, and film. Scholars may approach the study of speech communication from physiological, acoustic, linguistic, aesthetic, psychological, sociological, and humanistic vantage points.

Speech instruction has traditionally been the sort that seeks to help students develop their personal skills in oral communication. Thus, units and courses of instruction in speech attempt to improve the students' fundamental communication, speaking, listening, and media literacy skills. The first, and often the only, secondary school course in speech usually consists of bits and pieces from the various areas of public communication. Each student makes speeches, takes part in debate, reads a poem, listens effectively, and uses media in an appropriate way. In addition to the basic introductory course, advanced elective courses are often made available for students with special speech interests. Table 1 shows the NCA K–12 Standards from 1998 suggesting twenty areas in which students should be allowed the opportunity to gain skills.

## Cocurricular Speech Programs

In many high schools forensics, debate, and theater activities are as natural to the cocurricular program as band concerts, football games, and junior proms. The purpose of these activities is to give students with special aptitude an opportunity for more intensive and extended experience than is possible in the classroom. While the speech communication curriculum has moved away from total student performances, cocurricular speech programs will undoubtedly continue to make such experiences possible for interested and gifted students.

**Forensics.** The structure of forensic activities in high schools in the United States varies greatly from state to state. Some states have a well-defined and carefully organized system of forensic contests; others do not. Most states have a central agency responsible for the direction and control of forensic activities. In states with well-established forensic programs, a number of levels of contest activities exist. Most states offer some forms of impromptu and extemporaneous speaking, humorous interpretation, dramatic interpretation, original oratory, and poetry reading or literary programs. A number of states offer other events such as group acting, prose reading, radio and television speaking, after-dinner speaking, oratorical analysis, storytelling, pantomime, choral reading, student congress, informative speech, duet acting, expository speaking, and book reviewing.

**TABLE 1**

### Fundamentals of effective communication

**Competent communicators demonstrate knowledge and understanding of . . .**

1. The relationships among the components of the communication process.
2. The influence of the individual, relationship, and situation on communication.
3. The role of communication in the development and maintenance of personal relationships.
4. The role of communication in creating meaning, influencing thought, and making decisions.

**Competent communicators demonstrate the ability to . . .**

5. Show sensitivity to diversity when communicating.
6. Enhance relationships and resolve conflict using appropriate and effective communication strategies.
7. Evaluate communication styles, strategies, and content based on their aesthetic and functional worth.
8. Show sensitivity to the ethical issues associated with communication in a democratic society.

**Competent speakers demonstrate . . .**

9. Knowledge and understanding of the speaking process.
10. The ability to adapt communication strategies appropriately and effectively according to the needs of the situation and setting.
11. The ability to use language that clarifies, persuades, and/or inspires while respecting differences in listeners' backgrounds.
12. The ability to manage or overcome communication anxiety.

**Competent listeners demonstrate . . .**

13. Knowledge and understanding of the listening process.
14. The ability to use appropriate and effective listening skills for a given communication situation and setting.
15. The ability to identify and manage barriers to listening.

**Media literate communicators demonstrate . . .**

16. Knowledge and understanding of the ways people use media in their personal and private lives.
17. Knowledge and understanding of the complex relationships among audiences and media content.
18. Knowledge and understanding that media content is produced within social and cultural contexts.
19. Knowledge and understanding of the commercial nature of media.
20. The ability to use media to communicate to specific audiences.

SOURCE: National Communication Association. 1998. *The Speaking, Listening and Media Literacy Standards and Competency Statements for K–12 Education.* Washington, DC: National Communication Association.

The number of activities offered is also subject to great variation from state to state. Two national organizations sponsor contests for member schools. The National Forensic League offers contests in extemporaneous speaking, original oratory, humorous and dramatic interpretation, prose and poetry interpretation, student congress, and debate, with the latter including policy debate, Lincoln-Douglas debate, and Barbara Jordan debate (which concerns urban issues). The league has more than 1,000 chapters in the United States and a membership of approximately 240,000. The National Catholic Forensic League sponsors contests in extemporaneous speaking, original oratory, interpretation events, and Lincoln-Douglas and policy debate for its more than 500 member schools.

**Debate.** Debate is often listed as one of the forensic activities and is usually sponsored by the same state agency sponsoring the other forensic activities. Debate is frequently handled apart from the other school forensic activities, however; thus it may be considered separately.

Because debate is an intellectually rigorous activity, it is most appropriate for students who are above average in intelligence and possess strong interest in problems of social concern. Debate is credited with developing such skills as the ability to collect and organize ideas, the ability to subordinate ideas, the ability to evaluate evidence, the ability to see logical connections, the ability to speak convincingly, the ability to adapt, and the ability to think and speak in outline terms.

Because interscholastic debating activities must focus on common topics, a central national coordinating agency is necessary. The National Federation of High School Activities serves this important coordinating function with the help of an advisory council made up of a representative from each state with a speech league or similar organization, a representative from the National Forensic League, and a representative from the National Catholic Forensic League. At an annual meeting the advisory committee considers the various problem areas that are recommended for consideration as debate topics and selects three of these areas for possible adoption; the final selection is made by means of a national referendum. Because three alternative debate propositions are provided for the national topic area, each state must decide which of the three propositions within the national topic area selected it will use as a debate topic.

Once a state agency has determined the particular proposition to be debated, the state conducts a series of tournaments in which that proposition is debated. Most states sponsor a state tournament, and many offer district and regional elimination tournaments as well. In addition to state-sanctioned tournaments, individual schools and cooperating universities and colleges sponsor invitational tournaments. Near the end of the season, member schools of the National Forensic League engage in league-sponsored tournaments in which the national proposition is debated. Teams that win a district tournament are eligible to compete in the National Forensic League National Tournament. The National Catholic Forensic League sponsors a similar national tournament.

**Theater.** The vast majority of high schools in the United States have some form of cocurricular theater program. The quality and quantity of cocurricular dramatic activities differ a great deal from school to school. Some schools still limit dramatic activities to class plays, which are directed by teachers with limited experience and directorial talent. Other schools have active and balanced theater programs consisting of several full-length productions of various types, one-act play productions, play readings, theater trips, and formal and informal meetings, workshops, and discussion sessions. High school theater, both curricular and cocurricular, has strong national leadership through the International Thespian Society and the American Educational Theatre Association.

## Teacher Preparation

Nationally, a standards-based evaluation is used to measure how well teacher candidates meet quality indicators and competencies. According to a 2000 NCA document, *Communication Teacher Education Preparation Standards and Guidelines,* there are six quality standards used to assess the speech communication teacher preparation program: (1) structure of the program, (2) general studies component, (3) knowledge of communication, (4) professional education and pedagogical studies, (5) professional collaboration and growth, and (6) field-based experiences for communication.

*See also:* ENGLISH EDUCATION, *subentries on* PREPARATION OF TEACHERS, TEACHING OF; JOURNALISM, TEACHING OF; LANGUAGE ARTS, TEACHING OF; SECONDARY EDUCATION; SPEECH AND LANGUAGE IMPAIRMENT, EDUCATION OF INDIVIDUALS WITH.

### BIBLIOGRAPHY

ALLEN, RONALD R.; BROWN, KENNETH L.; and YATVIN, JOANNE. 1986. *Learning Language through Communication: A Functional Perspective.* Belmont, CA: Wadsworth.

BARKER, LARRY, et al. 1980. "An Investigation of Proportional Time Spent in Various Communication Activities by College Students." *Journal of Applied Communication Research* 8:101–109.

BOHLKEN, ROBERT. 1999. "Substantiating the Fact that Listening Is Proportionately Most Used Language Skill." *Listening Post* 70:5.

CHANEY, ANN, and BURK, TAMARA L. 1998. *Teaching Oral Communication in Grades K–8.* Boston: Allyn and Bacon.

COOPER, PAMELA, and MORREALE, SHERWYN, eds. 2002. *Creating Competent Communicators: Activities for Teaching Speaking, Listening, and Media Literacy in K–6 Classrooms.* Scottsdale, AZ: Holcomb Hathaway.

COOPER, PAMELA, and MORREALE, SHERWYN, eds. 2002. *Creating Competent Communicators: Activities for Teaching Speaking, Listening, and Media Literacy in 7–12 Classrooms.* Scottsdale, AZ: Holcomb Hathaway.

COOPER, PAMELA, and SIMONDS, CHERI. 1999. *Communication for the Classroom Teacher,* 6th edition. Boston: Allyn and Bacon.

COOPER, PAMELA J., ed. 1985. *Activities for Teaching Speaking and Listening: Grades 7–12.* Urbana, IL: ERIC Clearinghouse on Reading and Communication Skills and Speech Communication Association.

DANIEL, ARLIE, ed. 1985. *Activities for Teaching Speaking and Listening: Grades K–6.* Urbana, IL: ERIC Clearinghouse on Reading and Communication Skills and Speech Communication Association.

*Goals 2000: Educate America Act of 1994.* U.S. Public Law 103-227. *U.S. Code.* Vol. 20, secs. 5801 et seq.

HYNDS, SUSAN, and RUBIN, DONALD, eds. 1990. *Perspectives on Talk and Learning.* Urbana, IL: National Council of Teachers of English.

JOHNSON, KAREN E. 1995. *Understanding Communication in Second Language Classrooms.* Cambridge, Eng.: Cambridge University Press.

KOUGL, KATHLEEN. 1997. *Communicating in the Classroom.* Prospect Heights, IL: Waveland Press.

MORREALE, SHERWYN. 2002. "Preface." In *Creating Competent Communicators: Activities for Teaching Speaking, Listening, and Media Literacy in K–6 Classrooms,* ed. Pamela Cooper and Sherwyn Morreale. Scottsdale, AZ: Holcomb Hathaway.

NATIONAL COMMUNICATION ASSOCIATION. 1998. *The Speaking, Listening, and Media Literacy*

*Standards and Competency Statements for K–12 Education.* Washington, DC: National Communication Association.

NATIONAL COMMUNICATION ASSOCIATION. 2000. *Communication Teacher Education Preparation Standards and Guidelines.* Washington, DC: National Communication Association.

NATIONAL COMMUNICATION ASSOCIATION. 2000. *Guidelines for Developing Oral Communication Curricula in Kindergarten through Twelfth Grade.* Washington, DC: National Communication Association.

NATIONAL COUNCIL OF TEACHERS OF ENGLISH and INTERNATIONAL READING ASSOCIATION. 1996. *Standards for English Language Arts.* Urbana, IL: National Council of Teachers of English and International Reading Association.

O'KEEFE, VIRGINIA. 1995. *Speaking to Think, Thinking to Speak: The Importance of Talk in the Learning Process.* Portsmouth, NH: Boynton/ Cook.

PURDY, MICHAEL, and BORISOFF, DEBORAH. 1997. *Listening in Everyday Life,* 2nd edition. Lanham, MD: University Press of America.

SEILER, WILLIAM J., and BEALL, MELISSA L. 2002. *Communication: Making Connections,* 5th edition. Boston: Allyn and Bacon.

VANGELISTI, ANITA L.; DALY, JOHN A.; and FRIEDRICH, GUSTAV W. 1999. *Teaching Communication: Theory, Research, and Methods.* Hillsdale, NJ: Erlbaum.

ZAREFSKY, DAVID. 2002. *Public Speaking: Strategies for Success,* 3rd edition. Boston: Allyn and Bacon.

**INTERNET RESOURCES**

AMERICAN EDUCATIONAL THEATRE ASSOCIATION. 2002. <www.edta.org>.

NATIONAL COMMUNICATION ASSOCIATION. 2002. <www.natcom.org>.

INTERNATIONAL LISTENING ASSOCIATION. 2002. <www.listen.org>.

U.S. BUREAU OF THE CENSUS. 1997. "Americans with Disabilities: 1997—Table 2." <www.census.gov/hhes/www/disable/sipp/disab97/ds97t2.html>.

MELISSA L. BEALL

# SPELLING, TEACHING OF

Spelling has traditionally been considered to be a component of the English/language arts curriculum. Among most educators and the public, *spelling* retains its traditional definition: "the knowledge and application of the conventional written representation of words in the process of writing, and the instruction necessary to develop this knowledge." During the last few years of the twentieth century, however, many psychologists and educators extended this definition to include spelling knowledge, meaning an understanding of how the written form of words corresponds to their spoken counterparts and underlies the ability to decode words during the process of reading and to encode words during the process of writing. Because of this insight into the role of spelling knowledge in reading as well as in writing, spelling research and instruction were generating considerable interest and focus in the field of literacy at the beginning of the twenty-first century.

## The Nature of the Spelling System

English spelling balances a demand to spell units of sounds consistently from word to word with a demand to spell units of meaning consistently from word to word. In a large proportion of the words encountered in print beginning in the intermediate school years, however, the balance tilts most often toward consistent representation of meaning—"visual identity of word parts takes precedence over letter-sound simplicity" (Venezky, p. 197). Spellings that appear to be anomalous at the level of spelling-to-sound correspondences are usually logical when considered from the perspective of spelling-to-meaning correspondences in which the spelling visually retains the meaning relationships among words—*crumb* has a silent *b* to preserve its visual identity with *crumble,* in which the *b* is pronounced; the second syllable in *mental* is spelled -*al* rather than -*le, -el,* or -*ile* in order to retain its identity with the related word *mentality,* in which the spelling of the second syllable is clear and unambiguous; and *autumn* is spelled with a final silent *n* to preserve its visual identity with *autumnal,* in which the *n* is pronounced. "Words that are related in meaning are often related in spelling as well, despite changes in sound" (Templeton, p. 194).

Though the visual preservation of meaning is the most striking feature of English spelling, the manner in which sound is represented is more logical than often assumed, particularly when the position of a sound within a syllable is considered. For example, the sound /ch/ is always spelled with the letters *ch* at the beginning of a word, never *tch*. At the end of words, on the other hand, both spellings occur—usually determined by the sound that they follow. After a long vowel sound, /ch/ is usually spelled *ch* (poa*ch*, bea*ch*); after a short vowel sound, /ch/ is usually spelled *tch* (mat*ch*, pit*ch*). In two-syllable words, this logic occurs between syllables as well: A short vowel sound followed by a single consonant requires the consonant to be doubled before another syllable beginning with a vowel (*sitting, happy*) while a long vowel sound followed by a single consonant does not require this doubling (*siting, pilot*). Exceptions do exist, of course (consider ri*ch*, mu*ch* and *habit, cabin*) but these are few in relation to the consistency with which the patterns apply. As learners progress, they may learn that these exceptions become considerably fewer because they are explained in terms of the history of the word (the language from which it came), and by the tendency for visual preservation of meaning to override a consistent representation of sound.

## A Brief History of Spelling Instruction in the United States

From colonial times in America and continuing well into the nineteenth century, the teaching of beginning reading and the teaching of spelling were unified. Spelling was in fact the way in which beginning reading was taught. Instruction began with students learning the order and names of the letters of the alphabet; then individual sounds were blended to form simple syllables of the consonant-vowel and vowel-consonant forms; and finally words for reading were learned by spelling each word orally and then pronouncing it. The spelling books of Noah Webster (1758–1843), though not the first to be published in the United States, were the first that emphasized American pronunciation and spelling (most of which was determined by Webster himself, who would also publish the first dictionary of American English). Part I of Webster's *Grammatical Institute of the English Language* (1783) addressed spelling (Parts II and III addressed grammar and reading, respectively); immortalized ever after as the "old blue-backed speller," it was reissued as *The American Spelling Book* (1788), revised (1803), and revised again and retitled *The Elementary Spelling Book* (1829). Webster's lasting influence was the pre-

sentation of words in lessons according to frequency of occurrence in spoken and written language, as well as by type of spelling pattern.

By the 1840s the role of spelling books narrowed from that of ushering children into reading to that of focusing only on spelling (orthography) and pronunciation (orthoepy). Throughout the remainder of the nineteenth century, and well into the twentieth, spelling retained a separate niche in the language arts curriculum, embodied in separate spelling textbooks, or basals. Although the manner in which spelling was taught was criticized over the years, and on occasion the very necessity of teaching spelling as a separate subject was questioned, most classroom teachers embraced the necessity of a formal emphasis on spelling.

Though spelling basals continued to be published throughout the latter part of the twentieth century, the move towards integrating the reading and language arts curriculum resulted in the inclusion of spelling as a component in reading basal programs. The amount of time and emphasis on spelling as a subject decreased. To the degree that spelling was directly addressed, spelling words were pulled from reading selections with little or no emphasis on common patterns; often, these words were also new vocabulary words as well. Within the context of a *whole language* philosophy, spelling was often addressed during writing instruction—at point of need, on an incidental basis. Though some educational publishers offered new spelling programs during the 1980s, these programs did not enjoy a wide popularity until the late 1990s. Most of these basal programs organized their content in a scope and sequence that followed a developmental sequence, while, in notable contrast with series in previous years, some added explicit treatment of the spelling/ meaning connection. During the 1990s a considerable number of resource books intended for classroom teachers were published focusing on the teaching of spelling or word study (e.g. Bear et al. 1996; Pinnel and Fountas 1998).

## Spelling Development: Learning and Instruction

Research investigating the development of spelling knowledge has shown that knowledge about the nature and function of spelling begins to develop with the learning of the alphabet and may continue into college, though spelling instruction seldom extends into the middle grades and beyond. Young children's explicit understanding of how the spelling system works is based on the expectation that letters represent sounds in a spatial/temporal left-to-right match-up. Later, knowledge of the interactive relationship between sound and position is acquired, and later still, knowledge of the role that meaning plays. Most English/language arts educators concur with research that supports the importance of engaging students in as much reading and writing as possible and in encouraging young children to apply their knowledge of the alphabet and of letter/sound relationships in their writing. There is lack of agreement, however, concerning the degree and the nature of attention allocated to spelling instruction apart from ongoing reading and writing activities. Traditionally, the two common perceptions regarding how students may learn to spell have been either (1) rote memorization through repetitive practice or (2) acquisition through more natural engagements with reading and writing. In this latter conception, the need for the skill should be apparent to learners, therefore they will be motivated to acquire knowledge of conventional spellings. Most studies that have addressed this issue, however, support the need for students to examine words apart from the more natural contexts of reading and writing. In contrast with repetitive, low-level activities, however, this examination should include reading and writing the words in contexts that involve students in comparing and contrasting words in an active search for patterns. Although both the act of reading and the act of proofreading one's own writing for spelling errors involve the learner in the application of spelling knowledge, neither act—individually or in concert—appears to engage the learner in the types of explicit attention and thinking necessary for the abstraction of the logical patterns in the spelling system. For most older students (as well as adults), the role of meaning in the spelling system does not become apparent simply through reading and writing.

Advances in the assessment of spelling knowledge allow teachers to determine more effectively and efficiently the range of spelling ability among the students in their classroom, and thus to plan instruction accordingly. Such assessment may include spelling inventories and analysis of students' writing. Selection and organization of words for examination should be based on the developmental appropriateness of the words, the type(s) of spelling pattern they represent, and their familiarity in reading. In the primary grades, exploration will be directed towards the discovery of commonalities at the alphabetic,

within-syllable pattern, and later between-syllable patterns and morphological level (i.e., simple affixes and base words). For example, younger students who are moving from the beginning to the transitional phase of literacy development may compare and contrast words with a short vowel pattern, such as *grin* and *trim,* with words with a long vowel pattern, such as *line* and *time.* In the intermediate grades and beyond, exploration will be directed primarily towards extending between-syllable pattern knowledge, and then toward developing spelling knowledge in the context of more advanced morphological, or meaning, relationships. Older students may thus examine the spelling/meaning relationships in the known words *muscle* and *muscular* (thus remembering that *muscle* has a *c* in it because they hear the *c* pronounced in the related word *muscular*) and apply this knowledge to the unfamiliar word *muscularity* (because of the similar spelling they realize it is related in meaning to *muscle* and *muscular;* it also provides a clue to the spelling of the /er/ sound in *muscular*).

In the first edition of the *Encyclopedia of Education* (1971) Ralph M. Williams discussed the logical nature of the role of English spelling, noting the role of pattern, morphology (meaning), and etymology (word history). He noted the value of encouraging an inductive approach to instruction. The field has seen Williams's conclusions supported in the subsequent three decades and has added these additional insights:

1. Developmental research has provided a stronger foundation for crafting a scope and sequence for spelling instruction; there is a better understanding of when to teach which particular aspects of the spelling system.

2. Spelling knowledge plays a larger role in literacy than previously thought; it is the foundation for decoding words in reading as well as for encoding words in writing.

3. From an instructional standpoint, there is a clearer understanding of how the relationship between spelling and meaning at the intermediate grades and beyond can be developed and extended so that the areas of spelling and vocabulary—traditionally separate in the language arts curriculum—can be effectively blended.

These insights lead to the conclusion that spelling, as a topic, is no longer limited to being simply a skill in the writing process or an aspect of attention to the conventions of print. Rather, the range and focus of spelling instruction now impacts a broader terrain than it has in the past.

In order for students at all levels to arrive at the understanding of the role of pattern and meaning in the spelling system, their teachers must be knowledgeable about this system. In this regard, Hughes and Searle observed in 1997: "If we teachers do not believe that spelling has logical, negotiable patterns, how can we hope to help children develop that insight?" (p. 133). At the beginning of the twenty-first century, therefore, there is a renewed emphasis on developing teachers' knowledge base about the nature and structure of spoken and written language—and the relationships between the two. Such a foundation may help teachers in turn develop in their students a conscious attitude and habit of search that reflect the expectation that, most of the time, the nature and occurrence of sound and meaning patterns in spelling are logical and negotiable.

*See also:* ELEMENTARY EDUCATION, *subentries on* CURRENT TRENDS, HISTORY OF; HANDWRITING, TEACHING OF; LANGUAGE ARTS, TEACHING OF; READING, *subentry on* TEACHING OF; WRITING, TEACHING OF; WEBSTER, NOAH.

### BIBLIOGRAPHY

BEAR, DONALD R.; INVERNIZZI, MARCIA; and TEMPLETON, SHANE. 1996. *Words Their Way: Word Study for Phonics, Vocabulary, and Spelling Instruction.* Englewood Cliffs, NJ: Prentice-Hall.

CUMMINGS, DONALD W. 1988. *American English Spelling.* Baltimore: Johns Hopkins University Press.

HANNA, PAUL R.; HANNA, JEAN S.; HODGES, RICHARD E.; and RUDORF, HUGH. 1966. *Phoneme-Grapheme Correspondences as Cues to Spelling Improvement.* Washington, DC: U.S. Office of Education Cooperative Research.

HENDERSON, EDMUND H. 1990. *Teaching Spelling,* 2nd edition. Boston: Houghton Mifflin.

HUGHES, MARGARET, and SEARLE, DENNIS. 1997. *The Violent E and Other Tricky Sounds: Learning to Spell From Kindergarten Through Grade 6.* York, ME: Stenhouse.

MATHEWS, MITFORD M. 1966. *Teaching to Read, Historically Considered.* Chicago: University of Chicago Press.

MOATS, LOUISA. 2000. *Speech to Print: Language Essentials for Teachers.* Baltimore: Brookes.

PINNELL, GAY S., and FOUNTAS, IRENE. 1998. *Word Matters: Teaching Phonics and Spelling in the Reading Writing Classroom.* Portsmouth, NH: Heinemann.

TEMPLETON, SHANE. 1991. "Teaching and Learning the English Spelling System: Reconceptualizing Method and Purpose." *Elementary School Journal* 92:183–199.

TEMPLETON, SHANE, and MORRIS, DARRELL. 2000. "Spelling." In *Handbook of Reading Research,* Vol. 3, ed. Michael Kamil, Peter Mosenthal, P. David Pearson, and Rebecca Barr. Mahwah, NJ: Erlbaum.

VENEZKY, RICHARD L. 1999. *The American Way of Spelling: The Structure and Origins of American English Orthography.* New York: Guilford Press.

SHANE TEMPLETON

# SPORTS, SCHOOL

OVERVIEW
  Robert M. Malina
ROLE IN STUDENT'S SOCIAL AND EMOTIONAL
  DEVELOPMENT
  Sharon Shields
  Elizabeth Gilbert

## OVERVIEW

School sports refer to athletic programs in the context of the school setting. They refer most often to interschool competition at the middle/junior high school and high school levels in the United States. Interschool programs at the elementary level vary among communities. School sports also include intramural competition, but such programs are very rare. In the mid-1990s, intramural sports involved only about 450,000 middle, junior, and senior high school students, or 3 percent of the high school–aged population.

### Purposes of School Sports

The objective of school sports is the enrichment of the high school experiences of students within the context of the educational mission of schools. As such, school sports should be educational and contribute to the overall education of all students, not athletes only. Other objectives of school sports logically follow from the educational mission: citizenship, sportsmanship, fair play, teamwork, respect, and health and welfare of all students not only during the school years but continuing into adulthood.

## Origins of School Sports

Two major forces were involved in the development of interscholastic sports in the United States: the school program, specifically physical education, and students. The initial focus was almost exclusively on boys. Within the school program, Luther Gulick established the New York Public Schools Athletic League (PSAL) in 1903, and similar leagues were organized in 177 cities by 1915. The purpose was to encourage a healthy, strong body and mind through competitive exercises. The PSAL initially conducted "class athletics" in grades five through eight at specific times each year, not interschool competition as it is known today. Class athletics included seasonal track and field events (fall, standing long jump; winter, chinning the bar; spring, running sprints). PSALs also emphasized swimming, popular sports of the times (baseball, football, basketball), and several minor games.

Interscholastic high school sports for boys had their origins in student organizations in the 1880s. They were motivated in part by intercollegiate sports, especially football, baseball, and track and field. Activities of sports clubs attracted the attention of administrators and faculty, who had major reservations about the time and energy devoted to sports and effects on the schools, including the small number of boys involved, quality of coaching (clubs often hired their own coaches), unsportsmanlike conduct, use of "ringers" (nonstudents, professionals), out-of-town travel, length of schedule, interference with school work, lack of carry-over value, injury (especially in football), and emphasis on winning, among others. Although the welfare of high school athletes was a major issue, more important, perhaps, was concern of faculty and administrators for the reputations of the schools and the perceived need for adult control. These factors contributed to the formation of state high school athletic associations, such as those in Michigan (started in 1895) and Indiana (1903). State associations in Illinois, Indiana, Iowa, Michigan, and Wisconsin formed the Midwest Federation of State High School Athletic Associations in 1921, which became the National Federation of State High School Athletic Associations in 1923. The

name was subsequently changed to the National Federation of State High School Associations in the 1970s when the fine arts were established as a program area.

Two important factors in the acceptance, or perhaps tolerance, of interscholastic sports by administrators and faculty were the scholastic performance of boys and school retention. Boys did not do as well as girls in school, dropped out more often than girls did, and were commonly behind in grade level. Between 1890 and 1920, the majority of public school students (56%–58%) and graduates (61%–65%) were girls. Child labor and compulsory schooling laws, which were passed early in the twentieth century, contributed to increased school attendance.

A related factor was the emergence of progressive education and how it addressed the needs and problems of boys in a coeducational setting. The percentage of women teachers in high schools increased (65% in 1920), and an important role was attributed to interscholastic sports in meeting the needs of boys in this context. Educators "sought to instill a more masculine tone and temper in the schools, in part by co-opting the informal interscholastic athletics that the boys themselves had created" (Tyack and Hansot, p. 166).

Interscholastic sports spread rapidly from the 1930s through the 1950s, at a time when the medical and physical education communities were opposed to competitive sports for elementary and junior high, and occasionally high school, students. Sport opportunities for females also increased, but school sports were largely the domain of males. Title IX of the Education Amendments of 1972, which was implemented in 1975, increased sport opportunities for girls.

## Participation

The estimated number of participants in high school sports from 1971 to 2000 is illustrated in Figure 1. While the number of students enrolled in high school declined from the late 1970s to 1990, the number of athletes was rather stable after a slight decrease, 3.3 to 3.5 million males and 1.7 to 1.9 million females. Since 1990, numbers of high school students and athletes increased, but the increase in athletes was somewhat less in males (3.4 to 3.9 million) than in females (1.9 to 2.7 million). The larger increase in females reflected implementation of Title IX legislation and increased interest in sports for girls.

As a percentage of total students in grades nine through twelve, the number of male athletes was, with few exceptions, rather stable between 24 percent and 26 percent from 1971 to 2000 (see Figure 2). The percentage of female athletes increased from 2 percent in 1971 to 10 percent in 1975 and then more gradually from 12 percent in 1978 to 18 percent in 1999–2000. As a percentage of male athletes, the number of female athletes increased from 8 percent in 1971 to 53 percent in 1980 and then more gradually to 69 percent in 1999–2000.

Reported participation in high school sports in the Youth Risk Behavior Survey (YRBS) is consistent with trends in Figure 2. Weighted percentages of youth reporting participation in high school sports only in 1997 were 24.0 percent for males and 23.9 percent for females (see Table 1). Relatively more white males and females reported participating in school sports only than Hispanic and black males and females, and relatively more Hispanic students reported participating in school sports than black students. The YRBS also included nonschool sports. More males than females reported participation in both school and nonschool sports and the ethnic difference between black and white males was reversed. Participation in both school and nonschool sports is an issue among state high school associations, largely in terms of the time demands on youth as well as increasing demands and pressures from nonschool sport organizations for year-round participation in a single sport.

Corresponding estimates for other countries are not available. Intramural and to a lesser extent interschool sports competition are offered in some countries, but highly developed interscholastic sports programs as in the United States are not available. Most sports are organized in the context of specific clubs independent of the schools.

## Popular Sports

The ten most popular sports for boys and girls based on numbers of schools offering the sports in 1999–2000 are summarized in Table 2. Data for 1989–1990 are included for comparison. The most popular sport offerings have changed little. Competitive spirit squads replaced indoor track and field for girls. Soccer showed the largest gains over ten years, 99 percent in girls and 42 percent in boys. The same pattern was apparent for golf, 75 percent in girls and 26 percent in boys. With the exception of football

**FIGURE 1**

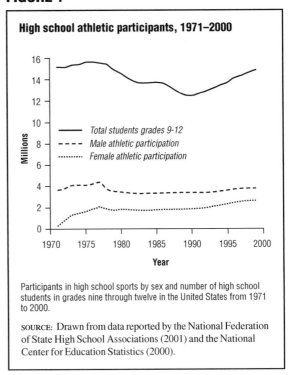

Participants in high school sports by sex and number of high school students in grades nine through twelve in the United States from 1971 to 2000.

SOURCE: Drawn from data reported by the National Federation of State High School Associations (2001) and the National Center for Education Statistics (2000).

(down 5%), all sports showed an increase in offerings over ten years.

Corresponding statistics for the ten most popular sports for boys and girls based on numbers of participants are summarized in Table 3. Football had the largest number of participants among boys, followed by basketball. Over the ten year interval, the number of participants in the top ten sports for boys increased and several sports changed rank. Baseball and wrestling declined, while track and field and soccer gained. The number of boys participating in soccer increased by about 50 percent in ten years. Other sports for boys that showed significant gains were golf (35%), outdoor track and field (18%) and cross country (17%).

Among girls, the number of participants in competitive spirit squads replaced golf in the top ten. The ranking of the top four sports (basketball, track and field, volleyball, and softball) did not change, while soccer moved to fifth. The number of participants in soccer increased by 142 percent, followed by fast pitch softball (67%), swimming and diving (63%), and cross country (47%). Overall and within the same or similar sports, relative increases in female participants were greater than corresponding increases in males.

**FIGURE 2**

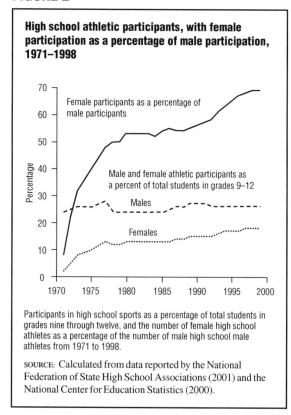

High school athletic participants, with female participation as a percentage of male participation, 1971–1998

Participants in high school sports as a percentage of total students in grades nine through twelve, and the number of female high school athletes as a percentage of the number of male high school male athletes from 1971 to 1998.

SOURCE: Calculated from data reported by the National Federation of State High School Associations (2001) and the National Center for Education Statistics (2000).

## Issues in School Sports

Although interscholastic sport program are popular, they are not without problems. Some are inherent to sports (such as injuries), whereas others span a range of issues.

**Safety and injuries.** Concern for the health and welfare of high school athletes is a primary objective of interscholastic programs. Nevertheless, risk of injury is inherent to sports. Comparison of injury rates for five sports in males (baseball, basketball, football, soccer, wrestling) and five sports in females (basketball, field hockey, soccer, softball, volleyball) during the 1995–1997 school years indicated the following trends (see Table 4). Football had the highest and baseball the lowest injury rates among the five sports for boys, whereas soccer had the highest and volleyball the lowest rates of injuries among the five sports for girls. Except for volleyball, injury rates were higher during games than practices in both genders. Sprains and strains, general trauma (including contusions), and fractures accounted for most of the injuries. About 90 percent of all reported injuries were new.

Estimated injury rates (per 100 athletes) in similar or the same sports were higher in girls than in boys for softball/baseball and soccer, but virtually identical for basketball. Rates of knee injuries were higher in female basketball and soccer players compared to male athletes in these sports, but only slightly more common in softball than in baseball players. Knee injuries required surgery more often in females than in males, and anterior cruciate ligament (ACL) surgery was especially more common in female basketball and soccer players than in male participants in these sports. The higher incidence of ACL injuries in adolescent and adult female athletes is well documented, and the issue of predisposing factors is an area of current study.

Among inherent risks in sport is the risk of death. Although deaths in sport are rare at young ages, they receive considerable media attention. Estimated rates for nontraumatic sport deaths in high school and college athletes thirteen to twenty-three years of age are less than one per 100,000 participants per year, but the ratio of males to females is about ten to one. Rates are higher among college than high school male athletes. Nontraumatic deaths in sport are due primarily to cardiovascular causes, but several noncardiovascular causes are also involved, including hyperthermia, electrocution due to lightning, and complications of asthma. These are preventable conditions. Corresponding data for traumatic deaths in high school athletes are less than one per 100,000 participants.

**Carry-over.** Benefits of participation in interscholastic sports should presumably carry over to other aspects of life during adolescence. Data from the YRBS indicate associations between sports participation and positive health behaviors related to physical activity, diet, cigarette smoking, illegal drug use, and reduced sexual intercourse (females). Associations were strongest for white and less consistent for black and Hispanic high school students. Other data indicate positive associations between sports participation and educational (higher grades, lower drop-out rates) and social (leadership roles, self-assurance) behaviors. Data relating high school sports participation to adult behaviors are generally lacking. Consequences of sport injuries for health in adulthood also need study.

**Coaches and coach education.** Qualifications for coaches vary among states and school districts. Many states and districts require coaches to have a teaching certificate, but there apparently is a lack of teachers with either an interest in coaching or the necessary credentials. As a result, an increasing number of coaches are not teachers and do not have faculty status. Nonteacher coaches are commonly required to complete a coach education program that includes principles of growth and development, coaching (theory, methods, psychology), and training (conditioning, nutrition); injury prevention, management and care; CPR and sports first aid; and risk management. Available courses vary in depth of content and mode of delivery. Coach education is required for nonteachers in 35 states and the District of Columbia and for all coaches in 15 states, but is not required in 15 states.

There is a lack of uniform standards for coaches education, although a comprehensive set has been recommended by the National Association for Sport and Physical Education. Professional coach education programs analogous to the systematic preparation and certification of teachers are not available in the United States.

**Programmatic issues.** School sport programs are currently affected by a number of issues, including schools that focus on a single sport ("rogue schools," "factories"); emphasis on "nationally ranked programs," which implies national travel during the school year; recruiting, especially for summer basketball; increasing numbers of international students; and threats to amateurism. International students are often concentrated in rogue schools for basketball and reported ages are commonly questioned. The United States Olympic Committee (USOC) has already foregone the rules of amateurism, and the National Collegiate Athletic Association (NCAA) may be moving in this direction.

High school programs generally emphasize competition and program success rather than developing skills for the next level of athletic competition. In contrast, many national sport governing bodies emphasize talent identification, development, and medals, and prefer that talented youth be passed along to a higher level of coaching and training than at the high school level. Talent identification programs in many sports are not consistent with objectives of school sports.

**College scholarships.** Unrealistic expectations for sport success beyond high school plague many programs and college scholarships are a major issue. The probability of receiving a college athletic scholarship is small. Of approximately three million

**TABLE 1**

**Weighted percentages of participation in high school sports and nonschool sports by gender and ethnicity, 1997**

| | High school sports only | Nonschool sports only | Both school and nonschool sports |
|---|---|---|---|
| **Male** | 23.3 | 12.8 | 33.8 |
| White | 24.1 | 12.1 | 34.6 |
| African American | 19.3 | 14.4 | 37.3 |
| Hispanic | 21.9 | 15.5 | 25.0 |
| **Female** | 21.6 | 8.7 | 23.1 |
| White | 23.9 | 9.0 | 25.5 |
| African American | 15.2 | 7.5 | 17.7 |
| Hispanic | 16.7 | 8.5 | 15.6 |

SOURCE: Adapted from Pate, Russell R.; Trost, Stewart G.; Levin, Sarah; and Dowda, Marsha. 2000. "Sports Participation and Health-Related Behaviors Among U.S. Youth." *Archives of Pediatric and Adolescent Medicine* 154:904–911.

eighth graders in 1988, only about 5 percent later reported participation in intercollegiate sports and only about 2 percent were in Division I schools. The number was further reduced when only those who received athletic financial aid was considered. Only 48 percent of all NCAA Division I athletes received athletic aid (scholarships) in 1992–1993.

The lure of college scholarships, especially for basketball and football, has resulted in widespread scouting at the middle or junior high school levels and commercially sponsored prep school football combines analogous to the National Football League. In the context of competition with professional leagues, the NCAA is also discussing a mentoring program for elite athletes as young as 12 years, specifically for basketball. One can question whose interests are best being served by such programs and their consistency with educational objectives of high school sports. Probability of success in sport beyond college is even more remote.

**Violence.** Violence at sporting events involving participants, coaches, and spectators is increasingly reported. The violence reflects interactions among several factors, including overemphasis on winning, lack of administrative supervision, lack of respect for authority, inconsistent officiating, social inequities in schools, and perhaps parental and community overinvolvement. Violence is also routinely tolerated and sanctioned in several highly popular sports, specifically ice hockey and football, and occasionally basketball and soccer (e.g., "professional fouls"). Re-

**TABLE 2**

Ten most popular interscholastic sports for boys and girls based on number of schools participating in the respective sports, 1989–1990 and 1999–2000

**Boys**

| 1989–1990 | | 1999–2000 | | Percent change |
|---|---|---|---|---|
| Basketball | 16,710 | Basketball | 16,852 | 0.9 |
| Track and field (outdoor) | 14,270 | Track and field (outdoor) | 14,664 | 2.8 |
| Football | 13,986 | Baseball | 14,610 | 7.2 |
| Baseball | 13,629 | Football (eleven-player) | 13,313 | -4.8[1] |
| Cross country | 10,311 | Golf | 12,391 | 26.3 |
| Golf | 9,773 | Cross country | 11,891 | 15.3 |
| Tennis | 8,941 | Tennis | 9,603 | 7.4 |
| Wrestling | 8,416 | Soccer | 9,330 | 42.2 |
| Soccer | 6,561 | Wrestling | 9,046 | 7.5 |
| Swimming and diving | 4,306 | Swimming and diving | 5,324 | 23.6 |

**Girls**

| 1989–1990 | | 1999–2000 | | Percent change |
|---|---|---|---|---|
| Basketball | 16,188 | Basketball | 16,526 | 2.1 |
| Track and field | 13,982 | Track and field | 14,587 | 4.3 |
| Volleyball | 11,996 | Volleyball | 13,426 | 11.9 |
| Cross country | 9,272 | Softball (fast pitch) | 13,009 | 49.7 |
| Softball (fast pitch) | 8,688 | Cross country | 11,277 | 21.6 |
| Tennis | 8,550 | Tennis | 9,468 | 10.7 |
| Swimming and diving | 4,227 | Soccer | 8,218 | 99.1 |
| Soccer | 4,128 | Golf | 7,090 | 75.0 |
| Golf | 4,052 | Swimming and diving | 5,536 | 31.0 |
| Track and field (indoor) | 1,936 | Competitive spirit squads | 3,497 | N/A |

[1]The earlier survey probably included schools offering six- and eight-player football programs.

SOURCE: Based on information from the National Federation of State High School Associations.

spect for opponents and sport and sportsmanship need stronger emphasis if the educational objectives of sport are to be attained.

Sport was allegedly a focus of attention in the violence that occurred in Littleton, Colorado, in the spring of 1999. The perpetrators of the violence allegedly identified athletes as targets and were described as being on the fringe of the high school social circles. These events raise important issues related to the preferential position and treatment of varsity athletes and the marginalization of some students by the social structure of high schools. Varsity sport is exclusive and schools offer few, if any, opportunities for youth who are not sufficiently skilled or who lack the size required for some sports. Schools and communities often indulge in varsity athletes in major sports and rank them among the socially elite. Administrators and coaches often tolerate unacceptable behaviors of athletes (physical, verbal, and social bullying; criminal activities), giving athletes a different status compared to other students. "Trash talk" and the "in-your-face" demeanor of many sports, which are essentially forms of non-physical violence, are commonly treated by coaches, administrators, and commentators as a form of strategy or "sport smarts." Does such verbal abuse contribute to poor sportsmanship, lack of respect for opponents and the sport, and physical violence? The data are suggestive.

**Nonschool sports.** Programs for talented young athletes (and by extension some coaches) to participate in a sport after the school season, but during the school year and in the summer, have expanded recently. High school eligibility can be compromised and young athletes face the risk of overtraining, injury, and exploitation. Some programs also compete directly with school sports. This is perhaps most apparent in elite youth soccer clubs that call for year-round training in the sport following the professional model. Further, professional soccer teams in the United States (in contrast to other professional sports) have signed players still in high school, a practice that is common in soccer and other sports throughout the world.

**Students with disabilities.** Most public schools practice inclusion of students with a disability in intramural and interscholastic sports programs according to the provisions of the Americans with

**TABLE 3**

Ten most popular interscholastic sports for boys and girls based on number of participants in the respective sports, 1989–1990 and 1999–2000

**Boys**

| 1989–1990 | | 1999–2000 | | Percent change |
|---|---|---|---|---|
| Football | 947,757 | Football (eleven-player) | 1,002,734 | 5.8 |
| Basketball | 517,271 | Basketball | 541,130 | 4.6 |
| Baseball | 413,581 | Track and field (outdoor) | 480,791 | 18.5 |
| Track and field (outdoor) | 405,684 | Baseball | 451,701 | 9.1 |
| Wrestling | 233,856 | Soccer | 330,044 | 49.5 |
| Soccer | 220,777 | Wrestling | 239,105 | 2.2 |
| Cross country | 155,806 | Cross country | 183,139 | 17.5 |
| Tennis | 136,939 | Golf | 165,857 | 34.9 |
| Golf | 122,998 | Tennis | 139,507 | 1.9 |
| Swimming and diving | 85,112 | Swimming and diving | 86,640 | 1.8 |

**Girls**

| 1989–1990 | | 1999–2000 | | Percent change |
|---|---|---|---|---|
| Basketball | 389,668 | Basketball | 451,600 | 15.9 |
| Track and field (outdoor) | 308,810 | Track and field (outdoor) | 405,305 | 31.3 |
| Volleyball | 293,688 | Volleyball | 382,755 | 30.3 |
| Softball (fast pitch) | 205,040 | Softball (fast pitch) | 343,001 | 67.3 |
| Tennis | 128,076 | Soccer | 270,273 | 141.9 |
| Soccer | 111,711 | Tennis | 159,740 | 24.7 |
| Cross country | 104,876 | Cross country | 154,021 | 46.9 |
| Swimming and diving | 84,760 | Swimming and diving | 138,475 | 63.4 |
| Field hockey | 50,237 | Competitive spirit squads | 64,319 | N/A |
| Golf | 40,418 | Field hockey | 58,372 | 16.2 |

SOURCE: Based on information from the National Federation of State High School Associations.

Disabilities Act (ADA) and the Individuals with Disabilities Education Act (IDEA). Disability accommodations depend upon the individual needs of the student.

*See also:* COLLEGE ATHLETICS; PHYSICAL EDUCATION; TITLE IX.

**BIBLIOGRAPHY**

BREWINGTON, PETER. 1997. "Scouts Keep Eye on 9th Graders." *USA Today,* July 9, p. 10C.

BREWINGTON, PETER. 2001. "Major League Soccer Is Signing Boys in High School Just Like Foreign Clubs." *USA Today,* April 17, pp.1A–2A.

GUTOWSKI, THOMAS W. 1988. "Student Initiative and the Origins of the High School Extracurriculum: Chicago, 1880–1915." *History of Education Quarterly* 28:49–72.

LOWMAN, CHARLES LEROY. 1947. "The Vulnerable Age." *Journal of Health and Physical Education* 18(9):535–636, 693.

MALINA, ROBERT M. 1999. "Sport, Violence, and Littleton: A Perspective." *Spotlight on Youth Sports* (Institute for the Study of Youth Sports, Michigan State University) 22(1):1–2.

MIREL, JEFFREY. 1982. "From Student Control to Institutional Control of High School Athletics: Three Michigan Cities, 1883–1905." *Journal of Social History* 16:83–100.

MITCHELL, ELMER D. 1932. "Trend of Athletics in Junior High Schools." *Journal of Health and Physical Education* 3(4):22.

MORAN, MALCOLM. 2001. "NCAA Looking to Mentor Youth." *USA Today,* March 30, p. 10C.

NATIONAL ASSOCIATION FOR SPORT AND PHYSICAL EDUCATION. 1995. *National Standards for Athletic Coaches.* Reston, VA: National Association for Sport and Physical Education.

NATIONAL FEDERATION OF STATE HIGH SCHOOL ASSOCIATIONS AND AMERICAN SPORT EDUCATION PROGRAM. 2001. *Blueprint for Success: 2001 National Interscholastic Coaching Requirements Report.* Champaign, IL: Human Kinetics.

OWINGS, JEFFREY; BURTON, BOB; and DANIEL, BRUCE. 1996. *Who Reports Participation in Varsity Intercollegiate Sports at 4-Year-Colleges.* NCES 97-911. Washington, DC: National Center for Education Statistics.

PATE, RUSSELL R.; TROST, STEWART G.; LEVIN, SARAH; and DOWDA, MARSHA. 2000. "Sports

**TABLE 4**

Injury rates (per 1,000 athlete exposures) in selected sports among high school boys and girls in the National Athletic Trainers' Association surveillance study

| Boys | Baseball | Basketball | Football | Soccer | Wrestling |
|---|---|---|---|---|---|
| Overall | 2.8 | 4.8 | 8.1 | 4.6 | 5.6 |
| Practices | 1.8 | 3.4 | 5.3 | 2.5 | 4.8 |
| Games | 5.6 | 7.1 | 26.4 | 10.2 | 8.2 |

| Girls | Basketball | Field hockey | Softball | Soccer | Volleyball |
|---|---|---|---|---|---|
| Overall | 4.4 | 3.7 | 3.5 | 5.3 | 1.7 |
| Practices | 3.2 | 3.2 | 2.7 | 3.1 | 2.8 |
| Games | 7.9 | 4.9 | 5.9 | 11.4 | 1.2 |

SOURCE: Adapted from Powell, John W., and Barber-Foss, Kim D. 1999. "Injury Patterns in Selected High School Sports: A Review of the 1995–1997 Seasons." *Journal of Athletic Training* 34:277–284.

Participation and Health-Related Behaviors among US Youth." *Archives of Pediatric and Adolescent Medicine* 154:904–911.

POINSETT, ALEX. 1996. *The Role of Sports in Youth Development.* New York: Carnegie Corporation of New York.

POWELL, JOHN W., and BARBER-FOSS, KIM D. 1999. "Injury Patterns in Selected High School Sports: A Review of the 1995–1997 Seasons." *Journal of Athletic Training* 34:277–284.

POWELL, JOHN W., and BARBER-FOSS, KIM D. 2000. "Sex-Related Injury Patterns among Selected High School Sports." *American Journal of Sports Medicine* 28:385–391.

REILLY, FREDERICK J. 1917. *New Rational Athletics for Boys and Girls.* New York: D.C. Heath.

RICE, EMMETT A. 1939. *A Brief History of Physical Education.* New York: A.S. Barnes.

TYACK, DAVID, and HANSOT, ELISABETH. 1992. *Learning Together: A History of Coeducation in American Public Schools.* New York: Russell Sage Foundation.

VAN CAMP, S. P.; BLOOR, C. M.; MUELLER, FREDERICK O.; CANTU, ROBERT C.; and OLSON, H. G. 1995. "Nontraumatic Sports Deaths in High School and College Athletes." *Medicine and Science in Sports and Exercise* 27:641–647.

WHITE, CAROLYN. 1997. "Football Combine Aids College Pool." *USA Today,* June 10, p. 8C.

INTERNET RESOURCES

ADAMS, LORRAINE, and RUSSAKOFF, DALE. 1999. "Dissecting Columbine's Cult of the Athlete." *Washington Post.* <www.washingtonpost.com/wp-srv/national/daily/june1999/columbine12.htm>.

KANABY, ROBERT F. 2001. "Some Perceptions of Our Present Circumstances." <http://nfhs.org/ADConf2k_rfk2gen.htm>.

MUELLER, FREDERICK O., and CANTU, ROBERT C. 2000. "National Center for Catastrophic Sport Injury Research Seventeenth Annual Report: Fall 1982–Spring 1999." <www.unc.edu/depts/nccsi/AllSport.htm>.

NATIONAL CENTER FOR EDUCATION STATISTICS. 2000. "Chapter 1. All Levels of Education." *Encyclopedia of ED Stats.* <www.nces.ed.gov>.

NATIONAL COLLEGIATE ATHLETIC ASSOCIATION. 2000. "Probability of Competing in Athletics Beyond the High School Interscholastic Level." *NCAA News Digest,* August 14. <www.ncaa.org.news/20000814/digest.html>.

NATIONAL FEDERATION OF STATE HIGH SCHOOL ASSOCIATIONS. 2001. "The Case of High School Activities." <www.nfhs.org/case.htm>.

NATIONAL FEDERATION OF STATE HIGH SCHOOL ASSOCIATIONS. 2001. "1999–2000 Athletics Participation Summary." <www.nfhs.org/part_survey99-00.htm>.

ROBERT M. MALINA

# ROLE IN STUDENT'S SOCIAL AND EMOTIONAL DEVELOPMENT

The role of sport in society, and more particularly in schools, has been debated for many decades.

There are divergent viewpoints on the value of sport, with proponents on one end of the continuum hailing sport as having the same goals and objectives as all of education and on the other end those who purport that sport is an entertainment enterprise that should be separated from education altogether.

## A Brief Historical Perspective

The development of organized sports and games in the United States has had an interesting history. Early settlers in the United States brought some games with them, but there was a minimal amount of organized athletics in communities and none in the schools until near the middle of the nineteenth century. Very little is known about the early history of sport development, but most authorities agree on the historical evolution of the major American sports that were developed in the eighteenth century. The first organized baseball team was founded in 1845, and the first college game was played between Amherst and Williams in 1859. The game of American football originated from soccer and rugby; the first game is claimed to have occurred in 1869 between Rutgers and Princeton. James Naismith created the game of basketball in 1891 to fill a need for play and sport during long winter months. Sports received mixed reviews, as the activities were usually conducted by citizens on a volunteer basis or by unsupervised high school and university students. By 1879 a need arose for systemization of sport and for a governing agent to oversee sports in the United States, which resulted in the formation of the Amateur Athletic Union in 1888. In 1906 the National Collegiate Athletic Association (NCAA) was founded as an outgrowth of meetings held by twenty-eight of the nation's colleges.

The NCAA and AAU have remained powerful governance boards in regulating college and all other amateur sports in America. As girls and women entered the sport arena, the formation of the National Association of Girls and Women in Sport in 1899 was instrumental in providing sound sport opportunities for all girls and women in a variety of sports at the elementary, high school, and collegiate levels. In 1971, with the impending passage of Title IX, representatives from 278 colleges and universities formed the Association of Intercollegiate Athletics for Women (AIAW), which governed women's intercollegiate sports until a takeover by the NCAA in 1981. The AIAW began to level the playing field for girls and women in sport. For the first time in American history, women's sports began to rival men's programs in the number of contests held, which increased the amount of publicity given to women's sports. When the NCAA took over as the governing body of women's intercollegiate athletics, it inherited a new era in women's participation. In 1971, only 31,000 women were engaged in varsity sports; a decade later there were 70,000, and the numbers have continued to escalate significantly.

In the United States, participation in organized sports has become a common rite of childhood. At the beginning of the twentieth century, agencies and schools provided sport opportunities as a means of providing wholesome leisure time activities for children and youth. Prior to 1954, most of these experiences occurred in Boys and Girls Clubs, Young Men's Christian Associations (YMCA), Young Women's Christian Associations (YWCA), Boy Scouts, and Girl Scouts. With the inception of Little League Baseball in 1954, sport for youth moved from social agencies and activities organized by youth themselves to adult-organized sport programs. In the early twenty-first century, schools have organized teams primarily for the "athletically elite," often to the exclusion of the majority of students. Opportunities for youth to engage in sport remain unequal across genders and social class.

The debate continues as to the value of sport in education. Sport is ingrained in society as both an educational fixture and an entertainment enterprise. The argument continues as to whether or not sport holds valued benefits for its youth and young adult participants and therefore warrants a prominent place in the educational system.

## Benefits of Sports to a Child's Development

A wide spectrum of outcomes has been attributed to modern-day sports and play. Critics have condemned sport for fostering excessive violence, an overemphasis on competition and winning, and the exploitation of individuals. Sport proponents have extolled the value of sport as a contributor to health, personal fulfillment, and community integration.

It is important to look at how sport has the potential for producing positive outcomes in educational and noneducational settings for children and youth. Mihaly Csikszentmihalyi has proposed a model for systematically assessing the potential positive outcomes of sports and the conditions necessary to produce them. The Csikszentmihalyi model is based on the premise that four main types of consequences are of importance when examining and/or evaluating any sport activity. Two of these consequences are present at the individual level: personal enjoyment and personal growth; and two are at the community level: social harmony/integration and social growth/change. In relation to this model, an ideal sport activity is one that contributes in significant ways to all four types of outcomes.

Leonard Wankel and Philip Kreisel have identified five factors that should be present for a child or youth to experience the benefit of personal enjoyment in sport: personal accomplishment, excitement of the sport, improving one's sports skills, testing one's skills against others, and just performing the skills. These factors are thought to contribute most to the enjoyment of sport.

Personal growth includes a variety of physical and psychological factors. Physical health can be maintained and improved through sport participation by enhancing the cardiovascular system; improving blood pressure and cholesterol levels; increasing muscular strength; improving muscular endurance, flexibility, and bone density; and weight management. Because sports are a major type of activity in which children and youth are involved, it is considered a viable method of promoting good health. Lifetime sports, such as golf, tennis, swimming, and cycling, are especially beneficial in meeting nationally established health objectives. Early childhood participation in sport can minimize the emphasis on competition and focus on skill instruction. However, sports may not be a sufficient substitute for physical education programs in the schools. Quality physical education curriculums that have developmentally appropriate physical activities which provide the necessary foundations in motor skill, movement acquisition, and behavioral development can enable children and youth to become successful participants in organized sport.

Numerous studies support the positive relationship that exists between psychological well-being and regular involvement in physical activity, especially in the areas of reduction of anxiety and depression. Conditions to maximize such outcomes are usually associated with individual preferences related to activity type; environmental factors; level of competition or intensity of activity; and individual versus group format.

Sport has also been shown to serve as a mechanism for the transmission of values, knowledge, and norms in creating social harmony. The specific values conveyed may be those of the dominant society, or they could be those of a subgroup. Therefore, sport could contribute to either differentiation and stratification or to integration into the overall society. Evidence indicates that different sports appeal to different social stratifications in the society and may reinforce cultural or societal differences. Sport also may serve to transmit general societal values, which leads many sport authorities to believe that sport has positive value for the participants in building character, discipline, a strong work ethic, and the ability to work in teams. The research literature supports the importance of de-emphasizing winning and competition and thereby moving young people into positive and enjoyable experiences. Unfortunately, the trend has been toward a more competitive, "win-oriented" framework, which has created increased aggression and violent behaviors among spectators and youth participants. This has led to many national forums at the high school, collegiate, and community levels to reassess the sport culture.

Positive outcomes related to socialization and social integration are also dependent upon appropriate leadership, as well as the creation of a climate for this to occur within the sport experience. Changes within sport and change in the general society have a symbiotic relationship—general societal changes affect sport, and changes in sport can also affect society.

## Conclusion

Youth sports participation can have many benefits for the individual and for society. However, it is evident that sports can produce negative consequences if quality programs are not developed. Schools and communities can strive for the highest standards by educating and training coaches, deterring the professionalization of youth sports programs, and abiding by the guidelines established by national sport governing bodies, so that sports programs have optimal benefit for all youth, regardless of age, gender, ethnicity, or ability.

*See also:* PHYSICAL EDUCATION.

### BIBLIOGRAPHY

CSIKSZENTMIHALYI, MIHALY. 1982. "The Value of Sports." In *Sport in Perspective,* ed. John T. Partington, Terry Orlick, and John H. Salmela. Ottawa, Ontario, Canada: Coaching Association of Canada.

GREENDORFER, SUSAN L. 1978. "Social Class Influence on Female Sport Involvement." *Sex Roles* 4:619–625.

MORGAN, WILLIAM P., and GOLDSTON, STEPHEN E., eds. 1987. *Exercise and Mental Health.* Washington, DC: Hemisphere.

NATIONAL COLLEGIATE ATHLETIC ASSOCIATION. 1981. *The Sports and Recreational Programs of the Nation's Universities and Colleges.* Mission, KS: National Collegiate Athletic Association.

SAVAGE, HOWARD J. 1929. *American College Athletics.* New York: Carnegie Foundation for the Advancement of Teaching.

SEIDEL, BEVERLY L., and RESICK, MATTHEW C. 1978. *Physical Education: An Overview,* 2nd edition. Reading, MA: Addison-Wesley.

SEEFELDT, VERN D., and EWING, M. (1997). "Youth Sports in America: An Overview." *Presidents Council on Physical Fitness and Sports Research Digest* 2(11):1–12.

WANKEL, LEONARD W., and BERGER, M. 1990. "The Psychological and Social Benefits of Sport and Physical Activity." *Journal of Leisure Research* 22(2):167–182.

WANKEL, LEONARD W., and KREISEL, PHILIP S. J. 1985. "Factors Underlying Enjoyment of Youth Sports: Sport and Age-Group Comparisons." *Journal of Sport Psychology* 7:51–64.

SHARON SHIELDS
ELIZABETH GILBERT

# STANDARDS FOR STUDENT LEARNING

*Standards,* as they are used in education, are verbal statements of goals or desired classes of outcomes. They describe *what* the goals of the system are. Standards-based educational reform has the intention of having most or all students reach identified standards and of organizing educational services, including teacher preparation and instructional interventions, to address such standards. The rhetorical linchpin of such a system is the standards themselves.

## Definitions and Descriptions

Standards differ according to function and have fallen into at least three overlapping classifications. *Content standards* are intended to describe domain-specific topics, for example, student performance in areas of mathematics, such as measurement or probability, or in physics, such as force and motion. National professional groups, such as the National Council of Teachers of Mathematics, the American Association for the Advancement of Science, and the American Historical Association, for example, have reached professional consensus about such standards. States have also put into place panels intended to recommend such standards for adoption to their state boards of education. School districts may choose to augment, focus, or redefine content standards adopted by their state. Content standards are often arrayed in a continuum of development, specifying, for instance, particular standards for eighth-grade students or for beginning readers or those standards thought to be necessary to meet high school graduation requirements. *Skill standards* are explications of either a fundamental skill, such as reading, or job-performance standards, such as the ability to work in teams. Skill standards are often, although not always, independent of a particular content domain.

*Performance standards,* unfortunately, is a term used to denote two very different concepts, and users often fail to be explicit about their interpretation. Some educators use performance standards as a means to describe the "what" of education further or to give examples of tasks that fit particular content standards. Performance standards of this type are intended to communicate more clearly the intention of general content or skill standards. Good performance standards should link up to the design of assessments intended to measure the standards, although they are usually at some distance from that process. For example, the content standard "to understand the causes of major historical events in American history" might be illustrated by a description that says "The student will be given primary source documents related to an important historical era, such as the American Revolution or the Great Depression, and be asked to identify alternative explanations for the causes offered by different historical writers." The student will evaluate these arguments and use source material to explain in an essay which perspectives are most reasonable. These performance standards might then be augmented with a sample task and scoring scheme for a set of such essays.

The second type of performance standard delimits the degree of proficiency, or the "how much" part, of performance. These performance standards are invoked following the development of assessments designed or selected to measure student performance of the standards. Frequently, these performance standards are described in terms intended to give a rough scale of competence, such as *basic, proficient,* or *advanced.* The operational definition of these standards is usually based on a cutscore—the dividing score between classifications—for example, "above 75 points." The underlying theory of standards-based reform is that it is criterion referenced. This means that performance of the system is judged in the light of attainment of the standards as measured by particular tests and assessments. Because the inferences drawn about educational improvement strongly depend on the validity of these achievement levels, or performance standards, they are of critical importance.

### Historical Context

In the United States the 1990s were the decade of educational policy on standards and assessments. Following on the educational reforms in Great Britain in the late 1980s, the movement in the United States was propelled by a connected and unprecedented set of events: the meeting of state governors at Charlottesville, Virginia, in 1989 establishing national educational goals; the release that same year of the National Council of Teachers of Mathematics standards, describing expectations for an integrated and applied form of mathematics learning; the 1992 report of the deliberations of the National Council on Education Standards and Testing; and the enactment of the Improving America's Schools Act of 1994, tying compensatory education resources to evaluations of progress toward standards.

The focus on educational standards as the basis for targeting and evaluating student learning seems the product of the 1990s but has, in fact, a venerable educational history. To understand the idea of standards for student learning, it is instructive to consider how the concepts of standards and assessments developed. The conception of standards and assessments can be traced to the 1951 writings of Ralph W. Tyler on curriculum and instruction in the "garden-variety schools." Tyler constructed the problem of improving education with admirable logic. In his

view, schools should organize themselves as entities seeking to produce learning and achievement. Outcome measures of learning and achievement should be considered the proximal ends of education. These ends, in order to be pursued in a reasonable way, required deliberate decisions made by educators and other interested parties. Tyler addressed the task of determining educational objectives in a systematic way. He described three potential sources for generating learning objectives: the subject matter discipline, the society, and the needs of learners. Because this process was sure to generate too many objectives, candidate objectives were to be filtered by using screens of two types. The first screen was the psychology of learning, to answer through the application of theory and empirical knowledge the question of feasibility. The set was to be winnowed by the question "Can the objectives be taught and learned?" The second screen to reduce and make coherent standards was to articulate and apply a simple but integrated philosophy of education. This philosophical screen was to answer questions of priority and coherence as well as value: "What goals are important and matter most?"

The remainder of Tyler's argument, called his *rationale,* focused on a systematic plan for teaching and learning and addressed criteria for the selection of learning opportunities, the creation of measures of achievement and other outcomes to match the objectives, and ways to involve feedback to improve the quality of education over time. Although there was considerable excess in the 1960s and 1970s in the focus on operational, behaviorally oriented objectives, there was some evidence that the system worked. The Tyler rationale was an object of study in the 1960s and the 1970s but is no longer in the working memory of many educators, who believe that the standards-based reform movement is a newly minted concept and revolutionary in its systemic focus.

### Comparing Past and Present

**Academic disciplines.** Two principal sources provided standards in the 1990s. The first was the academic disciplines, led by professional organizations, such as the National Council of Teachers of Mathematics in 1989, the joint effort of the International Reading Association/National Council of Teachers of English in 1994, the Mathematical Sciences Education Board of the National Research Council in 1995, and the National Council of Teachers of English in 1996. These groups either took on or were assigned the leadership position on the generation of standards (goals) for schools in their subject matters. The overwhelming use of this source made great sense because the rhetoric around standards pointed to the use of "new and challenging" standards intended to support the learning of all children. In the public's mind, challenging standards equaled academic- or discipline-based learning. The experts, as they had in the curriculum reforms in the late 1960s and 1970s, once again weighed in on what students should learn in school. Perhaps in response to behaviorism in goal statements, these statements of standards are often global and subject to multiple interpretations.

**Society.** The second source for the generation of standards was the society. This source was narrowed to standards that were regarded as important in the workplace. Reports of needed skills from the state of Michigan, from national research studies, from analyses of labor markets, and from the work of the U.S. Department of Labor Secretary's Commission on Achieving Necessary Skills devoted attention to requirements for success in employment. The argument for these sets of skills was tied to the importance of U.S. economic competition, and the sense, at the beginning of the 1990s, that the United States might be permanently eclipsed on the one hand by the economic dynamos in the Far East and on the other by the power of the emerging European community. This specter was bolstered by the reports of international comparisons of educational achievement showing that U.S. student performance was far lower than had been imagined and hovered in the not-so-good to truly miserable ranges. Consequently, societal sources of objectives took on four different varieties. The first was a set of new tasks, heretofore not emphasized in the academic side of schools; a good example was teamwork. In teamwork the emphasis was on roles and functions of team members rather than on "spirit." Second were fundamental skills, such as reading and computation, skills lacking in entry-level employees. Third, there was a new emphasis on applied problem solving, both the inventive type and the application or modifications of algorithms necessary for key procedures. The fourth category of standards was in the general affective area and involved responsibility, leadership, and service orientation. For the most part, these four strands of tasks were not reconciled.

**Students' needs.** A third source of Tyler's goals, the student's individual needs, found its way into standards through the focus on cognitive psychology, where the fundamentals of reading comprehension or mathematics problem solving, or the explanation of subject-matter content, and meta-cognition emphasized cognitive processes needed to display deep understanding. The promise of this approach was increased transfer. Such approaches often targeted integrative or project learning, but usually without addressing the transfer issue. For the most part, however, this source of objectives played out more directly in the application of the psychology screen and in the construction of assessments.

**Changing expectations.** A cynic might argue that the entire reform is explained by the psychological measure of paired associates, and that all that has been done is to substitute the term *standards* for goals and objectives, and the softer sounding *assessment* for the term *test*. Yet, the expectations for education have changed dramatically from the 1930s and 1940s. Education has become regarded as a right by society for a far greater proportion of learners than ever before. Society has changed scale and comprises greater numbers of individuals with different cultural, language, and economic backgrounds. Many differ substantially in their views of their own goals and prospects, the degree to which they embrace traditional American values, and the value they place on alternative ways to attain their own goals. It is clear that development of educational systems does not happen linearly on a cycle that supports achieving high levels of quality in one component (standards, for example) before attacking the next (e.g., the development of instruction). Paradoxically, it is probably best to act as if a logical, step-by-step process could guide the decisions about present or future practice, or at least as if superimposing a staged process were important. Without a framework as a guide for actions and understanding, it is difficult to think about such a complex system, in which institutions and organizations must respond to market pressures, to teacher-capacity variations, to economic shifts, technical advances, and the competitive strut of contending policy perspectives.

## Potential for Success

Will these standards work to improve education? Standards will be useful as a communication device to rally educators and the public. The system will fail programmatically and substantively, however, unless serious effort is taken to connect measures systematically to the standards, to set realistic priorities about what standards can be achieved (as opposed to the enormous numbers typically adopted by states and localities), and to emphasize the essential acts of teaching and learning in the system. Arbitrary standards for achievement are set, and are used to judge a school or system and to assign sanctions based on putative standards-based performance. This strategy attempts to assign uniformity to schools and systems that are inherently different—in governance, in capacity, and in development. For the system to succeed in the context of democratic educational institutions, policymakers will need to take steps to assure that growth in performance on measures is attributable to teaching and learning rather than to practices intended simply to raise test scores artificially. They will need to understand more systematically and procedurally what they mean when they claim a system is "aligned," and they will need to address forthrightly what requirements there may be to ensure the rising performance of all students.

*See also:* ASSESSMENT, *subentry on* PERFORMANCE ASSESSMENT; SCIENCE LEARNING, *subentry on* STANDARDS; STANDARDS MOVEMENT IN AMERICAN EDUCATION.

### BIBLIOGRAPHY

*Improving America's Schools Act of 1994.* 1994. H.R. 6, 103rd Congress, 2nd Session.

INTERNATIONAL READING ASSOCIATION/NATIONAL COUNCIL OF TEACHERS OF ENGLISH. 1994. *Standards for the Assessment of Reading and Writing.* Newark, DE: International Reading Association and National Council of Teachers of English.

NATIONAL COUNCIL OF TEACHERS OF ENGLISH. 1996. *Standards for the English Language Arts.* Urbana, IL: National Council of Teachers of English and International Reading Association.

NATIONAL COUNCIL OF TEACHERS OF MATHEMATICS. 1989. *Curriculum and Evaluation Standards for School Mathematics.* Reston, VA: National Council of Teachers of Mathematics.

NATIONAL COUNCIL OF TEACHERS OF MATHEMATICS. 1989. *Curriculum Standards for Teaching Mathematics.* Reston, VA: National Council of Teachers of Mathematics.

NATIONAL COUNCIL ON EDUCATION STANDARDS AND TESTING. 1992. *Raising Standards for American Education: A Report to Congress, the Secretary of Education, the National Education Goals Panel, and the American People.* Washington, DC: U.S. Government Printing Office.

NATIONAL RESEARCH COUNCIL. 1995. *National Science Education Standards.* Washington, DC: National Academy Press.

O'NEIL, HAROLD F., JR.; ALLRED, KEITH; and BAKER, EVA L. 1997. "Review of Workforce Readiness Theoretical Frameworks." In *Workforce Readiness: Competencies and Assessment,* ed. Harold F. O'Neil Jr. Mahwah, NJ: Erlbaum.

SMITH, MARSHALL, and O'DAY, JENNIFER. 1991. "Systemic School Reform." In *The Politics of Curriculum and Testing,* ed. Susan Fuhrman and Betty Malen. Philadelphia: Falmer.

TYLER, RALPH W. 1951. "The Functions of Measurement in Improving Instruction." In *Educational Measurement,* ed. Everet F. Lindquist. Washington, DC: American Council on Education.

U.S. DEPARTMENT OF LABOR. 1991. *What Work Requires of Schools: A SCANS Report for America 2000.* Washington, DC: U.S. Department of Labor.

EVA L. BAKER
HAROLD F. O'NEIL JR.

# STANDARDS MOVEMENT IN AMERICAN EDUCATION

The origins of the standards movement in American education are largely economic. For much of the twentieth century, most jobs in the United States could be done by people with an eighth-grade level of literacy. Only a minority of people needed more than that, and fewer still needed the kinds of knowledge and skill associated with the work of professionals and managers.

Then, in the late 1970s and early 1980s, everything changed. American business was assaulted by firms, mainly from Asia, that were making enormous inroads into American markets for goods and services at home and abroad. American business leaders discovered that many of these firms were paying 1/10 to 1/100 of the wages that they had to pay for people with a seventh- or eighth-grade level of literacy in the United States. Hundreds of thousands of jobs requiring relatively low literacy levels began moving offshore, never to return. The only way that firms could afford to continue to pay the prevailing wages in industrialized countries was if the people to whom those wages were paid could do the kind of highly skilled work that only highly educated people could do. In this new situation, eighth-grade levels of literacy would become a ticket to a life of economic struggle in the developed world.

## Governors Take the Initiative

State governors became very concerned about the jobs that were being lost to low-wage countries, and business leaders began to realize that skilled and educated people were vital to their future. All through the 1980s and 1990s, pressure grew to do something about this situation. The governors took the initiative. In a very unusual departure from prior practice, they devoted the 1986 meeting of the National Governors Association in Hilton Head, South Carolina, solely to education, declaring to professional educators, in effect, "We will give up regulating inputs and give you more flexibility and control over resources, in return for your commitment to be held more accountable for results."

## Standards-Driven Reform Models

**The business model of standards-driven reform.** The governors thus established the language of the new management revolution in business. The general approach that emerged was, roughly speaking: get your goals clear; communicate them clearly to everyone in the organization; create accurate measures of progress toward those goals; push decisions as to how to reach those goals as far down toward the people who make the product or render the service as you can; slice out most of the middle management in between; give the people on the front line the tools and training they need to do the job; and when all this is done, reward those who produce measured gains toward the stated goals and provide consequences for those who do not.

This model would have a powerful influence on the standards movement in education. Two other models came from analyses of the systems used in other nations that appeared to have more success than the United States in producing consistently high levels of achievement among the mass of their students: the accountability model and the ministry model. The accountability model came in two variants. The distinctions between them were subtle and terribly important.

**The educators' accountability model.** One emerging point of view held that American achievement could be greatly improved by adopting clear academic standards, and then mandating tests that closely matched these standards. Based on the European and Asian experience, the advocates of this view maintained that the annual release of school-by-school performance data would by itself create irresistible pressure on the schools to find effective curriculum materials, implement effective instructional strategies, and do the other things needed to raise student performance. The educators who came to this view typically advocated standards and assessments that would support a *thinking curriculum* that went far beyond the requirements of basic literacy to emphasize autonomous, thoughtful, informed, and reasoned behavior.

**The political accountability model.** This formulation resonated with many people in positions of political leadership, who were persuaded that the main challenge was to find a set of incentives to make professional educators do what they should have been doing all along. Many were furious that, all through the 1980s, large investments in elementary and secondary education had produced very little achievement gain for students. For many of these people, the content of the standards and assessments was much less important than the ability to use standards to call educators to account. In this model, all that was really important was to have standards, assessments, and a system of rewards and consequences that would provide strong incentives to the educators to raise dramatically the performance of public educators. Unlike those who embraced the educators accountability model, the people who held this view cared little about the specific character of either the standards or the assessments.

**The ministry of education model.** Some people who examined countries with highly successful education systems came to a different conclusion about the sources of their effectiveness. This perspective was put forth in a report of the National Center on Education and the Economy titled *America's Choice: High Skills or Low Wages!* (1990) and the report of the Third International Mathematics and Science Study (TIMMS) affirmed their view.

The researchers for the *America's Choice* study noted that high-performing countries had a common set of structural elements including: high and explicit standards that are the same for all students, as least through the age of fourteen; national examinations set to the standards; curriculum frameworks that specify the topics to be studied at each grade in the core subjects in the curriculum; and instruction and curriculum materials matched to the standards. The TIMSS researchers observed that, in contrast to the most successful nations, the curriculum they found in the United States was "a mile wide and an inch deep," a function of the fact that the states, and the nation as a whole, lacked formal curriculum frameworks specifying what topics are to be studied at each grade level in the core subjects of the curriculum.

The result has been that textbook publishers, given the need to sell their products to an unorganized market, cram many different topics into their texts, treating each one very superficially and leaving out much of the conceptual material that is needed for students to understand the subject. By this analysis, the fact that no level of government in the United States plays the role typically played by ministries of education in other countries in assuring the alignment of the whole instructional system to standards makes it impossible to have a truly standards-based system of education. In this conception of the standards movement, what lies at the core is a highly aligned instructional system, each component of which will support the development of the kind of high-level skills and knowledge needed in the high-wage economies.

### The Rise of the Standards Movement

In the three years following the governors' meeting at Hilton Head, events moved rapidly. By 1989, the National Council of Teachers of Mathematics (NCTM) had published *Curriculum and Evaluation Standards for School Mathematics.* In the same year, the chairman of the National Governors Association asked Governor Bill Clinton of Arkansas and Governor Carroll Campbell of South Carolina to co-chair a task force on educational goals. That fall, President George Bush asked the governors to join him in Charlottesville, Virginia in a meeting devoted solely to a discussion of educational goals.

When, in the following year, the White House announced a set of education goals for the nation, the governors responded once again with a call to establish a National Education Goals Panel, made up of governors and very senior representatives from the administration, to monitor the nation's progress toward the goals.

### The Politics of Standards

The story of the 1990s is the story of the ascendancy of the political accountability wing of the standards movement. As the decade began, the conversation about goals became a conversation about standards, and many people started looking for some way to establish a national entity to become the focal point for creating some sort of national system of standards and assessments. Republican and Democratic presidents took turns at various formulations of ways in which the federal government could take the lead, if not in setting national standards and requiring national exams, then at least in creating some mechanism by which the federal government could fund the development by the states of standards and exams, and then monitor and review the quality of what they produced. They wanted to assure the public that some sort of system of standards was being established that would enable the United States to compete in world commerce, and to graduate students with an education comparable to that offered by any nation in the world. As of 2001, however, all initiatives to create national exams or tests, to reference state tests to national tests, and to review state standards and tests at the national level had failed.

Political conservatives fear that entrusting these functions to the federal government could lead to the imposition of a national curriculum. Liberals, on the other hand, fear that the inevitable consequence of a system of national standards will be to deny graduation and other forms of opportunity to poor and minority students who could not meet the standards because of the inequitable distribution of resources in the American education system.

What the electorate was prepared to entrust to the federal government, during the first Bush administration, was the granting of funds to teachers' subject-matter associations to develop their own standards, following the example of the NCTM. Later, during the Clinton administration, there was a move to require the states to hold low-income students receiving federal funds to standards no lower than the standards to which all other students were held, which was tantamount to requiring all states to develop their own state standards.

### The Pivotal Role of the States

The most intense pressure to do something to use standards to raise educational achievement was falling, in any case, not on federal officials, but on top state officials. Many of these officials joined the New Standards Consortium, a gathering of twenty-two states, half a dozen cities, a university, and a not-for-profit organization, in an effort to develop standards and assessments of the kind and quality that many of the state leaders knew would be required. The New Standards Consortium did, in fact, produce performance standards and reference examinations that were later used as a quality benchmark by many states, and the ideas that emerged from it proved influential, but it did not become the nucleus of a national system of standards and examinations, as some of its originators had hoped.

Instead, each state went its own way. In the mid-1990s, as the state commissioners of education, sometimes in league with their governors, were leading the effort to establish state standards, they found themselves in a war zone. Despite the strong pressure from the business community, officials of general government, and the public at large to do something about establishing state standards, these state officials found themselves under heavy attack from conservative groups and liberal educators, for reasons such as those cited above. The only way they could survive these assaults was to appoint broad-based groups from within each state to create that state's standards. Even a hint that the standards had come from outside the state would have doomed them. In some states, the battle over the standards quickly became very heated, adding the phrases *math wars* and *reading wars* to the educators' vocabulary. These state-developed standards were rarely benchmarked to any standards outside the state. Some were tightly focused on narrow skills, most were very vague, and few provided the kind of guidance that would be required to construct a curriculum.

None of these standards included examples of the kind of student work that would meet the standard, the hallmark of the performance standards that had been created by the New Standards Consortium. This omission was important because it is virtually impossible to construct an instructional program to get students to the standard if neither the student nor the teacher know what sort of student work will meet the standard.

The state standards drew, in varying degrees, on the standards that had been developed by the teacher's disciplinary associations. But some of these standards had also drawn heavy fire. The social studies standards were assaulted on the grounds that they virtually ignored figures like George Washington and Robert E. Lee and gave much more space to women and minorities, whose role in the life of the nation was arguably less pivotal. Federal government support was withdrawn from the standards project of the English teachers because of its alleged failure to place sufficient weight on the conventions of English grammar, spelling, and other skills.

As the 1990s progressed, all but one of the states developed their own unique statewide standards, and most either bought off-the-shelf tests for state-wide use or, in the majority of cases, worked with commercial testing companies to produce custom tests, frequently of much the same design as the most popular off-the-shelf tests. In the main, the tests satisfied the needs of the accountability wing of the standards movement for an instrument that could be used to hold teachers accountable, but fell far short of the kind of assessment tool that would provide incentives to create a thinking curriculum in the schools.

## The Accountability Model Prevails

Professional educators experienced this both as a greatly increased burden of testing and, even more importantly, as the sharpest edge of a burgeoning accountability movement. State after state was using the tests mandated at three or more grade levels as the basis for publishing scores comparing schools within the states. As the twentieth century came to a close, the accountability movement came to dominate the standards movement in most states. As state after state devised different methods to construct *league tables* showing how schools compared to one another and to the state standards on the state tests, school districts everywhere began to find themselves under enormous pressure to improve student performance, as measured by the tests. This pressure was, of course, passed down to the schools.

## The Backlash

The pressure to improve performance produced predictable results. Teachers, either of their own volition or with the active encouragement of their principals, prepared their students for the tests by teaching them how to answer the general form of the questions they would get. A few, leaving nothing to chance, opened the tests before they were to be administered, and told their students the answers, and a few corrected wrong answers given by the students on the test after they took it.

Many of the state tests were narrowly focused on facts and skills, rather than on a real understanding of the subject or an ability to apply complex knowledge and skills to problems unlike those the students had practiced on. Because of this, teachers who focused almost wholly on test preparation ended up greatly narrowing the curriculum. Researchers found that this actually depressed the achievement of many students who would have achieved at higher levels if there had been no accountability system. This in turn produced a revolt among middle-class and upper-middle-class parents and the teachers of their children. The teachers felt that the new tests and the accountability system that went with them were destroying good teaching, and the parents felt that the accountability movement was responsible for "dumbing down" a rich curriculum and making it less, rather than more, likely that their children would be able to get into the selective colleges they would otherwise be destined for.

Though test makers claimed that their tests were closely aligned with the state standards, and makers of instructional materials claimed that their products were closely aligned with the tests and the standards of particular states, independent analysts repeatedly found otherwise. The instructional power that researchers associated with the highly aligned systems in other countries was therefore only rarely being exploited in the actual implementation of the system in the United States.

### The Future of the Standards Movement

The political accountability model, as mentioned previously, includes only three elements of the more complex business, ministry of education, and educational accountability models: the standards, the measures, and the accountability system (meaning the rewards for those who produced improved student performance and consequences for those who did not). Missing from this model, but part of the other models, was: (1) high standards that incorporate a "thinking curriculum," (2) assessments that teachers would like to teach to, (3) granting the school principals and others who will bear the burden of accountability the authority they need to do the job, (4) creating clear curriculum frameworks that would make it possible to build fully aligned instructional systems, and (5) making the heavy investments in the tools and training the school people would need to do the job.

The economic forces that have pushed American education toward explicit standards, the benchmarking of those standards against the standards in other countries, and the construction of league tables of school performance against common measures are unlikely to grow weaker in the foreseeable future. But the growing backlash among professional educators and suburban parents against the accountability version of the movement seems likely to grow, absent more thoughtful standards, tests that teachers feel comfortable teaching to, instructional materials closely aligned to standards that really support a thinking curriculum, and inclusion in the model of the missing elements of the business and ministry models of standards-driven education reform.

There are straws in the wind suggesting that this might happen. The national movement toward comprehensive school reform is beginning to produce organizations with the drive and resources to provide the training and technical assistance that schools need to bring students from many different backgrounds to high standards. Achieve (the organization founded by the governors and the business community to advance the cause of the standards movement in the United States) and the Southern Regional Education Board are working to assemble coalitions of states committed to the use of common examinations. Various organizations are working to develop instructional materials closely aligned to these frameworks that could become the basis for a thoughtful curriculum that good teachers will be pleased to teach. But there are other elements of the business and ministry models that are not much in evidence yet in the United States. The jury, therefore, is still out.

*See also:* BUSINESS INVOLVEMENT IN EDUCATION; CURRICULUM, SCHOOL; SCHOOL REFORM; STANDARDS FOR STUDENT LEARNING; STATES AND EDUCATION.

**BIBLIOGRAPHY**

KENDALL, JOHN, and MARZANO, ROBERT. 2000. "Content Knowledge: A Compendium of Standards and Benchmarks for K–12 Education." In *Mid-Continent Research for Education and Learning*, 3rd edition. Aurora, CO: Mid-Continent Research for Education and Learning.

Kohn, Alfie. 2000. *The Schools our Children Deserve: Moving Beyond Traditional Classrooms and Tougher Standards.* Boston: Houghton-Mifflin.

Meier, Deborah, ed. 2000. *Will Standards Save Public Education?* Boston, MA: Beacon Press.

National Center on Education and the Economy. 1990. *America's Choice: High Skills or Low Wages!* Rochester, NY: NCEE.

Ravitch, Diane, ed. 1995. *Debating the Future of American Education: Do We Need National Standards and Assessments?* Washington, DC: Brookings Institution.

Tucker, Marc S., and Codding, Judy. *Standards for Our Schools.* San Francisco: Jossey-Bass.

### INTERNET RESOURCES

Achieve. 2000. "High Standards: Giving All Students a Fair Chance, 2000." <www.achieve.org>.

Education Commission of the States. "Standards: What States Are Doing." <www.ecs.org>.

National Goals Panel. "The Road to Charlottesville: The 1989 Education Summit." <www.negp.gov>.

Marc S. Tucker

# STATE DEPARTMENTS OF EDUCATION

ROLE AND FUNCTION
William H. Roe
Carolyn D. Herrington
VOCATIONAL EDUCATION
Joanna Kister

## ROLE AND FUNCTION

In the United States, education has been established as a state function. Each state exercises this function completely or in part through a state department of education, within which there are varying degrees of responsibility. The state educational authority (usually known as the state department of education and personified by the state board of education and the chief state school officer and his or her staff) gains its powers and responsibilities specifically from the state's constitution and statutes. Much of its influence and authority, however, has developed as local school units, state governments, the federal government, and the courts have progressively looked to the state educational office as a source of professional advice and information.

In general, the growth and the specific roles of state departments of education have resulted from the state legislatures' responsibility to provide an adequate educational system; state education departments serve not only to interpret and facilitate the development of educational legislation, but also to observe its effect and to implement legislative mandates relating to education. The departments observe the school systems in operation and advise the legislatures of desirable changes and regulations. Moreover, there is a need for a central agent sufficiently knowledgeable about education to serve in a judicial capacity in controversies arising between school districts and local or regional educational agents and agencies of the state. State departments of education are needed to provide both voluntary services and services mandated by the legislatures to educational agents and state agencies. In general, the departments developed from the need to exercise leadership through both local government and the legislative and executive branches of state government and from the need to encourage positive improvement by uniting the educational forces within each state.

### Development

The concept of education as a state function is firmly rooted in the past, particularly in colonial laws that foreshadowed state laws and in ordinances regulating the territories that later became states. After the United States was formed, the concept of education as a state function was expanded through the general reservation of power to the states in the federal Constitution, through state constitutions, and through state statutory practice and judicial law.

**1812–1890.** State departments of education emerged and became firmly established during the period from 1812 to 1890. Although the first responsibilities of these departments during this period were advisory, statistical, and exhortatory, state departments of education began to come into their own with the swift expansion of public education following the Civil War. In these early days the extent of positive leadership exerted by the state agency depended a great deal on the quality of leadership exerted by the chief school officer. Some of the first state superintendents, such as Horace Mann of Massachusetts, Henry Barnard of Connecticut, John D. Pierce of Michigan, Calvin Wiley of North Carolina, Caleb Mills of Indiana, John Swett of California, Gideon Hawley of New York, and Robert Breckenridge of Kentucky, set the pattern for the development of modern state educational systems. In their respective states they consolidated the forces for education into movements that did not stop until free common school education became a reality.

These superintendents exerted a broad influence through dynamic leadership. They studied the weaknesses and strengths of the schools and interpreted the social forces that influenced education, and they kept the people and the legislators informed about education, becoming spokespersons not only for the teachers, but for all educational forces. These pioneering state superintendents, however, were aided by both social and economic movements and a growing democracy. Most important, there were individuals, groups, and organizations eager for a crusading leader who could present their ideas on education to the public.

**1890–1932.** The regulatory function of the state departments of education was expanded with the general acceptance of compulsory education, for it became apparent that only a state department of education could determine that compulsory attendance requirements were being enforced. The maintenance and operational functions of the state department of education were strengthened during the period from 1918 to 1932. Although compulsory attendance laws became universal and local school units stronger, it was apparent that local units varied greatly in their ability to provide education, in their educational burdens, and in their leadership—all of which resulted in startling inequities in educational offerings. This development demonstrated the need for a stronger state educational agency that could determine that minimum standards were being met. In some cases, it was the state that actively operated certain schools (e.g., schools for the blind, deaf, and similarly handicapped individuals; vocational-technical schools; and teacher-training institutions) as well as programs for the entire state.

**1932–1953.** The years from 1932 to 1953 saw the expansion of the service and support functions of the state department of education and the emergence of its leadership role. The rapid expansion of public education as a result of compulsory attendance and the

demand for equal education for all students increased the demands upon the states to provide greater support. Whereas city schools could supply and service a great variety of educational programs, rural schools could not. Therefore, numerous divisions and subunits within state departments of education were developed to provide instructional and professional assistance to rural schools. As states attempted to offset inequalities, it became apparent that a solution lay in the reorganization of rural schools into districts large enough to provide services. In fact, in most states the first significant leadership activities, which were aimed essentially at rural America, can be traced to statewide reorganization efforts. To a certain extent this rural emphasis precipitated the statewide neglect in urban education that became so apparent in the 1960s. During this period there was also an accelerating demand for new patterns of state financing that would provide a guaranteed minimum educational program to all children in all districts. The percentage of state support for public elementary and secondary education doubled from slightly more than 20 percent in 1930 to approximately 40 percent in 1950.

The influence of the federal government increased during this period, as World War II forced it to rapidly supply people trained in various fields. As a result of the national need, state departments of education directed, and in many cases operated, technical training programs during the war. After the war, when industrial expansion and the rapid increase, relocation, and migration of the population created massive school building problems, the federal government joined with state governments in stimulating long-range planning to provide adequate school buildings. It was also during the postwar period that the Council of Chief State School Officers (CCSSO), founded in 1928, achieved national influence and recognition. The council established the Study Commission of the Chief State School Officers, which took a leadership role in studying the major problems that were facing state departments of education.

**1953–1983.** Between 1953 and 1983 the federal influence on education increased, and state departments of education were strengthened through the federal-state partnership concept. This phase marked the beginning of the modern federal aid program for education. Social, economic, and demographic changes after World War II placed excessive demands on local school districts. In too many cases, states were unable to provide the help needed. Because there was such variation in the competency of the state departments of education, many people advocated abandoning the idea that the state department of education should maintain the balance of power between local and federal government, suggesting that the federal government assume leadership and control. In many ways federal involvement was encouraged by the National Defense Education Act (NDEA) of 1958, through which the federal government dealt directly with local school districts, colleges, and universities.

The NDEA, enacted after the launching of *Sputnik I* in 1957, actually resulted in an upheaval in the structure of state departments of education rather than in stability. An infusion of federal funds enabled a few states to move out of their former passive roles, but the most notable effect was an imbalance within the organization of the departments. By 1950 half of the professional staff members of state departments of education were assigned to federally subsidized programs. By 1960 that percentage had risen to more than 56 percent and in thirteen states to more than 70 percent. It was inevitable that personnel growth would take place in areas supported by federal funds. For example, in 1958 there were only fifteen state supervisors in mathematics, the sciences, and foreign languages in all the states combined. For English and social studies, there were twenty state supervisors in all the states. Title III of the NDEA offered financial assistance for strengthening science, mathematics, and modern foreign-language instruction. Thus, by 1963, five years after the act was passed, the number of state supervisors in those subjects had risen to 173, an increase of more than 1,100 percent. Because there was no federal support for English or social studies, the number of state supervisors in these subjects rose only slightly, to thirty-two for all states. In 1958 there were only three specialists in preschool education in all the states, and in 1963 there were still only three.

In spite of the massive increase in federal aid under the NDEA, state departments of education actually began to lose some of their strength and prestige. In 1963 the Advisory Council on State Departments of Education pointed out that most departments could not fully perform the duties expressly delegated to them by state legislation because of personnel shortages. Thus, when state education agencies were most needed, they were least prepared

to give the kind of statewide leadership necessary for improvement.

At the continued and insistent demands of educational, social, and political leaders, Title V of the Elementary and Secondary Education Act of 1965 included a five-year program of grants calculated to strengthen the capacity of state departments of education to meet their growing responsibilities. Three programs were established for this purpose. Section 503 provided basic grants to state educational agencies to develop, improve, or expand professional leadership activities. Section 505 supplied special project grants to support experimental programs and to develop special services to help solve problems common to several states. Section 507 provided for an interchange of professional personnel to develop and share leadership skills in both federal and state educational agencies. Though the percentage of the full-time staff in state departments of education paid entirely or in part by federal funds continued to rise, there was, nevertheless, greater balance in department staffs because general strength had been developed, rather than strength in specific subject areas.

**1983–2000.** The 1983 release of the landmark report of the National Commission on Excellence in Education, entitled *A Nation at Risk,* ushered in a period of sustained and intensive scrutiny of the quality of public schooling in the United States. The release of this federal document coincided with similar reports and commissions in many states. State departments, for the most part, were not the source of the thrust for reform. However, the renewed focus on academic achievement has had an extremely important impact on state departments. For example, state departments have been assigned much of the policy and program development work related to school reform. They have been charged by federal and state policymakers with responsibility for articulating the rationale, implementing the policies, and developing, overseeing, and monitoring state programs for school reform. These responsibilities have strengthened the importance of state departments while significantly challenging their capacity for overseeing school reform.

The implications of these responsibilities for the structure, personnel, and organizational behavior of state departments of education have been profound. Departmental units of testing and public information have increased in number and in size, and many departments have established offices of policy analysis and research. However, as pointed out by Susan Lusi in her 1997 study of the state departments of Vermont and Kentucky, state departments were not traditionally structured or staffed to engage in the complex work of instructional improvement, nor in the policy analysis or program development that has characterized school reform. Almost every state has developed statewide curricular standards, most states have developed tests for them, and a number of states have attached consequences to varying performance.

Such tasks, assigned to state departments by state legislatures, the courts, and the federal government, have drawn state departments into technically challenging and politically controversial roles. The state court in Kentucky abolished the state education department, requiring the legislature to re-establish it. In the early 1990s, the California Department of Education was the target of heated criticism for how it developed and informed the public about its state assessments. The governor subsequently vetoed the assessment program. Even more recently, state assumption of responsibility when local systems fail has put state departments in highly problematic relations with the local school districts: they are called up to implement sanctions; enforce school choice programs among local districts—and between local districts and private schools; take over failing schools or school districts; and interpret judicial pronouncements about what constitutes adequate and inadequate schooling. Nineteen states mandate that low-performing schools receive state assistance and thirteen of those states specify the assignment of a state staff person.

State education departments have also seen their roles challenged and their budgets vulnerable to other governmental reforms. Their authority and competence have been challenged by state oversight offices, which often have closer ties to governors and legislatures. State departments have suffered from attempts to downsize government and from budget-reduction exercises as proponents of smaller government have had success in legislative and gubernatorial races. A survey by *Education Week* found that at least 27 state education agencies had fewer employees in 1998 than they did in 1980. State departments have also been responsible for developing management information systems to support the new accountability systems, which has placed a large technical demand on the agencies. State departments are trying to respond to these new demands by in-

corporating new management styles and processes. For example, the Texas Department of Education increasingly has turned to privately contracted regional assistance centers for technical assistance duties.

## The Situation in the Early Twenty-First Century

Although there is still a great variation in the organization, operation, structure, staff, and influence of state departments of education, enough basic similarities exist so that one can generalize about their accepted roles and functions. In general, each state department of education has four major roles: regulation, operation, administration of special services, and leadership of the state program.

**Regulation.** The regulatory role consists of: (1) determining that basic administrative duties have been performed by local schools in compliance with state and local laws; (2) ascertaining that public school funds are employed properly; (3) enforcing health and safety rules for construction and maintenance of buildings; (4) enforcing and determining the proper qualifications and licensing of teachers and educational personnel; (5) ensuring that minimum educational opportunities are provided for all children through enforcement of compulsory school laws and child labor laws, and through pupil personnel services; (6) ensuring and monitoring the development of state educational standards and student performance measures and ascertaining that required procedures are used; and (7) ensuring that schools are organized according to the law. The regulatory function of all state departments of education is based on the acceptance of the fact that education is a state function and that local school districts have limited authority to act, except as state laws permit.

**Operation.** Operational roles of state education departments vary greatly from state to state. There is a general trend away from having the state department of education conduct direct operational functions.

Historically, states have accepted responsibility for the operation of educational agencies and services when no other agency could provide the necessary statewide direction, especially during the developmental stages of a particular program or enterprise. A state education department may operate teachers colleges, schools and services for students with disabilities, trade and correspondence schools, and agencies or institutions of a cultural nature (e.g., state libraries, museums, archives, historical agencies). It may also offer programs that other institutions are unwilling to offer, such as trade classes and programs for migrant workers.

**Administration of special services.** The state's role in the administration of special services developed in response to a need for statewide uniformity and efficiency in educational services. The state offers centralized services that improve education in general (e.g., teacher placement and retirement programs), and it provides services that, because of their scope, technical nature, or expense, can better be offered on a statewide basis (e.g., library services, centralized insurance, financial services, control of interscholastic athletics, statewide testing). The state also provides local school districts, the legislature, the executive office, and the general public with basic information about the status of education, such as comparative studies and statistical information and clarification of all statutes, rules, and regulations on education. As in the case of operational services, the state maintains administrative services only if they are not available through another institution or agency.

**Leadership.** According to the Council of Chief State School Officers, the important leadership functions of a state department of education include conducting long-range studies for planning the state program of education, studying ways of improving education, providing consultant services and advice in all areas of education, encouraging cooperation and promoting the proper balance among all units of the educational system, informing the public of educational needs and progress and encouraging public support and participation, and providing in-service education for all persons in the state engaged in educational work.

While all states have state departments of education, these departments differ in structure, organization, function, and size. All states have some type of state board of education, but there is a great variation in the amount of control exerted by the board on the department and on the overall state educational system. All states have a state school officer responsible for the department, but, again, the responsibilities of this officer vary among the states: some are political leaders and others are educational leaders; some are appointed and others are elected; some are regarded as the chief educational officer of the state; and others are one of many in the educational hierarchy who have state educational responsibilities.

At first, the chief state school officer discharged routine educational functions, sometimes with the help of a secretary. General office workers could easily carry out such tasks as compiling information pertaining to education, making annual and biennial reports, publishing school laws, and apportioning state financial aid.

In the early twenty-first century, the leadership function of the staff is not so easily determined, and there are a great variety of opinions as to how much leadership should be exerted by the state department of education. Compliance and regulatory functions remain important and substantial. The main objective remains to ensure that local school districts attain the minimum level of achievement required by the state. However, the goals of leadership and public aspirations for ever-increasing student achievement go above and beyond. The role of state department has expanded to incorporate increasing performance for all students and their function has evolved from monitoring compliance with state and federal laws and regulations to supporting school districts in pursuing this goal. As the new century begins, state departments face the daunting task of inspiring and stimulating local school systems to strive for the highest educational quality.

*See also:* FINANCIAL SUPPORT OF SCHOOLS, *subentry on* STATE SUPPORT; STATES AND EDUCATION; STATE EDUCATIONAL SYSTEMS.

### BIBLIOGRAPHY

GOERTZ, MARGARET E.; DUFFY, MARK C.; and LE FLOCH, KIRSTEN CARLSON. 2001 *Assessment and Accountability Systems in the Fifty States: 1999–2000.* Philadelphia: Consortium for Policy Research in Education.

LUSI, SUSAN FOLLETT. 1997. *The Role of State Departments of Education in Complex School Reform.* New York: Teachers College Press.

HERNDON, FRANK M. 1965. "State Supervision Through Leadership and Services." *National Business Education Quarterly* 33(4):20–25.

HERRINGTON, CAROLYN D., and FOWLER, FRANCES. 2002. "Rethinking the Role of States and Educational Governance." In *American Educational Governance on Trial: Change and Challenges,* ed. William Lowe Boyd. Chicago: National Society for the Study of Education.

LEMAHIEU, PAUL G., and LESLEY, BONNIE A. 1994. "State Education Agencies: Partners in Reform." In *Transforming State Education Agencies to Support Education Reform,* ed. Jane L. David. Washington, DC: National Governors' Association.

LARSON, CARL A. 1963 "The State Legislature, the State Department of Education, and Expertness." *Journal of Secondary Education* 38(4):248–252.

MASTERS, NICHOLAS A.; SALISBURY, ROBERT H.; and ELIOT, THOMAS H. 1964. *State Politics and the Public Schools.* New York: Knopf.

MINEAR, LEON P. 1968. "Some Unsolved Problems of Federal Aid to Education." *School and Society* 96(2304):135–137.

MORPHET, EDGAR L., and RYAN, CHARLES O., eds. 1967. *Implication for Education of Prospective Changes in Society.* Denver, CO: Bradford-Robinson.

SANFORD, TERRY. 1968. "The States: The Revitalized Senior Partners in Education." *National Association of Secondary-School Principals Bulletin* 50(309):41–44.

THURSTON, LEE M., and ROE, WILLIAM H. 1957. *State School Administration.* New York: Harper.

**INTERNET RESOURCE**

EDUCATION WEEK. 1999. "State Agencies Take Hands-on Role in Reform." <www.edweek.org/ew/vol-18/41power.h18>.

WILLIAM H. ROE
*Revised by*
CAROLYN D. HERRINGTON

# VOCATIONAL EDUCATION

Vocational education is a field in transition, undergoing changes prompted by an upward shift in the skill requirements for the workforce and by the call for increased standards and accountability in the education reform movement of the 1980s and 1990s. Vocational education programs are offered in comprehensive high schools, vocational schools or career centers, adult education centers, community and technical colleges, and proprietary schools.

In 1999 the national organization that represents vocational educators, the American Vocational Association, changed its name to the American Association for Career and Technical Education. Most states have also renamed their divisions and programs to career and technical education, or in some states, career and technology education.

## Purpose

Although the mission of vocational education remains to prepare people to prepare for work, historically the focus was on preparation for entry-level jobs in occupations requiring less than a baccalaureate degree. That mission has changed to a broadened purpose of preparing for work and continued education. Educational reformers and vocational education legislation both called for vocational education programs to maintain college entry as a viable option for students enrolled in career and technical education. The 1998 vocational education legislation explicitly stated that vocational education should contribute to students' academic and technical achievement.

The National Association of State Directors of Career Technical Education Consortium defined five key principles of career technical education.

1. To draw its curricula, standards, and organizing principles from the workplace.

2. To be a critical and integral component of the total educational system, offering career-oriented benefits for all students.

3. To be a critical and integral component of the workforce development system, providing the essential foundation for a thriving economy.

4. To maintain high levels of excellence supported through identification of academic and workplace standards, measurement of performance (accountability), and high expectations for participant success.

5. To remain robust and flexible enough to respond to the needs of the multiple educational environments, customers, and levels of specialization.

## Issues

Issues that are debated in vocational education include: (1) its role in secondary education; (2) the degree of specificity versus generality of occupational focus, that is, whether its focus should be education or training; and (3) whether it is intended for all students, as in career education, or for a subset of students who do not intend to pursue further education.

## Legislative Authority

The federal government has supported vocational education programs since 1917 when the Smith-Hughes Act was passed to help schools train workers for the country's rapidly growing economy. The Vocational Education Act of 1963 expanded the role of vocational education and funding was substantially increased. The Vocational Amendments in 1968 addressed the nation's social and economic problems and continued funding for students who were at risk or with disabilities.

The Carl D. Perkins Vocational Education Act of 1984 continued a focus on access for special populations, including women, minorities, and special needs, and added a focus on program improvement. The Carl D. Perkins Vocational and Applied Technology Education Act of 1990 (Perkins II) called for the integration of academic and technical instruction and introduced Tech Prep. The Carl D. Perkins Vocational and Technical Education Act of 1998 (Perkins III) continued the emphasis on academics in career and technical education and added a strong accountability requirement. The purpose of the act is to "develop more fully the academic, vocational, and technical skills of secondary students and postsecondary students who elect to enroll in vocational and technical education programs." Perkins III reflects major policy shifts from the set-asides and line items in earlier legislation that were prescriptive of how funds were to be spent, particularly for special populations and students at risk, to flexibility with increased accountability for results.

Two other legislative acts in the 1990s that influenced vocational education were the School-to-Work Opportunities Act in 1994 (STWOA) and the Workforce Investment Act (WIA) in 1998. The STWOA supplied funding to states to connect education and careers for all students. States could apply for five-year grants. The WIA provided a framework for a national workforce preparation and employment system designed to meet the needs of employers, first-time job seekers, and those looking to further their careers.

## Performance Standards

Historically, the primary measure of a program's performance was employment. The Carl D. Perkins Vocational and Technical Education Act of 1998 required states to meet four core indicators of performance: (1) student attainment of challenging state-established academic and vocational/technical skill proficiencies; (2) student attainment of a secondary school diploma or its recognized equivalent, a proficiency credential in conjunction with a secondary school diploma, or a postsecondary degree or credential; (3) placement in, retention in, and completion of postsecondary education or advanced training, placement in military service, or placement or retention in employment; and (4) student participation in and completion of vocational and technical education programs that lead to nontraditional training and employment. The act required each state to identify levels of performance for each indicator and report annually on its progress. States also develop additional state measures of performance.

## Magnitude of Vocational Education

Almost all high school graduates still complete at least one vocational course. More than half (58%) of public high school graduates take at least three vocational education courses, and virtually all (97%) take at least one vocational education course, according to figures obtained by the National Center for Education Statistics in 2000. Sixteen percent of all public high school credits are earned in vocational education. Forty-nine percent of all students seeking sub-baccalaureate degrees major in vocational fields. More than half (55%) of the public high school graduates who take concentrated vocational coursework enroll in a postsecondary institution within two years of high school graduation, according to the National Center for Education Statistics in 2000.

Between 1982 and 1994, there was a ninefold increase in the percentage of students completing both a vocational concentration and a college preparatory curriculum (from 2% to 18%). This trend suggests that students are increasingly integrating vocational and academic learning and that students in the high-tech fields of technology/communications and business are particularly likely to follow the broader course of study envisioned by recent federal legislation.

The postsecondary enrollment rates of public high school graduates showed a marked increase between 1982 and 1992. Among all sub-baccalaureate students, about one-half majored in a vocational program area in 1996.

## State Role in Vocational Education

State constitutions assign to each state its specific responsibility and legal authority for public education.

The state department of education coordinates activities among local school districts and between the federal government and local schools. State departments have shifted from an emphasis on compliance and monitoring of regulations to one of technical assistance to school districts.

Each state has a state board for vocational education. The organization and administration of vocational education varies in states. Thirty-six state directors of career-technical education are located in state departments of education or public instruction. Seven are located with higher education boards, and seven either have their own separate boards or are located with the state's workforce development board, according to Joanna Kister. State directors develop the state plan for vocational education that is approved by the U.S. Department of Education for distribution of federal funds. Local education agencies and postsecondary institutions are eligible recipients for subgrants. In addition, most state directors have responsibility for (1) policy (standards, budget); (2) program design and standards (including labor market data analysis); (3) curriculum frameworks and assessment; (4) professional/staff development and teacher education; (5) evaluation, accountability, and reporting; (6) strategic planning; (7) program and fiscal monitoring; (8) budget and personnel management; and (9) student organizations.

## Funding

Each year approximately $13 billion (federal, state, and local combined) is spent to support the vocational education system. Federal funding constitutes approximately seven percent of state vocational education spending. The relative cost for vocational education is estimated to be 20 percent to 40 percent greater than that of academic instruction, varying considerably by program area and content level. Most states provide some type of categorical funding for career-technical education. A national survey identified four broad categories for funding vocational education: (1) state foundation grants that are intended to ensure that all students in a state receive a minimum level of basic education services (states in this category do not budget additional supplemental funding for vocational education); (2) unit cost funding in which methods for determining funding formulas are based on unit cost by student participation, instructional unit, or cost reimbursement; (3) weighted funding per student; and (4) performance funding.

## Effectiveness of Vocational Education

There is strong evidence that the generic technical skills and occupationally specific skills provided in vocational education increase worker productivity, skill transfer, job access, and job stability when vocational graduates find training-related jobs. Large scale studies show that graduates who took a coherent sequence of vocational courses in high school (and did not enroll in postsecondary education) are likely to obtain more regular employment and higher wages than other non-college-going graduates, provided they are working in the field for which they were trained. Students with both a vocational concentration and a college preparatory curriculum outperformed vocational concentrators only. Performance of students who completed a college preparatory curriculum only was statistically indistinguishable from those with the combined vocational concentration and college preparation.

## Contemporary Role and Priorities

The principles for the contemporary career-technical education called for in legislation and by education reformers are reflected in the educational priorities in states. State directors of career and technical education reported the following as their priorities for change.

1. Integration of career-technical education in the total mission of education and education reform

2. Building a strong work force, economic development, and education partnership

3. Integration of academic and technical education through new delivery strategies, such as career academies, career pathway high schools, magnet schools, and linking of academic with technical curriculum

4. Development of business/industry certifications for all career-technical programs, at both secondary and postsecondary institutions

5. Implementation of a reliable and valid accountability system

6. Expansion of tech prep through secondary/postsecondary articulation

7. Expansion of career-technical education by providing access to all students

8. Increase of funding for career-technical education

9. Increase of use of technology

10. Addressing issues of teacher and administrator quality
11. Implementation of quality initiatives
12. Improvement of the image of career-technical education

State directors of career technical education are responsible for strengthening the relationship between education and work. They connect career and technical education to the larger high school reform movement, participate actively in both policy and practice realms in state workforce development systems, and ultimately contribute to economic development.

*See also:* VOCATIONAL AND TECHNICAL EDUCATION.

**BIBLIOGRAPHY**

BISHOP, JOHN. 1995. *Expertise and Excellence.* Ithaca, NY: Cornell University.

DELCI, MARIO, and STERN, DAVID. 1999. *Who Participates in New Vocational Programs?* Berkeley: University of California, National Center for Research in Vocational Education.

KISTER, JOANNA. 2001. *State Leadership for Career-Technical Education: Role and Nature of State Leadership; Developing Leaders.* Washington DC: National Association of State Directors of Career-Technical Education Consortium.

KLEIN, STEVE. 2001. *Financing Vocational Education: A State Policymaker's Guide.* Berkeley, CA: MPR Associates.

LEVESQUE, KAREN; LAUEN, DOUG; TEITELBAUM, PETER; ALT, MARTHA; and LIBRERA, SALLY. 2000. *Vocational Education in the United States: Toward the Year 2000.* Washington DC: U.S. Department of Education.

NATIONAL ASSOCIATION OF STATE DIRECTORS OF CAREER TECHNICAL EDUCATION CONSORTIUM. 2001. *Career Technical Education: An Essential Component of the Total Educational System.* Washington DC: National Association of State Directors of Career Technical Education Consortium.

NATIONAL CENTER FOR EDUCATION STATISTICS. 1999. *Issue Brief: Students Who Prepare for College and a Vocation.* Washington DC: U.S. Department of Education, Office of Educational Research and Improvement.

NATIONAL CENTER FOR EDUCATION STATISTICS. 2001. "The Data on Vocational Education (DOVE) System." *Education Statistics Quarterly* 2:4.

NATIONAL CENTER FOR EDUCATION STATISTICS. 2001. *The Condition of Education 2001.* Washington DC: U.S. Department of Education, Office of Educational Research and Improvement.

JOANNA KISTER

# STATE EDUCATIONAL SYSTEMS

The American system of public schooling is unusual for a modern state, as most nations rely upon education systems operated by the national government. The education system in the United States is actually a set of state-based systems. There is, however, a federal government role in education, and national education organizations and activities exist. But the ultimate authority—what is called *plenary* authority—for schooling in the United States resides with the individual states.

## The Legal Basis for State Control of Education

The U.S. Constitution omits any consideration of education or schooling—in fact, the words *education* and *schooling* do not appear in the document. James Madison's diary of the Constitutional Convention suggests that education was not even a topic of consideration at the Philadelphia deliberations. The only education topic of serious concern was whether or not to form a national university, which the delegates decided against.

The absence of any specific mention of education, coupled with the Constitution's Tenth Amendment, renders education a state function. The Tenth Amendment states that "The powers not delegated to the United States by the Constitution . . . are reserved to the States respectively, or to the people." This was a new and unique system, and it could be said that prior to formation of the United States, charters of liberty were granted by those with power, while in the United States, charters of power were now granted by those with liberty. The constitutions of all fifty states assume specific responsibility for education. Hence, the U.S. education system, by default, is a set of systems, not a single national system.

## School Organization Models

At the time of the nation's founding, transportation and communication were primitive by twenty-first-century standards. Consequently, states generally saw fit to delegate authority for school operation to local school districts. The United States has two major models for local school districts.

**The New England model of school organization.** The Massachusetts Commonwealth General Assembly enacted the Old Deluder Satan Act in 1647. This statute established township school districts. These were notable for three reasons: (1) schools were to be local or municipal, (2) the school boards that operated them were presumed to be made up of laypersons, and (3) these locally school boards were considered a form of "special" government, meaning that their authority was restricted to education. This New England model came to characterize most of the nation's educational systems. It spread west with the Northwest Ordinance, and eventually found its way into most of the states resulting from the Louisiana Purchase.

**The Southern model of school organization.** The Middle Atlantic and southern colonies existed under the sphere of influence of the Church of England. This body organized its operation into *parishes,* and parish lines were eventually transformed into county lines. Southern states came to rely far more heavily than the remainder of the nation upon county government, and in the twenty-first century many southern states continue to maintain county school districts or combinations of county and local school districts.

## The School District Consolidation Movement

The early twentieth century saw a wave of education efficiency efforts, as American education began to be viewed as ineffective due to its heavy reliance upon small local school districts. A coalition of academic and business leaders began to crusade in state after state for the elimination of small and rurally dominated school boards. The reform effort, which has come to be known as the *school district consolidate movement,* was reinforced by various other efficiency and good-government efforts. States sometimes simply eliminated districts, but more often they offered financial inducements for districts to combine into larger units.

By 1930, at the height of school district expansion, the United States had more than 125,000 local districts. School board members were then the nation's largest single segment of government officials. By 2000, the district consolidation movement had been dramatically effective, and the number of districts had been reduced to 14,000. Twenty percent of these were in only five states (California, New York, Illinois, Nebraska, and Texas), while the remaining forty-five states had fewer than 10,000 school districts. Some states, such as Maryland (24 districts), Florida (67 districts), Nevada (17 districts), and Delaware (7 districts), had very few.

School district consolidation has been effective in increasing the size of American school districts. By 2000, 25 percent of the nation's students went to school in only 1 percent of its districts, and 50 percent attended school in only 5 percent of the districts. The combination of district consolidation, population expansion, and urbanization has created some huge school districts, such as New York City (more than one million students), Chicago, Los Angeles, and Dade County (Miami), Florida.

The school district consolidation movement was premised upon a belief that larger districts were more efficient to operate economically and that they produced better education for students than rural districts. Neither premise has been proved. It could well be that there are substantial diseconomies of scale in these large districts, and the consolidation movement may in fact have done more harm than good. Whatever its outcome for students, it dramatically reduced the number of school board members. There was at one time a board member for every 250 citizens; in 2002 the ratio of representatives to citizens was twenty times that.

## The Modern Era of Big State Education Systems

In the period after World War II, states began to assume greater responsibility for education. They relied less upon local school districts, which had historically run the schools. This happened as small districts became larger and as communication and transportation rendered more direct state control possible. It was also a result of court decisions. Cases regarding racial desegregation, special education, and education finance, as well as school accountability and testing legislation, vested greater and greater authority in the states. By the turn of the twenty-first century, courts were beginning to take state constitutional statements regarding education literally, and they were holding state governments, not local school district officials, responsible for school quality.

In order to meet their legal and operational responsibilities for education, states rely upon several fundamental structural arrangements. All states have an executive, legislative, and judicial branch, paralleling the structure of the federal government. In addition, however, states also have education departments. These are generally bureaus reporting to the governor. In some instances, a state may have a state board of education that oversees the state education department. State structure is rendered more complicated by the position of chief state school officer, sometimes known as the superintendent of public instruction. In some states, the governor appoints a person to this office, in some states it is an elected office, and in a few instances the state board of education makes the appointment. If the chief state school officer is elected or appointed by an actor or agency other than the governor, he or she may have a statewide power base from which political opposition to the governor is possible.

The complicated nature of education governance hampers accountability. If a chief state school officer is not appointed by a state's governor, it is difficult to know who should be blamed or credited for results—the governor, the legislature, the chief state school officer, the state board of education, the state education department, local school boards, local school superintendents, or some other entity.

## State Education Department Structure

Each state has an education department among its executive branch bureaus. Some of these, such as in California and New York, are quite large, employing literally thousands of professional and staff members, while in a less populated state, such as Nevada, there may be fewer than a hundred employees. Regardless of size, one will usually encounter the following functions being undertaken. There will be an office of the superintendent with immediate staff and advisers, such as political liaison and public information specialists. There will be a budget office responsible for developing the state education department budget as a planning document. (The governor, often in cooperation with the chief state school officer, and the legislature will undertake the actual education budget and eventual appropriations of public revenues for education.) A budget office may also take responsibility for overseeing management of the department's own operating budget.

Other subunits will specialize in teacher certification, state testing, accountability, private school regulation, finance distribution, fiscal and performance audits, facilities construction, transportation, food service, preschool, accreditation of private and proprietary schools, and possibly higher education.

## Higher Education

States have historically relied upon a separate agency or structure to oversee public higher education. However, Florida and, to a slightly lesser degree, New York, provide models by which higher education is in many ways integrated into the larger education picture.

A conventional model is for a state to have a board of higher education, a board of regents, or both. Many states have two higher-education systems. One set of colleges reports to a state board of higher education, while the other is usually a more elite, usually research-oriented, system, comprised of one or multiple flagship campuses. When a state operates two systems of higher education, then invariably it will also have some kind of coordinating body that oversees the two or at least attempts to coordinate their budgets and facility construction efforts. Such coordinating mechanisms seldom prove effective. Colleges and universities often have such powerful alumni (and prestige to distribute) that they can evolve their own special relationships with governors and members of the state legislature.

Community colleges have evolved into a major component of American higher education, accounting for more than half of the nation's postsecondary enrollments. Increasingly, states have merged community college governance with that of their colleges and universities.

Private and religious colleges and universities have tended to be left unregulated by state government. The exception is when states utilize public funds for the tuition subsidy of private college students. Under such circumstances states may exercise a modicum of regulatory influence to protect the public's funds and interests.

As the United States has moved toward mass, rather than elite, higher education, the trend has been to treat colleges (particularly community colleges) and universities more and more like other education institutions and to try to integrate their management with that of K–12 education.

## The Role of the Federal Government

In the eighteenth and nineteenth centuries, the federal government assumed virtually no responsibility for overseeing or funding education. After the Civil War, Congress enacted the Morrill Acts, providing federal financial incentives for formation of state agricultural, mining, engineering, and military colleges. In 1946, Congress enacted the Lanham Act, which evolved into the Federal Impact Aid program, through which the federal government subsidizes local school districts in which there is a large federal presence (such as a military base).

In the post–World War II period, particularly during the 1960s, Congress enacted many education acts, the most important of which were the Elementary and Secondary Education Act (ESEA) of 1967 and the Higher Education Acts of 1965 and 1972. In the ESEA, the national government assumed added responsibility for providing local districts with monies for economically disadvantaged students, disabled students, and for student financial aid for higher education.

While the federal government does not have a large operational presence in education, there are still many national influences on American education. For example, there are literally hundreds of national education organizations, representing diverse groups and points of view (e.g., teachers, parents, textbook publishers, test manufacturers), all of which have a national presence and nationwide influence.

*See also:* Federal Educational Activities; Financial Support of Schools, *subentry on* State Support; States and Education.

**BIBLIOGRAPHY**

Bailey, Stephen K., et al. 1962. *Schoolmen and Politics.* Syracuse, NY: Syracuse University Press.

Cubberley, Ellwood P. 1934. *Public Education in the United States.* Boston: Houghton Mifflin.

Guthrie, James; Garms, Walter I.; and Pierce, Lawrence C. 1988. *School Finance and Education Policy: Enhancing Equality, Efficiency, and Choice.* Englewood Cliffs, NJ: Prentice Hall.

Theobald, Neil D., and Malen, Betty. 2000. *Balancing Local Control and State Responsibility for K–12 Education* (2000 Yearbook of the American Education Finance Association). Larchmont, NY: Eye on Education.

James W. Guthrie